Handbook on International Sports Law

Edited by

James A.R. Nafziger

Thomas B. Stoel Professor of Law and Director of International Programs, Willamette University College of Law, USA

Stephen F. Ross

Professor of Law, Director, Institute for Sports Law, Policy and Research, Lewis A. Vovakis Distinguished Faculty Scholar, The Pennsylvania State University, USA

RESEARCH HANDBOOKS IN INTERNATIONAL LAW

Edward Elgar

Cheltenham, UK • Northampton, MA, USA

Published by
Edward Elgar Publishing Limited
The Lypiatts
15 Lansdown Road
Cheltenham
Glos GL50 2JA
UK

Edward Elgar Publishing, Inc.
William Pratt House
9 Dewey Court
Northampton
Massachusetts 01060
USA

A catalogue record for this book is available from the British Library

Library of Congress Control Number: 2011922859

ISBN 978 1 84720 633 6 (cased)

Typeset by Columns Design XML Ltd, Reading
Printed and bound by MPG Books Group, UK

HANDBOOK ON INTERNATIONAL SPORTS LAW

RESEARCH HANDBOOKS IN INTERNATIONAL LAW

This highly original series offers a unique appraisal of the state-of-the-art of research and thinking in international law. Taking a thematic approach, each volume, edited by a prominent expert, covers a specific aspect of international law or examines the international legal dimension of a particular strand of the law. A wide range of sub-disciplines in the spheres of both public and private law are considered; from international environmental law to international criminal law, from international economic law to the law of international organisations, and from international commercial law to international human rights law. The *Research Handbooks* comprise carefully commissioned chapters from leading academics as well as those with an emerging reputation. Taking a genuinely international approach to the law, and addressing current and sometimes controversial legal issues, as well as affording a clear substantive analysis of the law, these *Handbooks* are designed to inform as well as to contribute to current debates.

Equally useful as reference tools or introductions to specific topics, issues and debates, the *Handbooks* will be used by academic researchers, post-graduate students, practicing lawyers and lawyers in policy circles.

Titles in this series include:

Handbook of Research on International Consumer Law
Edited by Geraint Howells, Iain Ramsay and Thomas Wilhelmsson with David Kraft

Research Handbook on International Environmental Law
Edited by Malgosia Fitzmaurice, David M. Ong and Panos Merkouris

Research Handbook on International Criminal Law
Edited by Bartram S. Brown

Research Handbook on the Law of International Organizations
Edited by Jan Klabbers and Åsa Wallendahl

Research Handbook on the Theory and History of International Law
Edited by Alexander Orakhelashvili

Handbook on International Sports Law
Edited by James A.R. Nafziger and Stephen F. Ross

Contents

Contributors

Paul M. Anderson – Associate Director and Adjunct Professor of Law, National Sports Law Institute, Marquette University Law School (USA).

Ian Blackshaw – International Sports Lawyer; Visiting Professor and Fellow, ASSER International Sports Law Centre; Member of the Court of Arbitration for Sport (UK).

Kerwin Clarke – Manager, Results Management/Legal Affairs, World Anti-Doping Agency (Canada).

Lucio Colantuoni – Prof. Avv., Attorney at Law; Professor in Sport Law, University of Milan Law School; Director of Sports Law Research Center, Milan; TAS/CAS Arbitrator, Lausanne, Switzerland (Italy).

Steve Cornelius – Professor, Department of Private Law, the University of Pretoria; Visiting Fellow, Anglia Ruskin University; Advocate of the High Court of South Africa (South Africa).

Timothy Davis – John W. and Ruth H. Turnage Professor of Law, Wake Forest University School of Law (USA).

Anthony J. Dreyer – Partner, Skadden, Arps, Slate, Meagher, & Flom, LLP; Adjunct Professor of Law, Fordham University School of Law and Cardozo Law School (USA).

Simon Gardiner Reader in Sports Law, Leeds Metropolitan University (UK).

Christine Graham – Trainee Solicitor, CMS Cameron McKenna LLP (UK).

Tone Jagodic – Secretary General, Olympic Committee of Slovenia; President, Supervisory Board of 'Sports Lottery,' Ltd (Slovenia).

Lewis Kurlantzick – Zephaniah Swift Professor of Law, University of Connecticut School of Law (USA).

Saskia Lettmaier – Research Assistant (2005–09), German and International Sports Law Research Unit, Institute for Law and Technology, University of Erlangen-Nuremberg (Germany).

Roberto Branco Martins – General Manager, European Football Agents Association (EFAA); Lecturer, Sports Labour Law, University of Amsterdam (The Netherlands).

Richard H. McLaren – Professor of Law, University of Western Ontario Faculty of Law; Arbitrator and Mediator; Member of the Court of Arbitration for Sport (CAS), attended five Olympic Games as an Ad Hoc Arbitrator for CAS (Canada).

Matthew J. Mitten – Professor of Law and Director, National Sports Law Institute and LL.M. in Sports Law Program for Foreign Lawyers, Marquette University Law School (USA).

James A.R. Nafziger – Thomas B. Stoel Professor of Law and Director of International Programs, Willamette University College of Law; Honorary President, International Association of Sports Law (USA).

Cristiano Novazio – Attorney at Law; Assistant Professor in Sport Law, University of Milan Law School; Administrative Secretary of Sports Law Research Center, Milan (Italy).

Richard Parrish – Professor of Sports Law, Edge Hill University (UK).

Richard W. Pound, Q.C. – Partner, Stikeman Elliot LLP; Chancellor *Emeritus*, McGill University; founding President, World Anti-Doping Agency; former Vice-President, International Olympic Committee (Canada).

Stephen F. Ross – Professor of Law, Lewis H. Vovakis Distinguished Faculty Scholar and Director, Penn State Institute for Sports Law, Policy, and Research, Dickinson School of Law, The Pennsylvania State University (USA).

Robert Siekmann – Professor, International and European Sports Law, Erasmus University Rotterdam; Director, ASSER International Sports Law Centre (The Netherlands).

Paul Singh – Chief Director of Client Support, Liaison, Events & Facilities, Sport and Recreation South Africa; Associate Professor, Department of Sport and Movement Studies, Faculty of Health Sciences, University of Johannesburg (South Africa).

Janwillem Soek – Senior Researcher, ASSER International Sports Law Centre (The Netherlands).

Klaus Vieweg – Professor (Chair of Civil Law, Business and Technology Law) and Director, German and International Sports Law Research Unit, Institute for Law and Technology, University of Erlangen-Nuremberg (Germany).

Chris Watson – Partner, CMS Cameron McKenna LLP (UK).

Preface

'*Citius, Altius, Fortius*' – faster, higher, stronger. To a great extent, this famous motto of the Olympic Movement expresses the aspirations that animate international sports law as well. For example, the ad hoc division of the Court of Arbitration for Sport (CAS) seeks to ensure *faster* resolution of disputes in the heated course of competition. Similarly, the CAS mediation facility provides a *faster* track for resolving out-of-competition disputes. CAS also aims for *higher* standards of dispute resolution and a *higher* level to review decisions of sports bodies bearing on such vital issues as the eligibility of athletes. As to the aspiration of '*fortius*', the World Anti-Doping Code and the UNESCO Anti-Doping Convention provide a *stronger* regime for ensuring a more level playing field free of drugs and other performance-enhancing abuse. As well, new rules of video surveillance and scoring established by international sports federations are directed toward *stronger* measures of trust in field-of-play decisions and the outcome of competition.

Socio-economic issues loom large in the international sports arena. 'This is how I fight', explained a women's soccer pioneer in Afghanistan, concisely referring to both gender equality and geopolitics. Whatever may be the role of sports as an instrument of global order, social issues such as discrimination and the protection of youth have been fundamental, as has the core principle of fairness.

Economic issues driven by globalization have also swept the sports arena. Transnational commercial issues bespeak the pervasive influence of the media and corporate sponsorship; the emergence of image, intellectual property, and other commercial rights; and the centrality of labour and anti-trust regulation. The application of competition law to commercial practices in the sports industry remains particularly controversial, hailed by some as essential to protect fans and players from monopolistic practices but criticized by others as unduly interfering in sporting decisions. It is clear, however, that the best practices and processes for addressing such fundamental issues are becoming more uniform across national boundaries. Moreover, open competition among amateur and professional athletes has led to a greater commonality of interests among all athletes and other stakeholders in sports. The two, historically separate tracks of the Olympic Movement and commercial activity are converging. This development is shaping an integrated process of international sports law, supported by more uniform national regulation and implementation.

This Handbook on International Sports Law presents a comprehensive collection of essays by leading scholars and practitioners in the burgeoning field of international sports law. From the World Cups in football/soccer and the Olympic Games to the rapidly expanding industry of sports management and promotion across national boundaries, it is apparent that international sports activity plays a central role in our daily lives. In addition, increased accessibility of reported cases and arbitral decisions facilitates a much broader exchange of ideas, as sports continue to globalize. It therefore should not be surprising that the evolving law applicable to international competition is of major importance.

We have been fortunate to recruit a first-rate group of authors from nine countries for this book. They address significant legal issues along the two converging tracks: the commercial sports industry, focused on professional competition; and the established institutional framework of the law that includes the International Olympic Committee, international sports federations, regional and national sports bodies, the Court of Arbitration for Sport, and the World Anti-Doping Agency.

Topics in this book include the institutional framework; fundamental issues, legal principles and decisions within those institutions; mediation, arbitration and litigation of disputes; doping; gambling; the expanding use and abuse of cameras and electronic technology in judging competitions; athlete eligibility requirements; discrimination; and protections of young athletes. The book also covers a broad range of commercial issues related to competition law and labor markets; media, image, and intellectual property rights; event sponsorships; and players' agents. Comparative analyses of sports models and practices in Europe, North America and elsewhere reinforce the general theme of international sports law.

The essays in this book comprehensively address the emerging process of international sports law. Comparative insights and analysis help define international custom and provide alternative solutions to problems. Laws and procedures in Europe, North America and South Africa receive particular attention. To be sure, the book does not include a few possible dimensions of the international process – taxation, for example – because of space limitations, relative unavailability of commentary, or the lack of pertinent processes of international law. Our hope, however, is that these essays will help expand both the geographical scope of commentary and the range of topics in this rapidly evolving field.

Our goal in producing this book is to offer up-to-date and accessible analysis of international sports law, broadly defined. We hope that these commentaries on some of the most controversial, cutting-edge issues will inform and inspire students of sports law, sports management, international law, comparative law and other subjects, as well as assist scholars, practicing lawyers and players' agents in their work. We also hope that the book will be useful to other professionals (not to mention amateurs) in the sports industry. Let the reading begin!

James A.R. Nafziger

Stephen F. Ross
July 2011

Acknowledgements

Paul M. Anderson – I would like to thank Marquette University Law school students Peter Barn, Carolina Dutriz, Peter Prigge, and Andre Salhab, and Attorney Nick Reider for their assistance in conducting research and drafting portions of this chapter.

Steve Cornelius – I wish to thank my academic assistants – Cara-Maeve Gilmour during 2007 and Esti Louw during 2008 – for their valuable contribution in the research for this article. However, I accept full responsibility for all the opinions expressed herein.

Timothy Davis – I wish to thank Ruger, Johansen, Lenard, Paul Anderson, Bruce Burton, James A.R. Nafziger, Stephen F. Ross, and Kenneth L. Shropshire for their review and comments; and to Brian Conley and David Ginzer for their research assistance.

Anthony J. Dreyer – I would like to thank Jordan Feirman, Andrew McClure, Shivram Sankar, Rebecca Silberberg, and Jamie Stockton for assisting with this chapter.

Christine Graham and Chris Watson – We acknowledge the assistance of Tarek Ben Brauer, Egon Engin Deniz, Sébastien Engelen, Ashley Halewood, Andriy Prykhodko, Gurinda Sandhu, and Hayley Stevenson.

Lewis Kurlantzik – I would like to thank James Goodfellow and Jason Hyne for research assistance; Jeremy Paul for research support; Kurt Strasser for critical suggestions; and Rosa Colón for secretarial aid.

Richard H. McLaren – I want to acknowledge the considerable assistance of my researchers, Geoff Cowper-Smith of the University of Western Ontario Law Class of 2009; and Erika Douglas, Morgan Borins, and Kit Scotchmer, all of Western Law Class of 2010. I would also like to acknowledge the input of Andreas Zaglis of Athens, Greece, and Erin McDermid of McKenzie Lake Lawyers LL.P., London, Canada, both of whom read and commented on earlier drafts of this chapter while each was serving as an ad hoc volunteer to the Court of Arbitration for Sport (CAS) at the Summer Olympic Games in Beijing, China.

Matthew J. Mitten – I dedicate this article to Coach Fred Beier, who taught me the importance of mental toughness and inspired me to always do my best. Thanks to Ruger, Johansen, Lenard, Paul Anderson, Bruce Burton, James A.R. Nafziger, Stephen F. Ross, and Kenneth L. Shropshire for their review and comments, and to Megan Ryther for her research assistance.

Abbreviations

AAA	American Arbitration Association
AALS	Association of American Law Schools
ACSU	Anti-Corruption and Security Unit of the ICC
ADA	Americans with Disabilities Act of 1990 (USA)
ADEA	Age Discrimination in Employment Act of 1967 (USA)
ADR	Alternative dispute resolution
AHD	Ad Hoc Division of the Court of Arbitration for Sport
AMS	Audiovisual Media Services Directive 2010/13/EC (EU)
ASA	Amateur Swimming Association (UK)
ATHOC	Organizing Committee of the Athens Olympic Games (2004)
ATP	Association of Tennis Professionals
BKS	Federal Communications Office (Austria)
BOA	British Olympic Association
BWF	Badminton World Federation
CAS	Court of Arbitration for Sport
CDPA 1988	Copyright, Designs and Patents Act 1988 (UK)
CEDR	Centre for Effective Dispute Resolution
CFI	Court of First Instance (EU)
CFL	Canadian Football League
CFO	Comité français d'organisation de la Coupe du monde de football
CJEU	Court of Justice of the European Union
CNN	Cable News Network
COC	Canadian Olympic Committee
CONI	Italian Olympic Committee
CYA	Canadian Yachting Association
DCMS	Department of Culture, Media and Sport (UK)
DDA	Disability Discrimination Act 1995 (UK)
DFB	German Football Association
EC	European Community
ECHR	European Convention on Human Rights
ECJ	European Court of Justice
EEA	European Economic Area
EFAA	European Football Agents Association
EP	European Parliament
EPAS	Enlarged Partial Agreement on Sport (Council of Europe)

EPFL	European Professional Football Leagues
ESC	European Sports Charter
EU	European Union
FA	Football Association (England)
FAO	Food and Agriculture Organization
FAPL	Football Association Premier League (England)
FASA	Football Association of South Africa
FEI	International Equestrian Foundation
FERG	Act on Exclusive Broadcasting Rights (Austria)
FIA	International Automobile Federation
FIBA	Federation Internationale de Basketball
FIFA	International Federation of Football Associations; Fédération Internationale de Football Associations
FIG	International Gymnastics Federation; Fédération Internacionale Gymnastique
FIH	International Hockey Association; Federation International de Hockey
FISA	International Rowing Federation; Fédération Internationale des Sociétés d'Aviron
FTAIA	Foreign Trade Antitrust Improvements Act of 1982 (USA)
IAAF	International Amateur Athletics Federation
ICANN	Internet Corporation on Assigned Namesand Numbers
ICAS	International Council of Arbitration for Sport
ICC	International Chamber of Commerce
ICC	International Cricket Council
ICPES	International Charter of Physical Education and Sport (UNESCO)
IF	International sports federation
IFWH	International Federation of Women's Hockey Associations
IIHF	International Ice Hockey Federation
ILO	International Labour Organization
IOC	International Olympic Committee
IP	Intellectual property
IPC	International Paralympic Committee
IPR	Intellectual property rights
IPTV	Internet streaming of television
ITC	Independent Television Commission (UK)
ITF	International Tennis Federation
ITTF	International Table Tennis Federation
ITU	International Telecommunications Union
LFP	Football League (Spain)

List, the	List of Prohibited Substances and Methods
MLB	Major League Baseball
MLBPA	Major League Baseball Players Association
MLS	Major League Soccer
NADO	National anti-doping organization
NASCAR	National Association for Stock Car Auto Racing
NBA	National Basketball Association
NBPA	National Basketball Players Association
NCAA	National Collegiate Athletic Association
NF	National federation
NFL	National Football League (North America)
NFLPA	National Football League Players Association (North America)
NGB	National governing body
NHL	National Hockey League
NHLPA	National Hockey League Players Association
NOC	National Olympic Committee
NPB	Professional Baseball League (Japan)
NSPCC	National Society for the Prevention of Cruelty to Children (UK)
NSWCA	New South Wales Court of Appeal
OASA	Olympic and Amateur Sports Act of 1998 (USA)
OCOGs	Organizing committees of the Olympic Games
OCR	Office for Civil Rights, Department of Education (USA)
Ofcom	Office of Communications (UK)
P2P	Peer-to-peer
PASPA	Professional and Amateur Sports Protection Act (USA)
PCCA	Prevention and Combating of Corrupt Activities Act 2004 (New Zealand)
PL	Premier League (football: England, Ukraine)
RA	Rehabilitation Act of 1973 (USA)
RICO	Racketeer Influenced and Corrupt Organizations Act (USA)
RLIF	Rugby League International Federation
RTSS	Real-time scoring system
SFT	Swiss Federal Tribunal
SOP	Streaming Over P2P
SROC	Sports Rights Owners Coalition
TAB	Totalisator Agency Board (New Zealand)
TFEU	Treaty on the Functioning of the European Union
TMA 1994	Trade Marks Act 1994 (UK)
TMO	Television match official

TOP	The Olympic Programme
TRIPS Agreement	Agreement on Trade-Related Aspects of Intellectual Property Rights
TUE	Therapeutic use exemption
TVWF	Television without Frontiers Directive 89/552/EEC (EU)
UCBSA	United Cricket Board of South Africa
UEFA	Union of European Football Associations
UIEGA	Unlawful Internet Gambling Enforcement Act (USA)
UNDP	United Nations Development Program
UNEP	United Nations Environment Program
UNESCO	United Nations Educational, Scientific, and Cultural Organization
UNHCR	United Nations High Commissioner for Refugees
UNODC	United Nations International Office on Drugs and Crime
UPU	Universal Postal Union
USADA	United States Anti-Doping Agency
USOC	United States Olympic Committee
USTA	United States Tennis Association
VfGH	Constitutional Court (Austria)
WADA	World Anti-Doping Agency
WADC	World Anti-Doping Code
WFL	World Football League
WHA	World Hockey Association
WHO	World Health Organization
WIPO	World Intellectual Property Organization
WIPO Center	Arbitration and Mediation Center of the World Intellectual Property Organization
WMO	World Meteorological Union
WTA	Women's Tennis Association
WTO	World Trade Organization

PART I

FOUNDATION AND STRUCTURE

1 International sports law

James A.R. Nafziger

I. INTRODUCTION

Law, like politics, has accompanied sports competition throughout history, and this law often has had a unique status. For example, the ancient Olympic Games relied on ad hoc officials – essentially judges – who were equipped with special sanctions to enforce both the rules of the game in a particular contest and the organizational rules of the Games as a whole. Notice to both the participating city-states and athletes of their obligations took the form of statues dedicated to Zeus (called *zanes*) that were financed from fines imposed on city-states and placed as reminders near the entrance to the stadium.[1] Two millennia later, in the eighteenth century, a court in Tuscany denied relief to owners of property damaged by stray balls from a traditional ball game. The court reasoned that sports took priority over torts because regularly scheduled public amusements created legal servitudes on neighboring property.[2] Today, the European Court of Justice (ECJ) struggles with a similar issue within the European Union, namely the extent to which sports activity is 'special' or has 'specificity' and is thus subject only to its own legal regime beyond the regulatory competence of the European Union.[3]

The contemporary legal regime governing sports blends normal rules and procedures transcending sports activity – general contract and tort law, employment law, competition (anti-trust) law, and so on – with a distinctive and coherent body of what has come to be known as 'sports law.' The justification for a specialized regime of law is partly cultural, partly historical, and partly practical. It must embrace both the rules of the game that define or circumscribe a particular field of play as well as the overarching organizational rules and practices that transcend the field of play and apply more broadly to organized sports activity. A 'non-interference rule,' to be discussed further in this chapter,[4] significantly limits judicial or arbitral review of complaints about breaches of game rules and field-of-play decisions by referees. Thus, athletes are entitled to 'honest "field-of-play" decisions, not necessarily correct ones.'[5]

---

[1] On the ancient Games and subsequent history in the West of organized international sports competition, see JAMES A.R. NAFZIGER, INTERNATIONAL SPORTS LAW 179 (2d ed. 2004).

[2] See Gino Goria, *A Decision of the Rota Fiorentina of 1780 on Liability for Damages Caused by the 'Ball Game,'* 49 TUL. L. REV. 346 (1975).

[3] See Commission of the European Communities, The EU and Sport: Background and Context: Accompanying Document to the White Paper on Sport, at Annex 1, COM (2007) 391 final (July 11, 2007) [hereinafter The EU and Sport].

[4] See text accompanying notes 85–96 *infra.*

[5] *Yang Tae Young* v. *Int'l Gymnastics Fed'n*, CAS 2004/A/704 (Oct. 21, 2004) (refusal by the Court of Arbitration for Sport (CAS) to overrule a field-of-play decision for failure to raise an objection to it in a timely manner).

The special status of sports activity, and hence of sports law, has gained particular recognition in public international law. Generally, the term 'international sports law' refers to a process that comprises a more or less distinctive body of rules, principles, and procedures to govern the conduct and consequences of transnational sports activity. This process is of recent origin, having emerged coherently only in the last quarter of the twentieth century. International sports law is certainly an idea whose time has come, in response to significant developments. These include, for example, the rampant growth of a sports industry heavily influenced by corporate investment, sponsorship and broadcasting, all of which threaten the autonomy and even integrity of sports; open competition between professionals and amateurs; a globalization of competition; the doping of athletes; playing field and spectator violence; and persistent (though much diminished) issues of international politics and nationality.

The still-evolving process of essentially public law that we call international sports law incorporates the applicable procedural rules and practices of private international law as well. These include, for example, the jurisdiction of national courts over the decisions of international sports federations, default rules for determining the applicable law to govern a dispute when parties to it have failed to exercise choice-of-law autonomy, and the role of comity in recognizing and enforcing foreign judgments in the absence of more formal requirements to do so. Thus, what might be characterized otherwise as an issue of private international law in an essentially private dispute – such as between an athlete and her sports organization related to international competition – falls within the public law of international sports.

II. STRUCTURE

A. The Framework of Inter-governmental Organizations

Among inter-governmental organizations, the United Nations Educational, Scientific, and Cultural Organization (UNESCO) has been instrumental in the development of international sports law. In 1978 UNESCO adopted the International Charter of Physical Education and Sport,[6] which sets forth a comprehensive set of rules and guidelines for national programs and transnational sports activity, overseen by an Inter-Governmental Committee for Physical Education and Sport. Within this framework, as further elaborated at conferences of sports ministers and sports officials that it has convened, UNESCO has adopted several resolutions calling upon states to enforce 'particularly the principles of non-discrimination, fair play, non-violence, and the rejection of harmful substances.'[7] In response to the latter problem, for example, UNESCO's International Convention Against Doping in Sport[8] entered into force in 2007.

---

[6] United Nations Educational, Scientific and Cultural Organization, Res. 1/5.4/2, 1 Records of the Gen. Conf., 20th Sess., at 31 (1978), available at http://www.unesco.org/humanrights/hrbe.htm.

[7] United Nations Educational, Scientific and Cultural Organization, Res. 1.20, Universality of the Olympic Games, 1 Records of the Gen. Conf., 25th Sess., at 91 (1989).

[8] United Nations Educational, Scientific and Cultural Organization, International Convention Against Doping in Sport, ED/2005/CONV-DOP rev.2, adopted Oct. 19, 2005 [hereinafter UNESCO Convention].

Other specialized agencies and special programs of the United Nations contribute to the inter-governmental framework. These include the Food and Agriculture Organization (FAO), establishing sports activity and recreational projects in poor rural communities; the International Telecommunications Union (ITU), encouraging satellite broadcasting of sports events; the United Nations Development Program (UNDP), financing sports and recreational facilities in developing countries; the United Nations Environment Program (UNEP), convening conferences to promote sustainable development, ranging from green procurement in the staging of sporting events to the design of environmentally friendly venues; the United Nations International Office on Drugs and Crime (UNODC), cooperating in efforts to control the use of drugs by athletes, particularly among youth; the United Nations High Commissioner for Refugees (UNHCR), distributing sports equipment in refugee camps; the Universal Postal Union (UPU), encouraging issuance of sports-related postage stamps to promote international competition; the World Health Organization (WHO), convening conferences on sports-related health issues; and the World Meteorological Union (WMO), providing forecasting assistance in staging events. The United Nations General Assembly has also been instrumental, though only sporadically, in the process of international sports law – for example, in adopting an influential declaration against apartheid in sports.[9] Its provisions mandated, for example, the denial of travel visas to representatives of sports bodies and athletes from any country practicing apartheid.

Outside the United Nations framework, noteworthy inter-governmental institutions include the Commonwealth Federation; the European Union; and the Supreme Council for Sports in Africa, which played a critical role in the erosion of apartheid in South Africa. An innovative amalgam of public and private parties is the World Anti-Doping Agency, whose World Anti-Doping Code,[10] to be discussed later, was adopted in 2003 by 73 states and 65 private sports organizations.

B. The European Region

The European region merits specific attention for at least three reasons. First, the origins, growth, and institutional leadership of modern sports law lie there. In particular, the European Union has generated important developments and decisions. For example, in its landmark *Bosman* decision,[11] the ECJ enforced the EC/EU Treaty's freedom-of-movement requirements by striking down the practice in football/soccer of requiring the payment of a transfer fee by a club to enable it to acquire a player from another club within the region. *Bosman* also struck down restrictions on nationality-restrictive formulas for the constitution of teams other than national teams that are organized to represent EC/EU member states in international competition. A European Convention on Spectator Violence[12]

---

[9]   Declaration of the International Conference on Sanctions Against Apartheid in Sport, held in London from June 27–29, 1983, U.N. Doc. A/38/310 (1983).

[10]   UNESCO Convention, note 8 *supra*, Appendix I.

[11]   *Union Royale Belge des Sociétés de Football Ass'n* v. *Bosman*, Case C-415/93 [1995] E.C.R. I-4921.

[12]   European Convention on Spectator Violence and Misbehavior at Sports Events and in Particular at Football Matches, 24 INT'L LEGAL MATERIALS 1566 (1985).

provides for extradition of suspects and other mutual assistance in criminal matters resulting from spectator violence.

Second, Europeans and European venues have dominated international sports organization, leadership, and competition itself. For example, since the 1894 Congress of Paris that initiated the modern Olympic Games, the President of the International Olympic Committee (IOC) has always been a European, with one exception. Over 60 percent of all venues for the Games (summer and winter) have been in Europe. Similarly, the venue for the quadrennial World Cup in football/soccer, since its beginning in 1930, has rotated on a 50/50 basis between Europe and the rest of the world. Moreover, European nationals disproportionately fill leadership positions ranging from 40 to 80 percent, in such institutions as the IOC, the international sports federations (IFs), and the Court of Arbitration for Sport (CAS). Of course, a variety of historical, cultural, economic, and meteorological factors help explain the European dominance, and it has been gradually diminishing. Even so, the Europeanization of international sports competition and authority continues to undermine the global reach and legitimacy of the international sports law process.

Third, European sports regimes are significant because they are conceptualized in terms of a distinctive, customary European Sports Model that has been regarded as a general practice within the region.[13] A Declaration of Sport annexed to the Treaty of Amsterdam[14] articulated the 'special' quality of sports activity and an 'open system' of sports organization. The Lisbon Treaty of 2009[15] is the first to incorporate provisions for regulation of sports, taking into account its specificity.

More precisely, the European system is said to entail a pyramidic structure that integrates professional and nonprofessional clubs and leagues in a single tiered hierarchy, annual promotion and relegation of teams between superior and inferior divisions on the basis of win-loss records, an encouragement of national identities in sports, and a reliance on communitarianism and voluntarism. Leaving aside obvious similarities with other national practices and regimes, the European Sports Model, particularly its pyramid structure, has been increasingly threatened by national licensing of teams, the formation of a powerful elite group of European football/soccer clubs outside the pyramid structure, and opportunities for investors to bypass the promotion-and-relegation system by purchasing higher-league teams and replacing them with aspiring but less successful

---

[13]   This topic will be explored further in Chapters 4 and 5. See generally LARS HALGREEN, EUROPEAN SPORTS LAW: A COMPARATIVE ANALYSIS OF THE EUROPEAN AND AMERICAN MODELS OF SPORT (2004); Stephen Weatherill, *Is the Pyramid Compatible with EC Law?*, INT'L SPORTS L.J. 2005/3-4, at 3; Stephen Weatherill, *Sport as Culture in EC Law*, in CULTURE AND EUROPEAN UNION LAW 113, 152 (Rachael Craufurd Smith ed. 2004); Stephen Weatherill, *Resisting the Pressures of 'Americanization': The Influence of European Community Law on the 'European Sports Model,'* 8 WILLAMETTE J. INT'L L. & DISP. RES. 37 (2000). For a summary of the White Paper issued by the Commission of the European Communities, which puts the European Sports Model in context, note 3 *supra*, see Remus Muresan, *Das 'Weissbuch Sport' der Kommission des Europäischen Gemeinschaften*, CAUSA SPORT, 3/2007, at 28.

[14]   Treaty of Amsterdam Amending the Treaty on European Union, the Treaties Establishing the European Communities and Certain Related Acts, Oct. 2, 1997, 1997 O.J. (C340) 1 (1997), 37 INT'L LEGAL MATERIALS 56 (1998).

[15]   Treaty of Lisbon Amending the Treaty on European Union and the Treaty Establishing the European Union, Dec. 17, 2007, 500 O.J. (C306) [hereinafter Treaty of Lisbon].

lower-league teams under common ownership or control. Therefore, the model may no longer be an entirely accurate description of European sports.

C. The Olympic Movement

Within the process of international sports law, the dominant institutional framework is not inter-governmental but rather non-governmental, as defined by the Olympic Movement. It is a fascinating example of a non-governmental organizational structure that has been accorded limited international legal personality as a chosen instrument of states whereby it contributes directly to the progressive development of international law. According to the foundational Olympic Charter, the structure of the Olympic Movement embraces the IOC, IFs, National Olympic Committees (NOCs), the organizing committees of the Olympic Games (OCOGs), 'other organizations and institutions as recognized by the IOC', such as the International Paralympic Committee and the World Anti-Doping Agency (WADA); national associations; local clubs, teams, and leagues; and athletes, referees, coaches, and other sports officials.

The Olympic Charter codifies general principles, custom, and authoritative decisions applicable to international sports competition and thereby forms a normative foundation of international sports law. By a gradual process of legitimization, its authority has expanded from the organization of periodic Olympic competitions among uncompensated 'amateurs' to governance of certain conduct and activity of both uncompensated and professional athletes as well as sports officials in a broad range of international competitions. Although the breadth of the Olympic Charter's authority may be questioned, its fundamental principles and operational rules generally satisfy the requirements of international custom involving the repetition, duration, and universality of practices, regarded as *opinio juris*.

The 'supreme authority' of the Olympic Movement is the IOC, headquartered in Lausanne, Switzerland.[16] Rule 19 of the Olympic Charter defines the IOC for legal purposes as an 'international non-governmental non-profit organization of unlimited duration, in the form of an association with the status of a legal person, recognized by the Swiss Federal Council.' Rule 2 stipulates that the IOC's primary mission is 'to lead the promotion of Olympism in accordance with the Olympic Charter.'

Under public international law, the special status of the Olympic Movement and its constituent organizations, especially the IOC, is well established. States acquiesce in decisions based on the Olympic Charter and conduct diplomacy with the IOC. For example, a federal appeals court in the United States, cautioning that 'a court should be wary of applying a state statute to alter the content of the Olympic Games,' observed as follows: 'The Olympic Games are organized and conducted under the terms of an international agreement – the Olympic Charter. We are extremely hesitant to undertake the application of one state's statute to alter an event that is staged with competitors from the entire world under the terms of that agreement.'[17] The United States Supreme Court has concluded that Congress officially adopted the Olympic Charter's aim 'to spread the

---

16   See generally ALEXANDRE MIGUEL MESTRE, THE LAW OF THE OLYMPIC GAMES (2009).
17   *Martin v. Int'l Olympic Comm.*, 740 F.2d 670, 677 (9th Cir. 1984).

Olympic principles.'[18] Four justices of the Court specifically described the IOC as 'a highly visible and influential international body.'[19] A Swiss statute accords the IOC special international status under Swiss tax and labor laws in view of its 'universal vocation in the world of sport.' A Belgian judgment, confirming earlier national and regional decisions in Europe, established that the sports rules derived from principles and practices of the Olympic Charter are controlling.[20] CAS has also pronounced that, in applying rules and principles of the Olympic Charter, it 'must [decide] disputes within the context of the law of sports.'[21]

III. ISSUES

A. Politics

In the early years of international sports law, its principal focus was on political issues such as boycotts of the Olympic Games – most notoriously of the Moscow Games in 1980 and the Los Angeles Games in 1984 – and of competition involving teams from South Africa, Rhodesia, and Taiwan. A secondary issue related to player eligibility for particular events, based on a traditional distinction between professionals and essentially uncompensated amateurs. Neither issue is any longer of much significance in an era of open competition that melds professionals and non-professionals alike. Today, the focus of international sports law has shifted toward such issues as the human rights of athletes, the fairness of in-play judging and use of electronic and photographic equipment for doing so, the widespread use of performance-enhancing agents (doping), violence in sports, transfer of players between clubs and teams, and the growing influence of commercial practices in the sports arena.

The transition in the content of international sports law became particularly clear in the 1992 Olympics at both the Winter (Albertville) and Summer (Barcelona) Games. For that reason, a closer look at those Games will be instructive. The Games were larger, more commercial, more professional, more visible because of expanded television coverage, and more highly regulated to deter and overcome doping by athletes. Also, the Games were far less political than in the past.

The Barcelona Games attracted a record number of 172 national teams. For the first time in many years, national teams from the Baltic States of the former Soviet Union and a South Africa free of apartheid, as well as a united German team, participated. Taiwanese athletes again competed as 'Chinese Taipei' with the concurrence of both the Taiwanese and Beijing-based Olympic Committees. Teams from Croatia, Slovenia, and Bosnia-Herzegovina rose from the ashes of Yugoslavia. Individual athletes from Serbia and the Former Yugoslav Republic of Macedonia as well as a Unified Team from the former Soviet Union accepted the Olympic flag and anthem as transitional symbols of their participation. For a while, playing fields competed with the battlefields of the former

---

[18]   *San Francisco Arts & Athletics, Inc.* v. *USOC & IOC*, 107 S. Ct. 2971, 2981 (1987).
[19]   *Ibid.* at 2988.
[20]   For brief references, see NAFZIGER, note 1 *supra*, at 25.
[21]   See, e.g., *R* v. *Int'l Olympic Comm.*, in Digest of CAS Awards 1983–1998, at 419 (Matthieu Reeb ed. 1998).

Yugoslavia on global television. Drawing upon the Fundamental Principles of the Olympic Charter, the IOC proclaimed an *ekecheiria* (truce) harkening back to the ancient Games, in a failed effort, unfortunately, to encourage the peaceful settlement of disputes and the suspension of armed conflict, most notably in Bosnia.

By 1992 the process of international sports law could claim several victories in the arena of international politics. The 'Chinese Taipei' compromise for designating Taiwanese teams not only worked but also set an example for eventual rapprochement between the two Koreas. Anti-apartheid sanctions imposed by the IOC and IFs, together with the Gleneagles Agreement of the British Commonwealth,[22] were instrumental not only in returning South African athletes to international competition, but also in gradually eliminating apartheid altogether and thereby democratizing South Africa. The IOC's firm refusal to reimpose a ban on transitional South Africa's participation in the 1992 Games, despite political pressures to do so, was impressive.

Also, the IOC played at least a minor role in the otherwise tumultuous reorganization of Eastern Europe following the Cold War. As new republics emerged from the wreckage of the Soviet Union and Yugoslavia, they quickly formed NCOs and sought the IOC's recognition of them, under the Olympic Charter, as a primary means of confirming their statehood. Meanwhile, the long-established recognition of Yugoslavian teams, by that designation, continued although it was increasingly limited to teams of Serbian-Montenegrin athletes. When the United Nations Security Council imposed sanctions against Yugoslavia on the eve of the Barcelona Games, the IOC successfully negotiated with the Sanctions Committee of the Security Council to allow the individual Serbian athletes to compete in Barcelona. Although a champion water polo team and competitive basketball, handball, and medley swimming teams from Serbia had to stay at home, the IOC clearly won the diplomatic game on behalf of individual athletes. Overall, the IOC's initiative was instrumental not only in ensuring the participation of individual Serbian athletes but also, more ambitiously, in confirming the statehood of those breakaway republics (Slovenia and Croatia) whose newly recognized independence enabled them to send national teams to Barcelona. The Barcelona Organizing Committee's adoption of the IOC compromises thereby gave content to the Committee's observation that '[t]he international community needs the Games to help it find itself.'[23]

The IOC's approach contrasted sharply with a decision by the Union of European Football Associations to bar the Yugoslavian team from the then eight-nation European Football championship matches. As runner-up for inclusion in the championship matches, Denmark then replaced the Yugoslavian team and surprisingly won the championship. To do so, Denmark ironically beat a team from Germany, whose government had initiated the diplomatic process of accepting the disintegration of Yugoslavia by its prompt (some would say premature) recognition of the breakaway republics of Slovenia and Croatia.

B. Commercialism

A prime example of the trend in the sports arena away from political issues and toward economic, social, and organizational ones includes the huge issue of commercialism. The

---

[22] See Nafziger, note 1 *supra*, at 251.
[23] OLYMPIC REV., Sept. 1992, at 438.

explosion of this issue has been fueled by extravagant contracts for television coverage of lucrative international competition, commercial endorsements by athletes, acquisition of clubs by billionaire investors, and prominent trademark displays of sponsors on athletic uniforms. Spending on star athletes is alarmingly out of control. Today, the Olympic Movement itself depends heavily on commercial revenues and a growing role in international marketing of consumer products.

Commercial disputes involving international sports competition are now a major focus of international sports law. Again, 1992 was a watershed year. To prevent a version of ambush marketing, a French court enjoined American Express from advertising in Albertville because its competitor, VISA, was an official sponsor of the Winter Games. Later in the year, the IOC threatened legal action against American Express for advertising in a manner that attempted to diminish the importance of VISA in Barcelona. A Spanish court enjoined the display of the Nike sportswear trademark, as an infringement of the intellectual property rights of a competing Spanish trademark.[24] The already-established trend toward commercialization of sports was perhaps symbolized by the IOC's earlier decision to convene the 1996 Games in Atlanta, the land of Cable News Network (CNN) and Coca-Cola, rather than Athens, the cradle of the ancient and modern Games.

C. Eligibility

As a general practice, the traditional bright line in sports competition between amateur and professional athletes has largely yielded to mixed, open competition. Moreover, the most widely accepted definition of an amateur athlete no longer depends upon the financial circumstances of the athlete. Although Gulag systems of training pseudo-amateurs largely disappeared with the communist regimes that created them, paid or subsidized athletes dominate the attention of the media and public today. Since its enactment in 1978, the Amateur Sports Act[25] that governs United States athletes in international competition and international competition in the United States simply defines 'amateur' in terms of sanctioned eligibility for such competition rather than in terms of financial circumstances. American basketball's Dream Team at the Barcelona Games in 1992 dramatized the arrival of open competition in Olympic and other arenas. What remains of amateurism is a legally restrictive rather than purely descriptive term in the original sense of noncompensated sports activity. No longer do IFs bar compensated athletes or generally manage trust accounts and other controls over the income of athletes.

Today the concept of eligibility, enshrined in amended provisions of the Olympic Charter, emphasizes a broader purpose: to put all athletes on an equal footing. Questions

---

[24]   See INT'L HERALD TRIB., July 23, 1992, at 9.

[25]   See, e.g., The Ted Stevens Olympic and Amateur Sports Act [popularly known and hereinafter cited as the Amateur Sports Law], 36 U.S.C. §§ 220501–220529 (2006). Despite its name, the Amateur Sports Act not only extends to professional athletes in open international competition, but otherwise influences developments and dispute resolution in purely professional competition. It is apparent that few truly uncompensated athletes remain in major competition if one considers the creeping professionalization of sport by athletic scholarships, free training facilities, travel funding, product endorsements and prize money for medalists.

of eligibility now involve complicated issues such as those related to doping, discrimination, and nationality. The latter issues arise, for example, out of the growing practice of granting instant citizenship to foreign athletes, given their potential for producing medals in international competitions. The rules of the International Federation of Football Associations (FIFA) on nationality, as well as age limitations, of football/soccer players are endlessly controversial.

Of course, it is still essential to draw a distinction between professional athletes governed by collective bargaining or other employment contracts and non-professional/amateur athletes who are not bound by such agreements. As we shall see in later chapters, the circumstances of contracted athletes raise a complex array of very important issues outside the general framework of international sports law.

D. Doping

Doping of athletes (and horses in equestrian events) has been a particularly troublesome and frequently disputed issue under international sports law. Not long after the problem emerged full-blown in the 1980s, the IOC's Medical Commission undertook to establish a controls regime. The resulting IOC Medical Code and Drug Formulary Guide was instrumental in establishing a list of prohibited substances, testing procedures, and sanctions.[26] Later, a series of awards by CAS further refined the parameters of a strict liability rule for the presence of a prohibited substance in an athlete as well as equitable relief for suspensions from future competitions ordinarily mandated by positive test results. Still, efforts to provide a legal playing field for competition by sanctioning and excluding abusers suffered from a lack of uniformity among national regulatory systems and different sports. Now, however, WADA, assisted by constituent national organizations, supervises the application of uniform rules, sanctions, and testing procedures according to a World Anti-Doping Code, to which both states and sports organizations have subscribed.[27]

The World Anti-Doping Code relies on a process of test distribution and planning, sample collection and handling, laboratory analysis, results management, hearings, and appeals. Most importantly, the Code identifies eight violations subject to sanctions namely the presence of a prohibited substance or its metabolites or markers in an athlete's urine; the use or attempted use of a prohibited substance or a prohibited method; refusing, failing to submit to, or evading sample collection; violations of requirements regarding athlete availability for out-of-competition testing, including missed tests and failures to provide required out-of-competition information about an athlete's whereabouts; tampering or attempted tampering with any part of doping control; possession of prohibited substances and methods; trafficking in them; and administration or attempted administration of them.

---

[26] Since then, the general testing practice has been to take two samples of urine from athletes. If sample 'A' is positive, the athlete involved may appeal the finding, as a result of which sample 'B' is analyzed. If it is negative, the athlete is cleared of a testable doping violation. If sample 'B' is also positive, however, the athlete is subject to sanctions but given the opportunity to present counter-evidence in a hearing. The 'B' sample must always be carefully sealed and stored for later review.

[27] World Anti-Doping Agency, World Anti-Doping Code (2010) [hereinafter WADA Code].

The use by athletes and others of performance-enhancing substances and methods that are undetectable or difficult to detect in the laboratory further complicates efforts to ensure a level playing field in sports competition. Alternative techniques include non-analytical positive evidence of doping by athletes in the form of e-mail communications with prohibited drug distributors, canceled personal checks for payment of drugs, and other extrinsic evidence. Such circumstantial evidence is, however, controversial, as is athletic profiling to establish violations on the basis of significant changes in an athlete's prototypical physical features over time. Frontier issues of genetic splicing and replacement already merit serious attention.

UNESCO's International Convention Against Doping in Sport[28] requires States Parties to comply with the principles of the Code, to support the World Anti-Doping Agency that administers the Code, and to undertake educational programs against doping. The Code, however, is not an integral part of the Convention, nor does it create binding obligations under international law for States Parties except as specifically provided in the cooperative terms of the Convention.

IV. DISPUTE RESOLUTION

A. The Network of Administrative Decisions

The institutional complexity of international sports law, as a process, invites confusion in resolving disputes. In recent years, the confusion has been compounded by a blurring of the distinction between professional and nonprofessional (or 'amateur') athletes. Historically, each of these categories of athletes generated its own legal regime. That is changing. For example, the Olympic Movement and its constituent institutions and law, though limited to amateur competition through most of its history, increasingly has an impact on professional sports activity as well. More than ever, therefore, the overlapping authority and concurrent jurisdiction between national governing bodies and IFs such as FIFA, on the one hand, and the IOC and NOCs, on the other, requires rules of priority. The role of national courts in the process is also problematic.

Although institutional decision-making and dispute resolution within the framework of international sports law constitute more of a network of authority than a coherent hierarchy, rules of priority have nevertheless developed along the following lines:

1.   *National governing bodies.* National governing bodies (or national sports organizations) have primary responsibility to avoid and resolve both field-of-play and organizational disputes as well as to apply sanctions, ranging from field-of-play infractions during competition to eligibility violations such as those involving doping. Disagreements between athletes and their respective sports bodies are typically resolved by internal administrative review, by independent arbitration, or by a combination of these two methods. National governing bodies are generally subject to the rules of their respective IFs, with whatever variations that may be prescribed by mandatory provisions of national laws.

---

28   Note 8 *supra.*

2. *International federations.* IFs review decisions of constituent national bodies concerning a broad range of issues involving field-of-play infractions and the eligibility of individual athletes. Arbitration generally resolves disputes between IFs and national governing bodies. Jurisdictional disputes between IFs and NOCs are generally resolved by the IOC itself or by CAS. The resulting decisions have usually favored the IFs. An example is a CAS advisory opinion to subordinate NOC decisions on doping of athletes to the primary jurisdiction of the IFs. Ultimately, the rules of the Olympic Charter are supreme, but within the general process of international sports law, it is somewhat unclear when IOC decisions trump IF decisions in the absence of an authoritative determination by the IOC.

3. *National Olympic Committees.* NOCs may intervene in disputes involving participation of athletes in sanctioned competition. National laws sometimes accord NOCs exclusive jurisdiction to sanction international competition and determine the eligibility of athletes to compete. These laws, however, sometimes limit the competence of NOC rulings on specific issues such as the duration of Olympic training, selection, and competition. Disputes within the Olympic Movement involving OCOGs are normally resolved by consultation between them, the IOC, and the pertinent NOCs.

4. *The International Olympic Committee.* The IOC, on its own initiative, that of an athlete, or that of an IF, may review a broad range of decisions by NOCs. Under Rule 28 of the Olympic Charter, the IOC recognizes the 'exclusive authority' of NOCs to represent their countries in fulfilling their obligation to send athletes to sanctioned competition. But Rule 27 grants power to the IFs to establish criteria of eligibility and to assume the responsibility for technical control and direction of their respective sports. The IOC nevertheless retains authority as a final arbiter of disputes within the Olympic Movement.

B. National Courts

The strength of international sports law has been sufficient to induce national courts to recognize and enforce rules and decisions of appropriate national governing bodies and IFs. Courts in the United Kingdom, the United States, and Canada, for example, have been reluctant to find either express or implied rights of action in claims by individual athletes against national governing bodies and IFs.[29] Instead, they have deferred to the

---

[29]   As a United States federal court wrote in the case involving the skater Tonya Harding, after she had allegedly conspired to cripple a competitor prior to the selection of the United States team for the 1994 Winter Games:

> The courts should rightly hesitate before intervening in disciplinary hearings held by private associations ... Intervention is appropriate only in the most extraordinary circumstances, where the association has clearly breached its own rules, that breach will imminently result in *serious* and irreparable harm to the plaintiff, and the plaintiff has exhausted all internal remedies. Even then, injunctive relief is limited to correcting the breach of the rules. The court should not intervene in the merits of the underlying dispute.

Harding v. *U.S. Figure Skating Ass'n*, 851 F. Supp. 1476 (D. Or. 1994). Similarly, in *Cowley* v. *Heatley* (1986) T.C.R. 430, an English court famously observed that: '[s]port would be better served

process of international sports law for resolving disputes.[30] Courts are particularly reluctant to intervene in disciplinary hearings by private bodies. There are limits to this deference of authority, however, in the face of countervailing statutory rules or strong public policy, due process challenges, and protections of the ability of professional athletes to earn a livelihood. Courts will, of course, enforce labor laws and uphold the collective bargaining process that helps define the rights of many professional athletes, particularly in North America, regardless of IF or other non-governmental rules to the contrary.

C.   *Lex Sportiva* and the Court of Arbitration for Sport

The concept of a *lex sportiva* refers to a limited body of emerging law that is roughly analogous to the *lex mercatoria* or law merchant in international commercial practice and commercial arbitration. These two bodies of law have numerous similarities, particularly in their origins of general practice and their development by arbitral tribunals. They also have numerous differences, particularly as the *lex sportiva* has matured.[31]

The scope of the *lex sportiva* has been variously defined, sometimes expansively to embrace most if not all of international sports law.[32] Ordinarily, however, the term is limited to its original definition as a body of rules and principles derived from awards

---

if there was not running litigation at repeated intervals by people seeking to challenge the decisions of the regulating bodies.'

[30]   For example, in a dispute between two competitive sailors and the Canadian Yachting Association (CYA) concerning their eligibility for the 1996 Olympic Games, a Canadian court refused to review the CYA's decision, deferring instead to what it described as the CYA's reasonable construction of its rules for elimination regattas. According to the court:

> [t]he bodies which heard the appeals were experienced and knowledgeable in the sport of sailing, and fully aware of the selection process. The appeals bodies determined that the selection criteria had been met[, the deciding judge expressing] profound regret that the parties have ended up in court when one realizes that all are genuinely concerned about encouraging our best athletes to achieve their highest level of skills for themselves and their country.

McCaig & McCaig v. *Canadian Yachting Ass'n*, Case # 90-01-96624 (Q.B. Winnipeg Centre 1996).

In *Akiyama* v. *U.S. Judo Inc.*, 181 F. Supp. 2d 1179 (W.D. Wash. 2002), a United States federal court reviewed a claim of religious discrimination, on the basis that the official rules for judo matches required athletes to bow to inanimate objects such as portraits and tatami mats. Ruling against the plaintiff, the court observed that: '[a] ruling abolishing the bowing ritual in this country would have no force over international organizations who are not parties to this litigation or in international competitions such as the Olympics and World Championships.'

[31]   See generally Boris Kolev, *Lex Sportiva and Lex Mercatoria*, INT'L SPORTS L.J. 2008/1–2, at 57 (noting similarities and differences between the ancient tradition and authority of the *lex mercatoria* and the recent development of a *lex sportiva*, in their respective origins and developments); Ulrich Haas, *Die Vereinbarung von 'Rechtsregeln' in Berufungs – Schiedsverfahren vor dem Court of Arbitration for Sport*, CAUSA SPORT, 3/2007, at 271, 272; LUC SILANCE, LES SPORTS ET LE DROIT 86, 87 (1998) (noting a difference in the reception of the term between Latin-based (Romance) languages and other languages and considering the term in the context of a transnational juridical order).

[32]   See, e.g., FRANCK LATTY, LA LEX SPORTIVA: RECHERCHE SUR LE DROIT TRANSNATIONAL (2007) (drawing upon Judge Philip Jessup's concept of transnational law that blends private and public processes and rules). See generally Richard H. McLaren, *The Court of Arbitration for Sport*, Chapter 2 of this volume.

made by the Court of Arbitration for Sport (CAS), primarily, and other formal pronouncements of general practice.

CAS, which is headquartered in Lausanne, Switzerland with branches in New York and Sydney, celebrated its twenty-fifth anniversary in 2009, having arbitrated well over 700 cases. Its purpose is to provide a specialized body of experts to decide a broad range of sports-related disputes. By contrast to litigation, the advantages of CAS, like other arbitral tribunals, include confidentiality, expertise, flexibility and simplicity of procedures, speed, reduced costs, and international effectiveness of an award by CAS. Its arbitral panels, however, do not resolve technical questions involving the rules of the game, scheduling of competition, or dimensions of the playing field, for example. Instead, they generally hear three kinds of disputes that transcend field-of-play and other technical questions: disciplinary measures against athletes, other issues involving the eligibility of athletes, and commercial issues.

Either individual athletes or sports organizations can bring disputes to CAS for arbitration. In disputes between athletes and their sports organizations, the interests of the athletes receive priority. On the issue of an athlete's strict liability for doping, for example, the interests of the athlete take precedence over those of an IF if questions of fact or legal interpretation arise. More generally, CAS will always have jurisdiction to overrule IF decisions and rules in order to protect the due process of athletes, even if the IF rules declare those rules and decisions under them to be nonappealable.[33]

CAS has three divisions: ordinary arbitration, involving such issues as media rights and contracts between athletes and their agents or sponsors; appeals arbitration to review decisions by sports bodies, often addressing issues that involve sanctions against athletes and typically based on choice-of-forum clauses mandated by sports bodies between them and athletes; and ad hoc arbitration during major sports competitions such as the Olympic Games, British Commonwealth Games, and World Cups. Alternatively, the parties may also submit their dispute to mediation or an expedited procedure organized by CAS. CAS also issues advisory opinions concerning any sports-related legal questions asked by designated organizations such as the IOC and international sports federations.

According to the CAS Rules of Procedure, the parties to ordinary arbitration may choose the governing law; in the absence of such choice, Swiss law applies. The parties may also authorize the arbitration panel to decide *ex aequo et bono*. In appeals arbitration, the parties may choose the governing law, in the absence of which the arbitration panel must apply the law of the country in which the federation, association or sports-related body which has issued the challenged decision is domiciled or according to the rules of law the application of which the panel deems appropriate, in which case the panel must give reasons for its decision. In ad hoc arbitration the arbitration panel must apply the Olympic Charter and applicable regulations, general principles of law and, as with appeals arbitration, the rules of law the application of which the panel deems appropriate.

Switzerland's Federal Act on Private International Law governs CAS arbitrations to the extent that the CAS Rules do not otherwise prescribe a particular procedural rule. With a few exceptions, awards generally are not appealable to courts of law. This is so as a matter of Swiss law regardless of the actual location of a CAS hearing and award insofar

---

[33] See, e.g., *Hellenic Olympic Comm. and Kaklamanakis* v. *Int'l Sailing Fed'n*, CAS 2004/Athens ad hoc. Div./009 (Aug. 24, 2004).

as the legal seat of CAS proceedings is always deemed to be in Lausanne, Switzerland. Those awards whose appeal to the Swiss Federal Tribunal has been possible have largely failed because of the tribunal's normal deference to CAS.

CAS awards are final and binding on the parties and are enforceable internationally under the New York Convention on the Recognition and Enforcement of Foreign Arbitral Awards to the extent that it binds a state where enforcement is sought (as it usually does among nearly 150 parties to the agreement).[34] Although the awards do not constitute precedent in the sense of the common law, they provide firm guidance in future cases[35] and are gradually forming the body of law that we call *lex sportiva*.

The emerging *lex sportiva* does not address all sports-related issues, however. As already noted, issues involving field-of-play decisions, rules of the game, or other technical provisions – the so-called *lex ludica* – generally are not susceptible to formal arbitration under international sports law. Instead, such issues are subject to the non-interference rule, which will be more closely examined later in this chapter. Also, such issues as the arbitrability of a dispute, the validity of an arbitration agreement, and judicial relief from arbitral awards do not normally fall within the *lex sportiva*. Instead, these issues are subject to the applicable rules of a particular arbitral tribunal, such as the *lex arbitrii* of Swiss law in the instance of CAS. Also, arbitral pronouncements on the civil rights of athletes or on labor law, anti-trust/competition law, and other regulatory laws generally fall outside the scope of the *lex sportiva*, as do any awards that are deemed to violate mandatory domestic law or public policy (*ordre public*).

In the end, the important point is that CAS awards are indeed creating 'a unique body of law known as *lex sportiva*.'[36] Although much of the general practice is still *lex ferenda* – that is, law still in the process of formation and acceptance – *lex sportiva* rules are evolving steadily, as is the larger process of international sports law itself.[37]

---

34   *Done* June 10, 1958, 330 U.N.T.S. 3.

35   See Int'l Ass'n of Athletics Fed'n v. U.S.A. Track & Field and Jerome Young, CAS 2004/A/628 (June 28, 2004) (making it clear that although CAS awards do not form a *stare decisis*, CAS will try to come to the same conclusion on matters of law as previous panels).

36   *2009 Annual Survey: Recent Developments in Sports Law*, 20 MARQ. SPORTS L. REV. 497, 541 (2010). For a retrospective on CAS by a leading expert, see Richard H. McLaren, *Twenty-Five Years of the Court of Arbitration for Sport: A Look in the Rear-View Mirror*, 20 MARQ. SPORTS L. REV. 305 (2010); Richard H. McLaren, *The Court of Arbitration for Sport: An Independent Arena for the World's Sports Disputes*, 35 VAL. U. L. REV. 379 (2001).

37   This overview of CAS and the *lex sportiva* draws from more extensive discussion in NAFZIGER, note 1 *supra*, at 40–3, 48–61. A definitive collection of essays on CAS is THE COURT OF ARBITRATION FOR SPORT 1984–2004 (Ian Blackshaw, Robert C.R. Siekmann, and Janwillem Soek eds. 2006). See also Richard H. McLaren, *The Court of Arbitration for Sport* in Chapter 2 of this volume.

IV. THE PRINCIPLE OF FAIRNESS

A. Introduction

A core principle, perhaps *the* core principle, to inform not only the *lex sportiva*, but also the larger body of international sports law, is *fairness*.[38] This commentary considers a broad range of sports-related contexts in which legal issues of fairness arise. The many examples are by no means definitive. They are intended only to stimulate further reflection about the role of fairness in guiding the decisions of CAS and other tribunals and in more broadly addressing fundamental issues of international sports law. Let us begin with two negative examples, that is, examples of dispute resolution that in one case rejected and in the other case ignored the principle of fairness in sports activity.

1. The *Mercury Bay* case

Twenty years ago, the most famous litigation in the history of the sport of sailing was tacking in and out of United States courts. *Mercury Bay Boating Club* v. *San Diego Yacht Club*[39] concerned an interpretation of the Deed of Gift that established the America's Cup in 1851. As later amended in 1887, it has served as the foundation for sailing's premier competition, which, in the words of Deed of Gift, is to be a 'friendly competition between foreign countries.' The winning yacht club becomes the trustee of the Deed and is thereby responsible for planning and conducting the next competition. The New York Yacht Club, having won every competition since the first race in 1851, became a sort of everlasting trustee until 1983, when the Royal Perth Yacht Club of Australia won the Cup. Since then, Australian, New Zealand, American, and Swiss clubs have served as trustees of this strangely established and organized competition.[40] The competition normally takes place only every few years, based on the initiation of a challenge under the Deed of Gift. In the 2010 competition, the Golden Gate Yacht Club of San Francisco won the Cup against a Swiss-based club that had been the trustee.[41] The victorious Golden Gate Yacht Club will therefore stage the next competition.

As of 1988, the load water-line lengths of the competing boats and other terms of the competition were defined by customary practices and mutual consent provisions. In that year, however, such stability of expectations and cooperation collapsed after the Mercury

---

[38]   For an excellent commentary on the concept of fairness, particularly in its relationship to field-of-play decisions, see Klaus Vieweg, *Fairness und Sportregeln – Zur Problematik sog. Tatsachenentscheidungen im Sport,*' in G. CREZELIUS, H. HIRTE, AND K. VIEWEG (HRSG.), FESTSCHRIFT FÜR VOLKER RÖHRICHT ZUM 65, GEBURTSTAG: GESELLSCHAFTSRECHT, RECHNUNGSLEGUNG, SPORTRECHT 1255–75 (2005), translated and reprinted as Klaus Vieweg, *Fairness and Sports Rules [and] Regulations – A Contribution to the Problem of 'Field of Play' Decisions*, in SPORTS LAW IMPLEMENTATION AND THE OLYMPIC GAMES 207 (Dimitrios P. Panagiotopoulus ed. 2005) (noting that 'the 'fairness' argument has become one of the most popular, most decisive forms of argumentation:' *ibid.* at 215, and that '[t]he volume of sports law literature on fairness and fair play is immense:' *ibid.* at 217.).

[39]   557 N.E.2d 87 (1990).

[40]   On the history and legal analysis of the America's Cup, see James A.R. Nafziger, *International Sports Law: A Replay of Characteristics and Trends*, 86 AM. J. INT'L L. 489, 510 (1992).

[41]   N.Y. TIMES, Feb. 25, 2010, at D10 (reports on the victory of the high-tech BMW Oracle trimaran of the Golden Gate Yacht Club over Alinghi of the Societé Nautique de Genève).

Bay Boating Club of New Zealand challenged the San Diego Yacht Club, which was then the trustee of the Cup. Mercury Bay announced that it would compete with a boat that was nearly three times as long as the customary length. The New Zealand gambit virtually invited a radical response by the San Diego Yacht Club, which obliged by announcing that it would compete with a multi-hulled catamaran. Mercury Bay then brought a civil action in a New York court against the San Diego Yacht Club, claiming that its selection of a catamaran for the race did not comply with the Deed of Gift. The trial and appellate courts disagreed, ruling that the Deed of Gift did not preclude the San Diego Yacht Club from entering a catamaran and that the club had satisfied its fiduciary responsibilities as trustee. The court rejected the admission of extrinsic evidence, ruling strictly within the four corners of the Deed of Gift.

It is noteworthy that the courts refused to consider the fairness of the strange race. Instead, the appellate court held that:

> [t]he question of whether particular conduct is 'sporting' or 'fair' in the context of a particular sporting event … is wholly distinct from the question of whether it is legal … Questions of sportsmanship and fairness with respect to sporting contexts depend largely upon the rules of the particular sport and the experience of those knowledgeable in that sport; they are not questions suitable for judicial resolution.[42]

A strong dissenting opinion[43] argued, however, that issues of fairness are fundamental to a proper interpretation of the Deed, particularly its requirement of 'friendly competition between countries.' This view echoed the words of a dissenting opinion in the trial court that: '[t]he 1988 America's Cup races were manifestly unfair in every sense. True sportsmanship and the integrity of this great sport demands far more.'[44] After all, the original settler of the trust had emphasized that 'the governing principle of America's Cup competition is fairness.'

Surely, the dissenting opinion is correct, not only on the facts of the *Mercury Bay* case itself, but more generally. If we expect fairness from athletes and officials on the playing field, we should likewise expect that the principle would play a central role in sports-related litigation. It is surprising, however, how limited the principle seems to be in guiding the decisions of courts and other decision-makers in sports-related disputes.

2.   The example of the Chinese gymnasts

Another example of a failure to give formal effect to the core principle of fairness occurred in a controversy concerning the actual ages of Chinese women gymnasts who won medals at the 2008 Games in Beijing.[45] They were widely suspected of being underage and therefore ineligible to compete in the Games. Although the International Federation of Gymnasts (FIG) and the IOC, after investigation, retroactively confirmed their eligibility, it is noteworthy that the FIG extended its investigation to earlier Olympic

---

[42]   557 N.E.2d at 92.
[43]   557 N.E.2d at 102 (Hancock, J., dissenting).
[44]   545 N.Y.S.2d 693, 710 (Kassal, J., dissenting).
[45]   See SPORTS ILLUSTRATED, Oct. 13, 2008, at 20; Juliet Macur, *I.O.C. Is Seeking Proof of Chinese Gymnasts' Ages*, N.Y. TIMES, Aug. 23, 2008, at B13; George Vecsey, *A Hint of Doubt in Every Shiny Medal*, N.Y. TIMES, Aug. 23, 2008, at B11; *Gymnast Only 13, Xinhua Said in '07*, INT'L HERALD TRIB., Aug. 16–17, 2008, at 27.

competition. As a result, the FIG stripped a Chinese gymnast of her medal, concluding that she was only 14 years old when she received a medal during the 2000 Games, contrary to the certification of her eligibility by the Chinese.[46] It is also noteworthy that at no time in the process of review was the standard of fairness explicitly invoked, even though it is embedded in China's own sports law. Article 34 of that law speaks of 'fair competition' and 'sports morality,' forbidding organizers of sports competitions from 'resorting to deception or engaging in improper practice for selfish ends.' Article 49, in the interest of fair competition, provides that: '[v]iolations of sports etiquette and rules in athletic contests, such as fraud and deception, shall be punished by sports associations in accordance with their respective rules.'[47] Even though China's Sports Law was not in itself capable of governing the outcome of the dispute, its provision for fair competition and related ethical prescriptions clearly obligated Chinese authorities to produce credible age documentation.

3.   The definition of fairness

But what exactly is 'fairness'? We all agree that 'fair play' in competition requires athletes, coaches, and referees to be in full compliance with the rules of the game on the playing field. Beyond that, however, definitions of the principle as applied to sports have been disappointing. For example, in 2001 the federal, provincial, and territorial sports ministers of Canada issued a lengthy and elaborate declaration entitled 'Expectations for Fairness in Sport,' but it is essentially meaningless because of its failure to come to grips with the term 'fairness.'[48]

In attempting to develop a meaningful principle of fairness as a core principle of the *lex sportiva* and international sports law as a whole, we can generally rely on standard definitions. According to a leading legal dictionary, 'fair' has 'the qualities of impartiality and honesty; free from prejudice, favoritism, and self-interest. Just; equitable; even-handed; equal, as between conflicting interests.'[49] We should add two additional elements: acting in good faith and what we can call 'coherence,' embracing the values of consistency and uniformity.

For further guidance, we can turn to public international law. A leading commentary on fairness in public international law emphasizes the substantive aspect of distributive justice and the procedural aspect of right process.[50] This distinction between substantive and procedural fairness is important. Turning first to procedural fairness, as a matter of due process or natural justice, we can identify two rules: the rule against bias and the right to a fair hearing. In turn, the right to a fair hearing can be seen to involve seven requirements: prior notice of a decision, consultation and written representation,

---

[46]   Juliet Macur, *Medal of Underage Chinese Gymnast Revoked*, N.Y. TIMES, Feb. 27, 2010, at Sports.

[47]   For an English translation of this legislation, which is subject to revision or replacement, see James A.R. Nafziger and Li Wei, *China's Sports Law*, 46 AM. J. COMP. L. 453, 474 (1998).

[48]   Federal-Provincial-Territorial Sports Ministers, Declaration: Expectations for Fairness in Sport, Aug. 10, 2001 (Canada).

[49]   BLACK'S LAW DICTIONARY 633 (8th ed. 2004). See also the historical development of the term, particularly its relationship to 'fair play,' in Vieweg, note 38 *supra*, at 216.

[50]   See THOMAS M. FRANCK, FAIRNESS IN INTERNATIONAL LAW AND INSTITUTIONS 7 (1995).

adequate notice of applicable sanctions, an oral hearing, a right to call and cross-examine witnesses, an opportunity for legal representation, and a reasoned decision.[51]

A definition of substantive fairness, in the sense of distributive justice, is more elusive. Of course, in some statutory contexts, such as that of labor and employment law governing claims of unfair dismissal, the principle of fairness is well elaborated in its application to sports.[52] But otherwise the meaning of fairness is somewhat less clear, varying as it does according to the issue. Moreover, many issues of fairness cannot be pigeon-holed as either 'procedural' or 'substantive,' particularly those involving organizational and institutional structures. Often issues are both procedural and substantive, such as in the resolution of disputes arising out of claims of discrimination. In any event, it will suffice for present purposes, within the framework of international sports law, simply to highlight the qualities of impartiality, equity, good faith, and coherence in the sense of consistency and uniformity.

4. Fairness in three contexts

Despite the obvious indeterminacy of the standard definition of fairness, it is worthwhile to consider its applicability in three contexts of international sports law: first, organizational and institutional structures; second, the eligibility of athletes and the conduct of competition; and third, dispute resolution. These three contexts roughly correspond, respectively, to the time framework before competition, during competition, and after competition.

Sometimes a determination of the appropriate context for applying the principle of fairness will in itself be significant. For example, the Lisbon Treaty of 2009[53] specifies the role of the European Union (EU) in sports for the first time in an EU treaty. Article 165 requires the EU to 'contribute to the promotion of European sporting issues, while taking account of the specific nature of sport, its structures based on voluntary activity and its social and educational function ... by promoting *fairness* and openness in sporting competitions'[54] and in other ways. It is unclear, however, whether this explicit mandate of fairness applies only to the field of play – that is, to actual competition, as a literal reading of the phrase would suggest. If so, then the EU mandate of fairness would largely lie beyond the competence of courts except to review issues involving governmental enforcement of the mandate. Or does the mandate apply more broadly to matters beyond field of play that impinge on sports competition but do not occur there – for example, to the organizational structure of the sports industry in ensuring a fair distribution of revenue, financial solidarity and stability, an acceptable nationality profile of clubs, and a general and competitive balance among sports clubs?[55] This is a likely but not obvious interpretation of Article 165. In any event, if the European Court of Justice and other EU authority expect to apply Article 165 properly, they will first need to explain its contextual scope.

---

[51]   See Ian Blackshaw, *The Rules of Natural Justice: What Are They and Why Are They Important in Sports Disciplinary Cases?*, INT'L SPORTS L.J., 2009/1–2, at 134.
[52]   See, e.g., SIMON GARDINER *ET AL.*, SPORTS LAW 580 (2d ed. 2001).
[53]   Treaty of Lisbon, note 15 *supra*.
[54]   *Ibid.* art. 165 (emphasis added).
[55]   See Stephen Weatherill, *Fairness, Openness and the Specific Nature of Sport: Does the Lisbon Treaty Change EU Sports Law?*, paper prepared for presentation at the International Conference on

B.   Fairness in Organizational and Institution Structures

1.   Match-fixing: corrupt betting and playing-field activity

Match-fixing is a serious problem. Corrupt sports betting and gambling activity by athletes, coaches, and other stakeholders in sports, particularly on the Internet, poses a serious threat to the fairness of sports competition and therefore to its very structure.[56] In addition, corrupt playing by athletes and the so-called 'black whistles' of referees have been all too common recently in the lesser leagues of European football/soccer. Sumo wrestlers in Japan have also been the subject of match-fixing controversy. In response to the general problem of corruption in and around the sports arena, the International Olympic Committee (IOC), as a leading stakeholder in the supervision of international sports law, has expanded its initiatives to detect and penalize match-fixing. It has employed International Sports Monitoring, a Swiss corporation, to monitor and track betting rings around the world. This effort involves the cooperation of some 400–450 odds-makers, betting firms, and lotteries, and will also involve an educational program for athletes and officials.[57]

2.   Selection of sports and sports events

A second problem of organizational and institutional fairness is a lack of coherent, impartial criteria for adding or dropping Olympic sports and sports events other basic rules of a general process. According to the Olympic Charter, each Session, as the IOC's Supreme Organ constituted as a general meeting, may add a limited number of sports to a 'core' list of sports in the Olympic program, so long as it does not exceed a maximum number of sports.[58] The Session may also drop sports from the core list. In 2007, the Olympic Charter was amended to eliminate more precise rules that were based on widespread practice and geographical representation on multiple continents. The unfortunate trend has therefore been to vest the IOC with even more discretion than it already enjoyed. The selection of sports and sports events for the Olympic program may seem

---

Lex Sportiva, Sept. 22, 2010, Universitas Pelita Harapan, Tangerang, Indonesia; Union of European Football Associations (UEFA) Club Licensing and Financial Fair Play Regulations (2010) (mandating, e.g., a 'break-even requirement on financial fair play,' according to which a club's relevant expenses must align with its 'relevant income' within stipulated margins in order to accomplish several purposes such as to better ensure that clubs are in a position to settle their liabilities with players and that they generally benefit football on a basis of fairness to other football clubs). See also European Parliament, Directorate General for Internal Policies, Policy Dep't B: Structural and Cohesion Policies, LISBON TREATY AND EU SPORTS POLICY STUDY, Sept. 6, 2010, at 37 (observing that art. 165 may discourage nationality discrimination in amateur sport).

[56]   See DECLAN HILL, THE FIX: SOCCER AND ORGANIZED CRIME (2008); see also Declan Hill, *The Usual Suspects: Fixers' Actions and FIFA's Inaction*, N.Y. TIMES, Dec. 6, 2009, at Sports 9; Rob Hughes, *Soccer Found Riddled with Corruption in Europe*, INT'L HERALD TRIB., Nov. 21–22, 2009, at 1; Hugh McIlvanney, *Video Refs Can Catch the Cheats*, SUNDAY TIMES, Nov. 22, 2009, at 18; Rory Smith, *Premier League Must Not Be Complacent on Match-Fixing, Expert Warns*, SUNDAY TELEGRAPH, Nov. 22, 2009, at 10.

[57]   See John Leicester, *IOC Sets Up System to Watch for Illegal Betting*, PITTSBURGH POST-GAZETTE, Oct. 4, 2009, at Sports; *IOC to Watch for Irregular Betting at Olympics Via a New Swiss-Based Company*, http://www.cbsnews.com/stories/2009/10/04/ap/sportline/main536.

[58]   These guidelines are established under OLYMPIC CHARTER Rule 46 (2007) and its bye-laws.

rather trivial, but it is a critical process, given the centrality and influence of Olympic sports, its nearly universal allure, and its specific role in shaping the aspirations of young people.

In 2004, the IOC established the Olympic Programme Commission to conduct systematic evaluations of each Olympic program, including recommendations to the IOC Executive Board and ultimately to the IOC itself for the inclusion and exclusion of particular sports and events within particular sports.[59] Supposedly, the Commission applies seven criteria: the history and tradition of a particular sport, its universality, its popularity, its general image, its implications for the health of participating athletes, the development of the sport's international federation, and the costs of staging a competition in the sport. In each instance, these criteria are to be considered in assessing the value that a particular sport or event in a sport may add to global competition. In practice, however, the process has proven to be arbitrary and shaped by financial considerations. As it turns out, the value added is expressed more in commercial than sporting terms.

An example of how unsatisfactory the selection process remains is the preliminary decision of the IOC, based on the International Cycling Union's recommendation, to eliminate from future Games cycling's signature endurance race of individual pursuit. The IOC President Jacques Rogge explained the decision in terms of a general shift from endurance events to sprint events. He hinted at the reason for the decision when he said it would be 'more appealing.'[60] Pat McQuaid, the President of the International Cycling Union, put it more candidly when he explained that individual pursuit events do not come across well on television. 'We have to think about what would be attractive to viewers.'[61]

Of course, the latest additions to the Olympic roster of mixed doubles in tennis, women's boxing, seven-a-side rugby, and golf are suitable. For example, insofar as mixed-gender events such as in tennis have come of age, adding women's boxing is only fair. But the inclusion of such sports as baseball and softball has also been suitable since they were added as Olympic sports in 1994. And yet they will be eliminated after the 2012 Games in London, having been in the Olympic program for less than 20 years after failing to be included in the 2012 Games in London or to make a comeback in the 2016 Games scheduled for Rio de Janeiro. Extraneous issues and the extraordinarily broad discretion that the revised Olympic Charter vests in the IOC seem to have influenced this result. As to baseball, the issues included the failure of organized baseball to ensure the participation of its best players (a problem shared with other sports in the Olympic program) and the failure of Major League Baseball (MLB) effectively to combat doping before 2002. On the other hand, softball, a women's sport in the program, seemed to suffer from a mistaken guilt by association with baseball, a men's sport. Why single out these two sports for exclusion? After all, baseball, at least, is a national pastime in such countries as the Dominican Republic, Nicaragua, Panama, Venezuela, Cuba, Taiwan, and Japan, and is a dominant sport in Mexico, the United States, Canada, Micronesia, and elsewhere.

---

[59]   See INTERNATIONAL OLYMPIC COMMITTEE, EVALUATION CRITERIA FOR SPORTS AND DISCIPLINES, Aug. 11, 2004 (658 kb).

[60]   SPORTS NEWS, Dec. 10, 2009.

[61]   Juliet Macur, *I.O.C. May Eliminate Phinney's Best Event*, N.Y. TIMES, Dec. 10, 2009, at Sports.

This is not to argue for or against particular sports and events, only for a coherent standard that will focus on the interests of the athletes themselves and, as much as possible, will resist the siren call of money and the media. One possible criterion for selection, among others, might be whether a particular competition such as the Olympics offers the pinnacle or signature championship in a particular sport. That certainly is not a criterion today. For example, both of the two most recent additions to the Olympic program, rugby and golf, have their own pinnacle or signature championship – the Opens in golf and the World Cup in rugby. Another criterion for selection might be the number of countries in which a particular sport is truly a national pastime or close to it. Above all, the selection of particular sports and events must be undertaken with greater integrity and transparency than exists today. We need to maintain the specificity or special nature of sport as distinct from pure entertainment.

3. The allocation of financial and other resources among different sports

A recent study surveyed presidents and executive directors of national sports bodies concerning their perceptions about the allocation of resources among different sports.[62] Although the respondents identified a 'need to be competitively successful' as the fairest principle for resource allocation, they perceived that 'equity based on medals won' was the most likely principle in practice, to the effect that 'the rich get richer' and sports such as team handball, archery, and curling suffer. The Chinese Olympic Committee achieved success in Beijing by targeting lower-visibility sports for long-range development, essentially on the principle of their comparative advantage and thus potential for competitive success. Whether that approach is taken or not, an over-allocation of resources on winning medals may run contrary to the broader vision of international sports law as a vehicle for promoting and encouraging physical fitness, public participation in sports, and athletic development.

The effort to allocate resources properly is seriously challenged and complicated, of course, by available funding for minor sports as well as pressures from the media and the public at large to emphasize the major or big-ticket sports. On the positive side, the experience at the domestic level indicates that as the major sports generate surplus revenue, integrated systems of sports such as among colleges and universities in the United States, have incentives to reallocate the surplus revenue for the development of minor sports.[63]

4. Leadership in organizing competition

Yet another fairness issue is the European dominance of the leadership of international sports federations, the IOC, the International Council of Arbitration for Sport, and CAS. Although some progress has been made in recent years to diversity leadership, *plus ça change, plus cést la même chose.*

---

[62] Stephen W. Dittmore *et al.*, Examining Fairness Perceptions of Financial Allocation in U.S. Olympic Sport (2009).

[63] See, e.g., Joe Drape and Katie Thomas, *As Athletic Directors Compete, Big Money Flows to All Sports*, N.Y. TIMES, Sept. 3, 2010, at A1 (reporting on reallocation of revenue of major sports to a broad range of minor sports by college and university sports directors competing for greater reputation and status of their comprehensive sports programs within the National Collegiate Athletic Association (NCAA)).

Of the IOC's 106 members, 46 (43 percent) are European, and all but one of the IOC presidents since 1894, in the run-up to the first Olympic Games, have been European. In CAS, it is much the same: of 270 members, 125 (46 percent) are European. In the International Council of Arbitration for Sport, of 19 current members, nine (47 percent) are European, and four of the five members (80 percent) of the Council's governing board are European.[64] What is more, the leadership of the IFs is also European-dominated.[65]

This is not at all to suggest that the European-dominated leadership of international sports organizations is monolithic in its decision-making, let alone corrupt, but only to suggest that the leadership is unrepresentative, not always geographically impartial in decision-making, and very slow to diversify. Perhaps as importantly, it just looks bad: the governance of international sports still looks like and operates as a disproportionately European network of old boys and a few girls.

C.   Fairness in Determinations of Eligibility and in the Conduct of Competition

1.   Doping issues

It is elementary that sports bodies must ensure both procedural and substantive fairness in determining the eligibility of athletes for competition. CAS has made that clear.[66]

Doping has been a particularly troublesome threat to eligibility. Sanctions for violations of anti-doping rules may result in both withdrawal of medals from athletes and suspensions of their eligibility. More broadly, it has been a persistent threat to an even playing field for all athletes and to overall fairness in sport. Trying to combat this threat is enormously challenging, however. One problem involves rapid advancements in pharmaceutical and genetic technology. Another concerns the due process and the rights of athletes.[67] Four of the most important current issues of fairness are, first, the 'whereabouts' rule; second, the use of circumstantial evidence against athletes; third, the standard of strict liability; and fourth, a piggyback sanction that enables the IOC to suspend the eligibility of athletes beyond the limits of sanctions under the World Anti-Doping Agency (WADA) Code,[68] even though it is the core of anti-doping efforts within the Olympic Movement. Let us briefly look at each of these issues.

The whereabouts rule requires that world-class athletes generally inform their sports organizations of their whereabouts at all times throughout the year in order to facilitate out-of-competition testing for performance-enhancing drugs or masking agents. Multiple failures to do so when such testing has been scheduled can result in suspension from eligibility for competition. The privacy rights of athletes implicated by this rule are, of

---

[64]   See http://www.tas-cas.org/arbitrators-genlist; http://www.tas-cas.org/icas-members (last visited Sept. 8, 2010).

[65]   See International Olympic Committee, OLYMPIC MOVEMENT DIRECTORY, passim (2010).

[66]   See, e.g., *Boxing Australia* v. *AIBA*, CAS 08/A/1455 (April 16, 2008) (insisting that international sports federations must announce all final qualifications for competition prospectively at a reasonably early stage of the qualification process).

[67]   See, e.g., Robyn R. Goldstein, *An American in Paris: The Legal Framework of International Sport and the Implications of the World Anti-Doping Code on [sic] Accused Athletes*, 7 VA. SPORTS & ENT. L.J. 149 (2007).

[68]   WADA Code, note 27 *supra*.

course, very serious and open to court challenge. Do we really want to establish a sort of police state in sports?[69] NO

Circumstantial evidence of doping, such as e-mail messaging and receipts for payments of drugs, in lieu of laboratory evidence of doping, is also controversial.[70] Is it fair? The answer may be 'yes,' in fairness to all athletes, by creating a level playing field. But we may need a more equitable and stable standard of proof than the current one of 'comfortable satisfaction.' As to the third issue – strict liability – the WADA Code establishes health, fairness, and equality as goals. On that basis, athletes, coaches, and other stakeholders in sports charged with violations of the Code must overcome an evidentiary presumption of strict liability regardless of the circumstances. The standard for burden of proof is: 'the comfortable satisfaction of the hearing body, bearing in mind the seriousness of the allegation which is made. This standard of proof in all cases is greater than a mere balance of probability but less than proof beyond a reasonable doubt.'[71] Is that standard rigorous enough? Is its application sufficiently coherent? In other words, is it equitable?

In *Quigley* v. *Int'l Shooting Union,*[72] CAS articulated the rationale for the strict liability standard as follows:

It is true that a strict liability test is likely in some sense to be unfair in an individual case, such as that of Quigley, where the athlete may have taken medication as the result of mislabeling or faulty advice for which he or she is not responsible – particularly in the circumstance of sudden illness in a foreign country. But it is also in some sense unfair for an athlete to get food poisoning on the eve of an important competition … Just as the competition will not be postponed to await the athlete's recovery, so the prohibition of banned substances will not be lifted in recognition of its accidental absorption. The vicissitudes of competition, like those of life generally, may create many types of unfairness, whether by accident or the negligence of unaccountable persons, which the law cannot repair.

Furthermore, it appears to be a laudable policy objective not to repair an accidental unfairness to an individual by creating an intentional unfairness to the whole body of other competitors. This is what would happen if banned performance-enhancing substances were tolerated when absorbed inadvertently. Moreover, it is likely that even intentional abuse would in many cases escape sanction for lack of proof of guilty intent. And it is certain that a requirement of intent would invite costly litigation that may well cripple federations – particularly those run on modest budgets – in their fight against doping.

The last specific issue of fairness in anti-doping efforts involves the piggyback sanction. With reference to the Olympic Charter's Rules 19 (3.10) and 45, this ruling of the IOC Executive Board provides that:

Any person who has been sanctioned with a suspension of more than six months by any anti-doping organization for any violation of any anti-doping regulations may not participate, in any capacity, in the next edition of the Games of the Olympiad and of the Olympic Winter Games following the date of expiry of such suspension.

---

[69] See, e.g., James Halt, *Where Is the Privacy in WADA's 'Whereabouts' Rule?*, 20 MARQ. SPORTS L. REV. 267 (2009).

[70] See James A.R. Nafziger, *Circumstantial Evidence of Doping: BALCO and Beyond*, 16 MARQ. SPORTS L. REV. 45 (2005).

[71] WADA Code, note 27 *supra*, arts. 2.1 (strict liability basis), 3.1 (burden of proof).

[72] CAS 94/129, 193.

Can this piggyback sanction be justified, given the understanding that the WADA Code provides a complete regime of doping control, including sanctions for violating the Code? Fortunately, a panel of the American Arbitration Association, in the case of the swimmer Jessica Hardy, noted the special precautions she took in order to avoid violating anti-doping rules as well as the absence of significant fault or negligence on her part, and therefore reduced a two-year suspension of her eligibility to one year. As to the piggyback rule, the panel ruled that its application to bar Hardy from Olympic competition would violate the fundamental principle of proportionality.[73] CAS dismissed WADA's appeal of this arbitral award, concluding that the one-year suspension was proportionate to the offense. As a matter of procedural fairness, CAS reiterated that when the measure of a sanction is at issue, it will overturn a disciplinary body of a sports federation in the exercise of its discretion only when the sanction is evidently and grossly proportionate to the offense.[74]

2.   Discrimination

a.   *The case of Oscar Pistorius*   Three prominent issues of discrimination in the global sports arena are instructive. The first issue involves Oscar Pistorius, a South African runner born without fibulae, who has worn prosthetic legs since he was 11 months old. The International Amateur Athletic Federation (IAAF) ruled, however, that competitive running on his 'cheetah' legs, which contain springs, violates IAAF rules. When Pistorius appealed this decision to CAS, the tribunal, after reviewing the results of scientific testing and analysis, concluded that he had no 'overall net-advantage' or metabolic advantage over his competitors.[75]

But what is the test of fairness, given what was acknowledged to be a substantial measure of indeterminacy in the scientific analysis? On the one hand, the 'cheetah' legs would seem to be as fair as oxygen tents, ice-filled vests for runners before a race to cool their core temperatures, and other technology employed by runners. Also, expensive medical procedures unavailable or unaffordable in much of the world, such as lasik eye surgery for golfers, would seem to be no less discriminatory than spring-assisted prosthetic legs. On the other hand, international sports federations have properly taken measures to avoid too much reliance by athletes on technology and facilitative wearing apparel. For example, FINA, the international swimming federation, now bans a large variety of body suits that were acceptable for a few experimental years, on the basis that the suits inordinately aid speed, buoyancy, and endurance, in violation of FINA's standards.[76] In doing so, FINA acted in part for reasons of fairness to earlier athletes who had not benefited from the body suits.

In the end, we are left wondering: what sports equipment, clothing, and training technology is fair and what is unfair? Clearly, international sports federations need to take the principle of fairness more seriously and interpret it more precisely.

---

[73]   *U.S. Anti-Doping Agency* v. *Hardy*, Am. Arb. Ass'n, AAA No. 77-190-00288-08 (May 2, 2009).

[74]   *World Anti-Doping Agency* v. *Hardy*, CAS 08/A/1870 (May 21, 2010).

[75]   *Pistorius* v. *IAAF*, CAS 2008/A/1480.

[76]   See *Record-setting Swimsuits Fail to Win FINA's Approval*, GLOBAL TIMES, May 21, 2009, at 22.

b.   The case of Caster Semenya   During the 2009 world championships in track and field, laboratory testing raised questions about the gender of South African runner Caster Semenya. The questions became front-page features when Semenya easily won the women's 800-meter race and the IAAF failed to protect the still-inconclusive laboratory results. Eventually, the IAAF concluded that Semenya had been eligible for the women's event, but questions of both procedural and substantive fairness remained.[77] Why had the IAAF allowed inconclusive test results to be leaked to the media? Why had Semenya not been granted a medically supervised, therapeutic-use exemption to enable her to boost her androgen level and suppress her testosterone level, from which both women and men athletes have benefited? Should naturally mixed-gender athletes be allowed to compete in their choice of either men's or women's events?

c.   The case of the women ski-jumpers   Finally, let us consider an issue of gender equality. Several world-class women ski-jumpers brought a civil action in the courts of British Columbia, Canada, claiming that the organizing committee of the 2010 Winter Games in Vancouver had violated Canada's Charter of Rights and Freedoms. Their claim was based on the Vancouver Olympic Committee's routine implementation of an IOC decision to bar women ski-jumpers from the Winter Games. In reaching a final judgment, the British Columbia Court of Appeal[78] first upheld findings of the provincial Supreme Court[79] that the gender-based bar to participation was, indeed, discriminatory; that the organizing committee's planning, organizing, financing, and staging of the 2010 Games was tantamount to a governmental activity under a Canadian constitutional test of an ascribed activity; and that the organizing committee was therefore subject to the anti-discrimination provisions of Canada's human rights Charter in making all local arrangements within its control for the Winter Games.

The courts held, however, that the organizing committee, in its contractual relationship with the IOC, could not control the selection of sports or sports events in the program; it therefore had no discretion to allow women's ski-jumping. The critical decision-maker was a non-party to the action, namely the IOC, to which the Charter did not apply. The class action brought by the women ski-jumpers therefore failed. Although the decision is technically reasonable in the context of a conflict between national and international authority and fully in conformity with the authority vested in the IOC under international sports law, it seems reasonable to ask whether the outcome was fair.

D.   Fairness in Dispute Resolution

The gold standard in resolving sports-related disputes has been set by CAS. The greatest value of the tribunal is one of ensuring fairness in terms of even-handedness, impartiality,

---

[77]   For an account of the controversy after its conclusion, see Robert Mackey, *South Africa Says Gender Controversy Is Over*, THE LEDE (N.Y. TIMES News Blog), Nov. 19, 2009. For discussion of the issues and policy options, including therapeutic use exemptions, see Alice Dreger, *Seeking Simple Rules in Complex Gender Realities*, N.Y. TIMES, Oct. 25, 2009, at Sports 8; see also Alice Dreger, *Swifter, Higher, Stronger? Science Adds a Variable,* N.Y. TIMES, Sept. 13, 2009, at 10. On gender-testing of athletes, see Jennifer Finney Boylan, *The XY Games*, N.Y. TIMES, Aug. 3, 2008, at 10.

[78]   *Sagen* v. *Vancouver Organizing Committee* [2009] B.C.C.A. 522.

[79]   *Sagen* v. *Vancouver Organizing Committee* [2009] B.C.J. 1393.

acting in good faith, and coherence. As a matter of distributive justice, it has often applied equitable doctrines such as the *lex mitior*. According to that doctrine, if newly applied sanctions against an athlete such as under the WADA Code are less severe than those in effect at the time of an offense, the new sanctions must be applied.[80] CAS panels have also contributed to coherence as an element of fairness by turning to the tribunal's prior awards for guidance. CAS has been at its best when, for example, it has taken fully into account its past awards and those of national tribunals to evaluate the fairness, on a comparative basis of equality, of a proposed sanction against an athlete.[81] As a matter of procedural justice, CAS has insisted that international sports federations provide for an appeals jury or some equivalent to review decisions involving issues of compliance with its rules.[82] Also, CAS has taken pains to avoid bias in dispute resolution. For example, in remitting issues for further fact-finding and other determination by sports bodies, CAS has insisted on reconstitution of decision-making panels and tribunals.[83]

Because CAS is an arbitral body, its decisions have no legal compulsion as precedent although they do provide firm guidance for future cases as part of an emerging *lex sportiva*. Even so, the gradual accretion of awards does not ensure consistency, an element of fairness, within the larger framework of international sports law. For example, although CAS itself has been careful to follow precedent in making decisions about reallocating Olympic medals after a medal winner has had to forfeit a medal, the IOC has not always followed CAS precedent. In 2009 the IOC decided not to award a gold medal to silver medalist Katrina Thanou of Greece that the sprinter Marion Jones had won at the 2000 Games in Sydney but had had to forfeit. The IOC's decision was based on Thanou's own disqualification from the 2004 Games in Athens. This rationale did not follow CAS precedent that had limited such a denial of a forfeited medal to only those athletes who had tested positive in the *same* Games.[84]

1.   THE NON-INTERFERENCE RULE   It has been difficult for CAS and other decision-makers to draw a sharp line between their normal competence to hear a sports-related dispute and the well-established rule of non-interference. As noted earlier, this rule significantly limits judicial or arbitral review of claims concerning breaches of game rules and field-of-play decisions. Such claims are left to a *lex ludica* beyond the scope of international sports law in the strict sense of the term 'law.'[85]

---

[80]   See *United States Anti-Doping Agency* v. *Brunemann*, Am. Arb. Ass'n/N. Am. CAS Panel, AAA No. 77–190-E-00447–08 JENF (Jan. 26, 2009) (noting that 'this doctrine is well-established *in lex sportiva* through many cases arising in several different sports,' and citing numerous previous decisions applying *lex mitior*).

[81]   *Brunemann*, note 80 *supra* (comparing a swimmer's negligent ingestion of a banned substance to the negligence of other athletes).

[82]   See, e.g., *SNOC* v. *FILA*, CAS, Ad Hoc Div. OG 08/007 (Aug. 23, 2008).

[83]   See, e.g., *Michael* v. *Australian Canoeing*, CAS 08/A/1549 (June 4, 2008).

[84]   See *A., B., C., D., & E.* v. *IOC*, CAS 2002/A/389, 390, 391, 392, & 393, and *COC & Scott* v. *IOC*, CAS 2002/A/372. On the reallocation of the medals initially claimed by Marion Jones, see Lynn Zinser, *Jones's Gold in 100 Meters Won't Go to Greek Sprinter*, N.Y. TIMES, Dec. 10, 2009, at B17.

[85]   Because the *lex ludica* refers to matters that are normally free of legal control, the '*lex*' is law only in a very loose sense of the word. For example, a bad call by a referee, though subject to the *lex ludica*, with possible private sanctions against the referee, is generally exempt from formal legal

In the interest of finality, the non-interference rule essentially represents a compromise between pure justice and the exigencies of fast-moving events organized and supervised by sports bodies. At the international level CAS has repeatedly confirmed that the technical rules of each sport, breaches of them by athletes, and field-of-play decisions are shielded from arbitral or judicial scrutiny unless they are malicious, in bad faith, or arbitrary. One other exception to the non-interference rule permits a nullification of post-event sanctions against athletes, even those that have been imposed because of field-of-play conduct, that appear to be grossly excessive or manifestly unfair. Otherwise, as an award of CAS made clear, athletes are entitled to 'honest "field-of-play" decisions, not necessarily correct ones.'[86] Three examples of the non-interference rule are noteworthy in disclosing problems that the rule may create but that can be corrected.

A first example, unrelated to CAS, is from organized baseball (MLB) in North America. Earlier this year, in what was called MLB's 'worst call, ever,'[87] an umpire's huge error denied pitcher Armando Galarrago of the Detroit (Michigan) Tigers a rare perfect game. After the game, when video replay confirmed the error, the umpire apologized profusely, but nothing could be done about it. That is because during a game MLB Rule 9.02(a) prohibits teams from questioning judgment decisions, and Rule 9.02(c) provides that '[n]o umpire shall criticize, seek to reverse, or interfere with another unless asked to do so by the umpire making it.'[88] The only official consolation for Galarrago, who himself was utterly gracious about the incident, came in the form of a proclamation by the governor of Michigan that he had, indeed, pitched a perfect game.[89] Although MLB's use of electronic replay is currently limited to disputed home-runs, the use of electronic replays will inevitably expand beyond home-run disputes. Until that happens, however, imperfect umpires will continue to be 'as much a part of this sport as imperfect fielders who muff a pop fly or imperfect runners who neglect to touch a base.'[90]

Another case in point involved the gold medal in men's gymnastics at the 2004 Olympic Games in Athens. A CAS decision confirmed the award of the medal to the American Paul Hamm despite a patent error in judging that, had it not occurred, would have given the gold medal to a Korean, Yang Tae Young, and relegated Hamm to a silver medal.

---

challenge. The *lex ludica* may be of true legal concern only when the rules of the game, or applications of them, violate established rules of tort or criminal law – e.g., in the unlikely event that the rules of the game actually encourage violence on the playing field – or, if rectification is possible after a controverted event, it can be shown, as another example, that a referee's decision was the product of a bribe. See Ken Foster, Lex Sportiva *and* Lex Ludica: *The Court of Arbitration for Sport's Jurisprudence*, in THE COURT OF ARBITRATION FOR SPORT 1984–2004, at 421 (Ian S. Blackshaw, Robert C.R. Siekmann and Janwillem Soek eds 2006) (noting that the *lex ludica* also refers to the 'sporting spirit' and covers ethical principles 'that should be followed by sports persons.' *Ibid.*).

[86]   Yang Tae Young, note 5 *supra* and text accompanying note 91 *infra* (refusing to overrule a field-of-play decision for failure to raise a timely objection). See also *Neth. Antilles Olympic Comm. v. IAAF*, CAS 2008/A/1641 (Mar. 6, 2009) (also refusing to overturn field-of-play decision).

[87]   See George Vecsey, *Worst Call Ever? Sure. Kill the Umpires? Never.*, N.Y. TIMES, June 4, 2010, at 1; see also Micheline Maynard, *Good Sportsmanship and a Lot of Good Will*, N.Y. TIMES, June 4, 2010, at B9; Alan Schwarz, *Replay Gets Another Look After a Gaffe Seen by All*, N.Y. TIMES, June 4, 2010, at B9.

[88]   Major League Baseball, Rule 9.02(a), (c) (2010).

[89]   Maynard, note 87 *supra*, at B11.

[90]   Vecsey, note 87 *supra*.

Although the technical basis of the award was the failure of the Korean Olympic Committee to raise a formal objection in a timely manner, the suspension of the judges by the International Gymnastics Federation (FIG) underscored the importance of their error. It was on this occasion that the tribunal also observed that field-of-play decisions must be honest but not necessarily correct.[91]

We should reflect further on the scope of this dictum as a matter of fairness.[92] In the football/soccer match between France and Ireland to fill the last qualifying slot for the 2010 World Cup, should FIFA have applied the non-interference rule despite the clear evidence of French team member Thierry Henry's hand all in violation of the rules?[93] Although at the time of the incident FIFA applied the rule strictly, it evidently has had some doubts since the 2010 World Cup. Although FIFA has continued to reject the immediate use of goal-line technology, it agreed after the 2010 World Cup to consider adding two goal judges, one at each end of the field, a practice that is already employed by the Europa League.[94] FIFA also holds open the possibility of installing goal-line technology before the 2014 World Cup.[95]

2.   THE TAINT (AGAIN) OF MONEY   A final example of an issue of fairness involves what was described as Formula One motor racing's 'worst scandal.'[96] It began when a member of the Renault team in the 2008 Grand Prix in Singapore[97] deliberately crashed his vehicle in a way that enabled a teammate to maneuver through the crash scene to victory. When the matter came before the International Automobile Federation (FIA), its disciplinary tribunal not surprisingly described the crash as one of 'unparalleled severity [that] not only compromised the integrity of the sport but also endangered the lives of spectators, officials and other competitors.' A severe penalty was therefore expected, including probable expulsion of Renault from Formula One racing. After all, the same tribunal had recently imposed a $100 million fine on the McLaren Mercedes Formula One team when it admitted stealing secret technical documents from its rival, Ferrari.

In the *Renault* case, however, the tribunal simply accepted Renault's apology for the deliberate crash, its offer to pay the costs of FIA's investigation, and its willingness to make other incidental contributions. The tribunal imposed no fine, however, and suspended its 2-year disqualification of Renault, saying that it would 'only activate this disqualification if the Renault F1 team is found guilty of a comparable breach in this

---

[91]   CAS 2004/A/704, notes 5 *supra*, at 86; Vieweg, note 38 *supra*, at 208.

[92]   See Vieweg, note 38 *supra*, at 224 (concluding that despite the disadvantages of interference in field-of-play decisions, '[f]airness should be accorded precedence!').

[93]   *Despite Uproar, FIFA Rejects Irish Call for Replay*, INT'L HERALD TRIB. , Nov. 21–22, 2009, at 8; Peter Berlin, *Irish Blood Up After the French Hand Ball*, INT'L HERALD TRIB., Nov. 20, 2009, at 12; Ian Hawkey, *Fallen Idol*, THE SUNDAY TIMES, Nov. 22, 2009, at 11.

[94]   See Jeff Z. Klein, *FIFA May Add Extra Officials*, N.Y. TIMES, June 29, 2010, at B11.

[95]   See *Referee System Faces Changes in 2014*, CHINA DAILY, July 10–11, 2010, at 7.

[96]   John F. Burns, *Renault Team Escapes Expulsion for Fixing Race*, N.Y. TIMES, Sept. 22, 2009, at B16. The quoted material in the paragraphs that immediately follow in the text is taken from this article.

[97]   This annual Grand Prix is one of five 'flyaways' (races outside Europe) that complete the Formula One season and is perhaps the most demanding of the flyaways. See Brad Spurgeon, *Closing of Formula One Season Is Race Around the World*, N.Y. TIMES, Sept. 26, 2010, at Sports 9; Javier Espinoza, *Formula 1 Is Racing to Bridge a Gap with Fans*, ASIAN WALL ST. J., Sept. 24–26, 2010, at 15.

time.' FIA President Max Mosely went so far as to assert that it would be wrong to impose an immediate penalty insofar as Renault had demonstrated that it had no moral responsibility for the crash. How can that be? What explains FIA's charitable attitude toward Renault? Quite simply, money is the explanation. More precisely, the earlier withdrawal of Honda and BMW from Formula One racing, this 'vast money-making machine' as it is known, had endangered the survival of Formula One racing or at least its capacity to maintain its customary level of financial support and media attention. Formula One racing therefore needed Renault more than it seemingly needed to punish Renault. Is that a fair basis for distinguishing the pseudo-sanction against the Renault team from the $100 million award against the Mercedes team? At the level of the athletes themselves, is a mere rap on Renault's knuckles fair to the competing drivers and teams in a Grand Prix race?

VI. CONCLUSION

The globalization of sports has been nurtured by the modern Olympic Movement, facilitated by communications technology, fueled by high-profile professional athletes and commercial interests, and challenged by difficult problems, such as the doping of athletes. International sports law, still in its youth, is growing along discernible lines of authority and dispute resolution such as the *lex sportiva* formed primarily by CAS awards.

The most prominent issues within the global sports arena in the immediate future are apt to include, roughly in general order of importance: (1) the development of effective prevention and control of doping; (2) the expanded role of international marketing, broadcast media, and other corporate influence; (3) the full merger of the separate legal regimes pertaining, respectively, to amateurs and professionals; (4) the further blurring of the line between true legal issues and field-of-play issues; (5) tensions between national law and national courts, on the one hand, and the decisions of international sports federations, on the other hand; and (6) the growing role of government in sports.[98] It is difficult to imagine how international sports law can respond effectively to any of these and other probable developments without full attention to the principle of fairness.

The issues discussed in this commentary might suggest that the principle of fairness is still too unsettled to be effective as a core principle of international sports law. Quite the contrary is true. On the basis of accepted attributes of fairness – impartiality, equity, good faith, coherence, and so on – the principle can be readily adapted to a broad range of sports and sports-related issues. Fairness should be fundamental in the future of sports and the growth of a creditable regime of international sports law. The challenge is simply to take the principle seriously and further develop it within a definitional and institutional framework that already exists.

---

[98] For further forecasting and commentary, see James A.R. Nafziger, *The Future of International Sports Law*, 42 WILLAMETTE L. REV. 861 (2006).

2 The Court of Arbitration for Sport

Richard H. McLaren

1. OVERVIEW OF CAS

In the early 1980s, the International Olympic Committee (IOC) perceived the need for an adjudicative tribunal that would be independent from international sports federations and capable of resolving international sports-related disputes. As IOC president H.E. Juan Antonio Samaranch described it, there was a need for 'a supreme court of world sport.'[1] Growing commercialization and globalization of sport meant sports-related disputes were becoming increasingly common and of a larger scale than previously seen. No one wanted to resolve such disputes in the opposite party's national legal system. The uniqueness of each nation and sport, with diverse rules, legal systems, opinions, principles and philosophies of law, and goals, made it a Herculean feat to create a dispute resolution system that would be fair to all parties involved.

Elite sport played at the global level depends upon nationalism, pride of spirit, and the sheer excitement of competition to support its ever-increasing popularity. The fleeting nature of sport makes expeditious, impartial, and independent dispute resolution essential to the continuing prosperity and growth of elite sport. These forces came together in the international world of sport and forced recognition of the need for a unifying body to assist in the development of sporting law principles. Such a body would ensure fairness and integrity in sport through sound legal control and the harmonization of diverse laws and reconciliation of differing philosophies. This was the challenge that the Court of Arbitration for Sport (CAS) faced from the outset. This chapter examines the extent to which the developments of CAS have recognized and achieved the demands and challenges of the sporting world.

i. History of CAS

In 1983, on the establishment of CAS,[2] the President of the IOC realized his dream of a single, independent forum for the world of sport to resolve its disputes. The goal of CAS was to provide a flexible, quick, and inexpensive procedure to resolve international sports disputes.[3] In its original form, CAS had both judicial and executive functions under a

---

[1] As cited in M Reeb, ed, 'Forward by H E Judge Kéba Mbaye', *Digest of CAS Awards 1986–1998* (The Hague, Staempfli Editions SA Berne, 1998) p. xii. Note that the three volumes of the CAS Digests will be referred for the remainder of this discussion as 'CAS Digests' preceded by the relevant volume number.

[2] The statutes creating the Court of Arbitration for Sport were officially ratified by the IOC in 1983. CAS became operational the following year. For a more detailed, official history of CAS, see M Reeb, ed, 'The Court of Arbitration for Sport (CAS)', 1 CAS Digests xxiii.

[3] 1 CAS Digests xxiv.

single umbrella. At the outset, the IOC controlled and financed CAS's operations. This changed in 1994, when a ruling from the Swiss Federal Tribunal raised questions about CAS's independence from the IOC.[4] Naturally, CAS's degree of impartiality was questioned. This landmark case led to reforms,[5] the most significant being the creation of an administrative and financial branch to oversee the judicial functions of CAS. This new branch, called the International Council of Arbitration for Sport (ICAS), replaced the IOC in the financing and administration of CAS.[6] The effectiveness of the reforms implemented in 1994 was affirmed by the Swiss Federal Tribunal when it recognized the independence of CAS from the IOC in the *Lazutina/Danilova* case in 2003.[7] The ICAS/CAS structure persists today. CAS's impartiality was raised again as a consequence of the death of the first president of CAS, H E Judge Kéba Mbaye. The rules concerning the replacement of the president were unduly deferential to the IOC until the 2010 amendments to Section 6 of the CAS Code. The Code now provides for a different procedure, which no longer mandates the selection of a president proposed by the IOC. However, before a president is selected, consultations with the IOC, as well as the Association of Summer Olympic International Federations, the Association of International Olympic Winter Sports Federations, and the Association of National Olympic Committees are to occur.

The stature of CAS has evolved as its case load has grown and its role at world sporting events such as the Commonwealth Games, European Cup, World Cup, and Summer and

---

[4]   *G v Fédération Equestre Internationale and Court of Arbitration for Sport (CAS)* (1993), Arrêt Du Tribunal Fédéral Suisse, 1st Civil Division, 15 March 1993. Elmar Gundel was a horse rider who appealed an International Equestrian Foundation (FEI) horse-doping sanction to CAS. CAS ruled against him and Gundel proceeded to appeal to the Swiss Federal Tribunal. He alleged that CAS did not meet the independence and impartiality requirement for an arbitration court in Swiss law. The Federal Tribunal found that CAS was sufficiently independent from the FEI. However, the more significant outcome of the case was the *obiter* statement of the Federal Tribunal that the links between the IOC and CAS were sufficiently strong that the independence of CAS would be questionable if the IOC became a party in proceedings before it. For the initial CAS decision that was appealed to the Swiss Federal Tribunal, see *G v Fédération Equestre Internationale*, CAS 92/63, 1 CAS Digests 115.

[5]   Reforms implemented in 1994 were: (i) the creation of ICAS, (ii) the division of the judicial branch of CAS into an appeals and an ordinary division, and (iii) the creation of the CAS Code (composed of the Statutes of the Bodies Working for the Settlement of Sports-related Disputes (CAS and ICAS) and the Procedural Rules) affirming all of these changes and governing the organization and arbitration procedures of CAS. The CAS Code was revised in 2003 (in force from 2004) to incorporate certain long-established principles of CAS case law and practices.

[6]   The restructuring of CAS was approved through the signing of the Agreement Concerning the Constitution of the International Council of Arbitration for Sport in June 1994.

[7]   *Lazutina and Danilova v International Olympic Committee* (IOC) (2003), Arrêt Du Tribunal Fédéral Suisse, 1st Civil Division, 27 May 2003. The Federal Tribunal assessed CAS's independence relative to the IOC in detail as part of an appeal by two Russian cross-country skiers, Larissa Lazutina and Olga Danilova, against a CAS award disqualifying them from an event at the Salt Lake City Winter Games. The court found CAS was sufficiently independent for the decisions it makes in cases involving the IOC to be considered as 'true awards, equivalent to the judgments of State courts.' For more on this case, see A Plantey, 'Independence of the CAS Recognized by the Swiss Federal Tribunal', in I Blackshaw, *et al*, eds, *The Court of Arbitration for Sport 1984–2004* (The Hague, T M C Asser Press, 2006) p. 50 [Blackshaw, *et al*, eds]; J A R Nafziger, 'Lex Sportiva', 1–2 *International Sports Law Journal* (2004) 3 at 4.

Winter Olympic Games has become a permanent fixture of those sporting events. All Olympic international federations and national Olympic committees have recognized the jurisdiction of CAS by including clauses in their statutes that refer relevant disputes to CAS. Some professional sports that are not Olympic-related, such as cricket, motor bike racing and rugby, have also placed themselves under the umbrella of CAS.[8] While others, such as men's and women's tennis, are only periodically included once every 4 years in the Olympic family. CAS has its seat of arbitration in Lausanne, Switzerland, but has two permanent branch offices located in the United States and Australia. These two offices may be venues for arbitrations carried on under its jurisdiction, and Ad Hoc Divisions (AHD) at major worldwide sporting events.[9] The adoption of the World Anti-Doping Code[10] (WADA Code) by the Olympic Movement and the adoption by national governments of its companion, the International Convention against Doping in Sport of the United Nations Education, Scientific and Cultural Organization (UNESCO), has made CAS the appeal court for most doping disputes worldwide.[11] The growth of CAS is also evident in the requests for arbitration or advisory opinions from the court, which has shot up from ten in 1986–87 to 252 in 2007.[12] This recognition of CAS affirms its importance as the institution for the final resolution of disputes within the global sporting community; subject only to the oversight of the Swiss Federal Tribunal under Switzerland's Federal Code on Private International Law.[13]

ii. Structure of CAS

The structure of CAS is governed by the CAS Code,[14] which provides for the establishment of the ICAS and CAS, and outlines both entities' responsibilities. The ICAS controls the administration and financing of the court,[15] and has a mandate to safeguard

---

[8]   Other organizations, such as the Professional Golf Association and the European Tour, while announcing in 2008 separate drug-testing regimes and adjudication procedures for the administration of any infractions of their regimes opted not to include CAS as their ultimate sport adjudication body (the Ladies Professional Golf Association, however, does permit appeals to CAS). Major League Baseball in the United States underwent a thorough examination of its doping control procedures culminating in the Mitchell Report of 13 December 2007. In its recommendations, the report elected not to adopt WADA Code standards, nor to have CAS as an independent appeals body of its internal collective bargaining arbitrations under its doping code.

[9]   CAS branch offices were opened in the United States and Australia in 1996. That year the ICAS also created the first AHD at the Atlanta Summer Olympic Games. Following the 2008 Summer Olympic Games in Beijing, consideration is now being given to the possibility of establishing a branch office in the People's Republic of China as well.

[10]   All references in this chapter are to the 2009 WADA Code unless specified otherwise.

[11]   Article 13 of the WADA Code makes CAS the appeals body for all international doping-related disputes. The WADA Code was created to advance and harmonize world anti-doping efforts. For more information on the WADA Code, see F Oschutz, 'Doping Cases before the CAS and the WADA Code', 12 *Marquette S L J* 2 (Spring 2002) 657.

[12]   Court of Arbitration for Sport, CAS Statistics, online, available at http://www.tas-cas.org/statistics. The numbers refer to the year when the request was made, not when a decision was rendered by CAS.

[13]   18 December 1987.

[14]   The CAS Code includes the Statutes of the Bodies Working for the Settlement of Sports-related Disputes (CAS and ICAS) and the Procedural Rules.

[15]   The CAS Code sets out the functions of the ICAS at § 6.

the independence and impartiality of arbitral adjudication by CAS. The ICAS is composed of 20 members from international federations, national Olympic committees, and the IOC.[16] The ICAS confirms by quadrennial election each arbitrator and appoints all CAS arbitrators.[17] There are now 277 arbitrators[18] appointed to the CAS pool, up from a mere 60 arbitrators in 1986. As set out in the statutes of CAS, the arbitrators serve renewable 4-year terms. Each member of CAS and the ICAS, including the arbitrators, must sign an undertaking to conduct their functions with 'total objectivity and independence, in conformity with the Code.'[19] To reinforce this independence, the ICAS decided that the members of the ICAS may not appear on the list of CAS arbitrators nor act as counsel to parties in proceedings before CAS.[20]

The 1994 restructuring of CAS also effected major changes to the structure of the adjudicative branch of the court. Two divisions were created, the Ordinary Arbitration Division,[21] for first-instance disputes, and the Appeals Arbitration Division,[22] for appeals of final decisions by international federations, national organizing committees, and other sports organizations recognizing the jurisdiction of CAS. Each division has a president, appointed by ICAS.

Since the 1996 Olympic Games in Atlanta, CAS has also established AHDs at each Olympic Games.[23] These AHDs are created to provide finality to time-sensitive decision-making during the Olympic Games, and to make the expedited CAS procedures accessible to those involved in the Games. Ad hoc tribunals are also set up for other major sporting events such as the Commonwealth Games,[24] UEFA European Championships,[25] and FIFA World Cups. The AHDs have played a significant role in raising awareness and developing the reputation of CAS among those involved in sport.

CAS's permanent judicial seat in Lausanne, Switzerland is established under the CAS Code.[26] Locating the seat in Lausanne has important legal implications, which are examined in the following discussion on the jurisdiction of CAS.

---

[16]   Each of these groups initially appoints four members. Four additional members are then appointed by the 12 original appointees, and this group then appoints the final four members.

[17]   See CAS Code, § 14 for the qualifications of arbitrators.

[18]   Statistics from the CAS website, online, available at http://www.tas-cas.org/arbitrators-genlist. This figure is accurate as of June 1, 2010.

[19]   CAS Code, §§ 5 and 18.

[20]   CAS Code, § 5.

[21]   For further information on the procedure of the Ordinary Division, see G Kaufmann-Kohler and P Bartsch, 'The Ordinary Arbitration Procedure of the Court of Arbitration for Sport', in Blackshaw, *et al*, eds, *supra* note 7 at 69.

[22]   For a discussion on the procedure of the Appeals Division, see C Krähe, 'The Appeals Procedure Before the CAS', in Blackshaw, *et al*, eds, *supra* note 7 at 99.

[23]   For a detailed account of CAS involvement at the Sydney, Nagano and Atlanta Olympic Games, see G Kaufmann-Kohler, *Arbitration at the Olympics Issues of Fast-track Dispute Resolution and Sports Law* (The Hague, Kluwer Law International, 2001) Chapters II–IV [Kaufmann-Kohler].

[24]   Ad hoc tribunals began at the Kuala Lumpur Commonwealth Games in 1998.

[25]   Ad hoc tribunals began at the UEFA Championships in 2000.

[26]   CAS Code, § 1.

iii.   Jurisdiction of CAS

CAS is 'competent to resolve all types of disputes of a private nature related to sport.'[27] The only limitation placed on the tribunals' competency is by the CAS Code, which stipulates that disputes must be 'related or connected to sport.'[28] However, as CAS Secretary General Matthieu Reeb notes, 'the Court has never found it did not have jurisdiction simply because a dispute was unrelated to sport.'[29]

CAS does not adjudicate disputes of a technical nature, such as referee calls on the field, and only occasionally considers the rules of sport.[30] CAS arbitrations instead focus on issues such as athlete eligibility, discipline, selection, doping, nationality, contractual breaches, and commercial disputes[31] regarding licensing, advertising,[32] and sponsorship.

---

[27]   M Reeb, 'The Role and Functions of the Court of Arbitration for Sport (CAS)', 2 *International Sports Law Journal* (2002) 21 at 31 [Reeb].

[28]   CAS Code, art. R27.

[29]   Reeb, *supra* note 27 at 21.

[30]   CAS will not generally interfere with decisions made in the course of competition. See, for example, *Mendy* v *Association Internationale de Boxe Amateur (AIBA)* CAS OG 96/006, 1 CAS Digests 413; *Segura* v *International Amateur Athletic Federation (IAAF)* CAS OG 2000/013, 2 CAS Digests 680; *David Calder & Christopher Jarvis* v *Fédération Internationale des Sociétés d'Aviron (FISA)* CAS OG 04/005, *CAS Awards – Salt Lake City 2002 & Athens 2004* (Lausanne, Court of Arbitration for Sport 2004) 121. Responsibility for such technical decisions is granted to international federations, under the Olympic Charter R. 47. In contrast, the interpretation of the rules of a given sport, which are set by the respective international federations, are frequently adjudicated by CAS. See, e.g., *Comité National Olympique et Sportif Français* v *Federation Equestre Internationale* CAS OG 04/007, *CAS Awards – Salt Lake City 2002 & Athens 2004* (Lausanne, Court of Arbitration for Sport 2004) 150, where CAS interpreted the FEI General Regulations to determine that the FEI Appeal Committee did not have the power to hear the appeal of the Ground Jury's ruling on a time penalty imposed on German equestrian Bettina Hoy. See also *Hellenic Olympic Committee & Mr. Nikolaos Kaklamanakis* v *International Sailing Federation* CAS OG 04/009, *CAS Awards – Salt Lake City 2002 & Athens 2004* (Lausanne, Court of Arbitration for Sport 2004) 179; *Italian Olympic Committee & Spanish Olympic Committee* v *International Sailing Federation & Danish Olympic Committee* CAS OG/08 008 & 009, where the CAS Panel found that it was within the power of the sailing jury to not sanction the Danish team for substituting their damaged boat immediately prior to the race. The jury was afforded a large degree of discretion under the applicable rules: *Swedish National Olympic Committee & Abrahamian* v *Fédération Internationale des Luttes Associées* CAS OG/08 007, where a Swedish wrestler and the Swedish National Olympic Committee challenged FILA's absence of a mechanism of appeal to resolve disputes regarding departures from FILA rules. The CAS panel interpreted FILA's rules to find that FILA was required, both under its own rules and under the Olympic Charter, to provide a procedure for an appeal jury (or some equivalent) to hear claims by athletes or others affected that in a competition the relevant officials have not complied with FILA rules and procedures. At the time of writing this chapter, the Swedish National Olympic Committee and the athlete had appealed to the appeal division of CAS in CAS/A/1647 but the matter had not yet been heard or adjudicated.

[31]   An interesting commercial dispute was heard at the Nagano 1998 Winter Olympic Games by the Ad Hoc Panel regarding trademarks displayed on the 'Klap skate.' The Dutch manufacturers of this unique new skate system complained to CAS that athletes using the skates were covering the Dutch company's trademarks with another company's mark. This made it appear as though the other manufacturer was producing the same 'Klap skate' technology. The Dutch manufacturer argued the Olympic Charter provisions regarding commercial marks were being violated. The claimant also alleged laws preventing unfair competition had been violated. However, CAS concluded that its jurisdiction did not include hearing the unfair competition dispute.

The topics that CAS addresses have constantly expanded to include a wider array of issues and sports, far beyond the classic disputes regarding sports doping.

Disputes may be brought before CAS by athletes, international or national federations, the IOC and its member national Olympic committees, as well as other sports organizations. However, arbitration can proceed 'only insofar as the statutes or regulations of the said sports-related bodies or a specific agreement so provide.'[33] In most cases, CAS arbitration is only possible because parties have an arbitration agreement that gives CAS jurisdiction to hear the matter. For example, the Olympic Charter provides that all participants in the Games sign an agreement requiring disputes to be submitted exclusively to CAS.[34] In the past, some international federations maintained their own separate arbitration tribunals.[35] The growing prestige of CAS led even the final holdout, FIFA, to begin using CAS to decide sports disputes as of late 2002. Now, all international federations that are a part of the Olympic Games place clauses in their regulations that require disputes to be submitted for arbitration with CAS.

Given the international nature of CAS disputes, the recognition of CAS's jurisdiction in relation to national courts is an ongoing issue. The New South Wales Court of Appeal (NSWCA) gave the jurisdiction of CAS a resounding affirmation in *Raguz v Sullivan*.[36] In this case, both athletes were Australian and the proceedings took place in Australia. Both athletes had signed a waiver giving authority over any disputes in the Olympic context to CAS. The athletes' application to the Australian courts was dismissed, and the NSWCA affirmed that the waiver signed by the athletes gave CAS exclusive jurisdiction to rule on the issue. The NSWCA found that it did not have jurisdiction because the arbitration agreement selected *international* arbitration, to be conducted between the athletes and their sports federation, and was, therefore, not a domestic arbitration agreement.[37] So, even though the ad hoc tribunal proceedings occurred in Australia, because the CAS Code made Lausanne the seat of arbitration, the arbitration agreement was not considered to be domestic. The deferment to the seat of arbitration in Lausanne, Switzerland was a remarkable result that greatly enhanced CAS's authority. In contrast to this approach, at the 2008 Beijing Olympic Games, the Supreme Court of the People's Republic of China (PRC) issued an edict to the inferior courts of the PRC that no sports-related disputes were to be entertained during the duration of the Olympic Games.[38]

---

[32] See *Fédération Française de Gymnastique (FFG)* v *Sydney Organizing Committee for the Olympic Games (SOCOG)* CAS OG 2000/014, 2 CAS Digests 685.

[33] CAS Code, § 1.

[34] Those involved in the Olympic Games agree that any 'dispute arising on the occasion of or in connection with my participation in the Olympic Games shall be submitted exclusively to the Court of Arbitration for Sport, in accordance with the CAS Code (Rule 59).' The question of the AHD's jurisdiction is specifically addressed in a case law analysis in Richard H. McLaren, 'Introduction the Court of Arbitration for Sport: The Ad Hoc Division at the Olympic Games', 12 *Marq Sports L Rev* (2001) 515 at 524.

[35] The International Amateur Athletic Federation (IAAF) and Fédération International de Football Association (FIFA) have maintained their own body of adjudicative experts in the past.

[36] [2000] NSWCA 240.

[37] *Ibid* at ¶ 108.

[38] As reported in comments delivered in Beijing to the Chinese International Economic and Trade Arbitration Commission (CIETAC) by the President of the ADH, Mr Robert Brinner, at a

Situating the seat of arbitration in Lausanne 'stabilizes the legal framework for resolving disputes'[39] by providing a uniform procedural regime for all CAS arbitration, regardless of the place of arbitration or national location of a dispute. The Lausanne seat also means CAS arbitrations are subject to the Swiss Federal Act on Private International Law,[40] and the only recourse for appeals is the Swiss Federal Tribunal.[41] The grounds for appeal to the Federal Tribunal are very limited. Since CAS became operational in 1984, only one case has been successfully challenged in the Tribunal.[42]

More recently, the jurisdiction of CAS was recognized by American courts in a decision regarding the eligibility of a track athlete to obtain an injunction of a CAS appeal decision, thereby clearing the legal blockade to his participation in the American Olympic tryouts leading to the selection of the American Olympic team for the 2008 Beijing Summer Games.[43] The US District Court found, pursuant to the New York

---

meeting between CIETAC and members of the ADH of CAS of which the author was a member and present when the speech was delivered on August 21, 2008.

[39]   Kaufmann-Kohler, *supra* note 23 at 101. For additional information on the Lausanne seat, see G Kauffmann-Kohler, 'Arbitration Procedure: Identifying and Applying the Law governing the Arbitration Procedure – the Role of the Law of the Place of Arbitration', in A J van der Berg, ed, 9 *ICCA Congress Series* (Kluwer, The Hague, 1999) 356.

[40]   18 December 1987. In the case of AHDs of CAS, the Federal Act on Private International Law applies to arbitration as a result of the express choice of law contained in Article 17 of the Olympic Games Rules and because of the choice of Lausanne, Switzerland as the seat pursuant to Article 7 of the Olympic Games Rules. See also the decision of the NSWCA before the Summer Olympic Games in Sydney, Australia: *Raguz* v *Sullivan* [2000] NSWCA 240.

[41]   Appeals to the Swiss Federal Tribunal were relatively rare until FIFA changed its rules to not implement CAS appeal decisions if there was an appeal to the Swiss Federal Tribunal that had not resulted in a judgment. As a consequence, a CAS decision may not be implemented for some time, if at all, when there is an outstanding appeal. As an example, see *Raducan* v *Comité Int'l Olympique* (2000) 5P 427/2000, Arrêt Du Tribunal Fédéral Suisse, December 4, 2000. The grounds of appeal are also limited to 'incorrect constitution of the arbitral tribunal, lack of jurisdiction, violation of the principle of equal treatment or incompatibility with public policy': M Reeb, 'The Role of the Court of Arbitration for Sport', in W P Heere, ed, *International Law and the Hague's 750th Anniversary* (The Hague, T M C Asser Press, 1999) p. 233 at 237.

[42]   *Cañas* v *Association of Tennis Professionals (ATP)*, CAS 2005/A/951. Argentinean tennis player Guillermo Cañas appealed a CAS ruling regarding his use of a banned diuretic during the Mexican Open in February 2005. The Swiss Federal Court ordered CAS to reconsider Cañas's case, finding that Cañas's right to be heard was not sufficiently regarded by the CAS Panel. The Swiss court also found the standard waiver of the right to file an appeal with the Swiss Federal Tribunal against a CAS award, which the ATP included in its agreements, was not enforceable. Upon reconsideration of the case, CAS arbitrators maintained the 15-month ban of the original decision (see *Cañas* v *Association of Tennis Professionals*, CAS 2005/A/951 Revised Arbitral Award of 23 May 2007), which was of itself a revision of the first-instance panel decision to impose the full 2-year sanction.

[43]   See *Justin Gatlin* v *United States Anti-Doping Agency* (Case No 3:08-cv-241/LAC/EMT U S District Court, Pensacola Division 24 June 2008). The CAS decision (6 June 2008) upheld American track and field athlete Justin Gatlin's ban from competition for a period of 4 years. He then appealed to the US District Court for an emergency injunction, pending his appeal, to allow him to compete in 100-meter trials for the US track and field's Olympic team. The key legal issue in this case was whether the US District Court can overrule a decision by the USOC regarding eligibility of an athlete. The District Court affirmed the USOC's exclusive jurisdiction over all matters concerning American athletes' participation in the Olympic Games.

Convention,[44] that 'claims that have been properly submitted to arbitration and ruled upon by entities such as CAS are barred from re-litigation in this forum.'[45] The US District Court begrudgingly noted that the jurisdiction to decide athlete eligibility belonged exclusively to the United States Olympic Committee (USOC), and endorsed the decision of CAS.

iv. Functions of CAS

The functions of CAS are set out in the CAS Code and the Arbitration Rules for the Olympic Games. CAS is best known for its Ordinary Arbitration and Appeals Arbitration Divisions. Because disputes heard by the Appeals Division are considered to be *de novo*, the evidence and legal arguments are not limited to those heard at the first instance.[46] Disputes come before both divisions through contractual arbitration clauses or by virtue of a special agreement to submit a particular dispute to CAS.

Beyond arbitration, the CAS Code also provides that CAS may offer mediation services and advisory opinions.[47] Advisory opinions can be given on any issue relating to sport practice or development. One such advisory opinion concerned the use of swimsuits at the Sydney Olympics.[48] The most significant difference between traditional arbitration and the advisory opinions or mediation services is that the latter two are not binding on the parties that request them.

---

[44] United Nations Convention on the Recognition and Enforcement of Foreign Arbitral Awards, opened for signature 10 June 1958, 330 U N T S 3, 21 U S T 2517.

[45] *Justin Gatlin* v *United States Anti-Doping Agency* (Case No 3:08-cv-241/LAC/EMT US District Court, Pensacola Division June 24, 2008).

[46] In *N, J, Y, W* v *FINA* CAS 98/208, 2 CAS Digests 234 at 239, CAS cited art. R57 of the CAS Code, and stated that a CAS appeal hearing is a rehearing. The panel was 'not limited to consideration of the evidence that was adduced before FINA [the federation whose decision was being appealed to the CAS] either at first instance or at the appellate stage, but had to consider all evidence, oral documentary and real, produced before it ...'. See also the interlocutory award of *French* v *ASC & CA* 2004/A/651, where the issue arose again.

[47] For more on the mediation and advisory opinion services of CAS, see Richard McLaren, 'CAS Advisory Opinions', in Blackshaw, *et al*, eds, *supra* note 7 at 180; I S Blackshaw, *Mediating Sports Disputes, National and International Perspectives* (The Hague, T M C Asser Press, 2002) p. 50, cited in the Advisory Opinion *WADA* v *FIFA* CAS 2005/C/976 & 986; Court of Arbitration for Sport, 'History of the CAS', online, available at http://www.tas-cas.org/history. For an interesting case where the CAS Panel suggested that the parties proceed by mediation rather than arbitration with the same Panel acting, see *Abernathy* v *International Luge Federation* CAS OG 06/005 & 007. A successful settlement was reached by mediation, and a consent arbitral award was issued to give effect to the mediation settlement.

[48] Advisory Opinion, *Australian Olympic Committee* CAS 2000/C/267, 2 CAS Digests 725. The Australian Olympic Committee (AOC) requested that CAS consider the decision of the Fédération Internationale de Natation to permit a novel type of full-body swimsuit to be used in competition. These swimsuits were designed to simulate shark skin, and supposedly increased swimmer speed, reduced drag, and increased buoyancy. The AOC was concerned that allowing this variation from the usual suits would result in claims of unfairness by athletes.

v.   Applicable Law and Enforcement of Awards

The parties to a dispute before CAS may agree upon a specific law to govern the proceedings. If the parties have not specified that a certain law will apply, the law that governs the proceedings will depend on the division of CAS where the case is heard. Ordinary Division proceedings are governed by Swiss law.[49] The parties may also agree that the arbitration panel may decide *ex aequo et bono*, meaning according to what the panel considers equitable regardless of the law.[50] When no law is specified by the parties, cases in the Appeals Division will be governed by the law of the country where the federation, sports body, or association is domiciled, or the law that the CAS panel deems appropriate.[51] The AHD at Olympic Games 'shall rule on the dispute pursuant to the Olympic Charter, the applicable regulations, general principles of law and the rules of law, the application of which it deems appropriate.'[52] This power to decide upon the applicable law is granted to the CAS panel to expedite the time-sensitive proceedings at the Games.

Once CAS has rendered an award, it is final and binding. The awards may be enforced by the parties internationally through the New York Convention.[53] The inclusion by international federations of a clause recognizing CAS as the sole arbitral body to which disputes may be submitted is recognition of the enforceability of CAS awards. In accordance with their own statutes, international federations must then rely on CAS for arbitration awards. The international federations would be unlikely to endorse an institution for which the awards are difficult to enforce. Locating CAS's seat in Lausanne makes the awards 'Swiss' for the purposes of enforcement under the New York Convention.[54]

vi.   *Lex Sportiva*

Defining the term *lex sportiva* is an unenviable task, for it has been construed to mean many things to many people, each of which will be examined in the following discussion. The term was first coined in 1990 or earlier, and has since gained increasing significance.[55]

---

49   See the CAS Code, art. R45. Swiss law grants the parties the autonomy to choose the law that will be applied to their dispute, and barring that, the law that will be applied is that which is most closely linked to the case. See art. 187 ¶ 1 of the Swiss Code on Private International Law of 18 December 1987. See also *B v International Basketball Federation (FIBA)* CAS 92/80, 1 CAS Digests 297.

50   CAS Code, art. R45.

51   CAS Code, art. R58. Where a CAS panel chooses the law that will be applied, they must provide reasons for doing so. For example, see *IAAF v OLV & Elmar Lichtenegger* CAS 2004/A/624.

52   CAS Arbitration Rules for the Olympic Games, art. 17.

53   United Nations Convention on the Recognition and Enforcement of Foreign Arbitral Awards, opened for signature 10 June 1958, 330 U N T S 3, 21 U S T 2517. Enforcement is possible in countries which have ratified the Convention. However, art. V(2)(b) allows a refusal to enforce an award on public policy grounds of the enforcing country. Enforcement can also be refused if the competent authority in the enforcing country determines that sport-related disputes are not capable of settlement by arbitration under that country's laws.

54   UN Convention, *ibid*. See Kaufmann-Kohler, *supra* note 23 at 101.

55   In Richard H McLaren, 'The Court of Arbitration for Sport: An Independent Arena for the Sports "Disputes"', 35 *Val U L Rev* (2001) 379 at n. 11 [McLaren], I noted that *lex sportiva* is 'a term coined by the Acting General Secretary of Court of Arbitration for Sport, Matthieu Reeb, at the time of the publishing of the first digest [1998] of Court of Arbitration for Sport decisions

Lex sportiva is considered by some to be a separate, and albeit inchoate but coherent, body of law with distinct legal principles of its own. Others are skeptical of such a grand, sweeping view and consider it to be merely a conglomeration of principles applicable to the specific sports disputes that are adjudicated by CAS from what have been accepted as discrete legal areas such as contract or general administrative law principles. Such an approach would mean that *lex sportiva* was nothing more than the aggrandizement of various legal principles applied in sports disputes and assembled piecemeal.[56]

Turning now to an examination of the differing views, some experts consider *lex sportiva* to be a subset of, or similar to, *lex mercatoria*. Others consider *lex sportiva*'s most salient feature to be its difference from *lex ludica*, or that it just exists in a *lex arbitri* or *lex specialis*. Still, others construe the concept more narrowly, considering only the constitutions of those federations that submit cases to CAS. More broadly, *lex sportiva* refers to the substantive output of CAS, functioning as a standards council; or, as the equitable principles that arise out of CAS decisions and such instruments subject to its interpretation, such as the WADA Code. Each of these views will be considered in turn, their merits and detractions considered, and then a tentative definition will be considered.

While some have held that the meaning of the term is not of great importance inasmuch as it has clearly permeated legal discussions around the globe,[57] the term *lex sportiva* can be found in CAS's official description of itself.[58] It has also been referred to in academic papers,[59] in CAS opinions,[60] in international law scholars' lexicon,[61] in law school textbooks,[62] and in presentations by sports officials.[63] Moreover, as the discussion on the desirability of *lex sportiva* will make clear, there is value in having a fully developed *lex*

---

stretching over the period from 1983–1998.' Teubner, however, quotes a 1990 source: G Simon, *Puissance sportive et ordre juridique etatique* (Paris, Dalloz-Sirey, 1990), in *idem*, '"Global Bukowina": Legal Pluralism in the World Society', in G Teubner, ed, *Global Law Without a State* (Andover, Dartmouth, 1997), for the proposition '*E mesmo no universo do esporte discute-se a emergência de uma lex sportiva internationalis*' Both Ken Foster and Allan Erbsen use this 1990 date as well. See Ken Foster, 'Is There a Global Sports Law?', 2 *ENT L* 1, 18 n. 16 (2003) and Allan Erbsen in 'The Substance and Illusion of Lex Sportiva', in Ian S Blackshaw, *et al*, eds, *supra* note 7 at 441, respectively. See also A Caiger and S Gardiner, eds, *Professional Sport in the EU: Regulation and Re-Regulation* (The Hague, T M C Asser Press, 2000) pp. 301–3, where they write of a 'distinct lex sportiva.' Regardless, the debate as to when the term was first coined is of little importance to its definition. There were considerably more cases heard after 1998, and so the period before 1998 is not very informative or determinative of how things have evolved.

56   Michael Beloff, 'Is There a Lex Sportiva?', 5 *I S L R* (2005) 49 at 49 [Beloff].
57   N Cox and A Schuster, *Sport and the Law* (First Law, Dublin, 2005) p. 5.
58   3 CAS Digest, at xiv (statement of CAS President Kéba Mbaye); 2 CAS Digest, at xxx (statement of CAS Secretary General Matthieu Reeb).
59   For example, McLaren, *supra* note 55.
60   See *Re CONI* CAS 2005/C/841, Slip Op at 12.
61   See Andreas Fischer-Lescano and Gunther Teubner, 'Regime Collisions: The Vain Search for Legal Unity in the Fragmentation of Global Law', 25 *Mich J Int'l L* (2004) 999 at 1036.
62   See Mathew J Mitten, *et al*, *Sports Law and Regulation: Cases, Materials and Problems* (New York, Aspen, 2005) p. 334.
63   See Craig A Masback, 'Leadership from the Trenches' (Presentation at Duke Law School, May 1999), available online at http://www.law.duke.edu/sportscenter/masback.pdf.

sportive; namely, in gaining efficiency of legal process, predictability and stability of expectations, and equal treatment of similarly situated persons.[64]

vii.   *Lex Mercatoria*

Use of the Latin moniker *lex sportiva* may not be merely pretentious, as some commentators maintain, for it echoes a much older and more established law: *lex mercatoria*. Lord Mansfield once described *lex mercatoria,* saying that 'it will not be the law of Rome or the law of Athens; not one law now, another hereafter; but one and the same law, for all people and for all times.'[65] More recently, the English Commercial Court described *lex mercatoria* as the 'general law of merchants a law to which some international tribunals have regard … but … not the law of a country which is capable of ascertainment by expert evidence from practitioners in the country.'[66] *Lex mercatoria* is an ancient source of law, which forms the basis for international commercial practice and commercial arbitration. It regulates 'the substantive rights and duties of parties to certain types of international transactions to the exclusion of substantive law.'[67]

Superficially, the analogy between *lex sportiva* and *lex mercatoria* seems to hold. Perhaps *lex sportiva* is nothing more than part of the *lex mercatoria*. After all, just as *lex mercatoria* is not particular to any one country or jurisdiction, *lex sportiva* has this same borderless characteristic. Both *lex mercatoria* and *lex sportiva* are applied almost exclusively through arbitration, and the parties to a particular dispute can be from different regions of the globe. This, however, is where the similarities end. *Lex mercatoria* has developed over hundreds of years and has evolved to enjoy the benefit of customary practice.[68] It comprehensively interpenetrates all of international commercial activity and institutions and is acknowledged in both the public and private sphere as a sound, separate legal system.

Lex sportiva, on the other hand, is a recent theory of only a few decades vintage. Whatever *lex sportiva* is taken to mean, it is the product of a few, principally CAS arbitrators, rulings on a narrow range of issues over a relatively short time compared to *lex mercatoria*. Moreover, *lex sportiva* does not enjoy the same cache as *lex mercatoria*. Not every sports dispute is decided by CAS, and those that are do not comprehensively address all points of law under examination. If the matter can be resolved without answering any particular issue, the practice is followed of not answering those questions. Sports-related decisions are not consistently published and are not binding on future disputes. The scope and sheer amount of precedent is minimal compared with *lex*

---

[64]   For a discussion of these benefits see the following discussion under the heading 'Desirability of *lex sportiva*.'

[65]   The original statement was in Latin as well: '*non edit alia lex Romae, alia Athenis; alia nunc, posthac; sed et apud omnes gentes et omni tempore, una eadem lex obtinebit.' Luke* v *Lyde*, 97 Eng Rep 787 (1759).

[66]   *Shamil Bank* v *Beximco Pharmaceuticals Ltd* [2003] EWHC 218, [2003] All E R (Comm) 849.

[67]   *Coppé-Lavalini SAN* v *Ken-Ren Chemicals* [1994] 2 All E R 449.

[68]   James A R Nafziger, *International Sports Law* 2nd ed (Ardsley, NY, Transnational Publishers Inc, 2004) p. 48 [Nafziger].

mercatoria, and the concept is best understood as being limited to CAS awards.[69] *Lex sportiva* cannot then be identical to *lex mercatoria.* This is tantamount to considering *lex sportiva* to be nothing more than the principles from the other various bodies of law – contracts, torts, administrative – that are used to decide cases. This position will be addressed and refuted shortly.

viii. *Lex Ludica*

While most writers are keen to point out that one of the emerging trends in the jurisprudence of CAS is a reluctance to interfere with field-of-play decisions, Michael Beloff Q.C. contends that *lex sportiva* might, at least in part, consist of occasional interference with field-of-play decisions,[70] or what has been called *lex ludica.*[71] These are the rules of the particular sport, as well as the enforcement of these rules by the game officials. The general trend of CAS jurisprudence has been to avoid interfering with field-of-play decisions and thereby not second-guessing rulings of referees, umpires, and other match officials.[72] It is this sense of the term that Beloff contends is part of *lex sportiva.*

Some writers equate the term *lex ludica* with *lex sportiva.*[73] Officials need to be free to make necessary calls exercising their judgment during the game and rest assured that these field decisions made of necessity at the moment the call arises not be questioned solely because a single participant does not like the result. However, the position is more nuanced. The rules of the game and the officials' application of those rules, the *lex ludica,* are not completely immune to legal intervention. There could be cases, and have been, where officials simply ignore or grossly misapply game rules.[74] There is now a lot of money in sport, and the outcome of competitions has serious financial consequences for athletes and owners. This has led some to argue that it is inevitable that the law will intervene in field-of-play decisions and the rulings of umpires, referees, and officials.[75] The claim is that CAS can and should second-guess the decisions of game officials.[76]

With respect, this may well be the case, but this does not mean *lex ludica* is synonymous with *lex sportiva,* or that the former forms a significant portion of the latter.[77] The inevitability of CAS's involvement with field-of-play decisions is a question that will be answered in time, and if CAS were to take a more active role in overturning the decisions

---

[69] Some have suggested that *lex sportiva* is synonymous with international sports law, free from any national rules, but this is prima facie unlikely: Jens Adolphsen, 'Eine lex sportive für den internationalen Sport?', *Jahrbuch Junger Zivilrechtles* 281, 282, 300 (2003), cited in Nafziger, *supra* note 68 at 49 (but not accepted by Nafziger).

[70] Beloff, *supra* note 56 at 54.

[71] Ken Foster, 'Lex Sportiva and Lex Ludica: The Court of Arbitration For Sport's Jurisprudence', in Blackshaw, *et al*, eds, *supra* note 7 at 420.

[72] For a detailed analysis of CAS's decision to avoid interfering in field of play disputes, see the discussion in the section entitled 'Development of *lex sportiva* to date,' below.

[73] Beloff, *supra* note 56 at 49.

[74] *Ibid* at 54.

[75] *Ibid* at 60.

[76] *Ibid* at 54.

[77] This is not really Beloff's contention, but more a logical implication of it. The article is more concerned with the inevitable nature of CAS's eventual interference with field-of-play decisions.

of game officials, then this would form a more important part of *lex sportiva*. With technology allowing a video or other review of a decision immediately after the fact – as in tennis, for instance – we may see increasing instances of review of field-of-play decisions.[78] However, it is very unlikely that CAS will begin to interfere with game official's decisions[79] – days, weeks, or even months after the fact. CAS has said that incorrect decisions by officials are a risk athletes just have to accept as part of the game unless the decision is malicious, made in bad faith, or arbitrary.[80] Rules of the game are not part of *lex sportiva*, and their application during the game should not be, either. At present, the field-of-play decisions that make up *lex ludica* remain an area that CAS is very reluctant to arbitrate, and as such do not form a significant part of *lex sportiva*.

There is another sense or meaning to the term *lex ludica*. This sense has been called 'sporting spirit.'[81] While this idea is not fully explored in the literature, it can perhaps be considered an 'internal law' of sport. Each sport has its own ethical principles, and these are best assessed by a specialized forum or system of arbitration particular to that sport. On this account, *lex ludica* might include not only a principle of autonomy for match officials, but also a distinction between those issues that CAS will and will not interfere with, regardless of their arising in a sports context. They are an 'internal law' of sport that is exempt from CAS's intervention. National courts can respect their internal governance by arbitration.[82] This idea is further addressed below.

---

[78]   An interesting example arose at the Beijing Olympics in the 400 meter race. An American athlete was running in first place, followed by a Dutch Antilles athlete in second, and then American athletes in the third and fourth position. Shortly after the race the track officials ruled out the third-place athlete on the grounds that he had stepped on the track lane line and therefore encroached on his competitor. The American Olympic officials in reviewing tapes of the race later in the evening noted that the Dutch Antilles athlete had done the same thing but the race officials at the time had not noticed that encroachment. The Americans protested as the rules of the IAAF permit suggesting that this athlete ought also to be disqualified thereby enabling the fourth-place American to be the silver medal winner. Some hours later, the IAAF official did eliminate that athlete as well. The Dutch Antilles Olympic Committee referred the matter to the AHD of CAS at the Games. The AHD ruled that because the matter was received on the closing Sunday of the Games, it would be referred to a single arbitrator of the AHD sitting later in Lausanne. See the press release issued by CAS on 5 September 2008: 'Athletics – Olympic Games Men's 200M Final: The Disqualification of Churandy Martina (Netherlands Antilles) Challenged Before the Court of Arbitration for Sport (CAS)'. The appeal of this decision was dismissed in *Netherlands Antilles Olympic Committee* v *IAAF & USOC*, CAS 2008/A/1641. CAS stated that field-of-play decisions are not granted review unless the decision was malicious, in bad faith, or arbitrary. See also CAS OG 02/007, Korean Olympic Committee.
[79]   See *Yang Tae Young* v *International Gymnastics Federation* CAS 2004/A/704.
[80]   See *Mendy* v *Association Internationale de Boxe Amateur* CAS OG 1996/006, 1 CAS Digests 413; *Hellenic Olympic Committee & Mr. Nikolaos Kaklamanakis* v *International Sailing Federation* CAS OG 04/009; *CNOSF, BOA, & USOC* v *FEI & NOCG* CAS OG 2004/007; *Italian Olympic Committee & Spanish Olympic Committee* v *International Sailing Federation & Danish Olympic Committee* CAS OG/08 008 & 009.
[81]   Foster, *supra* note 71 at 421.
[82]   *Ibid.*

ix. *Lex Arbitri* or *Lex Specialis*

Similar to the view that *lex sportiva* is really just a subset of *lex mercatoria*, *lex sportiva* might be cast as either *lex specialis* or *lex arbitri*. Parties can designate the seat of arbitration, and that entails the rules of arbitration – or *lex arbitri* – that govern the proceedings.[83] The Secretary General of CAS has suggested that the arbitrability of a dispute, the validity of an arbitration agreement, and judicial remedies against awards do not fall comfortably within the scope of *lex sportiva*; they fall within the *lex arbitri* of Swiss Law.[84] Since arbitration awards are never binding on future cases and parties, CAS decisions can be seen as a *lex specialis*[85] – that an earlier-enacted law governing a specific subject matter (*lex specialis*) is not overridden by a law subsequently enacted that only governs general matters. *Lex sportiva* concerns general principles derived from sports regulations, and their proper interpretation. But is this all *lex sportiva* amounts to?

In order to answer this question, it is helpful to consider all the senses in which *lex sportiva* is used.

x. Concept

While it is true that commentators disagree on what *lex sportiva* means, they generally agree that it exists in some fashion or other.[86] For example, *lex sportiva* might refer to:

- the comprehensive system of private law that comes about through the numerous agreements and bylaws that regulate athletes, national Olympic committees, national governing bodies for particular sports, international sports federations, and public and private anti-doping agencies;[87]
- a form of self-governance that sports officials endeavor to create by putting themselves beyond the reach of sovereign courts and regulators. This sense refers to the quasi-sovereign nature of interstitial arbitration awards, filling the void created by arbitration clauses that attempt to preclude litigation in national courts;[88] or
- those equitable doctrines that CAS arbitrators refer to when drafting specific holdings, or the body of precedent and jurisprudence that influences future CAS awards.[90]

It has been widely argued that *lex sportiva* is an imprecise term covering different concepts that glosses over these various senses, confusing each in turn.[90] The question as to whether *lex sportiva* is a set of unique legal principles particular to sports law has remained

---

[83] Kaufmann-Kohler, *supra* note 21.
[84] Reeb, *supra* note 41 at 236.
[85] Nafziger, *supra* note 68 at 48.
[86] Erbsen, *supra* note 55 at 441.
[87] *Ibid* at 444. Erbsen contends that an American swimmer in an elite-level international race is subject to no less than eight legal sources.
[88] Erbsen, *supra* note 55 at 444.
[89] *Ibid*.
[90] See Foster, *supra* note 71 at 441; Erbsen, *supra* note 55 at 444.

unanswered to date. Can any fundamental sports-specific innovations in the reasoning of the CAS awards be discerned?[91]

Absolutely. However, a very narrow definition of *lex sportiva* is necessary since CAS awards cover a limited range of sport-specific disputes. By reinforcing and building on existing established rules of international sports law, CAS awards are gradually forming a distinct body of law.[92] These awards are clearly the foundation of *lex sportiva*. If, as Beloff argues, the function of *lex sportiva* is to indicate who has what authority, then it is not merely the substantive sport-specific legal innovations in any of the CAS awards but also those issues that CAS chooses to abstain from deciding, such as *lex ludica*, that make up *lex sportiva*.

Lex sportiva is defined both by what it is and what it is not. *Lex sportiva* can be considered to refer to the body of CAS awards, or it can be interpreted more broadly to mean 'international sports law' as a whole.[93] Nafziger adopts the first interpretation, and this is more plausible than the latter. To equate *lex sportiva* with 'international sports law' is to expand its scope too far, including everything that might have a sports dimension.

The most obvious candidates for what these sport-specific innovations in the reasoning of the CAS awards would be are the 'sporting values' interspersed throughout the awards. Reminiscent of the second sense of *lex ludica*, these include equitable principles such as: that the best athlete should win; the referee's decision should be respected and not interfered with; the time, place, and result of a game once set should be respected; arbitrary discrimination is not acceptable; and the federations and governing bodies of sport should exercise fairness.[94] These principles accompany the general principles of law that are appropriately applied to cases. The width, depth, and breadth of *lex sportiva* will be more thoroughly discussed below.[95]

An ostensive definition of *lex sportiva* would point to the WADA Code, and the arbitration awards decided by CAS. Whatever else *lex sportiva* might mean remains an open question. Defining *lex sportiva* as global sports law[96] is problematic because this might include the statutes of all sporting federations and organizations. This goes too far, since any athlete can be bound by CAS if that athlete chooses (by choosing to be a member of a given sports federation that adheres to CAS). Perhaps because the WADA Code reflects a harmonization of many sports' anti-doping rules, it has a claim to be part of *the lex sportive*. However, its implementation is only mandatory in certain parts of its content and, more particularly, it is implemented through the rules of international federations that may choose to adopt the WADA Code in whole or part. Therefore, it is difficult to make a case that the WADA Code has a claim to be part of *lex sportiva*, while the international federations rules do not. While the WADA Code or international federations rules on anti-doping may not be said to form part of the *lex sportiva*, it may well be that the jurisprudence arising from the harmonization of those anti-doping rules is indeed a part of that body of principle.

---

[91] Erbsen, *supra* note 55 at 444.

[92] James A.R. Nafziger, 'Lex Sportiva and CAS', in Blackshaw, *et al*, eds, *supra* note 7 at 409.

[93] Nafziger, *supra* note 68 at 49.

[94] Michael Beloff, 'Drugs, Laws, and Versapacks', in John O'Leary, ed, *Drugs and Doping in Sport: Socio-Legal Perspectives* (London, Cavendish, 2001) p. 39 at 56.

[95] See the following section titled 'Development of *lex sportiva* to date.'

[96] See, e.g., Foster, *supra* note 55.

The concept of *lex sportiva* will most likely evolve over time, and as it does, so too will its definition. Therefore, any definition must be tentative at best. To count as part of *lex sportiva*, a statute or process of arbitration must have international reach, and be capable of being voluntarily entered into by any athlete, sport federation, or sport organization. The presence of the following factors would lend support to the inclusion in *lex sportiva* of a statute or process of arbitration: that the statute, decision, or arbitration award has been adopted by numerous agencies; that it is fair to all parties involved; that it is globally recognized; and that it is developed to promote and preserve the fairness, safety, and competitive spirit of sport. Any statute or process must also enhance the objectives of *lex sportiva* to be included within it. These objectives are to ensure predictability of outcomes, equal treatment of similarly situated persons, and the efficiency of the legal process.

2. DESIRABILITY OF A *LEX SPORTIVA*

However it may be defined, does *lex sportiva* make a difference in achieving dispute resolution in sport? Although there may be many positive aspects associated with its formation, the benefits of a *lex sportiva* could be countered by considerable drawbacks. Each side to the debate must be assessed to determine whether a *lex sportiva* is desirable. Favoring its development is the view that establishing a sound *lex sportiva* is advantageous to maintain certainty and predictability of dispute results throughout international sports law. The aim is that, with the progression of CAS awards, principles will develop and evolve so that precedents will be set with which to guide future decision makers in sport as well as the resolution of future disputes when decision makers are unable to resolve conflicts. *Lex sportiva* can, if nurtured and developed, assist in creating more predictable outcomes. Indeed, the development of a *lex sportiva* can contribute to the effectiveness of the WADA Code's harmonization role through the successful administration of anti-doping rules.[97] As a result, *lex sportiva* could potentially help to avoid a range of sports-related disputes,[98] since athletes and officials would base their actions with the guidance of previous cases and in their governing principles. A shared knowledge of CAS jurisprudence could act as an indicator for how those involved in sporting events should conduct themselves, and perhaps even present a deterrent in areas where questionable policies provide for discretion. Ideally, all parties would err on the side of caution to avoid being reprimanded, leading to a fairer and smoother running of competitions. For those who hold this view, the development of a body of principle is essential to the successful administration of the sports rules of international federations and games organizers such as the IOC.

An opposing minority view is that *lex sportiva* may have the contrasting effect of 'stunting the rationalization of jurisprudence that it purports to describe and justify.'[99] This viewpoint is more focused on the dispute resolution needs of sport rather than the day-by-day administration of sport through the application of its rules; the effect of which may be certain and predictable thereby making the administrative decisions easier

---

[97]   Nafziger, *supra* note 92 at 419.

[98]   *Ibid.*

[99]   Erbsen, *supra* note 55 at 445.

to determine. For example, CAS decisions may not be as well written or rationalized if the arbitrators proposing them merely state something because it falls within the standard of *lex sportiva*.[100] In this light, *lex sportiva* could create a trap for a narrow approach towards sports disputes; those making the decisions may place more emphasis on following the precedent previously set rather than on fully assessing the matter and providing their own new insights. The consequence of this systematic mode of decision making is that each case would be pooled within larger categories of similar matters, instead of being evaluated on its own individual merits and circumstances. This trade-off between certainty and predictability of results, on the one hand, with the aim of achieving justice in a particular case, on the other, is always a source of tension in dispute resolution.

Nafziger suggests that the principles of *stare decisis* would be served through a *lex sportiva* by the application of three values: efficiency of the legal process, predictability or stability of expectations, and equal treatment of similarly situated parties.[101] These values are fundamental to the adjudication process but do not emphasize sufficiently the sports administrators' need to use the results of arbitrations to make decisions about how to administer their sport, thereby potentially giving rise to the next arbitration with which the adjudication values ought to be applied. In this section, each of these three values will be assessed to gauge how effective an established *lex sportiva* would be in fulfilling both the adjudication and sports rule administration task, and whether or not it is something to be desired by the sporting world. Additionally, the concept of sports as increasingly more of a business with growing national interests will be discussed with respect to how this trend affects the development of *lex sportiva*.

i.   Efficiency of Legal Process

In order to assist in resolving sporting disputes, effective arbitration procedures must be deployed. CAS has been able to adapt its actions to the specificity of the rules in particular sporting events to provide effective adjudication by arbitration. Special procedural rules of arbitration are followed to combat such issues as time-sensitivity of the dispute.[102] Additionally, the trend in sport as increasingly more of a business with growing national interests will be discussed with respect to how such a trend affects the development of *lex sportiva*.[103] Given the nature and intensity of sporting events and competitions, these qualities are desirable to all those involved. The proper execution of sound decision making within the circumstances of each dispute will lead to a well-developed *lex sportiva* that can be followed in future matters.

Although *lex sportiva* could potentially create an efficient process for the application of sports sanctions, it remains unclear whether there would be any increase to the level of effectiveness in serving this aim; particularly, in doping cases where the arbitration panel has, with the introduction of the new WADA Code in 2009, considerably more discretion than in the past.[104] A developed *lex sportiva* could lead to heightened procedural

---

[100]   *Ibid.*
[101]   Nafziger, *supra* note 92 at 411.
[102]   R H McLaren and J P Sanderson, *Innovative Dispute Resolution: The Alternative* (Canada, Thomson Carswell, 2008) pp. 5–112.
[103]   *Ibid.*
[104]   For example, see Comment to Article 4.2.2 in the WADA Code 2009.

formality, additional evidentiary requirements, and other systematic adjustments that would result in longer hearings, a slower turnaround time for cases, and increased costs of the court – becoming more like court-based litigation.[105] These negative effects may offset any advantages gained through the increased efficiency discussed earlier, the consequence of which may be for CAS to lose credibility and recognition in the eyes of athletes, sporting federations, and other concerned or affected parties.

The adaptation of *lex sportiva* must be kept in check to ensure that it does not become overly rigid and doctrinaire. An artful balance needs to be maintained between reaching a systematic formality and preserving the speed of the process and low costs. CAS must continue dedicating adequate resources to settle each case with the fairest solution that is most agreeable to all those concerned. If this is achieved, then the resulting development of a *lex sportiva* will prove to be positive.

ii. Predictability and Stability of Expectations

The development of a *lex sportiva* through CAS is resulting in a harmonization of standards on a global level.[106] This is possible because of the ongoing 'transnational process arising from international arbitration.'[107] As more disputes are settled by CAS, the groundwork serving as a basis in later decisions will increase and therefore provide decision makers with frameworks from which to operate. Although an arbitration panel is not bound to follow precedent, in practice CAS awards provide guidance and influence towards later cases and even function as precedent as they must and should do in the anti-doping decisions.[108] From this, there will be a heightened level of familiarity in handling future cases of a like nature, and therefore a more effective approach based on the outcomes of past matters. There is also a public use, particularly of the doping cases, as a form of precedent not in the sense of being binding upon arbitration panels, but for the purpose of carrying out the day-to-day administration of sporting practice and procedure based on the rules of the sport, including doping rules.

The realization of these objectives could effectively 'strengthen the process of international sports law in attaining greater stability and integrity, [and] confidence in the consistency of outcomes among the cases.'[109] This is critical in doping cases, which need stability in their decisions in order to successfully administer the anti-doping rules and make decisions on how to apply those rules in future doping incidents based upon what CAS has enunciated in past awards. Further, it would benefit all areas of sports arbitration generally, since 'consistency of decision-making is a hallmark of any creditable method of dispute resolution'[110] and is essential to the effective sport administration decision-making process. This predictability feature is an important value to be preserved and encouraged in the future.

---

[105] Nafziger, *supra* note 92 at 412.
[106] Foster, *supra* note 71 at 437.
[107] *Ibid.*
[108] Nafziger, *supra* note 68.
[109] Nafziger, *supra* note 92 at 412.
[110] James A R Nafziger, *International Sports Law* (Dobbs Ferry, NY, Transnational Publishers, 1988) p. 50.

As CAS develops a definitive *lex sportiva*, the distillation of its principles will enable sports organizations to harmonize their own regulations and rules by basing them on the common principles arising out of CAS decisions. Ultimately, the interpretations provided through CAS proceedings may help in the broad development of international sports law.[111] The development will also shape the future of decision-making by international federations in both drafting and promulgating its rules and also interpreting the rules and applying them to athletes and others controlled by their content. This is best illustrated by the influence of CAS awards in shaping the WADA Code.

Predictability builds confidence for the parties relying on dispute resolution in sports cases. Any individual with a stake in competitive sports should desire 'to pursue these objectives for the sake of greater predictability and stability of expectations.'[112] With past results available to gauge the outcomes of future decisions, those affected by any sort of conflict would be able to predict the likelihood of how their own affairs would culminate. Such information could allow an affected party to decide whether or not it would be worthwhile to pursue a matter. CAS may be relieved from processing a new matter similar to a previous CAS decision. The party deciding whether to take up a new matter will be unlikely to do so if the *lex sportiva* makes success seem unlikely for the party in question. As a result, resources will be better allocated towards pressing and substantial issues that would further advance *lex sportiva*.

There are some disadvantages to the formalization of the CAS arbitration process. These would essentially be the same problems discussed in the previous section: mainly the threat of increased delays, transactional costs, and formality in the arbitration system.[113] However, additional problems may also arise while achieving the predictability and stability of results through *lex sportiva*, including a lack of confidentiality and an inability to allow flexibility towards the wishes of the parties.[114] If the outcomes of future cases are to become more predictable, then the decisions of past cases must be widely published and circulated. Additionally, flexibility towards the wishes of the parties in a dispute may become less realistic as a more formalized system grows.

iii.   Equal Treatment of Similarly Situated Persons

Justice systems should provide equal and fair treatment to all individuals through the application of their jurisprudence; sports law is no exception to this aim. In order for people to value and desire an established *lex sportiva*, they must feel confident in the protections it would afford them. By not differentiating or discriminating between the parties in various disputes, the persons affected by the system would receive its full benefits. Strict enforcement of this policy may be viewed as creating undue consequences, since it leaves no room for the considerations of unique circumstances.

An example would be an athlete with allergies who fails to pass a doping test after a team doctor has prescribed a medication containing a banned substance. CAS would apply the principle of strict liability in this case, placing this athlete in the same category as

---

[111]   *Ibid* at 51.
[112]   Nafziger, *supra* note 92 at 412.
[113]   Nafziger, *supra* note 110 at 52.
[114]   *Ibid*.

an athlete who knowingly ingested performance-enhancing substances.[115] In order to encourage compliance, policies must be strictly adhered to; it is better to set a stricter standard than a more lenient one. Athletes and other affected parties should therefore feel obligated to be extra careful to comply with the pertinent rules. This includes proper compliance with procedures in place that may allow for an exemption to use a banned substance for therapeutic purposes.[116] If all parties are aware that they must follow the rules strictly, then competitions will remain fair.

iv.   Corporate and National Interests in Sport

Today's sporting world can involve considerable monetary rewards,[117] placing the reputations of individual athletes, sporting federations, organizing committees, sponsors, and numerous other parties on the line. Organizing world games is still about competition and athletic prowess, albeit not just for recreation, but it has also become more of a business; 'national prestige can be at stake in a game's outcome.'[118] Indeed, world-level competitions cannot be run without considerable financial clout and organizational acumen requiring the introduction of business principles to achieve the sporting result. As the trend toward more business administration and management evolves, the need for legal regulation over private sporting bodies is increasing, which in turn generates more in the way of international sporting disputes generally. With the large emphasis on winning results and subsequent revenues, there also comes an increasing need for predictable outcomes in the legal administration of sport. An important aspect to this is the necessity for consistency by way of certainty of outcome and predictability of dispute resolution. There needs to be a shared understanding that the rules of the various sporting federations will be properly enforced and that any outcomes are stable. The level playing field and therefore the legitimacy of the level of competition is becoming an important selling point to effectively market events to the mass audiences created through television and the Internet mediums. The risk of ineffective regulations in sports could discourage sponsors and decrease commercial interests. If this is the case, it will be harder to convince national federations to sign on to arbitration under CAS or the WADA Code or continue with their current blanket adoption of CAS as their adjudication body. A more developed *lex sportiva* could help to improve the legitimacy of competitions, and therefore help maintain the multitude of reputations, investments and interests on the line.

---

[115]   See the following section titled 'Rules pertaining to doping offenses' below, for further discussion on strict liability.

[116]   For example, an athlete may be granted permission to use a banned substance pursuant to a therapeutic use exemption. Such an exemption will be granted without consequences only if the athlete complies with the relevant rules under the provision granting the exemption as outlined in the rules of the applicable sporting federation or event.

[117]   At the Beijing Olympic Games Prime Minister Putin of Russia announced that medalists would receive €100 000 for a gold medal, €60 000 for a silver medal, and €40,000 for a bronze medal. Similar rewards were offered by at least the United States and Australia and no doubt other countries of which the author was unaware at the time of writing.

[118]   Beloff, *supra* note 56 at 60.

3.   DEVELOPMENT OF *LEX SPORTIVA* TO DATE

The debate surrounding the existence of a CAS-driven *lex sportiva* is ongoing and heated. Proponents argue that the growing body of CAS opinions and awards has led to more clearly defined rules and principles, which have formed the foundation of the *lex sportiva*.[119] Those who take a contrary position regard nothing novel about any sports-specific law, and instead argue that general principles of law including contractual interpretation, due process, and equity principles can solve any sports-based legal problem.[120] While this argument is plausible, it is misleading. Merely because sport law decisions involve contractual interpretation as well as the application of due process and equity principles does not mean that those tools cannot be used within a specialized legal sporting context to help interpret *lex sportiva*. Indeed, an opponent of *lex sportiva* admits that 'even though CAS's interstitial common law relies on generally accepted due process and equity principles, these principles acquire a sports-specific flavor when filtered through arbitrators' collective sports-related experience.'[121] That 'flavor' should not be considered some kind of middle ground. Proposing a middle ground, even when argued eloquently, simply does not answer the question, but instead skirts it. Either there is a *lex sportiva* or there is not. As argued and explained below, CAS's collection of jurisprudence, specialized knowledge, and reliance on that jurisprudence and specialized knowledge, does indicate that a *lex sportiva* is applied to sporting disputes that fall within the grasp of CAS. There is clear evidence of such a *lex sportiva* through the examination of trends in decisions made by CAS panels and the development of statutory sources of rules applicable to sport such as the WADA Code.

i.   The Existence of a CAS-driven *Lex Sportiva*

That the number of disputes brought before CAS has risen dramatically since its inception is one positive indicator of its success.[122] While it is true that the rise in cases stems partially from the fact that many national sporting federations are forced to submit to CAS's authority if they wish to participate in international events such as the Olympics or the Pan-American Games, the international federations and Olympic organizing committees must be satisfied with the year-to-year results of CAS – at the very least – for it to continue to be the 'supreme court of world sport' that Antonio Samaranch envisioned when advocating its formation.[123] Recognition of CAS as a final authority is evidence of

---

119   See Nafziger, *supra* note 92 at 419; 2 CAS Digests, *supra* note 58 at xxx; Beloff, *supra* note 56.

120   Allan Erbsen argues that the common law created by CAS 'is not a novel branch growing away from general legal norms but rather a vine growing around them.' See Erbsen, *supra* note 55 at 443. Erbsen also believes that the concept of *lex sportiva* does not properly describe CAS's jurisprudence: *ibid* at 441. See also Foster, *supra* note 71.

121   See Erbsen, *supra* note 55 at 443.

122   For instance, CAS only heard approximately ten cases between 1986 and 1987. By 2007, the load had risen to 252 requests annually. See Court of Arbitration for Sport, CAS Statistics, online, available at: http://www.tas-cas.org/statistics. The numbers refer to the year when the request was made, not when a decision was rendered by CAS.

123   Antonio Samaranch was the Vice-President of the IOC from 1974 to 1978. The President of the IOC from 1980 to 2001, and was subsequently made an Honorary President for Life of the Olympic organizing body.

an acceptance of the *lex sportiva* it has created.[124] Presumably for one to be satisfied with the results of CAS and its application of *lex sportiva*, the court must instill confidence that the decisions made are fair, consistent, and relatively predictable. An assessment of these three factors can be made only by a review of prior CAS decisions, which each year increase in volume.[125] Given that those decisions are confined to sports-related issues, it is fair to say that CAS has developed a sports-specific body of jurisprudence.[126]

This CAS-derived jurisprudence has had the effect of developing principles and rules of the *lex sportiva* more precisely, thereby increasing certainty of results.[127] The gradual clarification of principles and rules is rooted in many CAS arbitrators' practice of referring to prior CAS decisions for guidance in shaping current decisions; effectively creating a standard that prior awards are, while technically non-binding, at least persuasive and capable of offering guidance. Although arbitrators are not bound to follow such precedent, in practice they do so on a regular basis.[128] The result has been the development of a relatively new body of law.

Embracing prior decisions as precedent is an indication that CAS is well on its way to achieving one of the stated interests of the court, which is to 'develop a jurisprudence that can be used as a reference by all the actors of world sport, thereby encouraging the harmonization of the judicial rules and principles applied within the sports world.'[129] Statements by CAS panels that its jurisprudence is a separate legal code strengthens the position that those decisions formulate a portion of *lex sportive*,[130] and trends in decisions are proof that arbitrators are embracing the *lex sportiva*, as evidenced by their use of it in shaping their decisions.

---

[124]   For instance, after years of refusal FIFA, one of the most steadfast detractors of CAS, finally began to recognize CAS in 2002. FIFA went so far as to request that CAS set up an AHD to deal with disputes during the World Cup tournament.

[125]   CAS decisions are now archived in a database accessible through its website: http://www.tas-cas.org.

[126]   See Nafziger, *supra* note 92 at 419.

[127]   *Ibid.*

[128]   For example, see *Italian Olympic Committee and Spanish Olympic Committee v International Sailing Federation* CAS OG 2008/008&009; *WADA, USADA, US Bobsled & Skeleton Federation & Zachery Lund v Fédération Internationale de Bobsleigh et de Tobogganing* CAS OG 2006/001.

[129]   See *2 CAS Digests*, note 58 *supra*, at p. xxx. This harmonization of judicial rules is on a global scale, specifically 'the primacy of international federations over their national members' has been argued to be the essence of a *lex sportiva* 'because it is a transnational process arising from international arbitration [which has created] principles that could not easily be formulated in any other forum of dispute resolution in international sport.' See Foster, *supra* note 71 at 436–7.

[130]   For instance, see *Norwegian Olympic Committee and Confederation of Sports (NOCCS) & Others v IOC* CAS 2002/O/372 at n14. The panel stated: 'CAS jurisprudence has notably refined and developed a number of principles of sports law, such as the concepts of strict liability (in doping cases) and fairness, which might be deemed part of an emerging "*lex sportiva.*" Since CAS jurisprudence is largely based on a variety of sports regulations, the parties' reliance on CAS precedents in their pleadings amounts to the choice of that specific body of case law encompassing certain general legal principles derived from and applicable to sports regulations.' In *B v IJF* CAS 1999/A/230, *2 CAS Digests* 369, the panel recognized CAS's deference to *lex sportiva*. The panel held that: 'CAS has to rule on the basis of sports law and cannot invent new sanctions. In other words, if regulatory documents define sanctions and how they should be applied to particular offenses, they should be strictly interpreted.'

ii.   CAS – Rules and Emerging Jurisprudence

A number of rules have emerged from CAS jurisprudence. These rules are exemplary of the *lex sportiva* that CAS applies to cases brought before it. These rules can be categorized into a number of discrete areas: (i) fairness of rules and procedures; (ii) rules pertaining to doping offenses; (iii) rules solving jurisdictional disputes; and (iv) rules governing CAS's power of review. Each of these is examined in turn in the following discussion.

Fairness of rules and procedures

CAS decisions suggest that the *lex sportiva* demands a general fairness of rules. This concept encompasses not only rules imposed by the sports federations and organizing committees, but also rules of procedural fairness before CAS. This idea aligns itself with the understanding that '[i]n sport, results should not only be fair, but be seen to be fair.'[131] To this end, CAS's application of *lex sportiva* will consistently uphold an athletes' right to be heard in a proceeding[132] and the athlete's assumption that their sports federation is acting in good faith.[133] Moreover, if a sports governing body rule is unclear, the benefit of the doubt is consistently given to the athlete.[134] Rules are likewise invalidated if they appear unreasonable or arbitrary.[135] As one commentator has observed,[136] examples of such prohibited rules are ones that give a club but not a player the option to extend a contract,[137] suspensions that run from a time other than that of the offense,[138] and disproportionate punishments.[139] When a federation decides to create new rules, it can only be made in compliance with that federation's existing rules.[140] Such newly enacted sanctions, when made within the confines of the guidelines of the federation, will be deemed to be retroactive when they are less severe than prior sanctions.[141] Rules created

---

[131]   Beloff, *supra* note 56 at 60.

[132]   But whether it is orally or in writing is inconsequential. See the decision CAS 1992/84.

[133]   An athlete can trust the information given to her by her sport's national federation. See *A C v Fédération Internationale de Natation Amateur* CAS 96/149, 1 CAS Digests 251. See also *CONI & COE v ISAF* CAS 2008/OG/008 & 009.

[134]   *US Swimming v FINA* CAS OG 1996/001, 1 CAS Digests 377. See also *S v International Equestrian Federation* CAS 91/56, 1 CAS Digests 93.

[135]   *AEK Athens v Union of European Football Associations* CAS 98/200, 2 CAS Digests 38; *Isabella Dal Balcon v Italian Olympic Team* CAS OG 2006/008.

[136]   Beloff, *supra* note 56 at 57–8.

[137]   See *Apollon Kalamaria v Morais* CAS 2004/A/678; *W v FEI* CAS 90/A/246.

[138]   See *Millar v VCI* CAS 2004/A/707.

[139]   In *Federazione Italiana Nuoto v FINA* CAS 96/157, 1 CAS Digests 351 the panel indicated it was a principle of sport law that a penalty must reflect the seriousness of the infringement. A compelling example of proportionate punishments arose in *Tsageav v International Weightlifting Federation* CAS OG 2000/010, 2 CAS Digests 658. The international wrestling federation had suspended an entire weightlifting team when only three of the athletes tested positive. The CAS panel indicated that the IWF could not punish those who had committed no offense. To do so, was after all, clearly disproportionate.

[140]   For example, see the advisory opinion made on the International Badminton Federation's attempt to change a scoring system, CAS 2003/C/45.

[141]   *Union Cycliste Internationale and Comité National Olympique Italien* CAS 1994/128, 1 CAS Digests 495.

by the provisions of a sports body's statutes may be used as texts of reference; provisions in accompanying guidelines cannot.[142]

The concept of procedural fairness has also been identified by both CAS itself and legal commentators as one of the unwritten principles of sport law.[143] But issues of procedural fairness within a sports body are generally moot insofar as a CAS proceeding is a hearing *de novo*.[144] Nevertheless, there are circumstances where a hearing *de novo* would not rectify a procedural irregularity. For instance, *lex sportiva* requires that when a person appears as an advocate against a party in one hearing, that person cannot then be an arbitrator in another hearing involving the same party, even if it is a completely separate hearing.[145] On these or other grounds, an objection to the arbitrator cannot come from a co-arbitrator, but instead must come from one of the parties to the proceedings.[146]

Rules pertaining to doping offenses   *Lex sportiva*'s clearest difference from other sources of law appears in the doping and doping sanctions context. The most contentious of these rules is that of strict liability, although that terminology is a misnomer of what the principle in doping cases really is about. Under the WADA Code, an athlete selected for testing is required to provide both an A and a B sample. When a prohibited substance is detected in the A sample, a provisional suspension is imposed, but the athlete may request that the B sample be analyzed. If the B sample confirms the existence of the prohibited substance found in the A sample, then an adverse analytical finding is declared by the WADA-accredited laboratory. The national federation or the national anti-doping organization seeks an explanation from an athlete before determining whether a doping offense has occurred. Once so declared and if the sample was taken at an in-competition site, strict liability applies so as to deprive the athlete of any related competition results and prize monies. Therefore, whether the doping substance was *intentionally* used is not a valid defense to the positive testing result. Otherwise, acceptable defenses to a doping charge are few and far between.[147] Generally, sports authorities and WADA will insist on this process (misnamed as 'strict liability'); for without it, catching cheating athletes would

---

[142]   Reeb, *supra* note 27 at 23–5.

[143]   For an example of CAS holding that procedural fairness is one of the unwritten principles of sports law, see *AEK Athens* v *Union of European Football Associations* CAS 98/200, 2 CAS Digests 38. Examples of legal thinkers supporting this proposition may be found in Beloff, *supra* note 56 at 56; Foster, *supra* note 71 at 430; Beloff, *supra* note 94 at 53–4.

[144]   Foster, *supra* note 71 at 431.

[145]   *Celtic PLC* v *Union of European Football Associations* CAS 98/201, 2 CAS Digests 106.

[146]   *N, J, Y, W* v *FINA* CAS 98/208, 2 CAS Digests 234. Note that CAS jurisprudence does not solve the problem of potential conflict of interests for advocates and arbitrators acting in dual roles. See the following section titled 'Key factors in the future development of *lex sportiva*,' below, for a further discussion on this issue.

[147]   Such as establishing that the testing procedures were faulty or that the athlete is subject to a therapeutic use exemption (TUE). Claiming that testing procedures were faulty is a common defense today. 'Attacks on the scientific methodology of various doping control tests have included calling into question the reliability of specific testing methods and have sparked changes in testing to keep up with the latest doping methods used by athletes. An athlete can call both the substantive and the procedural scientific aspects of drug testing into question because of the continuously evolving nature of the testing, where tests for substances like nandrolone and testosterone have been improved or new tests have evolved to identify blood transfusions, use of EPO, or even designer steroids like THG. As science progresses and testing procedures are refined, new information can be

be a nearly impossible task.[148] Commentators disagree, however, as to the direction of CAS jurisprudence in dealing with issues of strict liability. Some commentators argue that CAS will uphold strict liability for doping offenses completely,[149] whereas others disagree in part.[150] *Lex sportiva* confirms, at least, that athletes have a right to be provided the opportunity to present exculpatory rebutting evidence.[151]

The standard of review for doping offenses is 'to the comfortable satisfaction of the court,'[152] which is defined as 'less than the criminal standard, but more than the ordinary civil standard.'[153] Athletes convicted of a doping offense will be automatically disqualified from the competition in question without the opportunity to rebut that specific presumption of guilt. A further disciplinary sanction may be imposed as well, but it must reflect the degree of the violation.[154] A suspension sanction must commence from the first day that the offense would technically prevent the athlete from competing.[155] Simultaneous positive doping tests should be interpreted so that if the two are factually connected, the two positive results will not result in two separate disciplinary actions.[156]

---

used to rebut existing testing procedures.' See Richard H McLaren, 'WADA Drug Testing Standards', 18 *Marq Sports L Rev* (2007) 1 at 7. Another defense is establishing that the athlete held a TUE. TUEs are created under the WADA Code. Article 4.4 states that: 'athletes with documented medical conditions requiring [u]se of a [p]rohibited [s]ubstance or a [p]rohibited [m]ethod may request a therapeutic use exemption.' When an athlete has properly obtained a TUE for the specific prohibited substance in her or his system she or he may defend an accusation of using that prohibited substance by providing evidence that she or he is subject to a TUE.

[148]   For instance, Matthieu Reeb argues that 'if for each case the sports bodies had to prove the intentional nature of an act in order for it to be deemed an offense, the fight against doping would become virtually impossible.' See Matthieu Reeb, 'General Principles of CAS Case Law in Doping Issues', 26 *Olympic Rev* (1998) 67.

[149]   Erbsen argues that: '[d]espite the high stakes and conflicting values that strict liability implicates, CAS panels have been unwilling to second-guess regulator's decisions to adopt and enforce no-fault liability standards. Instead CAS has held that strict liability applies when controlling texts say it applies, but that strict liability does not apply if controlling texts do not affirmatively authorize it.' See Erbsen, *supra* note 55 at 446. Cases supporting this proposition are: *UCI* v *Moller* CAS 99/A/239; *USA Shooting & Quigley* v *International Shooting Union* CAS 94/129, 1 CAS Digests 187; *National Wheelchair Basketball Association* v *International Paralympic Committee* CAS 95/122; *C* v *FINA* CAS 95/141, 1 CAS Digests 215; *Lehtinen* v *FINA* CAS 95/142, 1 CAS Digests 225; *N, J, Y, W* v *FINA* CAS 98/208, 2 CAS Digests 234; *Bernhard* v *ITU* CAS 98/222, 2 CAS Digests 330; *Raducan* v *IOC* CAS 2000/011, 2 CAS Digests 665. It is important to note that strict liability in doping cases is different from the concept of strict liability in other legal contexts.

[150]   James A Nafziger argues that '[d]espite a prevailing rule among [international federations] of strict liability for doping, CAS awards generally disclose an inclination to avoid unnecessarily harsh results.' (Footnotes omitted.) Nafziger, *supra* note 92 at 415. Nafziger does not appear to disagree with CAS upholding the idea of strict liability so long as the consequences of such a finding are in line with the rule of general fairness that CAS panels will apply to disputes, specifically that the punishment should fit the crime.

[151]   See Reeb, *supra* note 148 at 68.

[152]   *N, J, Y, W* v *FINA* CAS 98/208, 2 CAS Digests 234. Article 3.1 of the WADA Code now explicitly incorporates CAS's common law 'comfortable satisfaction' standard.

[153]   *N, J, Y, W* v *FINA* CAS 98/208, 2 CAS Digests 234.

[154]   Reeb, *supra* note 148 at 68.

[155]   *Millar* v *British Cycling Federation* CAS 2004/A/707.

[156]   See *Union Cycliste Internationale* v *Federazione Ciclistica Italiana* CAS 98/203, 2 CAS Digests 221, where the panel held that different positive test results will not constitute separate offenses only when there is a close factual connection establishing that the two positive findings were

CAS's *lex sportiva* has also established rules for testing laboratories. A textual rule authorizing an accredited laboratory to conduct a given test is strong evidence that the test is reliable.[157] Accredited labs may validate their testing protocols[158] and their established procedures will be applied strictly by the court.[159] CAS will not accept an athlete's proposal that the lab be required to use additional testing procedures beyond what is already the established norm.[160] However, when a lab makes a mistake by deviating from its own testing rules, CAS will support an acquittal of the athlete unless another established rule by a sporting authority deals with the legal outcomes of such a mistake.[161] This reasoning reflects CAS's deference to the general principle of fairness as discussed above.

Rules for resolving jurisdictional disputes   CAS has developed a rule under the *lex sportiva* that international federations will have priority over national governing bodies in the event of a jurisdictional conflict.[162] For example, in the case where both an international federation and national federation of a sport have prescribed conflicting sanctions for a doping offense, the sanctions created by the international federation will prevail. This is a crucial rule. Without it, athletes from different countries caught cheating at an international competition could be subject to different penalties – a clearly inequitable result. For instance, if two athletes are caught doping at an international competition, and the sanction for the athlete from country A is 2 years' suspension from international events and the sanction for the athlete from country B is only a suspension of a mere 2 months, the inequitable consequences would actually encourage the athlete from country B to cheat. By allowing the international federation's sanctions to prevail, both athletes will suffer the same consequences for their misdeed with regard to *international* competitions. Clearly, those athletes may be subject to differing penalties with regard to their own national competitions, but that will not be unfair to the athlete with the stiffer penalty since the two will be in direct competition with one another only at international events.

Rules governing CAS's power of review   *Lex sportiva* determines the extent of the power CAS has to review decisions and to what extent certain types of decisions may be reviewed. These rules can be subcategorized into rules with regard to: (i) field-of-play decisions; (ii) non-interference with technical decisions; (iii) matters of criminal law; (iv) attempts to use the court to manipulate a sports authorities' rules; and (v) the degree of CAS's power of review. Each of these areas of *lex sportiva* is discussed in turn below.

---

based on the same single action. This was relied on by the panel in *Wilkins* v *UK Athletics* CAS 2002/A/455, 3 CAS Digests 454.

[157]   *Susin* v *Fédération Internationale de Natation* CAS 2000/A/274, 2 CAS Digests 389. See also *Tyler Hamilton* v *USADA & UCI* CAS 2005/A/884.

[158]   *Muehlegg* v *IOC* CAS 2002/A/374, 3 CAS Digests 286.

[159]   See *Floyd Landis* v *USADA* CAS 2007/A/1394, upholding the first level decision of the American Arbitration Association, *USADA* v *Landis* North American Court of Arbitration for Sport/AAA Case No: 30 190 00847 06.

[160]   *Haga* v *Fédération Internationale de Motocyclisme* CAS 2000/A/281, 2 CAS Digests 410.

[161]   *T* v *International Gymnastics Federation* CAS 2002/A/385, 3 CAS Digests 334.

[162]   *Union Cycliste Internationale and Comité National Olympique Italien* CAS 1994/128, 1 CAS Digests 495. See also *Fédération Française de Triathlon & International Triathlon Union* CAS 93/109, 1 CAS Digests 467.

Field-of-play decisions

CAS distinguishes between 'the "Rules of the Game" … [which] are the rules … intended to ensure the correct course of the game and competition respectively' and '[t]he "Rules of Law" … [which] are proper statutory sanctions that can affect the judicial interests of the person upon whom a sanction has been imposed other than in the course of the game or competition …'.[163] The rules of law, but not the rules of the game, constitute the *lex sportiva*. Each sport has internal regulations that constitute the rules of play that are distinct from any CAS-driven jurisprudence. These regulations are enacted by sports federations and are then enforced by the match officials during a competition. They are the field-of-play decisions. The two types of rules are distinguished by CAS in order to address what one scholar considers to be a paradox:

> [a]t the heart of the *lex sportiva* lies a paradox, namely that one of its key objectives of it is to immunize sport from the reach of law … [t]he referee … must be allowed free play within his own jurisdiction … he must be free to err, subject only to any corrective mechanism contemplated by the rules themselves.[164]

But the *lex sportiva* only immunizes field-of-play activity and not 'sport,' in a broader sense, from the reach of the law. To preserve the officiator's jurisdiction, it has become absolutely clear under *lex sportiva* that CAS panels will refuse to reverse field-of-play decisions except in the most exceptional of circumstances, such as when there is an element of arbitrariness or maliciousness or when an error of law has been made.[165] The theory contained in *lex sportiva* is to 'render under sports the things that are sports and to courts the things that are legal.'[166] The refusal to hear field-of-play decisions is based on the assumption that the officiator of the game or match is in a better position to apply technical rules of the game at the time, as opposed to a CAS panel after the fact.[167] Even if the official makes a mistake, CAS considers it a risk of the game that the athlete must accept.[168]

---

[163]   *WCM-GP Ltd* v *Fédération Internationale Motorcycliste (FIM)* CAS 2003/A/461, 471, 473, 3 CAS Digest 559.

[164]   Beloff, *supra* note 56 at 53.

[165]   In *Mendy* v *Association Internationale de Boxe Amateur* CAS OG 1996/006, 1 CAS Digests 413, the panel held that a technical decision would only be reviewed where there was an error of law or where a decision was arbitrary, made with malicious intent, or violated general principles of law or a social rule. See also *Bernardo Segura* v *IAAF* CAS OG 2000/013, 2 CAS Digests 680; *Rumyana Dimitrova Neykova* v *International Rowing Federation & IOC* CAS OG 2000/012, 2 CAS Digests 674; *Korean Olympic Committee* v *International Skating Union* CAS OG 2002/007, 3 CAS Digests 611.

[166]   Beloff, *supra* note 56 at 55.

[167]   The CAS panel elaborated on this idea in *Korean Olympic Committee* v *International Skating Union* CAS OG 2002/007, 3 CAS Digests 611 by suggesting that CAS would exercise self-restraint from making decisions on field-of-play issues for a number of reasons, including: the arbitrator's lack of expertise in the technical side of sport; the subjective nature of a referee's call, for example, from differences in physical perspectives, the disadvantages created by constant interruptions to the course of play for judicial reasons, and issues with re-writing the outcome of a competition after the fact given that it has many variables.

[168]   In *Mendy* v *Association Internationale de Boxe Amateur* CAS OG 1996/006, 1 CAS Digests 413, the panel held that an official's decision is final even if she or he makes a mistake as mistakes are simply part of the game which have to be accepted by competitors as a risk.

This desire to avoid arbitrating field-of-play decisions found in *lex sportiva* may find its foundations in a similar tradition, common to national legal systems. What occurs on the field of play, so long as it does not fall within the realm of criminal or civil law, is usually beyond the scope of what national courts will rule upon.[169] There are simply 'areas of human activity which elude the grasp of the law.'[170] Even so, arbitration of field-of-play decisions is not necessarily beyond the jurisdiction of CAS.[171] Challenges to field-of-play decisions are certainly within its prerogative of sports-related disputes. Nevertheless, CAS has considered its role in the world of sport, and noted that on the whole, it is more valuable to the sports community to allow games to go forth without unnecessary judicial interference.[172]

Non-interference with technical decisions

The principle of non-interference in technical decisions is contained in *lex sportiva*. For instance, the AHD of CAS gave an advisory opinion regarding a novel type of swimsuit that appeared at the 2000 Sydney Olympic Games.[173] FINA had approved the use of these technologically unique full-body swimsuits. CAS held that FINA had reached its decision in accordance with its own rules, and the decision was not reviewable on any basis of unfair procedure, bad faith, unreasonableness, or failure to adhere to general principles of law. The decision affirmed the discretion of international federations to govern technical standards and delineated the role of CAS in disputes concerning these decisions.[174]

Matters of criminal law

CAS has declared its own power of review in other areas as well, which has become part of the *lex sportiva*. The limits to the areas that CAS will review are often determined in keeping with what is justiciable in international law.[175] One such area is penal disputes. Although authors have suggested that some criminal laws should theoretically be applied in the sports arena,[176] the *lex sportiva* holds that application of penal laws is beyond CAS's

---

[169] For example, see *Agar v Hyde* [2000] HCA 41, 201 CLR 552. The Australian High Court considered whether a voluntary sporting association that makes the rules of a sport owed a duty of care to participants of the sport when drafting or altering the rules of the game. The High Court noted: 'The laws of a game like rugby football differ from norms of conduct enforced by the courts ...'

[170] *Yang Tae Young* v *International Gymnastics Federation* CAS 2004/A/704.

[171] As discussed above, CAS's jurisdiction to apply *lex sportiva* is wide. See the section titled '*Jurisdiction of the CAS*,' above.

[172] For a detailed discussion on this topic, see Beloff, *supra* note 56 at 53.

[173] Advisory Opinion, *Australian Olympic Committee* CAS 2000/C/267, 2 CAS Digests 725.

[174] See also *CNOSF, BOA, & USOC v FEI & NOCG* CAS OG 2004/007, where a panel declined to interfere in a time penalty that was meted out to a German equestrian athlete during competition as it was a field-of-play decision.

[175] For example, technical disputes are not heard in American or Swiss law.

[176] For instance, Professor Christo Lassiter of the University of Cincinnati College of Law argues that the introduction of a federal sports battery statute, limited to situations in which purposeful or knowing criminal misconduct during play leads to grievous bodily injury or death is long overdue, and that whether the criminal misconduct occurs during play or out of play should not be a conceptual barrier as long as the criminal prosecutor can demonstrate the requisite *mens rea*. See Christo Lassiter, 'Lex Sportiva: Thoughts Towards a Criminal Law of Competitive Sport' 22 *St John's J Legal Comm* (2007) 35 at 91. Professor Nafziger also suggests that 'perhaps serious

jurisdiction.[177] CAS has noted that it is 'not ... a criminal court and can neither promulgate nor apply penal laws ... [CAS] must decide within the context of the law of sports, and cannot invent prohibitions or sanctions where none appear.'[178]

It is neither necessary nor appropriate for CAS to rule on situations where there would be criminal charges for the conduct. This would be an unnecessary interference in the jurisdiction of national public law in an area it covers extensively. CAS fills a gap in sports law where international disputes previously had no authoritative body to resolve their issues; this is not paralleled in criminal law. The CAS arbitrator's competency does not lie in deciding issues of criminal law. The criminal laws of the various countries are diverse, and need not be harmonized for the integrity of sport, unlike the other sports disputes on which CAS rules.

Manipulation of rules
Another area where CAS has declined to intervene is in circumstances where one party is attempting to manipulate the rules and the power of the court to gain a strategic advantage.[179] CAS has refused to be used as a pawn in such cases. The exercise of an international federation's rules by a party who is not directly affected will be questioned by CAS, and 'an application by a party who is not directly affected by an event cannot be allowed to alter the competitive schemes of the Games.'[180]

Degree of review
CAS has limited its own power of review in *lex sportiva* by framing the capability of its powers to review a given issue to the same degree of the federation whose decision it is evaluating.[181] During the review, the standard of proof for guilt is, as noted above, 'less

---

physical assault should be treated the same in the sports arena and sports arbitration as on the streets.' See James A R Nafziger, 'Arbitration of Rights and Obligations in the International Sports Arena', 35 *Val U L Rev* (2000) 357 at 377.

[177]   This was made clear in *Rebagliati v IOC* CAS OG 1998/002, 1 CAS Digests 419, where the gold medalist snowboarder was found to have traces of marijuana in the testing sample he provided. Since the sporting authority, the Fédération Internationale de Ski, did not consider marijuana use to be a prohibited substance, CAS held it could not then create and apply penal sanctions not already in existence.

[178]   In *Rebagliati, ibid*, CAS noted that cannabis consumption is a concern both medically and ethically, and was clear that the court was not condoning its use. The FIS in this case also noted that it discourages cannabis consumption, although it has not prohibited its use by athletes. See also *Hall v Fédération Internationale de Natation* CAS 98/218, 2 CAS Digest 325, where the panel supported a sanction for the use of marijuana because FINA's rules prohibited its use.

[179]   See *Czech Olympic Committee, Swedish Olympic Hockey Committee and Samuelson v International Ice Hockey Federation* CAS OG 1998/004–005, 1 CAS Digests 435; *Azerbaijan Field Hockey Federation & Azerbaijan NOC v Federation Internationale de Hockey* CAS OG 2008/005. As I have previously suggested, '[t]he AHD will be reluctant to allow its adjudicative function to be used to achieve a strategic advantage, not otherwise obtainable on the field of competition.' See McLaren, *supra* note 34 at 541.

[180]   McLaren, *supra* note 34 at 541. See also *Azerbaijan Field Hockey Federation & Azerbaijan NOC v Federation Internationale de Hockey* CAS OG 2008/001, 003 & 005. These cases were at the time of writing this chapter the subject of an appeal to the Swiss Federal Tribunal.

[181]   The panel in *R. v International Basketball Federation* CAS 2000/A/262 held: 'the jurisdiction of the CAS can ... not go beyond the competence of the body whose decision the appeal is lodged against ... the panel itself is to be considered as an organ [of the federation it is reviewing].'

than the criminal standard, but more than the ordinary civil standard.'[182] It is also understood through *lex sportiva* that CAS will apply the axiom of *res judicata* only in cases where parties have been a direct part of the prior proceedings.[183] Finally, on a more specific note, when issues of athlete eligibility arise before CAS, those issues can be reviewed only on the basis of an arbitration agreement or specific IOC accreditation for competition of an athlete.[184]

iii. The WADA Code as an Indicator of *Lex Sportiva*

The WADA Code is the clearest indication of the existence of a *lex sportiva*. The WADA Code has been adopted by numerous international sports federations, international organizations, multi-sport organizations, national Olympic committees and associations, national Paralympics committees, Commonwealth Games associations, government-funded national anti-doping organizations, and a collection of other non-categorized organizations.[185] Essentially, it is a globally recognized commitment governing doping in sports. Much of CAS's jurisprudence has been accepted as forming the foundations in this code, further demonstrating the importance of CAS decisions in shaping *lex sportiva*.[186]

The introduction of the second generation of the WADA Code indicates the growing importance of WADA and its code. It has gained and will continue to gain greater acceptance towards its objective of leveling the playing field and harmonizing the rules against doping in sports between different countries; regardless of those countries' views on the use of performance-enhancing substances. Presumably, the success of the WADA Code suggests that other issues in sport, outside of doping, should be regulated through similar internationally recognized processes. Such potential statutes will find their foundation in CAS jurisprudence, as the issues that need to be tackled from a legislative point of view will likely have been identified in decisions made by CAS.

If such new organizations and their accompanying rules are eventually developed to promote and preserve the fairness, safety, and the competitive spirit of sport, the CAS will then defer to and rely on such sporting rules and regulations. Rather than applying the court's own understanding of those issues. There is already evidence of such deference today. For instance, when assessing strict liability sanctions made against athletes for

---

[182]   *N, J, Y, W* v *FINA* CAS 98/208, 2 CAS Digests 234.

[183]   McLaren, *supra* note 55 at 404. Cases supporting the proposition cited in this article are: *USOC & USA Canoe & Kayak* v *IOC* CAS OG 2000/001, 2 CAS Digests 595; *Arturo Miranda* v *IOC* CAS OG 2000/003, 2 CAS Digests 607; *Angel Perez* v *IOC* CAS OG 2000/005, 2 CAS Digests 625; *Dieter Baumann* v *IOC, National Olympic Committee of Germany and IAAF* CAS OG 2000/006, 2 CAS Digests 633; *Arturo Miranda* v *IOC* CAS OG 2000/008, 2 CAS Digests 645; *In The Matter of Angel Perez* CAS OG 2000/009, 2 CAS Digests 651.

[184]   *Ragheeb* v *IOC, IWF, National Olympic Committee of Bosnia and Herzegovina, and Weight-lifting Federation of Bosnia and Herzegovina* CAS 2000/A/297, 2 CAS Digests 761.

[185]   A list detailing all organizations, federations, and associations that recognize the WADA Code is available on the WADA website, online: 'The World Anti-Doping Agency', available at: http://www.wada-ama.org.

[186]   The 2009 WADA Code, which came into force on January 1, 2009, incorporated much of the CAS jurisprudence – effectively statutorily enacting this portion of *lex sportiva*.

doping, the CAS will rely on sporting rules and regulations such as the WADA Code instead of applying the court's own comprehension of doping standards and related sanctions.[187]

4. KEY FACTORS IN THE FUTURE DEVELOPMENT OF *LEX SPORTIVA*

A more precise and exhaustive *lex sportiva* would benefit the sporting world. However, in order to continue its progression in a positive fashion, CAS should consider taking a few proactive steps. First, an effective *lex sportiva* would require that CAS's jurisprudence develop substantially to become a more effective body of law.[188] One way to achieve this end is by ensuring that future CAS awards are made available to arbitrators, athletes, sports federations and organizations, lawyers, and academics. The publication of decisions has its inevitable drawbacks,[189] but those may be offset by the benefits that more predictable and equitable decision making would create. If decisions were widely published, the parties involved would be made known to the public at large, denying the actor's privacy. This could cause a flux of media attention given the significance of some of the larger decisions – a clearly undesirable outcome for many athletes. While preventing such results is seemingly fair to athletes, it is actually questionable given the public nature of sports.

Clearly, damage to the reputations of high-visibility athletes could be the consequence of enhanced media attention, but that is a risk for everyone in society, not just athletes. We rarely hold proceedings in private for other legal issues on the basis that if one is acquitted, they are publicly declared innocent and so should suffer no ill effects. Although there may be some drawbacks, why is it more important to protect an athlete from potential fallout of a public proceeding than a person accused of assault or a white-collar crime? The benefits outweigh the risks. Public proceedings would further the development of sports jurisprudence and would also further deter athletes, federations, and organizations from engaging in unsuitable behavior. Treating athletes like everyone else is a necessary step in bolstering the legitimacy of CAS awards as precedent or at least guidance for future panels.

Second, for *lex sportiva* to mature into a truly useful body of law, CAS must address nagging questions about its impartiality and institutional status, which may be affected by increased formalization of its proceedings.[190] CAS would need to strengthen its stature to withstand interference by domestic courts and to expect its decisions to be recognized under the New York Convention on Arbitral Awards.[191]

---

[187]   For example, see the *Rebagliati* decision, *Rebagliati v IOC* CAS OG 1998/002, 1 CAS Digests 419, where the panel held that the IOC could not disqualify a competitor for drug use that was not prohibited specifically in the governing federation's (in this case FIS) agreement with the IOC.

[188]   Nafziger, *supra* note 92 at 419.

[189]   For instance, part of the appeal of arbitration is the privacy the process can offer. See Ian S Blackshaw, 'Fair Play On and Off the Field of Play: Settling Sports Disputes Through the Court of Arbitration for Sport', 3&4 *International Sports Law Journal* (2006) 107 at 115.

[190]   Nafziger, *supra* note 92 at 419.

[191]   United Nations Convention on the Recognition and Enforcement of Foreign Arbitral Awards, opened for signature 10 June 1958, 330 U N T S 3, 21 U S T 2517. James A Nafziger proposed this recommendation. See Nafziger, *supra* note 92 at 414.

A third step CAS may take to further contribute to the growth of *lex sportiva* would be to constrain more aggressively the permissible scope of the textual rules such as a sport federation's rules and regulations governing sporting matters.[192] The court could, for instance, take measures to encourage federations and other sports organizations to have their own rules comply more strictly with what is provided for in the WADA Code.

A fourth step would be the creation of more extensive guaranteed procedural rights for parties to proceedings before CAS.[193] One procedural measure that is critical to *lex sportiva* is formally to prohibit arbitrators from sitting on a panel in one matter and then defending a client on another.[194] Currently, this prohibition is a part of CAS jurisprudence, but is still undeveloped.[195] As already emphasized, a lawyer who advocates against a party in one hearing may not then serve as an arbitrator involving the same party in another hearing, even if it is a completely separate hearing. Of course, this would not prevent a lawyer who appears *on behalf of* a party from subsequently being an arbitrator in a hearing involving the same party. Furthermore, an objection to the arbitrator can only come from one of the parties to the proceedings, not a co-arbitrator who may have a better idea of whom the other arbitrators have represented in the past.[196] It is difficult for any party to object because, given the confidentiality of prior proceedings, one party may have no knowledge that an arbitrator has a conflict of interest, not knowing who that arbitrator has represented in the past. Failing to prevent arbitrators and advocates from acting in dual roles will make it nearly impossible to project an image of unbiased decision-making and institutional impartiality.

Unfortunately, the development of a more effective and valuable *lex sportiva* may be extremely difficult for CAS to stimulate because the tribunal is at the wrong end of the process.[197] The tribunal cannot seize cases it wishes to hear. It can only receive them and thus address only the issues brought by others to be adjudicated. This makes it extremely difficult for the arbitral body to develop *lex sportiva* in areas that have been identified by lawyers, commentators, or sporting bodies as deficient unless the particular issue actually became the basis of a dispute. In a perfect world, an exhaustive *lex sportiva* would be able to *avoid* those disputes in the first place, by applying legal rules that could be understood by the parties in the conflict, who could then presumably attempt to solve their own problems knowing how CAS would apply the rule should they instead decide to take the matter to CAS. An international equivalent to legislative reform would be a better tool to further *lex sportiva* in this regard. Statutes such as the WADA Code could be improved and other statutes created to statutorily acknowledge the body of jurisprudence CAS creates and to fill in the gaps the case law does not formally address.

5. CONCLUSION

The subject of *lex sportiva* is difficult to characterize and define. At a minimum, however, it clearly encompasses the jurisprudence of CAS. Arguably, the term may encompass

---

[192] Erbsen, *supra* note 55 at 453.
[193] Nafziger, *supra* note 92 at 419.
[194] Professor Nafziger makes a similar recommendation. *Ibid* at 419.
[195] *Celtic PLC v Union of European Football Associations* CAS 98/201, 2 CAS Digests 106.
[196] *N, J, Y, W v FINA* CAS 98/208, 2 CAS Digests 234.
[197] Nafziger, *supra* note 92 at 418.

other sporting legislation and processes that have international reach and are capable of being voluntarily accepted by any athlete, sport federation, or sport organization. According to this expansive definition of the term, several factors would support the inclusion in *lex sportiva* of a statute, decision, or arbitration award; namely, whether it has been adopted by numerous agencies, is fair to all parties involved, and is globally recognized. In order to ensure their acceptance into *lex sportiva,* the principles enunciated must have been developed to promote and preserve the fairness, safety, and the competitive spirit of sport as well as to enhance the objectives of a *lex sportiva*. Those objectives are to ensure predictability of outcomes, equal treatment of similarly-situated persons, and the efficiency of the legal process. The concept of *lex sportiva* will evolve over time, and as it does, so to will its definition.

There are arguments for and against the desirability of a strong *lex sportiva*. Arguments supporting it suggest it will maintain certainty and predictability of dispute results throughout international sports law. As a result, *lex sportiva* could have the prophylactic effect of helping to avoid a range of sports-related disputes, since athletes and officials would base their actions according to previous cases and their underlying principles. The principles of *stare decisis* would be served through a stronger *lex sportiva* by contributing to the efficiency of the legal process, the predictability or stability of expectations, and the equal treatment of similarly-situated parties.

On the other side of the coin, *lex sportiva* could create a trap for a narrow approach towards sports disputes; those making the decisions may place more emphasis on routinely following precedent rather than fully assessing a particular matter and providing their own new insights.

Emerging rules of the *lex sportiva*, derived from CAS jurisprudence, may be categorized into discrete areas such as rules for determining the fairness of procedures and substantive rules, rules pertaining to doping offenses, rules solving jurisdictional disputes, and rules governing CAS's power of review. The WADA Code increasingly reflects much of CAS jurisprudence and is suggestive that a robust sports law is growing each year.

In order to further *lex sportiva* in a serious and effective manner, several steps must be taken. First, CAS awards must be made more readily available to arbitrators, athletes, sports federations and organizations, lawyers, and academics. The publication of decisions has its inevitable drawbacks, but those may be offset by the benefits that more predictable and equitable decision making would create. Second, CAS must address nagging questions about its impartiality and institutional status, which may be affected by increased formalization of its proceedings. Third, a more aggressive stance should be taken to constrain the permissible scope of the textual rules such as a sport federation's rules and regulations governing sporting matters. CAS could find ways to encourage federations and organizational bodies to have their own rules comply more strictly with what is provided for in the WADA Code. Finally, in order to further the development of *lex sportive*, more extensive and guaranteed procedural rights should be created for parties to CAS proceedings.

The exact extent of and technical definition for the concept of *lex sportiva* is not entirely clear. What is clear, however, is that the concept is alive and here to stay. We may not know exactly how to describe it just yet, but we can most definitely take clear and exact steps to make it stronger – and so serve the betterment of athletic competition and the pure entertainment value of those competitions around the globe.

3 Mediating sports disputes

Ian Blackshaw

I INTRODUCTORY

Sport is now big business – worth more than 3 per cent of world trade and more than 3.7 per cent of the combined GNP of the 27 European Union (EU) Member States, with a total population approaching 500 million. So, there is much to play for, in financial as well as sporting terms. Not surprisingly, therefore, sports disputes are on the increase. The sporting world prefers not to 'wash its dirty linen in public' but to settle disputes 'within the family of sport'.[1] And so the question naturally arises: how best to settle them? By traditional or modern means? Through the courts or by alternative dispute resolution (ADR)?

ADR, which may be defined as any process that leads to the resolution of a dispute through the agreement of the parties without the use of a judge, has become very popular over the years amongst companies, business people and organisations around the world, including sports bodies, such as the International Olympic Committee, which established the Court of Arbitration for Sport (CAS) in 1983 to settle sports disputes 'within the Olympic family'.[2]

Extra-judicial settlement of various kinds of disputes through ADR methods has developed because the courts – and, indeed, traditional arbitrations like those conducted through the International Chamber of Commerce in Paris, France – are often slow; procedurally complex, technical and inflexible; and quite expensive. Apart from all that, arbitration, which is designed to avoid litigation, often, in practice, results in litigation; and, because the outcomes of judicial proceedings are generally unpredictable, litigation is, therefore, something of a lottery! Added to which, judges are not always *au fait* with the background to certain kinds of business disputes, especially those involving highly technical matters. This is particularly true when it comes to sports disputes, in view of the special characteristics and dynamics of sport recognised by the European Commission in its recent 'White Paper on Sport'[3] – not least, the need for swift results where sporting deadlines are often in play – particularly recognised by the EU and referred to as the

---

[1] B. Foucher, '*La Conciliation comme Mode de Reglement des Conflits Sportifs en Droit Francais*' (2000), Paper presented at the Court of Arbitration for Sport Symposium on Mediation in Lausanne, Switzerland, 4 November, 2000.

[2] See further on the organisation and activities of the CAS: '*The Court of Arbitration for Sport 1984 – 2004*' by Ian S. Blackshaw, Robert C.R. Siekmann and Janwillem Soek (eds.), 2006 TMC Asser Press, The Hague, The Netherlands.

[3] European Commission 'White Paper on Sport' (COM(2007) 391 final), published on 11 July, 2007.

'specificity of sport'.[4] And, it should be added here, that the EU also promotes the use of ADR, especially mediation, for the settlement of all kinds of 'cross-border' disputes within the 27 Member States, and has recently issued a Directive on this subject.[5]

In England, there is a long established legal tradition that the courts do not generally intervene in sports disputes. They prefer to leave matters to be settled by the sports bodies themselves, considering them to be, in the words of Vice Chancellor Megarry, in the case of *McInnes* v. *Onslow-Fane* 'far better fitted to judge than courts'.[6] And, Lord Denning, the former swashbuckling Master of the Rolls, went further and expressed the point in the following succinct and characteristic way in *Enderby Town Football Club Ltd* v. *Football Association Ltd* 'justice can often be done in domestic tribunals better by a good layman than a bad lawyer.'[7] However, the English courts will intervene when there has been a breach of the rules of natural justice: *Revie* v. *Football Association*;[8] and also in cases of 'restraint of trade', where livelihoods are at stake: *Greig* v. *Insole*.[9]

A similar legal situation exists in the United States: see *Harding* v. *United States Figure Skating Association*;[10] and also in Canada: see *McCaig* v. *Canadian Yachting Association & Canadian Olympic Association*.[11]

In *Harding*, the Federal District Court made the following observations:

> The courts should rightly hesitate before intervening in disciplinary hearings held by private associations ... Intervention is appropriate only in the most extraordinary circumstances, where the association has clearly breached its own rules, that breach will imminently result in serious and irreparable harm to the plaintiff, and the plaintiff has exhausted all internal remedies. Even then, injunctive relief is limited to correcting the breach of the rules. The court should not intervene in the merits of the underlying dispute.

In *McCaig*, the judge made the following pertinent remarks about the role of the courts in the resolution of sports disputes:

> ... the bodies which heard the appeals were experienced and knowledgeable in the sport of sailing, and fully aware of the selection process. The appeal bodies determined that the selection criteria had been met ... [and] as persons knowledgeable in the sport ... I would be reluctant to substitute my opinion for those who know the sport and knew the nature of the problem.

---

4   See further generally on the value of resolving sports disputes by ADR, especially through mediation: '*Mediating Sports Disputes: National and International Perspectives*' by Ian Blackshaw, 2002 TMC Asser Press, The Hague, The Netherlands. See also the chapter on '*Alternative Dispute Mechanisms in Sport*' by Ian Blackshaw in '*Sports Law*' by Simon Gardiner, Mark James, John O'Leary, *et al.*, Third Edition, 2006 Cavendish Publishing, London, United Kingdom. On the psychological aspects of mediation, which are an important part of the mix, see '*Mediation: A Psychological Insight into Conflict Resolution*' by Freddie Strasser and Paul Randolph, 2004 Continuum, London and New York.

5   Directive 2008/52/EC of the European Parliament and of the Council of 21 May 2008 on certain aspects of Mediation in Civil and Commercial Matters: *Official Journal L 136, 24/05/2008 P. 0003–0008*.

6   [1978] 1 WLR 1520, at p. 1535.

7   [1971] 1 Ch 591, at p. 605.

8   *Times*, 19 December 1979.

9   [1978] 3 All ER 449.

10   [1994] 851 F Supp. 1476.

11   [1996] Case 90-01-96624.

In the US, courts have recognized that non-interference doctrines designed for purely voluntary private associations may not be fully applicable to dominant sports sanctioning organizations. In several cases, courts have suggested that more careful judicial review is appropriate when college athletes, who have no choice but to abide by rules of a national collegiate athletic association or individual collegiate conferences, challenge decisions as inconsistent with basic process or with the organization's own rules.[12]

A similar situation is developing in other parts of the world too, as sport is a global phenomenon, sports disputes are an increasingly common occurrence throughout the world and solutions need to be found quickly, informally, effectively and inexpensively. In other words, there is a widespread need to settle disputes outside the courts' system.

It should be added, however, that ADR is not a panacea for all ills and is not appropriate in cases where, for example, injunctive relief or a legal precedent is required to resolve the dispute. In such cases, the courts are the most appropriate forum for settling disputes.

The phenomenal rise of the Internet – not least in relation to sports content and sports-related websites – has spawned its own peculiar kind of disputes, including sports-related ones, and produced its own particular type of ADR process in domain name disputes pursuant to the Internet Corporation on Assigned Names and Numbers (ICANN) Uniform Domain Name Dispute Resolution Policy, administered by the Arbitration and Mediation Center of the World Intellectual Property Organization (WIPO Center), a specialised agency of the United Nations, based in Geneva, Switzerland.[13]

Other forms of ADR include 'med-arb' – a combination of mediation to identify the issues in dispute and, if necessary, arbitration finally to settle them. For example, the CAS offers this kind of dispute resolution method.

Another form of ADR, which is also useful as a means of settling sports disputes, is 'expert determination' whereby the parties in dispute appoint an acknowledged expert in the field of the dispute to settle the dispute and agree to be bound by the expert's decision. This is particularly apposite for settling financial disputes under sports marketing agreements, such as sponsorship and endorsement agreements, especially in the case of the latter, in relation to the abatement of fees under so-called 'morality clauses' because of misconduct by the athlete concerned – more often than not doping offences! For example, the WIPO Arbitration and Mediation Center offers 'expert determination' of all kinds of disputes – whether IP-related or not – including sporting ones. This is a new dispute resolution service offered by the WIPO Center, and the author of this chapter is a member of the WIPO Experts' Panel. CAS also offers a process analogous to 'expert determination' called 'Advisory Opinions', but these are not binding on the parties seeking them.[14]

---

[12]   See, e.g., *Gulf South Conference* v. *Boyd,* 369 So2d 553 (Ala. 1979); *California State Univ., Hayward* v. *Nat'l Collegiate Athletic Ass'n,* 121 Cal Rptr 85 (Cal. App. 1975).

[13]   See further on this in the new book '*Sport Mediation and Arbitration*' by Ian Blackshaw, 2009 TMC Asser Press, The Hague, The Netherlands.

[14]   See the CAS Badminton Advisory Opinion (CAS 2003/C/445) on new scoring rules introduced by the International Badminton Federation, rendered by the author of this chapter on 24 April, 2003, which, because of its non-binding nature, no order was made to force compliance with the opinion's findings.

Finally, one particular form of ADR that generally lends itself to and is especially useful in settling sports disputes – and is the subject of this chapter – is mediation. It is a confidential, flexible, speedy, relatively inexpensive and, perhaps most important of all, 'without prejudice' process with an overall general success rate of 85 per cent.

It is a form of assisted negotiation, whereby an independent third party, called a mediator, helps the parties in dispute to reach an amicable settlement of their differences. From this simple definition of mediation, it will be appreciated that mediation will only be successful when parties have a genuine desire to settle their disputes amicably. If this essential element is lacking, the mediation is more than likely to fail.

Before looking at mediation in detail and its relevance to the settlement of sports disputes, it would be useful to explain some general principles of negotiating.

II THE ART OF NEGOTIATING

Negotiating is an art – not a science – and put simply it is 'getting to yes'! There are a number of guidelines to be followed in order to negotiate effectively and successfully.

Like any other form of advocacy – persuading another person to accept your point of view – a negotiation needs to be carefully *planned*. Before you start, you need to know clearly what your *objectives* are and how you are going to achieve them. Make sure, however, that your objectives are *realistic* and reasonably achievable.

An important part of the planning process is to gather as much *intelligence* about the other side in the negotiation as possible. You will need to know, amongst other things, the kind of people you are dealing with; their strengths and weaknesses; and their aims and objectives.

Again, as part of the planning process, the negotiation needs to be *structured* into distinct phases. The first phase should identify any points of agreement and get those out of the way; the next, any points of disagreement and the reasons for them. The following phases should be to evaluate, from your own point of view and also that of the other side, the importance of these differences and the possibilities for any compromises. Try to identify the matters that are negotiable and the ones that are not negotiable. The points that be conceded and 'given away' and the ones that cannot – the ones that are 'deal breakers' if not agreed!

Watch out for and try to interpret any 'body language' – that is, non-verbal communications and gestures.

Negotiation also needs *time* and *patience* and should not, therefore, be rushed.

Every negotiation should be conducted in a courteous and conciliatory manner. When temperatures and blood pressures begin to rise, it is time to take a break! Shouting at people and losing one's temper never achieved anything!

The use of 'role play' – the 'hard' person and the 'soft' one – should be handled carefully. You should decide, in advance, on the particular roles to be played by each of the members of the negotiating team. And, having done so, you should stick to them. In particular, you should appoint one of the members of the team to lead the negotiations and someone else to take notes and keep a record of everything that is said and 'agreed' during them.

Likewise, the imposition of any *deadlines*, which are designed to move the negotiation along and reach a conclusion more speedily, should also be carefully managed. As in litigation, so also in a good negotiation, you should never issue a threat that you are not able or have no intention whatever of carrying out.

Timing is also very important. Choose your moment carefully to press home a particular point. Always know when and how to retreat.

In international negotiations, be aware of and allow for *cultural differences* and the need, where necessary, for the other side to 'save face'. This is especially important in negotiations with the Chinese and Japanese.

Always try to make it easy for the other side to say 'yes'.

In addition to all that other points that I have mentioned, there is one vital or 'golden rule' that should always apply to any negotiation and it is this:

> Do not insist on getting the last penny!
> Always remember that in a successful negotiation, everybody wins something!

III ADR GENERALLY

Before looking at mediation generally and its application in the sporting arena, it would be helpful to generally define ADR and describe its advantages and the different forms that it may take in order to put the subject matter of this Chapter into context.

ADR's Background and Advantages

ADR has been defined by the ADR Group, which is based in Bristol in the United Kingdom and claims to be the UK's first and largest private commercial dispute resolution service, as follows:

> Any process that leads to the resolution of a dispute through the agreement of the parties without the use of a judge or arbitrator.

The ADR Group was established in 1989 by a group of lawyers, businessmen and professional mediators to provide a:

> ... quick and inexpensive means of resolving disputes without the need to resort to the courts.

The ADR Group has affiliated offices in the United States, Canada and throughout the EU, and mediates in more than 12 000 cases annually, claiming a 94 per cent settlement rate. The Group offers services in dispute prevention and management and training courses in negotiation and mediation.

The other body providing ADR services in the UK is the Centre for Effective Dispute Resolution (CEDR), which is based in London. CEDR was established one year after the ADR Group in 1990. CEDR also offers training programmes and its members include leading lawyers and law firms and many 'blue chip' companies. CEDR claims an 85 per cent settlement rate.

ADR has grown out of the need to provide parties to a dispute with an alternative to litigation as a means of settling their disputes. Over the years, litigation has come to be regarded, especially by businessmen, as an expensive, inflexible and dilatory method of dispute resolution. Arbitration, originally seen and embraced by the commercial community as a quicker and less expensive way of settling disputes, is also now regarded as suffering from similar defects.

The English courts have responded to these complaints by promoting attempts to settle cases in the early stages of the litigation process as part of new reforms of the Civil Procedure Rules introduced on 26 April 1999 by Lord Woolf. Writing in *The Times* on 4 April 2000, Frances Gibb, the newspaper's legal editor, noted:

> Gladiatorial-style litigation is losing its appeal. In its place, mediation – a conciliatory way to tackle disputes outside the courtroom – is finally taking off. These are the findings of a survey [by MORI] into Lord Woolf's shake-up of civil justice. The message one year on is that the reforms have promoted a 'cultural shift' towards mediation.

In fact, to encourage attempts at mediation, the courts may impose an adverse order for costs on a party refusing to mediate who is considered to have acted unreasonably.

As the former UK Lord Chancellor, Lord Irvine of Lairg, told the CEDR Civil Justice Audit Conference, held in London on 7 April 2000:

> There is no doubt that ADR can provide quicker, cheaper and more satisfactory outcomes than traditional litigation. I want to see ADR achieve its full potential.

It is interesting to note, *en passant*, that, in the 1995 unreported case of *Lennox Lewis* v. *The World Boxing Council and Frank Bruno*, the High Court ordered Lewis to try to settle the dispute with Bruno and the WBC over a fight with Mike Tyson, as required by the WBC Rules, by compulsory mediation, which the judge considered would be 'a perfectly proper independent process of mediation'.

Like many other innovative business practices, ADR originated in the United States and has quickly spread around the world. For example, a number of US organisations, including one appropriately called 'JAMS', has been providing an ADR service to individuals and companies for more than 20 years, claiming a settlement rate of 90 per cent.

As CEDR puts it:

> All disputes, whether in difficult business negotiations or full-scale litigation, can become a drain on resources, sapping money, time and management focus, and destroying important commercial relationships.

So, what are the advantages of ADR? Again, according to CEDR, ADR offers:

- *Speed*. ADR processes can be set up quickly and usually last only one or 2 days.
- *Cost savings*. ADR costs a fraction of litigation.
- *Confidentiality*. ADR is confidential, thus avoiding any unwanted publicity.
- *Control and flexibility*. Unlike a court hearing, the parties themselves remain in full control of the ADR process and any settlement agreed. If no settlement is reached, the parties retain their rights to sue. In other words, the ADR process is conducted on a 'without prejudice' basis.
- *Commercial focus*. The parties' commercial and/or personal interests influence the outcome, thereby making more creative settlements possible.

- *Business relations.* ADR processes, being closer to business negotiations than adversarial courtroom procedures, can be better preserved or restored.
- *Independence.* Parties can benefit from rigorous and confidential analysis of their position by a genuinely independent mediator.

ADR can be used in conjunction with litigation and arbitration and in national and international disputes. It can also be used in almost any area of law or business (see later in this chapter).

But, as the Lord Chancellor, Lord Irvine of Lairg, has also pointed out in the Inaugural Lecture to the Faculty of Mediation and ADR in London on 27 January, 1999:

ADR is not a panacea, nor is it cost-free.

What forms of ADR are available?

Forms of ADR

As noted above, ADR takes various forms and these have been defined, again by the ADR Group, as follows:

- *Conciliation.* 'The intervention of an independent third party in order to bring the disputing parties together to talk.'
- *Mediation.* 'A voluntary private dispute resolution process in which a neutral person helps the parties to reach a negotiated settlement. The neutral third party would ordinarily play a more pro-active role than in conciliation. The mediator has no power to make any decision or award.'
- *The mini-trial.* A voluntary non-binding procedure allowing both parties to present their case before senior executives from each party. They would normally do so in the presence of a neutral 'expert' who would assist the parties to settle and who may if necessary give a legal or technical view of the merits of the case or likely litigation outcome. This procedure has been described as being 'structured to reconvert a legal dispute back into a business dispute'. The neutral 'expert' could also be a mediator.
- *Neutral evaluation.* The use of a neutral to evaluate the facts and offer an opinion designed to help the parties reach a settlement.

Although mediation and conciliation are similar, there is one important difference between them in theory and in practice. In conciliation cases, the conciliator is expected to suggest solutions to the parties for resolving their dispute, whilst in mediation, the mediator's role is solely to help the parties to negotiate and reach their own settlement, and only, if asked, will the mediator suggest a solution – and, even then, a good mediator is reluctant to do so!

The subject of this chapter is mediation, so we turn now to a discussion of mediation generally and then move on to look at mediation in sport.

IV MEDIATION GENERALLY

According to the ADR Group, CEDR, JAMS and other ADR service providers, the most popular form of ADR is mediation, with high success rates.

Mediation is also taking off in the rest of Europe, which, according to Jane Player, head of litigation at the London law firm, DLA:

> ... is more receptive to mediation because on the whole the continent is less adversarial [with] fewer large law firms with strictly litigation departments [and] lawyers [who] do both corporate and litigation.

Why is mediation so popular and successful? The ADR Group claims a settlement rate of 94 per cent of the mediation cases it handles; whilst CEDR and JAMS claim success rates of 85 per cent and 90 pre cent respectively.

Why Mediation?

Mediation enjoys the following main advantages:

- Mediation is quick – it can be arranged within days or weeks, rather than months or years as in the case of litigation, and can also be conducted in a very short time.
- It is less expensive – quick settlements save management time and legal costs.
- It is confidential – adverse publicity is avoided and unwanted parties, such as competitors or journalists, are not present.
- It covers wider issues, interest and needs – underlying issues and hidden agendas are exposed making creative solutions possible to satisfy the needs of all the parties.
- It is informal – a commonsense and straightforward negotiation results.
- It allows the parties to retain control – the parties make the decisions rather than control being handed over to a judge or an arbitrator.
- It is entirely 'without prejudice' – the parties have nothing to lose, their rights are not affected by the mediation, thus litigation can be commenced or continued if the mediation fails to produce an agreed settlement.

As Sam Passow, head of research at CEDR, has put it in a report, entitled, 'Hands across the table', by Kelly Parsons:

> ... mediation differs from other alternative dispute resolution methods, such as arbitration, because the outcome or solution is not imposed. It has to be concluded voluntarily by the parties on either side. The mediator facilitates by evaluating the dispute and proposing solutions, but does not make a judgment as happens in an arbitration or independent expert determination. This means the parties own the outcome, it is their problem but also their solution, therefore they are more likely to get an outcome that they can live with.[15]

So, what is mediation and how is a mediation conducted?

---

[15]   The European Lawyer, July 2000.

The Idea of Mediation

Mediation is not a new thing. People have been mediating – that is, trying to reconcile differences between individuals and groups – for thousands of years. The Bible and other ancient texts are full of examples. However, in the last 20 years or so, mediation, as a method of settling commercial disputes, has grown in popularity in the business community and has taken on certain features and characteristics.

Many learned books have been written and seminars given on the theory of mediation and the underlying principles of negotiation, as well as manuals published on its practical application to a range of disputes and issues.

Mediation, if not a science, is certainly an art, and there is a need for mediators to be properly trained in it. Many professional training and accreditation courses are available, and many litigators have taken or are taking advantage of them. Mediation is growing as a new legal practice area to satisfy a developing need amongst a wide range of clients.

The Mediation Process

What is mediation?
Mediation is a voluntary, non-binding, 'without prejudice' process that uses a neutral third party (mediator) to assist the parties in dispute to reach a mutually agreed settlement without having to resort to a court. It differs from litigation and arbitration in that a binding decision is not imposed on the parties by a judge or an arbitrator. The main advantage of the mediation process is to permit the parties to work out their own solution to their dispute with the assistance of the mediator.

Mediation is a natural extension of the most common method of resolving disputes, namely negotiation. However, negotiations either break down or cannot be commenced for a variety of reasons. Mediation gives the parties in dispute the option to start or continue negotiations in a controlled setting. If the mediation is not successful, the parties are still free to go to court or arbitration, so nothing has been lost.

Common concerns about mediation
Many people regard agreeing to mediation as an admission of failure. This is not the case. As previously mentioned, negotiations break down for various reasons, and so mediation gives the parties the chance of keeping the negotiations going. The negotiations have not failed until mediation has been attempted.

Putting the dispute in the hands of a mediator does not involve any loss of control by the parties. On the contrary, the control remains with the parties, as the mediator has no authority to render any decision or force any settlement. A settlement is only reached if and when the parties consider that the settlement proposed is fair and reasonable.

Mediation does not create extra work for the parties in dispute. In fact, in the long run, mediation saves time. The parties do have to invest some time and effort in the mediation, but most cases submitted to mediation settle, saving further time. Even in the minority of cases in which mediation does not lead to a settlement, the time spent on the mediation reduces the time needed for preparing for a trial.

Neither does mediation create extra costs. Mediation reduces costs related to litigation through the early settlement of the dispute. It also, as already mentioned, reduces the trial preparation time required in those cases which do not settle.

Many people shy away from mediation because they think that an opponent will use the mediation to gain more information about their case. In the mediation process, each party is completely in control of the information disclosed. If a party does not wish the other side to know something, they can keep it to themselves or disclose it to the mediator in confidence. However, if the information is something that might persuade the other party to accept a settlement, or is something they will find out about later on through discovery, there is little, in those particular circumstances, to be lost by disclosing that information.

The parties are entirely free to choose the mediator. In fact, they must agree on his or her appointment. Organisations, such as CEDR, that offer mediation services have a list of trained mediators with details of their qualifications and experience.

Most mediations are quick, lasting a few hours or a few days, but the mediator will continue to work with the parties as long as they wish to continue with the mediation.

It is often said that arbitration rather than replacing litigation tends to lead to litigation. On the other hand, mediation is not just an extra step in the dispute resolution process; it is usually the final step as most cases settle.

As already mentioned, nothing is lost if the mediation is not successful. Because the mediation process is conducted on a 'without prejudice' basis, the parties are free to go to court or arbitration. It is as if the mediation did not take place. Nothing revealed in the mediation can be used by either party and neither can the mediator be required to give evidence on behalf of either party in any subsequent court or arbitration proceedings.

When is mediation appropriate?
Mediation is not suitable for all kinds of disputes and in all circumstances.

Mediation will never work unless the parties are willing to reach an amicable settlement of their dispute.

Equally, not all types of dispute are suitable for mediation (more on this later when we look at the use of mediation for settling sports disputes).

Mediation should be seriously considered by parties in a dispute in the following circumstances:

- when they wish to control the outcome of the dispute rather than leave the decision to a judge or arbitrator;
- when they wish to preserve or restore a business relationship;
- when they wish to settle if they can get acceptable terms from the other side;
- when they wish to save the costs of preparing for a trial which may never take place;
- when they wish to avoid or limit the risks of going to trial;
- when they wish to have a quick settlement, including preferring to settle for less now than perhaps more later;
- when they consider that the legal and/or technical complexities of the case are in danger of eclipsing the economic and commercial realities;
- when they prefer to settle a dispute in private;
- when they feel that an injection of common sense or communication is needed to reach a settlement;

- when they believe that a few hours of concentrated effort is likely to produce an acceptable settlement.

When should a dispute be referred to mediation?

A dispute can be referred to mediation at any time, but certain times have been identified by experience as being opportune.

According to the ADR Group, there are four 'windows of opportunity' for referring a dispute to mediation. They may be summarised as follows:

- When each party to a dispute has taken legal advice and before the dispute escalates. A process called a mediated pre-litigation review can be helpful at this stage. The parties meet to decide whether they really wish to litigate and what information they need in order to make an informed decision
- When a writ has been served. Until then the defendant may not recognise the seriousness of the dispute to warrant mediation.
- When discovery has taken place and the parties have a clear idea of the situation.
- When the case is ready for trial and before the parties have incurred the heavy costs of a trial.

However, it is possible to mediate at any stage of a dispute and, if the mediation proposal is refused, there is no reason why it cannot be proposed again at a later stage.

How to start a mediation

In practice, the party interested in mediation contacts one of the mediation service providers, such as the ADR Group or CEDR, and discusses, in complete confidence, the nature of the dispute and its suitability for mediation. If the case is considered to be suitable, the next step is to discuss the possibility of mediation with the other side. This is often done through solicitors or the mediation service provider. According to the ADR Group, an indirect suggestion to mediate is often more effective than a direct approach by one of the parties.

If the other side agrees to mediate, the parties need to choose a mediator who is acceptable to them. The mediation service providers maintain lists of qualified mediators with details of their qualifications and experience to help the parties to decide on the most suitable mediator for their particular dispute.

The next stage is to set a date, time and place for the mediation to commence, which is mutually convenient to the parties. This date should be as far ahead as necessary to give the parties the time they need to prepare fully for the mediation.

The parties are asked to sign an Agreement to Mediate. They are also required to confirm that they have authority to settle the case at the mediation if agreement is reached.

About a week before the date on which the mediation is scheduled to commence, the mediator will call the parties to introduce him- or herself and to answer any preliminary questions the parties may have on the mediation.

The next step is to mediate.

Before describing how mediation works in practice, it would be useful to set out the sort of qualities that a mediator should possess.

Qualities required by a mediator

Much has been discussed and written on what makes a good and effective mediator. For example, writing as long ago as 1688 – mediation is not, in fact, that new! – the Prior of St. Pierre had this say:

> ... to be a good mediator you need more than anything patience, common sense, an appropriate manner, and goodwill. You must make yourself liked by both parties, and gain credibility in their minds. To do that, begin by explaining that you are unhappy about the bother, the trouble and the expense that their litigation is causing them. After that, listen patiently to all their complaints.

Although, as in the above quotation, a number of general qualities and attributes have been identified, much depends on the nature of the dispute and the context in which it has arisen. In the final analysis, to use a sporting metaphor: it is a question of 'horses for courses'!

However, in an insightful article, entitled '*Strategic Considerations in Choosing a Mediator*', published by JAMS/ENDISPUTE, an appropriately named Washington, DC-based provider of mediation and arbitration services, which describes itself as 'The Resolution Experts', Dr David S. Ross, an attorney and mediator with 10 years' experience, sets out some of the main considerations in selecting a mediator.

In this article, he points out upfront that: 'Because the mediation process is only as effective as the mediator who manages it, choosing the right mediator is critical.'

According to Ross, the most important qualities needed in a mediator are the following:

- mediation experience;
- mediation process skills;
- substantive expertise;
- reputation for neutrality;
- creativity;
- strong interpersonal skills; and
- the ability to help parties reach agreements.

He strongly advocates obtaining references on any mediator proposed, pointing out that most mediators provide references on request. He goes further than this, however, and advises that parties should take the time to speak directly to individuals who have used the mediator proposed and obtain their feedback on the mediator's abilities and competence, especially strengths and weaknesses and mediation style.

He also underscores the need for the mediator to have 'substantive expertise', that is, specialist knowledge in the particular field in which the dispute arises. He notes that, as more mediators are specialising in specific substantive areas, parties are able to choose a mediator with both 'substantive expertise' and 'mediation process skills', regarding both as essential qualities.

He also stresses the importance of mediator 'empathy' and defines the ability to 'empathize' as the capacity to 'demonstrate an understanding of the feelings and needs of another person'. And he adds:

> Empathic mediators can build strong, trusting relationships with parties, leading to more open and effective communication ... [which] drives the mediation process, creating opportunities for joint problem solving ...

Finally, he addresses the tantalising gender issue: do female mediators have particular advantages over male mediators? Although he ducks the issue, he does seem to imply that, again, it depends on the nature of the dispute and the gender of the parties themselves. But what he does say with more certainty is that if a party is 'highly emotional, then a mediator with strong interpersonal skills should be a priority'. He also adds for good measure that the parties have a common interest in choosing a mediator who makes them 'feel comfortable and confident'. We will return to this and other qualitative issues when we take a look at mediating sports disputes later.

Professor Karl Mackie, the Chief Executive of CEDR, a leading authority on ADR in the UK (he is Professor of ADR at Birmingham University), has also opined on the essential qualities of a good mediator. In an article in the Maritime Review of 1997, he wrote:

> Mediation is the ADR technique which enables the parties to resume, or sometimes to begin, negotiations. The very presence of a mediator changes the underlying dynamic of the negotiating process. The mediator brings negotiating, problem-solving and communication skills to the process, deployed from a position of independence and neutrality, making real progress possible where direct negotiations have stalled.

So, a good mediator needs to be a skilled negotiator, trouble-shooter and communicator as well.

On the subject generally of the qualities required of a mediator, one further important matter needs to be addressed. That is, the professionalism of the mediator. Mediation is still a relatively new method of dispute resolution and many parties may be reluctant to try it because they are not sure of the professional status of the mediator.

To what extent, for example, can the parties rely on the mediator acting impartially and avoiding any conflicts of interest? If the mediator is a lawyer, he will presumably be bound by the Rules of the Law Society or The Bar Council in discharging his duties as a mediator. In such a case, if the mediator contravenes those rules, he or she can be disciplined. But mediators are drawn from a variety of professions and none. So, to protect the public from an unscrupulous mediator and ensure high standards amongst mediators, many of the organisations providing mediation services have anticipated this and issued their own codes of conduct.

The ADR Group Code of Conduct covers such matters as impartiality, confidentiality, conflicts of interest, disclosure of fees and advertising and promotion. Also, where a solicitor mediator is involved, the Code requires him or her to take out professional indemnity insurance covering his or her practice as a mediator.

Standards in mediation have also caught the attention of the European Commission; and the EU also promotes and encourages the use of ADR, especially mediation, for the settlement of all kinds of 'cross-border' disputes within its 27 Member States. In fact, it has recently issued an important and trail-blazing Directive on this subject.[16] The background to these major initiatives is as follows: In April 2002, the European Commission published a discussion paper on alternative dispute resolution. In July 2004, the

---

[16]   Directive 2008/52/EC of the European Parliament and of the Council of 21 May 2008 on certain aspects of Mediation in Civil and Commercial Matters: *Official Journal L 136, 24/05/2008 P. 0003–0008.*

Commission organised the launch of a Code of Conduct for Mediators, which was approved and adopted by a large number of mediation experts, and in October 2004, the Commission adopted and submitted to the European Parliament and the Council a proposal for a Directive on certain aspects of mediation in civil and commercial matters. This Directive, which interestingly does not apply to Denmark, was adopted on 21 May 2008. The aims and rationale of the Directive are set out in paragraphs (5) and (6) of its Preamble as follows:

> (5)   The objective of securing better access to justice, as part of the policy of the European Union to establish an area of freedom, security and justice, should encompass access to judicial as well as extrajudicial dispute resolution methods. This Directive should contribute to the proper functioning of the internal market, in particular as concerns the availability of mediation services.
>
> (6)   Mediation can provide a cost-effective and quick extrajudicial resolution of disputes in civil and commercial matters through processes tailored to the needs of the parties. Agreements resulting from mediation are more likely to be complied with voluntarily and are more likely to preserve an amicable and sustainable relationship between the parties. These benefits become even more pronounced in situations displaying cross-border elements.[17]

How to Prepare for Mediation

As with negotiating, preparation is crucial to success. In a helpful practical booklet, entitled, 'Making the Most of Mediation', the ADR Group devotes a section on how to prepare for mediation. It points out that a common reason for mediation not producing a settlement agreement is that one side or the other has failed to prepare sufficiently for the mediation.

Although preparing for a mediation is less time-consuming and expensive than for a trial or arbitration, mainly because there is no formal presentation of evidence or cross-examination of witnesses, the parties need to be clear about what they wish to achieve and be ready to evaluate settlement offers from the other side. The ADR Group offers a preparation strategy, which, it says, will enable parties to go into a mediation with 'confidence'.

This strategy may be summarised as follows:

- Check that you have all the information needed to value your case (e.g. expert reports, counsel's opinion, medical evidence, a keen understanding of the law, and so on).
- Make sure you know all the facts and what witnesses you can call on if the case goes to trial.
- Determine the particular questions you wish the mediator to ask the other side (mediators only have the power the parties give them).
- Identify and analyse the legal issues.
- Consider what you wish the mediator to have in advance – ideally a two-page summary of the facts and the arguments.

---

[17]   See further on the content and effect of this Directive, 'Mediating Business and Sports Disputes in Europe' by Ian Blackshaw, Entertainment and Sports Law Journal (ESLJ), Vol. 6, No. 2, 2009.

- Decide on your tactics – what you wish to disclose to the other side. If you are not sure of its relevance or value, discuss in confidence with the mediator.
- Consider how best you can use the mediator – not only is the mediator a channel of communication, but he or she can also play devil's advocate, be a problem solver and source of new ideas and approaches.
- Work out a mediation plan and how best you can persuade the other side to your point of view and position.
- Be realistic about what you want and how best to persuade the other side that you are being realistic.
- With this in mind, prepare your opening statement, which should be designed to impress the other side with your grasp of the facts and the strength of your arguments.
- Decide who is to do what, especially if you are represented by a solicitor, but be ready to participate actively in the private meetings.

In other words, as in any kind of negotiation – and mediation essentially is an assisted negotiation – careful planning and structuring of the process pays dividends.

How mediation works in practice

Most mediations start rather formally. In the early stages, the parties, who may act alone or with their legal representatives (if one party is legally represented and the other not, the mediator normally encourages the unrepresented party to obtain independent legal advice), tend to argue about the facts of the dispute and state their respective legal positions. Later on, in the private sessions with the mediator, the mediation usually becomes more informal, with the parties discussing settlement options and trading settlement positions back and forth.

The mediator acts as a facilitator to get the parties to open up and discuss matters and try to reach a settlement of their dispute. As one satisfied client of a CEDR organised mediation put it:

> The mediator did a first class job – facilitating the discussion rather than trying to take charge.

And added for good measure:

> I think we would have regarded the mediation process as productive even if it had not culminated in a settlement.

The mediator controls the procedural aspects of the mediation, but there are no formal rules of procedure or evidence. In international mediations, the mediator decides on the language in which the mediation is conducted and whether and what documents should be translated.

The mediator holds individual meetings (known in mediation speak as 'caucuses') and joint meetings with the parties and, in consultation with them, fixes the time and place of each session and the agenda. The mediation is to be conducted expeditiously. Only if authorised by the party concerned to do so, does the mediator disclose to the other side anything that is discussed or revealed to the mediator by that party.

Like any kind of negotiation, the mediation is a developing and evolving process and its success depends on the skills of the mediator to bring the parties closer together to try to reach a settlement. As a satisfied client of the ADR Group put it:

> The mediation was principally to discuss quantum and try and resolve the enormous gap between the two sides ... We must say, before it took place we were a little sceptical but we were impressed by the way the negotiations were handled by the mediator ... We feel that we secured a very reasonable settlement when balancing the risks for costs and damages ... We therefore feel that in the sort of case where the parties have reached an impasse and their valuations are poles apart, mediation is worth trying before the last resort of trial.

However, the mediator does not impose any solution on the parties. But, if they are unable to reach a settlement and, if all the parties and the mediator agree, the mediator will produce for the parties a non-binding written recommendation on settlement terms. The mediator will not attempt to anticipate what a court might decide, but, based on all the circumstances of the particular case, will set out what the mediator would suggest could be appropriate terms on which to settle the dispute.

No formal record or transcript of the mediation proceedings is made – the mediation is conducted on an entirely confidential basis. Only the parties can agree to disclose or publish anything.

Any settlement reached, as a result of the mediation, will not be legally binding on the parties until it has been incorporated in a Settlement Agreement signed by or on behalf of the parties.

Although each mediation is unique and follows its own particular course, most mediations tend to follow a certain broad general framework, which Professor Karl Mackie of CEDR has usefully identified as follows:

1. Preliminary contact between the parties and the mediation organisation (or mediator) to:
    agree to mediation;
    agree terms of mediation including dates, duration, location, representation, legal framework;
    costs documentation;
    agree on a named mediator.
2. Limited, brief written summaries of the case submitted by the parties in advance to:
    inform the mediator
    focus the parties on the real issues.
3. Initial joint meeting at which:
    the mediator clarifies the process and establishes the ground rules;
    the parties present a summary of their case to each other;
    the issues are clarified.
4. Private, confidential meetings between the mediator and each party separately to:
    examine important issues and needs of each party;
    encourage openness about weaknesses as well as strengths;
    discuss options for settlement.

Although the success or failure of the mediation process largely depends upon the skills of the mediator, the attitude, co-operation and preparedness of the parties also play an important part. With this in mind, the ADR Group has issued some guidelines to help parties get the most out of mediation. These throw further light on the nature of the mediation process and are worth summarising as follows.

Ensure that whoever attends the mediation is totally prepared and has authority to make decisions, and all who need to attend are present.

- Allocate sufficient time for the mediation: start early and stay as long as it takes.
- Be punctual at sessions: being late may give a wrong impression.
- Your opening statement should deal with the facts of the case and, if the other side has gone first, indicate where you agree or disagree with them.
- Stay calm and be realistic.
- Only use emotive language, if you feel genuinely aggrieved about something and wish the other side to know it.
- Avoid making your opening demands too specific. For example, if you say 'I will only settle for x amount', the other side will stop listening and start thinking why you should not get it.
- Keep an open mind throughout. Mediation is a creative process and often reveals possibilities for agreement of which the parties may not be aware.
- Be persistent. Every mediation has a 'low point' when agreement seems unlikely. This is normal and most cases go on to settle. A break for reflection by the parties often helps in such cases.

V MEDIATION IN SPORTS DISPUTES

Mediation has proved to be a useful method of settling sports disputes, where the parties have been ready to engage in the process, including sports business disputes, where often mega sums are at stake, as the following *Woodhall/Warren* case clearly demonstrates.

Woodhall/Warren Dispute

In general, mediation is swift: a particular advantage to sports persons, who often have pressing event and other commitments and commercial deadlines to meet.

And this was one of several factors why a dispute between Frank Warren, the boxing promoter, and Richie Woodhall, the former WBO super middleweight world champion, was successfully resolved by mediation.

In April 1999, Richie Woodhall sought to terminate his management and promotion agreements with Frank Warren, claiming that Warren was in breach of them and also that the agreements were unenforceable. Woodhall refused to fight for Warren, and also started approaches to other boxing promoters.

On the other hand, Warren refused to let Woodhall go, claiming that contracts were valid; that there was still some considerable time to run on them; and that he was not in breach of them. The parties were adamant in their respective positions.

Woodhall, therefore, started proceedings in the High Court in June 1999. He requested an early hearing of the case to enable him to fight the defence of his world title by September, as required by the rules of the World Boxing Organisation. As the agreements required that any disputes were to be referred to the British Boxing Board of Control, Warren, for his part, sought an order from the court to that effect.

This dispute had all the makings of a full-blown legal fight in the courts, with lots of blood on the walls – and in the full glare of the media. As such, it would not only be time-consuming and expensive to both parties, but also potentially damaging for their reputations. In addition, Woodhall was anxious to get back in the ring and, if he were to continue to be of any value to Warren, he needed to fight his mandatory defence to his world title shortly. So, in all these circumstances, the question arose whether the court was the best forum in which to resolve this bitter dispute. It was decided to refer the dispute to mediation. And the court was prepared to adjourn the proceedings, for a short time, to enable the parties to see if they could, in fact, settle their differences by this method.

A hastily arranged mediation was set up and conducted under the auspices of CEDR. Within 72 hours, the dispute was resolved, and Woodhall signed a new deal with Warren.

Unfortunately, as mediation is confidential and there is no official record or transcript of the process, it is not possible to have a 'blow-by blow' account of what was said, what arguments were adduced and exactly why a settlement was reached (e.g. what leverage the mediator was able to apply to reach a compromise) and what precisely were its actual terms.

One thing can, however, be deduced from the brief facts and circumstances of this dispute – there were some sporting and commercial deadlines to concentrate the minds of the parties and act as a spur to reaching a compromise. There was also a pressing need for the parties not to 'wash their dirty linen in public'!

Mediation by Sports Bodies

Mediation is not only offered by commercial organisations, such as CEDR, but also by sports bodies, such as the Court of Arbitration for Sport (CAS), based in Lausanne, Switzerland, the former UK Sports Dispute Resolution Panel (SDRP), now known as Sports Resolutions UK, based in London,[18] the Sport Dispute Resolution Centre of Canada and the FIFA Dispute Resolution Chamber. Unfortunately, the Australian National Sports Dispute Centre has been wound up, largely as a result of the establishment of the CAS Oceania regional outpost based in Sydney.[19]

The mediation services provided by these and other sports bodies are a complete subject in their own right and worthy of further study. But, within the confines of this chapter, we will concentrate on CAS, which is the best known and in 2008 celebrated the twenty-fifth anniversary of its foundation by the International Olympic Committee; and which is also the model for many of the other sports bodies around the world offering dispute resolution services to their sporting constituents.

CAS Mediations

CAS also offers a mediation service,[20] which was introduced on 18 May 1999.[21] And, as Ousmane Kane, Former Senior Counsel to the CAS and formerly responsible for CAS Mediations has remarked:

---

[18]   See the Chapter on '*Alternative Dispute Mechanisms in Sport*' by Ian Blackshaw in '*Sports Law*' by Simon Gardiner, Mark James, John O'Leary, *et al.*, Third Edition, 2006 Cavendish Publishing, London, United Kingdom. See also '*Sport Mediation and Arbitration*' by Ian Blackshaw, 2008 TMC Asser Press, The Hague, The Netherlands.

[19]   See Brian Doyle, '*Sports dispute resolution in Australia*', 2000 3(4) Sports Law Bulletin, at p. 13.

[20]   See the booklet 'Mediation Guide' published by and available from CAS.

[21]   There are currently some 65 CAS mediators.

The International Council of Arbitration for Sport [the Governing Body of CAS] took the initiative to introduce mediation alongside arbitration. As the mediation rules encourage and protect fair play and the spirit of understanding, they are made to measure for sport.[22]

Article 1, paragraph 1 of the CAS Mediation Rules (the Rules) defines mediation in the following terms:

CAS Mediation is a non-binding and informal procedure, based on a mediation agreement in which each party undertakes to attempt in good faith to negotiate with the other party, and with the assistance of a CAS mediator, with a view to settling a sports-related dispute.

Article 2 of the Rules defines a 'mediation agreement' as follows:

A mediation agreement is one whereby the parties agree to submit to mediation a sports-related dispute which has arisen or which may arise between them.
A mediation agreement may take the form of a mediation clause inserted in a contract or that of a separate agreement.

In other words, an express or an 'ad hoc' mediation reference clause (see later in this chapter).

Although mediation is expressly excluded (in paragraph 2 of Article 1 of the Rules) for disciplinary and doping cases, for obvious reasons, mediation is very appropriate for settling the commercial/financial issues and consequences (e.g., loss of lucrative sponsorship and endorsement contracts), which often follow from a doping case, particularly where the sportsperson concerned was wrongly accused of being a drugs cheat. For example, Dianne Modahl would probably have been better advised to try to settle her claims for compensation against the British Athletic Federation through mediation rather than through the courts.[23]

In that case, Modahl was able to establish that the testing procedure was flawed, because of the failure of the laboratory to store the samples properly; and sought – unsuccessfully – to sue her governing body in the English High Court and Court of Appeal, for the financial losses she had suffered as a result of the governing body's wrongful accusations and conduct.

If the parties in dispute prefer to settle their differences by mediation – and many do because of the special characteristics and dynamics of sport[24] – the CAS model mediation clause is as follows:

---

[22]   On the value of mediation generally for settling sports disputes, see '*Mediating Sports Disputes – National and International Perspectives*' by Ian S. Blackshaw, 2002 TMC Asser Press, The Hague, The Netherlands; and on CAS mediation, see Ian Blackshaw, '*Settling sports disputes by CAS mediation*', CAS Newsletter No. 3, November 2005, at pp. 4–7.

[23]   *Modahl* v. *British Athletic Federation* [2001] All ER (D) 181 (Oct). See also 'Modahl Loses Appeal For Compensation' by I Blackshaw, November/December, 2001 issue of the 'Sports Law Bulletin', Vol. 4, No. 6, at pp. 1, 3 and 4.

[24]   See the case of Richie Woodhall and Frank Warren involving a time-critical dispute under certain management and promotion agreements entered into between them, which was settled within 72 hours by mediation, discussed at p. 182 in '*Mediating Sports Disputes – National and International Perspectives*' by Ian S. Blackshaw, 2002 TMC Asser Press, The Hague, The Netherlands.

> Any dispute, any controversy or claim arising under, out of or relating to this contract and any subsequent of or in relation to this contract, including, but not limited to, its formation, validity, binding effect, interpretation, breach or termination, as well as non-contractual claims shall be submitted to mediation in accordance with the CAS Mediation Rules.

If mediation proves to be unsuccessful, although mediation providers usually claim a success rate of 85 per cent, CAS recommends the following additional clause to be inserted in a contract to cover the above contingency:

> If, and to the extent that, any such dispute has not been settled within 90 days of the commencement of the mediation, or if, before the expiration of the said period, either party fails to participate or continue to participate in the mediation, the dispute shall, upon the filing of a Request for Arbitration by either party, be referred to and finally settled by CAS arbitration pursuant to the Code of Sports-related Arbitration. When the circumstances so require, the mediator may, at his own discretion or at the request of a party, seek an extension of the time limit from the CAS President.

Thus, the CAS offers disputing parties the possibility of a 'med-arb' dispute resolution process: mediation to identify the issues; and arbitration to settle them.

'Med-arb' can prove to be useful in those cases in which the parties finally agree on compromising their dispute through the good offices of the mediator but leave some technical details, such as the apportioning of liability or the quantum of the claim, to be decided by an arbitrator. Depending on the particular circumstances of the case, it may be advisable for the arbitrator not to be the mediator, but a different person, who comes fresh to the issues which the mediation have brought to life.

It may be noted, *en passant*, that in a recent landmark ruling in the English Courts in the case of *Cable & Wireless PLC* v. *IBM United Kingdom*,[25] Mr Justice Colman held that an agreement to refer disputes to mediation is contractually binding. In this case, IBM called on Cable & Wireless to mediate a dispute that had arisen under a contract in which the parties had agreed to mediate future disputes. Cable & Wireless refused to do so, claiming that the reference to mediation in the contract was legally unenforceable because it lacked certainty and was like an unenforceable agreement to negotiate. The judge rejected this argument, holding that the agreement to try to resolve a dispute, with identification of the procedure to be used, was sufficient to give certainty and, therefore, legal effect to the clause. It may be added that, in England too, parties, who, under court rules, refuse to try to settle their disputes by mediation at an early stage in the litigation process, may run the risk of being denied their legal costs if ultimately successful, contrary to the normal rule that 'costs follow the event'.[26]

In other words, generally speaking, the successful party in any litigation can expect to be awarded by the judge its legal costs. In case the successful party unreasonably refuses to try to settle the dispute by mediation, then it is not unreasonable for the other party, who was willing to give mediation a try, should not be financially prejudiced by the extra costs incurred by that party that a successful mediation might have avoided. Of course, any form of enforced or mandatory mediation goes against the basic general principle that

---

[25]   [2002] 2 All ER (Comm) 1041.

[26]   See *Susan Dunnett* v. *Railtrack PLC* [2002] EWCA Civ 302.

mediation, in order to be successful and effective, should be a voluntary process. A fine dividing line in practice!

Because of its popularity in the sporting world, many international and national sports federations now include specific provisions for mediation of appropriate sports disputes in their statutes and constitutions. As to the legal validity of a so-called CAS arbitration or mediation 'clause by reference' in such statutes and constitutions, see the decision of the Swiss Federal Tribunal of 31 October 1996 in the case of *N.* v. *Federation Equestre Internationale*.[27] In that case, the court held that by agreeing to abide by the rules of the Federation, which included a provision to refer all disputes exclusively to the CAS, the sportsperson concerned was bound to submit the dispute to CAS, even though he had not expressly agreed to CAS arbitration or mediation. So-called 'sports association law' applied in such a case.

Procedural Aspects of CAS Mediations

Under Article 3 of the Rules, except where the parties agree otherwise, the version of the Rules in force at the time the written request for mediation (required under Article 4 of the Rules) is filed at the CAS court office shall apply.

Article 4 provides that the written request shall contain:

> ... the identity of the parties and their representatives (name, address, telephone and fax numbers), a copy of the mediation agreement and a brief description of the dispute.

Upon filing the mediation request, the administrative fee stipulated in Article 14 of the Rules (see below) must be paid; and the day on which this request is received by the CAS court office shall be considered as the date on which the mediation proceedings commenced.

Pursuant to Article 6 of the Rules, the CAS President chooses the mediator from the list of CAS mediators drawn up in accordance with the provisions of Article 5. The mediator appointed must be and remain independent of the parties (*ibid.*). The parties may be represented or assisted at their meetings with the mediator (Article 7). The representative must have full authority to settle the dispute alone, without consulting the party whom he or she is representing (*ibid.*).

Under Article 8 of the Rules, the procedure to be followed in the mediation shall either be agreed by the parties themselves or determined by the mediator. This is a slight deviation from the general principle that the mediator is the one who controls the procedural aspects of the mediation. But the parties are required to 'cooperate in good faith with the mediator and ... guarantee him the freedom to perform his mandate to advance the mediation as expeditiously as possible.'

The role of the mediator is laid down in Article 9 of the Rules, which recognises the basic concept of mediation, namely, that the mediator acts as a facilitator and may act in any manner 'he believes to be appropriate' but may not impose any solution of the dispute on either of the parties.

---

[27] *Nagel/FEI*, CAS-Digest I, p.585.

Article 10 of the Rules provides for the confidentiality of the mediation process subject to the normal exception of making any disclosure as required by the law. And further provides that:

> No record of any kind shall be made of the meetings ... [and] [a]ll the written documents shall be returned to the party providing these upon termination of the mediation and no copy therefore shall be retained.

Article 10 also makes provision for the mediation to be conducted on a 'without prejudice' basis, expressed in the following terms:

> The parties shall not rely on, or introduce as evidence in any arbitral or judicial proceedings:
> a.   views expressed or suggestions made by a party with respect to a possible settlement of the dispute;
> b.   admissions made by a party in the course of the mediation proceedings;
> c.   documents, notes or other information obtained during the mediation proceedings;
> d.   proposals made or views expressed by the mediator;
> e.   the fact that a party had or had not indicated willingness to accept a proposal.

Article 11 of the Rules deals with the questions of when and how the mediation may be terminated and provides as follows:

> Either party or the mediator may terminate the mediation at any time.
> The mediation shall be terminated:
> a.   by the signing of a settlement by the parties;
> b.   by a written declaration of the mediator to the effect that further efforts at mediation are no longer worthwhile; or
> c.   by a written declaration of a party or the parties to the effect that the mediation proceedings are terminated.

Article 12 of the Rules requires that any settlement of the mediation must be in writing and signed by the mediator and the parties, and further provides that:

> Each party shall receive a copy thereof. In the event of any breach, a party may rely on such copy before an arbitral or judicial authority.
> A copy of the settlement is submitted for inclusion in the records of the CAS Court Office.

Article 13 of the Rules deals with the question of failure to settle and includes the following important provision – absolutely fundamental to the process of mediation:

> In the event of failure to resolve a dispute by mediation, the mediator shall not accept an appointment as an arbitrator in any arbitral proceedings concerning the parties involved in the same dispute.

CAS Mediation Costs

Article 14 of the Rules deals with the equally important subject of the costs of CAS mediations. Until the CAS administrative fee is paid by each party, the mediation proceedings cannot be started; and the CAS court office may require the parties to deposit an equal amount as an advance towards the CAS mediation costs.

The parties are required to pay their own mediation costs and, unless otherwise agreed, share equally the other final costs, which include the CAS fee, the mediator's fees, calculated on the basis of the CAS fees scale, a contribution towards the costs of the CAS, and the costs of witnesses, experts and interpreters.

CAS Mediations to Date

To date, there have been a number of mediations conducted by CAS in relation to administrative sporting disputes involving sports federations and the exercise of their regulatory functions. Details are sketchy because of the confidentiality requirements.

There have also been a number of commercial disputes settled by CAS mediation. These cases have included a dispute with a sports management agency over the commercialisation of a cyclist's image rights and some financial disputes between athletes and their advertising agencies in relation to substantial commission payments.

As the CAS mediation service becomes more widely known, it is expected that more sports disputes, including commercial and financial ones, will be referred to CAS for settlement under the Mediation Rules, thus proving the suitability of mediation for resolving sports disputes quickly, confidentially and relatively inexpensively.

VI CONCLUSIONS

As previously mentioned, mediation is essentially an assisted negotiation and is particularly suitable, generally speaking, for settling sports disputes. One of its main advantages in this context is that mediation helps to preserve and maintain personal and business relationships. This is something which is particularly important in the comparatively small world of sport, as the *Woodhall/Warren* mediation case, discussed above, clearly demonstrated.

Again, another valuable feature of Mediation is that it is a 'without prejudice' process, which means that if, in the statistically unlikely event, the mediation is not successful, the parties are entirely free to seek redress through arbitration or the courts, but without being burdened by or bringing with them any – so to speak – 'legal baggage' which might inhibit them in achieving a fair result in any subsequent legal proceedings.

Also, mediation is likely to work, in practice, and produce a good result, because the parties themselves determine the outcome and do not have the result imposed upon them by someone else – a judge or an arbitrator – so have 'ownership' – so to speak – of the settlement they reach, with the help of the neutral mediator, whose impartiality and expertise, one should add, are crucial in the process.

Other advantages of this process and its particular suitability for settling sports disputes, including its flexibility and confidentiality, have been noted in the course of this chapter and need not be repeated here.

However, the following caveats should be added. Mediation is not suitable in all circumstances, not least where injunctive relief is sought; and the success of mediation will always depend upon the willingness of the parties to seek an amicable settlement of their dispute, without which the process is almost certainly bound to fail; and, finally, mediation will only succeed by observing the following so-called 'golden rule of negotiation', namely:

Do not go for the last penny – in a good negotiation everybody wins something!

4 European and North American models of sports organization

James A.R. Nafziger

I. INTRODUCTION

Comparative legal commentary on the organizational structure of sports, particularly of professional sports, has been of substantial interest in recent years. In particular, the commentary has compared European and North American models of organization.[1] This chapter first describes the two models and then considers whether they are accurate and whether they remain divergent or are converging. Both models are largely European constructs. It is not surprising, therefore, that they are widely known among policymakers, practitioners, and scholars in Europe, especially the European Sports Model, but are relatively unknown in North America. It is also not surprising that, given the primacy of the European Sports Model, the North American Sports Model may simply be that which the European Sports Model is not. Even so, the models are useful in analyzing characteristics and trends in national and regional organization of sports. Comparing the models highlights divergent values and characteristics, sharpens analysis, and yields new insights.

A few preliminary observations may be useful in defining the models. First, they are just that: models – that is, general representations of reality rather than precise descriptions of organizational structures. We should not expect too much of them. Also, we should not overlook significant variations within each of the two regions. The European Sports Model is based largely on a single sport, football/soccer, which dominates public attention on that continent. Other sports, however, have their own distinctive structures. For example, contrary to the monolithic structures of football/soccer in European countries, several competing organizations stage championship boxing matches there. Also, a few European rugby leagues, contrary to the European Sports Model, maintain caps on the salaries of players that each club is allowed to spend. There are also important variations even among the structures of national football/soccer organizations in Europe. Moreover, although the European Sports Model has been replicated widely around the world, it is by no means universal. In addition to the North American Sports Model, some Asian and Caribbean organizational structures, for example, are distinctive.

The North American Model is likewise diversified. There are important variations among the major professional sports leagues (baseball, basketball, hockey, and football),

---

[1] See, e.g., LARS HALGREEN, EUROPEAN SPORTS LAW: A COMPARATIVE ANALYSIS OF THE EUROPEAN AND AMERICAN MODELS OF SPORT (2004). See also Stephen Weatherill, *Resisting the Pressures of 'Americanization': The Influence of European Community Law on the 'European Sports Model,'* 8 WILLAMETTE J. INT'L L. & DISP. RES. 37 (2002). For an earlier version of this chapter focused on these models, see EU, SPORT, LAW AND POLICY 35 (Simon Gardiner, Richard Parrish, and Robert C.R. Siekmann eds. 2009).

between Canadian and US structures, and between these similar national structures and others elsewhere in North America such as in Mexico, Central America, and the Caribbean.[2]

Second, a functional analysis and evaluation of the European Sports Model inevitably must take account of European Community/European Union (EC/EU) law. Of particular significance are the tensions between the exigencies of economic integration and the so-called specificity of sport, according to which the special nature of sport – the 'sporting exception,'[3] with its own complex structure of regulation and dispute resolution, merits a reserved domain of authority beyond EU supervision and regulation.

Finally, the actual structure of professional sports in Europe continues to evolve. Consequently, the European Sports Model may no longer reflect the realities of football/ soccer (if it ever did) in an era of global marketing, sponsorships, inflated salaries, and so on.

II. THE EUROPEAN SPORTS MODEL

What, then, is the European Sports Model? In 1997 the Treaty of Amsterdam, which amended the Treaty Establishing the European Economic Community, attached several single-paragraph declarations, including Declaration 29 on Sport.[4] It was the first to acknowledge the economic and social roles of sport in the process of European integration. Later, in preparation for a 1999 Conference on Sport in Olympia, Greece, the European Commission expanded on this declaration by publishing a detailed consultation document entitled 'The European Sports Model.'[5] The same year, the Commission

---

[2] Throughout this chapter, discussion of the North American Sports Model will be limited to the features of sport in the United States and Canada, drawing heavily on examples from the United States. The Canadian structure is similar to that of the United States so that a few Canadian teams and their players in binational professional leagues are thereby subject to the same rules as United States teams and their players.

[3] For a thorough, highly informative exploration of this topic, see RICHARD PARRISH AND SAMULI MIETTINEN, THE SPORTING EXCEPTION IN EUROPEAN UNION LAW (2008). In his Foreword to the book, Stephen Weatherill, *ibid.* at vii, observes as follows:

> In my view the correct way to understand the so-called 'sporting exception' in EC law is simply to regard it as the space allowed to sports governing bodies to show that their rules, which in principle fall within the EC Treaty where they have economic effects, represent an essential means to protect and promote the special character of sport. There is no blanket immunity. There is case-by-case scrutiny. EC law applies, but does not (necessarily) condemn.

On the 'specificity of sport,' see also Ian Blackshaw, *The 'Specificity of Sport' and the EU White Paper on Sport: Some Comments*, 2007/3–4 INT'L SPORTS L.J., at 87.

[4] Declaration 29, Treaty of Amsterdam Amending the Treaty on European Union, the Treaties Establishing the European Communities and Certain Related Acts, Oct. 2, 1997, 1997 O.J. (C340) 1 [hereinafter Declaration 29 on Sport]. The entire Declaration 29 appears in the text at note 19 *infra*. See also Treaty of Nice, Feb. 6, 2001, O.J. (C80) 1. Both of these treaties amended the Treaty of the European Economic Community [hereinafter EC/EU Treaty].

[5] European Commission, Directorate-General X, THE EUROPEAN MODEL OF SPORT (1999) [hereinafter Consultation Document]; RICHARD PARRISH, SPORTS LAW AND POLICY IN THE EUROPEAN UNION (2003); Weatherill, *supra* note 1. For a cogent analysis of current problems and possible solutions related to the model, see Thomas M. Schiera, *Balancing Act: Will the European*

published the Helsinki Report on Sport[6] in response to which the European Council published a definitive statement, the 2000 Nice Declaration on Sport.[7] Neither of these latter two documents specifically reiterates the features of the European Sports Model although they both confirm values closely associated with the model. Then, in 2007, the Commission issued a White Paper on Sport[8] that put several features of the model in the larger context of sport as an economic and social phenomenon of fundamental importance to human welfare.

The comprehensive Lisbon Treaty of 2009[9] is the first formal agreement among EU member states to incorporate a specific provision on sport. The agreement as a whole is intended to strengthen the institutional structure and decision making of the European Union. Article 165 establishes that '[t]he Union shall contribute to the promotion of sporting issues, while taking into account the specific nature of sport, its structure based on voluntary activity and its social and educational function.' Among other provisions, the same Article emphasizes the aim of 'developing the European dimension in sport.'

The European Commission's Consultation Document identified six specific features that form the core of the European Sports Model, as follows.

A. Pyramid Structure

In each country, a single, comprehensive structure for each sport includes four integrated, interdependent levels of professional and nonprofessional organizations. This structure is described as a pyramid. At its base are the largely autonomous and nonprofessional *clubs* that are said to be fundamental institutions in European society from the smallest communities on up. For example, it is estimated that 39 percent of the population in

---

Commission Allow European Football to Reestablish the Competitive Balance That it Helped Destroy?, 32 BROOK. J. INT'L L. 709 (2007); Gritt Osmann, *Das Europäische Sportmodell*, SPURT, 6/1999, at 228; 2/2000, at 58. Pertinent documents may be found in THE EUROPEAN UNION AND SPORT: LEGAL AND POLICY DOCUMENTS (Robert Siekmann and Jan Willem Soek, eds. 2005).

6   Report from the Commission to the European Council with a View to Safeguarding Current Sports Structures and Maintaining the Social Function of Sport Within the Community Framework, The Helsinki Report on Sport, COM (1999) 644 final.

7   Declaration on the Specific Characteristics of Sport and its Social Function in Europe, of Which Account Should be Taken in Implementing Common Policies, No. 13948/00 of Dec. 2000 (EC).

8   Commission of the European Communities, White Paper on Sport, COM (2007) 391 final. [hereinafter White Paper]. PARRISH AND MIETTINEN, note 3 *supra*, at 43, observe as follows:

> The White Paper was not designed to act as the basis for legislative proposals but to state the Commission's current policy position on sport. In doing so the White Paper acts as another communication with sports organizations and also as an orientation document sensitizing the other Commission DG's and EU institutions to the current debates within sport. The White Paper is structured around three themes: the societal role of sport, its economic dimension and its organization in Europe.

With respect to the European Sports Model, the White Paper adopts the concept of the specificity of sport, *ibid.* at 44, but advances a rather noncommittal view that in defining that concept, a case-by-case method is preferable to a uniform model. *Ibid.* at 50.

9   Treaty of Lisbon Amending the Treaty on European Union and the Treaty Establishing the European Community, Dec. 17, 2007, 500 O.J. (C306).

Austria belongs to a sports club.[10] At the next higher level are *regional federations* within each country. They are responsible for organizing competition among the constituent clubs in a particular sport. At the third level up are *national federations.* They are responsible for overseeing the work of the regional federations, organizing competition among clubs from different regions, staging national championships, and regulating sports activity. For each sport, there is a separate national federation, each of which therefore enjoys both a monopolistic position in a particular sport and the competence to regulate itself, subject to national legislation. At the top of the pyramid are the *European federations*, again, one for each sport, such as the Union of European Football Associations (UEFA), with one member from each country. They organize European championships in each sport, based on the rules of international sports federations (IFs) and with their approval, such as the Fédération Internationale de Football Associations (FIFA) in football/soccer.

Theoretically, a primary function of this pyramid structure is to facilitate an equitable distribution of revenue among the constituent sports clubs so as to encourage mass participation and competitive balance among clubs. In practice, however, an equitable distribution of revenue relies less on the pyramid structure than simply on discretionary funding by national federations from the income of the national teams that represent each country in international competition.

B. Promotion and Relegation

In Europe's open system of promotion and relegation, clubs may move up or down from year to year depending largely on their win-loss records. The purposes of this system are primarily to give small- or medium-sized clubs a better chance to reward merit and generally to enhance competition.[11] A dynamic, hierarchical system therefore operates at all levels of the pyramid. The English Football Association (FA) hierarchy, for example, consists of seven tiers. Each year, the best-performing teams on any of the bottom six tiers may advance to a higher tier and, if they are consistently successful, end up in the National Football Conference, the highest tier of competition. The FA itself is the exclusive, recognized national federation in English football and is therefore a member of UEFA.

The specific rules and criteria for the process of promotion and relegation are defined by the national federations such as the FA in England, but they all seek to reward merit and promote equality of opportunity and balanced competition among teams. In addition, the promotion-and-relegation system performs an ethical function by mandating relegation to a lower tier of any team that has engaged in specified questionable practices.

Thus, for example, English football clubs finishing in the last four places of the National Football Conference at the top are relegated to either of two second-tier leagues for the following season. Two clubs are therefore relegated to the North League and two clubs to the South League. Conversely, the top team in each of these second-tier leagues is promoted to the geographically undifferentiated National Football Conference. Its remaining two spots for promoted clubs, one from each league, are filled after a series of

---

[10] *Sport for All*, SPORTS INFO. BULL. 19 (1997).
[11] On the benefits of this system, generally see PARRISH AND MIETTENEN, note 3 *supra*, at 207.

play-off games among clubs finishing second through fifth in each of the leagues. These play-offs not only add to the excitement of competition each year, but also offer an equitable second chance to some clubs, particularly late bloomers and non-champions. Promotion and relegation of teams in the lower tiers is also merit-driven, but clubs must affirmatively request promotion upward if they qualify.[12]

Overall, the European Commission:

> '... has taken the position that the pyramid structure of sport, along with promotion and relegation, are important aspects of the culture of sport in Europe, and that preservation of [such cultural] institutions (and presumably after such cultural aspects of sports) is an important interest that should be considered in determining whether the rules and policies of leagues and governing bodies are lawful under EU law, including competition law.'[13]

As we shall see, this is the crux of what we might call an ongoing legal rivalry or tournament in Europe, involving substantial litigation.

C.   Grassroots Involvement

Another feature of the European Sports Model is a strong commitment to voluntary, grassroots participation and leadership. Some 700 000 clubs at the local level are expected to be actively involved in training athletes and organizing competition in their communities, usually by enlisting volunteers (an estimated 10 million throughout Europe) rather than paid professionals.[14] Such grassroots involvement is a foundation of European sports. For example, Portuguese football/soccer clubs rely on approximately 70 000 unpaid coaches.[15] While there may be some funding and other involvement at the grassroots from the regional and national federations, the clubs bear most of the responsibility for developing players and putting together teams.

The role of sports is idealized in Europe as a vital means for communities to bind their citizens together, from the grassroots to the top professional level. Indeed, throughout the world, '[s]port is central enough to the experience of the vast majority of people to be a useful tool to break down the barriers which divide citizens.'[16] It is unclear, however, how to define a genuine sports community above the level of highly localized, essentially

---

[12]   Football Association, National League System Regulations (2006); see also Roger G. Noll, *The Economics of Promotion and Relegation in Sports Leagues: The Case of English Football*, 3 J. SPORTS & ECON. 169 (2002).

[13]   Gary Roberts, *The Legality of the Exclusive Collective Sale of Intellectual Property Rights by Sports Leagues*, 3 VA. SPORTS & ENT. L.J. 52 (2001).

[14]   See *Commission of the European Communities, Commission Staff Working Document*, THE EU AND SPORT: BACKGROUND AND CONTEXT, ACCOMPANYING DOCUMENT TO THE WHITE PAPER ON SPORT 14, SEC (2007) 935.

[15]   See Consultation Document, note 5 *supra*, at 2.

[16]   John Wunderli, *Squeeze Play: The Game of Owners, Cities, Leagues and Congress*, 13 SPORTS LAW & REGULATION 24 (1999). Thus:

> A professional sports team should be a tool to be used to improve the quality of life of the members of the community. A sports team can be a very effective educational and communicative tool. The intangibles of a sports franchise can be good or bad, but sports is definitely a powerful medium. It may sound trite, but it is nevertheless true, that a sporting contest has metaphorical qualities which [lend themselves] to shared observation, evaluation, and discussion. It also has

neighborhood competition. Consequently, it is unclear whether the vaunted grassroots involvement ever comes close to achieving the ideal of communitarianism championed by the European Sports Model. Even if that ideal is generally achievable, sports communities are not always coterminous with municipalities. Sports therefore divide some municipalities.[17] For example, football/soccer loyalties in Glasgow and Liverpool, British bastions of the sport, have historically been divided between Protestant and Catholic-oriented clubs. That kind of division is certainly not an optimal outgrowth of grassroots participation in sports activity.

D. National Identity

The European Commission has described sport in Europe as: 'one of the last national passions. The commitment to national identity, therefore, is one of the features of sport in Europe.'[18] Declaration 29 on Sport, annexed to the Treaty of Amsterdam, articulated this principle as follows:

> The Conference emphasises the social significance of sport, in particular its role in forging identity and bringing people together. The Conference therefore calls on the bodies of the European Union to listen to sports associations when important questions affecting sport are at issue. In this connection, special consideration should be given to the particular characteristics of amateur sport.[19]

The Commission's 2007 White Paper amplifies this appeal by noting the reciprocal roles of patriotic emotions and solidarity, on one hand, and of personal commitments to physical exercise and healthy social relationships, on the other.

E. International Competitions

The European Commission, acknowledging an apparent psychological need for people to confront one another physically, promotes sports competition as an alternative to conflict, if not bloodshed, and as a safeguard of cultural diversity.[20] International competitions therefore are seen as a means of harnessing national identity in the production of regional harmony and integration.

---

romantic qualities which frame idealistic thoughts and memories ... A sports franchise is a powerful tool that a city can use to improve the quality of life of its citizens.

Ibid. at 25.
[17]

[It] must be strongly noted that a professional sports team does not automatically have a unifying effect by virtue of being a professional sports team. In fact, the same power a sports team has to unify, it has to divide, if it is perceived as only for a particular race, economic class, or culture ... Professional sports can also bring to the fore pettiness, greed, divisiveness, and an exaggerated emphasis on athletic victories.

Ibid. at 24, 25.
[18]   Consultation Document, note 5 *supra*, at 4, 5.
[19]   Declaration 29 on Sport, note 4 *supra*.
[20]   Consultation Document, note 5 *supra*, at 5.

F. Negative Aspects

The last of the six features of the European Sports Model candidly acknowledges the negative aspects of competition, particularly as a byproduct of efforts to forge national identities. Specifically, the European Commission's Consultative Document recognized that the formation of national identities often inspires ultra-nationalism, racism, intolerance, and hooliganism related to sports events.[21]

III. THE NORTH AMERICAN SPORTS MODEL

In general, the European Sports Model reflects an *open* system of national competitions in which individual clubs, organized comprehensively from the grassroots to the top professional tier in a pyramid structure, move up or down in status generally based on merit at the end of a season. The North American Sports Model, as a European construct, is less easily defined because there is little agreement on what exactly it is other than what, to some extent, the European Sports Model is not. For the most part, it largely restates what is seen to be a creeping Americanization of sport, a view that is variously inspired by European nativism, disapproval of American culture, and misunderstanding of it.[22]

This creeping Americanization, as it has been called, is closely identified with commercialism but has other distinctive characteristics. For example, the European Commission's Consultation Document claimed that sport in North America is not a pastime and way of contributing to society, as it is said to be in Europe, but only a business 'operated mainly by professionals.'[23] On the other hand, the same document concluded that the negative features of the European Sports Model – ultra-nationalism, racism, intolerance, and hooliganism – 'are unknown in the U.S.'[24] Despite the questionability of such generalizations about the sports culture in North America, the model merits consideration as a creditable attempt to represent reality. As sketched out in the literature,[25] it has, like the European Sports Model, six principal characteristics, as follows.

---

[21] *Ibid.*

[22] The perception of creeping Americanization has been described as follows:

Indeed, it seems as if the British find every aspect of the sporting world's Americanization fearful. Thus, for example, *The Guardian* reported complaints in 1995 that British stadiums have increasingly come to resemble those in America and are now equipped with good seats, restaurants, and even dance floors: Abolishing those infamous standing-room sections, or 'terraces,' where nearly 100 people lost their lives in riots at Hillsborough in Sheffield, has made the sport too 'nice.' In 1998 *The Independent* intoned: 'The creeping Americanisation of British sports, in terms of ubiquitous coverage and potential for earning, means that niceness is at a higher premium than ever before.' Americanization has also been blamed for taming fans, who previously cared passionately about whatever game they were watching; now they allegedly attend events primarily to see and be seen.

Andrei S. Markovits, *Western Europe's America Problem*, CHRON. HIGHER ED., Jan. 19, 2007, at B6, B8. See also Weatherill, note 1 *supra, passim*.

[23] Consultation Document, note 5 *supra*, at 4.

[24] *Ibid.* at 5.

[25] See especially HALGREEN, note 1 *supra*, at 7.

A.   A Sharp Distinction between Amateur and Professional Sports

The pyramid structure of European sports organizations merges professional and non-professional sports into a hierarchy governed for the common good by vertically integrated associations and federations. The North American Sports Model, however, is said to distinguish sharply between 'amateur' and 'professional' sports, each with its own unintegrated structures. On the one hand, professional sports are governed primarily by their own league rules and employment agreements reached by collective bargaining. Amateur sports, on the other hand, are governed by several layers of authority in the United States: community leagues, school athletic associations, state and national regulatory boards, the National Collegiate Athletic Association (NCAA) and other supervisory organizations at the non-professional level, the Amateur Sports Act, and the rules and processes of the Olympic Movement. The precise definition of an 'amateur' varies, from the NCAA's strict prohibitions on contracts for compensating athletes to the inclusive eligibility rules of the Amateur Sports Act and the Olympic Movement that have little to do with compensation of athletes.

The important point is that the distinction between amateur and professional sports that Europeans attribute to North American sports is fundamental in highlighting the European commitment to an open, integrated structure of competition. Once the distinction has been made, however, it has tended to be exaggerated so as to obscure the strong role of non-professional competition in North American sports culture and its role in training professional athletes. Instead, in the words of a leading European expert, the core of the North American Model is 'synonymous with the way professional sports has been organized in the four Major League Sports.'[26]

B.   The Role of Schools and Colleges

The fundamental role of schools and colleges in the organization of sport, and the characteristic combination of sport with academic education, is another fundamental feature of the North American Sports Model,[27] indeed, an essential building block of both non-professional and professional sports. It is therefore surprising how little attention this feature of North American sports culture has received in the comparative legal commentary.[28] Without understanding the role of the schools and colleges as building blocks, however, the division between 'amateur' and 'professional' sports appears to be far more pronounced than it really is.

C.   A Closed System of Competition

The structure of sports organization in North America is said to involve a *closed* system of competition. In contrast to the European Sports Model's pyramid structure and its open

---

[26]   *Ibid.*

[27]   'This direct interrelationship between the education system and professional sports leagues is quite unique for the U.S. in comparison to Europe.' *Ibid.* at 73.

[28]   But see HALGREEN, *ibid.* at 72 ('The very strong sports tradition among U.S. high schools and colleges is also a very significant feature in the American Model of sport compared to the situation in Europe').

system of promotion and relegation, the major sports leagues in the United States are generally closed and autonomous, each with an average of 30–32 teams. Within the framework of governmental regulation, the teams in each league co-opt their own membership. They define which teams are to be included within a league, and once teams are so included, they may remain in the league with little fear of expulsion.[29] Indeed, membership in a league is an essential and definitive requirement for a team. Member teams thus have only derivative rights from a league and must satisfy distinct obligations[30] to other members to protect mutual market opportunities as well as the league itself. It has been said, quite aptly, that although in Europe there are no leagues without teams, in the United States there are no teams without leagues.

> [It] is the league, not the teams, that generates the fundamental market opportunity to produce professional sports games within the league territories. The league transfers derivative rights in the naked market opportunity, a property interest, to enable the member clubs to gain economic rewards by enhancing the inherent value of the business opportunity through team marketing and other operations.[31]

The North American Sports Model implies that membership in the league is essentially a gift from other members of the league, although membership normally entails the payment of a substantial fee. Expansion and contraction of teams is controlled solely by cooptation. Unlike the generally open system within the pyramid of the European Sports Model, the lowest levels of organized *professional* sports in North America – farm teams and minor leagues in such sports as baseball and hockey – are fundamentally recruitment mechanisms to help train and provide the major leagues with seasoned players.

Thus, the professional leagues operate as joint ventures among the constituent teams. While competing with each other on the field, teams work together off the field in order to promote their mutual economic interests. The teams are horizontally integrated, whereas the European hierarchy of clubs, associations, and federations is vertically integrated.

The North American Sports Model, as constructed in European documents and professional commentary, emphasizes that its constituent leagues operate as cartels of team owners. This point can be exaggerated, however, particularly because the players' unions place a substantial restraint on the hegemony of the owners. The issue of synthetic

---

[29]   The North American sports structure is said to be both 'closed' and 'hermetic,' as follows:

The structure and organization of sporting leagues in the US also differs on other essential points. The major leagues are generally considered to be 'hermetic,' meaning that new teams are seldom admitted to a league and there is no annual promotion or relegation between junior leagues and senior leagues. Expansion franchises are admitted only on agreement between existing league members, and there is a substantial entry fee for new franchisers, which is divided among existing league members. The league structure is not just hermetic, it is also 'closed' in the sense that member teams do not compete simultaneously in different competitions. And apart from occasional exceptions, such as the consecutive NBA-dominated 'dream teams' at the Olympic Games, nor do teams release players to compete in national team competitions. This means that especially the World Cup in ice hockey is often deprived of the best players, who have to play championship games at the same time in the NHL.

HALGREEN, *ibid.* at 77.
[30]   See, e.g., *Hollywood Baseball Ass'n* v. *Commissioner*, 42 T.C. 234 (1964).
[31]   RAY YASSER, JAMES R. MCCURDY, C. PETER GOPLERUD, *ET AL.*, SPORTS LAW: CASES AND MATERIALS 231 (2006).

basketballs is a case in point. When players complained about the replacement by the National Basketball Association (NBA) of leather-covered basketballs, their union promptly filed a grievance with the National Labor Relations Board, claiming that the NBA had violated agreements by failing to consult the players. The union's initiative prompted David Stern, the NBA Commissioner, to acknowledge and respond to the players' complaints.[32]

D. Commercialization of Sport

The composition of the closed leagues that comprise the North American Sports Model is based not on promotion and relegation of teams, but rather on a combination of owner preferences, usually for commercial reasons, and approval by the other established teams that together form a joint venture. Major league teams are called franchises, a commercial term, and investment in them is protected by the closed, horizontally integrated system. The product is sometimes described as little more than packaged entertainment. This is the heart of the argument by Europeans that the North American Sports Model is the product solely of profit-maximization rather than of grassroots social activity and a mix of commercial and non-commercial participants, as the European Sports Model purports to be.[33]

E. An Extensive System of Labor Market Restraints

The European Sports Model has not relied on team and player restraints to enhance competitive balance among clubs. Indeed, several decisions of the European Court of Justice, to be discussed later,[34] have struck down restraints on conditions for a club's employment and transfer of players that had been imposed by sports associations and federations. In North America, however, restraints on teams and players are important, especially various combinations of contractual restraints, the draft system for player recruitment, salary caps, luxury and payroll taxes, and revenue sharing.[35]

Contractual restraints are best understood against a background of free agency by which players may be released or otherwise freed of their contractual obligations with a team. Free agency has been qualified, however, by reserve clauses in particular. Accordingly, a player declining to sign with a team that has drafted him may be restricted from playing on other teams for a period of time. Such free agency restrictions vary from league to league and often change with new collective bargaining agreements. Generally, though, they impose conditions on a player's freedom to transfer, based on the length and terms of service the player has provided a team.

---

[32] WR NEWS, Edition 3, Jan. 26, 2007.

[33] See generally Weatherill, note 1 *supra*; see also John Doyle, *Toronto's M.L.S. Team is Testing Patience of its Fans*, N.Y. TIMES, Oct. 17, 2010, at Sports 10 (observing that with respect to Major League Soccer in Canada, as in the United States, 'every club is a business franchise, created, owned and operated by a corporation. The fans are customers, not stakeholders,' thereby presenting a contrast to Europe and South America, 'where most clubs are historically rooted in a community and begin as an affiliation of players and supporters.').

[34] See text at notes 55–9 *infra*.

[35] See Stephen F. Ross, *Player Restraints and Competition Law Throughout the World*, 15 MARQ. SPORTS L. REV. 49 (2004).

Also, in the past teams even had the right to prolong a player's contract indefinitely under a reserve clause, or, temporarily, under an option clause. The former 'Rozelle Rule' of the National Football League (NFL), for example, represented the use of reserve clauses as a basis for imposing transfer fees on teams acquiring players from other teams, often with the intent and effect of locking a player into service with a single team for his entire career. The 'right of first refusal' was later developed, which enabled a free agent's former team to match any offer made to him by another team in order to retain his services. Ordinarily, if the team elected not to exercise the right of first refusal, the Rozelle Rule still applied and the NFL Commissioner could himself impose a transfer fee.

A second type of player restraint in North America is the draft system. Although procedures vary from one professional league to another, an annual draft generally serves as the primary mechanism for recruiting players. The Commissioners of each professional league assign priority numbers to teams to determine the order in which they may select from the rosters of available new players. In the interest of balancing among teams, the poorest performers from the previous season generally have the first right to pick rookies, thereby helping allocate new talent in the league in reverse proportion to performance. These drafts largely define the access of teams to the pool of new players and to exclusive contracting of them.

The third type of player restraint is the salary cap, which sets a limit on the maximum amount a team can pay its players. The purpose, again, is to encourage balance among teams by limiting the ability of the wealthiest teams to pick off the choicest cherries in the league. A luxury tax has a similar purpose but operates differently so as to impose a penalty on salary payments above a set limit.

F. Collective Bargaining System

In North America, professional team and player restraints, and formal relationships between them, are largely premised in labor agreements. Indeed, the collective bargaining system has been described as a 'very essential difference compared with Europe, where the "sports industry" concept is not yet as developed and player unions have been relatively weaker and not equipped with the necessary bargaining powers.'[36] Although restraints on a market such as that of the sports industry may violate US anti-trust law, two exemptions remove restraints on labor from this general policy. The 'statutory exemption' is an express statement in the Clayton Act[37] that labor is not a commodity or article of commerce, thereby removing labor agreements from the reach of anti-trust law. The 'nonstatutory exemption' establishes that the Wagner Act and later labor-relations legislation preempt applications of the anti-trust laws. These exemptions, however, have not always been applied consistently.

---

[36] HALGREEN, note 1 *supra*, at 79.
[37] 15 U.S.C. § 12 *et seq*. (2000).

IV. COMPARISON: CONTINUING DIVERGENCE OR GRADUAL CONVERGENCE?

A. Commonalities

1. Ends

In practice, how accurate are the two sports models? Do the current organizational structures on the two sides of the Atlantic remain divergent or are they converging? Let us begin to answer these questions by noting some commonalities between the two models as means to accomplish certain ends, not as ends in themselves. We shall see that because the ends help shape the means and are largely the same on both sides of the Atlantic, the models, as means toward those ends, are gradually converging.

The first of the common ends is to encourage competition at the highest level for the public benefit, whether we define that level as one of pure entertainment or not. Consequently, for example, both Europe and North America employ 'anti-siphoning' regulations to restrict the media in its ability to control public access to broadcasted competition. In other words, the ability of the media to 'siphon off' events by blackouts or pay-for-view requirements is limited, though not prohibited by any means, on both sides of the Atlantic. Second, both systems seek to find the right balance between the necessary values of cooperation and competition in the sports arena. Striking this balance in a social enterprise with 'no analogous models in other industries,'[38] however, can be difficult. Third, the two models both seek competitive balance among clubs or teams based on two principles of competition: equality of teams and uncertainty of outcome.[39] Opposing teams should be roughly equal on a given day. Dominance by a single team, in the opinion of the Seventh Circuit Court of Appeals, 'would be like one hand clapping,'[40] and the sound of even two or three hands clapping would also be disappointing to the spectator public. Perhaps a better metaphor, however, involves the sound of music: 'Sport without uncertainty of result would be like opera. You would know who is going to die in the end. It might be entertaining, but it would not be sport.'[41]

One might think that the so-called closed system in North America, in which the same teams compete against each other year after year, would not encourage the adjustments in the composition of leagues upon which competitive balance relies. It might seem that the rich, flush with success, would tend to get richer and the poor, poorer. To some extent, this is true and poses a serious risk, but mostly in the short run. Generally, the professional leagues maintain competitive balance. Even the well-endowed New York Yankees in Major League Baseball (MLB) lose games and pennant races. A variety of factors, such as

---

[38] MATTHEW J. MITTEN, TIMOTHY DAVIS, RODNEY K. SMITH, *ET AL.*, SPORTS LAW AND REGULATION: CASES, MATERIALS, AND PROBLEMS 399 (2005).

[39] See White Paper, note 8 *supra*, at 4.1 For further discussion of the unique balancing required, see Stephen Weatherill, *Fairplay Please!: Recent Developments in the Application of EC Law to Sport*, 40 COMMON MKT. L. REV. 51, 52–7 (2003).

[40] *Chicago Professional Sports LP* v. *N.B.A.*, 95 F.3d 593, 598 (7th Cir. 1996).

[41] Weatherill, note 39 *supra*, at 76.

robust players' unions, the annual players' drafts, salary caps (both hard and soft[42]), and revenue-sharing of broadcast revenue, help promote equality.

In European football/soccer, however, a traditional reluctance to adopt such restraints has led to competitive imbalances. Well-established, large-market clubs dominate the sport,[43] and newly formed consortia of elite clubs[44] reinforce the imbalances. Competition within the European-wide Champions League is now far more popular than that among the leagues within each country. Thus, the top clubs view the redistribution of revenue to improve competitive balance as a threat to their opportunity to participate in the elite Champions League and thereby, they argue, to accommodate the public preference in each country.

In part, the upsetting of competitive balance among European clubs may be attributable to decisions of the European Court of Justice and other applications of EC/EU law,[45] but, overall, increased economic regulation of the clubs should have the effect of minimizing commercial disparities among the clubs. The EC/EU regulatory machinery has been unable to keep up with the steady, if not rampant, commercialization of European football/soccer, however.

In both Europe and North America, it must be acknowledged that many fans prefer dominant teams. For such fans, having some assurance of a championship may be more important than watching exciting matches.[46] Thus, the principles of equality and uncertainty of outcome[47] not only may be frustrated but may actually run contrary to the preferences of sports fans. In sum, although competitive balance remains a shared goal of both sports models, there are clearly limitations on its achievement and questions about its popularity.

Finally, the two models seek to insulate sport as much as possible from political and harmful economic manipulation. For example, the European Commission secured an agreement that limits the role of the International Automobile Federation (FIA), which governs Formula One Racing, in response to complaints that the FIA had been using its regulatory power to favor its own economic interests.[48]

---

[42] The hard cap, employed by the NFL, specifically and absolutely limits the total amount that a team may pay its players, whereas a soft cap, as employed by the NBA, likewise sets a limit on compensation but allows exceptions, for example, to enable a team to sign again its own veteran free agent without a salary cap limitation. Players anticipating a transfer to another team may negotiate a salary with their current team cap-free. Thus, soft caps encourage players to remain with their teams. See Alan M. Levine, *Hard Cap or Soft Cap: The Optimal Player Mobility Restrictions for the Professional Sports Leagues*, 6 FORDHAM INTELL. PROP. MEDIA & ENT. L.J. 243 (1995).

[43] Stratis Camatsos, *European Sports, the Transfer System and Competition Law: Will They Ever Find a Competitive Balance?*, 12 SPORTS L.J. 155, 178 (2005).

[44] The first of these was the erstwhile G14 consortium of 14 elite European clubs.

[45] See notes 55–9 *infra*. For a discussion of the effect of these decisions in shifting power from clubs to players and thereby triggering a dramatic increase in players' salaries so as to favor dominant teams, see Schiera, note 5 *supra*, at 718.

[46] See James D. Whitney, *Winning Games Versus Winning Championships: The Economics of Fan Interest and Team Performance*, 26 ECON. INQUIRY 703 (1988).

[47] For an influential articulation of these principles, see Simon Rottenberg, *The Baseball Players' Labor Market*, 64 J. POL. ECON. 242 (1956).

[48] In the United States, by contrast, the National Association for Stock Car Auto Racing (NASCAR), which sets standards and organizes competition for the most popular form of

2. Means: the models themselves

To what extent do the basic features of the two models, respectively, conform to reality in this era of globalization and commercialization? To what extent are the models similar despite the apparent differences between their respective features? In seeking answers to these questions, it will be helpful to note several characteristics of sport as it actually operates on both sides of the Atlantic, in terms of the six basic features of the European Sports Model.

a. *Pyramid structure* In the closed, horizontally integrated system of the North American Sports Model, a kind of pyramid structure, though not the same or as formally organized as that of the European Sports Model, is nevertheless apparent. That is due to several factors: the profound role of schools and colleges in training and recruiting professional players, the annual drafts for recruiting new players, and the importance of semi-professional teams and leagues in thousands of communities. Moreover, a closed system generates lasting long-term loyalties to particular teams as well as close cultural identifications with them, perhaps to a greater extent than is possible for communities hosting non-elite clubs in the European system of promotion and relegation – here one day, gone the next. Also, the establishment of open competition in sports, involving non-professionals and professionals alike, has further blurred the distinction between amateur and professional sports in North America.

b. *Promotion and relegation* In the North American Model, team success also serves to a limited extent as a basis for reconstitution of league membership. To be sure, the process of recomposition or reconstitution of team membership in leagues is not established by formal rules, as in the European Sports Model, nor is it routine, and the process is very gradual. But there is a kind of slow, haphazard version of promotion and relegation, in which a team's competitive standing, by influencing ticket sales and other commercial revenue, helps determine the long-term sustainability of a particular franchise. In recent years, the relocation to Washington, D.C. of the less-than-successful Montreal Expos in MLB is one example of this phenomenon; another involves the relocation within the NBA of the underperforming Seattle Sonics to Oklahoma City. The latter relocation is noteworthy because the team, contradicting the theory of commercialization, moved from a large population center and media market to a much smaller one. Perhaps only a community-owned team such as the Green Bay Packers in the NFL is virtually unaffected by this incremental process of promotion and relegation.

More significantly, however, Europe's promotion-and-relegation system for football/soccer may no longer be absolute. It is under attack by both institutional reforms and commercialism. UEFA's new system for comprehensive licensing of teams, following a French practice, challenges the merit-based system of promotion and relegation. Relying on a licensing system to certify teams may engender a semi-closed tournament system akin to the North American Model. Also, the decision of the Court of Arbitration for Sport (CAS) in the *Granada 74* case[7], which upheld the purchase, renaming, and relocation of a team, opens up a major crack in the system. In addition, the elite European

---

automobile racing in the country, is a family controlled, for-profit enterprise that is independent of FIA regulation.

clubs have formed and reformed their own revenue-generating dream league. This league, replacing the defunct G14 organization of elite clubs, threatens the vertically integrated, promotion-and-relegation-driven hierarchy of the European pyramid structure, crowned by its own championship competition.

c.   *Grassroots participation and leadership*   Grassroots participation and leadership in sports is alive and well, not only in Europe, but also in North America. Such hallowed traditions as Little League baseball, competition among schools and colleges, and community leagues in many sports bear witness to the vitality of voluntary, grassroots organization of sports in North America. As we have seen, this grassroots activity provides the basic foundation for training and recruiting professional players. To be sure, some college and other amateur competition is more commercial than sandlot, but that is true in both Europe and North America.

Meanwhile in Europe, 'much professional sport is rapidly distancing itself from the social and educational context of recreational sport.'[49] Foreign acquisition of elite clubs has accelerated this development. In effect, commerce has trumped the interests of the community. For example, in describing the Hicks Sports Group's acquisition of Liverpool F.C., its chief operating officer spoke of a 'gold rush to English soccer' by investors who sought 'low-hanging fruit,' 'brand exploitation,' and 'synergies in cross-fertilizing opportunities.'[50] The commercial marketing of sports now permeates European football/soccer. To summarize, grassroots organization of sports remains strong in Europe, but the same is true in North America, where a robust system of non-professional competition among schools, colleges, and community leagues remains a fixture of the sports culture. In both regions the sports arena is becoming less communitarian and more commercial.

d.   *National identities, international competitions, and negative aspects*   In terms of professional sports, the remaining three features of the European Sports Model – national identities, international competition, and negative aspects – are considerably less important in North America, primarily because the North American Sports Model encompasses only two countries – the United States and Canada. Moreover, only three of the four major leagues in North America – the MLB, the NBA, and the National Hockey League – have any teams at all in Canada; and only one, the NHL, has substantial Canadian membership.

The feature of national identity in the European Sports Model is itself problematic. Indeed, 'the traditional structures of European sports will most likely continue to create problems simply because they are by nature based on the importance of nationality and thus contain an inherent element of potential discrimination.'[51] The 'inherent element of potential discrimination' too often takes the form of spectator violence and hooliganism, all of which constitute the 'negative aspects' of the European Sports Model.

Also, as the clubs employ more and more foreign nationals, there is a growing disconnect between them and the national identity of the clubs. In response, sports

---

49   Weatherill, *supra* note 39, at 92.
50   Casey Shilts, *Remarks*, Conference on the Increasing Globalization of Sports: Olympic, International and Comparative Law and Business Issues, National Sports Law Institute, Marquette University (Sept. 28, 2007).
51   HALGREEN, note 1 *supra*, at 64.

organizations have imposed new requirements on their members that are intended to restore the national identity of teams while conforming to EC/EU law. For example, FIFA, although not a European-only organization, has certainly had Europe primarily in mind in formulating the 6+5 rule as a compromise between the inclusion of talented non-nationals (often non-Europeans) in clubs, on the one hand, and, on the other, the responsibility of professional clubs, in terms of the European Sports Model, to train local players for national teams. The 6+5 rule requires a football club to begin a game with at least six players entitled to play for the national team of the country in which the club is located. Thus, a maximum of five players can be used at the beginning of the match who are not entitled to play for that national team. An alternative approach in the English Premier League of football/soccer, beginning in the 2010–11 season, establishes a squad cap of 25 players, of whom at least eight must be 'home grown.' The definition of 'home grown' is a player who has been registered and thereby trained in either the English or Welsh professional associations for a period of 3 years under the age of 21, regardless of his nationality.

New pressures to relocate clubs and establish feeder clubs in other countries further challenge the national identity of football/soccer competition. Moreover, the nature of the international competition at the apex of the European pyramid no longer promotes national identity. Although the European Cup in football/soccer, based on fully national teams vying for the championship, is still paramount, the growing, separately organized competition among elite clubs offers an alternative structure at the apex of the pyramid that is *not* based on national rivalries.

It is not at all clear that over a half-century of European integration has led to any continent-wide sense of community in sport. Indeed, many English football fans often cheer for Brazilian and Argentinean teams in their World Cup matches with French and Italian teams rather than for their fellow Europeans. This is particularly puzzling in a region committed to social as well as economic integration. Why, indeed, are there so few European-wide teams? If European integration is important enough to trump the autonomy of sports as something 'special,' why is the impulse of integration missing in the actual composition of teams? The Ryder Cup team in golf is a unique example of a European wide team.[52]

B. Institutional Differences and the Great Legal Rivalry or Tournament in Europe

Despite the commonalities shared in varying degrees by the two systems of sports organizations, important institutional differences between them are also profound. We have already seen that their structures differ, though perhaps more in theory than in practice. Of increasing significance, however, has been the framework of external regulation. Although both European and North American systems are subject to similar legal constraints such as anti-trust/competition law, some constraints are more distinctive of one system than the other – for example, labor and collective bargaining law as a fundamental element in North American professional sports. Moreover, the framing of regulatory issues has been quite different.

---

[52]   See Mark Rice-Oxley, *Common Currency? New Flag? Nope. Try Golf to Unify Europe*, CHRIST. SCI. MON., Sept. 17, 2004, at 1.

Unlike the North American practice, the distinctive framework within which important issues have been addressed within the EU involves a dichotomy between 'pure' sporting activity exempt from economic regulation and sports-related activity that is subject to economic regulation. Despite an abiding recognition that sport is 'special' and therefore worthy of an exemption from regulation when it does not threaten the process of economic integration in Europe, the need for regulation and support for it have expanded as the European sport arena has become more commercialized. The sale of English football/soccer clubs to investors has heightened public distaste for commercialization of the sports arena.[53] Sport no longer seems so 'special.' This development poses a threat to the European Sports Model. When the requirements of EC/EU law are interpreted to countermand the practices of sports associations and federations, however commendable those requirements may be in themselves, they challenge the integrity of the pyramid of sports organizations. The resulting legal tournament in Europe concerning regulatory authority in the sports arena versus the autonomy of clubs and associations has been described as the 'crux of sports law'[54] in Europe.

The state of play in this legal tournament is reflected in four cases, three that have been decided by the European Court of Justice (ECJ) and one by the Court of Arbitration for Sport (CAS), as follows:

1. *Bosman*

The first of these cases, *Union Royale Belge des Sociétés de Football Ass'n v. Bosman*,[55] remains the *cause célèbre* related to European sports. A Belgian player, Bosman, who had become a free agent, sought a transfer from his former team to a French team. When his former team failed to pay a required transfer fee to the new team, thereby preventing the transfer, Bosman brought legal action against the team and the Belgian football association. The transfer-fee requirement, long a fixture in European sports, had been justified as a means of ensuring balanced competition and uncertainty of results, as well as an equitable means of compensating a team for the cost of training a player. Ultimately, however, the ECJ struck down the player transfer system under Article 39 of the EC/EU Treaty, which provides for freedom of movement among member states. On the same basis, the ECJ also struck down a provision that, in the interest of national identity, had strictly limited the number of players from other EU member states who could become members of a team. The *Bosman* decision was later extended to benefit players from non-EU states having special agreements with the EU – that is, the so-called 'Europe agreements' states that are in the process of applying for membership in the EU.[56]

---

[53]   See, e.g., Ola Olatawura, *The 'Theatre of Dreams'? – Manchester United, FC Globalization, and International Sports Law*, 16 MARQ. SPORTS L.J. 287, 289 (2006) (corporate raider Malcolm Glazer's purchase of Manchester United); John Cassidy, *The Red Devil*, NEW YORKER, Feb. 6, 2004, at 47 (Russian billionaire Roman Ambromovich's takeover of Chelsea).

[54]   HALGREEN, note 1 *supra*, at 396.

[55]   Case C-415/93, [1995] E.C.R. I-4921. For a thorough analysis of pertinent European Union law, see STEFAN VAN DEN BOGAERT, PRACTICAL REGULATION OF THE MOBILITY OF SPORTSMEN IN THE EU POST *BOSMAN* (2005).

[56]   See *Deutscher Handballbund eV v. Kolpak*, Case C-438/00, [2003] E.C.R. I-4135. For a discussion of judicial and other developments in the EU regulation of sports after *Bosman*, see Roberto Branco Martins, *The* Kolpak *Case*: Bosman *Times 10?*, 2004–1/2 INT'L SPORTS L.J. 26.

In response to controversy after the *Bosman* decision, FIFA and the UEFA reached an agreement with the European Commission in 2001 that provides for a revenue-redistribution mechanism between teams in compliance with EU law. The new mechanism involves two elements. The first is a provision for training compensation whereby, if a player under age 23 who has trained with one club transfers to another club, training compensation is due from the transferee to the transferor club. The ECJ suggested the rationale for this system in *Bosman* by noting that a system of compensation to teams for expenses incurred in training players might not run afoul of Article 39, even, as in the FIFA regulations, after the expiration of a player's contract. The second element in the agreement is a so-called 'solidarity mechanism,' which requires that if a player is transferred during the course of his contract, a small portion of any fees paid by the transferee to the transferor team must be redistributed to other teams for which a player has played previously. The agreement applies only to transfers during the course of a player's contract.

2. *Meca-Medina*

In *Meca-Medina & Majcen* v. *Comm'n of the Eur. Communities*,[57] two swimmers claimed that the anti-doping rules of the Olympic Movement, as specified by the international swimming federation (FINA), violated provisions of the EU Treaty that protect freedom of movement and void collusive arrangements among organizations. The ECJ confirmed earlier decisions to the effect that EU law generally applies to sports-related issues, just as it would to other issues with economic implications. Thus, to avoid the prohibitions of the EU Treaty, contested sporting rules must be limited to sporting necessities. In the dispute itself, however, the ECJ ruled that EU law did not bar the controverted anti-doping measures. Instead, the swimmers' claim was 'at odds with the Court's case law,' and their argument that anti-doping rules were imposed not only for health considerations but also to safeguard the economic potential of international competition was 'not sufficient to alter the purely sporting nature of the legislation.' It is disappointing that *Meca-Medina* failed to clarify what is economic and what is not in defining the contours of sports organizational autonomy within the EU.

3. *Charleroi*

In *Charleroi* v. *FIFA*,[58] a Belgian football/soccer club, the Royal Charleroi Sporting F.C., joined by the G14 group of elite clubs, challenged rules of FIFA. These rules require clubs to release players for so-called 'international duty' on national teams and insure them against the risk of injury in FIFA-sponsored or recognized international matches without compensation from FIFA, even when players are injured in the course of such 'mandatory release' competition.[59] A Moroccan national, Abdel Majid Oulmers, was badly injured in

---

[57]   Case C-519/04P, [2006] E.C.R. I-6991.
[58]   Case C-243.96 (*withdrawn*).
[59]   The ECJ's precise framing of the question presented is as follows:

Do the obligations on clubs and football players having employment contracts with those clubs imposed by the provisions of FIFA's statutes and regulations providing for the obligatory release of players to national federations without compensation and the unilateral and binding determination of the coordinated international match calendar constitute unlawful restrictions of

the course of a mandatory release competition to play on the Moroccan national team. The injury resulted in demonstrable losses to the club during Oulmers' prolonged period of recovery from his injury. The Charleroi club therefore requested damages for these losses. More ambitiously, the G14 elite group requested €860 million in damages as compensation for costs incurred by elite clubs over a period of 10 years to implement the FIFA mandatory release requirements to their detriment. FIFA responded, first, that there was no connection between the injury of Oulmers and Charleroi's eventual league standing; second, that it is the national associations, not FIFA or UEFA, that should reimburse clubs for the cost to them of player injuries; and third, that 75 percent of the profits from major tournaments are returned to national associations for use in their discretion, such as to compensate them for player injuries as in *Charleroi* itself.

The case was initially brought before a Belgian commercial tribunal, the Tribunal de Commerce de Charleroi. It rejected the G14 demand for damages but decided to refer two questions to the ECJ: (1) whether the club's obligation to release players without compensation, as FIFA mandated, violated freedom-of-movement and anti-trust competition provisions of the EU treaty; and (2) whether FIFA's binding determinations of a coordinated match calendar, which is an essential foundation of the pyramid construction of European sports, complied with those provisions.

The case was eventually settled. What is important about it is, once again, the question of where to draw the line between the autonomy of sporting activity and regulation of it by the EU in the interest of economic integration. Had the petitioning club and the G14 won, the pyramid and its vertical integration of European clubs, under the supervision of FIFA and UEFA, might have crumbled further. It was also feared that a decision in favor of the petitioners would all but end the coordination of professional, non-professional, and national team competition in conformity with the European Sports Model. If that should happen, not only would the pyramid be quite hollow as a formal consideration, but it would be especially difficult, if not impossible, for national teams from poorer countries to compete internationally if they cannot count on a coordinated calendar of matches that ensures the availability of star players employed by high-paying European clubs. The settlement of the action appears to have avoided a serious threat to the pyramid structure of sports in Europe.

4. *Granada 74 SAD*

In 2007 FIFA and UEFA asked the Court of Arbitration for Sport to enjoin the Spanish Football Federation from allowing a new club, Granada 74 SAD, to compete in the second division of Spanish football. A wealthy investor purchased a second-division football/soccer club, Ciudad Murcia, renaming it Granada 74 SAD and relocating its headquarters to a coastal town, Motril, south of Granada and west of Murcia. FIFA and UEFA claimed that the club's registration by Spain's Football League (LFP) violated the normal promotion-and-relegation system for gaining membership in the second division, based on sporting results on the field of play rather than a commercial transaction.

---

competition or abuses of a dominant position or obstacles to the exercise of the fundamental freedoms conferred by the EC Treaty and are they therefore contrary to Articles 81 and 82 of the Treaty or to any other provision of Community law, particularly Articles 39 and 49 of the Treaty?

Ibid.

The sole CAS arbitrator, however, endorsed the club owner's view that Granada 74 SAD was not a new legal entity that had replaced Ciudad Murcia. Instead, it was the same entity with a different owner, name, and location. He also found that Granada 74 SAD had been duly recognized by the LFP. Thus, the new ownership, the name change from Ciudad Murcia to Granada 74 SAD, and the club's relocation did not breach any applicable rules. Insofar as the Ciudad Murcia team had obtained the right to play in the Second Division on sporting merit, its mere sale and conversion into Granada 74 SAD did not breach FIFA and UEFA regulations that are designed to prevent a different range of practices – namely, all methods or practices that jeopardize the integrity of matches or competitions. The CAS arbitrator therefore concluded that the owners of the upstart club had engaged in a perfectly legal business transaction by purchasing 100 percent of the shares of a registered sports company whose renaming and change of registered address was protected by Spanish law. Finally, the CAS arbitrator ruled that the similarity of the newly formed club's name, Granada 74 SAD, with that of another club, Granada 74 CP, was immaterial insofar as the LFP had duly registered the name of Granada 74 SAD.[60]

C. Specific Legal Issues

So far, we have seen that despite the contrasting features of the European and North American Sports Models, they are converging insofar as they share some fundamental commonalities and structural characteristics in practice, but they remain divergent institutionally and in certain specific practices. In particular, the EC/EU framework of law is materially different insofar as it understandably puts overwhelming emphasis on issues of economic import in the interest of European integration. Thus, inspired by the objective of regional integration, a unique effort continues in Europe to distinguish 'pure' sporting activity from sporting-related activity subject to economic regulation. The resulting disputes play out in a sort of legal rivalry or tournament centered in the ECJ.

Other legal issues involving professional sports highlight both the continuing divergence and emerging convergence between the two models. As one example, the following comparative summary of anti-trust (competition) regulations, with specific reference to broadcasting rights, is instructive.[61]

1. Regulation under Anti-trust/Competition Laws

a. United States The structure of professional sports leagues in the United States is shaped in no small measure by a combination of labor law and anti-trust law: 'The common ground for attack is found in application of the antitrust law.'[62] Most claims arising in this area are based on the Sherman Act,[63] alleging collusion between owners of separate teams. What, then, are the main anti-trust ramifications of the organizational structure for professional sports in North America?

---

[60] Case Granada 74, The Claim, C.A.S. Press Release, Sept. 7, 2007.
[61] Another important set of issues, involving the licensing of sports merchandise, lies beyond the scope of this chapter but merits mention. (In North America almost all licensing is collective, unlike the European practice. See Roberts, note 13 *supra*.)
[62] YASSER *ET AL.*, note 31 *supra*.
[63] 15 U.S.C. § 1 *et seq.* (2000).

I)   JOINT VENTURE/HORIZONTAL INTEGRATION STRUCTURE   Whenever   a   professional league is classified as a joint venture of separate and independent teams, economically profitable collusion between them is open to attack under the Sherman Act. In
defense, the leagues have asserted that they do not constitute prohibited cartels but rather
a single entity [64] Thus, any collusion is 'internal' and beyond the reach of the Sherman
Act. Under this single-entity approach, teams can no more illegally collude with one
another in violation of the law than could members of the board of a corporation.
Unfortunately for the professional leagues, however, US courts have not been very
receptive to classifying professional sports leagues as single entities or to allowing a
single-entity defense to what would otherwise be a restraint of trade or commerce in
violation of the Sherman Act.

In *Copperweld* v. *Independence Tube Corp.*,[65] the Supreme Court held that a parent
company and its wholly owned subsidiary constituted a single entity that withstood an
anti-trust challenge. In reaching that conclusion, the court adopted a 'unity of interest'
test to differentiate between strictly 'internal' agreements to manage the affairs of a single
entity and illegal anti-competitive agreements that established relationships between
teams. The court drew a sharp distinction between prohibited 'concerted action' in
restraint of trade or commerce and acceptable 'independent action' of constituent entities
within a formally established single entity. While this test suggested new hope for the
single-entity defense, courts have been reluctant to accept it so as to relieve the leagues of
anti-trust regulation.

Recently, Major League Soccer (MLS), the newest professional sports league in North
America, was deliberately structured so that it would resemble a single entity. All teams
are owned by the league, with investors/operators having very limited control over the
actual decision making. Many predicted that this would be a new model for successful US
sports leagues, but this aspiration is still uncertain. In *Fraser* v. *Major League Soccer
L.L.C.*,[66] a federal appeals court did not rule, as had been hoped, on the question of
whether the MLS structure passed the 'unity of interest' test of *Copperweld*, but rather
decided the case on other grounds. Under the Sherman Act's prohibition of monopolies,
the court ruled that, although sports leagues are generally not treated as single entities, the
trial court's contrary holding in this case had been harmless error, given a fatal lack of
evidence to determine the relevant market for anti-trust purposes.

Then, in *American Needle, Inc.* v. *National Football League*,[67] the Court unanimously
refused to apply the single-entity defense to bar the applicability of the Sherman Act and
the normal Rule of Reason under it in determining the validity of an exclusive license
granted by National Football League Properties (NFLP) for the manufacture and sale of
apparel bearing insignias of the constituent teams of the NFL. In reaching this decision,

---

[64]   On the single-entity defense, see, e.g., Nathanial Grow, *There's No 'I' in 'League': Professional
Leagues and the Single Entity Defense*, 105 MICH. L. REV. 183 (2006); L. Kaiser, *The Flight from
Single-Entity Structured Sports Leagues*, 2 DEPAUL J. SPORTS L. & CONTEMP. PROBS. 1 (2004);
Karen Jordan, *Forming a Single Entity: A Recipe for Success for New Professional Sports Leagues*, 3
VAND. J. ENT. L. & PRAC. 235 (2001); Brad McChesney, *Professional Sports Leagues and the
Single-Entity Defense*, 6 SPORTS L.J. 125 (1999).

[65]   104 S. Ct. 2731 (1984).

[66]   284 F.3d 47 (1st Cir. 2002).

[67]   130 S.Ct. 2201 (2010).

the court used a functional rather than formalistic approach, relying on substance not form, to determine whether a prohibited conspiracy existed. Quoting *Copperweld*, the court articulated the relevant inquiry to be: 'whether there is a "contract, combination ... or conspiracy" amongst "separate economic actors pursuing separate economic interests," such that the agreement "deprives the marketplace of independent centers of decision-making," and therefore of diversity of entrepreneurial interests ... The question is whether the agreement joins together "independent centers of decisionmaking."'[68] Concluding that the constituent NFL teams are separate, profit-making entities and that their interests in licensing team trademarks are not necessarily aligned, the court remanded the case to the federal district court for further proceedings consistent with the rule of reason.

Historically, the anti-trust law has applied comprehensively to all sports organizations except that of baseball (MLB). In *Federal Baseball Club of Baltimore Inc. v. National League of Professional Baseball Clubs*,[69] the Supreme Court famously ruled that organized baseball did not fall within the scope of anti-trust law. Despite criticism by later courts and judicial invitations for Congress to modify the statute to change this rule, the exemption still exists to a great extent. Indeed, it remained absolute until 1998 when Congress, in response to an incident involving a pitcher, Curt Flood, nearly 30 years earlier, extended the anti-trust law partially to baseball. Most importantly, the court decided that the law applies to employment issues, but only employment issues, involving MLB (but not minor league) players, thereby giving those players rights comparable to those of other professional athletes.

II) BROADCASTING RIGHTS Television and media rights engage a complex of collective league rights and individual club rights. The essential question for analysis of legal issues surrounding the sale and distribution of television and other media rights for professional sports is: who owns the rights in the first instance? If the rights are viewed as belonging to the individual teams, then the collective selling of them is subject to review as possible 'concerted action' under anti-trust law. If, however, the rights actually belong to a league of teams, the anti-trust law does not apply. The common law supports the former view.

> Under the common law, the home team has a fundamental right to telecast its own game. Thus, any rights sales by a club-run league constitutes an agreement among competing clubs to jointly sell valuable rights, which is subject under anti-trust law to the rule of reason analysis. Any sale that demonstrably raises prices, reduces viewership, or renders output unresponsive to consumer demand would be unlawful.[70]

The Sports Broadcasting Act of 1961,[71] however, created an exemption from anti-trust regulation for the collective selling by professional leagues of the rights to broadcast professional baseball, hockey, basketball, and football games. This exception has been justified by the necessity of a collective sale and corresponding distribution of revenues in

---

[68]   *Ibid.* at 2212.
[69]   259 U.S. 200 (1922).
[70]   Stephen F. Ross and Stefan Szymanski, *Antitrust and Inefficient Joint Ventures: Why Sports Leagues Should Look More Like McDonald's and Less Like the United Nations*, 16 MARQ. SPORTS L. REV. 213, 229 (2006).
[71]   15 U.S.C. §§ 1291–4 (2000).

order to maintain equality and competitiveness between small-market and large-market franchises. Only the NFL, however, sells the collective exclusive rights to every game. The other major leagues sell exclusive television rights for some games, but games not sold by the league may be sold by the teams playing in the games within their own assigned territories.

b.   Europe   In the European system, competition law and regulations are also fundamental.[72] Articles 81 and 82 of the EC/EU Treaty, much like Articles 1 and 2 of the Sherman Act upon which the European provisions were based, prohibit anti-competitive agreements and market dominance. As applied to sports, the ECJ has ruled, for example, that the Greek motorcycling federation violated the treaty by serving as both a government-designated regulator and authorizing authority of competition as well as a competitor of other motorcycling associations in organizing events in that sport.[73] Articles 81 and 82 therefore constitute the main vehicles for challenges to arrangements that set up exclusive broadcast and distribution rights.

Article 81(3) of the EC/EU Treaty, however, gives the Commission the power to allow exemptions from anti-trust challenges if doing so could be reasonably expected to improve production or distribution in the interest of regional economic integration while benefiting consumers, so long as otherwise prohibited arrangements include only restrictions that are indispensable to the attainment of acceptable objectives and do not afford the possibility of substantially eliminating competition. Under Article 81(3) the collective sale of television rights is acceptable. In the terminology of US anti-trust law, but as a matter of EC/EU jurisprudence, UEFA acts as a single entity, selling the pooled broadcast rights of the constituent clubs. In practice, however, the arrangements for collective sales have encountered problems:

> [In Europe, transaction costs inhibit] club-run leagues from maximizing profits from the sale of broadcast and internet rights. Owners have passed up profitable opportunities because, unable to agree among themselves on how to divide the proceeds, a requisite super-majority cannot agree to proceed with a valuable rights sale. In the English Premier League in football/soccer, for example, rights have traditionally been sold collectively. In reviewing a government challenge to an agreement to sell television rights for only sixty of the league's 380 possible games, a tribunal found that the league's limitation on television sales actually reduced revenues. However, the clubs could not agree on how to share revenue gained from additional sales, whether negotiated individually or collectively. Unlike English soccer, television rights to NBA games not collectively sold by the league may be sold by each club within a team's assigned territory.[74]

Starting in 1999, therefore, UEFA sought clearance from the Commission for its pooled sale of the right to broadcast Championship League games between constituent football/soccer clubs. The result is a revised selling arrangement approved by the Commission in 2003 with several essential elements. First, a bidding process establishes broadcast rights. Rights to broadcast matches that have not been so acquired by a certain deadline revert to the clubs, giving them the ability to exploit the residual rights within their respective

---

[72]   See generally ELEANOR M. FOX, THE COMPETITION LAW OF THE EUROPEAN UNION (2002).

[73]   *Motosykletistiki Omospondia Ellados NPID* v. *Elliniko Dimosio*, Case C-49/07, Judgment of July 1, 2008, 46 C.M.L.Rev. 1327 (2009).

[74]   Ross and Szymanski, note 70 *supra*, at 239.

media markets and thereby increase the likelihood of events being televised to their fan base. Second, contracts for broadcast rights may not exceed a period of three years, at which time a new bid process is to be initiated. Third, opportunities for exploitation of new media, such as Internet broadcasts, are to be marketed separately in response to the Commission's concern that the so-called 'bundling' of those rights with the television broadcast rights would inhibit the development of the new media.

V. CONCLUSION

'Globalization and commercialism are not just American inventions.'[75] These trends continue on both sides of the Atlantic,[76] accelerating a convergence of the European and North American Sports Models in many respects and on all levels of competition. In sharper focus, the formation of a group of elite European football/soccer clubs, the licensing of clubs, and opportunities for investors in clubs to bypass the promotion-and-relegation system are among the developments that threaten the pyramid system which the European Sports Model describes. On the other side of the Atlantic, the variations in practices among the several North American professional leagues as well as the much-neglected similarities between features of the European Sports Model and the actual characteristics of sports organization in North America further call into question both the reality of a North American Sports Model and the extent to which its features differ materially from those of its European sibling. The two models are therefore becoming a bit more like caricatures today.

Traditionalists may lament the changes that are occurring rapidly in the organization of European sports, such as the creeping Americanization, as it has been dubbed, of English football. But the current developments are often positive. For example, the perennial issue among NCAA schools in North America of allocating funds between money-making and money-spending sports is becoming significant in Europe as the more monolithic, single-sport structure of its organizational pyramid falls apart. Also, European sports will likely continue moving toward a collective bargaining system and an exemption from EC/EU competition law for labor agreements. These developments should certainly accrue to the benefit of players even as they threaten to undermine the carefully crafted vertical integration of the European sports pyramid. The more the models stay the same in theory, the more they change in reality.

---

[75]   *Ibid.* at 81.
[76]   See, e.g., Stephen Weatherill, *Is the Pyramid Compatible with EC Law?*, 2005/3–4 INT'L SPORTS L.J., at 3.

5   Models of sport governance within the European Union

Robert Siekmann and Janwillem Soek

1. INTRODUCTION

In 2004 André-Noël Chaker published a study on 'Good governance in Sport – A European survey' which was commissioned by the Council of Europe.[1] The Council of Europe was the first international organisation established in Europe after the Second World War. With 46 Member States, the Council of Europe currently represents the image of a 'wider Europe'. Its main objective is to strengthen democracy, human rights and the rule of law. The Council of Europe was the first international intergovernmental organisation to take initiatives, to establish legal instruments and to offer an institutional framework for the development of sport at European level.[2] The study covers the sport-related legislation and governance regulations of 20 European countries. The aim of this study was to measure and assess sport governance in each of the participating countries. For the purposes of the study the term 'sport governance' had been given a specific meaning. Sport governance is the creation of effective networks of sport-related state agencies, sport's non-governmental organisations and processes that operate jointly and independently under specific legislation, policies and private regulations to promote ethical, democratic, efficient and accountable sports activities. The legislative framework of the countries under review was analysed according to whether they have references to sport in their constitutions and whether they have a specific law on sport at national level. There are two distinctive approaches to sports legislation in Europe. Countries have adopted an 'interventionist' or a 'non-interventionist' sports legislation model. An interventionist sports-legislation model is one that contains specific legislation on the structure and mandate of a significant part of the national sports movement. All other sports-legislation models are deemed to be non-interventionist.

In December 2009, the European Commission (Employment, social affairs and equal opportunities DG) commissioned the T.M.C. Asser Instituut (ASSER International Sports Law Centre) to undertake a study on 'The Role of Member States in the Organising and Functioning of Professional Sport Activities'. The background of the study is as follows.

Article 39 of the European Community Treaty (EC Treaty) establishes the free movement of workers in what became the European Union (EU). It prohibits all discrimination on the basis of nationality. The European Court of Justice (ECJ) has confirmed that professional and semi-professional sportsmen are workers within the meaning of this

---

[1] Council of Europe Publishing, Strasbourg, September 2004.
[2] See Robert C.R. Siekmann and Janwillem Soek Eds, The Council of Europe and Sport: Basic Documents. T.M.C. Asser Press, The Hague 2007, at p. XIX.

Article and consequently, Community law applies to them.[3] This implies the application of equal treatment and the elimination of any direct or indirect discrimination on the basis of nationality. The Court particularly stated that Article 39 EC Treaty not only applies to the action of public authorities but also extends to rules of any other nature aimed at regulating gainful employment in a collective manner and that obstacles to freedom of movement for persons could not result from the exercise of their legal autonomy by associations or organisations not governed by public law.[4]

In light of recent developments in the field of sport, however, certain international sport authorities have advocated the adoption of rules that might be contrary to Community law and in particular to the free movement-of-workers principle. National sport authorities, being members of the international sports authorities, should also apply the rules adopted at the international level. Therefore, the implementation at the national level of such rules would be contrary to EC law.

For example, the European Commission has published an independent study on the 'home-grown players' rule' adopted by the European football governing body. This rule requires clubs participating in the European-wide club competitions – Champions League and Union of European Football Associations (UEFA) Cup (as from the 2009–10 season: Europa League) – to have a minimum number of 'home grown players' in their squads. Home grown players are defined by UEFA as players who, regardless of their nationality or age, have been trained by their club or by another club in the same national association for at least 3 years between the age of 15 and 21. Compared with the '6+5' rule adopted by the world football governing body, the International Federation of Football Associations (FIFA), which is incompatible with EU law, the Commission considers that UEFA has opted for an approach which seems to comply with the principle of free movement while promoting the training of young European players.[5] The '6+5' rule provides that at the beginning of each match, each club must field at least six players who are eligible to play for the national team of the country of the club.

The European Commission, as guardian of the EC Treaty and within the framework of its competences, can initiate infringement proceedings before the ECJ against Member States that have breached Community law. According to the case law, an infringement procedure can be initiated against a Member State if government authorities of that Member State are at the origin of the infringement.[6] As to the actions of private entities, the ECJ has indicated that Member States might be responsible for breach of EC law by private entities, recognised as having legal personality, whose activities are directly or indirectly under state control. Possible criteria that are mentioned in this context are, in particular, the appointment of the members of the entity's management committee by State authorities and the granting of public subsidies which cover the greater part of its expenses.[7]

---

3   Case 13/76 *Donà*, ECR 1976, p. 1333 and Case C-415/93 *Bosman*, ECR 1995, I-4921.
4   Case C-415/93 *Bosman*, ECR 1995, I-4921.
5   Cf., IP/08/807 of 28 May 2008.
6   Case C-95/97 *Région wallone* v. *Commission*, ECR 1997, I-1787.
7   Case C-249/81 *Commission* v. *Ireland*, ECR 1982, 4005.

Therefore, the fundamental element authorising the Commission to initiate an infringement procedure against a Member State is the existence of behaviour breaching Community law that can be attributed to the State. The same reasoning applies also in the field of professional sports activities, where in order for the services of the Commission to launch the infringement procedure, behaviour – breaching Community law attributed to the State must be present. Consequently, it is essential to determine whether, and to what extent, Member States participate directly or indirectly in the organisation of professional sports activities.

Community law on the free movement of workers, and in particular Article 39 of the EU Treaty being directly applicable in the Member States' legal orders, means that every EU citizen who considers that his or her rights have been violated might go and seek a redress in front of the national administrative authorities and jurisdictions. If the application of EU law is at stake, national courts may request a preliminary ruling from the EECJ, which is entitled to give rulings about the compatibility of sporting rules with the EU legal order.

In the White Paper on Sport, adopted in 2007,[8] the Commission reaffirmed its acceptance of limited and proportionate restrictions (in line with EU Treaty provisions on free movement and the ECJ's rulings) to the principle of free movement in particular as regards:

- the right to select national athletes for national team competitions;
- the need to limit the number of participants in a competition; and
- the setting of deadlines for transfers of players in team sports.

In order to improve knowledge of the functioning of sport regulations across the EU and to outline the general trends in Europe, analysis of national sport legislation is required in order to determine whether, and to what extent, Member States participate directly or indirectly in the organisation of professional sport activities, with a view of clarifying the different levels of responsibility. This country-by-country analysis is to cover:

a)   *Organisation of professional sport activities.* The way in which professional sport activities are organised with particular focus on whether the organisation is:
   –   part of general organisation of sport activities or whether there are separate special rules regulating professional sport activities;
   –   underpinned by general law, framework law or specific rules governing sectoral sport activities;
   –   at the level of the state, or has devolved to, for example, the regional/local level.
b)   *Organisation and functioning of sport authorities.* The way in which sport authorities are organised and function, with particular focus on whether the sport authorities:
   –   are private actors or whether they act or operate under the auspices of the State;
   –   have State participation in any of their responsibilities for the organisation of professional sport activities (for example, nomination of members of governing

---

bodies, financing, and adoption of regulations governing professional sport competitions).

c)   *Discrimination*. Whether there are direct or indirect discriminatory rules and/or practices with regard to Community citizens. The following fields of professional sport activities must be covered: football, basketball, volleyball, handball, rugby and ice-hockey (as to both men and women championships, and in both first and second divisions).

The final purpose of the study was to determine, on the basis of the information gathered and the research undertaken, to what extent the organising and functioning of professional sport activities might be attributed to the State in the EU.

In this contribution we present a summary of the results of the study in a comparative form, that is, in relation to the issues above under a) and b). We do not discuss the issue of c) since we are mainly interested in the current 'abstract' relationship between state and sport authorities in the EU from the perspective of the 'interventionist'/'non-interventionist' models of sport governance. Of course, this perspective is relevant also for the determination of whether states may be considered responsible for the behaviour of the national sport-governing bodies.

2.   STATE INFLUENCE ON THE LEGAL ORGANISATION OF PROFESSIONAL SPORT ACTIVITIES

2.1.   The Non-interventionist Sports Legislation Model

In Austria, Belgium, the Czech Republic, Denmark, Estonia, Finland, Germany, Ireland, Luxembourg, Malta, the Netherlands, Slovakia, Slovenia, Sweden and the United Kingdom the sports federations set up according to the act of association are active private actors; they are not under control, responsibility or supervision of State authorities. Also, in Lithuania the sports federations have full autonomy, even though they must be recognised by the Department of Physical Education and Sports, which sets out the procedure and criteria for recognition. In Hungary other criteria for the legal existence of a sports federation are applicable. A sport federation will only be recognised in cases where, first, it has at least ten sport organisations operating in a particular sport as members; second, it operates a national contest scheme (championship) continuously for at least 3 years; and, third, it has a contest scheme involving at least 100 sportsmen having a contest permit.

2.2.   The Interventionist Sports Legislation Model

The situation of the sports federations in the remainder of the EU Member States contrasts strongly with that in the above-mentioned countries. There, the interference of the State in the doings and dealings of the federations is more or less immanent.

In Bulgaria, according to the Law on Physical Education and Sport, one of the requirements for granting a licence to a sport federation is that it presents rules for the organisation of sport competitions. The licence is issued for a period of 4 years and encompasses the right to organise and carry out sport competitions.[9] Every 4 years a commission appointed by the head of the State Agency for Youth and Sport assesses the sport organisation with regard to renewal of its licence.

In Cyprus, the sports federations are under control of the State, both in respect of their financial status and rules for operation. The semi-governmental organisation, the Cyprus Sports Authority, supervises sporting activities, advises sports federations and ensures the functional implementation of all athletics programmes. Furthermore, the Cyprus Sports Authority organises the sport representation of Cyprus abroad, regulates the federations, runs competitions and imposes sanctions to sports federations for violation of sports law and international regulations.

In France, the law provides for separate structures to manage professional activities in disciplines to whose federations responsibilities have been allocated by the Minister of Sports. The French Sports Code covers the legal existence of the professional leagues, bodies charged with the representation, management and coordination of professional sporting activities. The sports federations act under the control and supervision of the State authorities insofar as the State delegated their powers to them through legislative measures and the State can therefore cancel these powers as provided by law. The sports federations operate independently but under the control of the Minister of Sport.[10] Before powers can be delegated to them, the sports federations must fulfil certain conditions: first, to be responsible for the organisation of one sport only or related sports; second, to have been approved beforehand by the State under the conditions of the Sports Act; and, third, to have an internal regulation that contains specific provisions as defined in the Sports Act.

In Greece, the State exercises supervision. The competent authorities control the legality of the statutes of association, and financial control is applied to all federations and clubs participating in a professional league. The delegation of the powers by the State to the sport authorities is provided by law. This delegation concerns the possibility to take decisions on every matter concerning the regulations of sport competitions.

In Italy, all sport activities are controlled by the Italian Olympic Committee (CONI), which is a public body. CONI is independent although it is under State control (the Undersecretary for Sport). Although the governing authority of each sport is the sports federation, the technical, organisational and managerial autonomy of the federations is supervised by CONI.[11]

In Latvia, the Council of Latvian Sports Federations controls the activities of the sports federations in the field of the organisation and management of particular sport activities according to the procedure provided by regulations of the Cabinet of Ministers (although such regulations have so far not been adopted).[12] Also the Ministry of Welfare, the Ministry of Interior, the Ministry of Defence and the Ministry of Justice have certain competencies in the field of sport.[13]

---

[9]   Law for the Physical Education and Sport, amend. SG. 96/29 Oct 2004, Art. 19(1).
[10]   Loi n° 2003–708 du 1er août 2003 relative à l'organisation et à la promotion des activités physiques et sportives, Art. 16.
[11]   Legge N. 91/81 sul Professionismo Sportivo, Art. 14.
[12]   Latvian Sports Law, Published: 'Vestnesis', 13 November 2002, No. 165 (2740), S. 10(3).
[13]   *Ibid.* S. 6.

In Poland, the organisation of top sports competitions falls within the competence of the Polish sports federations, which are managed autonomously. However, their activity is subject to the supervision of the Minister of Physical Education and Sport. The Minister exercises control in order to verify the compliance of the activity with the applicable regulations, statutes and rules of procedure.

In Portugal, sports bodies responsible for the organisation and functioning of professional sport competitions – the professional leagues – are established as privately registered non-profit associations. On the basis of the Sports Act, in order to exercise those functions, the professional leagues must conclude a contract with the federations. The activities of the federations, as well as the professional leagues, are supervised by State authorities though enquiries and inspections.

In Romania, the Ministry of Youth and Sport is the specialised body of the central public administration coordinating activity in the field of sport, according to the Law on Physical Education and Sports. The national sport federations are given competence to establish, by means of their own regulations, the conditions for practising professional sport. These regulations have to be approved by the Ministry of Youth and Sport. This Ministry may also supervise and control compliance with the legislative provisions in force and the rules and statutes within all sport structures.

In Spain, although the sports federations are private entities with their own legal personality, they also exercise public functions which have been delegated to them by central administration. They act as partners of the public authorities. The articles of association and regulations of the sports federations have to be approved by the Higher Sports Council. In addition, the Higher Sports Council has the competence to conclude agreements with the Spanish sports federations on their objectives and sports programmes, in particular those concerning high-level sport, and on the organisational functions of the federations. Such agreements are governed by administrative law.

National umbrella organisations

In all EU countries, sports federations are affiliated with a national umbrella organisation. The main purpose of these umbrella organisations is to act as intermediaries between the sports federations and the public authorities in order to establish a coherent sports policy. In various countries, however, the tasks of the umbrella organisation are more comprehensive, and certain public powers are delegated to them in their relations with sports federations.

In Latvia, the State has authorised the Council of Latvian Sports Federations to assume the responsibility of recognising activities of the sports federations. The Council of Latvian Sports Federations gives sports federations the right to manage and coordinate activity in their respective fields of sports as well as to represent the State in the relevant international sports federation.

In Italy, the State has assigned to CONI all regulatory powers in the sports sector. More specifically, CONI manages the organisation of national sports and promotes the strengthening of national sports, deals with training of the athletes and makes available appropriate means for Olympic Games and any other national or international sporting event, fosters the practice of sporting activities and takes and supports any initiative necessary for fighting doping, discrimination and violence in sport. All CONI's tasks are listed in a Legislative Decree. These provisions state that CONI's National Council regulates and coordinates national sports activities, harmonising the action of national federations, in accordance with deliberations and directives of the International Olympic Committee (IOC). Among its various tasks, the CONI National Council adopts the CONI statutes and any regulations within its competence and issues decisions aimed at the recognition of national sports federations, affiliated sporting activities and other sporting bodies. The National Council also establishes the fundamental principles to which national sports federations' statutes must conform in order to be recognised. Moreover, the CONI National Council establishes, in line with international sporting rules and within each sport federation, the criteria for distinguishing professional sport from amateur sport. In addition, the National Council sets out conditions and criteria governing the exercise of its controlling powers over federations and any other sports bodies.

In Malta, the sports federations can opt to register with the Malta Sports Council. All sport organisations that register with the Malta Sports Council are entitled to receive assistance or benefits under the Malta Sports Act. Registration also entitles them to make use of State-run sport facilities at a subsidised rate or to receive by legal title or rent a sport facility to be administered by them.

In Slovenia, the Sports Act authorises the National Olympic Committee to implement the licensing system and to manage the benefits that come with the status of elite athlete (medical examinations, health insurance, social security, scholarships, special education and studying conditions, and so on).

In Sweden, the Sports Confederation has the authority to distribute State grants to sport.

2.3.   Extent of State Control

As Chaker observed in his 2004 study, ' "interventionism" should not be taken to mean undue state control or governmental infringement of the basic freedoms of sports NGOs'.[14] The Council of Europe's member states have accepted the European Sport Charter.[15] One of the essential prerequisites the Charter has achieved is to provide the necessary balance between governmental and non-governmental action and to ensure the complementarity of responsibilities between them. This is given expression in the fact that – even in interventionist countries – the law has bestowed upon the sports federations some public powers. Normally the State does not delegate powers or responsibilities to the sports federations through laws or regulations except in France, Greece, Romania and Spain. In Cyprus, these powers are mostly found in the competences that the State has given to the federations in order for them to have their own legal and arbitration committees as well as control of their own programmes. In Portugal, on basis of the Sports Act, the State delegates to the sporting authorities some disciplinary and regulatory powers. In Slovenia, the sporting authorities can appoint eight members to the Council of Experts. Among other tasks, this council can make proposals for new laws and

---

[14]   André-Noël Chaker, Good Governance in Sport – A European Survey, Council of Europe Publishing, Strasbourg, September 2004, p. 9.
[15]   Recommendation No. R(92)13 Rev. of the Committee of Ministers to Member States on the Revised European Sports Charter (adopted by the Committee of Ministers on 24 September 1992 and revised on 16 May 2001).

regulations in the field of sports. In Spain, the Sports Act establishes that sports federations, under the coordination and guidance of the Higher Sports Council, will, among other things, exercise disciplinary authority on the terms laid down in the Act and its implementation rules.

A State could most effectively intervene in the organisation and functioning of professional sport competitions if it is involved in the appointment of members of the sporting authorities. However, there are no EU countries where the public authorities have this right of appointment or participation in any way in the composition of the management bodies.[16] To help avoid electoral irregularities, however, the Electoral Guarantees Board of the Spanish Higher Sports Council is responsible for overseeing the electoral processes in the governing organs of the sports federations.

Another indication of the limits of the influence of the State on the organisational freedom of national federations can be found in the degree of autonomy of those federations to adopt regulations governing competitions. In almost all EU countries (25 out of the 27), the supreme authorities of the sports federations (according to their statutes) are entitled to adopt regulations, rules and other provisions in line with international rules and the domestic general legal framework but independent of State intervention. Although in Poland the state is not involved in establishing the federations' statutes, they are subject to the control of the Minister of Physical Education and Sport, in respect of their compliance with applicable regulations. In Romania, conditions for practising professional sport are established by the national sport federations, by means of own norms, but the conditions must be approved by the Ministry of Youth and Sport. A specialised central public body is entitled to supervise and control the way the national sport federations observe these norms.

National Sports Acts do not necessarily imply the adoption of an interventionist sports legislation model. Indeed, 22 EU countries have promulgated sports legislation, of which 17 favour the non-interventionist approach.

3. STATE INFLUENCE ON THE FINANCING OF PROFESSIONAL SPORT ACTIVITIES

Article 12 of the revised European Sports Charter[17] reads that: '[A]ppropriate support and resources from public funds, that is, at national, regional and local levels, shall be made available for the fulfilment of the aims and purposes of this Charter. Mixed public and private financial support is to be encouraged, including the generation by the sports

---

[16]   Most statutes of the international sports federations contain provisions relating to the independence of member associations and the independence of the decision-making process of the governing body in each country. State involvement in appointment and approval procedures may conflict with these provisions and could lead to national associations being suspended by the international federation. In Recommendation Rec(2005)8 of the Committee of Ministers to Member States on the principles of good governance in sport (adopted by the Committee of Ministers on 20 April 2005) it was recommended that the governments of Member States adopt effective policies and measures of good governance in sport, which include – inter alia as a minimum requirement – democratic structures for non-governmental sports organisations based on clear and regular electoral procedures open to the whole membership.

[17]   See note 2 *supra*.

sector itself of resources necessary for its further development.' The sports authorities are thus expected to generate resources for themselves. In all EU countries, the first matter of importance is that the professional competitions are funded through the governing body. Principally the financing of sport associations consists of membership fees, sponsorship agreements, income from business activities such as owning property and selling fan products, the sale of broadcasting rights or even public listing on the stock exchange.[18] The popularity of only a few sport disciplines is great enough to render sports federations financially self-supporting. By contrast, the segments of the population that the majority of sports disciplines attract are too narrow to ensure their own funding. These sports federations are dependent on direct and/or indirect public financial support.

In Austria, the legal basis for public financing is to be found in the Federal Sports Promotion Act.[19] Sport authorities can be financed through benefits from annuities, interests and credits, loans by the State or subsidies through grants under private law.[20] Decisions on such financial support are made by the Chancellor in an annual plan, after consulting with the respective sport governing bodies.[21] If one single sport-related grant exceeds 2/100 000 of the total annual budget of Austria, it has to be expressly authorised by the Federal Minister of Finance.[22] In principle, the State exercises financial control, but the Chancellor is empowered to transfer the financial control to the Federal Austrian Sport Organisation (BSO) by a contract that must contain a reporting obligation for the BSO.[23]

In Belgium, the professional bodies are dependent on commercial activities for their funding. The State does not participate directly or indirectly in their financing. In the Flemish community, the sporting authorities do not receive any direct financial support from or experience any financial control by the Flemish government either. The State participates indirectly in their financing through granting subsidies to the Flemish sports federations under a decree concerning sports federations.[24] The Flemish government only exercises financial control over the Flemish sports federations within the framework of this decree.

In Bulgaria, according to Article 18 of the Law on Physical Education and Sport:[25] 'The sport clubs and associations, members of a licensed sport federation, shall acquire the right ... to receive state support and to use sport grounds and facilities which are state

---

[18]   The activities of sports federations are in principle twofold: besides being charged with the organisation of a specific sport, they pursue a commercial activity. However, the sports performance is their priority and the financial aspects serve as constraints for their ambitions on the field.

[19]   Bundesgesetz Vom 12. Dezember 1969, Betreffend Förderungen des Sportes aus Bundesmitteln (Bundes-Sportförderungsgesetz) Stf: Bgbl. Nr. 2/1970.

[20]   *Ibid.* § 2. and § 4.(3).

[21]   *Ibid.* § 3.(1), (2).

[22]   *Ibid.* § 19.

[23]   *Ibid.* § 10.

[24]   Décret relatif à un mouvement de rattrapage en matière d'infrastructure sportive par le biais du financement alternatif of 23 May 2008, Moniteur Belge of 06-08-2008, no. 2008202798, p. 41071.

[25]   Law for The Physical Education and Sport. Prom. SG. 58/9 Jul 1996, amend. SG. 53/4 Jul. 1997, amend. SG. 124/27 Oct. 1998, amend. SG. 51/4 Jun. 1999, amend. SG. 81/14 Sep. 1999, amend. SG. 53/30 Jun. 2000, corr. SG. 55/7 Jul 2000, amend. SG. 64/4 Aug. 2000, amend. SG. 75 2 Aug. 2002, amend. SG. 95 8 Oct. 2002, amend. SG. 120 29 Dec. 2002, amend. SG. 96/29 Oct. 2004.

and municipal property, according to the regulations for this purpose.' The State participates directly and indirectly in the financing of sports authorities responsible for the organisation of professional competitions. In compliance with the aims and tasks underpinning the programme for the development of physical education and sport and the Law on Physical Education and Sport, the State (1) finances (funds) the duly approved programmes and projects for public sport and youth activities; (2) supports and promotes non-profit legal entities to implement public sport and youth activities through tax, credit-interest, customs and other financial and economic concessions (relief), as well as different kinds of financing provided in various legal documents; and (3) establishes, maintains, modernises and manages sports sites and facilities which are State property and controls the conditions for their use for this purpose only. The State exercises financial control over the funding so provided.[26]

In the Czech Republic, only the Ministry of Education, Youth and Sport offers financing, by allocating grants to the associations with a country-wide competence in the field of sport.[27] Regional authorities also give financial support to sport activities, and there is the possibility of funding through a special procedure that operates annually and through which the deputies of the Lower Chamber of the Czech Parliament present proposals for financial support, some of which may involve the financing of a volleyball court, a football field, or similar facilities. If the State decides to support an activity in this way, control is very rigorous.

In Denmark, one of the characteristics of sport is the large amount of public funding that may indirectly or directly be granted in support of professional sport. In addition to this, the Danish sport sector benefits from specific rules on VAT taxation. The State subsidy for sport is based on the Act on Football Pools, Lotteries and Betting Games, which stipulates the allocation of the National Lottery's profits to a number of different cultural and humanitarian purposes, such as sport organisations.[28] The subsidies allocated to the Ministry of Culture are primarily granted to the main sport organisations[29] and the Danish Foundation for Culture and Sports Facilities. The Ministry of Culture exercises financial control in pursuance of the Executive Order on Accounts and Audit of Beneficiaries of Subsidies.[30] The Danish Foundation for Culture and Sports Facilities manages public venture capital and acts as an independent expert council under the Ministry of Culture. The mission is to develop and support construction in the field of sport, culture and leisure not based on interests of personal finance.[31] The Danish Foundation for Culture and Sports Facilities acts as the secretariat for the Elite Facility Committee, established as a self-governing institution with the purpose of supporting construction in the area of elite sport with a view to international sport events. The

---

[26]   *Ibid.* Art. 64e (1) and (2).
[27]   Act No. 115/2001 on Support of Sport, dated 28th February 2001 § 3 (1) c).
[28]   Consolidation Act No. 273 of 17 April 2008.
[29]   Namely the organisations mentioned above under Section 2.1 and the Horse Race Finance Foundation, cf. S. 6B. Apart from the fixed allocation laid down in S. 6B earmarked for specific sport organisations, the Ministry of Culture also receives an allocated fixed amount which is not earmarked other than for 'cultural purpose', which includes sport.
[30]   Executive Order No. 924 of 28 September 2005.
[31]   By Act No. 349 of 9 June 1993, amending the Act on Football Pools, Lotteries and Betting Games (*Tips- og lottoloven*), cf. the Regulations on the Foundation.

Ministry of Culture exercises financial control in pursuance of the Executive Order on Accounts and Audit of Beneficiaries of Subsidies.[32] The Act on the Promotion of Elite Sport regulates elite sport in general by establishing the framework for Team Denmark.[33] Team Denmark is a self-governing State institution with the overall responsibility of developing elite sport in a socially justifiable manner through subsidies. Team Denmark must also procure commercial income for elite sport through media agreements in cooperation with the National Olympic Committee and Sports Confederation of Denmark (DIF). In addition, municipalities may support elitist sport where this is not actual business. Again, The Ministry of Culture exercises financial control in pursuance of the Executive Order on Accounts and Audit of Beneficiaries of Subsidies. Sport Event Denmark was established as a self-governing institution with the purpose of attracting major international sport events to Denmark through financial support and acts as an advisory to national federations, municipalities and others. Sport Event Denmark is owned and financed by DIF, Team Denmark, the Ministry of Economics and Business Affairs and the Ministry of Culture, the State being the largest sponsor. Moreover, a number of municipalities have established public-funded event offices.[34] Here too, the Ministry of Culture exercises financial control in pursuance of the Executive Order on Accounts and Audit of Beneficiaries of Subsidies.

In Estonia, sports activity is financed from several sources: State budget, local budgets, foundations, sponsors and an organisation's financing.[35] Support from the state budget is paid to sports organisations that have a development plan and have timely submitted an official statistics report to the agency conducting official statistical surveys which complies with the relevant requirements. The procedure for the distribution of funds allocated from the State budget to support sport organisations is established by a regulation of the Minister of Culture. The Ministry of Culture concludes a contract with the sport authority receiving the support, stipulating the purpose for which the support may be used, the rights and obligations of the parties, the procedure for reporting proper purpose use of the support and sanctions for breach of contract.

In Finland, sport associations may apply for State subsidies for their activities. The Ministry for Education allocates the State subsidies to associations that have applied for them after obtaining an opinion from the National Sport Council. The grounds for granting State subsidies are set forth in the 1998 Sports Act[36] and the 1998 Sports Regulations. State subsidies can be used, among other things, for financing youth work, organising competitions at different levels and covering the costs of participating in international competitions and tournaments. In addition to this, the State exercises financial control through tax law.

---

[32]   Executive Order No. 924 of 28 September 2005. As for the Elite Facility Committee, this is stipulated in the Regulations, S. 10.

[33]   Consolidation Act No. 1332 of 30 November 2007.

[34]   Formerly named *Idrætsfonden Danmark*.

[35]   Sports Act, passed 6 April 2005 (RT1 I 2005, 22, 148), entered into force 1 January 2006, Chapter 4 – Financing of Sports, § 14 Sources of financing and § 15 Principles of financing from state budget.

[36]   Chapter 2 – State financing, Section 5 – Statutory state grants for local sport provision (Amendment 662/2002) and Chapter 3 – Miscellaneous provisions, Section 11 – Financing of state subsidy and grants.

In France, according to the Sport Act, the sport associations can obtain public funding for missions of general interest.

In Germany, the sporting authorities finance themselves from the revenues that they earn. The State is neither directly nor indirectly involved in financing them and does not exercise any financial control.

In Greece, Article 16 of the Constitution states that sports shall be under the protection and the ultimate supervision of the State. The State shall make grants to and control all types of sport associations, as specified by law. The use of grants in accordance with the purpose of the associations receiving them shall also be specified by law. However, this financial support concerns only the national sport federations and not the sporting authorities in charge of the organisation of professional competitions. Law 2725/1999[37] provides that no state aid is available to professional athletes' unions. In reality, however, the State indirectly supports professional sports through broadcasting rights of public television and sponsorship from a betting company, which is also controlled by the State. The professional sporting authorities are financially controlled by the Ministry of Trade.

In Hungary, the State is involved in financing the sports authorities – sports organisations and sports associations – appointed to organise professional competitions. Financing takes place both directly – State aid pursuant to the Sports Act,[38] Act XXXVIII of 1992 on public finances, the Government Decree[39] on State financial procedures and the Ministerial Decree on State support for sports purposes – and indirectly by tax allowances. Besides the national government, local government also takes part in financing the sport authorities. This financing may be carried out through tenders, in the form of sponsoring, by the municipality's own business activity, and so on. Regarding the monitoring of the use of State support, the State acts in accordance with the provisions of Act C of 2000 on accounting. In addition, pursuant to subsection (2) of Section 13/A of Act No XXXVIII of 1992 on public finances, all organisations or private persons financed from any subsystem of public finances or from EU funds or receiving any aid from those resources must account for the proper use of any amount granted to them for any special purpose other than as a social allowance. The funded institution shall verify the use of and account for the amounts. Should the organisation or private person financed or subsidised fail to meet this obligation in due time, then any further financing or assistance shall be suspended until the obligation is fulfilled. In case of illegal or improper use of any assistance, the user shall be subject to reimbursement as laid down in separate laws. In addition, the State Audit Office and the Government Audit Office are entitled to carry out auditing activities concerning the use of central State aids.

In Ireland, there is some State financing. The Department of Arts, Sport and Tourism administers the Sports Capital Programme, which is funded by the National Lottery. Funding is also provided to specific national sporting bodies by the Irish Sports Council, acting under the Irish Sports Council Act 1999.[40] The Irish Sports Council sees itself as a resource for these bodies, with a priority of strengthening and developing their capabilities.

---

[37] Ν 2725/1999/Α-121 Ερασιτεχνικός – Επαγγελματικός Αθλητισμός και άλλες διατάξεις ΦΕΚ Α' 121/17.6.1999, ΝΟΜΟΣ ΥΠ' ΑΡ. 2725.
[38] See Chapter VIII of the Sports Act.
[39] 217/1998 (XII.30.) Korm.
[40] Number 6 of 18 May 1999.

Eligibility criteria establish minimum requirements for bodies wishing to apply for support. This eligibility process is currently under review. The Sports Council has to report before the Minister for Sport, Tourism and Recreation about each spending.[41] The State exercises financial control insofar as financial support is targeted, and the bodies concerned must show that they have delivered on key objectives. The Irish Sports Council sees this as a process of dialogue.

In Italy, CONI performs all its tasks and activities through a limited company called *Coni Servizi*.[42] *Coni Servizi* has a share capital amounting to €1 000 000, and all shares are assigned to the Ministry of Economic and Financial Affairs.[43] Any further increase in the capital is decided by the Minister of Economic and Financial Affairs in agreement with the Minister of Cultural Heritage and Activities. The relationship between CONI and *Coni Servizi*, including the financial one, is governed by an annual service contract. The president and the other members of the board of directors are appointed by CONI. The president of the board of statutory auditors is appointed by the Minister of Economic and Financial Affairs, and all other members are appointed by the Minister of Cultural Heritage and Activities. *Coni Servizi*'s accounts are controlled by the Court of Accounts in accordance with Article 12 of Act no. 259 of 1958.[44] The State finances CONI directly and directly controls *Coni Servizi*. The Court of Accounts is also competent to control national federations' accounts.[45] This is due to the public character of the service relationship between national sport federations and CONI, which directly or indirectly finances the national federations, and also to the public nature of CONI's resources.

In Latvia, the State budget funds for sport have been allocated in accordance with the annual State budget law. The Financial Commission of the Ministry of Education and Science assesses financial proposals submitted by the sports federations in accordance with the internal regulations of the Ministry of Education and Science, by which State budget funds are to be allocated to sports. The Financial Commission submits the financial proposal to the Latvian National Sports Council, which develops recommendations for the division of the State budget funds in the field of sport and submits such recommendations to the Ministry of Education and Science.[46] The State participates indirectly in professional sports financing since State budged funds have been allocated to the specialised sports organisation – the limited liability company 'Latvian Olympic Team' – which further contracts athletes.[47] The financing system provides a transparent process for monitoring the expenditures of the State allocations. The agreements on State budget funding signed for each sports organisation stipulate that a financial report shall be submitted on a regular basis. The Ministry of Education and Science monitors the flow of finances and whether expenditures correspond to the particular objective stated in the agreement.

---

[41]   Irish Sports Council Act, 1999, s. 26.

[42]   Law-Decree no. 138 of 2002, *Interventi urgenti in materia tributaria, di privatizzazione, di contenimento della spesa farmaceutica e per il sostegno dell'economia anche nelle aree svantaggiate*, Art. 8.1.

[43]   *Ibid.* Art. 8.4.

[44]   *Ibid.* Art. 8.10.

[45]   See Corte dei Conti, Lazio sez., judgment of 23-01-2008 no. 120 at pages 9–12 (doc. 06).

[46]   Sports Law, Published: 'Vestnesis', 13 Nov. 2002, No. 165 (2740), S. 9(3), 2).

[47]   *Ibid.* S. 14(1) and (2).

In Lithuania, sports may be financed by allocations from the State budget and municipal budgets, by funding derived from lotteries, as well as other financing legally obtained. The State can participate directly in the financing of sporting authorities. Non-governmental physical education and sports organisations may receive funds from the State and municipal budgets for the implementation of physical education and sports programmes and projects.[48] A State institution or the municipal administration shall sign contracts for the use of such funds with the organisations involved. The procedure and format for the conclusion of such contracts as well as the procedure for accounting for funds used are laid down by the Department of Physical Education and Sports. If the State and the municipal institutions allocate funds, they have the right to check how these funds are used. The organisations which have received funds from the State and municipal budgets must submit a report on the use of these funds to the institutions which have allocated the funds.

In Luxembourg, the Sports Act provides that the funds that the State grants for sporting activities, for technical supervision and for sports administration are to be determined annually in the State budget.[49] State funding is divided into subsidies and financial contributions for a specific expense, the latter requiring supporting documentation. The State provides subsidies and financial contributions for competitive and leisure sports and sports infrastructure. The State provides ordinary subsidies to sports clubs and federations, based on a point system that takes into account the number of licensed members, particularly young members, the qualifications of club trainers and the federation's participation in official competitions. With respect to the federations, the State is more inclined to provide financial contributions for the federations' operating expenses than ordinary subsidies.

In Malta, a company may prove to the satisfaction of the Commissioner that it has made a cash donation to an athlete or sports organisation participating in national or international sports events and such events are approved by the Malta Sports Council. Such donation may then be claimed as a deduction against income for the year of assessment in which it is made, provided that a certificate is issued in this respect by the Malta Sports Council and the said athlete or sports organisation is not in any way related to the donor company. The State participates indirectly through the schemes made available by the Malta Sports Council to those sport organisations that are registered.[50] There are several incentive schemes for improvement of facilities, equipment and education to help grassroots athletes, including the maintenance and upgrading of sport facilities. The State, through its Sport Authority, verifies that the public funds received by the organisations were used for the purpose for which they were granted. At the end of their financial year, sport organisations registered with the Malta Sports Council must submit their audited accounts so that the Council can verify that the organisation has not become profit-making.

In the Netherlands, a general framework for subsidising the sport sector is laid down in the Public Welfare Act of 1994. National sports associations can file an application with

---

[48]   Law on Physical Culture and Sport of the Republic of Lithuania, December 20, 1995 No. I-1151, Arts. 10, 3), 11, 2) and 5), 38 and 40.
[49]   Loi du 3 août concernant le sport, Mémorial A-N° 131, 17 August 2005, Art. 9.
[50]   Sports Act, Sports [CAP. 455. 1], Chapter 455, 27 January 2003, Act XXVI of 2002, PART II.

the Ministry of Health, Welfare and Sport for an annual subsidy for performing their activities. Occasionally they may apply to other ministries for subsidies, for example, to finance special projects in the field of sports. Besides this, municipalities and provinces spend many millions of Euros to maintain sporting facilities, to organise major events and to fund special projects, but also to stimulate elite sport. The associations and/ or clubs are accountable for their expenditures. In addition to public financing, the National Olympic Committee (NOC*NSF) provides subsidies to regular members. This money comes from the revenue generated by the National Lottery, which is involved in organising games of chance. Some of the funds that are available for sport are paid directly to sports associations. Another portion goes to umbrella organisations. These umbrella organisations receive funds in order to maintain themselves and to carry out activities for the purpose of supporting the sport associations.

In Poland, the sports federations are funded from different sources, that is, membership fees, voluntary contributions by sponsors and the State budget, that is, by means of subsidies from the central budget, special purpose funds and the funds provided by local governments. The special purpose subsidies are aimed at financing certain tasks, such as the organisation of sports competitions or Olympic preparations. Some funds allocated from the subsidies may be spent on the administrative activity of sports associations. The use of public funds is subject to control of the national or local government that grants the subsidy and by the Supreme Chamber of Control.

In Portugal, professional leagues are registered non-profit associations that have financial, technical and administrative autonomy[51] The State is not allowed directly to participate in financing the organisation of professional sport competitions, except for the improvement of sport facilities. The financial activities of the federations and the professional leagues are supervised by State authorities though enquiries and inspections.[52]

In Romania, the Sports Act contains provisions regarding the financing of sports activities.[53] National sport federations can request support from the budget of national or local public authorities. The budget of public sport structures is determined by local or national public authorities. It is very important that all non-governmental sport structures are exempt from local contributions and taxes. Based on special contracts, the non-governmental sport associations and the Romanian Olympic Committee may receive funding from the State budget or from the budget of local authorities for organising sport competitions or other sport events. The State, by means of its specialised bodies, can thereby exercise financial control over the activities of the national sport federations.

In Slovakia, according to the Law on Physical Culture, the sources of financing of sport are, among others, the State budget to a minimum of 0.5 per cent of the annual budget; the State budget under a special Act on Support of Sport; profit from lotteries and other forms of betting; and support from municipalities.[54] The State participates directly in the

---

[51]　Lei no 5/2007 de 16 de Janeiro, Lei de Bases da Actividade Física e do Desporto, Art. 22(1).

[52]　*Ibid.* Art. 21.

[53]　Legea Educatiei Fizice şi Sportului, Law no. 69/2000, Title XI, Arts 67–75.

[54]　300/2008 Z.z., ZÁKON z 2. júla 2008 o organizácii a podpore športu a o zmene a doplnení niektorých zákonov, Zmena: 462/2008 Z.z., Art. 13.

financing of sport, which is regulated by the Sports Act.[55] Financing of sports from the State budget is implemented through grants that may be provided for securing the organisation of sport competitions.[56] The beneficiary of a grant is obliged annually to publish the amount and type of grants received if the income from grants exceeds €33 194 a year.[57] The law does not provide for any other specific means of financial control by the State.

In Slovenia, the State directly finances the sporting authorities if they organise competitions which fall under the National Sports Program and/or annual sports programme and if that programme is of a 'public interest' as defined by the law.[58] Competitions can also be financed by local municipalities.[59] In the case of professional competitions that are financed by public funds, financial control is carried out by the Court of Auditors.

In Spain, the public authorities – State, autonomous regions and local authorities – may grant subsidies to sports associations. State subsidies are awarded by the Higher Sports Council. The grounds for granting State subsidies are laid down in a Ministerial Order.[60] Moreover, groupings of clubs at national level may receive State subsidies. The Higher Sports Council is not only responsible for granting these financial subsidies to the sports federations and other sports bodies and associations, but also for authorising the multi-annual budgets of the Spanish sports federations, determining the use of the federations' net capital in the event of their dissolution, controlling the subsidies that have been granted and authorising the levying and conveyance of their property assets, where these have been wholly or partially financed through State public funds.

In Sweden, the State contributes to the financing of sport activities. Subsidies are paid to sport associations on different levels. In principle, the State pays financial contributions to the national sport federation, which transfers money to different levels of the national sport associations.[61] In general the State transfers money to the national federation, and most of that money is transferred to local sport clubs as operating grants. Beyond that, most subsidies for sport derive from the State-regulated organisation dealing with lotteries and other forms of betting. However, in a government proposal presented in January 2009 it was suggested that the financial contribution via this National Lottery be replaced by a more stable and predictable financial contribution directly from the State.[62] Regional county councils also pay contributions to the sport associations at the regional level, independently of State subsidies. At the local level, municipalities give direct or indirect financial support to sport clubs. For instance, a sport club could receive funding from the local authorities depending on the number of members. Furthermore, the local authorities are often in charge of football grounds, sports centres, and so on. Indirectly, this amounts to support for local sport activities since clubs can thereby rent time for

---

[55]   *Ibid.* Arts. 10–18.
[56]   *Ibid.* Art. 11 (1) (b).
[57]   *Ibid.* Art. 18 (5).
[58]   The Law on Sport of the Republic of Slovenia, Srt. 3.
[59]   *Ibid.* Art. 7.
[60]   Ministerial Order ECI/2768/2007, of 20 September, respecting the rules for awarding subsidies and financial grants by the Higher Sports Council.
[61]   See Ordinance Förordning (1999:1177) om statsbidrag till idrottsverksamhet.
[62]   The Government's proposition 2008/09:126 Statens stöd till idrotten. See also Official Report SOU 2008:59 Föreningsfostran och tävlingsfostran – En utvärdering av statens stöd till idrotten.

playing, training, and so on, at a reasonable price. The State monitors the financial support to sport. Reports from the Swedish National Audit Bureau and the Swedish Agency for Public Management account for financial contributions to non-profit associations. One conclusion of such reports has been that there is no common basic policy for financial support from State authorities. Further, it was noted that there is no common policy or regulations governing financial support at the regional and local level and that monitoring systems were insufficient.[63] In 2009, government proposals were presented for the establishment of a new monitoring system.[64] According to these proposals, the Centre for Sport Research (CIF) would be responsible for the annual monitoring activities whereby certain criteria – formulated in rather general terms related to general goals for State support – have to be used, such as sport as a 'popular movement', the importance of sport for public health, sport and its relevance for children and youth, equal participation of men and women, training in democracy, and so on.[65] Before, monitoring was carried out by means of reports from national sport federations on different aspects of the use of financial contributions to sport. These reports, focusing on quantitative data, are now to be completed within the terms of the new monitoring instruments.

In the United Kingdom, the Department of Culture, Media and Sport (DCMS) advised that it undertakes the following funding activities in respect of sport: 'DCMS provides significant funding for sports provision, improving the quantity and quality of sporting opportunities at every level, from the playground to the podium. Our aim is to encourage wider participation in sport, helping to create a more active nation through sport and improve performance.' In June 2008 the DCMS published 'Playing to Win – a new era for sport', which sets out the government's ambition to become a truly world-leading sporting nation, capitalising on the 2012 Olympic Games and Paralympic Games. The main funding elements in connection with professional sports are:

- *Sport England*. The DMCS funds Sport England, which is responsible for delivering the government's sporting strategy in England in the same way as the sports councils do for the devolved home countries of the UK. It distributes exchequer and lottery funding and advises the DCMS on sports policy. Designated sports authorities such as governing bodies, clubs and local authorities may receive such funding. The government's equality agenda in sport and its community programmes are channelled through Sport England.
- *UK Sport*. Established by Royal Charter in 1996, UK Sport works in partnership with the home country sports councils and other agencies in an effort to lead sport in the UK to world-class success. UK Sport is responsible for managing and distributing public investment and is a statutory distributor of funds raised by the National Lottery. UK Sport is focussed on elite sporting success. It develops and funds performance and events programmes.

---

[63]   Riksrevisionen, Offentlig förvaltning i privat regi – statsbidrag till idrottsrörelsen och ideella organisationer (RIR 2004:15). See also Bidrag till ideella organisationer – kartläggning, analys och rekommendationer, Statskontoret, Rapport 2004:17, Stockholm 2004.

[64]   Note 62 *supra*.

[65]   The Government's proposition 2008/09:126 Statens stöd till idrotten, p. 32 ff.

- *Sports facilities*. The DCMS funds new or refurbished public sports facilities. For example, the government partly financed the construction of Wembley Stadium.

The State exercises financial control directly through the normal rules on taxation and indirectly through the funding programmes mentioned above.

4. CONCLUSION

To what extent are the public authorities of the EU countries involved in the organisation and functioning of professional sport competitions? Have they adopted an attitude of aloofness or do they intervene on the basis of sports legislation? In other words, have they adopted a 'non-interventionist' or an 'interventionist' model of sport governance? Another interesting question is whether and to what extent the legislators in the various EU countries have provided the public authorities with powers to control the financial situation of the sport sector. Apart from legislation, another means available to governments to exercise control over the sports movement is access to funding.[66] By regulating the flow of money into the sports movement, a government with a non-interventionist sports legislation model can have as much or more of an impact on the sports movement than an interventionist-type country. In the Appendix below the findings of the T.M.C. Asser Instituut's research study for the European Commission are summarised concerning these issues, country-by-country.

The European Model of Sport has as main feature its pyramid structure of sport organisations. Sport clubs are members of one national federation (known as the *One-Association-Principle*); that federation forms part of an international federation. The regulations of the international federation must be implemented in the regulations of the lower echelons. Where an Olympic sport and a pre-Olympic or Olympic event are concerned, the international federation is subject to the rules and regulations of the IOC. National federations in interventionist countries could be sandwiched between the sports legislation of the country and the rules and regulations of the higher echelons. Serving those two masters, normally, does not give way to conflicts, because – as said before -interventionism should not be taken to mean undue State control or governmental infringement of the basic freedoms of sports non-governmental organisations. However, the occurrence of conflicts is not a purely academic question. This was, for example, proven in 2006, when FIFA suspended the European football champion Greece and its member clubs from international competition because of government interference in the sport. The Hellenic Football Federation was suspended for not being in line with the principles of the FIFA statutes regarding the independence of member associations and the independence of the decision-making process of the football-governing body in each country. In the shortest possible time the Greek Parliament approved an amendment to the relevant legislation to make the Greek Football Federation more independent; FIFA's emergency committee then lifted the suspension.

---

[66] André-Noël Chaker, Good governance in sport – A European survey, Council of Europe Publishing, Strasbourg, September 2004, p. 11.

APPENDIX

Sports legislation framework and sports financing in EU countries

Country	Sport in the Constitution	Sports Act	Type of sports legislation	Direct/indirect financing by the State
Austria	Yes	Yes	Non-interventionist	Direct and indirect
Belgium	No	No	Non-interventionist	No
Bulgaria	Yes	Yes	Interventionist	Indirect
Cyprus	Yes	Yes	Interventionist	Indirect
Czech Republic	No	Yes	Non-interventionist	Direct
Denmark	No	Yes	Non-interventionist	Indirect
Estonia	No	Yes	Non-interventionist	Direct
Finland	No	Yes	Non-interventionist	Direct
France	No	Yes	Interventionist	Indirect
Germany	No	No	Non-interventionist	No
Greece	Yes	Yes	Interventionist	Direct
Hungary	Yes	Yes	Non-interventionist	Direct
Ireland	No	Yes	Non-interventionist	Direct
Italy	Yes	Yes	Interventionist	Indirect
Latvia	No	Yes	Interventionist	Direct
Lithuania	Yes	Yes	Non-interventionist	Direct
Luxembourg	No	Yes	Non-interventionist	Direct
Malta	No	Yes	Non-interventionist	Indirect
Netherlands	No	No	Non-interventionist	Direct and indirect
Poland	Yes	Yes	Interventionist	Direct
Portugal	Yes	Yes	Interventionist	No
Romania	No	Yes	Interventionist	Direct
Slovakia	No	Yes	Non-interventionist	Direct
Slovenia	No	Yes	Non-interventionist	Direct
Spain	Yes	Yes	Interventionist	Indirect
Sweden	No	Yes	Non-interventionist	Direct
United Kingdom	No	No	Non-interventionist	Indirect

PART II

PROTECTION OF COMPETITION AND ATHLETES

6 Doping in sport

Richard W. Pound, Q.C. and Kerwin Clarke

A BRIEF OVERVIEW OF DOPING IN SPORT

Doping is the term used to describe the prohibited practices within sport relating to substances and methods used with the objective of enhancing performance. The term has been developed to distinguish sport-related activity from what is often referred to as social or recreational drug use as well as to incorporate expansion of the concept from the use of prohibited substances to include certain methods and manipulations.

The purpose of this chapter is to provide a brief historical review of the context of doping in sport, the establishment, legitimacy and extent of the applicable anti-doping rules, their enforcement within national and international theatres and the resolution of disputes arising from application of the rules.

Doping, as a concept in sport, is relatively recent. Sport as an organized activity is governed by rules which are accepted by participants. Without the agreed-upon rules, the activity does not constitute sport. The rules define the sport or game, describe the field of play, determine the extent of the game or contest, establish the scoring parameters, prescribe the equipment to be used, provide penalties for rule infractions; in short, identify everything the participants need to know in order to practice the sport.

For centuries there have been stories of athletes who have lived on special diets, taken drugs and used other substances with the objective of improving their performances. Some undoubtedly had no effect whatsoever, some probably did and others may have merely provided a psychological boost. There is recent evidence that placebos can induce improved performance, if the athlete believes that he or she has ingested the 'real' substance. There is also little doubt that many of the substances used were inherently dangerous or became dangerous when used in sufficient quantities. Such use was, in many cases, reckless, undertaken with no understanding whatsoever of the possible side effects. Whatever the physical dangers involved, such activity was not contrary to the established rules of the sport and was, therefore, imbued with no disapprobation.

It was not until the mid-twentieth century that serious attention began to be accorded to what was recognized as increasing use of performance-enhancing substances in sport. The initial focus grew out of concerns for the health of the athletes who ingested the substances. Some international sports federations (IFs) adopted rules to prevent or discourage the use of certain substances. The International Olympic Committee (IOC) was also concerned, although it had no administrative role in the governance of international sport, other than its control of the Olympic Games, an event that occupied 2 weeks every 4 years. Acceleration of the IOC's consideration of the problem occurred following the death of a Danish cyclist during the road race at the Rome Olympics in 1960. The IOC formed a Medical Commission, which in turn created a sub-commission on doping and biochemistry and recruited scientists with experience relating to the use of doping substances, many of whom were directors of research laboratories. Based on their experience, the Medical Commission developed the first list of prohibited substances.

Drug testing was introduced by the IOC at the 1968 Olympic Games, in Grenoble and Mexico City, and this has continued ever since, including at the Beijing Games in 2008. Over time, all the Olympic IFs adopted anti-doping rules of various degrees of sophistication, usually based on the IOC rules and normally using the IOC 'List', which became the reference list for anti-doping. Most rules were directed at testing during competitions, where 'race-day' drugs such as stimulants could be detected. The rules did not address the problem of drugs that might be taken during training periods, which, though cleared from the systems of the users, nevertheless provided a residual advantage at the time of competition. Chief among these, at the time, were anabolic steroids. The initial lack of focus on out-of-competition drug use may have resulted from the lack of IOC jurisdiction to conduct tests on athletes between Olympic Games. Other reasons included the fact that until 1974, there was no reliable test for anabolic steroids and most IFs were small, impecunious organizations with insufficient resources to institute a comprehensive testing program.

Until the advent of rules prohibiting the use of certain substances, there were no sport constraints attaching to such use. There may have been some general legal prohibitions, particularly with respect to cannabinoids, but there was no separate issue to be addressed by the sports authorities. The advent of prohibitions within sport and imposition of penalties for infractions of the rules led to a dramatic change in the legal landscape, as well as to the behavioral patterns amongst athletes and their entourages. What had previously been openly acknowledged within sport became clandestine. Sports authorities were faced with the ongoing problem of attempting to discover what substances and methods were being used. Such knowledge was only part of the puzzle, since, barring an admission from the athlete, there had to be scientifically reliable proof of the use or practice before any penalties could be imposed. Rules were added to require the provision of a urine sample by athletes upon request of the appropriate sport authority. A process of gas chromatography-mass spectrometry was adapted to identify and analyze the prohibited substances or their metabolites in the urine samples. If use of a prohibited substance was detected, the athlete was confronted with the evidence and was liable to disciplinary action. The new consequences, however, required a new system of rules that would set out the duties of athletes, the responsibilities of the sports authorities, the standards of scientific analysis, the rights of an accused athlete and the extent of any applicable sanctions.

In the early days of anti-doping, the agenda was carried by the scientists, with minimal attention paid to the legal framework within which the anti-doping rules would operate. The possibility of challenge to the scientific outcome was extremely limited. In days when the role of athletes was to accept whatever decisions a paternalistic sport authority might make, there was a certain practical validity to that approach. As the professional athletes began to become more important and the economic consequences of a suspension for a doping infraction became more significant, there was a sea-change in the legalistic approach. The IOC had referred for years in the Olympic Charter to an IOC Medical Code. In fact, the IOC had never adopted such a code and what was regarded as the IOC Medical Code was a series of scientific and quasi-scientific reflections, occasionally bordering on mere speculation, on a variety of doping and scientific issues. Had any serious challenge been mounted in respect of a doping-related disqualification at the Olympic Games, the IOC might have been hard-pressed to demonstrate any statutory basis for the disqualification. The IFs, for the most part, had at least adopted anti-doping rules as part of their internal governance rules and could point to such rules in the event of a challenge.

The IOC was in the process of filling this lacuna at the time of the Festina cycling scandal during the Tour de France in 1998. It had first contemplated adoption of the IOC Medical Code, already referred to in the Olympic Charter, but altered that approach to consider an IOC Anti-Doping Code, which was, in fact, a more accurate description of what was needed and intended. As the extent of the implications arising from the Festina scandal became more apparent, there was a further effort to expand the code to an Olympic Movement Anti-Doping Code, with the support of the Olympic IFs. Events overtook even this initiative when the First World Conference on Doping in Sport, held in Lausanne in February 1999, supported the creation of an independent international anti-doping agency, which led to formation in November 1999 of the World Anti-Doping Agency (WADA), with the unusual governance structure of equal representatives of the Olympic Movement and of governments. The role of WADA was to coordinate and lead the fight against doping in sport.

WADA undertook the complex task of analyzing all of the existing anti-doping rules and developing a consensus on a single set of rules, the World Anti-Doping Code (WADC), to be applicable to all sports, all athletes and all countries. This consensus was achieved in March 2003 at the Second World Conference on Doping in Sport. By the time of the Olympic Games in Athens in 2004, the entire Olympic Movement had adopted the WADC and had incorporated it into their appropriate internal governance rules. Governments, somewhat slower to react, nevertheless negotiated and adopted an international convention under the aegis of the United Nations Educational, Scientific, and Cultural Organization (UNESCO), obtaining the unanimous approval of 191 member states at the 33rd session of the UNESCO General Conference on 19 October 2005. The Convention came into force in February 2007 when the requisite number of instruments of ratification had been deposited with UNESCO. The Convention requires member states, inter alia, to use the WADC as the basis for their fight against doping in sport. With this circle closed, for the first time in history, the sports authorities and the public authorities were dealing with doping in sport based on the same set of rules.

An important exception to the universal application of the WADC is the refusal of many professional sports leagues and organizations outside the Olympic Movement to adopt and implement it in the governance of their own enterprises. This is discussed at greater length towards the end of this chapter.

The next section of this chapter examines various aspects of the legal structures within which anti-doping activities occur, the anti-doping rules and the responsibilities of the various parties to which the rules apply.

STRUCTURAL ISSUES IN INTERNATIONAL SPORT

The international structures in sport have their origins in the late nineteenth century. As organized sport began to emerge as an international phenomenon, efforts were required to ensure that the rules for each sport were standardized and that competitions were properly organized. These were the early, primarily European, beginnings of today's IFs. The IOC was another early example of an organization concerned with the internationalization of sport, albeit with a significantly different governance philosophy regarding the roles and responsibilities of its members.

IFs have the self-assumed responsibility for adopting and enforcing the rules governing their sports. They operate on a quasi-diplomatic basis, according 'recognition' to organizations deemed best able to regulate the particular sport in their respective countries, thereby becoming national federations (NFs) under the general authority of the IF. NFs participate in the general assemblies or congresses of the IFs and elect the members of their executive organs. Voting may be on the basis of one vote per country or may be weighted to give some additional effect to the importance of larger NFs. NFs are responsible for application of the rules governing their sports, as established by the IF. Should they fail to do so, they may be suspended and, if they are unable to govern the sport in their countries, their recognition may be withdrawn by the IF and new recognition may be granted to a different organization that is deemed to be more able to carry out the responsibilities.

The IOC was established in 1894, with the specific short-term objective of organizing the first edition of the modern Olympic Games in Athens 2 years later. From this modest beginning and with some early near-disasters, the IOC has emerged as the organization which leads what has become known as the Olympic Movement. Its governing document is the Olympic Charter, which is amended periodically by its members meeting in general session. In relation to the Olympic Games, the IOC determines, inter alia, which sports will figure on the program of the Games, where and when the Games will be held and what events will be contested. The IOC also operates on much the same quasi-diplomatic recognition system as that used by the IFs. It recognizes IFs as well as national Olympic committees (NOCs) in countries (with a few post-colonial exceptions which might not qualify as 'countries' as measured by current international standards) throughout the world that meet certain specified conditions, including membership of NFs recognized by their respective IFs. Voting control of NOCs must rest with the members representing the NFs, a policy decision to ensure that the NOCs are closely connected with the sport organizations in their countries.

Unlike other sports governing bodies, whose members were designated representatives of their national organizations and who were expected to represent their respective national interests, the IOC members were specifically chosen to be independent of national concerns. It was, therefore, the IOC which co-opted its own members and gave them lifetime appointments, to ensure that they could not be changed should they decide something that might displease their country or its sports authorities.

The IFs governing Olympic sports are responsible for the technical arrangements of their sports at the Olympic Games, including the results of the competitions. The NOCs are responsible for the delegations from their countries at the Games and the selection of their athletes. Some aspects of the latter responsibilities have effectively been taken out of their hands as part of the effort to keep the size of the Games under control. Team sports are limited to a specified number of teams in the Olympic competitions and the IFs organize various pre-Olympic competitions and establish other criteria (often geographic) to arrive at the limit established by the IOC. In other sports, minimum performance criteria can be established by the IFs, as well as a maximum number of athletes from a single country per event or per sport. The performance criteria can, on occasion, become a matter of contention for the national delegations, especially when the NOC may decide to adopt higher standards than those set by an IF. In theory as well, though seldom in practice, a NOC might decide not to enter a team that would otherwise qualify in a particular sport, should it believe that the team's performance will not meet the general standards expected from its athletes.

In addition to these basic structural blocks, there are many multi-sport organizations, including the worldwide Association of National Olympic Committees, continental associations of NOCs and certain IFs, the General Association of International Sports Federations, associations of summer and winter Olympic IFs, Fédération Internationale du Sport Universitaire, Commonwealth Games Federation, recognized IFs, International Paralympic Committee (IPC), all having varying connections and interactions with the Olympic Movement and each with its own jurisdictional issues and responsibilities.

RULE-MAKING

As indicated above, rules are the very essence of sport. The authority for making them has always been consensual, in the sense that those who participate determine and accept certain rules as governing for purposes of their participation. The basic validity of the established rules, from a legal perspective, is that those who do not agree with them are free not to participate. No persons are forced to take part in any sport activity in which the conditions of participation are unacceptable to them.

Important from a legal perspective is the extent of the jurisdiction of the organization as a whole, as well as the constitutional process by which rules are adopted. Care must be taken to ensure that what purports to be a governing rule has been properly adopted. Some legislative powers in that regard belong to the plenary session of members as a whole, others may fall within the power of the executive body and still others to specified officers of the organization, such as the president. For example, within the IOC, decisions on the selection of host cities may be made only by the session of members, as are amendments to the Olympic Charter and the admission or removal of sports on the Olympic program. Specified majorities must be achieved, for example, to effect an amendment of the Olympic Charter.

Once a sport has been admitted to the Olympic program, however, disciplines and events within that sport which will be included in the Games are determined by the IOC Executive Board. Procedural decisions, some of which may have a profound effect on the affairs of the IOC, are generally the responsibility of the president. IFs and NOCs operate along the same general constitutional lines. Rules can only be enforced if they are constitutionally valid. This is the first question any lawyer must ask when confronted with any purported rule.

DOPING RULES AS SPORT RULES

The anti-doping rules contained in the WADC and adopted by the relevant sports organizations become, through that process, sport rules. Anyone in the position of having to enforce them or argue in favor of them will almost certainly have encountered lawyers and other advocates who would have decision-makers regard the rights of someone charged with a doping offence as more sacred than any constitutional safeguard. In fact and in law, however, they are nothing more than sport rules and are subject to the same principles of interpretation as any administrative law. Principles of natural justice, procedural fairness, unbiased decision-making and proportionality of sanctions for offences are all part of these universal principles, since sport rules, while specific to their particular context, do not exist in isolation from general legal systems, whether domestic or international.

The portion of the WADC which deals with interpretation provides that the official text shall be maintained by WADA and be published in English and French. If a conflict exists between the English and French versions, the English version prevails (Article 24.1). The comments annotating various provisions of the WADC shall be used to interpret it. The WADC shall be interpreted as an independent and autonomous text and not by reference to the existing law or statutes of the signatories or governments (Article 24.3). The purpose, scope and organization of the World Anti-Doping Program and the WADC and definitions shall be considered as integral parts of the WADC (Article 24.6).

There have been many examples in the past (and there will undoubtedly more in the future) in which decisions of sports organizations have been referred to various governmental courts when parties have disagreed with a particular outcome. While there is often a natural tendency to afford some deference to the expertise residing within the sport organization, governmental courts have not hesitated (nor should they have) to step in to protect rights that have been ignored or abused, or when principles of natural justice have not been followed. Even within the dispute resolution system relating to doping, described below, the courts are willing to intervene when there has been a breach of the applicable rules, when the proper procedures have not been observed or when there has been a failure of natural justice. For the most part, however, governmental courts generally recognize and accept that their judges should not normally be put into the position of selecting athletes for teams or determining the outcomes of sporting contests.

The formal process by which the WADC becomes part of the applicable sport rules is described in the WADC. Signatories first accept the WADC by signing a declaration of acceptance, upon approval by their respective governing bodies. Signatories contemplated in the WADC are WADA, the IOC, the IPC, the IFs, the NOCs, the national Paralympic committees, major event organizations (the continental associations of NOCs and other international multi-sport organizations that function as the ruling body for any continental, regional or other international event) and national anti-doping organizations (NADOs) (Article 23.1.1). Other sport organizations that may not be under the control of a signatory may, upon invitation by WADA, also accept the WADC. The list of all acceptances is made public by WADA (Article 23.1).

Following acceptance, signatories are required to implement applicable provisions of the WADC through policies, statutes, rules or regulations according to their authority and within their relevant spheres of responsibility (Article 23.2.1). Certain articles of the WADC must be implemented without substantive change, including the definition of doping, anti-doping rule violations, proof of doping, WADA's determination of the prohibited list, automatic disqualification of individual results, sanctions on individuals, consequences to teams, statute of limitations, interpretation of the WADC and definitions.

No additional provision may be added to a signatory's rules which changes the effect of these identified articles. Signatories are encouraged to use the models of best practice recommended by WADA in implementing the WADC (Article 23.2.2). Until signatories have accepted and implemented the WADC, they are not considered to be in compliance with the WADC (Article 23.3.2).

Signatories are always free to withdraw acceptance of the WADC after providing WADA with 6 months' written notice of their intent to withdraw (Article 23.7).

INCORPORATION OF WADC INTO INTERNAL SPORT RULES

WADA, although governed by sport and government stakeholders in representative capacities, is nevertheless separate and distinct from them as a matter of law. The adoption of the WADC by WADA has no juridical significance and leads to no consequence whatsoever to any of the stakeholders, unless and until the stakeholders act, in accordance with their own rules, to include the WADC as part of those rules or to adopt it by reference. An IF, for example, has no jurisdiction to discipline one of its constituents for breach of a rule of another organization unless the IF first takes the necessary steps to make that rule one of its own. The IOC amended the Olympic Charter to make the WADC part of its own rules, including the provision that only sports which adopt and implement the WADC can be admitted to or remain on the program of the Olympic Games.

When the original version of the WADC was adopted by WADA during the course of the Second World Conference on Doping in Sport, held in Copenhagen in March 2003, the Olympic Movement representatives undertook to cause the IOC, the IFs and the NOCs (together with accredited laboratories and national anti-doping agencies) to adopt the WADC prior to the Opening Ceremony of the 2004 Olympic Games in Athens. By means of signing the non-legally binding (but effectively politically binding) Copenhagen Declaration, governments undertook to use the WADC as the centerpiece of their own actions in anti-doping prior to the Opening Ceremony of the Olympic Winter Games in Torino in 2006. Legal 'delivery' on that political promise was achieved with adoption of the UNESCO International Convention against Doping in Sport.

DEFINITION OF DOPING

It has proved impossible to date to arrive at a legally satisfactory conceptual definition of doping, so the default position has been to fall back, to some degree, on the scientific approach and to define doping as the use or attempted use of any of the prohibited substances or methods described in the List of Prohibited Substances and Prohibited Methods incorporated by reference into the WADC. From the perspective of decision-makers, certainty in the application of the WADC was considered far more important than elegant philosophical descriptions, which might be open to a variety of interpretations. The strong consensus was for the decision-maker not to be required to wrestle with philosophical concepts, in the interests of a harmonized approach to the problem.

Thus, 'doping' is defined in Article 1 of the WADC as the occurrence of one or more of the anti-doping rule violations set forth in Article 2, namely:

(a) presence of a prohibited substance or its metabolites or markers in an athlete's sample; [It is each athlete's duty to ensure that no prohibited substance is present in his or her body. It is unnecessary that intent, fault, negligence or knowing use be demonstrated in order to establish an anti-doping rule violation (Article 2.1). Sufficient proof of an anti-doping rule violation is established by either (i) the presence of a banned substance or its metabolites or markers in an 'A' sample when a 'B' sample has been waived and subsequently not analyzed or (ii) the 'B' sample confirms the presence of the prohibited substance or its metabolites or markers found in the athlete's 'A' sample (Article 2.1.2). Exceptions are provided for certain qualitative thresholds (Article 2.1.3) and special criteria for prohibited substances which can also be produced endogenously (Article 2.1.4).]

(b) use or attempted use by an athlete of a prohibited substance or a prohibited method; [This may be established by any reliable means, including admission by the athlete, witness statements and longitudinal profiling. Success or failure in terms of use does not matter. It is enough that the effort was made (Article 2.2).]

(c) refusing or failing without compelling justification to submit to sample collection after notification as authorized in applicable anti-doping rules, or otherwise evading sample collection; [This includes hiding from a doping control officer to escape notification for testing (Article 2.3).]

(d) violation of applicable requirements regarding athlete availability of out-of-competition testing, including failure to file required whereabouts information and missed tests based on rules which comply with the international standard for testing (Any combination of three missed tests and/or filing failures within an eighteen-month period as determined by anti-doping organizations with jurisdiction over the athlete shall constitute an anti-doping violation); [In certain situations, a missed test or filing failure can constitute an anti-doping rule violation (Article 2.4).]

(e) tampering or attempted tampering with any part of doping control (Article 2.5);

(f) possession of prohibited substances or prohibited methods, including 'purchasing it for a friend' (Article 2.6);

(g) trafficking or attempted trafficking in any prohibited substance or prohibited method (Article 2.7); or

(h) administration or attempted administration to any athlete in-competition of any prohibited method or prohibited substance, or administration or attempted administration to any athlete out-of-competition of any prohibited method or prohibited substance that is prohibited out-of-competition, or assisting, encouraging, aiding, abetting, covering up or any other type of complicity involving an anti-doping rule violation or any attempted anti-doping rule violation (Article 2.8).

THE PROHIBITED LIST

WADA has the responsibility of preparing and publishing on its website as often as needed, and at a minimum once per year, the annual List of Prohibited Substances and Methods (the List). Unless otherwise provided, each new List comes into effect 3 months after publication by WADA (Article 4.1).

There are two categories of substances and methods which are prohibited. One is those which are prohibited at all times, because of their potential to enhance performance in future competitions (or their masking potential), and the other is those that are prohibited in-competition only. Inclusions on the List may be by general category (e.g., anabolic agents) or by specific reference to a particular substance or method (Article 4.2).

The criteria to be considered with respect to inclusion of a substance or method on the List are:

(a) medical or other scientific evidence, pharmacological effect or experience that the substance or method, alone or in combination with other substances or methods, has the potential to enhance or enhances sport performance (Article 4.3.1.1);

(b) medical or other scientific evidence, pharmacological effect or experience that the use of the substance or method represents an actual or potential health risk to the athlete (Article 4.3.1.2);

(c) WADA's determination that the use of the substance or method violates the spirit of sport described in the introduction of the WADC (Article 4.3.1.3).

(d) WADA's determination that there is medical or other scientific evidence, pharmacological effect or experience that the substance or method has the potential to mask the use of other prohibited substances or prohibited methods (Article 4.3.2).

WADA's determination of the prohibited substances and methods included on the List and the classification of substances into categories on the List is final and may not be challenged based on an argument that the substance or method was not a masking agent or did not have the potential to enhance performance, represent a health risk or violate the spirit of sport.

The spirit of sport is a more elusive concept, attempting to describe what is intrinsically valuable about sport (hence the 'spirit' of sport). It is the essence of Olympism and is how one – to use the WADA motto – plays true. It is the celebration of the human spirit, body and mind and is characterized by the following values: ethics, fair play and honesty; health; excellence in performance; character and education; fun and joy; teamwork; dedication and commitment; respect for rules and laws; respect for self and other participants; courage; and community and solidarity. Doping is fundamentally contrary to the spirit of sport.

SPECIFIED SUBSTANCES

One of the most frequently expressed concerns with the first version of the WADC, which came into effect on 1 January 2004, was that in some adverse analytical findings of prohibited substances, there may well have been no intention to have doped, but there was an adverse analytical finding that could not be ignored and a normative sanction, in the interest of harmonization, of 2 years of ineligibility for a first offence. The legal principle of proportionality was not offended by the consequences, but there was a strong body of opinion (principally within the IFs and some hearing panels) that the outcome in some cases was felt to be too severe in the circumstances. The response was to add a new rule dealing with 'specified substances' and to provide greater flexibility to move lower on the sanction scale if the circumstances pointed to inadvertence and no intention to dope. The amendment provides, for purposes of applying the sanctions, that all prohibited substances are to be considered as specified substances, except substances in the classes of anabolic agents and hormones and those stimulants and hormone antagonists so identified on the List. Prohibited methods, however, are not to be considered as specified substances (Article 4.2.2). To preserve a degree of flexibility for the future, if a new class of prohibited substances is added to the List, the WADA Executive Committee shall determine whether or not it is to be considered as a specified substance (Article 4.2.3).

WHEREABOUTS SYSTEM

Testing during competitions is a necessary element in an effective anti-doping program, but even more important is the ability to test athletes during the periods of preparation for competition. Experience has shown that most doping activity occurs out-of-competition, with the joint objective of achieving the performance enhancement (e.g., from anabolic steroids, the hormone erythropoietin (EPO) – human growth hormone)) and having time for the detectable metabolites or other indications of the use to clear from the athletes' systems. Experience has also shown that it takes remarkably little time to be able to interfere with tests. It is essential, therefore, that tests be unannounced and that athletes be chaperoned from the moment that a request is made to provide a sample. For the unannounced out-of-competition element of the anti-doping program to work, it has to be possible to find the athletes wherever they may be and whenever they are to be tested. This, in turn, requires that they provide sufficient information as to where they will be located during the training periods.

Detailed rules are provided in the international standard for testing. Article 14.3 requires athletes who have been identified by their IF or NADO for inclusion in a registered testing pool to provide accurate, current location information. The IFs and NADOs are required to coordinate the identification of the athletes and the collection of current location information and submit these to WADA. The information can be made available to other ADOs having jurisdiction to test the athletes, but is otherwise maintained strictly confidentially at all times and is used solely for purposes of planning, coordinating or conducting testing. Laboratory information or test results are to be destroyed after they are no longer relevant for those purposes (Article 14.3).

TESTING

Testing is either in-competition or out-of-competition. There are certain jurisdictional rules, designed to prevent duplication, pursuant to which the WADC establishes a priority of responsibility for initiating and directing testing during the period of a sport event. In general for testing purposes the international body which is the ruling body for the event, for example the IF for world championships, the IOC for the Olympic Games and the Pan American Sports Organization for the Pan American Games will direct testing. For national events, the NADO in that country (Article 15.1) will typically oversee testing. An additional rule provides that an ADO which wishes to conduct testing at an event must first confer with the ruling body for the event and obtain its permission to conduct and to coordinate any additional testing. If an unsatisfactory response is received, the ADO may ask WADA for permission to test and to determine how to coordinate the additional testing. WADA shall not grant approval before consulting and informing the ruling body for the event (Article 15.1.1).

Out-of-competition testing is required to be initiated and directed by both international and national organizations. It may be done by WADA, the IOC or IPC in connection with the Olympic Games and Paralympic Games, the IF or any other ADO that has testing jurisdiction over the athlete (Article 15.2).

Subject to the jurisdictional limitations described above, each NADO has testing jurisdiction over all athletes who are present in that country or who are nationals, residents, license-holders or members of sports organizations of that country. IFs have jurisdiction over athletes who are members of their national federations or who compete in their events. Athletes are required to comply with any request by an ADO with testing jurisdiction (Article 5.1). ADOs are required to plan and conduct an effective number of in-competition and out-of-competition tests on athletes over whom they have jurisdiction. IFs are required to establish a registered testing pool for international-level athletes in their sport and NADOs have a similar obligation to establish a registered testing pool at the national level. Athletes included in a registered testing pool are subject to the whereabouts requirements (Article 5.1.1). Except in exceptional circumstances, all out-of-competition testing is required to be undertaken with no advance notice (Article 5.1.2). Target testing is to be a priority (Article 5.1.3) and tests are to be conducted on athletes serving a period of ineligibility or a provisional suspension (Article 5.1.4). Testing is to be conducted in conformity with the international standard for testing (Article 5.2).

Results management for such tests and any hearings arising from the procedures fall to the responsible ADO which initiated the test and will be governed by its procedural rules. Where there may be no authority to conduct results management, the default rules will be those of the IF (Article 15.3). Results management and the conduct of hearings arising from a test by or discovered by a NADO involving an athlete who is not a national, resident or license-holder or member of a sport organization of that country are administered as directed by the rules of the applicable IF. Results management and the conduct of hearings from a test by the IOC, the IPC or another major event organization are referred to the applicable IF with respect to sanctions over and above disqualification from the event or the results of the event (Article 15.3.1).

ACCREDITED LABORATORIES

WADA inherited and has added to a system of accredited laboratories originally established by the IOC. The accreditation process begins with a request for accreditation and is followed by a thorough analysis of the laboratory, its equipment, its director and personnel, as well as tests to determine the level of expertise and the ability of the laboratory to detect prohibited substances in samples prepared by WADA for the purpose. Regular tests are built in to the continuing accreditation, which is granted on an annual basis. Failures to detect or unsatisfactory performance can lead to withdrawal of accreditation or down-grading the laboratory with respect to certain substances. Laboratories are obliged to analyze samples and report results in conformity with the international standard for laboratories (Article 6.4).

Only WADA-accredited laboratories are permitted to perform the analysis for prohibited substances, other than by exception approved by WADA (Article 6.1). ADOs responsible for results management are free to use any accredited laboratory. Sample analysis covers prohibited substances and methods, substances that may be part of a monitoring program (substances that are not currently prohibited, but where there may be patterns that suggest misuse and to profile parameters in urine, blood or other matrix, including DNA or genomic profiling, for anti-doping purposes) (Article 6.2). Rules exist to prevent samples from being used for any purpose other than those described without the written consent of the athlete and such use (for research purposes, e.g.) requires that any identification be removed which could allow tracing a sample back to a particular athlete (Article 6.3). Re-testing is, however, permitted for anti-doping purposes (Article 6.5).

THERAPEUTIC USE EXEMPTIONS

There is a recognized understanding that, merely because a person is an athlete, he or she should not be precluded from access to medical treatment, even when such treatment may involve the use of a prohibited substance or method. An international standard has been developed for the process of granting therapeutic use exemptions (TUEs) in appropriate circumstances. Each IF is required to ensure that its international level athletes or any athlete entered in an international event with documented medical conditions which require use of a prohibited substance or method can benefit from a process which allows the request for a TUE, to be issued (or not) pursuant to the rules established by the IF. Similar rules exist at the national level for national level athletes. The IFs are required to advise WADA of each TUE issued, as are NFs in respect of TUEs to athletes registered in a NADO's registered testing pool. WADA has the right to review, at any time, acceptance or refusal of a TUE application and may reverse the decision.

The presence of a prohibited substance or the metabolites or markers, the use or attempted use of a prohibited method, the possession of the substances or methods and the administration of a prohibited substance or method will not be considered anti-doping rule violations (Article 4.4) provided that the method or administration is consistent with the provisions of an applicable TUE issued pursuant to the international standard for TUEs. Central to that outcome, of course, is that the usage, attempt or administration complies with the terms of the TUE.

Decisions by WADA reversing the grant or denial of a TUE may be appealed exclusively to the Court of Arbitration for Sport (CAS) by the athlete or the ADO whose decision was reversed. Decisions by ADOs other than WADA denying TUEs, which are not reversed by WADA, may be appealed by international athletes to CAS and by other athletes to the national-level reviewing body. If that body reverses the decision to deny a TUE, that decision may be appealed to CAS by WADA. When an ADO fails to take action on a properly submitted TUE exemption application within a reasonable time, the ADO's failure to decide may be considered a denial for purposes of the appeal rights (Article 13.4).

RESULTS MANAGEMENT

Basic principles are established to ensure that each ADO has in place a process for dealing with pre-hearing administration of potential anti-doping rule violations. These processes include:

(a) An initial review to confirm that a TUE has been issued or that there has been no departure from the international standards that might have caused the adverse analytical finding (Article 7.1).

(b) Where a TUE has not been issued and the initial review has not disclosed anything which might have caused the adverse analytical finding, prompt notification of the athlete regarding the finding, the anti-doping rule violated, the right to request analysis of the 'B' sample, the scheduled date for the 'B' analysis (unless such analysis has been waived), the opportunity for the athlete and/or a representative to be present when the 'B' analysis is to be performed and the right to obtain copies of both the 'A' and 'B' laboratory documentation packages (Article 7.2).

(c)   Where the initial review shows the presence of a prohibited substance which may also be produced endogenously (an atypical finding), the anti-doping agency is required to conduct an investigation to determine whether the case will be brought forward as an adverse analytical finding, in which event the process referred to in (b) above is engaged. No notice of an atypical finding is provided until the investigation has occurred, unless it is determined that the 'B' sample should be analyzed or unless an event organizer or organization concerned with selecting a team requests information as to whether any atypical findings exist with respect to anyone on the proposed list of competitors. Notification can be given, after first notifying the athlete (Article 7.3).

(d)   Provisional sanctions are required to be imposed on the basis of the 'A' sample, provided notice is given and either a provisional hearing is afforded or an expedited right to a hearing is granted. Should that occur and the 'B' sample analysis fails to confirm the 'A' sample analysis, if it is still possible to be reinserted in the competition, the athlete may continue to take part (Article 7.5).

(e)   If an athlete retires from competition during the course of a results management process, jurisdiction is nevertheless retained by the ADO which began the process. If the process did not begin before the athlete retired, the organization which should have had the results management responsibilities will assume them (Article 7.6).

SELECTED ISSUES IN RELATION TO DOPING

Strict Liability

The nature of doping is, apart from accidental ingestion of a prohibited substance or inadvertent use of a prohibited method, a practice that is deliberately clandestine. Evidence, including that of intention, is all but impossible to obtain. The rule which has emerged over time and which has been accepted by participants, despite occasional desultory challenges, is that of strict liability. Athletes have a responsibility to be knowledgeable of and comply with all applicable anti-doping policies and rules adopted pursuant to the WADC, to be available for sample collection, to take responsibility, in the context of anti-doping, for what they ingest and use, to inform medical personnel of their obligation not to use prohibited substances and prohibited methods and to take responsibility to make sure that any medical treatment received does not violate anti-doping policies and rules adopted pursuant to the WADC (Article 21.1).

The offence of doping is complete, insofar as analytical positives are concerned, when the prohibited substance or its metabolites are found in the bodily specimen (sample) provided by the athlete. It is not necessary for the sport authority to demonstrate any intention on the part of the athlete, nor to establish that the prohibited substance would, in fact, have resulted in enhanced performance. The same is true, with appropriate variation, in the case of prohibited methods. The offence is complete when it is established that the method was used or was attempted. It is not required to show that performance was enhanced. Nor is it necessary to demonstrate that there was intent, fault, negligence or knowing use on the athlete's part in order to establish an anti-doping rule violation (Article 2.1.1, 2.2.1). The success or failure of the use or attempted use of the prohibited substance or method is not material (Article 2.2.2).

There are certain cases in which doping may be established by means other than adverse analytical findings. Included in this category are any reliable means of establishing facts, such as admissions, documentary and circumstantial evidence and the testimony of third party witnesses. As governments take a greater interest in doping, their powers of investigation, their ability to seize evidence and their ability to compel the giving of evidence under oath are likely to produce substantially more cases of non-analytical positive cases of anti-doping rule violations than will result from sample collections. This will be especially effective for non-athletes involved in doping, since until such investigations became prevalent, it was normally only athletes who were sanctioned for anti-doping rule violations, given the difficulties of obtaining evidence regarding the role of third parties.

Burdens and Standards of Proof

The onus of proof in doping matters rests with the ADO (Article 3.1). The ADO is required to produce evidence that reaches the level of a 'comfortable satisfaction' of any hearing panel called upon to make a determination. Comfortable satisfaction lies somewhere between a balance of probabilities on the low side and proof beyond a reasonable doubt on the high side. Hearing panels have specifically declined to apply the criminal onus in doping matters, even prior to the existence of the WADC, but the reasoning they have demonstrated in decisions suggests that comfortable satisfaction is likely considerably closer to the higher standard than the lower. Rebuttal evidence on the part of a person charged with the doping offence is specifically set at the lower standard of balance of probabilities, with two exceptions: first, whenever an athlete seeks to have a lesser sanction in respect of the use of certain specified substances where there was no intention to enhance performance (Article 10.4) and, second, whenever there are aggravating circumstances that might lead to a 4-year suspension for a first violation rather than the normal 2-year suspension (Article 10.6). In both of these circumstances, the athlete has the 'comfortable satisfaction' burden.

Exculpatory Defenses

The WADC contemplates a gradation of substances and methods. In respect of some, once use of the substance or method has been established, there is no further discussion, apart from the sanction to be applied in the circumstances. In other cases, there may be some defenses that can go to the issue of whether doping has been established. These include, for example, certain stimulants, in which there are thresholds provided in the WADC, below which there is no doping, and an upper limit, in which there is an irrefutable presumption that doping has occurred. In between the two limits, there is scope for the athlete to demonstrate the circumstances that led to the presence of the substance in the biological sample provided and the lack of intention to have committed an anti-doping rule violation.

In other cases, an athlete may be able to establish that while the substance was present in the sample provided, he or she had obtained a TUE in order to permit medical use of an otherwise prohibited substance or method.

There are several procedural and other defenses that may be relied upon, including lack of proper identification of the sample as related to the athlete charged, failure to maintain a chain of custody of the sample that would prevent manipulation of the sample, failure of the 'B' sample analysis to confirm the 'A' sample analysis, improper procedures in the laboratory performing the analysis and scientific unreliability of the test used to determine the presence of the prohibited substance. Important for such purposes is that the person or athlete raising the defense must show (on a balance of probabilities) that a departure from the international standard for laboratories could reasonably have caused the adverse analytical finding. If that preliminary burden is satisfied, the onus shifts back to the ADO to establish that the departure did not cause the adverse analytical finding (Article 3.2.1). Similarly, departures from any other international standard or other anti-doping rule or policy do not invalidate such results. If, however, the athlete or person establishes (on a balance of probabilities) that the departure could reasonably have caused the adverse analytical finding or other anti-doping rule violation to have occurred, the onus again shifts to the ADO to establish that such departure did not cause the adverse analytical finding or the factual basis for the anti-doping rule violation (Article 3.2.2).

Other defenses may not apply in relation to the establishment of the anti-doping rule violation, in the sense that the anti-doping rule violation exists, but the defenses could nevertheless be relevant in determining the extent of any sanction that may be imposed in respect of the anti-doping rule violation. These include no fault on the part of the person affected or no significant fault. The impact of these latter defenses is discussed below.

Presumptions

The WADC includes several presumptions. First and foremost is the presumption that no person is guilty of doping until the anti-doping rule violation has been established or proven. This is, of course, a rebuttable presumption. Another is that the presence of a particular substance or method on the List is not open to challenge based on an argument that the substance or method was not a masking agent or did not have the potential to enhance performance, represent a health risk or violate the spirit of sport (Article 4.3.3). A further rebuttable presumption is that the scientific analysis of a sample and the custodial procedures by a laboratory accredited by WADA has been properly performed in accordance with the international standards for laboratories (Article 3.2.1) and that the results as determined by the laboratory are scientifically correct. An irrebuttable presumption is that athletes or persons are responsible for knowing what constitutes an anti-doping rule violation and the substances and methods which have been included on the prohibited List (Article 2).

Absent proof that the decision violated principles of natural justice, the facts established by a decision of a court or professional disciplinary tribunal of competent jurisdiction that is not the subject of a pending appeal, shall be irrebuttable evidence of those facts against the athlete or person to whom the decision applied (Article 3.2.3). Not unlike the civil practice regarding inferences, hearing panels are entitled to draw adverse inferences concerning an athlete or person from a refusal, after a request, made a reasonable time prior to the hearing, to appear at the hearing (in person or by telephone, as directed by the panel) and to answer questions directed by the panel or the ADO asserting the anti-doping rule violation (Article 3.2.4).

Sanctions for Anti-doping Rule Violations

An anti-doping rule violation occurring during a competition mandates automatic disqualification of the result obtained in that competition and the forfeiture of any medals, points and prizes, plus any other consequences, if the athlete is in an individual sport (Article 9). Sanctions on individuals when an anti-doping rule violation occurs during or in connection with an event (e.g., the Olympic Games) may, upon the decision of the ruling body of the event (in the case of the Olympic Games, the IOC), lead to the disqualification of all the individual results of the athlete in that event, including all medals, points and prizes, unless the athlete establishes the he or she bears no fault or negligence for the violation, in which case the other competition results will not be disqualified unless the other results were likely to have been affected by the anti-doping rule violation (Article 10.1).

The next level of sanction for an anti-doping rule violation is that of ineligibility. The period of ineligibility for a first violation arising from use, attempted use or possession of prohibited substances or methods, absent reduction or elimination – or possibly increase (as discussed below) – is 2 years (Article 10.2). For other violations, such as refusing or failing to submit to sample collection or tampering with doping control, the same 2-year sanction applies unless there is a reduction or increase (Article 10.3.1). For still others, such as trafficking or attempted trafficking and administration or attempted administration, the minimum is 4 years, up to lifetime, unless a reduction can be obtained. Anti-doping rule violations involving minors are considered to be particularly serious violations and, if committed by support personnel in relation to anything other than specified substances, will lead to lifetime ineligibility. Infractions which may violate non-sporting laws and regulations shall be reported to the competent administrative, professional or judicial authorities (Article 10.3.2). In the case of whereabouts information failures or missed tests, the sanction is a minimum of one year and a maximum of 2 years, depending on the athlete's degree of fault.

The WADC contains a number of provisions which allow for mitigation of sanctions (Article 10.4). In each of these circumstances, the premise is that the anti-doping rule violation has been established. The only issue remaining is whether the normative sanction should be applied or whether there are circumstances which would justify a lesser sanction. If the violation involved a specified substance and the athlete or person can establish how the substance entered his or her body or came into his or her possession and that it was not intended to enhance sport performance or mask the use of a performance-enhancing substance, and it was a first violation, the 2-year period of ineligibility may be replaced with, at a minimum, a reprimand and no period of ineligibility and, at a maximum, 2 years. This requires the athlete or person to provide corroborating evidence, in addition to his or her word, which establishes to the comfortable satisfaction of the hearing panel that there was no performance enhancing or masking intention. The degree of fault is the key criterion to be considered in assessing the factual background of the case and determining whether a reduction in the sanction should be made (Article 10.4).

Exceptional circumstances may also be considered. Where an athlete can establish that there was no fault or negligence, the period of ineligibility is eliminated. If a prohibited substance has been found, the athlete must establish how it entered his or her system in order for the ineligibility period to be eliminated. The finding of no fault or negligence requires the athlete to establish that he or she did not know or suspect, and could not reasonably have known or suspected even with the exercise of utmost caution, that he or she had used or been administered the prohibited substance or prohibited method. If the provision is applied, the violation will not count as a violation in the event of any subsequent violation, for purposes of determining the applicable sanctions (Article 10.5.1). The next variation on this theme is the ability to establish no significant fault or negligence, in which event the period of ineligibility may be reduced, but not below one-half of the otherwise applicable period. In this case as well, the athlete must also establish how a prohibited substance entered his or her system (Article 10.5.2). To benefit from this provision, the athlete must establish that his or her fault or negligence, when viewed in the totality of the circumstances and taking into account the criteria for no fault or negligence, was not significant in relation to the anti-doping rule violation.

Because a significant part of the objective of an anti-doping program is to eliminate doping as a practice, the WADC also provides for the possibility of reduced penalties where an athlete or other person provides substantial assistance to an ADO, criminal authority or professional disciplinary body which results in the ADO discovering or establishing an anti-doping rule violation or the criminal or professional authority discovering or establishing a criminal offense or a breach of professional rules (Article 10.5.3). This provision is nuanced, depending on whether a final appellate decision has or has not already been taken. In the latter case, the anti-doping organization may act on its own initiative, whereas in the former, it may act only with the concurrence of WADA and the relevant IF. In either event, notice must be given to each ADO which has a right to appeal against such a decision. The limit of any reduction of suspension is three quarters of the otherwise applicable period. Substantial assistance requires that the person involved must fully disclose in a signed written statement all information he or she possesses in relation to anti-doping rule violations and fully cooperate with the investigation and adjudication of any case related to that information, including, for example, presenting testimony at a hearing if requested to do so by an ADO or hearing panel. The information must be credible and must comprise an important part of any case which is initiated or, if no case is initiated, must have provided a sufficient basis on which a case could have been brought.

When a voluntary admission of an anti-doping rule violation occurs prior to receipt of notice of a violation and the admission is the only reliable evidence of the violation at the time of the admission, the period of ineligibility may be reduced by up to one-half of the otherwise applicable period (Article 10.5.4). There is a further possibility of reduction if an athlete or person demonstrates that relief should be available under two or more provisions, for example, no significant fault, as well as provision of substantial assistance, the period then may be reduced by up to three-quarters of the otherwise applicable period (Article 10.5.5).

Increased sanctions are contemplated where aggravating circumstances are involved (other than in cases of trafficking or attempted trafficking and administration or attempted administration), in which event the period of ineligibility for a first offence can be increased up to a total period of 4 years, unless the athlete or person can prove to the comfortable satisfaction of the hearing panel that he or she did not knowingly commit the anti-doping rule violation. The increased sanction may be avoided if there is prompt admission of the anti-doping rule violation after notification of it (Article 10.6).

Sanctions for anti-doping rule violations beyond first offenses are, as one might expect, significantly more severe, ranging from double the period of ineligibility to life (Article 10.7.1). The mitigating circumstances provisions may still apply, but only after the offense has been established and the new applicable period of ineligibility has been determined. The reductions, calculated using the same principles described above, are from the new (higher) period (Article 10.7.2). Where a lifetime sanction may have been pronounced, the reduction cannot be to a period of less than 8 years (Article 10.7.3). A series of rules is included to deal with various cases of multiple offenses, bearing in mind that some may be discovered to have preceded a case which has already been concluded. Multiple offenses may be considered as a factor in determining aggravating circumstances (Article 10.7.4). For offenses to be considered as multiple, each must occur within the same 8-year period (Article 10.7.5).

Unless fairness requires otherwise, in addition to disqualification of results in the competition which produced a positive sample, all other competitive results obtained from the date of the sample collection or the date another anti-doping rule violation occurred shall also be disqualified, with the resulting forfeiture of any medals, points and prizes (Article 10.8). In order to regain eligibility after having been found to have committed an anti-doping rule violation, an athlete must first repay all prize money forfeited (Article 10.8.1). Unless the rules of the IF provide that forfeited money be reallocated to other athletes, such money shall be allocated first to the ADO that performed the necessary steps to collect back the prize money, then to reimburse the expenses of the ADO that conducted results management in the case, with the remaining balance (if any) allocated in accordance with the IF rules (Article 10.8.2).

Ineligibility Issues in Doping Cases

Prior to adoption of the WADC, there was often confusion and inconsistency regarding the appropriate commencement date for periods of ineligibility. The general rule now is that the period will start on the date of the hearing decision providing for the ineligibility or, if a hearing has been waived, on the date ineligibility is accepted or otherwise imposed. Any period of provisional suspension (whether imposed or voluntarily accepted) is credited against the period of ineligibility imposed (Article 10.9). If there have been substantial delays in the hearing process or other aspects of doping control, not attributable to the athlete or other person, the body imposing the sanction may start the ineligibility period at an earlier date that date may commence as early as the date of the sample collection or that date on which another anti-doping rule violation may have occurred (Article 10.9.1), as is the case where there has been timely admissions of violations (Article 10.9.2), provided in the latter case that the ineligibility period shall be at least one-half of the period of ineligibility from the date of acceptance, hearing decision or date the sanction was otherwise imposed. Credit is given for the periods of provisional suspensions, whether imposed (Article 10.9.3) or voluntarily accepted (Article 10.9.4), where the acceptance has been accepted in writing, but no credit is given for any period prior to the provisional suspension (imposed or accepted), regardless of whether an athlete elected not to compete or was suspended by his or her team (Article 10.9.5).

The status of an athlete or person during a period of ineligibility has often been unclear. The harmonized rules now provide that an athlete or other person may not participate in any capacity in any competition or activity (other than authorized anti-doping or educational programs) authorized or organized by any organization that has adopted the WADC. Where a period of longer than 4 years has been imposed, after 4 years the athlete or person may participate in local sport events other than in the sport in which the anti-doping rule violation had occurred, provided that such event is not at a level which could otherwise qualify the athlete or other person, directly or indirectly, to compete in or accumulate points toward a national championship or international event (Article 10.10.1). If there is a violation of such rule, the period of ineligibility recommences, subject to possible reduction if it can be demonstrated that there was no significant fault or negligence for having violated the prohibition against participation (Article 10.10.2). In respect of any anti-doping rule violation not involving a reduced sanction for specified substances, some or all sport-related financial support or other sport-related benefits may be withheld by any organization which has adopted the WADC (and its member organizations and clubs) and governments (Article 10.10.3).

During any period of ineligibility, an athlete must, as a condition of eventually regaining eligibility, make him or herself available for out-of-competition testing and must, if requested, provide current and accurate whereabouts information. If an athlete retires and is removed from the testing pools, but subsequently seeks to return to competition, any reinstatement shall not occur until the athlete has notified relevant ADOs and has been subject to out-of-competition testing for a period of time equal to the period of ineligibility remaining as of the date of retirement (Article 10.11).

Financial sanctions may be imposed in accordance with the rules of ADOs. No financial sanction may, however, be considered as a basis for reducing the period of eligibility or other sanction otherwise applicable under the WADC (Article 10.12).

TEAM SPORTS

Team sports are subjected to a significantly lower standard of doping controls and consequences than is the case with individual sports. There are limitations in the rules of the IF as to the number of players who can be selected for doping controls in competition and how the players are selected for the purpose. If more than one member of a team has been notified of an anti-doping rule violation in connection with a particular event, the ruling body for the event (e.g., the IOC for the Olympic Games or FIFA for the World Cup) shall conduct target testing of the team during the event period (Article 11.1). If more than two members of a team are found to have committed an anti-doping rule violation during an event period, the ruling body shall impose an appropriate sanction on the team, such as loss of points, disqualification from the competition or event, or other sanction, in addition to any consequences which may be imposed upon the individual athletes who committed the anti-doping rule violation (Article 11.2). Some flexibility is afforded to the ruling body of an event, which may impose stricter consequences for purposes of the event (Article 11.3). Thus, for example, rules for the Olympic Games could be stricter for team sports than for events organized under the authority of the particular IF.

RIGHT TO A FAIR HEARING

Any athlete or person charged with an anti-doping rule violation has a right to a fair hearing. ADOs are required to provide a hearing process to address whether an anti-doping rule violation was committed and, if so, the appropriate consequences. Such process is required to respect the following principles: timeliness; a fair and impartial hearing panel; the right to be represented by counsel (at the person's own expense); the right to be informed in a fair and timely manner of the asserted violation; the right to respond to the asserted violation and resulting consequences; the right to present evidence, including the right to call and question witnesses (subject to the discretion of the hearing panel to accept testimony by telephone or in writing); the right to an interpreter at the hearing (the hearing panel to determine the identity and the responsibility for the costs of the interpreter); and receipt of a timely, written, reasoned decision, specifically including an explanation of the reasons for any period of ineligibility (Article 8.1).

Hearings held during the course of an event (e.g., a world championship or the Olympic Games) may be conducted by an expedited process as permitted by the relevant ADO and the hearing panel (Article 8.2). Should a hearing be waived, expressly or by failure to challenge the assertion of an anti-doping rule violation in a timely manner, the responsible ADO submits a reasoned decision, explaining the reasons to the athlete or other person who is the subject of the decision, the other party (if any), the IF, the NADO of the country where the person resides or is licensed, the IOC or IPC if the decision may have an effect in the Games subject to their jurisdiction and WADA (Article 8.3).

APPEALS AND DISPUTE RESOLUTION

As indicated earlier, a degree of confusion within sport often resulted when governmental courts issued rulings that were at odds with sanctions pronounced by sport organizations. Further complications occurred where a governmental court, having jurisdiction only within its own territory, might reduce or eliminate a sanction imposed by an IF. The anomalous outcome could be that an athlete might be able to compete in the country in which the governmental court judgment was enforceable, but nowhere else in the world. Considerable tensions could be generated where the IF might have a rule to the effect that anyone competing against another athlete suspended by the IF could lose his or her own eligibility, even if the competitions were to occur in the country whose courts had reduced or eliminated the IF-imposed sanction. Governmental courts have limited experience in matters of sport and, arguably, even less in matters of doping. This is not to suggest that a governmental court, faced with a competently presented and argued case, is incapable of reaching a perfectly reasonable outcome, but only to observe that these cases tend to be specialty matters which lend themselves to resolution by experts familiar with the field of international sports law.

In 1984, the IOC established the Court of Arbitration for Sport (CAS) as a Swiss-based forum for resolution of sport-related disputes. Initially funded solely by the IOC, such funding has evolved to allocation among the IOC, the IFs, the NOCs and some specialized users of CAS. Governance rests with the International Council of Arbitration for Sport (ICAS), which consists of representatives of the IOC, IFs, NOCs, athletes and some appointed senior judges. A panel of potential arbitrators is established from names recommended by all stakeholders. The Swiss Federal Tribunal has accorded to CAS considerable deference in all matters within CAS's sphere of jurisdiction as an independent tribunal. The IOC and other components of the Olympic Movement generally agree that the resolution of any disputes will be referred to CAS. For example, all decisions taken by the IOC during the Olympic Games, relating to such matters as disqualifications, eligibility and nationality, are referred to an ad hoc division of CAS established specifically to deal with matters arising at the Games. Decisions on such occasions are normally reached by the panels within 24 hours of a case being submitted.

When the WADC was adopted in 2003, the Olympic Movement representatives, already familiar with CAS, had no conceptual difficulty with the idea of using CAS as the court of final resort for doping matters. Representatives of the public authorities, recognizing the essentially technical nature of anti-doping rule violations, the need for swift resolution of them and not wishing to add to the already heavy case loads of their own governmental courts, also accepted the concept that CAS should be the court of final resort. Governmental courts, including the Swiss Federal Tribunal, will intervene if CAS does not follow its own procedures, but otherwise will accord deference to CAS and treat its decisions as definitive.

Decisions made under the WADC or rules adopted pursuant to it may be appealed. The decisions against which the appeal is taken remain in effect while under appeal unless the appellate body orders otherwise. Prior to institution of any appeal, any post-decision review provided for in the rules of the ADO must be exhausted (Article 13.1). If WADA has a right to appeal and no other party has appealed a final decision within the ADO's process, WADA may appeal such decision directly to CAS without having to exhaust other remedies in the ADO's process (Article 13.1.1).

Appeals lie from decisions that:

(a)   an anti-doping rule violation was committed;
(b)   impose consequences for an anti-doping rule violation;
(c)   no anti-doping rule violation was committed;
(d)   an anti-doping rule violation proceeding cannot go forward for procedural reasons (including, e.g., prescription);
(e)   involve violations of a prohibition of participation;
(f)   an ADO lacks jurisdiction to rule on an alleged anti-doping rule violation or it consequences;
(g)   involve a refusal by an ADO not to bring forward an adverse analytical finding or an atypical finding as an anti-doping rule violation;
(h)   involve a failure to go forward with an anti-doping rule violation after an investigation; and

(i)   impose a provisional suspension as a result of a provisional hearing or in violation of the requirements for a provisional hearing.

Where international-level athletes are involved or a matter arises from participation in an international event, the decision may be appealed exclusively to CAS in accordance with the CAS rules (Article 13.2.1). Those entitled to appeal to CAS are (Article 13.2.3):

(a)   the athlete or other person who is the subject of the decision being appealed;
(b)   the other party to the case in which the decision was rendered;
(c)   the relevant IF;
(d)   the NADO of the person's country of residence or countries where the person is a national or license-holder;
(e)   the IOC or IPC, as applicable, where the decision may have an effect in relation to the Olympic Games or Paralympic Games, including decisions affecting eligibility for either; and
(f)   WADA.

In the case of national-level athletes who do not have a right to appeal to CAS, the decision must be appealed to an independent and impartial body in accordance with rules established by the NADO. In such cases, the parties having the right to appeal to the national-level reviewing body shall be as provided in the NADO's rules, but at a minimum, shall include:

(a)   the athlete or other person who is the subject of the decision being appealed;
(b)   the other party to the case in which the decision was rendered;
(c)   the relevant IF;
(d)   the NADO of the person's country of residence; and
(e)   WADA.

In addition, WADA and the relevant IF also have a right to appeal to CAS with respect to the decision of the national-level reviewing body. Rules for such national-level appeals must respect the principles of a timely hearing, a fair, impartial and independent hearing panel, the right to be represented by counsel at the person's own expense and a timely, written, reasoned decision (Article 13.2.2).

The most interesting aspect of appeals is WADA's right to appeal or intervene which must be in the interest of making certain that harmonization occurs within the anti-doping system and that ADOs pursue doping infractions in accordance with the provisions of the WADC, whether at the international or national level. Special delays are afforded for such purposes. The delay is the later of 21 days after the last day on which any other party in the case could have appealed and 21 days after WADA's receipt of the complete file relating to the decision (Article 13.2.2). WADA has an additional right to appeal directly to CAS where an ADO fails to render a decision with respect to whether an anti-doping rule violation that was committed within a reasonable deadline set by WADA. WADA's appeal in such circumstances is based on the premise that the ADO had found that no anti-doping rule violation had occurred. If the CAS hearing panel determines that an anti-doping rule violation was committed and that WADA acted reasonably in deciding to appeal directly to CAS, then WADA's costs and attorneys fees in prosecuting the appeal are to be reimbursed to WADA by the ADO (Article 13.3).

MONITORING FUNCTION

Compliance with the WADC is monitored by WADA or as otherwise agreed by WADA. Each signatory is required to report to WADA on compliance with the WADC every second year and explain reasons for any non-compliance. Failure to provide compliance information requested by WADA or failure to submit information to WADA as required pursuant to other provisions of the WADC may be considered non-compliance with the WADC (Article 23.4.3). WADA compliance reports shall be approved by its Foundation Board. WADA is required to 'dialog' with a signatory of the WADC before reporting the signatory as non-compliant, however. A WADA report which concludes that a signatory is non-compliant must be approved by the WADA Foundation Board at a meeting after the signatory has been given the opportunity to submit its written arguments to the Foundation Board. The conclusion by the WADA Foundation Board that a signatory is non-compliant may be appealed to CAS. WADA makes reports on compliance to the IOC, IPC, IFs and major event organizations, which reports are also made available to the public. In extraordinary situations, WADA may recommend to the foregoing signatories that they provisionally excuse the non-compliance (Article 23.4).

WADA itself has no power to do anything more than to monitor activities of the signatories, request information as necessary and report cases of non-compliance to the appropriate organizations. It has no separate sanctioning power. The WADC contains provisions setting forth the responsibilities of the IOC, the IPC, IFs, NOCs, national Paralympic committees, NADOs and major event organizations (Article 20), which clarify the consequences (principally exclusion) of non-compliance. Additional consequences of non-compliance may include forfeiture of offices and positions within WADA, ineligibility or non-admission of any candidature to hold any international event in a country, cancellation of international events, symbolic consequences and other consequences pursuant to the Olympic Charter. Imposition of such consequences may be appealed to CAS by the affected signatory (Article 23.5).

Although not technically a monitoring function, WADA is also responsible for overseeing the evolution and improvement of the WADC, a process in which athletes, all signatories and governments are invited to participate. WADA therefore initiates proposed amendments to the WADC and ensures a consultative process to both receive and respond to recommendations and feedback on proposed amendments. Amendments must be approved by a two-thirds majority of the WADA Foundation Board, including a majority of both the public sector and Olympic Movement members casting votes. Unless otherwise provided, amendments come into effect 3 months after such approval.

PROFESSIONAL SPORT LEAGUES

While doping has become a major concern within the Olympic Movement, no similar sense of urgency in dealing with the problem has been generated within many professional sports leagues, associations and organizations. These are, for the most part, unregulated businesses, organized for profit, which are not directly integrated into the Olympic Movement. They have only a limited inclination to adopt or embrace the WADC or any serious anti-doping programs within their organizations. Standard public positioning of such organizations is that there is no doping problem within their sport or that there is already another effective anti-doping program in place. In the United States, some professional leagues argue that the relationship is one of contractual employment between consenting players and owners and that no one has any right to interfere in such relationships. Collective agreements are negotiated which prevent testing from taking place or which limit testing to circumstances that all but assure no positive cases will result. Even when doping is proved, the sanctions are so minimal that the obvious conclusion is that it is not regarded as a serious offense. In Europe some continental tribunals have premised their decisions on an athlete's right to work and therefore have eliminated or significantly reduced sport sanctions.

The policies involved are not essentially legal in nature, but rather social and national health. There can be little doubt that behavior is influenced by sports stars. If the stars are using drugs or methods of performance enhancement, the message is that if you want to be a star, you will have to do the same things or, at the very least, that such practices are acceptable. These messages filter down to the level of secondary education, where teenagers become involved in uncontrolled use of substances the consequences of which they either ignore or have no idea. The effects on the physical and mental health of such youth (as well as others) can be devastating. Governments have been reluctant to confront the obvious use of such drugs by professional sport, despite the mounting evidence of increased use throughout the sports and by the public at large.

APPENDIX

SANCTION DECISION MATRICES

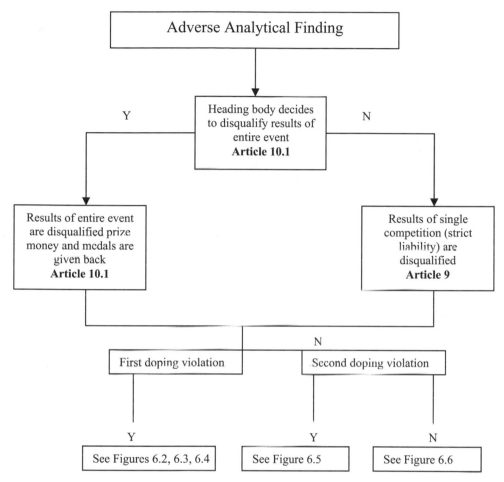

Figure 6.1 Disqualification of results due to an in-competition adverse analytical finding (AAF)

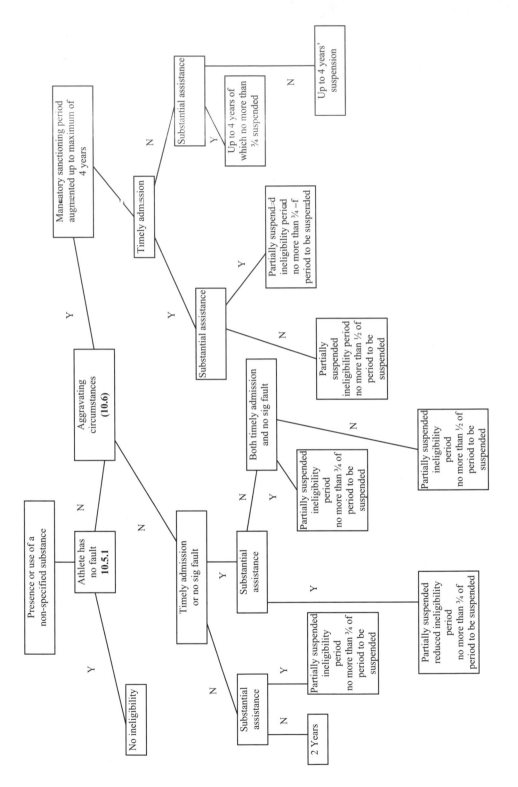

Figure 6.2 AAF non-specified substance

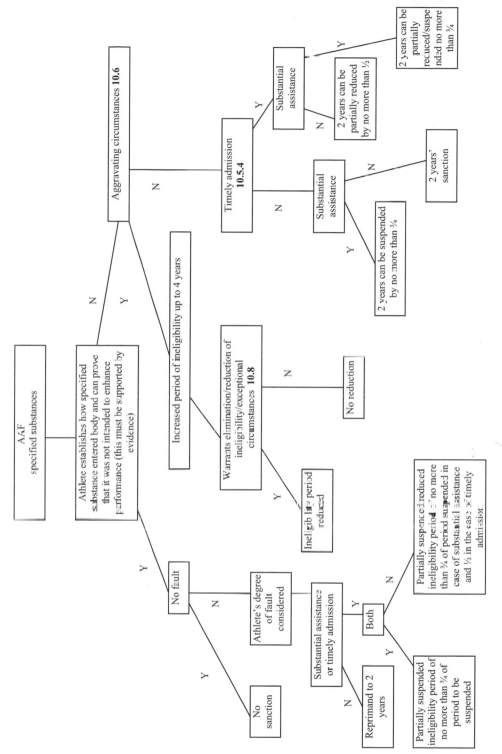

Figure 6.3 AAF specified substance

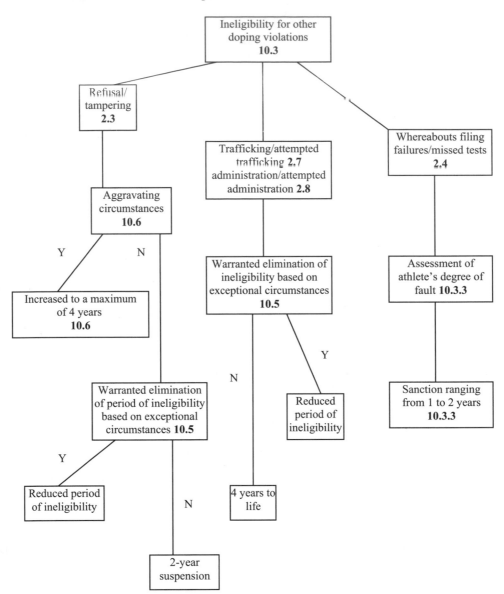

Figure 6.4 Non AAF anti-doping rule violations (ADRVs)

2nd Violation / 1st Violation	RS	FFMT	HSF	St	AS	TRA
RS	1–4	2–4	2–4	4–8	8–10	10–Life
FFMT	1–4	4–8	4–8	6–8	10–Life	Life
HSF	1–4	4–8	4–8	6–8	10–Life	Life
St	2–4	6–8	6–8	8–Life	Life	Life
AS	4–5	10–Life	10–Life	Life	Life	Life
TRA	8–Life	Life	Life	Life	Life	Life

Figure 6.5 Second ADRV

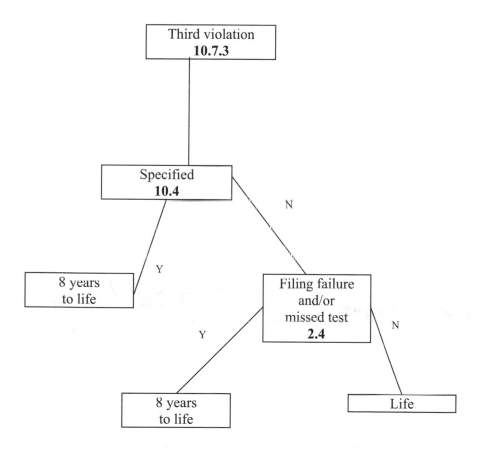

Figure 6.6 Multiple ADRVs

7 Gambling on sports

Paul M. Anderson

I. INTRODUCTION

On November 5, 2010, a Major League Baseball (MLB) betting scandal came to light when New York Mets clubhouse manager Charlie Samuels was suspended by the club and surrendered to authorities for placing bets on baseball and football games with a mob ring.[1] This incident culminated a larger, five-year investigation of illegal betting by Mets employees.[2] It originated when authorities determined that the team's head grounds-keeper had been part of a $360 million gambling ring. The specific investigation of Samuels began when the Mets contacted the police and district attorney because they suspected he was 'misappropriating funds in a number of ways'[3] and may have raided the team's accounts and sold memorabilia to help cover his gambling debts.[4]

Unfortunately, this example is not unique. The sports arena is frequently shaken by scandal when players and employees bet on their events or contests. In response, legislators, courts, and sports organizations throughout the world have taken measures to combat the problem of corrupt gambling on sports, while at the same time promoting controlled, revenue-producing gambling activity. This chapter focuses broadly on the regulation of sports-related gambling by the United States, several other countries, and international sports organizations. What follows is essentially a comparative study of alternative regulatory institutions and instruments. Before we turn to this body of law, however, it will be helpful to ask why regulation is essential to the integrity of sports competition.

A. The Need for Regulation

In general, betting or gambling on sports is typically perceived as a serious threat insofar as it may influence the result of a contest outside the normal field of play. Moreover, gambling entails serious social costs, often referred to as the 'ABCs' of gambling: addictions, bankruptcies, and crime.[5] Adverse social impacts of gambling include 'addiction to

---

[1] Alison Gendar and Teri Thompson, Sources: New York Mets Clubhouse Manager Charlie Samuels Caught On Wiretaps Placing Bets, NYDAILYNEWS.COM, Nov. 5, 2010.

[2] The Queens New York District Attorney's Office and the New York Police Department's Crime and Control Bureau conducted the investigation. *Ibid.*

[3] Samuels admitted to MLB that he had bet on MLB games and had been taped by authorities making bets on college and professional football games with organized crime associates who were photographed in $400 seats that Samuels had provided at Mets games. *Ibid.*

[4] Fanhouse Staff, Charlie Samuels, Mets Clubhouse Manager, Reportedly Bet on Baseball, MLB.FANHOUSE.COM (2010).

[5] See John Warren Kindt and John K. Palchak, Legalized Gambling's Destabilization of U.S. Financial Institutions and the Banking Industry: Issues in Bankruptcy, Credit, and Social Norm Production, 19 BANKR. DEV. J. 21, 25 (2002).

gambling, neighborhood crime, political corruption, and infiltration of gambling by organized crime.[6] On the other hand, revenues from sports gambling based on lotteries or other state-run exercises may provide needed funding for other state-run activities.

In the United States, the legislative history to the Professional and Amateur Sports Act of 1992 is instructive. A Senate report supporting its passage noted that, '[s]ports gambling threatens to change the nature of sporting events from wholesome entertainment for all ages to devices for gambling. It undermines public confidence in the character of professional and amateur sports.'[7] Moreover, the Report noted that:

> [s]ports gambling is a national problem. The harms it inflicts are felt beyond the borders of those States that sanction it. The moral erosion it produces cannot be limited geographically ... We must do everything we can to keep sports clean so that the fans, and especially young people, can continue to have complete confidence in the honesty of the players and the contests. Scandals in the sporting world are big news and can have a devastating effect on the outlook of our youth to whom sports figures are heroes and idols.[8]

In the United Kingdom, the Gambling Review Report, prepared in 2001 by the British Department for Culture, Media and Sport and presented to Parliament, seems to have similar concerns. Part three of the report, entitled 'Why regulate?,' provides rationales behind the regulation of gambling in sport.[9] The first rationale, in Chapter Fifteen: Keeping Crime Out of Gambling, is expressed as follows:

> Gambling involves the circulation of money, mainly anonymously, which provides opportunities for money laundering. Also, athletes can be vulnerable and may be easily cheated, games can be rigged, and improper attempts can be made to influence the outcomes of events. Moreover, the profitability of gambling encourages attempts to limit potential competition.[10] These costs then 'spill over into costs for society through recourse to health and social services and the criminal justice system.'[11]

Another rationale is provided in Chapter; Seventeen: Protecting the Vulnerable. This chapter provides many potential social costs associated with gambling.[12]

B.   The Opinions of Sports Bodies

In addition to these governmental concerns, many sports organizations have also determined that it is necessary to regulate gambling in the sports that they oversee respectively and even to challenge permissive laws.

---

[6]   *Ibid.* at 55.
[7]   Professional and Amateur Sports Protection, Senate Rep. 102–248, Nov. 26, 1991.
[8]   *Ibid.*
[9]   United Kingdom, Department for Culture, Media and Sport, Gambling Review Body, Gambling Review Report, July 2001, at 73.
[10]   *Ibid.* at 74.
[11]   *Ibid.*
[12]   These costs include job loss, absenteeism, poor work/study performance, stress, depression and anxiety, suicide, poor health, financial hardship, debts, assets losses, exposure to loan sharks, bankruptcy, resorting to theft, imprisonment, neglect of family, impacts on others, relationship breakdown, domestic or other violence, burdens on charities, and burdens on the public purse. *Ibid.* at 94.

1.   United States bodies

At the level of collegiate sports, the National Collegiate Athletic Association (NCAA) first discussed the perils of sports gambling in 1939 when it created its unethical conduct legislation, now known as Bylaw 10 of the Division I Manual.[13] Today, the NCAA's 'Don't Bet On It' program specifically focuses on the dangers of sports wagering, as the NCAA, 'opposes all forms of legal and illegal sports wagering, which has the potential to undermine the integrity of sports contests and jeopardizes the welfare of student-athletes and the intercollegiate athletics community.'[14] This opposition is based on the NCAA's position that:

> Sports wagering can be a serious crime that threatens the well-being of student-athletes and the integrity of the game. Financially troubled student-athletes are viewed by organized gambling as easy marks for obtaining inside information or affecting the outcome of a game. Student-athletes who gamble are breaking the law and jeopardizing their eligibility. The NCAA believes sports should be appreciated for the benefits of participating or watching, not the amount of money that can be won or lost depending on the outcome of the games.[15]

At the professional sports level, perhaps the best evidence of the perceived threat of gambling can be found in the testimony that various commissioners of professional sports leagues provided to Congress in its consideration of proposed legislation to regulate sports gambling. This testimony focused on protecting the integrity of the game.[16] NBA Commissioner David Stern asserted that, 'sports betting places athletes and games under a cloud of suspicion, as normal incidents of the game give rise to unfounded speculation of game-fixing and point-shaving.'[17]

In 2009, when the state of Delaware passed a Sports Lottery Act[18] that authorized sports betting and gaming at existing and future facilities there, it was immediately sued by MLB, the National Basketball Association (NBA), the NCAA, the National Football League (NFL), and the National Hockey League (NHL). All of these sports organizations claimed that this new form of sports-related betting would violate the Professional

---

[13]   NATIONAL COLLEGIATE ATHLETIC ASSOCIATION, NCAA CONVENTION PROCEEDINGS (1939).

[14]   National Association of Basketball Coaches, Gambling Awareness: NCAA Position on Sports Wagering, available at http://www.nabc.org/nabc_programs/nabc_programs-gambling-awareness.html.

[15]   NCAA Press Release, NCAA Behind the Blue Disk – Gambling on College Sports – What's the Big Deal?, Apr. 1, 2009.

[16]   For example, then MLB Commissioner Fay Vincent testified that:

> The intense feelings with which I approach betting on Baseball might best be understood if one remembers that the Office of the Commissioner of Baseball was created in direct response to the 1919 'Black Sox' scandal. Protecting the integrity of the game is our primary job. State-sponsored sports betting runs the real risk of undermining public confidence in the honesty of what transpires on the field ... No state should be permitted to create an environment that is conducive to a major sports betting scandal ...

Hearings on S. 474 Before the Senate Subcommittee on Patents, Copyrights and Trademarks, 102d Cong., 1 (1991).

[17]   *Ibid.*

[18]   Delaware Sports Lottery Act, 29 Del. C. § 4801 *et. seq.* (2010), cert. denied, *Markell* v. *OFC Comm. Baseball et al.*, 130 S. Ct. 2403 (2010).

and Amateur Sports Protection Act. Within its initial brief, each of the major American professional sports leagues and the NCAA argued that if Delaware were allowed to initiate its new law, their sports would all suffer irreparable harm.[19] The court agreed.[20]

Overall, both collegiate and professional sports organizations in the United States restrict their participants and employees from gambling in any manner. The organizations are consistent in focusing on the dangers of gambling to their participants and to the perceived integrity of a sport or event.

2.   International sports organizations

Interestingly, some international sports federations recognize that gambling activity offers a valuable source of funding for other purposes. As a report on money-laundering on football/soccer noted, '[t]here is an ambiguous relationship between betting and sport. On one hand, betting has historically been an important revenue source for sport in many countries. On the other hand, betting has also been associated with attempts to fix matches and alter results of sporting competitions.'[21]

3.   Regional (European) sports bodies

The opinions of European sports bodies such as the European Union of Football Associations (EUFA) on betting and gambling in sports has found expression in several pronouncements by the European Union and private organizations. The European Commission's White Paper on Sport, for example, noted that, '[i]n many Member States sport is partly financed through a tax or levy on state-run or state-licensed gambling or lottery services.'[22] The Remote Gaming Association, a gambling trade association in London and Brussels, recognized that, '[s]ports seek to control the betting product and to

---

[19]   *OFC Comm. Baseball et al.* v. *Markell & Lemons, Appellants' Opening Brief in Support of Their Appeal of the Denial of Their Motion for a Preliminary Injunction*, No. 09-3297, 2009 WL 2609334, at 21 (3rd Cir. 2009):

The spread of sports gambling, including sports lotteries involving single game betting, threatens the integrity of professional and amateur sports and are fundamentally at odds with the principle – essential to the success of MLB, the NBA, the NCAA, the NFL and the NHL – that the outcomes of professional and collegiate athletic contests must be perceived by the public as being determined solely on the basis of honest athletic competition ... Professional and amateur sports are an integral part of American culture, particularly among the country's youth who often look up to professional athletes as role models and heroes. The implementation of a comprehensive sports betting scheme in Delaware would irreparably harm professional and amateur sports by fostering suspicion and skepticism that individual plays and final scores of games may have been influenced by factors other than honest athletic competition ... the proliferation of sports betting ... threatens to harm the reputation and goodwill of MLB, the NBA, the NCAA, the NFL and the NHL, and to adversely affect the way the public views professional and amateur sports.

[20]   *OFC Comm. Baseball et al.* v. *Markell & Lemons*, 579 F.3d 293 (3rd Cir. 2009), *cert. denied*, *Markell* v. *OFC Comm. Baseball, et al.*, 130 S. Ct. 2403 (2010).
[21]   FINANCIAL ACTION TASK FORCE, FATF REPORT: MONEY LAUNDERING THROUGH THE FOOTBALL SECTOR 24 (2009).
[22]   COMMISSION OF THE EUROPEAN COMMUNITIES, WHITE PAPER ON SPORT, COM(2007) 391 final [hereinafter WHITE PAPER].

obtain increased revenues from the betting industry.'[23] To this end, a recent report estimated that €3.4 billion is contributed annually to European Union sport by public- and private-sector gambling operators.[24]

Aside from gambling's funding capacity, the focus of European sports bodies still relates to the effect of gambling on the integrity of sport. For example, the Council of Europe's Code of Sports Ethics focuses on 'fair play' and provides that, 'ethical considerations leading to fair play are integral, and not optional elements, of all sports activity, sports policy and management, and apply to all levels of ability and commitment, including recreational as well as competitive sport.'[25] Gambling activity is often understood to foster corruption in sports, whereas the principle of fair play is 'concerned with the elimination of cheating, gamesmanship, doping, violence (both physical and verbal), the sexual harassment and abuse of children, young people and women, exploitation, unequal opportunities, excessive commercialization and corruption.'[26] Similarly, the European Sports for All Charter seeks 'to protect and develop the moral and ethical bases of sport and the human dignity and safety of those involved in sport, by safeguarding sport, sportsmen and women from exploitation for political, commercial and financial gain ...'[27]

The White Paper on Sport identified several 'threats and challenges' that are often connected with gambling in sport, 'such as commercial pressure, exploitation of young players ... corruption and money laundering.'[28] It recognized that '[c]orruption, money laundering and other forms of financial crime are affecting sport at local, national and international levels. Given the sector's high degree of internationalisation, corruption in the sport sector often has cross-border aspects. Corruption problems with a European dimension need to be tackled at the European level.'[29]

The Commission also pointed to the 2006 Independent European Sport Review, recognizing that one of the reasons for the review was that it identified many problems in sport including 'doping, corruption, racism, illegal gambling, money-laundering and other activities detrimental to the sport.'[30] Initiated by the Sports Ministers of France, Germany, Italy, Spain, and the United Kingdom, and focused on European football,[31] the Review advocated a formal structure between the European Union and the governing bodies for football, in particular because 'several European countries (such as Belgium, Finland, Germany, Italy, Portugal etc.) have been shaken by matchfixing and corruption

---

[23]   REMOTE GAMBLING ASSOCIATION, SPORTS BETTING: LEGAL, COMMERCIAL AND INTEGRITY ISSUES 121 (2010).

[24]   Europe Economics (Executive Summary), The Funding of Sports in the EU by Private Sector Gambling Operators (2010).

[25]   Council of Europe, Committee of Ministers, Appendix to Recommendation No. R (92) 14 rev, Code of Sports Ethics: Fair Play – The Winning Way (1992).

[26]   *Ibid.*

[27]   Council of Europe, Committee of Ministers, Appendix to Recommendation No. R (92) 13 rev, European Sports Charter, art. 1 (1992).

[28]   WHITE PAPER, note 22 *supra*, at 2.

[29]   *Ibid.* at 16.

[30]   COMMISSION OF THE EUROPEAN COMMUNITIES, COMMISSION STAFF WORKING DOCUMENT, The EU and Sport: Background and Context, accompanying document to the White Paper on Sport, COM(2007) 391 final, §§ 932, 934, 936, at 52 (2007).

[31]   JOSE LUIS ARNAUT, INDEPENDENT EUROPEAN SPORT REVIEW (2006).

scandals, linked to betting and to players' agents.'[32] Specific sections of the Review related to match-fixing, corruption and betting also pointed to a 'strong need to issue a directive on betting in order to control betting on sports.'[33]

C. The Prevalence of Sports Gambling

1. The United States

In 1996, due to the rise in legalized gambling at the state and local level, the growth of Internet gambling, and questions regarding the social and economic impacts of gambling, the United States Congress enacted the National Gambling Impact Study Commission Act.[34] This legislation established the National Gambling Impact Study Commission. The Commission's role was to conduct a comprehensive legal and factual study of the social and economic impacts of gambling in the United States. In its 1999 report, the Commission estimated that Americans illegally wager between $80 and $380 billion annually on sporting events.[35] Although this is the latest national study of sports betting within the United States, the estimated wagering has surely increased substantially since the report's publication.

Gambling on collegiate and other amateur sports is permitted only in Nevada, which is the only state that permits non-tribal, statewide gambling. An estimated $2.5 billion is wagered annually in Nevada on college sports, $197 million of which is attributed to bets surrounding the NCAA's Division I men's basketball tournament.[36] In total, betting related to the NCAA basketball tournament is approximately $50 billion each year, which is slightly less than the estimated $60–70 billion that is illegally gambled on college football annually.[37] In a survey of student athletes, the NCAA found that 30% of males and 7% of females reported wagering on sporting events within the past year.[38] In addition, illegal bookmaking rings involving college students have been found at universities in Michigan, Florida, South Carolina, Texas, Arkansas, Iowa, Maine, and Rhode Island.[39]

In professional sports the amount of illegal wagering is also very high. According to a CNBC study in 2009, the following amounts are spent on illegal sports gambling each year: NFL – $80–100 billion ($10 billion alone is bet annually on the Super Bowl, featuring the top teams from the American and National Football Conferences); NBA – $35–40 billion; MLB – $30–40 billion; and hockey, golf, the National Association for Stock Car Auto Racing (NASCAR), and other sports – $1–3 billion.[40]

---

[32]   *Ibid.* at 139.
[33]   *Ibid.* at 121.
[34]   National Gambling Impact Study Commission Act, Pub. L. 104–169, 110 Stat. 1482 (1996).
[35]   National Gambling Impact Study Commission, Final Report (1999), at 2–14.
[36]   Stephanie Armour, Anti-Gambling Groups Seek Moratorium on Office Pools to Curb Addiction, USA TODAY, Mar. 28, 2007.
[37]   Center for the Study of Sports Betting, The Big Business of Illegal Gambling: Top Sports for Illegal Wagering (2009).
[38]   NCAA Press Release, note 14 *supra*.
[39]   Douglas Engwall, Robert Hunter, and Marvin Steinberg, Gambling and Other Risk Behaviors on University Campuses, 52 J. AMER. COLLEGE HEALTH 245 (2004).
[40]   The Big Business of Illegal Gambling, note 37 *supra*.

2. Europe and New Zealand

Overall information on the amount of gambling outside of the United States is also staggering. One recent estimate put the size of the global gambling market at €228.8 billion, with €13.3 billion devoted to sports betting alone.[41] Another put the total gambling market in the European Union at around €51,528 million in 2004.[42] In the United Kingdom, gambling was an £84 billion industry for 2006–07.[43] In Germany, sports betting constituted 5% of the gambling market, according to a recent study conducted for the European Commission.[44] In New Zealand, almost NZ$15 921 billion is wagered annually.[45]

II. RECENT SPORTS GAMBLING CONTROVERSIES

A. United States

Perhaps due to a premise or presumption throughout much of the United States that gambling is illegal in any form, gambling scandals have not been a particularly serious threat to the integrity of sports. Still, there are numerous cases of illegal sports gambling,[46] and, as we shall see, betting on sports is a major industry.

1. Collegiate athletics

A recent study reviewed 12 different gambling incidents at the NCAA level since 1990, noting that between 2003 and 2008 alone there were 27 other reported cases of NCAA violations by student-athletes, coaches, and administrators who gambled on college or professional sports.[47] Two recent examples in 2007, for example, involved the University of Toledo and Ohio University. At Toledo, suspicious gambling activity led to an investigation that revealed that a football player and a gambler from Detroit, Michigan had schemed to point-shave several games during the 2005 season.[48] The football player was removed from the team and later charged criminally, although the case was later dropped by investigators.[49] Similarly, an investigation at Ohio University revealed that five baseball players had violated NCAA rules by accepting professional sports wagers, placing bets, and bookmaking; three of the athletes were then declared ineligible for sanctioned competition.[50]

---

[41]   REMOTE GAMBLING ASSOCIATION, note 23 *supra*, at 9.

[42]   SWISS INSTITUTE FOR COMPARATIVE LAW, STUDY OF GAMBLING SERVICES IN THE INTERNAL MARKET OF THE EUROPEAN UNION, Final Report 1465 (2006) [hereinafter STUDY].

[43]   GAMBLING COMMISSION, ANNUAL REPORT 2008–09, at 10.

[44]   PROBLEM GAMBLING FOUNDATION OF NEW ZEALAND, GAMBLING IN NEW ZEALAND: THE OUTCOMES (2009).

[45]   STUDY, note 42 *supra*, at 1196, 1462.

[46]   See, e.g., text at notes 1–4 *supra*; text at notes 49, 50, 52–7, 103, 112, 113, 114, 119, 125 *infra*.

[47]   Adam Epstein and Bridget Niland, Gambling and Collegiate Athletics, 2009 INT'L SPORTS L.J. 80, 82–5.

[48]   *Ibid.* at 85.

[49]   *Ibid.*

[50]   *Ibid.*

2. NBA referee scandal

Like most professional sports leagues in the United States, the NBA prohibits its players and employees from betting on professional sporting events.[51] In recent years a scandal involving referee Tim Donaghy came to light. During the 2003–04 season, he began to provide a friend with betting recommendations for NBA games, including games he officiated. The friend then placed bets on Donaghy's behalf for about 30 to 40 games annually.[52] Eventually, other gamblers became aware of Donaghy's bets and convinced him to work with them to provide picks using his access to private information including 'the identity of the officiating crews for upcoming games, the interactions between certain referees and team personnel, and the physical condition of the players.'[53] Instead of betting his own money, Donaghy was paid a fee of up to $5,000 for each correct pick. Soon after, the Unites States government became aware of the betting conspiracy, and Donaghy agreed to cooperate with the government's investigation. He pled guilty to conspiracy to commit wire fraud and to transmit wagering information.[54]

After the Donaghy controversy came to light, fans and commentators criticized the NBA, wondering how it could have let this situation happen and whether more referees were gambling on the sport. In response, the NBA hired a New York law firm to review the League's officiating program independently and to report its findings to the league and the public.[55] The report found no information showing that any other NBA referee was involved in betting on NBA games or leaking any confidential information to gamblers. The report did find, however, that many other referees had placed bets in other sports, contrary to NBA rules.[56] Specific to Donaghy, he repeatedly denied making any calls to influence the outcome of an NBA game, a claim the government supported, and the report found no evidence to contradict this claim.[57]

B. South Africa, Europe, and Japan

1. The Cronjé scandal in South Africa

At the turn of the twentieth century, the sport of cricket faced an international betting scandal that revealed a level of corruption 'threatening to tear the fabric of the game apart.'[58] In 2000, the Code of Conduct Commission of the International Cricket Council (ICC)[59] discovered a betting scandal involving four South African cricket players, including former captain Hansie Cronjé.[60] Cronjé was discovered to have accepted bribes for

---

51 NATIONAL BASKETBALL ASSOCIATION, CONSTITUTION, arts. 35A(g), 35(f).
52 *U.S.* v. *Donaghy*, 570 F. Supp. 2d 411 (E.D.NY 2008).
53 *Ibid.* at 416.
54 *Ibid.*
55 Lawrence B. Pedowitz, Report to the Board of Governors of the National Basketball Association (Oct. 1, 2008).
56 *Ibid.* at ES 2.
57 *Ibid.* at ES 3.
58 Urvasi Naidoo and Simon Gardiner, On the Front Foot Against Corruption, 2007 INT'L SPORTS L.J. 21, 21 (2007).
59 See *ibid.* at 22.
60 *Ibid.* at 23; JAMES NAFZIGER, INTERNATIONAL SPORTS LAW 33 (2nd ed. 2004); Rochelle Le Roux, The Cronjé Affair, 2002(2) INT'L SPORTS L.J. 11 (2002).

match-fixing during a competition against India in March of 2000.[61] To determine the full extent of the scheme, the United Cricket Board of South Africa (UCBSA) combined with the South African government to establish the King Commission.[62] Its report resulted in severe disciplinary action against each person involved in the scandal.[63] Cronjé, in particular, was banned for life.[64] He subsequently challenged his suspension all the way to the South African High Court, where it was ultimately upheld.[65]

Despite the investigation conducted by the King Commission, the ICC was still concerned about possible corruption resulting from betting. As a result, Lord Condon, a former Commissioner of Metropolitan Police in London, was appointed the chairman of the ICC's Anti-Corruption and Security Unit (ACSU), then called the Anti Corruption Unit.[66] While Condon was head of the ACSU, he led an international commission designed to determine the root causes of betting scandals in cricket. The resulting Condon Report is considered to be 'the most comprehensive study to date as it tried to get to the heart of the problem.'[67] The report lists 24 recommendations to combat corrupt betting activity.[68] Specifically, it noted the susceptibility of cricket to betting due in part to the number of statistics and game events on which persons can bet.[69] The report also sparked the creation of the renamed ACSU as a means for eliminating corrupt betting practices. The ICC's Anti-Corruption Code will be discussed later in this chapter.[70]

The ACSU is charged with two principal goals: '[t]o assist the ICC Code of Conduct Commission and the Members of ICC in the eradication of conduct of a corrupt nature prejudicial to the interest of the game of cricket, [and t]o provide a professional, permanent security infrastructure to act as a long-term deterrent to conduct of a corrupt nature.'[71] The ASCU's work in furtherance of these goals is divided into education, physical security, and appointment of security personnel. Its techniques include placing security cameras to detect corrupt practices and requiring regional security managers, who act as a 'police force,' to attend every international cricket match to ensure compliance with the anti-corruption rules.[72]

To avoid a future relapse into past bad practices, the ICC, working through the ASCU, has worked to establish ties with various entities, governments, police forces, betting exchanges, gambling boards, and other sports entities.[73] The ICC has worked with these

---

[61]   *Ibid.* at 11.

[62]   *Ibid.* at 11.

[63]   Naidoo and Gardiner, note 58 *supra*, at 23. In addition, the King Commission made several recommendations to rectify many of the problems then plaguing the sport. See COMMISSION OF INQUIRY INTO CRICKET MATCH FIXING AND RELATED MATTERS 13 (June 2001).

[64]   *Ibid.*

[65]   *Ibid.*

[66]   *Ibid.*

[67]   *Ibid.* See also International Cricket Council, Report on Corruption in International Cricket (2010).

[68]   *Ibid.*

[69]   NAFZIGER, note 60 *supra*, at 33.

[70]   See text at notes 343–51 *infra*.

[71]   Naidoo and Gardiner, note 58 *supra*, at 24.

[72]   *Ibid.*

[73]   *Ibid.* at 25.

groups by means of memoranda of understanding that enable a fast transfer of information better to detect and prevent corrupt betting practices from occurring.[74]

2. European football/soccer

On April 15, 2010, UEFA imposed one of its harshest penalties ever when it was discovered that FK Podeba, a Macedonia member club, was found to have violated the anti-betting laws.[75] The club, its president, Aleksandar Zabrcanec, and one of its former players, Nikolce Zdraveski, were found to have participated in an elaborate match-fixing scheme during the first qualifying round of the 2004–05 UEFA Champions League tournament.[76] The club was suspended from all UEFA competitions for 8 years. Both Zabrcanec and Zdraveski were banned for life.[77] The parties appealed the suspension to the Court of Arbitration for Sport (CAS), but CAS upheld the suspensions on the basis that UEFA had presented sufficient evidence to demonstrate that the matches in question were, in fact, fixed by the suspended parties.[78]

The Podeba scandal demonstrated the serious gambling problems facing UEFA in recent years. Match-fixing and betting by referees has been a particular scourge. In September 2009, UEFA conducted an investigation into match-fixing that allegedly occurred in 40 separate cases involving referees and others.[79] Like other sports, UEFA faces particular difficulty controlling illegal betting and match-fixing because of the unique nature of football.[80] In a practice called 'in running' wagers, bettors can place bets on various activities in the game that do not necessarily affect the outcome of the game and are thus more difficult for enforcement personnel to detect.[81] For example, a bettor may wager on the first player to receive a yellow card or the first player to perform a corner kick.[82]

UEFA rules specifically prohibit betting not only by direct participation, but also indirectly through, for example, ownership or other connections with companies that broker gambling activities.[83] In order to detect and oversee violations of the anti-betting rules better, FIFA established the Early Warning System GmbH (EWS).[84] The EWS was created in partnership with various national governing bodies better to detect and prevent gambling violations.[85] The system was so successful that it was used by the IOC as part of the 2008 Olympic Games in Beijing.[86] The EWS is not a new invention, but in 2007 the program was expanded to include monitoring of the preliminary competitions in the 2010

---

[74]   *Ibid.*
[75]   *FJ Podeba v. UEFA*, CAS 2009/A/1920 (Apr. 15, 2009).
[76]   *Ibid.* at 3–4.
[77]   *Ibid.* at 4–5.
[78]   *Ibid.* at 24–5.
[79]   Rob Harris, UEFA Investigating 40 Match-Fixing Cases, Mainly Involving Eastern European Clubs, DAYTON DAILY NEWS, Sept. 25, 2009.
[80]   Lester Munson, Scandal, Slurs, Sex … Happy Holiday!, ESPN.COM, Nov. 25, 2009.
[81]   *Ibid.*
[82]   *Ibid.*
[83]   FIFA CODE OF ETHICS 5 (2009).
[84]   FIFA to Monitor Sports Betting at National Level, GAMBLING UPDATE, Mar. 25, 2009.
[85]   *Ibid.*
[86]   *Ibid.*

World Cup in football/soccer. FIFA expanded the program with the dual purpose of preventing illegal sports betting and to raise awareness of the issue.[87]

3. Japan

The sport of sumo wrestling, centered in Japan, holds a significant, traditional spot in Japanese history and culture. In recent years, however, the sport's connections to organized crime and illegal sports betting have removed a significant amount of its luster and prestige.[88] In response, public broadcaster NHK decided to cancel its live broadcast of the 2010 Nagoya Grand Sumo Tournament after allegations that numerous sumo wrestlers had engaged in a broad illegal sports-betting scheme. NHK had aired the tournament on television since 1953 and on radio since 1928.[89] Interestingly, the alleged illegal sports betting was not for sumo wrestling but for baseball.[90] In Japan, betting is prohibited except on horse racing and certain types of motor sports.[91]

Japan's Metropolitan Police Department (MPD) raided numerous sumo stables and other locations to determine the extent of the illegal operation.[92] The resulting revelations were met with outcry and frustration by fans and critics against both the Japanese Wrestling Association (JWA), the governing authority in sumo, and the wrestlers themselves.[93]

As for long-term solutions to the scandal, only time will tell.[94] Some critics argue that the sport's connection to various Japanese organized crime syndicates is to blame and that the appropriate response is to sever the sport from these seedy connections.[95] These critics levy the blame on the JWA for not having a regulatory system in place that is capable of handling the depth and extent of the problem.[96]

III. THE LEGAL REGULATION OF GAMBLING

A. The United States

In the United States gambling is regulated by an extensive network of federal law, complemented by state laws.

---

[87]   FIFA Extends Early Warning System for Monitoring Sports Betting, FIFA.COM, Aug. 16, 2007.

[88]   Yauo Matsubara, Investigation Focusing on Gangster Connections, YOMIURI.CO.JP, July 8, 2010.

[89]   Editorial, Sumo's Fight to Regain Fans' Trust Starts Now, YOMIURI.CO.JP, July 8, 2010.

[90]   Police Search Sumo Stables over Betting, YOMIURI.CO.JP, Jul. 8, 2010.

[91]   Kimiko de Freytas-Tamura, Japan's Sumo Bodyslammed by Scandal, YOMIURI.CO.JP, July 8, 2010.

[92]   Matsubara, note 88 *supra.*

[93]   Sumo Fans Shocked By Raids / JSA Officials Avoid Reporters; Supports Demand Wrestlers 'Shape Up,' YOMIURI.CO.JP, July 8, 2010.

[94]   See, e.g., Ken Marantz, Rantz n Raves: Does Sumo See Writing on Wall Yet?, YOMIURI.CO.JP, July 14, 2010.

[95]   *Ibid.*

[96]   *Ibid.*

1. Federal law

The starting point for understanding the regulation of sports betting in the United States is the following survey of the many federal laws that have been put in place to enforce this regulation. It is important to recognize that virtually all federal laws that regulate gambling within the United States are based on Congress' authority under the Commerce Clause of the United States Constitution.[97] In addition to federal laws under this provision, the states are left to create their own independent regulations of many activities.

a. *Wire Act.* Federal regulation of gambling began in 1961. The Wire Act essentially prohibits people from using a 'telephone facility' to receive bets or send gambling information while engaged in interstate commerce.[98] As the United States Court of Appeals for the Fifth Circuit explained, the purpose of the Wire Act:

> ... is to assist the various States, territories, and possessions of the United States and the District of Columbia in the enforcement of their laws pertaining to gambling, bookmaking, and like offenses and to aid in the suppression of organized gambling activities by prohibiting the use of or the leasing, furnishing, or maintaining of wire communication facilities which are or will be used for the transmission of certain gambling information in interstate and foreign commerce.[99]

The first part of the Act criminalizes certain types of gambling behavior.[100] Accordingly, it is illegal in the United States to transmit bets or wagers, use information assisting betting or wagering on a sports event or contest, or engage in any communication that entitles the recipient to receive money or credit resulting from betting or wagering. Individual liability hinges on conduct using a 'wire communication facility.'[101]

The second section of the Act contains a safe harbor provision providing that:

> (b) Nothing in this section shall be construed to prevent the transmission in interstate or foreign commerce of information for use in news reporting of sporting events or contests, or for the transmission of information assisting in the placing of bets or wagers on a sporting event or

---

[97]   This clause provides that Congress has the authority 'to regulate commerce with foreign nations, and among the several states, and with the Indian tribes.' U.S. CONST., art. 1, § 8, Cl. 3.

[98]   18 U.S.C. § 1084 (2011).

[99]   *Martin* v. *United States*, 389 F.2d 895, 895 n.6 (5th Cir. 1968).

[100]   18 U.S.C. § 1084(a):

(a) Whoever being engaged in the business of betting or wagering knowingly uses a wire communication facility for the transmission in interstate or foreign commerce of bets or wagers or information assisting in the placing of bets or wagers on any sporting event or contest, or for the transmission of a wire communication which entitles the recipient to receive money or credit as a result of bets or wagers, or for information assisting in the placing of bets or wagers, shall be fined under this title or imprisoned not more than two years, or both.

[101]   This term is defined as:

... any and all instrumentalities, personnel, and services (among other things, the receipt, forwarding, or delivery of communications) used or useful in the transmission of writings, signs, pictures, and sounds of all kinds by aid of wire, cable, or other like connection between the points of origin and reception of such transmission.

Ibid. § 1081.

contest from a State or foreign country where betting on that sporting event or contest is legal into a State or foreign country in which such betting is legal.[102]

This section includes an exemption from liability for news reporting of information from sporting events and another exemption when the information used or the bet placed is transmitted from a state or country where gambling is legal to another jurisdiction where gambling is also legal.

The *McLeod* case explains how the Wire Act specifically applies to sports betting. Barbara McLeod was involved in a football parlay card business that operated out of Indianapolis, Indiana.[103] Although the business operated out of Indianapolis, McLeod worked from Las Vegas by phone. While McLeod was making phone calls from a public telephone in Las Vegas, a government official stood about 4 feet from her and heard her give out the football line information. A check of the phone records revealed that McLeod had made phone calls to various phone numbers in Indiana. She was then arrested for violating the Wire Act.

McLeod claimed that the evidence obtained against her by the agent listening to her phone calls was a violation of her constitutional rights to be free from unreasonable searches because the government agent did not obtain the proper authorization to intercept her communication. In addition, she claimed that the evidence against her was not sufficient to show that she made the disputed calls because the agent did not provide adequate evidence from phone records. The court found that the government agent did not need a listening device to hear her conversation and those constitutional protections did not extend to conversations on public telephones as they are 'conversations knowingly exposed to the public.'[104] The court also found that there was enough evidence to substantiate the charges against her, because, although phone records did not provide any evidence that phone calls had been made across state lines, as required by the statute's interstate commerce language, the court ruled that reasonable inferences could be made about the phone calls actually being made from Las Vegas to Indiana.[105]

Most cases under this Act are similarly easy for the government to prosecute. As long as a suspect has engaged in some form of prohibited betting activity as defined in the Act, and as long as that activity took place in interstate commerce, the suspect will typically be found to have violated the federal law. Overall, any form of sports betting within the United States can be found to violate the Wire Act and therefore result in criminal prosecution, as long as the activity does not take place between states that have legalized sports betting (to be discussed at the end of this chapter – see Section III(A)(2)).

b.   Travel Act. In conjunction with the Wire Act, in 1961 the United States Congress also passed the Travel Act. Most cases contesting gambling activities charge the claimant under both Acts. In general terms, the Travel Act prohibits interstate travel or the use of mails or other methods, including the Internet, to convey illegal gambling materials such as winnings from an illegal betting operation, as well as the use of a credit card over the

---

102   *Ibid.* § 1084(b).
103   *United States* v. *McLeod*, 493 F.2d 1186 (7th Cir. 1974).
104   *Ibid.* at 1188.
105   *Ibid.*

telephone or Internet to make an illegal bet.[106] For purposes of the Travel Act,[107] an 'unlawful activity' includes illegal gambling, which can include sports betting.

In the *McLeod* case, the defendant was also convicted of violating the Travel Act because she 'traveled' across state lines to help 'facilitate' gambling operations. McLeod argued that her information was not essential to those operations because line information was available in Indiana as well. The court ruled, however, that 'the use of any facility in interstate commerce need not be essential to the gambling operation; "it need only facilitate" the carrying on of illegal gambling.'[108] The court explained that 'facilitate' means to 'make easy or less hard.'[109] Therefore, the court determined that the information at issue helped contribute to the success of the gambling operation because it allowed the operator to distribute their cards before other sources would have been available.

In another case, Thomas Wilkinson and Broadus Stewart operated a sports bookmaking business in Jackson, Mississippi. On November 20, 1976, a search warrant was executed to search Wilkinson and Stewart's place of business, where government agents found gambling and phone records from people who wanted to place bets or wanted betting line information. At trial, the court affirmed the jury's decision that the defendants had violated the Travel Act, finding that they were involved in interstate commerce because at least one customer had called from outside Mississippi.[110]

c.   Illegal Gambling Business Act. In 1970, in a shift from attempting to regulate only individuals who engage in gambling activities, Congress passed the Illegal Gambling Business Act, a law prohibiting people from running an illegal gambling business. In the end, the Illegal Gambling Business Act has expanded the reach of federal regulation of sports betting in order to curb larger gambling businesses and activities.

The law specifically provides that, '(a) Whoever conducts, finances, manages, supervises, directs, or owns all or part of an illegal gambling business shall be fined under this

---

[106]   18 U.S.C. § 1952 (2011).

[107]   The Travel Act specifically provides that:

(a)   Whoever travels in interstate or foreign commerce or uses the mail or any facility in interstate or foreign commerce, with intent to –

(1)   distribute the proceeds of any unlawful activity; or
(2)   commit any crime of violence to further any unlawful activity; or
(3)   otherwise promote, manage, establish, carry on, or facilitate the promotion, management, establishment, or carrying on, of any unlawful activity,

and thereafter performs or attempts to perform –

(A)   an act described in paragraph (1) or (3) shall be fined under this title, imprisoned not more than 5 years, or both; or
(B)   an act described in paragraph (2) shall be fined under this title, imprisoned for not more than 20 years, or both, and if death results shall be imprisoned for any term of years or for life.

Ibid.

[108]   493 F.2d at 1189.
[109]   *Ibid.*
[110]   *United States v. Wilkinson*, 601 F.2d 791, 796 (5th Cir. 1979).

title or imprisoned not more than five years, or both.'[111] In order to find that a business is an 'illegal gambling business,' the government must prove there is a gambling operation that violates a state or local law where it is conducted; involves five or more persons who conduct, finance, manage, supervise, direct, or own all or part of the business; and remains in substantially continuous operation for more than 30 days or has a gross revenue of $2000 in any given day.

Courts have liberally determined who can be counted towards the minimum of five persons. In one case, that number included anyone involved in the business to any degree, except those merely betting,[112] while in another case, it included everyone 'from layoff bettors and line services to waitresses who serve drinks.'[113] In one last case, Robert Mick and his girlfriend, Harriet Brodzinski, ran a bookmaking business out of a trailer in Alliance, Ohio for over 10 years. During a 2-month period in 1997, the FBI ran a surveillance, which found over 3400 calls on the fax machine and over 6400 calls on the other two lines. About 98% of the fax machine calls were outgoing and about 90% of the telephone calls were incoming. In addition, Mick had a friend in Kentucky maintain a telephone line in her house to help with the betting operations. This allowed bettors in Kentucky to make a local call, which was then forwarded to one of Mick's lines in Ohio. Mick and Brodzinski, along with Mick's two sons, answered the phone calls, which were mainly people calling to place bets on various sporting events. Mick was charged with violating the Illegal Gambling Business Act, among other federal laws, for running an illegal gambling business.[114] The court included bookmakers who regularly placed bets, the friend who set up a phone line in Kentucky, and the bar owner who distributed parlay sheets on Mick's behalf, which put the amount of people regularly involved in the business well above the necessary five to classify as an illegal gambling business for purposes of the Act.[115]

d.   Racketeer Influenced and Corrupt Organizations Act.   Also in 1970, in a package of federal laws aimed at controlling organized crime including the Illegal Gambling Business Act, Congress enacted the Racketeer Influenced and Corrupt Organizations Act (RICO).[116] RICO was intended to combat organized crime by attacking the sources of its revenue, such as gambling and bookmakers. The law imposes both criminal and civil sanctions on those who engage in certain prohibited activities. First, the Act makes it unlawful to invest funds derived from a pattern of racketeering activity or collected from an unlawful debt.[117] Next, the Act forbids an entity from acquiring or maintaining an interest in an enterprise that affects commerce through a pattern of racketeering activity or through collection of an unlawful debt. And finally, as a catch-all, the Act forbids any person from being employed in or associated with these types of activities.[118]

---

[111]   18 U.S.C. § 1955 (2011).
[112]   *Sanabria* v. *United States*, 437 U.S. 54 (1978).
[113]   *United States* v. *Heacock*, 31 F.3d 249, 252 (5th Cir. 1994).
[114]   *United States* v. *Mick*, 263 F.3d 553 (6th Cir. 2001).
[115]   *Ibid.* at 569.
[116]   18 U.S.C. § 1962 (2011).
[117]   *Ibid.*
[118]   *Ibid.*

A group of notorious Chicago gangsters was involved in a sports bookmaking business in Chicago during the 1980s and early 1990s.[119] The group often moved its operations from place to place in order to keep government agents off its trail. The mobsters took bets from people on various professional sporting events and horse races. All bets were allowed to be taken on credit, but in an effort to make sure that all bets were collected, the bookies were held personally responsible for any of their customers' past-due accounts; they, in turn, threatened to harm or kill customers who owed money. This evidence served to convict the defendants of violating RICO by racketeering in sports.[120]

e. *Professional and Amateur Sports Protection Act.* The next major piece of federal legislation to impact sports betting came in 1992 with the enactment of the Professional and Amateur Sports Protection Act (PASPA).[121] This Act prohibits a person or government entity from operating or authorizing any betting or wagering scheme based on 'competitive games in which amateur or professional athletes participate.'[122] Four states (Nevada, Oregon, Montana, and Delaware) have statutes predating PASPA that allow sports wagering. These states therefore were not affected by the Act. Thus, Nevada continued to offer legalized sports wagering, Oregon and Delaware continued their sports lotteries, and Montana created a sports lottery.

Of particular interest to those within the sports industry, PASPA applies to both amateur and professional sports organizations. It defines 'amateur sports organizations' vaguely as '(A) a person or governmental entity that sponsors, organizes, schedules, or conducts a competitive game in which one or more amateur athletes participate, or (B) a league or association of persons or governmental entities described in subparagraph (A).'[123] 'Professional sports organizations' are then defined as '(A) a person or governmental entity that sponsors, organizes, schedules, or conducts a competitive game in which one or more professional athletes participate, or (B) a league or association of persons or governmental entities described in subparagraph (A).'[124] As a result, amateur sports organizations such as the NCAA and state associations of school sports, along with professional organizations including the NBA and the NFL, are all subject to the provisions of the Act.

Although it has been in place since 1992, to date there is only one reported judicial decision involving PASPA. In 2007, a citizen of New Jersey, James Flagler, challenged the constitutionality of the Act, but the United States District Court for the District of New Jersey ruled the statute constitutional.[125] Flagler had alleged that the United States Constitution did not specifically mention gambling, so that any laws related to gambling are to be reserved for the states. His claims were dismissed for lack of standing because he was not able to show that the right to gamble on professional and amateur sports was a legally protectable interest, nor was he able to show that he had suffered any harm.[126]

---

[119]   *United States* v. *Zizzo*, 120 F.3d 1338 (7th Cir. 1997).
[120]   *Ibid.* at 1346.
[121]   28 U.S.C. § 3701, *et. seq.* (2011).
[122]   *Ibid.*
[123]   *Ibid.* § 3701(1).
[124]   *Ibid.* § 3701(2)).
[125]   *Flagler* v. *U.S. Attorney, D.N.J.*, 2007 U.S. Dist. LEXIS 70916 (D.N.J. Sept. 25, 2007).
[126]   *Ibid.* at *7.

f. Unlawful Internet Gambling Enforcement Act. In general, the Unlawful Internet Gambling Enforcement Act (UIGEA)[127] prohibits the transfer of funds from a financial institution, such as a bank or credit card company, to an Internet gambling website. The law does not make it illegal for a person to participate in Internet gambling. Instead, in order to regulate Internet gambling activities,[128] the law focuses on financial institutions and Internet service providers by prohibiting the transfer of funds from bettors to operators of most online gambling websites.[129] Financial institutions must then adopt procedures and policies designed to block the flow of prohibited funding to the operators of affected online gambling websites.[130] Interestingly, the law exempts participation in fantasy sports online.[131]

The impact of UIGEA is still to be seen. Immediately after its passage, many Internet gambling sites stopped taking bets from United States gamblers using United States financial institutions. However, the application of the law to gambling and gamblers is less clear as there has been little litigation involving the Act. A few cases, however, have tested the waters. In 2008, Interactive Media Entertainment & Gaming (Interactive Media), a non-profit group that collects and disseminates information on Internet gambling, claiming that UIGEA was unconstitutional, moved to enjoin the Act from being enforced. Interactive Media claimed that it violated the First Amendment by burdening the plaintiff's freedom to express itself about Internet gambling.[132] The New Jersey District Court held, however, that the Act does not do so because it does not prevent a group from

---

[127]   31 U.S.C. § 5361, *et. seq.* (2011). The Act defines a bet or wager as:

(A) ... the staking or risking by any person of something of value upon the outcome of a contest of others, a sporting event, or a game subject to chance, upon an agreement or understanding that the person or another person will receive something of value in the event of a certain outcome;
(B) ... the purchase of a chance or opportunity to win a lottery or other prize (which opportunity to win is predominantly subject to chance);
(C) ... any scheme of a type described in [The Professional and Amateur Sports Protection Act of 1992);
(D) ... any instructions or information pertaining to the establishment or movement of funds by the bettor or customer in, to, or from an account with the business of betting or wagering.

Ibid. § 5362(1). The Act was scheduled to go into effect on December 1, 2009; however, financial institutions, thoroughbred racing organizations, and gambling interests pressured the Treasury Department and Federal Reserve to grant a 6-month delay to allow legislators an opportunity to clarify the existing Act.
[128]   The term 'unlawful Internet gambling' means to:

... place, receive, or otherwise knowingly transmit a bet or wager by any means which involves the use, at least in part, of the Internet where such bet or wager is unlawful under any applicable Federal or State law in the State or Tribal lands in which the bet or wager is initiated, received, or otherwise made.

Ibid. § 5362(10)(A).
[129]   *Ibid.* § 5363.
[130]   *Ibid.* § 5364.
[131]   *Ibid.* § 5362(I)(E)(ix).
[132]   *Interactive Media Entertainment & Gaming Association* v. *Gonzales*, 2008 U.S. Dist. LEXIS 16903, Civ. Act. No. 07–2625 (D.N.J. Mar. 4, 2008).

expressing its views about Internet gambling.[133] In fact, nothing in the Act prevents the plaintiffs from continuing to promote Internet gambling. As the court explained, 'the plaintiff and its members remain free to promote Internet gambling; nothing in the challenged statute implicates the plaintiff's expressive activities in this regard.'[134] Another recent case focused on whether online fantasy sports leagues violate UIGEA. The court unsurprisingly answered 'yes.'[135]

g. Other federal laws. The federal laws discussed so far provide an extensive structure that can significantly regulate all forms of gambling in the United States. A few other federal laws add to the general framework of gambling regulations within the United States.

While not directly related to the regulation of gambling, the Bribery in Sporting Contests Act[136] makes it a crime to bribe or attempt to bribe an individual in a scheme to influence the outcome of a sporting event. The actual scheme involved must take place in interstate commerce but can involve athletes at any level of sports participation, as the act defines a 'sporting contest' as 'any contest in any sport, between individual contestants or teams of contestants (without regard to the amateur or professional status of the contestants therein), the occurrence of which is publicly announced before its occurrence.' Violations of this law can lead to fines and imprisonment. As many sports gambling schemes involve allegations that players, referees, or other participants were bribed in order to affect the outcome of a game in order to meet or change bets made, this Act can have a wide impact on behalf of the federal government's efforts to combat gambling.

The Money Laundering Control Act[137] criminalizes money laundering activities when bettors or gamblers try to disguise where the money involved has originated. The statute criminalizes (1) financial transactions where the defendant involved knows that the proceeds involved are from some form of unlawful activity; (2) the intentional transportation, transmission, or transfer (or attempts to do the same) of funds are known to be the proceeds of an unlawful activity; or (3) whenever the defendant intentionally conducts or attempts to conduct a financial transaction involving property represented to be the proceeds of, or used to conduct or facilitate, a specified unlawful activity.

The Illegal Money Transmitters Act[138] makes it a crime to conduct, control, manage, supervise, direct, or own all or part of a business, knowing the business is an illegal money transmitting business. This type of business is one that involves the transmission of money, affects interstate commerce in any manner, and fails to comply with either state law or the registration requirements for such a business. Specific to gambling, 'money transmitting' includes transferring funds on behalf of the public by any and all means. The Act therefore covers money transfers as part of a sports betting scheme.

---

[133]   *Ibid.* at *22.
[134]   *Ibid.*
[135]   *Humphrey* v. *Viacom, Inc.*, 2007 U.S. Dist. LEXIS 44679, No. 06–2768 (DMC) (D.N.J. June 19, 2007).
[136]   18 U.S.C. § 224 (2011).
[137]   18 U.S.C. § 1956 (2011).
[138]   18 U.S.C. § 1960 (2011).

The Interstate Transportation of Wagering Paraphernalia Act[139] prohibits an individual from knowingly carrying or sending in interstate or foreign commerce any record, paraphernalia, ticket, certificate, bills, slip, token, paper, writing, or other device used, or to be used, or adapted, devised, or designed for use in (a) bookmaking; or (b) wagering pools with respect to a sporting event; or (c) in a numbers, policy, bolita, or similar game. The statute focuses on the actual paraphernalia used within betting transactions and specifically includes materials used within wagering pools for sporting events.

The Federal Anti-Lottery Act[140] bans the transmission of lottery-related materials and paraphernalia within interstate commerce. In 1994 its general prohibitions were modified to allow states to create their own lotteries. Many of these state-level lotteries have been used to fund the construction of sports facilities.

The Bank Records and Foreign Transactions Act,[141] also known as the Bank Secrecy Act, requires 'financial institutions' and casinos outside of Nevada to report all currency transactions greater than $10 000 as a means of detecting money laundering.

The Gambling Devices Transportation Act[142] makes it unlawful to knowingly transport a gambling device to a state where that device is prohibited by state law. The Gambling Ship Act[143] prohibits offshore gaming except on certain voyages beyond the territorial waters of the United States.

By contrast to these laws prohibiting or regulating gambling, federal laws support horse racing and Indian gaming. The Interstate Horseracing Act[144] supports state-specific gambling and wagering connected with horse racing in order to further the horse-racing and legal off-track betting industries in the United States. The Indian Gaming Regulatory Act[145] allows Indian tribes to control their own gaming activities. It allows Indian tribes to conduct gaming activities that could otherwise be found to be illegal forms of gambling, from bingo and electronic games to slot machines and other similar high-stakes games of chance. According to the National Indian Gaming Association, 233 tribes across 28 states participate in gaming, which has grown into a $25.9 billion industry.[146]

2. State law

Each state in the United States has created its own scheme to regulate gambling. For example, in Wisconsin a person can be criminally liable for making a bet; entering a gambling place with the intent to make a bet; participating in a lottery; playing a gambling machine; or conducting, intending to conduct, or possessing the facilities necessary to conduct a lottery.[147] In addition, participants in contests (including sports contests) are liable for illegal gambling. The applicable statute provides that, 'any participant in, or any owner, employer, coach or trainer of a participant in, any contest of skill, speed, strength

---

[139]   18 U.S.C. § 1953(a) (2011).
[140]   18 U.S.C. § 1301, *et. seq.* (2011).
[141]   Pub. L. No. 91–508, Titles I, II, 84 Stat. 114, 1970.
[142]   15 U.S.C. § 1171, *et. seq.* (2011).
[143]   18 U.S.C. § 1081, *et. seq.* (2011).
[144]   15 U.S.C. § 3001, *et. seq.* (2011).
[145]   25 U.S.C. § 2701, *et. seq.* (2011).
[146]   National Indian Gaming Association, The Economic Impact of Indian Gaming in 2008 (2009).
[147]   Gambling, WIS. STAT. § 945.02 (2011).

or endurance of persons, machines or animals at which admission is charged, who makes a bet upon any opponent in such contest is guilty …'[148] Similarly, bribery of participants 'with intent to influence any participant to refrain from exerting full skill, speed, strength or endurance' is also illegal.[149] This example is typical of state laws.

A few states allow limited forms of sports-related gambling, however. In Nevada, for example, sports pools are legal. A sports pool is defined as 'the business of accepting wagers on sporting events by any system or method of wagering.'[150] In order to operate a legal sports pool or book, an individual or organization must simply obtain a proper license.[151] In Montana, sports pools and sports tab games are authorized by statute.[152] It is also legal to participate in a fantasy sports league in Montana, but it is still illegal for individuals to bet or wager on the outcome of a sports event.[153]

Also, it might be noted that several state legislatures have considered gambling as a possible source of revenue to offset budget shortfalls. In Alabama, for example, a bill was introduced to allow state-regulated casinos to offer the same games as Native American casinos.[154] New Jersey considered a bill to legalize most gambling, including sports gambling on the Internet.[155] Missouri, Rhode Island, and Delaware urged the United States Congress to lift its ban on sports gambling. Such initiatives at the state level have been open to judicial attack. For example, Delaware's Sports Lottery Act, which was discussed earlier,[156] authorized sports betting and gaming at existing and future facilities. As noted earlier, the MLB, NBA, NCAA, NFL, and NHL all sued the state, claiming that the new law would violate the Professional and Amateur Sports Protection Act. The court agreed, striking down the Delaware law insofar as it attempted to develop new forms of sanctioned sports betting in Delaware, in violation of the federal law.[157]

Before UIGEA, several states passed laws specific to Internet gambling: Illinois, Indiana, Louisiana, Montana, Nevada, Oregon, South Dakota, Washington, and Wisconsin. Louisiana's law is a prime example.[158] Oregon and South Dakota also have

---

[148]   *Ibid.* § 945.07.
[149]   *Ibid.* § 945.08.
[150]   NEV. REV. STAT. ANN. § 463.0193 (2011).
[151]   *Ibid.* § 463.160.
[152]   MONT. CODE ANN., § 23-5-502 (2011).
[153]   *Ibid.* §§ 23-5-802, 23-5-806.
[154]   Alabama House Bill 154 (2011).
[155]   State of New Jersey, 214th Legislature, Senate Resolution, No. 19 (2010).
[156]   Text at notes 18–20, *supra.*
[157]   579 F.3d at 304.
[158]   In its general statute that criminalizes gambling, Louisiana defines prohibited 'Gambling by computer' as:

> … the intentional conducting, or directly assisting in the conducting as a business of any game, contest, lottery, or contrivance whereby a person risks the loss of anything of value in order to realize a profit when accessing the Internet, World Wide Web, or any part thereof by way of any computer, computer system, computer network, computer software, or any server.

LA. REV. STAT. ANN. § 14:90.3 (2011).

specific statutory provisions for 'Internet gambling' and 'Gambling by computer.'[159] Other states license some forms of Internet gambling.[160]

Overall, the regulation of Internet gambling at the state level is a relatively recent and sparse development. Unlike federal legislation, most state laws specifically target and criminalize the actual activity of Internet gambling. Coupling these laws with the federal laws already discussed leads to an overall scheme that prohibits most Internet gambling within the United States.

B.   The United Kingdom

The United Kingdom's laws on gambling have remained 'fairly uniform'[161] and consistent with the country's historical concern for the criminal component of sports betting.[162] 'Betting by the poor led to debt, which led to crime. Even where crime was avoided, deterioration of character was not, especially among the young and women.'[163] Additionally, gambling's historical relationship with sport has also served 'as a motive for malpractice and corruption and as a source of finance for sporting activities.'[164] As a consequence, the United Kingdom law has severely restricted the scope of gambling in general.

In 1999, England established an independent review commission ('the Commission') to determine the effectiveness of its restrictive law and to suggest revisions.[165] At first, the Commission recognized that gambling involves large sums of mostly anonymous money and that games, both sporting and casino-based, can be rigged.[166] The Commission made several determinations regarding the state of gambling as it then existed. In particular, it noted that it was a better practical policy to use 'administrative rather than criminal powers'[167] to combat the problems associated with gambling. To that end, the Commission made a total of 181 recommendations, covering a wide range of gambling issues, notably granting powers of entry, seizure, and search to the Gambling Commission. In all,

---

[159]   OR. REV. STAT. § 167.109 (2009). The South Dakota statute focuses exclusively on 'Internet gambling,' providing that no one in the state can engage in or establish a website that conducts Internet gambling activities. A person engaged in gambling business is prohibited from betting online: S.D. CODIFIED LAWS § 22–25A-7–8 (2010).

[160]   For example, within its definition of regulated gambling, Montana defines Internet gambling as follows.

'Internet gambling', by whatever name known, includes but is not limited to the conduct of any legal or illegal gambling enterprise through the use of communications technology that allows a person using money, paper checks, electronic checks, electronic transfers of money, credit cards, debit cards, or any other instrumentality to transmit to a computer information to assist in the placing of a bet or wager and corresponding information related to the display of the game, game outcomes, or other similar information.

MONT. CODE ANN. § 23-5-112 (2011).

[161]   STUDY, note 42 *supra*, at 904.

[162]   SIMON GARDINER, MARK JAMES, JOHN O'LEARY, *ET AL.*, SPORTS LAW 343 (3d ed. 2006).

[163]   *Ibid.*

[164]   *Ibid.* at 344.

[165]   DEP'T FOR CULTURE, MEDIA, AND SPORT, GAMBLING REVIEW BODY, GAMBLING REVIEW REPORT 74 (2001).

[166]   *Ibid.*

[167]   *Ibid.*

159 of the Commission's recommendations were adopted by the Department for Culture, Media, and Sport.[168]

A new United Kingdom law based on the Commission's recommendations was drafted in 2003.[169] Parliament's initiative was 'a product of its time – an attempt to stifle the proliferation of illegal gambling which had begun to become a feature of the UK market and to arrest the development of a relationship between the gambling industry and organized crime.'[170] The draft legislation went quickly through a number of revisions in the House of Commons and the House of Lords.[171] The most vehement objections to the bill were the speed at which it went through Parliament and the corresponding inability to review its provisions fully.[172] Despite the objections to the pace at which the bill was passed, the bill was enacted in 2005 and officially came into effect in 2007.[173]

The Gambling Act 2005[174] has three central objectives: '(1) preventing gambling from being a source of crime or disorder, being associated with crime or disorder or being used to support crime; (2) ensuring that gambling is conducted in a fair and open way; and (3) protecting children and other vulnerable persons from being harmed or exploited by gambling.'[175] Not surprisingly, the objectives of the Act reflect England's historical approach towards gambling in general. The express goal, however, is to 'strike an appropriate balance between increasing consumer choice for adults, affording greater protection for the minority who have problems with their gambling and ensuring that those who provide commercial gambling observe high standards of probity and social responsibility.'[176] The Act provides for a Gambling Commission that, among other duties, is intended to oversee the operation of the Act, issue regulations, and issue licenses for operating a gambling establishment.[177] The Commission was also designed to respond to new problems that a static act would not be able to protect against.[178]

Section 42 of the Gambling Act 2005, although it does not specifically mention sports, prohibits a person from doing 'anything for the purpose of enabling or assisting another person to cheat at gambling.'[179] The provision was 'aimed at catching match fixers who, regardless of whether of not they have accepted money, attempt to influence the outcome of a game or race, or some aspect of it.'[180] Often the allure of gambling in sport is the wide variety of components that can be bet upon, such as the number of corner kicks that may

---

[168]   Carl Rohsler and Katherine Conlon, An Analysis of the Chief Features of the Gambling Act 2005, 16(8) ENT. L. REV. 226, 227 (2005).

[169]   *Ibid.* at 226.

[170]   *Ibid.*

[171]   *Ibid.*

[172]   *Ibid.* (noting that '[t]he passage of the Bill through Parliament was accompanied by what could only be called a reactionary campaign from certain quarters of the press under the general headline "Kill the Bill."').

[173]   *Ibid.*

[174]   Gambling Act 2005, s. 19 (England).

[175]   ADAM LEWIS AND JONATHAN TAYLOR, SPORT: LAW AND PRACTICE 1270 (2d ed. 2008).

[176]   David Clifton, The UK Gambles on its Future, 44 EURO. LAW. 10, 10 (2004/05).

[177]   *Ibid.*

[178]   *Ibid.* (noting that '[i]f there is evidence of problems emerging as a result of the reform, tougher protections will be introduced.').

[179]   Gambling Act 2005 2005, ss. 19, 42.

[180]   *Ibid.*

occur in a game. That number may have no impact on the result of the game, so it can be harder to detect. As a result, gamblers may be able to avoid detection if they influence these aspects of the game. Section 42 tries to eliminate this by prohibiting gambling activity even if the cheater does not participate in the fixed match.[181]

Significantly, the Gambling Commission addressed the advertisement and sponsorship of teams by gambling companies.[182] The specific concern is that if a gambling company sponsors a team, the fans of that team, children in particular, will be more susceptible to addiction to gambling.[183] After taking public and industry comments, the Gambling Commission recommended – and the industry subsequently adopted – standards of conduct aimed at reducing these concerns. These standards include a prohibition on logos of gambling companies on children's replica shirts, a requirement to add public awareness messages within advertisements, and a general practice of demonstrating social responsibility in advertisement and sponsorship deals.[184]

The Department for Culture, Media, and Sport also issued a ten-point plan designed as a code of practice for sports authorities.[185] It is a rough outline of basic policies that sports authorities should follow. Unfortunately, it is written so that a sports authority is not required to take any specific action. For example, '[t]he sports authority will *not avoid* taking necessary action when they suspect, or are aware of betting activity which threatens the integrity of the sport and objectives of this code of practice.'[186] Furthermore, the plan need not be adopted as is; rather, sports authorities are free to use it as a 'starting point to develop more detailed policies and rules of their own.'[187]

Most recently, the Department for Culture, Media, and Sport released a report on sports betting integrity, which was designed as a set of recommendations to sports authorities, the Gambling Commission, police, and other government entities.[188] The report notes that there have been recent problems with sports betting, particularly in horse racing, cricket, and tennis. To remedy these problems, the report makes several recommendations, which include three main elements: 'the adoption of robust rules and disciplinary procedures, the implementation of a comprehensive education programme for all participants, and the creation of an integrity unit which has the capability to gather and analyse intelligence.'[189]

---

[181]   *Ibid.*
[182]   LEWIS AND TAYLOR, note 175 *supra*, at 1271.
[183]   *Ibid.*
[184]   *Ibid.*
[185]   DEPARTMENT FOR CULTURE, MEDIA, AND SPORT, INTEGRITY IN SPORTS BETTING: A 10-POINT PLAN (2005).
[186]   *Ibid.* (emphasis added).
[187]   *Ibid.*
[188]   SPORTS BETTING INTEGRITY PANEL, REPORT OF THE SPORTS BETTING INTEGRITY PANEL (2010).
[189]   *Ibid.* at 6.

C. Germany

In Germany, sports bets are defined simply as transactions in which money is placed on the outcome of a certain sporting event,[190] typically as entertainment or for profit of either a private or a state organization. Sports bets are generally considered gambling and not 'games of skill,' which are regulated differently, because the average participant cannot foresee the outcome of sports matches or events.[191]

Betting is one of the most controversial sports-related topics in Germany.[192] Traced back to the fourteenth century, gambling in Germany was initially promoted by public gaming houses.[193] Germany slowly adapted to the gambling market, which eventually was used to attract wealthy aristocrats as a means of raising tax revenues.[194] As the gambling market grew, the government interest in controlling the sports betting and gambling market developed,[195] leading to regulations on both state (*länder*) and national levels. The role of the courts in the regulatory process has generated much controversy. Conflicts also exist between the state-sponsored market and the private market for sports betting as to whether private entities should be unregulated or require specific licensing.

1. State and national regulation of gambling

The justifications for gambling regulation at the *länder* and national levels, respectively, are different. The overriding reasons for gambling regulation on the national level relate to public interest and social order.[196] Specifically, the national government wants to avoid an increase of the human passion for gambling and its exploitation for private or commercial profits[197] and to control the course of gaming activity within Germany.[198] The national government seeks to avoid the risks of crime and fraud within a private market, advocating a system of official licensing according to European Commission law.[199]

Justifications for state-level regulation are both similar to and different from those at the national level. As at the national level, the state's main interest in controlling the sports betting and gambling market rests on control of the human passion for gambling.[200] The state also justifies its regulation on the avoidance of excess and abuse of profit-making opportunities in the private market, assurance that gambling institutions comply with the

---

[190] Wolfgang Freiherr Raitz Von Frentz and Christian L. Masch, Gambling, Sports Bets, Games of Skill, Lotteries, Entertainment Games, Gambling Houses, Amusement Arcades and Raffles in Germany: An Overview about the Latest Developments of the German Gaming Law, 17(7) ENT. L. REV. 196–203 (2006).

[191] *Ibid.*

[192] STUDY, note 42 *supra*, at 269.

[193] INTERNATIONAL CASINO LAW 255 (Anthony N. Cabot, William Thompson and Andrew Tottenham, eds. 1991).

[194] *Ibid.*

[195] *Ibid.*

[196] STUDY, note 42 *supra*, at 269.

[197] *Ibid.*

[198] *Ibid.*

[199] *Ibid.*

[200] *Ibid.* at 1025.

rules of use, and a determination that proceeds accrue to public interests.[201] States also want to control gambling to prevent crime due to unlimited private gambling activities while also minimizing the dangers of gaming addictions.[202] Whatever the justifications may be, the Interstate Agreement Concerning Lotteries clarifies that the fiscal interests of state monopolies alone are not enough to justify withholding private market participation.[203]

2.   Conflicts between legal regimes

The *länder*[204] control the market for sports betting by using 'interstate agreements' to establish a common framework for the operation of sports bets between the *länder*.[205] A license is granted by the respective *land* in which the operator wishes to exercise his activity, and that activity will be limited strictly to the *land*.[206] Licenses are not granted to private operators for commercial lotteries and sports betting except in special circumstances, which itself is controversial.[207] Exclusive licenses are often granted to state operators, thereby creating 'state monopolies' for the majority of sports betting and gambling games under the *länder* legislation. This restriction on private operators has created a black market for sports betting operations trying to sneak into the market by claiming they are only providing 'horse race' betting, which is legal.[208]

At the national level, the German Criminal Code provides that, '[w]hoever, without a license granted by the relevant public authorities, organizes or runs a game of chance for the general public or makes the equipment therefore available, shall be punished with imprisonment for not more than two years or a fine.'[209] This provision obliges operators to hold a German license, most often specific to a particular *land*, leaving the operation of sports betting to the state or state-held companies.[210] Anyone who advertises a game of chance without a license may be punished by a fine and no more than one year in jail.[211]

Evaluating the current sports betting regime in Germany is problematic because courts have made only a limited number of authoritative decisions and the applicable legal regimes sometimes conflict, particularly between the laws of the *länder* and European Union law.[212] The states are apt to view the latter as an interference. That is because the European Council decided that restrictions on gambling should be dealt with on a

---

[201]   *Ibid.*

[202]   *Ibid.*

[203]   *Ibid.* at 269.

[204]   *Ibid.* at 268.

[205]   *Ibid.*

[206]   *Ibid.* at 269.

[207]   *Ibid.* There is some controversy regarding whether former East German states hold valid licenses to operate in other countries. The *länder* assert that the licenses should not be valid, and the states that hold the licenses from the GDR (former East Germany) feel that they should be valid because they were declared valid by the European Union after the reunification.

[208]   *Ibid.*

[209]   *Ibid.* at 265–6.

[210]   *Ibid.* at 325.

[211]   *Ibid.* at 326.

[212]   See, in particular, Consolidated Version of the Treaty on the Functioning of the European Union, OFF. J. EUR. UNION, C 115/47 (Sept. 5, 2008).

national level in each member state, a concept known as subsidiarity.[213] Thus, the European Union and those advocating for sports betting and gambling market regulation on a national level consider state laws (in the sense of states in a federal union) to be unduly restrictive of trade. The states, on the other hand, are inclined to oppose the European Union legislation that allows non-state-sponsored gambling. Basically, they view such activity as a threat to their capacity to generate revenue though state-sponsored gambling activities.[214]

3.   Court decisions

A later section of this chapter[215] will discuss a line of decisions by the European Court of Justice (ECJ) that have addressed issues of gambling. The following paragraphs, however, will summarize decisions that pertain to German sports.

In *Her Majesty's Customs and Excise* v. *Schindler*[216] – the first case involving the application of 'national' gambling laws to come before it[217] – the ECJ upheld the prohibition of private gambling operations and provided the rationale for state exceptions to gambling. The court held that the justifications for restrictions on the private market of gambling were related to the public interest and did not interfere with the freedom to provide services, as protected by the Rome Treaty.[218]

A second case, *Questore di Verona* v. *Zenatti*, confirmed that member states could impede the cross-border provision of gaming services within the European market so long as the restrictions are compatible with European law.[219] Thus, after *Schindler* and *Zenatti*, it is clear that states may restrict markets as long as the means of restriction are non-discriminatory, justified by imperative reasons of general interest, and proportional and necessary for achieving state objectives such as avoiding gambling addictions.[220]

A landmark decision that gave rise to the current conflict in German sports betting is the *Gambelli* decision.[221] Piergiorgio Gambelli was arrested in Italy for transmitting sports wagers online without a license. He claimed that the Italian law violated the European Union's freedom to provide services.[222] The court reaffirmed its two prior decisions, stating that a state prohibition on 'taking, booking, and forwarding ... bets on sports events without a license or authorization from the member state concerned constitutes a restriction on the freedom of the establishment and the freedom to provide services

[213]   Philippe Vlaemminck and Pieter De Wael, The European Union Regulatory Approach of Online Gambling and Its Impact on the Global Gaming Industry, 7 GAMING L. REV. 177, 177 (2003).

[214]   Matthew W. Mauldin, The European Union, State-Sponsored Gambling, and Private Gambling Services: Time for Harmonization?, 36 GA. J. INT'L & COMP. L. 413, 414 (2008).

[215]   See text at notes 371–94 *infra*.

[216]   Case C-275/92, 1994 E.C.R. I-1039.

[217]   Thibault Verbiest and Ewout Keuleers, Cross-Border Gaming: The European Regulatory Perspective, 7 GAMING L. REV. 185, 188 (2003).

[218]   1994 E.C.R. I-1039, at ¶¶ 34–5.

[219]   *Questore di Verona* v. *Diego Zenatti*, Case C-67/98, 1999 E.C.R. I-7289, at ¶ 30.

[220]   Thibault Verbiest and Ewout Keuleers, Gambelli Case Makes It Harder for Nations to Restrict Gaming, 9 GAMING L. REV. 9, 10 (2004).

[221]   *Criminal Proceedings Against Gambelli and Others*, Case C-243/01, 2003 E.C.R. I-13031.

[222]   *Ibid.*

provided by the Rome Treaty,'[223] such that a 'state monopoly' must be legitimately related to the public interest. The court, however, did not create any bright line rule or criteria to determine the validity of particular state restrictions.

The German sports-betting market took another turn 2 years after the ECJ's *Gambelli* judgment when the Federal Constitutional Court declared that the state monopolies and the prohibition imposed on private individuals and entities organizing sports betting are unconstitutional.[224] The court found that the statutory provisions of the *länder* did not sufficiently combat gambling addiction;[225] instead, the *länder* prohibited the private sports-betting market for strictly fiscal purposes, which has not been identified as a legitimate state interest.[226] Although the court did find that the monopolies were unconstitutional, it did not declare the existing statutes null and void, thus creating a confusing environment for the states.[227] The court simply left the *länder* with two options: they could retain existing monopolies if they renounce their fiscal policy goals and legitimately try to combat gambling, or they could continue their fiscal policy goals of state monopolies as long as they opened the market to private enterprises.[228]

The German sports-betting market remains in a state of flux. The *länder* monopolies claim to be able to control the private markets for gambling and sports betting based on legitimate state interests, such as controlling gambling addiction. However, the European courts have decided that private entities should be allowed to operate in the German sports-betting market in competition with state entities. The Federal Constitutional Court has also determined that the *länder*, on behalf of legitimate public interests, want to regulate and prohibit private enterprises from entering the gambling market. Meanwhile, however, the *länder* are actually doing the contrary by aggressively advertising state-sponsored gambling activity, thereby undermining their own rationale for regulation and prohibition of gambling.

D. New Zealand

In New Zealand sports gambling is highly regulated by both the Racing Act 2003 and the Gambling Act 2003. The Racing Act 2003[229] was enacted to effectively control the racing industry and any related betting. The Gambling Act 2003[230] was enacted to control gambling in a way that promotes healthy gambling, reduces problem gambling, and produces benefits to the community from gambling earnings. The Racing and Gambling Acts each have a substantial legislative history.

---

223   *Ibid.*
224   Michael Winkelmuller, The German Sports Betting Market in Flux: Germany Faced by New Statutory Provisions and ECJ Rulings, 19(2) ENT. L. REV. 29 (2008).
225   *Ibid.*
226   *Ibid.* at 29.
227   *Ibid.*
228   *Ibid.*
229   Racing Act 2003, 2003 No. 3, § 3 (N.Z.).
230   Gambling Act 2003, 2003 No. 51, § 3 (N.Z.).

Horse racing in New Zealand stretches as far back as 1835.[231] The first successful Act to regulate betting at the racetrack was the Gaming and Lotteries Act 1881. Under this Act, betting contracts were held to be void, but not illegal.[232] The Gaming Act 1908 limited all betting to the physical racecourse.[233] Under this Act, a bookmaker had to be licensed, and all communications to the racecourse, either by telephone or telegraph, were illegal.[234] In 1910, Parliament prohibited bookmaking from the racecourse. Off-course betting was authorized via referendum in 1949; this referendum also created the Totalisator Agency Board (TAB), which set up a system for authorized on- and off-course betting. New Zealand was the first country to establish a system of this sort. The Racing Act 1971 responded to criticism of the TAB by creating a New Zealand Racing Authority, redirected more taxes to the TAB, and relaxed government control.

The Racing Act 2003 replaced the Racing Act 1971.[235] It established the New Zealand Racing Board,[236] which promotes the racing industry, racing betting, and sports betting.[237] Members of the Board, who must all be acceptable to the Minister of the Crown, include one independent chairperson, one member of the New Zealand Thoroughbred Racing Incorporated, one member of the Harness Racing New Zealand Incorporated, one member of the New Zealand Greyhound Racing Association, and three individuals appointed by the nomination advisory panel.[238] The responsibilities of the Board include preparing financial statements for the year, distributing accumulated funds to the appropriate racing codes, creating a business plan at the commencement of each racing year, delivering an annual report to the Minister, and ensuring that each racing code is maintaining and enforcing its regulating rules.[239] The Board is also responsible for creating a racing calendar and issuing betting licenses for the pertinent days.[240]

The Racing Act 2005 grants a broad range of authority to the Board.[241] It may 'make, alter, and revoke rules providing for the establishment of a system or systems of racing betting'[242] or sports betting.[243] Before the Board may authorize sports betting on any sporting event, it must obtain the written agreement of the appropriate New Zealand national sporting organization.[244] The Board may operate as a totalisator for purposes of gambling, but the operation of the totalisator is subject to the provisions of the Gambling Act 2003.[245] Only persons above 18 years of age may engage in betting, fines related to a violation of this age restriction range from $500 for the minor committing the offence to

---

[231]   DAVID GRANT, TWO OVER THREE ON GOODTIME SUGAR: THE NEW ZEALAND TAB TURNS 50 (2000), at 11.

[232]   Gaming and Lotteries Act 1881 (N.Z.).

[233]   Gaming Act 1908 (N.Z.).

[234]   *Ibid.*

[235]   Racing Act 2003, § 4.

[236]   *Ibid.* § 7(1).

[237]   *Ibid.* § 8.

[238]   *Ibid.* § 11.

[239]   *Ibid.* §§ 13(1), 16, 17, 20, 21, 29(1).

[240]   *Ibid.* §§ 42, 45.

[241]   *Ibid.* § 50.

[242]   *Ibid.* § 52(1).

[243]   *Ibid.* § 54(1).

[244]   *Ibid.* § 55(1).

[245]   *Ibid.* § 61(1) and (2).

$5000 for racing clubs or agents of the Board who permit a bet to be made for or on behalf of a minor.[246] The Act makes it clear that '[b]etting contracts authorized by or under this Act are enforceable at law.'[247]

The Board's regulatory authority is not exclusive under the Act. The Governor-General is given authority to make regulations to prevent harm.[248] The Governor-General may require the Board to provoke awareness of problem gambling by training supervisors of racing and sports betting.[249] The Governor-General may also make regulations prohibiting admission to certain Board venues for purposes of betting; if a person breaches this regulation, he may be charged with trespassing.[250] Aside from prohibiting general admission to a Board venue, the Governor-General may also prohibit problem gamblers from entering Board venues and enact procedures for removing identified problem gamblers from Board venues.[251] The Act also abolished the TAB as it was then constituted.[252] The TAB name continues to be used, however, as a betting corporation run by the New Zealand Racing Board.[253]

The Gambling Act 2003, in accordance with its purposes,[254] prohibits gambling unless it is specifically authorized by or under the Act, authorized by or under the Racing Act 2005, or constitutes private gambling.[255] The Act also strictly prohibits bookmaking and remote interactive gambling.[256] Only those gambling contracts that are authorized by the Act will be enforceable at law.[257] The Act prohibits any overseas gambling advertisement unless it meets one of the exceptions, such as health messages concerning gambling or advertisements about gambling equipment intended for distribution.[258] Fines for engaging in illegal gambling are substantial.[259]

The Gambling Act 2003 divides gambling activity into six classes.[260] It also authorizes private gambling, sales promotion schemes, and gambling authorized by the Racing Act 2005. Class 1 gambling, which does not require a license, cannot have a prize or turnover larger than NZ$500 and must not utilize a gaming machine. Also, the turnover of the gambling plus interest must be awarded to the winner of a gamble if the gambling is

---

246   *Ibid.* § 63(5).
247   *Ibid.* § 64.
248   *Ibid.* § 65F.
249   *Ibid.* § 65F(d).
250   *Ibid.* § 65G(1) and (3).
251   *Ibid.* § 65H(1)(b) and (c).
252   *Ibid.* § 73.
253   NZ Racing Board, About the NZ Racing Board (2010).
254   These purposes are to control the growth of gambling; prevent and minimize the harm caused by gambling, including problem gambling; authorize some gambling and prohibit the rest; facilitate responsible gambling; ensure the integrity and fairness of games; limit opportunities for crime and dishonesty associated with gambling; ensure that money from gambling benefits the community; facilitate community involvement in decisions about the provision of gambling. Gambling Act 2003, note 230 *supra*, § 3.
255   *Ibid.* § 9(1).
256   *Ibid.* § 9(2).
257   *Ibid.* § 14(2).
258   *Ibid.* § 16(1) and (2).
259   *Ibid.* § 19(3).
260   *Ibid.* § 20(1) and (2).

conducted by an individual.[261] Class 2 gambling, which also does not require a license, cannot have prizes offered exceeding NZ$5000 and a turnover over NZ$25 000, must not utilize a gaming machine, and must be conducted by a recognized society.[262] Class 3 gambling must have prizes exceeding NZ$5000, the gambling must not utilize a gaming machine, and it must be conducted by a society that holds a class 3 operator's license.[263] Class 4 gambling utilizes gaming machines and must be conducted by a society that holds a class 4 operator's license.[264] The final two legal classes are casino gambling, which requires a casino venue license and a casino operator's license, and gambling conducted by the Lotteries Commission.[265] Racing betting or sports betting in a casino that is conducted by the New Zealand Racing Board and that is authorized by and complies with the Racing Act 2005 must not be treated as casino gambling and, accordingly, is not subject to casino gambling provisions.[266] The Gambling Act 2003 also has provisions similar to the Racing Act 2005 relating to harm prevention.[267]

Animal fight betting is illegal in New Zealand, pursuant to the Animal Welfare Act 1999,[268] which prohibits knowingly owning an animal 'for the purposes of having that animal participate in an animal fighting venture.' This legislation defines an animal fighting venture as 'any event that involves a fight between at least two animals and is conducted for the purpose of sport, wagering, or entertainment; but does not include any activity the primary purpose of which involves the use of one or more animals in hunting or killing an animal in a wild state.'[269]

In sum, New Zealand allows gambling only under a strict regulatory structure that nevertheless allows citizens to participate in what the law deems to be 'healthy' gambling.

E. South Africa

In South Africa, the National Gambling Act 1996 created the National Gambling Board and established regulations on gambling activities.[270] In 2004, the Act was amended and became the National Gambling Act 2004.[271] The changes include stronger protection of players at casinos, exclusion of minors, probity standards, and other compliance measures.[272] The purpose of the National Gambling Act is to ensure uniformity, harmonization, and integrity of the gambling industry in South Africa.[273] Activities such as

---

[261] *Ibid.* §§ 22, 23.
[262] *Ibid.* §§ 24, 25, 26.
[263] *Ibid.* §§ 27, 28, 29.
[264] *Ibid.* §§ 30, 31.
[265] *Ibid.* §§ 20(1)(e) and (f), 34.
[266] *Ibid.* § 120(1).
[267] *Ibid.* §§ 313–25.
[268] Animal Welfare Act 1999, 1999 No 142, § 31 (N.Z.).
[269] *Ibid.* § 31.
[270] Andre Louw, South Africa, in INTERNATIONAL ENCYCLOPEDIA OF LAWS 152 (Prof. Dr. F. Hendrickx, ed., 2009).
[271] World Casino Directory staff, African Gambling Law, WORLD CASINO DIRECTORY.
[272] *Ibid.*
[273] NATIONAL GAMBLING BOARD, The National Gambling Act (2010).

gambling, casinos, racing, and wagering on sporting events are regulated under the Act,[274] and nine other statutes created by the National Gambling Board.

To prevent corruption in wagering on sporting events and races, the National Gambling Act 2004 requires the licensing of wagering operations and operators through provincial gambling boards. Licensees may take bets interactively by 'the conducting or operation of an interactive game of chance or skill, or of an interactive game with a combination of skill and chance or interactive wager, where the players are not in the same premises as the gaming equipment, pursuant to these Regulations.'[275] Any person who provides or accepts a wager on a sporting event or a race without acquiring a license through the required gambling boards is guilty of committing a criminal offense. In addition, an individual who is connected to the management, control, or administration of a gambling business, or a business where gambling occurs in any form or in any other business operated by the same licensed holder, is prohibited from participating in gambling activities at any of these businesses. Unfortunately, although the National Gambling Act 2004 seems clear, there is a need for improvements.[276] For example, as it stands, illegal operators can escape legal sanctions by conducting their activities outside of New Zealand.

The Prevention and Combating of Corrupt Activities Act 2004[277] (PCCA) was enacted because previous measures to combat corruption in sports failed to combat gambling activity, which has been a major corrupting influence on sports in South Africa.[278] It covers all 'sporting events,'[279] including those that are most closely associated with

---

[274]   More specifically, the legislation seeks:

[t]o provide for the co-ordination of concurrent national and provincial legislative competence over matters relating to casinos, racing, gambling and wagering, and to provide for the continued regulation of those matters; for that purpose to establish certain uniform norms and standards applicable to national and provincial regulation and licensing of certain gambling activities; to provide for the creation of additional uniform norms and standards applicable throughout the Republic; to retain the National Gambling Board; to establish the National Gambling Policy Council; to repeal the National Gambling Act, 1996; and to provide for matters incidental thereto.

World Casino Directory staff, note 271 *supra*.

[275]   Interactive Gaming and Interactive Wagering Regulations, SOUTH AFRICA GAMING REGULATIONS (2010).

[276]   Louw, note 270 *supra*, at 154.

[277]   See INTERNATIONAL CENTRE FOR ASSET RECOVERY, PREVENTION AND COMBATING OF CORRUPT ACTIVITIES 2004.

[278]   Steve Cornelius, South African Measure to Combat Match Fixing and Corruption, THE 2007(3/4) INT'L SPORTS L.J. 68 (2007).

[279]   Section 1 of PCCA defines 'sporting event' as:

... any event or contest in any sport, between individuals or teams, or in which an animal competes, and which is usually attended by the public and is governed by rules which include the constitution, rules or code of conduct the of any sporting body which stages any sporting event or of any regulatory body under whose constitution, rules or code of conduct the sporting event is conducted.

Ibid.

corrupt practices in South Africa, such as horse racing, show jumping, polocrosse, pigeon racing, and others.[280]

Corruption, a pivotal component of PCCA, is defined as 'the improper prospect or passing of some monetary or other benefit, not ordinarily due, to direct the recipient's conduct, in a certain way as directed by the person offering or passing the benefit.'[281] Corruption in sporting events can occur in multiple ways. One example occurs when an individual is persuaded to commit an act that constitutes a threat or undermines the integrity of a sporting event, such as match-fixing. Another example is when an individual attempts to influence the outcome of a sporting event. Still a third example is when an individual is persuaded to aggravate the reporting of a corrupt act to the managing director, chief executive officer, or any other person in a similar position. Under § 15 of the Act, an offense is defined as a 'scheme' that threatens or undermines the integrity of a sporting event.[282] The several stipulated punishments for those convicted of committing an offense can be severe.[283] The court can also choose to impose a fine equal to five times the value of the gratification derived from the offense.[284]

The issue of match-fixing and corruption in sports began to receive public attention after the former captain of the South African cricket team admitted involvement in manipulating matches. In *Cronjé* v. *United Cricket Board of South Africa*, discussed earlier in this chapter,[285] Cronjé admitted that he received tens of thousands of dollars on five different occasions from bookmakers in exchange for information about cricket matches.[286] During his confession, he also admitted offering teammates money in exchange for commitments to underperform in matches. The court imposed a lifetime ban from the country's cricket team on Cronjé. The ban extends to all matches affiliated with the United Cricket Board.[287]

Another example of corruption in South African sports involved violations by a referee. In October 2006, Premier Soccer League referee Enoch Radebe became the first match official in South Africa to be convicted of match-fixing.[288] Evidence showed that Radebe had bribed another referee and the other referee's assistant to influence a match. Both declined the offer and notified the court of Radebe's actions. Radebe received a huge fine.[289]

---

[280] *Ibid.*
[281] *Ibid.*
[282] *Ibid.* at 69.
[283] Any person who is convicted of an offence under PreCCA, is liable in the case:

... of a sentence to be imposed by a High Court, to a fine or to imprisonment up to a period of imprisonment for life; in the case of a sentence to be imposed by a regional court, to a fine not exceeding R360,000 or to imprisonment for a period not exceeding 18 years; in the case of a sentence to be imposed by a magistere's court, to a fine not exceeding R100,000 or to imprisonment for a period not exceeding five years.

Ibid. at 71.
[284] *Ibid.*
[285] See, text at notes 60–5 *supra.*
[286] South Africa Hands Cronje Life Ban, THE INDEPENDENT CRICKET (2000).
[287] *Ibid.*
[288] Cornelius, note 278 *supra*, at 71.
[289] Carvin Goldstone, First Referee Fined for Match-Fixing, SAFETY & SECURITY DIRECTORY (2006).

In sum, the addition of the PCCA to the regulatory scheme created by the National Gambling Act 2004 has helped tremendously in the fight against match-fixing and corruption in South Africa.[290]

IV. REGULATION BY SPORTS ORGANIZATIONS

In addition to the regulation of sports gambling by the state, many sports organizations have their own regulations to combat gambling activity by participants and employees under their authority

A.   United States Sports Organizations

1.   The National Collegiate Athletic Association (NCAA)
The NCAA governs the majority of collegiate athletics competitions played in the United States. Major teams within the NCAA are governed by Division I rules that are embodied in a manual. Similar rules can be found in the Division II and III manuals. Sports gambling is covered by Article 10 of the NCAA Bylaws, which delineates 'Ethical Conduct.'[291] The overriding principle of this article is 'honesty and sportsmanship.' Specifically, administrators, coaches, and student athletes must act 'with honesty and sportsmanship at all times' and 'shall represent the honor and dignity of fair play and the generally recognized high standards associated with wholesome competitive sports.'[292] Sports wagering[293] specifically violates these notions of fair play, honesty, and sportsmanship. A 'wager' is defined as 'any agreement in which an individual or entity agrees to give up an item of value (for example, cash, a shirt, or dinner) in exchange for the possibility of gaining another item of value.'[294]

Student athletes, athletic department and conference staff members, including coaches, and others connected with intercollegiate athletics programs are then prohibited from 'knowingly participat[ing] in sports wagering activities or provid[ing] information to individuals involved in or associated with any type of sports wagering activities concerning intercollegiate, amateur or professional athletics competition.'[295] This prohibition

---

[290]   Cornelius, note 278 *supra*, at 71.
[291]   NATIONAL COLLEGIATE ATHLETIC ASSOCIATION, 2009–2010 NCAA DIVISION I MANUAL (2009).
[292]   *Ibid.* 10.01.1.
[293]   Sports wagering is defined as:

… placing, accepting or soliciting a wager (on a staff member's or student-athlete's own behalf or on the behalf of others) of any type with any individual or organization on any intercollegiate, amateur or professional team or contest. Examples of sports wagering include, but are not limited to, the use of a bookmaker or parlay card; Internet sports wagering; auctions in which bids are placed on teams, individuals or contests; and pools or fantasy leagues in which an entry fee is required and there is an opportunity to win a prize.

Ibid. 10.02.1.
[294]   *Ibid.* 10.02.2.
[295]   *Ibid.* 10.3, at 48.

applies to any practice or competition involving any intercollegiate, amateur, or professional team.[296]

Students athletes who violate these rules through point-shaving – 'engag[ing] in activities designed to influence the outcome of an intercollegiate contest or in an effort to affect win-loss margins' – or betting on their own institution will permanently lose all of their eligibility to participate in collegiate athletics.[297] Student athletes who gamble online or through a bookmaker or parlay card will lose one year of eligibility, and will completely lose their eligibility if they are found to violate the rules a second time.[298] Employees of athletic departments who violate these rules can also be subject to disciplinary or corrective action according to the NCAA's enforcement procedures.[299]

Violations of the NCAA rules are classified as secondary – 'a violation that is isolated or inadvertent in nature, provides or is intended to provide only a minimal recruiting, competitive or other advantage and does not include any significant recruiting inducement or extra benefit' – or major – 'All violations other than secondary violations are major violations, specifically including those that provide an extensive recruiting or competitive advantage.'[300] Universities and their athletic departments can face serious sanctions if the NCAA finds that their employees or student athletes have committed either type of violation. An example of a secondary violation occurred in a 2005 incident at Tulane University. Several track and field athletes agreed to participate in a professional football pool run by a non-athlete.[301] The school's investigation found that no money had changed hands and that the students were unaware that NCAA rules prohibited gambling on professional and amateur sports.[302] As a result, and because of the one-time nature of the violation, the NCAA determined that this was a secondary violation. The student athletes were therefore reinstated after performing community service.[303]

An example of a major gambling violation involved former University of Washington coach Rick Neuheisel. In April 2002, a confidential source contacted the NCAA enforcement staff and reported that Neuheisel had bet close to $15 000 in a 'March Madness' gambling pool.[304] Based on investigations by the NCAA and the university, Neuheisel was suspended and soon fired as head coach.[305] The case then went before the NCAA's Committee on Infractions, which found that Neuheisel had violated the NCAA's gambling rules by participating in the gambling pool. The Committee therefore sanctioned the university for Neuheisel's violations.[306]

---

[296]   *Ibid.* 10.3.1.
[297]   *Ibid.* 10.3.2(a).
[298]   *Ibid.* 10.3.2(b).
[299]   *Ibid.* 10.4.
[300]   *Ibid.* 19.02.2, at 289–90.
[301]   Epstein and Niland, note 47 *supra*, at 82.
[302]   *Ibid.*
[303]   *Ibid.*
[304]   *Ibid.* at 83.
[305]   *Ibid.*
[306]   *Ibid.* NCAA, University of Washington Public Infractions Report, Oct. 20, 2004.

2. Professional leagues

In general terms, each of the United States' professional sports leagues regulates its players and employees by prohibiting them from gambling on their sport. These prohibitions are typically found in the league's constitution, bylaws, and collective bargaining agreement with players. NBA regulations are typical of all United States professional sports leagues.

Article 35 of the NBA Constitution and By-Laws, labeled 'Misconduct,'[307] provides as follows:

> Any Player who, directly or indirectly, wagers money or anything of value on the outcome of any game played by a Team in the league operated by the Association shall, on being charged with such wagering, be given an opportunity to answer such charges after due notice, and the decision of the Commissioner shall be final, binding and conclusive and unappealable. The penalty for such offense shall be within the absolute and sole discretion of the Commissioner and may include a fine, suspension, expulsion and/or perpetual disqualification from further association with the Association or any of its Members.[308]

A similar provision applies to all team owners and employees, including coaches, and League employees, including referees.[309] Taken together, these provisions provide the NBA Commissioner with 'absolute and sole discretion' to punish any players or other individuals involved with wagering on NBA games.

The NBA's Collective Bargaining Agreement also addresses gambling by players. Initially, Article VI requires players to attend mandatory educational programs that include information on 'gambling awareness.'[310] Players who do not attend these programs are subject to a large fine. The agreement is not specific, however, about banning gambling activities. Instead, this type of ban is implied as a banned activity that affects the integrity of the game and can be punished by the Commissioner within the discretion vested in him under Article 35 of the NBA Constitution and By-Laws.[311] If the Commissioner punishes a player who gambles on NBA games, the player can then turn to the agreement's provisions dealing with grievance arbitration and disputes over player discipline.[312] The Uniform Player Contract, Exhibit A to the agreement, supplements these provisions.

---

[307]   NATIONAL BASKETBALL ASSOCIATION, CONSTITUTION AND BY-LAWS, Apr. 18, 2008.
[308]   *Ibid.* art. 35(f).
[309]   Any person who, directly or indirectly, wagers money or anything of value on:

… the outcome of any game played by a Team in the league operated by the Association shall, on being charged with such wagering, be given an opportunity to answer such charges after due notice, and the decision of the Commissioner shall be final, binding, conclusive, and unappealable. The penalty for such offense shall be within the absolute and sole discretion of the Commissioner and may include a fine, suspension, expulsion and/or perpetual disqualification from further association with the Association or any of its Members.

Ibid. art. 35A(g).
[310]   NATIONAL BASKETBALL ASSOCIATION AND NATIONAL BASKETBALL ASSOCIATION PLAYERS ASSOCIATION, COLLECTIVE BARGAINING AGREEMENT 88 (July 29, 2005).
[311]   Anita Moorman, Gambling and Professional Athletics, 2009 INT'L SPORTS L.J. 90, 93 (2009).
[312]   *Ibid.*

By signing the Uniform Player Contract, each NBA player agrees to 'give his best services, as well as his loyalty, to the Team … conduct himself on and off the court according to the highest standards of honesty, citizenship, and sportsmanship; and … not to do anything that is materially detrimental or materially prejudicial to the best interests of the Team or the League.'[313] By signing the Uniform Player Contract, each NBA player agrees to be subject to Article 35 and therefore subject to the Commissioner's right to penalize or suspend him if he is found to have gambled on NBA games.[314]

The NBA also prohibits all of its employees, including coaches and referees, from disclosing confidential League or team information that might be used in gambling activities, particularly under the League's Legal Compliance Policy and Code of Conduct.[315] NBA referees are also subject to more specific regulations related to gambling.[316] In addition, the Work Rules for NBA Officials make clear that referees are prohibited from engaging in any type of gambling activity or disclosing any confidential information.[317] Overall, the NBA, typical of all professional sports leagues within the United States, has an extensive regulatory scheme that attempts to stop players, referees, team employees, and other stakeholders from engaging in NBA-related gambling activities.

3. United States Olympic Committee (USOC)

The USOC, which was reconstituted under the Amateur Sports Act in 1978,[318] enjoys the same special status of all National Olympic committees under international sports law, as described in Chapter I.[319] The USOC Code of Conduct[320] includes a prohibition of gambling within a section on 'computer networks and information.'[321]

---

[313] *Ibid.*, Exhibit A: National Basketball Association Uniform Player Contract, at A-2.

[314] *Ibid.* at A-2–A-3.

[315] NBA LEGAL COMPLIANCE POLICY AND CODE OF CONDUCT, § II.C.

[316] The collective bargaining agreement between the NBA and its referees provides:

No Referee shall participate in any gambling or place bets of any kind; nor shall any Referee visit or attend any race track, off track betting establishment, casino, or gambling establishment of any kind; provided, however, that a Referee may, during any Off-Season (i) visit and place bets at race tracks; and (ii) attend a show at a hotel/casino, provided that the Referee may, at no time, be present in the 'gaming' area of such hotel/casino.

NATIONAL BASKETBALL ASSOCIATION AND NATIONAL BASKETBALL REFEREES ASSOCIATION, COLLECTIVE BARGAINING AGREEMENT, Art. XI, § 2 (2010).

[317] Pedowitz, note 55v, at 23–4, citing 2006–07 Work Rules for NBA Officials (internal citations omitted).

[318] 36 U.S.C. §§ 220501 *et seq.* (2010).

[319] The USOC is recognized by the International Olympic Committee (IOC) as the National Organizing Committee for the United States and oversees the process under which United States cities seek to host future Olympic Games.

[320] United States Olympic Committee, Code of Conduct, Jan. 1, 2010.

[321] *Ibid.* at 9. In addition to a general policy regarding the use of these networks, the Code of Conduct provides that:

… the following activities are highly inappropriate and strictly forbidden; in certain situations, they may also be illegal and subject the USOC and the individual(s) involved to litigation and possible civil and/or criminal sanctions:

…

Gambling online or by email; …

4.   National governing bodies (NGBs)

NGBs provide only limited specific regulation of gambling activities. Some NGBs focus their prohibitions against participants participating in gambling activities only on gambling connected with NGB events. For example, in its regulations governing participant conduct, USA Cycling provides that, '[n]o person with official responsibilities at a race (including, but not limited to, race officials, race announcers, marshals, or organizers) may lay a wager on the outcome of the race they are participating in.'[322] The rule covers not only the participants in any particular event, but also includes, and is 'not limited to, race officials, race announcers, marshals, [and] organizers.'[323]

The United States Tennis Association (USTA), the United States' national governing body for tennis provides that:

> A player shall not associate with professional gamblers; bet or act as a bookmaker on matches; accept money or other consideration for losing a match or for winning by only a particular margin, or be a party to any payment of money or other consideration to another person to induce the person to lose a match or to win by only a particular margin.[324]

The USTA handbook also imposes 'an obligation to avoid acts which may be considered detrimental to the game of tennis.'[325] Acts that are considered 'detrimental' to the game include the gambling activities outlined above.[326] As a result, not only are the specific gambling activities noted by the handbook prohibited, but potentially any gambling activity that would have a detrimental affect on the game. Other United States-based NGBs generally do not regulate or focus on sports gambling by their participants, perhaps as a reflection of the extensive legal regulatory structure under both federal and state law.

B.   International Sports Organizations

1.   International Olympic Committee (IOC)

As the supreme authority on international sports competition, it is not surprising that the IOC would have specific concerns related to sports betting. The Fundamental Principle of Olympism, as articulated in the Olympic Charter, provides that:

> 4. The practice of sport is a human right. Every individual must have the possibility of practicing sport, without discrimination of any kind and in the Olympic spirit, which requires mutual understanding with a spirit of friendship, solidarity and fair play. The organisation, administration and management of sport must be controlled by independent sports organisations.
> 5. Any form of discrimination with regard to a country or a person on grounds of race, religion, politics, gender or otherwise is incompatible with belonging to the Olympic Movement.[327]

---

[322]   USA Cycling, General Regulations ch. I, at 64.
[323]   *Ibid.*
[324]   UNITED STATES TENNIS ASSOCIATION, FRIEND AT COURT: TENNIS RULES & REGULATIONS HANDBOOK 120 (2009 ed.).
[325]   *Ibid.* at 116.
[326]   *Ibid.* (explaining that '[s]uch detrimental acts include, but are not limited to, the acts set for in USTA Regulation IV.C,' which includes the prohibition on gambling activities).
[327]   International Olympic Committee, OLYMPIC CHARTER (2007).

These fundamental notions of anti-discrimination and fair play highlight the IOC's concern for 'dignity' found in its Code of Ethics. Under this principle of 'dignity,' the IOC Code of Ethics provides that, '[a]ll forms of participation in, or support for betting related to the Olympic Games, and all forms of promotion of betting related to the Olympic Games are prohibited.'[328]

In addition, the Common Position of the Olympic and Sports Movement on the Implementation of the Treaty on the Functioning of the European Union (TFEU) on Sport[329] commented on 'gambling and betting' within a section devoted to 'the integrity of sporting competitions.' This statement, noting that gambling can threaten the 'integrity of competitions,' asked European Union institutions to 'pay more attention to the integrity aspects of this issue by taking into account the international dimension of this problem.'[330] The statement then asked the European Union institutions to assist sports bodies directly with important information.[331] Finally, recognizing the international use of gambling proceeds to fund many sports enterprises, the statement sought to ensure that 'the funding of sports federations will not be jeopardised by this new betting and gambling context.'[332] In the end, the IOC recognizes '[t]he fight against illegal and irregular betting as well as corruption induced by betting activities requires common efforts from all stakeholders even at international level.'[333]

2. International federations (IFs)

The following examples disclose different ways in which IFs address sports gambling.

a. Badminton World Federation (BWF). The stated purpose of the Badminton Players' Code of Conduct is to 'ensure and maintain an orderly and fair administration and conduct for [BWF]-sanctioned tournaments, and to protect players' rights and the respective rights of the BWF, sponsors, and the public' and 'to uphold the good name of the BWF and the integrity of the sport of Badminton world-wide.'[334] In accordance with this general purpose, the Players' Code of Conduct specifically prohibits wagering. This includes 'wagering anything of value in connection with an [sic] tournament in which one will be, or is, competing.'[335]

---

[328]   *Ibid.* Code of Ethics 1 (2007).
[329]   International Olympic Committee, Common Position of the Olympic and Sports Movement on the Implementation of the New Treaty on the Functioning of the European Union (TFEU) on Sport, Jan. 2010.
[330]   *Ibid.* at 5.
[331]   *Ibid.* Accordingly, sports bodies are to be consulted:

… on the type of bet and subjects of betting that are possible to be made on their events in order to preserve the integrity of sport. This is also to ensure that gambling and betting operators, without any distinction (physical or on-line betting operators), provide sufficient and appropriate guarantees to safeguard the integrity of sports competitions and the protection of the sports organisations' property rights as well as intellectual property rights.

[332]   *Ibid.* at 6.
[333]   *Ibid.* at 8.
[334]   BADMINTON WORLD FEDERATION, LAWS OF BADMINTON AND REGULATIONS 120 (2010/2011) (citing sections 1.1 and 1.2).
[335]   *Ibid.* at 123.

Wagering is not only prohibited by the code; it is one of only three offenses that the code lists as a 'major offence.'[336] The other two are 'conduct contrary to the integrity of the game,' which includes criminal law violations, and 'bribes or other payments,' which prohibits a variety of activities that would 'influence any player's efforts or the result of a match in any BWF-sanctioned tournament.'[337] In effect, the BWF considers wagering or sports gambling to be as serious an offense as a criminal conviction that would result in a prison sentence.

b.　Fédération Internationale de Football Association (FIFA).　The latest version of FIFA's Code of Ethics[338] binds any official (defined as anyone responsible for the 'technical, medical and administrative matters in FIFA,' and including coaches, referees, and trainers). All officials:

> … are forbidden from taking part, either directly or indirectly, in betting, gambling, lotteries and similar events or transactions connected with football matches. They are forbidden from having stakes, either actively or passively, in companies, concerns, organisations, etc. that promote, broker, arrange or conduct such events or transactions.[339]

This prohibition is then enforced within FIFA's Disciplinary Code. Section 6 on 'Corruption' sets forth disciplinary measures applicable to both players and officials who bet on matches.[340]

c.　International Cricket Council (ICC).　As we have seen,[341] the ICC has attempted to combat gambling and its impact on the integrity of cricket matches. Its Anti-Corruption and Security Unit (ACSU) focuses on three objectives: investigation, education, and prevention.[342] The ICC's Anti-Corruption Code for Players and Players Support Personnel[343] makes clear that it is 'committed to taking every step in its power to prevent corrupt

---

[336]　*Ibid.*
[337]　*Ibid.*
[338]　Fédération Internationale de Football Association, Code of Ethics (2009).
[339]　*Ibid.* ¶13, at 9.
[340]　FIFA Disciplinary Code, Art. 62, at 35–6 (2009):

> 1. Anyone who offers, promises or grants an unjustified advantage to a body of FIFA, a match official, a player or an official on behalf of himself or a third party in an attempt to incite it or him to violate the regulations of FIFA will be sanctioned:
>
> a) with a fine of at least CHF 10,000,
> b) with a ban on taking part in any football-related activity, and
> c) with a ban on entering any stadium.
>
> 2. Passive corruption (soliciting, being promised or accepting an unjustified advantage) will be sanctioned in the same manner.
>
> 3. In serious cases and in the case of repetition, sanction 1b) may be pronounced for life.
>
> 4. In any case, the body will order the confiscation of the assets involved in committing the infringement. These assets will be used for football development programmes.

[341]　See, text at notes 59–74 *supra*.
[342]　See International Cricket Council, Anti-Corruption Overview (2010).
[343]　*Ibid.*

betting practices undermining the integrity of the sport of cricket, including any efforts to influence improperly the outcome or any other aspect of an International Match or ICC Event.'[344] Under this code, betting is a specific offense.[345]

The ICC Anti-Corruption Code also prohibits players and support personnel from using inside information for betting purposes[346] or attempting to bet or assisting a coach, trainer, manager, agent, or others in betting and thereby violating the code.[347] The sanctions for a betting offense of this type start at a 2-year period of ineligibility and can extend to a maximum of 5 years of ineligibility.[348] In addition, the Anti-Corruption Tribunal can impose a fine on a player or support personnel 'up to a maximum of the value of any Reward received ... out of, or in relation to, the offence committed ...'[349]

The ICC supplements this code by banning the use of any 'betting logo' on clothing and equipment used in cricket. A 'betting logo' is defined as 'a Logo which is either perceived, or likely to be perceived, by spectators and viewers, as being associated or connected in some way with betting, gaming or gambling of any kind.'[350] A breach of the regulations related to clothing and equipment may result in a fine.[351]

C.   European Union

1.   Treaties

Many specifically European bodies have put forth statements or regulations regarding gambling in sport. The Treaty on the Functioning of the European Union (the Lisbon Treaty) provides that the Union itself should be competent to 'support, coordinate or supplement the actions of the Member States,' in regard to several activities, including 'education, vocational training, youth and sport.'[352] Accordingly, Article 165 of the

---

[344]   International Cricket Council, ICC Anti-Corruption Code for Players and Players Support Personnel, art. 1.1.5, at 360 (2010).
[345]   'Betting' is defined as follows:

> 2.2.1 Placing, accepting, laying or otherwise entering into any Bet with any other party (whether individual, company or otherwise) in relation to the result, progress, conduct or any other aspect of any International Match or ICC Event.
>
> 2.2.2 Soliciting, inducing, enticing, instructing, persuading, encouraging, facilitating or authorising any other party to enter into a Bet for the direct or indirect benefit of the Player or Player Support Personnel in relation to the result, progress, conduct or any other aspect of any International Match or ICC Event.
>
> 2.2.3 Ensuring the occurrence of a particular incident in an International Match or ICC Event, which occurrence is to the Player or Player Support Personnel's knowledge the subject of a Bet and for which he/she expects to receive or has received any Reward.

Ibid. art. 2.2, at 363.
[346]   *Ibid.* art. 2.3, at 364.
[347]   *Ibid.* art. 2.5, at 365.
[348]   *Ibid.* art. 6.2, at 377.
[349]   *Ibid.*
[350]   International Cricket Council, Clothing and Equipment Rules and Regulations, at 403 (2010).
[351]   *Ibid.* at 417.
[352]   Consolidated Version of the Treaty on the Functioning of the European Union, OFF. J. EUR. UNION, C 115/47, art. 5.

Lisbon Treaty provides that the EU 'shall contribute to the promotion of European sporting issues, while taking account of the specific nature of sport, its structures based on voluntary activity and its social and educational function.'[353] The European Union is to take actions aimed at 'developing the European dimension in sport, by promoting fairness and openness in sporting competitions and cooperation between bodies responsible for sports, and by protecting the physical and moral integrity of sportsmen and sportswomen, especially the youngest sportsmen and sportswomen.'[354] Also, Article 43 of the EC Treaty[355] applies to gambling 'in the event that restrictions are imposed on the activities of a company pursuing gaming activities established or wishing to establish in one Member State.'[356] In addition, the European Court of Justice has interpreted Article 49 of the same treaty, which relates to the 'freedom to provide and receive services,' in terms of 'remuneration [involving] activities of an economic nature.' [357] Services therefore cover such activities as lotteries, sport betting, and gaming, including the cross-border provision of such services via telephone.[358] The European Court of Justice has found that gambling activities fall within the scope of this article as economic activities because these activities involve the provision of a particular service for remuneration and the intention by the parties to make a profit.[359]

2.   European Parliament (EP)

Initially, in 2008, the EP adopted a resolution welcoming the European Commission's White Paper on Sport.[360] The EP initially recognized that sport is 'confronted with new threats and challenges,' including 'match fixing, corruption, betting fraud and money laundering.'[361] In addition, it noted that 'sports betting activities have developed in an uncontrolled manner ... a growing number of matches have been fixed and ... betting-related scandals have recently come to light in Member States, threatening the integrity of sport and sporting competitions.'[362] Regardless, after acknowledging this threat, the EP recognized that sports organizations in Europe 'consider the contribution made to the financing of non-professional sport by state-run lotteries and licensed gambling bodies operating in the general interest as indispensable.'[363] The EP then called upon Member States and the European Commission to address problems related to sports betting by adopting regulatory measures that will ensure that sport is protected from any improper influence related to betting.[364] Specifically, it asked that these bodies create a 'workable,

---

[353]   *Ibid.* art. 165.

[354]   *Ibid.*

[355]   Consolidated Version of the Treaty Establishing the European Community [hereinafter EC Treaty], Art. 43.

[356]   STUDY, note 42 *supra*, at 970.

[357]   The European Court of Justice's Rulings on the Definition of Educational Services, May 4, 2006.

[358]   Anastasios Kaburakis, ECJ Jurisprudence and Recent Developments In EU Sport Betting, Saint Louis University – John Cook School of Business Working Paper (2009).

[359]   STUDY, note 42 *supra*, at 969.

[360]   Resolution of 8 May 2008 on the White Paper of Sport, EUR. PARL. Doc. 2007/2261 (INI).

[361]   *Ibid.* ¶C.

[362]   *Ibid.* at ¶AC.

[363]   *Ibid.* ¶AB.

[364]   *Ibid.* ¶¶70, 89.

equitable and sustainable framework to ensure that all sports in the European Union remain free from illegal betting practices and that public confidence in their integrity is retained.'[365]

Another EP resolution related to gambling and sport focused on online gambling.[366] This resolution recognized that the revenues which EU Member States realize from gambling are 'by far the most important source of income for sports organizations in many Member States.'[367] However, this resolution also recognized that the dangers associated with match-fixing and other problems associated with sports betting are particularly problematic online. The EP then acknowledges that each Member State has an 'interest and right to regulate and control their gambling markets ... in order to protect consumers against addiction, fraud, money-laundering and match-fixing in sports.'[368] The resolution then devoted an entire section to 'tackling fraud and other forms of criminal behavior,' noting that in order to protect the integrity of sporting events from the dangers associated with online gambling, several stakeholders – athletes, coaches, referees, online betting operators, and public authorities – must work together.[369] The resolution went further by advocating the creation of new form of intellectual property right that could be given to competition organizers to protect their right in the competition itself.[370]

3. European Court of Justice (ECJ)

The ECJ's primary function is to decide cases on the basis of European Union law and to resolve disputes between the organization's institutions.[371] The court typically hears cases involving 'failure of a member state or EU body to fulfill its treaty obligations, judicial review of laws passed by EU bodies and preliminary rulings on cases handed up by national courts.'[372]

Before the ECJ dealt with sports betting cases, it decided a few cases that played a crucial role in the its subsequent decisions relating to sports betting.[373] Two of these cases set the standard for the way the court would interpret the term 'services' within the scope of the freedom of provision of services. In the *Schindler* case,[374] which was briefly noted earlier in this chapter,[375] the Schindlers were independent agents for a German lottery. They issued advertisements and applications for it, urging individuals to participate. Arguably, this activity should not be considered an economic activity within the meaning of the EC Treaty because participation was purely for entertainment purposes. The court rejected this view, concluding that the lottery activity fell within the scope of the treaty's

---

365   *Ibid.* ¶90.
366   Resolution of 10 March 2009 on the Integrity of Online Gambling, Eur. Parl. Doc. 2008/2215 (INI).
367   *Ibid.* ¶B.
368   *Ibid.* ¶1.
369   *Ibid.* ¶8.
370   *Ibid.* ¶10.
371   European Court of Justice (ECJ), Britannica Encyclopedia (2010).
372   European Court of Justice, Civitas EU Facts (2010).
373   See Marios Papaloukas, Sports Betting and European Law, 2010(1/2) Int'l Sports L.J. 86 (2010).
374   *Her Majesty's Customs and Excise* v. *Schindler*, Case C-275/92, 1994 E.C.R. I-1039.
375   See text at notes 216–18 *supra*.

protection of freedom to provide services.[376] The court reasoned that even though participants were not promised any money as in a normal economic transaction, the activity still had economic purposes. The court noted that the nature of entertainment is not determinative.

In the *Laara* case,[377] Finnish legislation allowed one licensed public body to operate slot machines and other gaming services, for 'the carrying-on of casino activities, with a view to the collection of funds for various public interest initiatives.'[378] The court found that, 'the Treaty provisions relating to freedom to provide services do not preclude national legislation such as the Finnish legislation which grants to a single public body exclusive rights to operate slot machines, in view of the public interest objectives which justify it.'[379] Such public interests that could justify a monopoly on these services include 'preventing the risk of fraud or crime … and using the resulting profits for public interest purposes.'[380]

In *Zenatti*,[381] the court found that restrictions to protect consumers from deception or a scam as well as social policies would not constitute a monopoly in violation of European Union law. The court noted, however, that the country's national court must have ruled that the restrictions were created because foreign gambling companies were not doing a good job protecting of consumers from fraud.[382] After *Schlinder* and *Zenatti*,[383] the pertinent cases have included *Anomar* (2003),[384] *Gambelli* (2003),[385] *Lindman* (2003),[386] and *Palcanica, Palazzese, and Sorricchio* (2007).[387] In *Gambelli*,[388] the ECJ examined the principle of proportionality, which it had done in numerous non-gambling cases in the past. The principle of proportionality must be taken into consideration before setting the restrictions on freedom to provide services and freedom of establishment. The ECJ found that restrictions on gambling by a Member State 'must be justified by imperative requirements in the general interest, be suitable for achieving the objective which they pursue and not go beyond what is necessary in order to attain it … [and] [t]hey must … be applied without discrimination.'[389]

Generally, the ECJ has accepted three reasons that can justify restriction of gambling and its control by the state: moral, religious, or cultural implications when gambling is simply a source of private profit, the increased rate of crime and fraud because of the size

---

[376]   1994 E.C.R. I-1039, at ¶27.
[377]   *Markku Juhani Laara, Cotswold Microsytems Ltd, Oy Transatlantic Software Ltd, and Kihlakunnansyytaja (Jyvaskylaw), Suomen Valtio (Finnish State)*, Case C-124/97, 1999 E.C.R. I-06067.
[378]   *Ibid.*
[379]   *Ibid.* ¶4.
[380]   *Ibid.* ¶37.
[381]   *Questore di Verona* v. *Diego Zenatti*, Case C-67/98, 1999 I-07289. See text at notes 216–20, 374–6, 381–2 *supra*.
[382]   *Ibid.* ¶¶35–8.
[383]   See text at notes 216–20, 374–6, 381–2 *supra*.
[384]   *Associacão Nacional de Operadores de Maquinas Recreativas (Anomar) and Others* v. *Estado portugues*, Case C-6/01, 2003/02/11.
[385]   Case C-243/01, 2003 E.C.R. I-13031.
[386]   *Diana Elisabeth Lindman* v. *Skatterattelsenamnde*, Case C-42/02, 2003/04/10.
[387]   *Criminal proceedings against Massimiliano Placanica* (Case C-338/04), *Christian Palazzese* (Case C-359/04), *Angelo Sorricchio* (Case C-360/04) (Joined Cases).
[388]   Case C-243/01, 2003 E.C.R. I-13031.
[389]   *Ibid.* ¶65.

of money at stake, and the damaging effects of individual and social consequences.[390] In a consolidated set of cases that considered such restrictions, the ECJ ruled that they were a breach of European Union law.[391] As in *Gambelli*, the court confirmed that a monopoly on gambling is only acceptable if the monopoly extends to all forms of gambling.[392] The ECJ therefore decided that a controverted monopolization of online gambling by the German government did not aim to protect the public interest and instead focused on growing profits,[393] thereby breaching European Union law.[394]

With specific reference to *Gambelli*, the ECJ has consistently applied the proportionality principle in betting cases. To return to an initial observation, the only exceptions have been where a Member State has imposed restrictions in order to combat illegal matters, when it has dealt with moral or religious issues, or when it has sought to prevent social or individual damaging consequences.

D. Council of Europe

The Council of Europe's Code of Sports Ethics and European Sports Charter establishes a framework for fair play and integrity in sport competition. In 2007, the Council established the Enlarged Partial Agreement on Sport (EPAS), 'in order to give fresh momentum to pan-European sports co-operation and address the current challenges facing sport in Europe.'[395] Currently, 33 countries are parties to the EPAS and seven sports organizations are non-governmental partners. In a resolution entitled Ethics in Sport, the Council of Europe recognized 'the problem of corruption, match fixing and illegal betting in sport' and invited the EPAS and other organizations to 'promote best practices to tackle the challenges to sports ethics posed notably by match fixing, corruption, illegal betting' and to draw up a new resolution related to these challenges.'[396]

E. The Court of Arbitration for Sport (CAS)

As the leading tribunal for resolving international sports disputes, CAS has decided several disputes related to sports gambling. In one decision, CAS relied on the conclusion of sports authorities that wagering by professional athletes in their own sport is likely to harm the legitimacy of the sport and enable individuals to exploit athletes who are involving in betting.[397] Tennis has generated a disproportionate number of cases, quite likely because the individual nature of the sport makes it possible for a single corrupt player to fix a match's outcome.[398]

---

[390]   See Papaloukas, note 373 *supra*.

[391]   Joined Cases C-316/07, C-358/07 to C-360/07, C-409/07 and C-410/07.

[392]   Michael F., German Court Ruling Causes Gambling Law Confusion, GAMINGZION.COM (2010).

[393]   European Court of Justice, Rules Against German Online Gambling Laws (2010).

[394]   *Ibid.*

[395]   Enlarged Partial Agreement on Sport (EPAS), Fact Sheet, EPAS (2010) 10, Feb. 2010.

[396]   Council of Europe, Eleventh Conference of Ministers Responsible for Sport, Resolution 1, reprinted in ETHICS IN SPORT, Dec. 10–12, 2008, at 2.

[397]   *Montcourt* v. *Association of Tennis Professionals*, CAS 2008/A/1630.

[398]   *Ibid.*

When considering whether to reduce a sanction for gambling on sports, CAS takes into consideration factors such as a misunderstanding by the athlete, the organization's failure to communicate the rules to players and make sure players comprehend the rules, the organization's inconsistencies, an athlete's lack of intent, an athlete's admission of the offense, an athlete's cooperation, and a finding that the gambling activity was the athlete's first such offense. In the two examples that follow, the court examined these mitigating factors to determine whether the penalty imposed was appropriate.

In *M.* v. *Association of Tennis Professionals Tour, Inc.*,[399] a professional tennis player obtained an online account with an online betting organization. He claimed that he never placed bets on any of the tennis matches in which he had competed, but he did admit to online betting on other tennis matches. He claimed, however, that he had not realized that there was a rule against this type of betting. After learning of his actions, the Association of Tennis Professionals (ATP), which certifies tennis tournaments and provides govern-ance and support to the tournaments and team members, charged him with an offense. The ATP's anti-corruption hearing officer (AHO) found that the appellant had violated the ATP's Tennis Anti-Corruption Program, specifically a provision[400] pledging 'to maintain the integrity of tennis and to protect against any efforts to impact improperly the rules of a match.'[401] This provision specifically states that, '[n]o Player nor any of his Player Support Personnel shall, directly or indirectly, wager or attempt to wager money or anything else of value to enter into any form of financial speculation on the outcome of any other aspect of any event.'[402] The AHO imposed a penalty of 9 months' ineligibility from tennis and a $60 000 fine on the player. CAS disagreed with the severity of the AHO's punishment, however. According to CAS, the penalty handed to the appellant did not justify the estimated 2-year time period for the player to work his way back through the rankings. CAS also factored in the player's age and noted that he had been grossly negligent rather than acting with intent. CAS therefore deducted 2 months from the overall sentence and reduced the fine to $20 000.[403]

In a similar case, *Montcourt* v. *Association of Tennis Professionals*,[404] another tennis player had wagered on several tennis events through an online betting organization. After receiving notice from the ATP, he admitted to gambling on a few occasions, but he explained that he had not been aware of the 2005 Rules that prohibited gambling, was not aware of the consequences for his actions, and had stopped wagering as soon as he discovered the rules pertaining to wagering.[405] Regardless, the ATP recommended a suspension of 10 weeks and a fine of $15 000. The tennis AHO challenged the decision, reducing the penalty to 8 weeks of ineligibility for any ATP event and a fine of $12 000.[406] On review, CAS concluded that the player had committed the infractions and should be

---

[399]   *M.* v. *Association of Tennis Professionals*, CAS 2007/A/1427.
[400]   See Association of Tennis Professionals, Tennis Anti-Corruption Program, Rule 7.05 C.1.a. AHO (2010).
[401]   *Ibid.*
[402]   *Ibid.*
[403]   *Ibid.*
[404]   *Montcourt* v. *Association of Tennis Professionals*, CAS 2008/A/1630.
[405]   *Ibid.* at 2–3.
[406]   *Ibid.* at 3.

held responsible for his action[407] but determined that he had been ready to have the case heard at an earlier time. It was thus arbitrary to deprive the player of the possibly of participating in a major competition because of something that had been out of his control.[408] The tribunal therefore partially upheld the AHO's decision, ruling that the player's ineligibility period should be reduced to 5 weeks, but the fine of $12 000 should remain.[409]

V. CONCLUSION

In the end, national and state governments, international sports organizations, and local sports organizations are all instrumental in regulating the global problem of sports gambling. Athletes and other stakeholders in sports are therefore subject to numerous sanctions under country-specific laws as well as participation rules or codes of sports bodies. But the extent of the gambling problem, unfortunately, is endless.

---

[407] *Ibid.* at 8.
[408] *Ibid.* at 9–10.
[409] *Ibid.*

8 Adjudicative technology in sports

Simon Gardiner

INTRODUCTION

Judges, on the one hand, and sports umpires and referees, on the other, share many similarities. They all hold positions of power and responsibility in the adjudicative roles that they perform. They are applying both specific written laws and rules and more abstract principles. Their rulings are 'interpretations' of how the laws/rules should be applied to a determined factual situation. They also both assume something of a solitary and detached role; their function is to be one of objectivity. Within liberal democracies, both for the legal judge and the sporting umpire or referee, the 'rule of law' and all of its inherent values is an overriding guide to their deliberation: there should be a lack of bias, everyone is equal in the eyes of the laws/rules and participants must accept the rules and norms of conduct. However, it is unclear to what extent those subject to adjudication should also have *some* recourse. This is where perhaps some distinctions can be drawn. Rights of appeal in the law are not an absolute right but a privilege: there is finality in what circumstances legal decisions can be reviewed.

In sport, there is a powerful discourse that, contrary to any specific provisions in sporting rules, the decisions of officials are absolute and decisive. For example, in cricket, the traditionally white-coated umpire is constructed as the 'man in white is always right' (even when he gets a decision wrong). Within the preamble to the Laws of Cricket, it is stated that is against the Spirit of the Game, 'to dispute an umpire's decision by word, action or gesture'.[1]

Modern sport is witnessing a reformation with an ever-increasing quest for certainty. This can be observed amongst other things in the playing rules and location of sporting activity, the endorsement for fairness of sporting endeavour and in verification of on-field decisions. The common theme in these issues is the role of technology in facilitating this search for certainty. This chapter will provide the context of this increased standardization of sporting activity and specifically question the tension between sporting and legal adjudication and the use of new technology such as video replays particularly in determining, verifying and in some instances replacing on-field decisions by sports adjudicative officials (hereafter to be known as 'officials').[2] The role of what could be collectively called the Robo-Ref is to be evaluated.

---

[1] Available at: htttp://www.lords.org/laws-and-spirit/laws-of-cricket/ (accessed 15 May 2009).

[2] Common terms are referees and umpires – these terms will be used together with term 'officials'.

STANDARDISATION OF SPORTS PLAY

The last two decades have seen an increasing conformity among the playing rules of various sports. This has been identified by sports academics including sports sociologists such as Norbert Elias who identify a 'civilizing trend' within sport from past unruly and unstructured folk games to the codification of organized sports with the formalisation of playing rules.[3] Elias presents an historical view of sport as having increasingly become codified, regulated and a part of civil society.[4] He uses the term 'sportisation' to refer to a process in the course of which the framework of rules applying to sport becomes stricter, including those rules attempting to provide for fairness and equal chances to win for all. The rules become more precise and explicitly differentiated, and the supervision of rule-observance becomes more efficient. This perspective is analogous to the project of legal positivism within twentieth century Anglo-American jurisprudence with the reification of the legal rule.

A major issue is to what extent and frequency the rules of games should be modified. One argument is that changes are merely tinkering and are often carried out with the aim of short-term expediency. This is often to placate external pressures such as sponsors and television, for example, the introduction of the back-pass rule in soccer to speed the game up; or to curb the excellence of particular participants, for example, the changes in the rules of Formula One motor racing largely to curb the past dominance of Michael Schumacher and the Ferrari team. Rules certainly do have an elasticity, and, together with the players 'playing culture', are only part of the regulation of the sport. Without this acknowledgment and the ability to modify rules, sport is subject to unwanted predictability and ossification. But in most sports, rule changes have significantly accelerated in the last 30 years. Increasing external pressures may well be the cause. Too many changes can be counterproductive and damage the balance of particular sports. Some sports such as rugby and North American Football have numerous and complex rules. Others such as soccer have a simplicity that is derived from a small number of rules. Coherent rule changes are made for these reasons: to promote safety, assist the fluidity of the game and allow the skilful to shine. Some are not fundamental changes in the rules but different interpretations of existing ones. There is, however, a danger that rule changes in sport are aimed at developing increasingly sanitized and commodified games for mass global consumption.

This mission for certainty has also manifested itself in standardisation of the playing environment. Sports geographers have identified that new rules or laws of the game have produced an increasingly uniform activity in terms of locale through the development of rules governing play and the increasingly standardised spatial dimensions of play. For

---

3   See Elias, Norbert (1939), *The Civilising Process* Oxford, Blackwell; and Dunning, Eric (1999) *Sport Matters: Sociological Studies of Sport, Violence and Civilisation*, London, Routledge. Also see Agozino, B. (1996), 'Football and the Civilizing Process: Penal Discourse and the Ethic of Collective Responsibility in Sports Law' 24 *International Journal of the Sociology of Law* 163–88. This theoretical paradigm is known as Figurational theory.

4   For example, in Britain, rule structures and elite governing bodies began to emerge in the 1860s and 1870s: the Football Association in 1863, the Amateur Athletic Club in 1865, boxing's Queensbury Rules in 1867, the Rugby Union in 1871 and the Wimbledon Lawn Tennis Tournament in 1877.

example, football pitches need to be within certain size limits, international boxing rings need to meet a number of criteria on surface and size and environmental factors such as wind velocity need to be inside certain parameters to protect the validity of international records in athletics. Certain sports facilities are increasingly regulating environmental factors, for example, the Sky Dome in Toronto, one of the first stadiums to have a retractable roof. The term 'placelessness' describes this process of increasing standardisation of the places where sport is played: 'the modern sports landscape can be described as tending towards placelessness in its geographical sense of places looking and feeling alike with "dictated and standardized values".'[5]

Finally it is worth noting that although fairness of sporting activity has been an inherent value within the history of organized sport, promoted by values such as the requirement of a 'level-playing field' and the 'uncertainty of outcome', the modern era in sport has seen a fixation with mechanisms in response to activities that seem to contradict these values. The creation of the World Anti-Doping Agency (WADA) is an example of this, central to the stated 'war on drugs in sport'. More problematic is the regulation of developments such as improved playing equipment and sportswear that provide a competitive advantage using sports equipment, so-called technological doping.[6]

THE JURIDIFICATION OF SPORT

The quest for certainty in sport has been augmented with the emergence of law as a major agent of sports regulation. Compliance with legal norms provides a context of certainty through the process of juridification. What are intrinsically social relationships between humans within a 'social field' become imbued with legal values and are understood as constituting legal relationships. Thus social norms become legal norms.[7] If a dispute then befalls the parties, a legal remedy is seen as the primary remedy. This invariably changes the nature and perception of the dispute and the relationship between the parties.[8]

Not only is compliance with general legal rule important, but also the law's role within the context of regulatory regimes, such as in Europe as the European Community increasingly engages with sport. It can be strongly argued that law is best understood in contemporary society, not in the classic formulation of Anglo-American jurisprudence as a collection or model of rules but as a form of 'governance' or regulation. And as has been already illustrated, sport has increasingly attempted to re-appropriate self-regulation through initiatives such as WADA and the engagement of drugs in sport as well as the

  [5]   Bale, John (1994), *Landscapes of Modern Sport,* Leicester, Leicester University Press, p. 94.
  [6]   See, for example, Heshka, J. and Lines, K. (2008), 'Swimming – Credibility Crisis or Tempest in a Teapot?' 16(3) *Sport & Law Journal* 15.
  [7]   See Bourdieu, Pierre (1987), 'The Force of Law: Towards a Sociology of the Juridical Field' 38 *Hastings Law Rev.* 814.
  [8]   Foster, K. (1993), 'Developments in Sporting Law' in Alison, L. (ed.) *The Changing Politics of Sport*, Manchester, Manchester University Press, p. 108. For juridification in other social fields, see Flood, J. and Caiger, A. (1993), 'Lawyers and Arbitration: The Juridification of Construction Disputes' 56(3) *Modern Law Rev.* 412 and Gardiner, S., James, M., O'Leary, J., *et al.* (2006), *Sports Law,* London, Routledge Cavendish, p. 84.

Court of Arbitration for Sport.[9] In sport as in society generally, it can be argued that there is a diversity of legal and quasi-legal phenomena. 'Law exists as an increasingly detailed and particularistic regulation of ever more specific situations and relations in which any boundary between law and non-law is difficult if not impossible to identify.'[10]

In sport there has been a diversification and pluralisation of law and regulation and an identified 'turf war' as to competing forms of governance. Together with the complexity of both organisational and playing rules, the emergence of a plethora of codes of ethics and conduct and the complex playing cultures surrounding specific sports, this overarching legal and quasi-legal governance provides a complex normative rule milieu.

EMERGENCE OF THE ROBO-REF

Within this rule-bound world of modern sport, there is also a complex interaction between the playing rules and the adjudicative officials that enforce them. It is a highly dynamic interface, where at particular points in time, governing bodies instruct referees or umpires to enforce the rules more or less strictly. This can lead to disquiet from players censored for rule infringements and fouls during the game. Match statistics may indicate a fall or increase in foul play but it is unlikely to be primarily about changes in the style of play, becoming more violent, for example. It is as much about official attitudes towards policing of actual and potential perpetrators during the game.

Increasingly, the human vulnerability of officials is being questioned. A number of sports are using various forms of technology to aid officials in coming to decisions. In sports such as horse racing and athletics, cameras have been used for many years in determining who has crossed the finish line in 'dead heats'. In tennis, line decisions have been determined electronically for some time. The use of video cameras as an aid to the officials on the field of play or as a guide to a 'third umpire' as the final arbiter have been used in sports such as cricket and rugby league in the United Kingdom for some years. In the United States, their use has been more recent. In a range of sports, officials are wired up, with the ability to communicate with colleagues both on and off the field. We are witnessing the emergence of the 'Robo-Ref' and an increasingly technological determination of decisions.[11] Table 8.1 at the end of the chapter presents the current position in a number of team sports, although on a sport-to-sport basis, the use of technology is subject to change and modification.[12]

Views differ on the efficacy of adjudicative technology. Supporters of the use of technology argue that within the business of professional sport, there is now such a thin line between success and failure involving huge sums of money and heartache that we

---

[9]   This has been conceptualized as the emergence of a 'global sports law' and as such a continued mechanism of self-regulation of a number of issues including doping within the domain of sport, see Foster, K. (2003), 'Is There a Global Sports Law?' 2(1) *Entertainment and Sports Law Journal* 1.

[10]   Hunt, Alan (1993), *Explorations in Law and Society: Towards a Constitutive Theory of Law*, London, Routledge, chapter 13, 'Law as a Constitutive Mode of Regulation', p. 307.

[11]   'The Robo Ref: High-tech officiating is ready to rule, but can we handle the call?', available at: http://sports.espn.go.com/espnmag/story?section=magazine&id=3633879 (accessed 15 May 2009).

[12]   See Table 8.1. This is clearly not an exhaustive list but provides information on the use of adjudicative technology in a number of team sports.

have to accept a more contemporary and formal approach. If the technology is available it should be used. For example, it is accepted in professional tennis that technology adjudicating on-line decisions is essential. This is predicated on the basis that the balls are hit so hard and fast that it is impossible for line judges to be exact in their determination. Human error needs to be minimised as much as possible when a wrong decision may have an enormous financial cost. The argument is that technology such as video replays provides 'objective truth' within the image. 'Technology allows umpires, referees and other officials to apply the law to the "facts", as objective reality, law and justice become one.'[13]

Detractors argue that video replays and other technologies are themselves only just another representation of what actually happened, to be interpreted not alone but along with all the other evidence. Additionally, there is a view that the officials' authority runs the risk of being undermined. Also, it is argued that the greater use of technology has contributed to lower ethical norms in sport whereas formerly, often the word of a player would be taken primarily in constructing the truth. A more abstract but significant view is that technology makes a game too clinical; human error is part of sport and as with players, umpires and referees should be allowed to make mistakes. As Alexander Pope exclaimed, 'to err is to be human'. Video technology mistakenly provides a belief 'that certainty now reigns in cricket [sports] adjudication ... [and] is based in the epistemological error that insists that television (the image) is truth'.[14]

This reification for the human element in adjudication is often repeated, especially in those sports such as soccer, where such technology has been resisted, where determination of whether the ball has crossed the goal line to award a goal continues to be in the domain of the referee and his assistants on the touchline. Indeed, this type of incident can illustrate the argument that attempts to perfect such decisions will leave sport poorer. If you are an England soccer fan, there are a number of disputed goals indelibly fixed in the memory. The issue of whether Geoff Hurst's winning goal for England in the 1966 International Federation of Football Associations (FIFA) World Cup Final against West Germany did cross the goal line has been long discussed. More painful is the 'Hand of God' and the scoring of a goal by Diego Maradona which should have been disallowed for handball in the quarter final of the World Cup in Mexico in 1986. And of course the disallowed goal for England in the match against Germany at the 2010 World Cup when the ball had clearly crossed the line is yet another example. Also Ireland fans have their own grievance concerning the handball incident of Thierry Henri in the lead up to the goal that contributed to the victory of France over Ireland in the World Cup play-off match in 2009. This view is that such controversies make sport richer.

FIFA has deliberated for many years over the use of goal-line technology involving a chip in the ball. An experiment took place in 2004, where the referee received a visual signal on his watch when the ball containing a microchip crossed the goal line in the Club World Cup. However, in March 2008 the International Football Association Board, the FIFA body which oversees rule changes, decided to halt evaluation of those uses of technology in the context of 'the questions of the human aspect of the game, the universality of the Laws of the Game, as well as the simplicity and efficiency of the

---

13   Fraser, David (2005), *Cricket and the Law* London, Frank Cass, p. 113.
14   *Ibid.* p. 121.

technology'.[15] After the goal line incident at the 2010 World Cup discussed above, pressure is on FIFA again to reconsider its position.

ADJUDICATIVE TECHNOLOGY IN SPORT EXPLAINED

In those sports that have adopted technology to various degrees, an ongoing concern is how disruptive such adjudication is to the dynamics of the play, especially when an off-field official evaluates an on-field incident or decision. The use of the electronic system called 'Hawk-Eye' in international cricket and tennis is instructive. The Hawk-Eye system of cameras and computer provides predictions of the flight and movement of the ball. The system is based on the principles of triangulation using the visual images and timing data provided by at least four high-speed video cameras located at different locations and angles around the area of play. The system rapidly processes the video feeds by a high-speed video processor and ball tracker. A data store contains a predefined model of the playing area and includes data on the rules of the game. In each frame sent from each camera, the system identifies the group of pixels which corresponds to the image of the ball. It then calculates for each frame the 3D position of the ball by comparing its position on at least two of the physically separate cameras at the same instant in time. A succession of frames builds up a record of the path along which the ball has travelled. It can also predict, using the laws of physics, the future flight path of the ball and where it will interact with any of the playing area features already programmed into the database. The system can be used to interpret these interactions to decide infringements of the rules of the game. In such circumstances, the system generates a graphic image of the ball path and playing area, which means that information can be provided to adjudicative officials, television viewers or coaching staff in near real time. Additionally, the pure tracking system is combined with a database and archiving capabilities so that it is possible to extract and analyse trends and statistics about individual players, games or ball-to-ball comparisons.

The technology was first used by the UK broadcaster, Channel 4, in an international cricket Test Match in 2001. Today, the majority of television networks use it to track the trajectory of balls in flight, for example, for 'leg before wickets' (LBW), one form of dismissal of the batsman. The likely path of the ball can be projected forward, through the batsman's legs, to see if it would have hit the wicket. However, this information has for a significant period only been visible to television viewers to add value to the action.[16] In 2004, the International Cricket Council, the world governing body, introduced a series of trials where the third (video off-field) umpire has been able to use an image of the flight of

---

[15] http://www.fifa.com/aboutfifa/federation/bodies/media/newsid=707751.html (accessed 15 May 2009). In the UEFA Europa League during the 2009–10 season, in addition to the match referee and two assistant referees on the touchline, two extra assistants were placed behind the goal line, with the mission of focusing on incidents taking place in the penalty area, such as fouls or misconduct.

[16] Two other technological aids are used in many international matches: 'Snicko', where a microphone is used to identify the ball hitting the edge of the bat very faintly and being caught behind the wicket and therefore a dismissal, and 'Hot Spot', which is the use of an infra-red camera to show faint contact between bat and ball which will leave a friction-heat mark. Both are only currently used for the enjoyment of TV viewers.

the ball produced by Hawk-Eye produced image of the ball up to the time it hits the batsman's body when a decision has been referred to him from one of the on-field umpires.

The Hawk-Eye technology has also been introduced into international tennis, replacing other electronic technologies such as 'Cyclops' and 'Autoref' for aiding line calls. The Australian Open in 2007 was the first grand slam tournament to use it and there are now common rules that limit the number of challenges that a player using Hawk-Eye to judge can make against an officials' call.[17] However, there are questions as to its role and reliability. For example, at the 2008 Wimbledon final match between Roger Federer and Rafael Nadal, Nadal challenged a shot which was called out. Hawk-Eye 'proved' it otherwise, with the ball just clipping the line by a millimetre. The reversal agitated Federer enough for him to request (unsuccessfully) that the umpire turn off the Hawk-Eye technology for the remainder of the match.[18] The fallibility of technology, however, can be illustrated by another incident at the 2009 BNP Paribas tournament at Indian Wells in a match between Andy Murray and Ivan Ljubicic, in which a Hawk-Eye replay showed the ball bouncing centrally on the line after a 'drop shot' when in fact it had been called out. The ball in fact had been out by some distance, but the spin had caused the ball to bounce a second time on the line; it was this second bounce that Hawk-Eye displayed.[19] The umpire had no power to overrule the Hawk-Eye decision, much to the disquiet of all the participants in the match. Clearly, in this instance the technology produced an erroneous result. This example suggests the danger of identifying technological determinations with 'objective truth'.

A major issue is whether the use of adjudicative technology improves the dynamics of the game and whether it will actually create greater opportunities legally to challenge decisions of officials. How are the interests of sporting justice to be addressed? Will new technology deliver a new type of absolute justice to sporting uncertainties? The reality is that the interstices between laws/rules and justice are complex. As in the law itself, the notion that absoluteness and truth can be exposed is part of a discourse that is fundamentally flawed. Legal theory, from the classical theorists of natural law onwards, the legal positivism of the twentieth century and the contrary views of the realist movement, provides opposing views of being able to provide a 'right answer' in the law. Whether it is in the adjudication of the law generally or of sport specifically, technology can positively assist adjudication, but it cannot by itself reveal truth. The one reality is that the process of adjudication within sport, as within the law, is based on the construction of contingencies in making decisions.

---

17   From March 2008, the International Tennis Federation (ITF), Association of Tennis Professionals (ATP), Women's Tennis Association (WTA), announced a uniform system of rules: three unsuccessful challenges per set, with an additional challenge if the set reaches a tie-break.

18   The Hawk-Eye Innovations website (http://www.hawkeyeinnovations.co.uk/) states that the system has an average error of 3.6 mm (it does not indicate what the maximum error is). The standard size of a tennis ball is reportedly 65–68 mm. This means that there is a 5 per cent error relative to the diameter of the ball. This could throw into doubt the accuracy of such calls as the one mentioned in the Nadal–Federer 2007 Wimbledon final. For the sake of comparison, approximately 5 per cent of the diameter is the fluff on the ball.

19   'Murray gets lucky as HawkEye goes blind', http://www.guardian.co.uk/sport/2009/mar/20/andy-murray-ivan-ljubicic (accessed May 2009).

THE JURISPRUDENCE OF THE ROBO-JUDGE

A useful analogy can be made with the attempts to promote the use of technology in legal adjudication. Legal thinkers have considered the application of computer technologies within the law so as to remove the vagaries of adjudication and the construction of the law based on contingencies. With roots in the American Realist movement, Lee Loevinger developed the theory of Jurimetrics by claiming 'man's progress must be from jurisprudence (which is mere speculation about law) to jurimetrics – which is the scientific investigation of legal problems'.[20] Although Loevinger was at pains to stress that 'science offers us neither ultimate nor certain answers to legal problems',[21] during the 1950s, the invention of a judgment machine or Robo-Judge was mooted. Lasswell predicted: 'when machines are more perfect [*sic*] a bench of judicial robots ... can be constructed.'[22] One scholar speculated on the replacing of human judges by computer technology as follows:

> Would we lose a judge's 'judgment', and how important would such a loss be to our legal system? Surely computers do not make 'judgments' the way humans do, and so we would lose the 'human' aspect of legal judgments. But what specifically do we lose when we lose humanness of judgments? Is human judgment just a euphemism for arbitrariness, discretion, or bias?[23]

Jurimetrics continues as a sub-discipline within jurisprudence in which the debate has shifted from the possibility of a judicial machine to what role 'legal expert systems ... not designed to pass judgment, but to provide legal advice',[24] can play in the legal process. Technology that may ensure a utopian future where the vagaries of judicial behaviouralism and discretion will be eradicated and law sanitized of human error has been viewed as unworkable.

COURTS AND SPORTS ADJUDICATION

National law courts have provided very limited opportunities for individuals to challenge decisions of adjudicative officials for on-field decisions. A major issue has been what legal standing an action might have. Actions in breach of contract, administrative law or in the law of tort are possible alternatives, insofar as analogies can be found in case law concerning other non-sporting matters.[25] Others argue that decisions within sport involving so-called 'game-rules' are 'virtually certain to be held non-reviewable by the courts ... so obvious is the above proposition that one ought not to need authority to support it; it

---

[20] Loevinger, L. (1949), 'Jurimetrics: The Next Step Forward' 33(5) *Minnesota Law Rev.* 455, 483.

[21] Loevinger, L. (1961), 'Jurimetrics: Science and Prediction in the Field of Law' 46(2) *Minnesota Law Rev.* 259.

[22] Lasswell, H. (1955), 'Current Studies of the Decision Process: Automation versus Creativity' 8(3) *The Western Political Quarterly* 398.

[23] D'Amato, A. (1977), 'Can/Should Computers Replace Judges?' 11(5) *Georgia Law Rev.* 1280.

[24] Popple, James (1996), '*A Pragmatic Legal Expert System* Aldershot, Dartmouth (Ashgate), p. 49.

[25] Cornelius, S. (2004), 'Liability of Referees (Match Officials) at Sports Events' [1–2] *International Sports Law Journal* 52.

simply goes without saying'.[26] Arguing that this view is simplistic, one writer states that 'as with all other matters, judicial remedies may be suitable and available in certain cases, yet unsuitable and unavailable in others',[27] and concludes:

> [T]hat the question of whether judicial or other intervention in decisions taken by officials at a sports events is possible, is more complex than a simple 'yes' or 'no' would permit   officials who act reasonably and in good faith, should not have to fear legal action. However, it is equally clear that officials who act in bad faith or in way that is grossly unreasonable, may have to answer to the courts.[28]

In the United Kingdom, although case law has developed in the connected area of referee liability in negligence for injury caused to participants,[29] there are no authorities concerning successful challenges of officials' decisions concerning play. Any arguments along these lines have been given short shrift. In the Australian case of *Sinclair* v. *Cleary*,[30] an action in negligence failed when it was brought by the owner of a horse against a horse racing official on the grounds of the failure to place his horse as winner. The judge held that the plaintiff was contractually bound to accept the official's decision, the official was independent, and no wrongdoing was found on his part. In the US case of *Bain* v. *Gillespie*,[31] a vendor of team apparel brought an action against the umpire in a basketball match for an alleged wrong decision contributing to a victory by the opponent team and consequential loss of business for the vendor. The judge commented: 'Heaven knows what the uncharted morass a court would find itself in if it were to hold that an athletic official subject himself to liability every time he makes a questionable call ... the possibilities are mind boggling.'[32]

This reluctance to intervene into decisions of sports adjudicative officials is also evident within the jurisprudence of the Court of Arbitration for Sport (CAS) where decisions of match officials will not be questioned when they take place within their specific jurisdiction of play. In essence, CAS recognizes subsidiarity as far as match officials are concerned.[33] Cases in this area have generally been heard as appeals during Olympic tournaments when CAS is sitting in its ad hoc jurisdiction.[34] It has been consistently ruled that decisions made on the field of play should not be questioned and this is premised on the understanding that: 'any contract that the player has made in entering the competition

---

[26]   Beloff, M., Kerr, T. and Demetriou, M. (1999), *Sports Law* Oxford, Hart Publishing, p. 107.

[27]   Cornelius, note 25 *supra*, p. 65.

[28]   *Ibid.* p. 61.

[29]   *Smoldon* v. *Nolan and Whitworth* (1997) *Times* December 18 (2007); *Vowles* v. *Evans and the Welsh Rugby Union Ltd* [2003] EWCA Civ. 318.

[30]   *Sinclair* v. *Cleary* (1946) St. R. Qld. 74, discussed in Kelly, G.M. (1987) *Sport and the Law*, Sydney, Law Book Company, p. 183.

[31]   *Bain* v. *Gillespie* 357 N.W. 2d 47 (1984).

[32]   *Ibid.*

[33]   Oschutz, Frank (2006), 'The Arbitrability of Sports Disputes and the Rule of the Game' in Blackshaw, I., Siekmann, R. and Soek, J. *The Court of Arbitration for Sport 1084–2004*, The Hague, Asser Press.

[34]   For a general analysis of this areas see Nafziger, James (2004), *International Sports Law* 2nd ed., New York, Transnational Publishers, pp. 109–18 and Foster, K. (2006), 'Lex Sportiva and Lex Ludica: The Court of Arbitration for Sports Disputes' in Blackshaw, Siekmann and Soek, note 33 *supra*.

is that he or she should have the benefit of honest "field of play" decisions, not necessarily the correct ones.'[35]

In *Mendy* v. *Association Internationale de Boxing Amateur (AIBA)*,[36] CAS ruled that it would not review an allegation that an official had made a wrong ruling, in this case disqualifying a boxer who had hit his opponent 'below the belt'. The tribunal reasoned that it was 'less well placed to decide than the referee in the ring or the ring judges'.[37] CAS further held that:

> [T]raditionally, doctrine and judicial practice have always deemed that game rules, [i.e. technical field of play rules] in the strict sense of the term, should not be subject to the control of judges, based on the idea that 'the game must not be constantly interrupted by appeals to the judge[38] ... [And further] in comparative law the game rule is not shielded from the control of judges, but their power of review is limited to that which is arbitrary or illegal ... [39]

In *Korean Olympic Committee (KOC)* v. *International Skating Union (ISU)*,[40] CAS stated that before it would review a field of play decision, there must be:

> ... evidence, which generally must be direct evidence, of bad faith. If viewed in this light, each of those. CAS accepts that this places a high hurdle that must be cleared by any applicant seeking to review a field of play decision. However, if the hurdle were to be lower, the flood-gates would be opened and any dissatisfied participant would be able to seek the review of a field of play decision.[41]

In this case and others, however, this autonomy of adjudicating officials is clearly not a policy of 'complete abstention' but rather one of 'self-restraint'. Technical rules can be reviewed where there were actions that could be characterized as being ' "arbitrary", a "breach of duty" and "malicious intent" '.[42] Essentially, there needs to be some evidence of preference for, or prejudice against, a particular team or individual and 'decisions are taken in violation of ... social rules or general principles of law'.[43] CAS arbitrators do not review the determinations made on the playing field by judges, referees, umpires or other officials as they are not, 'unlike on-field judges, selected for their expertise in officiating the particular sport' [44]

CAS guidance on the issue of challenging technology-based decisions is instructive. In *Neykova* v. *International Rowing Federation (FISA) & International Olympic Committee*[45] the applicant was a participant in the women's single sculls event final during the Sydney

[35]   *Yang* v. *Hamm* CAS 2004/A/704, 37, award dated 21 October 2004.
[36]   *Mendy* v. *Association Internationale de Boxing Amateur (AIBA)*, CAS Ad Hoc Division, Atlanta, OG 96/006.
[37]   *Ibid.* para. 13.
[38]   *Ibid.* para. 5.
[39]   *Ibid.* para. 11.
[40]   *Korean Olympic Committee (KOC)* v. *International Skating Union (ISU)*, OWG 02/007 award of 23 February 2002.
[41]   *Ibid.* para. 16.
[42]   *Ibid.* para. 17.
[43]   *Mendy*, note 36 *supra*, para. 13.
[44]   *Segura* v. *International Amateur Athletic Federation (IAAF)* CAS OG Sydney 2000/13 Digest Vol.2 p. 680. para. 17.
[45]   *Neykova* v. *International Rowing Federation (FISA) & International Olympic Committee* Arbitration CAS Ad Hoc Division OG Sydney 00/012.

Olympics. Following a photo finish, the first place for the women's single sculls was awarded to Karsten from Belarus (time 7:28.141) and second place to Neykova from Bulgaria, (time 7:28.153) on the basis of evidence produced by the official 'Scan"o"vision' photo finish system using two special Swatch photo finish cameras fixed permanently to the structural steel frame of the finish tower. The Bulgarian Olympic Committee challenged the result based on video evidence provided by television cameras. These cameras were set up in an approximate manner for the television audience and served no official purpose. So the question facing the panel was to what extent video evidence that had been presented as contradicting the official photographic technology might be used to override the stated result.

Essentially, *Neykova* concerned a challenge to the accuracy of the official technical equipment that determined placings in the race. Because the panel found that on this question, the applicant had not proved that the technical equipment was deficient, it dismissed the application. The case had not been based on evidence questioning the reliability of the official photographic equipment, but rather on the basis of images produced by TV cameras primarily positioned to produce pictures for viewers. In fact, expert evidence argued that the TV cameras were:

> ... located 10 centimeters ahead of the finish line. When this 10 centimetre discrepancy is projected across the 200 metre width of the course, it is not surprising that the television camera's perspective is different to that of the Scan'o'vision photo finish. This was therefore 'different to that of a typical official's field of play decision'.[46]

The limitations of video imagery from single or multiple cameras is highlighted by the facts that:

> ... it is obvious that a camera can only show what it sees from its particular angle. What it shows will depend upon where it was in relation to the particular incident when that incident took place. A different camera showing the same incident from a different position may well give an entirely different perspective of the same incident.[47]

In the subsequent case of *Canadian Olympic Committee* v. *International Skating Union (ISU)*,[48] the Canadian Olympic Committee (COC) filed an application with the CAS Ad Hoc Division the day after the final of the ladies' short track speed skating. The COC requested CAS to order the ISU to instruct its referee to review the race's videotape. The COC was seeking determination of whether a 'kicking out' infraction was committed by the winner of the race, Radanova, a Bulgarian skater. Possible disqualification of Radanova would have resulted in Canadian athletes advancing to the second and third places. The view of the panel was that:

> ... there is a more fundamental reason for not permitting trial, by television or otherwise, of technical, judgmental decisions by referees. Every participant in a sport in which referees have to make decisions about events on the field of play must accept that the referee sees an incident from a particular position, and makes his decision on the basis of what he or she sees. Sometimes

---

[46]   CAS OG Sydney 2000/12 Digest Vol. 2 p. 674. para. 13.

[47]   *KOC* v. *ISU*, note 40 *supra*, para. 11; also see Gardiner, S. (1999), 'The Third Eye: Video Adjudication in Sport' 7(1) *Sport and the Law Journal* 20.

[48]   CAS OG 06/006 *Canadian Olympic Committee* v. *ISU*.

mistakes are made by referees, as they are by players. That is an inevitable fact of life and one that all participants in sporting events must accept. But not every mistake can be reviewed. It is for that reason that CAS jurisprudence makes it clear that it is not open to a player to complain about a 'field of play' decision simply because he or she disagrees with that decision.[49]

The view of CAS continues to be that decisions by officials, irrespective of whether or not technology is involved, will only be reviewed in narrow circumstances where there is evidence helping to evaluate the decision which can be characterized as being clearly in bad faith, however that might be constructed within the specific case.[50]

CONCLUSION

This chapter has indicated the increasing prevalence of technology to determine on-field decisions. The dynamic between human deliberation and the exercise of judgment, on the one hand, and the view of the 'electronic eye', on the other, is clearly changing. The mantra supporting an increased role for technology is that it can improve on human error and provide objectivity. However, what is crucial to comprehend is that technology, or at least technology as we know it, does not provide an absolute truth. Video replays and systems such as Hawk-Eye therefore should be seen merely as an 'interpretive tool' to aid the official exercising judgment. Illustrations involving the use of technology to determine sporting decisions, discussed above, highlight the danger of accepting that technology provides objective truth.

Of course, this discussion might be criticized as an overtly academic debate that provides little in the sense of real conclusions for administrators involved in running contemporary sport who pragmatically see technology bringing certainty and precision to sporting decisions within a sporting industrial complex. Interestingly though, some sports such as soccer and its governing body, FIFA, have resisted the introduction of video replay and Hawk-Eye-type technology, preferring greater human monitoring.

The debate about the increased role of technology generally and adjudicative technology specifically can be seen as being part of a continuum of a codifying and 'civilising process'. Increased legal regulation of sport is also central in this process. Whether law is national, supra-national or international, it brings familiar values and principles to 'play within sport', any of which are beneficial to sport and sports athletes, especially within the liberal discourse of the enforcement of individual rights. Controversies will of course continue to occur in sport and adjudicative officials and technology will often be central to them. Only time will tell whether tribunals will be more or less likely to intervene when a more prominent role of technology is at issue. What is instructive is that the legal community, in its deliberations concerning legal adjudication, has acknowledged the limitations of technology and dismissed a potential role for the 'Robo-Judge' and a 'Judgment machine'.

Sporting justice is the key: use of both the law and technology support fairness and equity. But sporting adjudication is often concerning complex deliberation. In both sport

---

[49]   See *KOC* v. *ISU*, note 40 *supra*, para. 11 – 'arbitrary', 'a breach of duty' and 'malicious intent'.

[50]   *Mendy*, note 36 *supra*.

and the law, adjudication is often in the context of 'hard cases', where the outcome is unclear and is based on contingencies. It is difficult to argue that technology should not be allowed in such 'hard case' sporting adjudication – the Robo-Ref has a role but it needs to have limitations. The relationship between technological and human deliberation is crucial and the former should, as argued earlier, be an 'interpretive tool', helping to manage human error. Human deliberation can still exercise a qualitative skill not possible by computers and with sport being one of the most instinctive, unreserved and joyful activities: *viva* the traditional umpire and referee.

Table 8.1 Use of Video Technology in a number of team sports circa 2010

Sport	Use of video technology
North American football: National Football League – North America	The referee has 60 seconds to watch the instant replay of the play and decide if the original call was correct. The referee must see 'incontrovertible visual evidence' for a call to be overturned. If the challenge fails, the original ruling stands and the challenging team is charged with a timeout.
Baseball: Major League Baseball – North America	Major League Baseball implemented a system from the last month of the 2008 season and beyond. Instant replay may only be used to review boundary home run calls to determine: fair (home run) or foul or whether the ball was subject to spectator interference. A technician and an official (either an umpire supervisor or former umpire) monitor all games occurring at any given time from the MLB Commissioner's office in New York City. Though a player or coach may argue for a review, final determination of whether a review will occur lies solely with the umpire crew chief, usually after consultation with the rest of the umpiring crew. If a crew chief believes a replay is warranted, he will go to a special console installed at every ballpark – accompanied by one or more members of the umpiring crew – and call the technician using the phone attached to the console. The technician in turn will feed the appropriate footage to the television screen. Upon reviewing the footage, the umpire must see 'clear and convincing evidence' that the call on the field was incorrect in order to reverse it.

Sport	Use of video technology
Cricket: International Cricket Council (ICC) – worldwide	In international cricket matches the third umpire (or TV Umpire) is an off-field umpire who makes the final decision in questions referred to him by the two on-field umpires. Television replays are available to the third umpire to assist him in coming to a decision. An on-field umpire, at his own discretion, can use a radio link to refer any close decision concerning dismissals (catches, run outs or stumpings) or boundaries to the third umpire. The third umpire will make the decision. The ICC decided to trial a referral system during the Indian tour of Sri Lanka through late July and August 2008. This new referral system allows players to seek reviews, by the third umpire, of decisions by the on-field umpires on whether or not a batsman has been dismissed. Each team can make three unsuccessful requests per innings, which must be made within a few seconds of the ball becoming dead; once made, the requests cannot be withdrawn. Only the batsman involved in a dismissal can ask for a review of an 'out' decision; in a 'not out', only the captain or acting captain of the fielding team. In both cases players can consult on-field teammates but signals from off the field are not permitted. A review request can be made by the player with a 'T' sign; the umpire will consult the TV umpire, who will review TV coverage of the incident before relaying back fact-based information. The field umpire can then either reverse his decision or stand by it; he indicates 'out' with a raised finger and 'not out' by crossing his hands in a horizontal position side to side in front and above his waist three times. The TV umpire can use slow-motion, ultra-motion and super-slow replays, sound from the microphones in the stumps at the end of the wicket and approved ball tracking technology, which refers to Hawk-Eye technology that would only show the TV umpire where the ball pitched and where it hit the batsman's leg. It is not to be used for predicting the height or the direction of the ball. This 'Decision Review System' has been used in all Test Matches worldwide after October 2009 where the technology has been available.
Field hockey: International Hockey Association (FIH) – worldwide	Video referee can be asked by on-field referee to assist in helping determine whether a goal has been scored or not. The on-field umpire has the final decision.

Sport	Use of video technology
Ice hockey: International Ice Hockey Federation (IIHF) – worldwide	The video goal judge reviews replays of disputed goals. As the referee does not have access to television monitors, the video goal judge's decision in disputed goals is taken as final. In IIHF matches and the North American National Hockey League matches, goals may only be reviewed in the following situations: a puck crossing the goal line completely and before time has expired, a puck is in the net prior to goal frame being dislodged, a puck has been directed into the net by hand or foot, a puck is deflected into the net off an official, and a puck is deflected into the goal by the high stick (stick above the goal) by an attacking player.
Rugby union: International Rugby Board – worldwide	In rugby union the video referee is officially referred to as the television match official (TMO) and is used mainly in international and professional games. The TMO can only be used in the situation where the referee is unsure whether a try or goal attempt has been scored, or in the event of foul play in-goal The TMO will make the decision and relay it to the on-field referee.
Rugby league: Rugby League International Federation (RLIF) – -worldwide	Video referees are also used in rugby league in the domestic National Rugby League (Australia/New Zealand) and Super League (Europe) as well as in international matches. In rugby league the video referee can be called upon by the match official to determine the outcome of a possible try. The 'video ref' can make judgments on knock-ons, offside, obstructions, hold-ups and whether or not a player has gone dead, but cannot rule on a forward pass. If a forward pass has gone unnoticed by the on-field officials it must be disregarded by the video ref, as such judgments cannot reliably be made due to camera angle effects.
Soccer: Fédération Internationale de Football Association (FIFA) – worldwide	No use of video referee or goal-line technology.

9 Athlete eligibility requirements and legal issues
Matthew J. Mitten and Timothy Davis*

I. INTRODUCTION

This chapter compares and examines the existing legal frameworks governing athletic eligibility rules and dispute resolution processes for Olympic and international sports as well as United States professional, college, and high school sports from both private law and public law perspectives. At all levels of sports competition, monolithic sports leagues and governing bodies[1] establish eligibility requirements and conditions that must be satisfied for an individual to participate in athletics. Most sports governing bodies have broad, exclusive authority to regulate a single sport or group of sports on either an international, national, or state-wide basis, which provides the corresponding power to exclude or limit athletic participation opportunities. In some instances, unilaterally established eligibility rules either completely preclude an individual from athletic participation or condition his or her right to participate upon compliance with substantial requirements. Given the many tangible and/or intangible benefits that athletes derive from athletic participation at all levels of competition, this chapter assesses whether the developing discreet bodies of international and United States national and state law appropriately regulate the promulgation of athlete eligibility rules and their application by monolithic sports leagues and governing bodies having broad, plenary authority to oversee Olympic, professional, college, and high school sports respectively. In conducting our analysis and making recommendations, we consider whether athletes have an effective voice and/or voting rights in the eligibility rule making process; the nature and effect of the eligibility rule; and the nature and scope of judicial or arbitral review of a sports governing body's eligibility rules, application, and enforcement. Our analysis reveals that International and United States law do not recognize any fundamental right to participate in Olympic, international, or professional sports. Nevertheless, in each of these areas,

---

*   This chapter is based on Matthew J. Mitten and Timothy Davis, *Athlete Eligibility Requirements and Legal Protection of Sports Participation Opportunities*, 8 VA. SPORTS & ENT. L. J. 71 (2009).

[1] Athletes often have no alternative opportunities to participate in a sport at the subject level of competition. For example, the National Football League is the sole purchaser of the services of major league professional football players in the United States. *USFL* v. *NFL*, 644 F. Supp.1040, 1042 (S.D.N.Y. 1986), *aff'd*, 842 F.2d 1335 (2d Cir. 1988). The International Olympic Committee has 'supreme authority' over Olympic sports competition, and its recognized international federations are the worldwide governing bodies for their respective sports. Olympic Charter, Chap. 1, Rul. 1(1) (11 February 2010) available at http://www.olympic.org/Documents/olympic_charter_en.pdf (last visited May 16, 2011). The National Collegiate Athletic Association has plenary nationwide governing authority over its approximately 1200 member universities and colleges and 400 000 student-athletes. Each of the 50 state school athletic governing bodies has exclusive, broad authority to regulate interscholastic sports competition within its state.

athletes are provided a means to seek independent review of eligibility decisions, usually through a system of private arbitration. In contrast, despite the significant benefits to participation in intercollegiate or interscholastic competition, high school and college athletes lack any of these procedural protections. We offer some suggestions for reform of this anomaly in the law of athlete eligibility.

II. OLYMPIC AND INTERNATIONAL SPORTS COMPETITION

A. International Legal Framework

Global athletic competition is an essential part of the world's culture. The Games of the Olympiad and Winter Olympic Games occur every 4 years, with thousands of participating athletes and hundreds of millions of worldwide spectators and viewers.[2] Despite geographical distance and language barriers among participating athletes and fans, sports provide a forum for maximizing unique physical talents and enhancing personal growth as well as for increasing understanding, appreciation, and respect among diverse cultures and societies.[3]

Major international competitions, including the Olympics and various 'world cups' in other professional sports, help achieve the United Nations' goal of using sports to further understanding among people of different cultures and to provide hope to millions of disadvantaged persons throughout the world. Since the 1950s, the United Nations Educational, Scientific, and Cultural Organization (UNESCO) has actively sought to encourage and promote the worldwide development of sport. UNESCO recognizes that, '[p]hysical education and sport form an important part of educational systems and are key contributors to social, human and intellectual development.'[4] UNESCO's 'Education through sport' information sheet notes that sports participation transmits inherent values such as respect for rules and rejection of cheating as well as respect for the winner and loser of an athletic competition, which provide the foundation for living together peacefully in a diverse society while respecting our differences.[5]

In 1978, UNESCO adopted the International Charter of Physical Education and Sport (ICPES). Article 1.1 states that, 'Every human being has a fundamental right of access to

---

[2] World Cup competition in men's and women's soccer (or 'football' as this popular game is called outside of the United States) is another major international sports competition that also occurs every 4 years, as do the Paralympic Games and Special Olympics. Other major trans-national sports events, including the Asian Games, Commonwealth Games, and Pan American Games, also are regularly held.

[3] Willye White, an African-American woman who was a member of four United States Olympic teams who competed in international track and field competitions in more than 150 countries, said: 'Before my first Olympics, I thought the whole world consisted of cross burnings and lynchings. The Olympic Movement taught me not to judge a person by the color of their skin but by the contents of their hearts. Athletics was my flight to freedom ... my acceptance in the world. I am who I am because of my participation in sports.' Fred Mitchell, *Olympian's Finest Work Came Long After Games*, CHI. TRIB., Feb. 10, 2007, at 1.

[4] Sport for Social and Human Development, http://www.unesco.org/shs/sport.

[5] http://www.unesco.org/bpi/pdf/memobpi45_educationsport_en.pdf.

physical education and sport, which are essential for the full development of his personality. The freedom to develop physical, intellectual, and moral powers through physical education and sport must be guaranteed both within the educational system and in other aspects of social life.'[6]

Similarly, Article 1 of the European Sports Charter (ESC) states that, '[g]overnments, with a view to the promotion of sport as an important factor in human development, shall take the steps necessary ... to enable every individual to participate in sport ...'[7] While acknowledging that '[v]oluntary sports organizations have the right to establish autonomous decision-making processes within the law,' the ESC seeks to ensure non-discriminatory equal opportunities to participate in sports competition.

Although the individual benefits of athletic participation and corresponding collective benefits to our global society resulting from widespread sports competition are widely acknowledged, there is no right to engage in sport under international human rights agreements or other international laws.[8] The international and European sports charters create aspirations for widespread athletic participation based on the ideal of sport for all persons, rather than a legally enforceable right to participate in sports with effective remedies for its denial. Even though the constitutions of a few countries (e.g., Brazil and Ecuador[9]) establish and legally recognize an individual right to participate in sports, most countries (including the United States[10]) do not have national laws that do so. Thus, there is no internationally recognized right to participate in sports competition based on, or arising out of, an international custom to create and protect this right under national law.[11]

1. A fundamental principle of Olympism: 'The practice of sport is a human right' – a canard?

The Olympic Charter[12] codifies the fundamental principles, rules, and bye-laws adopted by the International Olympic Committee (IOC) that govern the Olympic Movement.[13] All members of the Olympic Movement, which include the IOC, international sports federations (IFs), national Olympic committees (NOCs), and national sports governing

---

[6] http://www.unesco.org/education/educprog/eps/EPSanglais/EVENTS_ANG/international_charter_ang.htm.

[7] *Ibid.* Article 3(3), however, recognizes that, '[v]oluntary sports organizations have the right to establish autonomous decision-making processes within the law.'

[8] JAMES NAFZIGER, INTERNATIONAL SPORTS LAW (2d ed.) at 126–7 (Transnational Publishers, Inc. 2004).

[9] *Ibid.* at 130.

[10] See notes 100–102 and 186–8 and accompanying text *infra*.

[11] NAFZIGER, note 8 *supra*, at 130–1.

[12] OLYMPIC CHARTER, note 1 *supra*. Most of the IOC's current 110 members (whose responsibilities include drafting the Olympic Charter) reside in civil law countries, whose laws are primarily embodied in codes. See Official Website of the Olympic Movement, International Olympic Committee Members, http://www.olympic.org/content/the-ioc/the-ioc-institution1/ioc-members-list/ (last visited May 16, 2011).

[13] Paragraph 3 of the Fundamental Principles of Olympism defines the 'Olympic Movement' as 'the concerted, organised, universal and permanent action, carried out under the supreme authority of the IOC, of all individuals and entities who are inspired by the values of Olympism.' *Ibid.* at 11. All organizations, athletes, and others belonging to the Olympic Movement must be recognized by the IOC and comply with the Olympic Charter. *Ibid.* at 11.

bodies or federations (NGBs), are bound by a series of interlocking agreements to comply with the Charter. The IOC, an international private non-profit organization domiciled in Lausanne, Switzerland, is the 'supreme authority' of the Olympic Movement and its decisions, including interpretations of the Charter, generally are final.[14] Each IF is a non-governmental organization (most are based in a European country) that functions as the worldwide governing body for a particular sport (or group of sports). For example, the International Amateur Athletic Federation governs track and field, and its member NGBs (e.g., USA Track & Field) have national regulatory authority over that sport in their respective countries. Each NOC (e.g., the United States Olympic Committee) has exclusive authority regarding the representation of its country or IOC recognized geographical territory in connection with the Olympic Games.

Pierre de Coubertin, the founder of the modern Olympic Games, said '[s]port is part of every man and woman's heritage and its absence can never be compensated for.'[15] The 4th Fundamental Principle of Olympism embodied in the Charter expressly provides that, '[t]he practice of sport is a human right. Every individual must have the possibility of practicing sport without discrimination of any kind and in the Olympic spirit, which requires mutual understanding with a spirit of friendship, solidarity and fair play.'[16] The 5th Principle prohibits '[a]ny form of discrimination with regard to a country or a person on grounds of race, religion, politics, gender or otherwise,' which is deemed to be 'incompatible with belonging to the Olympic Movement.'[17] The 'right' to practice sport codified in the Olympic Charter protects athletes only from being discriminated against on enumerated grounds by any member of the Olympic Movement.[18] Rule 45(2) of the Charter expressly states '[n]obody is entitled to any right of any kind to participate in the Olympic Games.'[19] An athlete may participate in the Olympic games only if he or she satisfies several requirements and conditions specified in the Charter's Eligibility Code.[20]

Among the more important eligibility requirements a athlete must satisfy are: 1) to comply with the Olympic Charter; 2) to comply with the relevant IF rules (including the sport's specific eligibility criteria as applied by an IF, NOC, and NGB) as approved by the IOC; 3) to be entered in the Olympic Games by his or her NOC; 4) to respect the spirit of fair play and non-violence, and behave accordingly; and 5) to comply fully with the World

---

[14]   Rule 15(4) states: 'The decisions of the IOC are final. Any dispute relating to their application or interpretation may be resolved solely by the IOC Executive Board and, in certain cases, by arbitration before the Court of Arbitration for Sport (CAS).' OLYMPIC CHARTER, note 1 *supra*, at 29.

[15]   Commission of the European Communities, White Paper on Sport at 2 (2007).

[16]   OLYMPIC CHARTER, note 1 *supra*, at 11.

[17]   *Ibid.* Age limits for Olympic Games competitors are prohibited unless prescribed in an IF's competition rules as approved by the IOC's Executive Board. *Ibid.* Rul. 43, at 83. This Rule's predecessor prohibited age limits 'other than as prescribed for health reasons in the competition rules of an IF,' which appears to be a narrow ground for permissible age discrimination. NAFZIGER, note 8 *supra*, at 126–7.

[18]   Each NOC enters athletes into Olympic events based on the recommendations of the NGB for the particular sport in its country and has a duty to ensure no athlete is excluded for 'racial, religious or political reasons or by reason of other forms of discrimination.' OLYMPIC CHARTER, note 1 *supra*, Rul. 45(3), at 83.

[19]   *Ibid.* Rul. 45, at 83.

[20]   *Ibid.* Rul. 41, at 80–81.

Anti-Doping Code.[21] In addition to these eligibility requirements, an athlete must be a 'national of the country of the NOC' entering him or her.[22] The NOC shall enter only athletes 'adequately prepared for high level international competition.'[23] Notwithstanding an athlete's compliance with these requirements, the IOC has the discretion 'at any time' to refuse to accept entry of any athlete 'without indication of grounds.'[24] While these detailed provisions seem to indicate that the broad language of the 4th Olympic principle ('sport is a human right') may be a canard, Olympic sport governing bodies do not have unlimited discretion because their athlete eligibility decisions are subject to independent review.

2. Athlete eligibility dispute resolution process

The Court of Arbitration for Sport (CAS) is a private, specialized arbitral body based in Lausanne, Switzerland (and thus subject to Swiss law) that was established by the IOC on April 6, 1983 to resolve sports-related disputes.[25] Despite the first word of its name, the CAS, whose jurisdiction and authority as an arbitration tribunal is based on agreement of the parties, is not an international court of law. It 'provides a forum for the world's athletes and sports federations to resolve their disputes through a single, independent and accomplished sports adjudication body that is capable of consistently applying the rules of different sports organizations ...'[26] Its creation recognizes the need for international sport's governance to be uniform and protective of the integrity of athletics competition,

---

[21] The Introduction to the World Anti-Doping Code states that 'Anti-doping rules, like *Competition* rules, are sport rules governing the conditions under which sport is played. *Athletes* or *Persons* accept these rules as a condition of participation and shall be bound by these rules.' See WORLD ANTI-DOPING AGENCY, WORLD ANTI-DOPING CODE 17 (2009), available at http://www.wada-ama.org/rtecontent/document/code_v2009_En.pdf (last visited May 16, 2011).

[22] OLYMPIC CHARTER, note 1 *supra*, Rul. 42, at 81.

[23] *Ibid.* Rul. 45(4), at 83.

[24] *Ibid.* Rul. 45(2), at 83. This rule was added after the CAS ad hoc Division at the Olympic Winter Games in Salt Lake City determined that the IOC had no authority under the then-current Charter to refuse to allow an otherwise qualified athlete to compete in the Games. Based on its view that an IF's improper reduction of the athlete's doping sanction violated the World Anti-Doping Agency (WADA) Code and was simply a device to enable him to compete in the Olympic bobsled competition, the IOC had declared him ineligible. Arbitration CAS ad hoc Division (O.G. Salt Lake City 2002) 001, *Sandis Prusis* v. *IOC*, award of 5 Feb. 2002 in VOL. 3 DIGEST OF CAS AWARDS 2001–2003 573 (Matthew Reeb 2004). See notes 45 and 58–9 and accompanying text *infra*.

[25] The International Council of Arbitration for Sport (ICAS), a group of 20 high-level jurists that currently includes two United States members, Michael B. Lenard and Judge Juan R. Torruella, now oversees the CAS and appoints its member arbitrators. CAS arbitrators are representative of the world's continents and are appointed for 4-year renewable terms by ICAS based on recommendations from the IOC, IFs, NOCs, and athletes' groups. They must have legal training and knowledge of sport, be objective and independent in their decisions, adhere to a duty of confidentiality, and have good command of at least one CAS working language (i.e. English or French). The ICAS is obligated to 'wherever possible, ensure fair representation of the continents and of the different juridical cultures.' COURT OF ARBITRATION FOR SPORT, CODE OF SPORTS-RELATED ARBITRATION, S16, available at http://www.tas-cas.org/d2wfiles/document/3923/5048/0/Code%202010%20(en).pdf (last visited May 16, 2011). The Code of Sports-Related Arbitration, which is drafted by ICAS, governs the organization, operations, and procedures of the CAS. The IOC, IFs, and NOCs fund the operations of ICAS and the CAS.

[26] Richard H. McLaren, *The Court of Arbitration for Sport: An Independent Arena for the World's Sports Disputes*, 35 VAL. U. L. REV. 379, 381 (2001).

while also safeguarding all athletes' legitimate rights and adhering to fundamental principles of natural justice.[27]

To ensure 'fast, fair, and free' resolution of disputes involving an athlete's eligibility to participate in the Olympic Games,[28] a CAS ad hoc Division operates at the site of the Games and provides expedited adjudication (usually within 24 hours of the filing of a claimant's request for arbitration),[29] which provides athletes with the procedural right to be heard before an independent tribunal. Rule 59 of the Olympic Charter states that all disputes 'arising on the occasion of, or in connection with, the Olympic Games,' including an athlete's eligibility to participate in the Olympics, must be submitted to the CAS ad hoc Division for final and binding resolution.[30] The substantive 'law' governing an athlete's eligibility to participate in the Olympic Games is the Olympic Charter, relevant IOC rules, or general principles of law.[31]

The CAS also may resolve non-Olympics athlete eligibility disputes arising out of appeals from the final decisions of an IF pursuant to its *appeals arbitration* procedure.[32] These cases normally must be decided within 4 months after the filing of an appeal.[33] In athlete eligibility disputes other than those arising out of the Olympic Games, the relevant IF rules and the law of the country in which the IF is domiciled generally apply.[34]

In either CAS ad hoc Division or appeals arbitration, the involved athlete may be represented by counsel. A panel of three arbitrators[35] (or, at times, a single arbitrator) adjudicates the athlete eligibility dispute by majority decision and issues a written award setting forth the reasons for the decision, which is final and binding on the parties and usually publicly disclosed. Regardless of its geographical location, the 'seat' of all CAS

---

[27]   Tricia Kavanagh, *The Doping Cases and the Need for the International Court of Arbitration for Sport*, 22 UNSW L. J. 721 (1999).

[28]   Statement of Michael B. Lenard, an ICAS member who was instrumental in the establishment of the first CAS ad hoc Division at the 1996 Olympic Games in Atlanta, Georgia. The CAS ad hoc Division was created so that, 'no athlete can be left knocking on the door to the gates of the Olympic village.' *Ibid.* In other words, all IFs are bound by CAS ad hoc Division awards regarding an athlete's eligibility to participate in the Olympics. Final and binding arbitration in a single proceeding provides athletes with a legal process superior to multi-stage litigation in a national court, which even if successful, may not provide an effective legal remedy. See, e.g., *Reynolds v. IAAF*, 23 F.3d 1110 (6th Cir. 1994).

[29]   See generally Richard H. McLaren, *Introducing the Court of Arbitration for Sport: The Ad Hoc Division at the Olympic Games,* 12 MARQ. SPORTS L. REV. 515 (2001).

[30]   OLYMPIC CHARTER, note 1 *supra*, Rul. 59, at 104. As a condition of participating in the Olympic Games, athletes must agree that all eligibility disputes will be finally resolved by the CAS.

[31]   COURT OF ARBITRATION FOR SPORT, ARBITRATION RULES FOR THE OLYMPIC GAMES, art. 17 available at http://www.tas-cas.org/adhoc-rules (last visited May 16, 2011).

[32]   CODE OF SPORTS-RELATED ARBITRATION, note 25 *supra*, S20(b).

[33]   *Ibid.* R59.

[34]   *Ibid.* R58.

[35]   For the appeals arbitration procedure, each party selects one arbitrator, and the President of the appeals arbitration procedure appoints the third arbitrator who serves as the president of the panel. CODE OF SPORTS-RELATED ARBITRATION, note 25 *supra*, R48, R53, and R54. Ad hoc Division arbitrators come from a pool of CAS arbitrators chosen by ICAS for the Olympic Games. ARBITRATION RULES FOR THE OLYMPIC GAMES, note 31 *supra*, art. 3.

arbitration proceedings is always Lausanne, Switzerland.[36] This ensures uniform procedural rules and substantive law for all CAS arbitrations, which provides a stable legal framework and facilitates efficient dispute resolution in locations convenient for the parties.

The Swiss Federal Tribunal (SFT), which has the exclusive authority to review all CAS awards and decisions,[37] has ruled that, 'the CAS is a true arbitral tribunal independent of the parties, which freely exercises complete juridical control over the decisions of the associations which are brought before it' and 'offers the guarantees of independence upon which Swiss law makes conditional the valid exclusion of ordinary judicial recourse.'[38] Subsequently, the SFT held that the CAS now is sufficiently independent from the IOC for its decisions 'to be considered true awards, equivalent to the judgments of State courts.'[39] It concluded: '[a]s a body which reviews the facts and the law with full powers of investigation and complete freedom to issue a new decision in place of the body that gave the previous ruling ... the CAS is more akin to a judicial authority independent of the parties.'[40]

i. Emerging principles of CAS jurisprudence　Unlike common law judicial precedent, '[i]n CAS jurisprudence there is no principle of binding precedent, or stare decisis.'[41] Nevertheless, although the CAS is an arbitral tribunal and the majority of its arbitrators have a civil law background, it is ironic that CAS awards are forming a developing body of *lex sportiva*.[42] Different panels of CAS arbitrators (like appellate courts in a common law system) may reach different conclusions regarding the meaning of a rule and its application in a particular case.[43] However, 'a CAS Panel will obviously try, if the evidence permits, to come to the same conclusion on matters of law as a previous CAS Panel.'[44] Thus, a developing *lex sportiva* is shaping the nature and scope of legal protection of an athlete's opportunity to participate in the Olympic Games and other international sports

---

[36]　CODE OF SPORTS-RELATED ARBITRATION, note 25 *supra*, R28.

[37]　COURT OF ARBITRATION FOR SPORT, 20 QUESTIONS ABOUT THE CAS, available at http.//www.tas-cas.org/en/20questions.asp/4-3-231-1010-4-1-1/5 0 1010 13 0 0/ (last visited May 16, 2011).

[38]　*G.* v. *Federation Equestre Internationale* (Swiss Federal Tribunal 1993) in VOL. 1 DIGEST OF CAS AWARDS 1986–1998 561, 568–9 (Matthiew Reeb 1998).

[39]　*A._ and B._* v. *IOC*, at 3.3.4 (Swiss Federal Tribunal 2003).

[40]　*Ibid.* at 3.3.3.2.

[41]　Arbitration CAS 2004/A/628, *IAAF* v. *USA Track and Field & Jerome Young*, award of 28 June 2004 ¶73 at 18 [hereinafter *Jerome Young*].

[42]　Professor Jim Nafziger has observed that CAS awards 'provide guidance in later cases, strongly influence later awards, and often function as precedent,' which reinforce and help elaborate 'established rules and principles of international sports law.' NAFZIGER, note 8 *supra*, at 48. Professor Allan Erbsen asserts that, 'the gradual accretion of CAS precedent that is often labeled as Lex Sportiva can more helpfully be understood as comprising several distinct approaches to legal analysis that rely on diverse sources of governing principles'. Allan Erbsen, The Substance and Illusion of *Lex Sportiva*, in THE COURT OF ARBITRATION FOR SPORT 1984–2004 at 452 (I.S. Blackshaw, R.C.R. Siekmann, and J.W. Soek, eds., 2006).

[43]　Advisory Opinion CAS 2005/C/976 and 986, FIFA and WADA Advisory Opinion, 21 Apr. 2006, ¶84 at 31 (observing that different CAS panels may have a 'different understanding' when applying same fault standard in doping cases).

[44]　*Jerome Young*, note 41 *supra*, at ¶73.

competitions, although our conclusions are necessarily tentative because all CAS awards currently are not generally available for review and analysis.

Whenever an athlete's eligibility to compete may be adversely affected, the CAS imposes an obligation on the IOC and other international sports governing bodies to provide the athlete with a fair opportunity to be heard during an internal proceeding. Thus, the CAS recognizes an athlete's procedural 'right to be heard as one of the fundamental principles of due process.'[45]

In reviewing a sports governing body's interpretation or application of rules affecting an athlete's eligibility to compete pursuant to the ad hoc Division or appeals arbitration procedure, the CAS conducts a *de novo* hearing. [46] If the athlete was denied due process in the sports governing body's internal proceeding, this violation is remedied by providing a full and fair opportunity to be heard during the CAS arbitration.[47] Moreover, to provide 'a safeguard for athletes [that] substantially ameliorates the possibility of flawed or arbitrary decision-making' [48] by international sports governing bodies, 'it is the *duty* of the [CAS panel] to make its independent determination of whether the Appellant's contentions are correct, not to limit itself to assessing the correctness of' the award or decision from which the appeal was brought.'[49] In other words, 'it is to be a completely fresh rehearing of the dispute and not one narrowly focused on finding error in the original decision.'[50]

In defining the nature and scope of an athlete's substantive participation rights, the CAS has not construed the Olympic Charter as creating an absolute right to participate in a sport. The CAS also has concluded: 'there is no rule of "fairness," to be derived from the Olympic Charter's acknowledgment that the practice of sport is a fundamental human right, which would under circumstances create an outer time limit of Olympic ineligibility.'[51] Rather than applying a 'fairness' requirement in athlete eligibility disputes on a case-by-case basis, the CAS appears to provide a significant degree of deference to international sports governing bodies regarding the establishment, application, and interpretation of eligibility rules and has not relied on this fundamental principle of Olympism in the Olympic Charter to substitute its judgment for IOC or IF eligibility determinations. For example, one CAS panel concluded that, although a particular

---

45   Arbitration CAS 2000/A/317, *A.* v. *Federation Internationale des Luttes Associees*, award of 9 July 2001, in VOL. 3 DIGEST OF CAS AWARDS 2001–2003 159, 162 (Matthiew Reeb 2004); Arbitration CAS ad hoc Division (O.G. Salt Lake City 2002) 001, *Sandis Prusis* v. *IOC*, award of 5 Feb. 2002 in VOL. 3 DIGEST OF CAS AWARDS 2001–2003 573 (Matthiew Reeb 2004).

46   CODE OF SPORTS-RELATED ARBITRATION, note 25 *supra*, Rul. 57 (applicable to appeals arbitration), states that the CAS 'shall have full power to review the facts and the law.' ARBITRATION RULES FOR THE OLYMPIC GAMES, note 31 *supra*, Art. 16 (for ad hoc Division arbitration, '[t]he Panel shall have full power to establish the facts on which the application is based.').

47   *Ibid.* See also Arbitration CAS 94/129, *USA Shooting & Q.* v. *UIT*, award of 23 May 1995, in VOL. 1 DIGEST OF CAS AWARDS 1986–1998 187, 203 (Matthiew Reeb 2004).

48   Arbitration CAS 2008/A/1574, *D'Arcy* v. *Australian Olympic Committee*, award of 7 July 2008 at 22.

49   *Ibid.* at 18.

50   *Ibid.* at 22.

51   Arbitration CAS ad hoc Division (O.G. Sydney 2000) 001, *USOC and USA Canoe/Kayak* v. *IOC*, award of 13 Sept. 2000, in COURT OF ARBITRATION FOR SPORT, CAS AWARDS – SYDNEY 2000, 13, 21 (2000).

eligibility rule may work hardship in individual cases, it does not 'prove the rule was not enacted in the pursuit of legitimate general interest.'[52]

The CAS has ruled that the monolithic position of an international sports governing body imposes a 'duty of confidence' owed to athletes whose eligibility to compete may be adversely affected by its exercise of disciplinary authority.[53] This legal duty requires the governing body not to act in 'bad faith,' which means acting in a 'completely arbitrary, blatantly, unsustainably, unreasonably or abusively manner.'[54] The CAS determined that this duty is satisfied if the sports governing body fully complies with its own rules when making athlete eligibility determinations.[55] At the same time, CAS *de novo* review assures that athletes incorrectly ruled ineligible by governing board officials in a manner inconsistent with applicable rules will be reinstated.

The CAS has implicitly applied this standard by requiring that doping rules must provide clear notice of the prohibited conduct,[56] and that disqualification or suspension of an athlete must be an authorized sanction for the rule violation.[57]

For example, during the 2002 Salt Lake City Olympics, a CAS ad hoc Division panel ruled that the then-current Olympic Charter did not authorize the IOC to reject a Latvian bobsledder's entry into the Olympic Games.[58] The athlete's 3-month suspension for a

---

[52]   *Ibid.*

[53]   Arbitration CAS 95/142, *L. v. FINA*, award of 14 Feb. 1996, in VOL. 1 DIGEST OF CAS AWARDS 1986–1998 225, 243–44 (Matthiew Reeb 2004).

[54]   *Ibid.* at 243.

[55]   *Ibid.* at 244.

[56]   See, e.g., Arbitration CAS ad hoc Division (O.G. Nagano 1998) 002, *R. v. IOC*, award of 12 Feb. 1998 in VOL. 1 DIGEST OF CAS AWARDS 1986–1998 419 (Matthiew Reeb 2004) (overturning alleged doping violation because neither IOC nor international skiing federation rules banned athlete's usage of marijuana); Arbitration CAS 96/149, *A.C. v. FINA*, award of 13 Mar. 1997 in VOL. 1 DIGEST OF CAS AWARDS 1986–1998 251 (Matthiew Reeb 2004) ('[I]t is incumbent both upon the international and the national federation to keep those within their jurisdiction aware of the precepts of the relevant codes.'). *Ibid.* at 262, A full analysis of doping rules and the process for imposing sanctions for doping is outside the scope of this chapter. For scholarly commentary concerning these issues, see Hayden Opie, *Drugs* in *Sports and the Law-Moral Authority, Diversity and the Pursuit of Excellence*, 14 MARQ. SPORTS L. REV. 267 (2004); see also Michael Straubel, *Enhancing the Performance of the Doping Court: How the Court of Arbitration for Sport Can Do Its Job Better*, 36 LOY. U. CHI. L.J. 1203 (2005).

[57]   See, e.g., *USOC and Athletes v. IOC & IAAF*, Arbitration CAS 2004/A/725, award of 20 July 2005 [hereinafter *USOC and Athletes*] (disqualification of team's race results because one team member ineligible to compete because of doping violation not an authorized sanction under applicable International Amateur Athletic Federation rules); Arbitration CAS ad hoc Division (O.G. Sydney 2000) 010, *Tzagaev v. IWF*, award of 25 Sept. 2000 in COURT OF ARBITRATION FOR SPORT, CAS AWARDS – SYDNEY 2000, 101 (2000) (disqualification of entire weightlifting team, including innocent athletes, not an enumerated sanction for other team members' doping violations). Sanctions for doping violations also must be proportionate to an athlete's fault, see, e.g., *A. v. FILA*, Arbitration CAS 2000/A/317, award of 9 July 2001 in VOL. 3 DIGEST OF CAS AWARDS 2001–2003 159 (Matthiew Reeb 2004), which principle has been incorporated into WADA. WORLD ANTI-DOPING CODE, note 21 *supra*, §10.5. The CAS has observed that the WADA, which is domiciled in Switzerland, did so to ensure that doping sanctions affecting athletes' eligibility to compete in Olympic and international sports competitions will be proportionate, which is required by Swiss law. See *Mariano Puerta v. ITF*, CAS 2006/A/1025, award of 12 July 2006.

[58]   Arbitration CAS ad hoc Division (O.G. Salt Lake City 2002) 001, *Sandis Prusis v. IOC*, award of 5 Feb. 2002 in VOL. 3 DIGEST OF CAS AWARDS 2001–2003 573 (Matthiew Reeb 2004).

doping violation ended before the bobsled competition would begin, but the IOC's Executive Board declared him ineligible to compete in the Olympics based on its members' belief that the International Bobsleigh and Tobogganing Federation's reduction of his suspension from the normal 2 years for a first doping offense was improper. Determining that the athlete was eligible to participate in the Games, the CAS panel explained: 'an athlete has a legitimate expectation that, once he has completed the punishment imposed on him, he will be permitted to enter and participate in all competitions absent some new reason for refusing his entry.'[59]

The CAS will construe ambiguous eligibility rules in favor of athletes, thereby requiring that a sports governing body's limits or conditions on an athlete's right to participate must be clearly defined. 'If a text may be interpreted in two ways,' the CAS will resolve any ambiguity 'in favour of an athlete who is guilty of neither wrong-doing nor even negligence in terms of the Olympic Charter.'[60] On the other hand, absent 'clear proof of abuse or ill will,' the CAS has declined to review a sports governing body's discretionary refusal to waive an unambiguous eligibility rule and permit an athlete to compete in a sports event.[61]

ii. Swiss Federal Tribunal Review of CAS Awards   The Swiss Federal Code on Private International Law[62] provides for judicial review of a CAS arbitration award by the SFT on very narrow grounds. The SFT will vacate an arbitration award if the CAS panel was constituted irregularly, erroneously held that it did or did not have jurisdiction, ruled on matters beyond the submitted claims, or failed to rule on a claim. An award also may be vacated if the parties are not treated equally by the CAS panel, if a party's right to be heard is not respected, or if the award is incompatible with Swiss public policy.[63]

---

[59]   *Ibid.* at ¶35.

[60]   Arbitration CAS ad hoc Division (O.G. Sydney 2000) 005, *Perez v. IOC*, award of 19 Sept. 2000, in COURT OF ARBITRATION FOR SPORT, CAS AWARDS – SYDNEY 2000, 53, 62 (2000).

[61]   See, e.g., Arbitration CAS ad hoc Division (O.G. Sydney 2000) 003, *Miranda v. IOC*, award of 13 Sept. 2000 in COURT OF ARBITRATION FOR SPORT, CAS AWARDS – SYDNEY 2000, 29 (2000) [hereinafter *Miranda I*]. (upholding COC's affirmance of Canadian Olympic Committee's rigid refusal to exercise permitted discretion to allow immigrant who had previously represented Cuba to participate on the 2000 Canadian diving team). Although the CAS panel dismissed his appeal, it recognized that the COC's 'inexplicable' decision imposed 'considerable hardship' on Miranda, who was ineligible to compete for the Cuban Olympic team under FINA rules because he did not reside in Cuba during the 12 months before the Sydney Olympics. *Ibid.* at 40. Characterizing Miranda's ineligibility to participate 'in light of the principle that the interests of *athletes* "constitute a fundamental element" of the Olympic Movement,' the CAS requested that the IOC ask the COC to reconsider its decision. *Ibid.* at 40. The CAS also recommended that the IOC consider modifying Rul. 46 to avoid unintended hardship to individual athletes in circumstances such as the present one. The IOC did so, which may reflect the ability of the CAS to influence IOC rule-making in the same manner that courts may affect the legislative process. Bye-law 2 to Rul. 42 (formerly Rul. 46) now provides that an athlete who changed his nationality or acquired a new one is eligible 'to represent his new country [in the Olympic Games] provided that at least three years have passed since the competitor last represented his former country.' See OLYMPIC CHARTER, note 1 *supra*, Rul. 42, Bye-law 2, at 82.

[62]   Switzerland's Federal Code on Private International Law, available at http://www.tas-cas.org/en/arbitrage.asp/4-3-292-1023-4-1-1/5-0-1023-3-0-0/ (last visited May 16, 2011).

[63]   *Ibid.* art. 190.

The SFT exercises judicial review of CAS awards regarding athlete eligibility issues because 'suspension from international competitions is far more serious than simple sanctions designed to protect the smooth running of a sport and constitutes a statutory punishment that affects the legal interests of the person concerned.'[64]

Thus, in *Canas* v. *ATP Tour*,[65] the SFT refused to enforce the Association of Tennis Professionals' insistence that athletes waive their right to appeal a CAS award as a condition of participating in any events organized or sponsored by the ATP Tour. The SFT initially found that the athlete's agreement to arbitrate a doping dispute before the CAS is enforceable because it 'promotes the swift settlement of [sports] disputes ... by specialized arbitral tribunals that offer sufficient guarantees of independence and impartiality.' However, the SFT observed that it is important to ensure that 'the parties, especially professional athletes, do not give up lightly their right to appeal awards issued by a last instance arbitral body before the supreme judicial authority of the state in which the arbitral tribunal is domiciled.' The SFT explained this apparent contradiction by stating 'this logic is based on the continuing possibility of an appeal acting as a counterbalance to the "benevolence" with which it is necessary to examine the consensual nature of recourse to arbitration where sporting matters are concerned.' The SFT vacated the CAS award, which violated the athlete's right to a fair hearing by not providing a reasoned decision for rejecting his arguments that his doping sanction violated United States and European Union laws.[66]

However, the SFT thus far has uniformly rejected challenges to the substantive merits of a CAS panel's decision.[67] Although a CAS award may be challenged on the ground that it is incompatible with Swiss public policy, no athlete has successfully asserted this argument. The SFT has ruled that this defense 'must be understood as a universal rather than national concept, intended to penalize incompatibility with the fundamental legal or moral principles acknowledged in all civilized states.'[68] According to the SFT, 'even the

---

[64] *A._ and B._* v. *IOC*, at 2.1 (1st Civil Chamber May 27, 2003).

[65] 4P.172/2006, (1st Civ. Law Ct., Mar. 22, 2007).

[66] On remand, the CAS panel briefly considered but rejected these claims in its award while reaching the same decision. *Guillermo Canas and ATP Tour*, CAS 2005/A/951, award of 23 May 2007, at 18.

[67] A CAS award also can be attacked if it is incompatible with procedural public policy that 'guarantees the parties the right to an independent ruling on the conclusions and facts submitted to the arbitral tribunal in compliance with the applicable procedural law; procedural public policy is violated when fundamental, commonly recognised principles are infringed, resulting in an intolerable contradiction with the sentiments of justice, to the effect that the decision appears incompatible with the values recognised in a State governed by the rule of law.' *A._ and B._* v. *IOC*, at 4.2.1 (1st Civil Chamber May 27, 2003).

[68] *N., J., Y., W.* v. *FINA*, 5P.83/1999 (2d Civil Court, Mar. 31, 1999) at 779. To achieve the desired objective of a uniform, worldwide body of law governing athlete eligibility disputes, a valid CAS award, which is a foreign arbitration award in all countries except Switzerland, should bar re-litigation of the merits of athlete eligibility disputes under national or transnational law in a judicial forum. See *Slaney* v. *IAAF*, 244 F.3d 580 (7th Cir. 2001), *cert. denied*, 534 U.S. 828 (2001) (athlete's state law claims seeking to relitigate same issues decided by a valid foreign arbitration award are barred by the New York Convention on the Enforcement of Foreign Arbitration Awards, a treaty to which the United States is a signatory). But see *Meca-Medina and Majcen* v. *Comm'n of European Communities* [2006] 5 C.M.L.R. 18 (ECJ 3rd Chamber 2006) (despite final and binding CAS award not appealed to SFT, European Court of Justice allows two Slovenian professional

manifestly wrong application of a rule of law or the obviously incorrect finding of a point of fact is still not sufficient to justify revocation for breach of public policy of an award made in international arbitration proceedings.'[69] This standard is 'more restrictive and narrower than the argument of arbitrariness.'[70] In *N., J., Y., W.* v. *FINA*,[71] the SFT upheld 2-year suspensions for doping violations, rejecting a claim that the CAS award failed to comply with the principle of proportionality and thus is incompatible with Swiss public policy because the disciplinary sanction imposed on four Chinese swimmers was the maximum provided by the applicable rule and the quantity of the banned substance found in their urine was very low. Rejecting this argument, the court concluded that the CAS award did not 'constitute an attack on personal rights which was extremely serious and totally disproportionate to the behavior penalized.'[72]

A CAS award also may be attacked on the ground it violates the principles of good faith and equal treatment, contrary to Swiss public policy. Although CAS panels are required to treat like cases alike, which facilitates the development of a consistent body of *lex sportiva*, materially different facts may justify different CAS awards without contravening these principles.[73]

3. Analysis and conclusions

The Olympic Charter's explicit statement that, 'the practice of sport is a human right' protects an athlete's opportunity to participate in the Olympic Games and other international sports competition *only if* several enumerated athlete eligibility requirements and other conditions are satisfied. There are, however, several safeguards. First, the Olympic Charter expressly prohibits exclusion of individual athletes because of class-based discrimination. Second, former and current athletes have an important voice in rule-making and governance decisions. For example, the IOC Athlete Commission provides a means for Olympic athletes to have a voice in IOC affairs.[74]

---

swimmers to challenge FINA sanctions for positive doping test at world championship in Brazil under European Union law).

[69]   *FINA*, 5 P.83.1999 at 799.

[70]   *G.* v. *Int'l Equestrian Fed'n (FEI)*, CAS 92/63, award of Sept. 10, 1992 (translation), in DIGEST OF CAS AWARDS 1986–1998 115 (Matthieu Reeb ed., 1998). The SFT held that doping rules prohibiting the usage of substances that allegedly are not likely to affect a horse's racing performance do not violate public policy simply because 'the norms prescribed by the regulations … might be incompatible with certain statutory or legal provisions.' *Ibid.* at 575.

[71]   5P.83/1999 (2d Civil Court, Mar. 31, 1999).

[72]   *Ibid.* at 780.

[73]   *Raducan* v. *IOC*, 5P.427/2000 (2d Civil Court, Dec. 4, 2000) (prior CAS award absolving athlete of alleged doping violation because a jar containing his urine sample was not properly closed and raised the possibility contamination, different from case where athlete admitted banned substance in her system).

[74]   Several current IOC members are former Olympians (i.e. 36 of 110). See Official Website of the Olympic Movement, note 12 *supra*. For example, IOC President Jacques Rogge was a three-time member of the Belgium Olympic yachting team; IOC member Anita DeFrantz was a United States Olympian. *Ibid.* This Commission, which was created on October 27, 1981, consists of eight elected athletes who participate in summer Olympic sports, four elected athletes who participate in winter Olympic sports, and seven athletes to ensure diversity by sport, geographical region, gender, and ethnicity. John W. Ruger, *Athletes* in *Olympic Administration*, OLYMPIC REV. (Dec. 1993), available

Third, CAS arbitration provides an independent and impartial forum for quickly and finally resolving the often complex issues arising in athlete eligibility disputes by an international pool of arbitrators with specialized expertise in sports law, which increases the likelihood that fair and just resolutions will occur. The CAS ad hoc Division provides a fast, fair, and free on-site means of resolving eligibility disputes arising in connection with the Olympic Games. The CAS appeals arbitration process also provides an efficient and impartial means of adjudicating athlete eligibility issues arising in other international sports competitions. The costs of CAS arbitration are relatively low in comparison with litigation, which facilitates access to this method of dispute resolution for all athletes, including those with limited financial resources.[75]

The evolving *lex sportiva* suggests that CAS arbitration panels, while respecting governing bodies' authority to promulgate athlete eligibility rules, recognize the primacy of athletes' interests in the Olympic Movement and require international sports governing bodies to have clear rules that are fairly and consistently applied without discrimination. Although the CAS is authorized to provide *de novo* review of the merits of athlete eligibility decisions by the IOC or other international sports governing bodies,[76] it appears actually to usually apply no more than a deferential arbitrary and capricious standard of review. Because of the monolithic authority of the IOC and IFs and the importance of an elite athlete's opportunity to participate in worldwide sports events, we believe it would be appropriate for the CAS to provide closer scrutiny of sports governing body rules and decisions that adversely affect an athlete's eligibility to compete in the Olympic Games or other international sports competitions.

A positive development in this regard is the recent CAS award ruling that Oscar Pistorius, a South African athlete who is a double amputee, is eligible to run in IAAF-sanctioned track events with 'Cheetah' model prosthetic legs.[77] An IAAF rule prohibited the use of 'any technical device that incorporates springs, wheels or any other element that provides the user with an advantage over another athlete not using such a device.' The CAS panel rejected the IAAF's argument that the use of a technical device providing an athlete 'with any *advantage*, however small, in any part of a competition ... must render that athlete ineligible to compete regardless of any compensating disadvantages.' It concluded that the use of a passive device such as the 'Cheetah' prosthetic legs does not violate this rule 'without convincing scientific proof that it provides him with *an overall net advantage* over other athletes.' The panel concluded that, because scientific evidence did not prove that Pistorius obtained a metabolic or biomechanical advantage from using the

---

at http://www.la84foundation.org/OlympicInformationCenter/OlympicReview/1993/ore313/ORE 313zi.pdf (last visited Feb. 15, 2008).

[75] CAS ad hoc Division arbitration is free of charge to the parties. ARBITRATION RULES FOR THE OLYMPIC GAMES, note 31 *supra*, art. 22. An athlete must pay the required fee to submit an appeal under the CAS appeals arbitration procedure, with the arbitrators determining how the costs of arbitration are apportioned among the parties as part of their award. CODE OF SPORTS-RELATED ARBITRATION, note 25 *supra*, R64. Athletes are responsible for paying the costs of their own legal representation, witnesses, experts, and interpreters, although the rules governing the appeals arbitration procedure authorize the arbitrators to grant the prevailing party a contribution towards its legal fees and other costs. *Ibid.*

[76] See note 46 *supra*.

[77] *Pistorius* v. *IAAF*, CAS 2008/A/1480, award of 16 May 2008.

'Cheetah' prosthetic legs, his exclusion would not further the rule's purpose of ensuring fair competition among athletes.

Athletes have the right to have an adverse CAS award reviewed by the SFT, although its scope of judicial review is very limited. Nevertheless, this provides a means for judicially invalidating a CAS award if an athlete's right to be heard is denied, if he or she is not treated equally and in good faith, or if the merits of the decision violate fundamental international legal or moral principles. Of course, all CAS appeals arbitration and ad hoc Division awards must be publicly available and readily accessible for athletes to exercise their right to be heard effectively and for their legal counsel to ensure they are treated equally.

B.   United States Legal Framework

The United States Olympic Committee (USOC) is authorized by the IOC to represent the United States in all matters relating to its participation in the Olympic Games. The USOC selects an NGB as the governing authority for each Olympic sport within the United States, which is a member of the corresponding IF that governs the sport on a worldwide level. Pursuant to a series of hierarchical contractual agreements with the IOC and IFs, the USOC and its NGBs are required to adopt, apply, and enforce IOC and IF rules that determine or affect Unites States athletes' eligibility to qualify for, or participate in, Olympic or other international sports competitions. For example, the USOC and NGBs must comply with the IOC Charter's athlete eligibility requirements and anti-discrimination provisions protecting athlete participation opportunities. They also must comply with CAS awards resolving issues concerning the eligibility of American athletes that arise in connection with the Olympic Games or in disputes with an IF or WADA.

As previously discussed, CAS arbitration generally is the agreed forum for resolving eligibility disputes between a United States athlete and the IOC or an IF. The New York Convention on the Enforcement of Foreign Arbitration Awards[78] requires United States courts to recognize and enforce valid foreign arbitration awards, including CAS awards. In *Slaney* v. *IAAF*,[79] the Seventh Circuit held that a valid foreign arbitration award precludes a United States athlete from relitigating the merits of an eligibility dispute. The court concluded that, '[o]ur judicial system is not meant to provide a second bite at the apple for those who have sought adjudication of their disputes in other forums and are not content with the resolution they received.'[80]

---

[78]   9 U.S.C. § 201.

[79]   *Slaney*, 244 F.3d 580.

[80]   *Ibid.* at 591. A United States court may be unable to provide effective relief to a United States athlete whose eligibility to participate in sports competition is adversely affected by an IOC or IF rule or decision because its judicial authority is not binding on foreign sports governing bodies outside its jurisdiction. *Michels* v. *U.S. Olympic Comm.*, 741 F.2d 155, 159 (7th Cir. 1984) (noting that an IF 'can thumb its collective nose' at the USOC and ask the IOC to disqualify the entire United States Olympic weightlifting team if the USOC placed an athlete suspended by the IF on the team). *Gahan* v. *U.S. Amateur Confederation of Roller Skating*, 382 F. Supp.2d 1127 (D. Neb. 2005) (observing that a United States court is unable to protect athletes from decisions of international sports governing bodies).

1. Ted Stevens Olympic and Amateur Sports Act

The USOC, a federally chartered corporation created by Congress, and all NGBs must comply with the Ted Stevens Olympic and Amateur Sports Act ('Amateur Sports Act'),[81] which establishes a legal framework for protecting the participation opportunities of Olympic sport athletes. Although current Olympic athletes are not eligible to be members of the USOC, the Amateur Sports Act requires that an Athletes' Advisory Council be established to represent their interests and to ensure open communication with the USOC.[82] It also requires the USOC to ensure that athletes have at least 20% of the membership and voting power held by its Board of Directors[83] and committees[84] as well as each NGB.[85]

To be eligible to be recognized by the USOC as the NGB for an Olympic sport, an amateur sports organization must provide all amateur athletes with an equal opportunity to participate 'without discrimination on the basis of race, color, religion, sex, age, or national origin.'[86] Each NGB has an affirmative duty to encourage and support athletic participation opportunities for women and those with disabilities.[87] An NGB's eligibility and participation criteria for United States athletes to participate in the Olympic, Paralympic, and Pan American Games must be consistent with those of the IF for its sport.[88] Athletes must be allowed to compete in international amateur athletic competitions unless the organization conducting the competition does not meet the applicable sanctioning criteria.[89] The Amateur Sports Act requires the USOC to establish a procedure for investigating and resolving complaints by athletes alleging that an NGB has violated these requirements, which adversely affects their eligibility to compete.[90]

---

[81]   36 U.S.C. §220501. The USOC has a statutory obligation to ensure, directly or by delegation to the NGBs for the various sports (which normally occurs), 'the most competent representation possible' for the United States in each event of the Olympic, Paralympic, and Pan-American Games. 36 U.S.C. §220503(4). Its mission is '[t]o support United States Olympic and Paralympic athletes in achieving sustained competitive excellence and preserve the Olympic ideals, and thereby inspire all Americans.' UNITED STATES OLYMPIC COMMITTEE, BYLAWS OF THE UNITED STATES OLYMPIC COMMITTEE, section 2.1 (2010), available at http://assets.teamusa.org/assets/documents/attached file/filename/31256/FINAL_ADOPTED_BYLAWS_9.25.10.pdf (last visited May 16, 2011).

The Amateur Sports Act also requires the USOC to encourage participation opportunities for women, racial and ethnic minorities, and disabled athletes and to provide assistance necessary to achieve this objective. 36 U.S.C. §220503(12)–(14).

[82]   36 U.S.C. §220504(b)(2). Members of the USOC Athlete Advisory Committee 'must have represented the United States in the Olympic, Pan American, or Paralympic Games, World Championships, or an event designated as an Operation Gold event within the ten (10) years preceding election.' BYLAWS OF THE USOC, note 81 *supra*, section 14.4. The Council's members are elected by United States athletes who meet these criteria. *Ibid.*

[83]   36 U.S.C. §220504(b)(2). At least two members of the USOC's Board of Directors must have 'competed in the Olympic Games at some time during their lives.' BYLAWS OF THE USOC, note 81 *supra*, section 3.2.

[84]   36 U.S.C. §220504(b)(2).

[85]   36 U.S.C. §220522(a)(10).

[86]   36 U.S.C. §220522(a)(8). However, an NGB has no authority to regulate high school or college athletic competition. 36 U.S.C. §220526(a).

[87]   36 U.S.C. §220524(6)–(7).

[88]   36 U.S.C. §220522(a)(14).

[89]   36 U.S.C. §220524(5).

[90]   36 U.S.C. §220509(a). If the USOC finds that an NGB is not in compliance, it is authorized to place the NGB on probation or revoke its recognition.

The Amateur Sports Act also mandates that the USOC establish a procedure for 'swift and equitable resolution' of disputes 'relating to the opportunity of an amateur athlete ... to participate' in the Olympics, Paralympics, Pan-American Games, and world championship competitions (hereinafter 'protected competitions').[91] The USOC is required to hire an athlete ombudsman to provide independent advice to athletes (free of charge) regarding resolution of disputes regarding their eligibility to participate in these competitions.[92]

Section 9 (formerly Article IX) of the USOC's Bylaws creates some important procedural and substantive rights for an 'amateur athlete,'[93] which protect 'professional' athletes who now are eligible to participate in the Olympic Games and other international sports competitions. No member of the USOC, such as an NGB, 'may deny or threaten to deny any amateur athlete the opportunity to participate' in a protected competition.[94] An athlete may seek to protect his or her opportunity to participate by filing a complaint with the USOC against an NGB that declares him or her ineligible to participate.[95] The USOC is required 'by all reasonable means at its disposal' to 'protect the right of an amateur athlete to participate if selected (or to attempt to qualify for selection to participate) as an athlete representing the United States' in any protected competition.[96] The USOC must 'seek information from the parties' if an athlete files a complaint alleging a denial of his or her participation rights by an NGB and attempts to resolve the matter.[97] The Act gives an athlete the right to submit an eligibility dispute to final and binding arbitration in accordance with the Commercial Rules of the American Arbitration Association (AAA) if it is not resolved by the USOC to his or her satisfaction.[98] The USOC has a right to participate in the arbitration proceeding, 'but it cannot be involuntarily joined by a party.'[99]

2.　Athlete eligibility dispute resolution process

A United States athlete has no federal constitutional right to participate in the Olympic Games.[100] The Amateur Sports Act[101] does not create any substantive athletic

---

[91]　*Ibid.*

[92]　36 U.S.C. §220509(b). John Ruger, a member of the 1980 United States Olympic biathlon team, currently serves as the USOC athlete ombudsman.

[93]　An 'amateur athlete' is defined as 'any athlete who meets the eligibility standards established by the [NGB] or Paralympic Sports Organization for the sport in which the athlete competes.' BYLAWS OF THE USOC, note 81 *supra*, section 1.3(a).

[94]　BYLAWS OF THE USOC, note 81 *supra*, section 9.1.

[95]　*Ibid.* sections 9.2 and 9.3.

[96]　*Ibid.* section 9.1.

[97]　*Ibid.* section 9.6.

[98]　*Ibid.* section 9.7. See also 36 U.S.C. §220522(a)(4)(B) (as a condition of being recognized as an NGB, it must agree to submit to binding arbitration in any dispute regarding an amateur athlete's opportunity to participate in a competition).

[99]　BYLAWS OF THE USOC, note 81 *supra*, section 9.7.

[100]　In *DeFrantz* v. *USOC*, 492 F. Supp. 1181 (D.D.C. 1980) a group of athletes selected to be members of the U.S. Olympic team sought injunctive relief enabling them to compete in the 1980 Moscow Olympic Games. The Carter administration urged a boycott of the Moscow Games to protest the Soviet Union's 1979 invasion of Afghanistan. *Ibid.* Faced with political pressure from the federal government, threatened legal action by President Carter, and the possible loss of its federal funding and federal tax exemption, the USOC decided not to enter a United States team in the Moscow Games. The court found that, under IOC rules, the USOC has the exclusive and

participation rights that athletes can enforce in a private litigation against the USOC or an NGB.[102] As one Seventh Circuit judge remarked, 'there can be few less suitable bodies than the federal courts for determining the eligibility, or the procedures for determining the eligibility, of athletes to participate in the Olympic Games.'[103] Consistent with this view, federal courts have ruled that the Amateur Sports Act immunizes an NGB from antitrust liability for rules and decisions that adversely affect an athlete's eligibility to participate in a protected competition.[104] The Amateur Sports Act, which requires that all amateur athletes be given an equal opportunity to participate in protected competitions without discrimination, does not expressly nullify or supersede any applicable federal civil rights statutes that protect Olympic sport athletes against prohibited disability,[105] gender,[106] race,[107] and religious discrimination.[108] However, even if an award of damages against the USOC or an NGB is an appropriate remedy for civil rights violations, courts are reluctant to grant requested injunctive relief that would interfere with the USOC's exclusive jurisdiction regarding all matters regarding eligibility to participate in the Olympics or other protected competitions.[109]

---

discretionary authority to decide whether to enter a United States team in Olympic competition. *Ibid.* The court held that, despite being federally chartered, the USOC is a private organization rather than a state actor; therefore, its conduct is not subject to the constraints of the United States Constitution. *Ibid.* Even if the USOC's decision constituted state action, athletes have no federal constitutional right to participate in the Olympic Games. The Supreme Court subsequently confirmed that the USOC is not a state actor. *San Francisco Arts & Athletics, Inc. v. U.S. Olympic Comm.*, 483 U.S. 522 (1987). Consistent therewith, courts have held that an NGB also is not a state actor. *Behagen v. Amateur Basketball Ass'n of U.S.*, 884 F.2d 524 (10th Cir. 1989).

[101]   In 1998, the Amateur Sports Act was renamed the Ted Stevens Olympic and Amateur Sports Act and, *inter alia*, amended expressly to provide that, although the USOC may sue and be sued in federal court, nothing in the Act 'shall create a private right of action.' 36 U.S.C. §220505(b)(9).

[102]   See, e.g., *Slaney v. IAAF*, 244 F.3d 580 (7th Cir. 2001). Courts also generally hold that athletes had no private right of action under the Amateur Sports Act. *Martinez v. USOC*, 802 F2d 1275 (10th Cir. 1986); *Oldfield v. Athletic Congress*, 779 F.2d 505 (9th Cir. 1985); *Michels v. USOC*, 741 F.2d 155 (7th Cir. 1984); *Lee v. U.S. Taekwondo Union*, 331 F. Supp.2d 1252 (D. Haw. 2004). But see *Sternberg v. USA Nat'l Karate-Do Fed'n, Inc.*, 123 F. Supp.2d 659 (E.D.N.Y. 2000) (athlete allegedly excluded from participating in a protected competition because of her sex has an implied private right of action for damages against an NGB for violating the Amateur Sports Act's prohibition against gender discrimination).

[103]   *Michels*, 741 F.2d at 159. See also *Abdallah v. U.S. Ass'n of Taekwondo, Inc.*, 2007 WL 2710489 (S.D. Tex. 2007).

[104]   *Behagen v. Amateur Basketball Ass'n of United States*, 884 F.2d 524 (10th Cir. 1989). See also *JES Properties, Inc. v. USA Equestrian, Inc.*, 458 F.3d 1224 (11th Cir. 2006); *Eleven Line, Inc. v. North Texas State Soccer Ass'n, Inc.*, 213 F.3d 198 (5th Cir. 2000).

[105]   *Shepherd v. USOC*, 464 F. Supp.2d 1072 (D. Colo. 2006), *aff'd, Hollonbeck v. USOC*, 513 F.3d 1191 (10th Cir. 2008).

[106]   *Sternberg*, 123 F. Supp.2d 659.

[107]   *Lee*, 331 F. Supp.2d 1252.

[108]   *Akiyama v. United States Judo Inc.*, 181 F. Supp.2d 1179 (W.D. Wash. 2002).

[109]   See, e.g., *Gatlin v. USADA*, 2008 WL 2567657 (N.D. Fla. 2008); *Lee*, 331 F. Supp.2d at 1260, n. 2. As one court observed, although the Amateur Sports Act requires the USOC and its NGBs to submit unresolved eligibility disputes to binding arbitration, the statute does not require an athlete to do so. *Sternberg*, 123 F. Supp. at 666. Although a court must give effect to both the Amateur Sports Act and a federal civil rights statute if they can be reconciled, judicial application of a federal

Courts have ruled that the Amateur Sports Act preempts state law claims by athletes arising out of eligibility disputes regarding protected competitions except for a breach of contract action to require the USOC or an NBG to follow its own internal dispute resolution procedures.[110] United States judges recognize the need for a uniform national procedure for resolving athlete eligibility issues, which is necessary to further Congress' 'grant of exclusive jurisdiction to the USOC over all matters pertaining to United States participation in the Olympic Games.'[111] Thus, 'only a very specific claim will avoid the impediment to [a court's] subject matter jurisdiction' established by the Amateur Sports Act.[112]

In summary, courts hold that the Amateur Sports Act limits the nature and scope of judicial authority in athlete eligibility disputes. The role of the judicial system is to ensure that the USOC and NGBs follow their own rules and provide a minimum level of procedural due process consistent with this federal statute.[113] The merits of disputes regarding an athlete's eligibility to participate in the Olympic Games and other protected competitions are to be resolved by AAA arbitration, not courts.

Section 9 of the USOC Bylaws gives an athlete the right to submit an eligibility dispute to binding AAA arbitration. The athlete must submit a list of persons that he believes may be adversely affected by the arbitration (e.g., other athletes).[114] The AAA's Commercial Arbitration Rules govern, with an expedited procedure available to ensure that a timely

---

civil rights law to resolve the merits of an eligibility dispute would conflict with the Amateur Sports Act's grant of exclusive authority to the USOC in such matters. Arbitration, not judicial intervention, is the best means of finally resolving the merits of all athlete eligibility disputes in a timely and efficient manner.

[110]   See *Harding* v. *U.S. Figure Skating*, 851 F. Supp. 1476 (D. Ore. 1994), *vacated on other grounds*, 879 F. Supp. 1053 (D. Ore. 1995); *Slaney*, 244 F.3d 580.

[111]   *Slaney*, 244 F.3d at 594.

[112]   *Ibid.* at 595. In *Harding*, a federal district court held that judicial intervention in athlete eligibility disputes: 'is appropriate only in the most extraordinary circumstances, where the association has clearly breached its own rules, that breach will imminently result in *serious* and irreparable harm to the plaintiff, and the plaintiff has exhausted all internal remedies. Even then, injunctive relief is limited to correcting the breach of the rules. The court should not intervene in the merits of the underlying dispute.' 851 F. Supp. at 1478 (emphasis original).

[113]   The Amateur Sports Act, in relevant part, provides: 'In any lawsuit relating to the resolution of a dispute involving the opportunity of an amateur athlete to participate in the Olympic Games, the Paralympic Games, or the Pan-American Games, a court shall not grant injunctive relief against [the USOC] within 21 days before the beginning of such games if [the USOC], after consultation with the chair of the Athletes' Advisory Council, has provided a sworn statement in writing ... to such court that its constitution and bylaws cannot provide for the resolution of such dispute prior to the beginning of such games.' 36 U.S.C. §220509 (a). As one court observed, this statutory provision 'is designed to prevent a court from usurping the USOC's powers when time is too short for its own dispute-resolution machinery to do its work.' *Lindland* v. *USA Wrestling Ass'n*, 227 F.3d 1000, 1007 (7th Cir. 2000).

[114]   BYLAWS OF THE USOC, note 81 *supra*, section 9.8. This provision was added after the conclusion of multiple arbitration proceedings and subsequent litigation in *Lindland*, which illustrates the need for all affected athletes to have a fair opportunity to be heard in a single arbitration. *Lindland* v. *U.S. Wrestling Ass'n Inc.*, 227 F.3d 1000 (7th Cir. 2000).

award that will 'do justice to the affected parties' can be made.[115] The dispute, which is an arbitration proceeding between the athlete and the NGB (the USOC generally is not a party), is resolved by a single impartial arbitrator or panel of arbitrators selected by the AAA (usually an attorney, retired judge, or other individual familiar with the particular sport).[116] Like CAS arbitration, the AAA panel's review is *de novo*, and its award must be in writing and include findings of fact and conclusions of law.[117]

Because the AAA is bound by confidentiality obligations, it does not publicly release Article IX arbitration awards. Although we are unable to draw any definitive conclusions based on our 2008 review of only a limited sample of recent Section 9 arbitration awards obtained from sources other than the AAA,[118] these awards illustrate that arbitration panels have required that: 1) athletes have a fair opportunity to qualify for protected competitions;[119] and 2) an NGB's selection procedures must be fair, reasonable, and consistently applied to all athletes.[120]

---

[115] American Arbitration Association Online Library, *Sports Arbitration, Including Olympic Athlete Disputes* ('AAA Sports Arbitration'), available at http://www.adr.org/si.asp?id=4135 (last visited Dec. 20, 2007).

[116] *Ibid.*

[117] *Ibid.* The arbitrator has no authority to review 'the final decision of a referee during a competition regarding a field of play decision,' which may determine or materially influence whether an athlete is selected to participate in a protected competition, unless it was outside the referee's authority to make or was 'the product of fraud, corruption, partiality, or other misconduct.' BYLAWS OF THE USOC, note 81 *supra*, section 9.12.

[118] Copies of the limited sample of awards reviewed by the authors are on file with Professor Mitten. A complete index of Section 9 arbitration awards from 1987 to 2011 now is available on the USOC website at http://www.teamusa.org/legal/arbitration-hearing-panel-cases/section-9-formerly-article-ix (last visited May 16, 2011).

[119] *In the Matter of Arbitration between Sean Wolf and U.S. Rowing Association*, Case No. 30 190 00635 02 (AAA, Aug. 9, 2002) (finding that the NGB had granted a waiver to another rower who was unable to participate in one of the national selection regattas because he was taking a law school exam, the arbitrator ruled that the NGB improperly refused to grant claimant a waiver for a similar reason).

[120] *In the Matter of Arbitration between Rebecca Conzelman*, Case No. 30 190 404 04 (AAA, Apr. 6, 2004) (arbitrator concluded that time standards used to select United States competitors for World Cup cycling event have a rational basis and are valid).

There is a special arbitration process for resolving doping disputes that affect a United States' athlete's eligibility to participate in protected competitions. See generally Travis T. Tygart, *Winners Never Dope and Finally, Dopers Never Win: USADA Takes Over Drug Testing of United States Olympic Athletes*, 1 DEPAUL J. SPORTS L. & CONTEMP. PROBS. 124 (2003); Anne Benedetti and Jim Bunting, *There's a New Sheriff in Town: A Review of the United States Anti-doping Agency*, I.S.L.R. 19 (2003). The United States Anti-Doping Agency (USADA), an independent anti-doping agency for Olympic sports in the United States, provides drug education, conducts drug testing of Unites States athletes, investigates positive results, and recommends charges and sanctions for violations of the World Anti-doping Code or an IF's doping rules. See UNITED STATES ANTI-DOPING AGENCY, http://www.usantidoping.org/ (last visited Nov. 25, 2007). If a United States athlete is dissatisfied with the USADA Review Board's proposed disposition of an alleged doping offense, he or she may request a hearing before a single arbitrator or a panel of three arbitrators who are qualified as both AAA and North American CAS arbitrators. In this arbitration proceeding, USADA and the athlete are adversarial parties. Special AAA supplementary procedures apply to a USADA doping arbitration before the AAA/North American CAS panel. See *Jacobs* v. *USA Track & Field*, 374 F.3d 85 (2d Cir. 2004) (rejecting athlete's petition to compel arbitration pursuant to AAA Commercial Rules). The arbitrators' decision is published and available on the USADA website. An athlete may

A court will provide only limited scrutiny of an AAA arbitration award affecting an athlete's eligibility to participate in a sport, which is subject to review and enforcement under the Federal Arbitration Act.[121] In *Gault* v. *United States Bobsled and Skeleton Federation*,[122] a New York appellate court explained: '[a]lthough we also may disagree with the arbitrator's award and find most unfortunate the increasing frequency with which sporting events are resolved in the courtroom, we have no authority to upset it when the arbitrator did not exceed his authority.' However, a court will vacate or refuse to confirm an arbitration award that is 'the result of "corruption," "fraud," "evident partiality," or any similar bar to confirmation.'[123]

3.   Analysis and conclusions

The Amateur Sports Act has several provisions that advance the rights of United States athletes to participate in Olympic sports. The statute requires athlete voting power on the USOC's Board of Directors and committees and each NGB as well as establishing an athletes' advisory council. Second, the Act establishes some important procedural safeguards and substantive protections against discrimination to protect United States athletes' opportunities to participate in (and qualify for) Olympic and other protected international amateur sports competitions. Although there is no United States constitutional or Amateur Sports Act right to participate in the Olympic Games or other protected competitions, athletes receive free independent advice from an ombudsman and have the right to submit the dispute to final and binding arbitration through the AAA, which features impartial arbitrators with legal training and knowledge of the subject sport to resolve athlete eligibility disputes promptly. This arbitration process appears to effectively protect athletes' participation opportunities.

Courts have a very limited role in resolving athlete eligibility disputes. Although a court will not resolve the merits of the dispute, it will ensure that the USOC and NGBs follow their own rules and provide an athlete with the procedural due process protections required by the Amateur Sports Act and the USOC Bylaws. A court also will provide limited scrutiny of a Section 9 athlete eligibility award to ensure that the arbitrator did not exceed his or her authority and that it is not the product of corruption or bias.

III.   PROFESSIONAL SPORTS: THE PRIMACY OF CONTRACT AND COLLECTIVE BARGAINING

Unionized professional athletes have an effective voice in the promulgation of athlete eligibility requirements.[124] In addition, similar to the process for resolving eligibility

---

appeal an adverse AAA/North American CAS arbitration award to a different panel of three CAS arbitrators, whose decision is final and binding. Although generally not parties to USADA doping arbitrations, the USOC and United States NGBs effectively are bound by the resulting awards pursuant to the Amateur Sports Act. *Gahan*, 382 F. Supp.2d 1127.

[121]   9 U.S.C. §1 *et seq.*

[122]   578 N.Y.S.2d 683, 685 (N.Y. App. Div. 1992).

[123]   *Lindland*, 227 F.3d at 1003.

[124]   In the major United States professional sports leagues (e.g., MLB, NBA, NHL, NFL, and Major League Soccer), players unions represent athletes and possess exclusive authority to negotiate on behalf of athletes over terms and conditions of employment such as minimum salaries,

disputes involving Olympic athletes, *de novo* arbitration before independent arbitrators with specialized sports law expertise often is used to resolve athlete eligibility disputes arising in unionized professional team sports. Otherwise, the legal framework governing athlete eligibility issues and disputes arising in the United States professional sports industries[125] differs significantly from those for Olympic sports and other worldwide athletic competitions.

For most professional athletes, playing a sport is their primary occupation and source of income. In team sports, professional athletes generally are employees of their respective clubs who are paid an agreed salary, which typically is a substantial sum for National Football League (NFL), Major League Baseball (MLB), National Basketball Association (NBA), and National Hockey League (NHL) players.[126] Professional athletes who participate in individual performer sports such as golf and tennis usually are independent contractors who must satisfy the event organizer's qualifying criteria in order to participate in organized competitions. Their compensation is based on their respective individual performances in competitions.

In professional sports, the legal framework establishing the parameters of permissible athlete eligibility requirements and protecting an athlete's opportunity to participate is a mix of contract, labor, antitrust, and civil rights laws. In general, the legal relationship between a producer of professional sports competition and an athlete is established by the terms of their contract, with state contract law and federal labor, antitrust, and civil rights law limiting its boundaries. United States professional sports leagues and governing bodies are private entities that are not subject to the constraints of the United States Constitution,[127] and, therefore, are not obliged to comply with, for example, the requirements of the Due Process and Equal Protection Clauses. The Constitution's dormant Commerce Clause[128] precludes direct state regulation (other than by contract law) of the legal relationship between a professional athlete and a national or multi-state professional sports league or governing body.[129]

---

pension benefits, playing conditions, eligibility rules, and grievance procedures. MATTHEW J. MITTEN, TIMOTHY DAVIS, RODNEY K. SMITH, *ET AL.*, SPORTS LAW AND REGULATION: CASES, MATERIALS, AND PROBLEMS 743 (2d ed. 2009). Negotiations between players' representatives and management representatives result in collective bargaining agreements.

[125] Professional team and individual performer sports are a very popular form of entertainment in the United States. The producers of professional sporting events such as sports leagues and other organizations have strong market incentives to create a brand of athletic competition that attracts elite, highly skilled athletes, is commercially appealing to the public, and is profitable. Major professional team sports such as the NFL, MLB, NBA, and NHL as well as individual performer professional sports such as golf and tennis collectively attract millions of event attendees and viewers and generate billions of revenues annually.

[126] As of 2010, estimated average annual player salaries for the four major US professional sports leagues were as follows: NBA – $5.85 million; MLB – $3.25 million; NHL – $2.4 million; and NFL – $1.9 million.

[127] See, e.g., *Long* v. *NFL*, 870 F. Supp. 101 (W.D. Pa. 1994), *aff'd*, 66 F.3d 311 (3rd Cir. 1994).

[128] See generally JOHN E. NOWAK AND RONALD D. ROTUNDA, PRINCIPLES OF CONSTITUTIONAL LAW sec. 8.1 (Concise Hornbooks, 2nd ed. 2005); ERWIN CHEMERINSKY, CONSTITUTIONAL LAW PRINCIPLES AND POLICIES sec. 5.3 (2nd ed. 2002).

[129] See, e.g., *Partee* v. *San Diego Chargers Football Co.*, 668 P.2d 674 (Cal. 1983). An early case, *Neeld* v. *American Hockey League*, held that state human or civil rights laws such as those prohibiting disability discrimination can be applied to multi-state professional sports leagues.

To satisfy public demand for competition among a sport's best athletes, producers and organizers of professional sports events have a strong economic incentive not to base eligibility requirements on factors other than an athlete's ability, skill, or proficiency. However, historically some athletes with the requisite talents were discriminated against and denied an opportunity to participate in most professional sports solely because of their race or ethnicity. For example, for many years during the twentieth century, African-American,[130] Native American,[131] and to a lesser extent Latino American[132] athletes were excluded from professional sports; such blatant discrimination is now clearly prohibited by federal civil rights laws.[133] Today, a majority of athletes in some professional sports such as football and basketball are African-American.[134]

A. Team Sports

1. Initial eligibility requirements
In the past, professional team sport athletes successfully challenged on antitrust grounds league-wide eligibility requirements (other than medical and physical fitness requirements[135]) that prevented member clubs from employing them. For example, courts have enjoined a professional sports league from enforcing eligibility rules requiring that a prospective player attain a minimum age or that a specified number of years have elapsed from his high school graduation; these rules were found to unreasonably restrain trade in the market for player services.[136]

Today, a disability discrimination claim by a professional athlete against an interstate professional sport league or association is likely to be brought under the federal Americans with Disabilities Act. *Neeld* v. *American Hockey League*, 439 F. Supp. 459 (W.D.N.Y. 1977); see, e.g., *PGA Tour, Inc.* v. *Martin*, 532 U.S. 661 (2001).

[130] See generally Timothy Davis, *Race and Sports* in *America: An Historical Overview*, 7 VA. SPORTS & ENT. L.J. 291 (2008); WILLIAM C. RHODEN, FORTY MILLION DOLLAR SLAVES: THE RISE, FALL, AND REDEMPTION OF THE BLACK ATHLETE (2006); KENNETH L. SHROPSHIRE, IN BLACK AND WHITE: RACE AND SPORTS IN AMERICA (1996); ARTHUR ASHE, A HARD ROAD TO GLORY (1988).

[131] Sally Jenkins, *The Team That Invented Football*, SPORTS ILLUS., Apr. 23, 2007, at 60.

[132] Latinos endured a double standard. During major league baseball's period of segregation, fair-skinned Latinos were permitted to play, while those with dark skin were not. Timothy Davis, *Breaking the Color Barrier*, in COURTING THE YANKEES (ed. Ettie Ward 2003).

[133] See Title VII, 42 U.S.C. § 2000(e) *et seq.* (2006); Americans with Disabilities Act, 42 U.S.C. § 12101 *et seq.* (2006).

[134] MITTEN, *ET AL.*, note 124 *supra*, at 741–2.

[135] *Neeld*, 594 F.2d 1297 (upholding league rule prohibiting one-eyed player from playing for member clubs because its primary purpose and effect is to promote safety and has *de minimis* anticompetitive effect).

[136] *Linseman* v. *World Hockey Ass'n*, 439 F. Supp. 1315 (D. Conn. 1977); *Denver Rockets* v. *All-Pro Management, Inc.*, 325 F. Supp. 1049 (C.D. Cal. 1971). See also *Boris* v. *USFL*, No. Cv. 83–4980 LEW (Kx), 1984 WL 894 (C.D. Cal. Feb. 28,1984) (holding that league rule requiring player to exhaust college football eligibility or to earn college diploma or that at least 5 years elapse since he entered college unreasonably restrains trade). Other courts have enjoined a league and its member clubs from collectively refusing to employ players who formerly played for a defunct rival league. *Bowman* v. *NFL*, 402 F. Supp. 754 (D. Minn. 1975). Cf. *Gardella* v. *Chandler*, 172 F.2d 402 (2d Cir. 1949) (alleged agreement among 'organized baseball' clubs in United States not to employ

In *Denver Rockets* v. *All-Pro Management, Inc.*,[137] the court granted a preliminary injunction against enforcement of a bylaw making a person ineligible to play in the NBA until 4 years after he graduated from high school based on its finding of a substantial probability that the bylaw violated the federal antitrust laws. Because it was undisputed that plaintiff was well qualified to play NBA basketball, the court observed that the challenged bylaw 'is an arbitrary and unreasonable restraint upon the rights of [Spencer] Haywood and other potential NBA players to contract to play for NBA teams until the happening of an event ... fixed by the NBA without the consent or agreement of such potential player.'[138] Recognizing that professional basketball players generally have short careers, the court concluded that plaintiff would suffer irreparable harm if he was unable to play NBA basketball immediately because his physical condition and skills would deteriorate without high level competition. Consequently, a substantial part of his playing career will be lost.

Similarly, in *Linseman* v. *World Hockey Association*, the court found that 'the loss of even one year of playing time is very detrimental.'[139] It preliminarily enjoined the World Hockey Association from enforcing a rule prohibiting its clubs from drafting players who were not at least 20 years old. Characterizing the rule as 'a blanket restriction as to age without any consideration of talent,'[140] the court found 'no need for concerted action as to which specific players will be employed,' which 'determination, under our free market system, ought to be left up to each individual team.'[141]

It is significant that the player eligibility requirements successfully challenged in *Denver Rockets* and *Linseman* were established by agreement between the member clubs of a league, without the consent of a union representing the league's players during collective bargaining negotiations. Currently, MLB, NFL, NBA, NHL, and Major League Soccer players have unionized. Their respective unions have both the exclusive authority to represent all players and a duty to fairly represent all players[142] in collective bargaining negotiations with the leagues. All current and prospective players are bound by the terms of the union's collective bargaining agreement with the league, which has led to litigation by some players not yet members of the union who have asserted that the union did not adequately protect their interests by agreeing to terms that harmed them.[143]

In *Clarett* v. *National Football League*,[144] the Second Circuit held that the non-statutory labor exemption immunizes player eligibility requirements that are the product of a lawful collective bargaining process from antitrust scrutiny. Claiming an antitrust violation, Maurice Clarett, a star football player in his sophomore year at Ohio State University,

---

player who played professionally in Mexico contrary to reserve clause states antitrust claim because conduct 'unreasonably forbids any one to practice his calling.').
[137]   325 F. Supp. 1049 (C.D. Cal. 1971).
[138]   *Ibid.* at 1056. But see discussion of a collective bargaining agreement's effect on the legality of age restrictions at notes 142–53 and accompanying text *infra*.
[139]   439 F. Supp. 1315, 1319 (D. Conn. 1977).
[140]   *Ibid.* at 1323.
[141]   *Ibid.* at 1321.
[142]   *Steele* v. *Louisville & Nashville Railroads*, 323 U.S. 192 (1944).
[143]   See, e.g., *Wood* v. *Nat'l Basketball Ass'n*, 809 F.2d 954 (2d Cir. 1987).
[144]   369 F.3d 124 (2d Cir. 2004), *cert denied*, 544 U.S. 961 (2005).

challenged an NFL rule stipulating that players are eligible to be drafted only if 'at least three full college seasons have elapsed since their high school graduation.'[145]

The Second Circuit ruled that the union has the exclusive authority to negotiate the terms and conditions of prospective NFL players' employment. Eligibility rules are a mandatory subject of collective bargaining between the league and the players union because they pertain to players' 'wages, hours, and other terms and conditions of employment.'[146] As part of its efforts to obtain a collective bargaining agreement providing the best overall deal for all NFL players, federal labor law gives the union 'the ability to advantage certain categories of players over others, subject ... to [its] duty of fair representation.'[147] For example, the union may 'favor veteran players over rookies ... and can seek to preserve jobs for current players to the detriment of new employees and the exclusion of outsiders.'[148]

Although the eligibility rule temporarily excluded Clarett from the NFL regardless of his ability and readiness to play professional football, the Second Circuit held: 'the NFL and its players union can agree that an employee will not be hired or considered for employment for nearly any reason whatsoever so long as they do not violate federal laws such as those prohibiting unfair labor practices ... or discrimination ...'[149]

Clarett, although binding precedent only in the Second Circuit,[150] is consistent with general labor law principles providing a union with exclusive and plenary authority to negotiate all terms and conditions of its members' employment, including restrictions and limits favoring existing workers over those initially seeking to work for a unionized employer.[151] It also is consistent with *Brown* v. *Pro Football Inc.*,[152] in which the Supreme Court held that the non-statutory labor exemption bars an antitrust challenge to an employment term that is a mandatory subject of collective bargaining – even by players who are not currently eligible for membership in the union. In other words, it is inappropriate to impose antitrust liability for agreements or conduct that is permitted by federal labor law. In addition, *Clarett* follows Second Circuit precedent that broadly construes the scope of the non-statutory labor exemption as applied to professional sports.[153]

---

145   *Clarett*, 369 F.3d at 127.
146   *Ibid.* at 140 .
147   *Ibid.* at 139.
148   *Ibid.*
149   *Ibid.* at 141.
150   Nevertheless, so far it is being followed by other circuit courts. *Nat'l Hockey League Players Ass'n* v. *Plymouth Whalers Hockey Club*, 419 F.3d 462,474 (6th Cir. 2005) (citing *Clarett*, 369 F.3d 124 with approval).
151   *Trans World Airlines, Inc.* v. *Indep. Federation of Flight Attendants*, 489 U.S. 426 (1989); *Fibreboard Paper Products Corp.* v. *NLRB*, 379 U.S. 203 (1964); *Ford Motor Co.* v. *Huffman*, 345 U.S. 330 (1953).
152   518 U.S. 231 (1996).
153   *Caldwell* v. *ABA*, 66 F.3d 523 (2d Cir. 1995); *NBA* v. *Williams*, 45 F.3d 684 (2d Cir. 1995); *Wood* v. *NBA*, 809 F.2d 954 (2d Cir. 1987). See also *Zimmerman* v. *NFL*, 632 F. Supp. 398, 405 (D. D.C 1986) ('Not only present but potential future players for a professional sports league are parties to the bargaining relationship.'). In contrast, the *Clarett* district court relied on Eighth Circuit authority, *Mackey* v. *NFL*, 543 F.2d 606 (8th Cir. 1976), adopted by two other circuits in ruling that the NFL's draft eligibility requirement is not immune from antitrust scrutiny. *Clarett* v. *NFL*, 306 F. Supp.2d 379, 391 (S.D.N.Y. 2004).

On the other hand, *Clarett* fails to consider that there is only one major professional league (i.e. source of employment) for each sport in the United States. Because there is only one major United States professional league for sports such as football, basketball, hockey, baseball and soccer, blanket eligibility requirements wholly unrelated to individual skill and ability may have much greater exclusionary and economically detrimental effects on team sport professional athletes than those on employees in other industries. For example, electricians, plumbers, and carpenters have the option of seeking employment with non-union employers. Other courts, including the *Clarett* district court,[154] have recognized that professional athletes may not have any alternative employment that is a reasonable substitute for a United States major professional sports league.[155] Because most professional athletes have very short playing careers, even short-term league-wide exclusion for reasons not reasonably related to individual skill and ability or health and safety may cause irreparable harm to athletes' ability to use and develop their unique talents.[156] On the other hand, in the future, due to the increasing globalization of sports, major league professional sports employment options may be more readily available (e.g. European basketball for United States athletes who do meet the NBA's minimum age requirements).

In *Brown*, the Supreme Court conceded that professional athletes, unlike most unionized workers, often have unique individualized talents and skills. Nevertheless, the court refused to characterize professional sports as 'special in respect to labor law's antitrust exemption'[157] or to provide professional athletes with an antitrust remedy not available to employees in other industries. Thus, athletes excluded from participating in unionized professional sports generally are limited to labor and civil rights law remedies,[158] which may not adequately protect their athletic participation interests in individual circumstances.

A labor union has a duty to represent all current and prospective players fairly, but only conduct that is 'arbitrary, discriminatory, or in bad faith' breaches this duty.[159] In *Air Line*

---

[154] '[T]he NFL represents an unparalleled opportunity for an aspiring football player in terms of salary, publicity, endorsement opportunities, and level of competition.' *Clarett*, 306 F.2d at 384

[155] *Linseman*, 439 F. Supp. at 1319; Denver Rockets, 325 F. Supp. at 1053.

[156] For example, Maurice Clarett, despite being drafted in the third round of the 2005 NFL draft by the Denver Broncos, was unable to make the club. *Denver Done With Clarett; Broncos Cut Ties With Ex-Ohio State RB; Their 3rd-round Pick*, CHI. TRIB., Aug. 29, 2005, at 6. Being ineligible to play NFL football during the 2004 season (combined with his suspension that precluded him from playing college football for Ohio State during the 2003 season) likely caused his playing skills to deteriorate significantly, with corresponding irreparable harm to his once-promising potential career as an NFL player. Clarett subsequently served a prison term for armed robbery. See *Denver Rockets*, 325 F. Supp. at 1057 (finding player will suffer irreparable injury from being excluded from NBA for one year because 'a substantial part of his playing career will have been dissipated, his physical condition, skills and coordination will deteriorate from lack of high level competition ...').

[157] *Brown v. Pro Football, Inc.*, 518 U.S. 231 at 248 (1996).

[158] However, a player may have an antitrust remedy if it he can satisfy the difficult burden of proving that a professional league's minimum age limits or *de facto* equivalents are the product of conspiracy with an economically interested third party not part of the collective bargaining relationship such as the NCAA. *Boris*, 1984 WL 894 at *2; *Denver Rockets*, 325 F. Supp. at 1063; See also *Linseman*, 439 F. Supp. at 1320.

[159] *Peterson v. Kennedy*, 771 F.2d 1244, 1253 (9th Cir. 1985).

Pilots Association International v. *O'Neill*, the court held that this standard applies to the collective bargaining process and explained:

> Congress did not intend judicial review of a union's performance to permit the court to substitute its own view of the proper bargain for that reached by the union. Rather, Congress envisioned the relationship between the courts and labor unions as similar to that between the courts and legislature. Any substantive examination of a union's performance, therefore, must be highly deferential, recognizing the wide latitude that negotiators need for the effective performance of their bargaining responsibilities ... For that reason, the final product of the bargaining process may constitute evidence of a breach of duty only if it can be fairly characterized as so far outside a 'wide range of reasonableness.'[160]

In determining employment eligibility the union has a duty not to agree to arbitrary or irrational terms that constitute 'invidious' discrimination against some individuals it represents.[161] An exclusionary eligibility requirement does not breach a union's duty of fair representation unless it discriminates illegally against a protected class. For example, collective bargaining terms allowing exclusion from employment based on one's race violates this union duty.[162] On the other hand, labor law precedent permits a union to agree to seniority-based employment eligibility preferences.[163]

Because professional athletes have different levels of playing skills and experience and compete among themselves for a limited number of jobs, a players union needs wide latitude in determining how to further their collective best interests. Agreeing to initial employment eligibility requirements based on a prospective player's minimum age or the passage of a particular period of time as a method of allocating a limited number of jobs in a professional sports league does not violate the union's duty of fair representation. In *Clarett*, the Second Circuit, applying well-established labor law principles, observed that the union 'may, for example, favor veteran players over rookies ... and can seek to preserve jobs for current players to the detriment of new employees and the exclusion of outsiders.'[164]

Under existing law a minimum age eligibility rule (or a *de facto* equivalent) for professional athletes is not a form of prohibited discrimination that breaches a players union's duty of fair representation. The federal Age Discrimination in Employment Act of 1967 (ADEA)[165] protects only persons who are at least 40 years old. Although the ADEA 'forbids discriminatory preference for the young over the old,' it does not prohibit 'favoring the old over the young.'[166] For example, although such eligibility rules categorically exclude young athletes for reasons unrelated to their individual talent, skills, and maturity, these rules do not violate federal labor or civil rights laws.

---

[160]   499 U.S. 65, 78 (1991).

[161]   *Ibid.* at 79–82.

[162]   *Steele* v. *Louisville & N.R. Co.*, 323 U.S. 192 (1944). See also *Air Line Pilots Ass'n* v. *O'Neill*, 499 U.S. 65 at 73–8 (summarizing judicial development of labor union duty to represent all members' interests without hostility or discrimination).

[163]   *Air Line Pilots Ass'n*, 499 U.S. 65; *Local 357, Int'l Brotherhood of Teamsters, Chauffeurs, Warehousemen and Helpers of America* v. *NLRB*, 365 U.S. 667 (1961); *Ford Motor Co.* v. *Huffman*, 345 U.S. 330 (1953).

[164]   369 F.3d at 139.

[165]   29 U.S.C. §621 *et seq.* (2006).

[166]   *General Dynamics Land Systems, Inc.* v. *Cline*, 540 U.S. 581, 584 (2004). See also *Detroit Police Officers Ass'n* v. *City of Detroit*, 214 N.W.2d 803 (Mich. 1974).

In some individual cases, league-wide minimum age rules or their functional equivalent appear unfair and arbitrary when applied to extraordinarily talented young athletes who have both the physical skills and maturity to play a major professional sport. They may have no other options to participate in a sport at a comparable level of competition and no effective means of legal redress under current law.[167] On the other hand, a minimum age eligibility requirement is only a temporal limitation or restriction. Such eligibility restrictions exclude relatively few athletes having the requisite current ability and skills to play a professional sport. All things considered, the establishment of threshold eligibility standards by collective bargaining between the players union and league representatives (the parties that are most knowledgeable about the relevant factors to consider) is superior to case-by-case antitrust adjudication by non-expert courts, which only have authority to invalidate player eligibility rules found to be unreasonable rather than to establish 'reasonable' eligibility rules.

2. Disciplinary sanctions affecting athlete eligibility and dispute resolution process
Disciplinary sanctions adversely affecting a player's current or future eligibility to participate (usually with corresponding economic consequences) are mandatory subjects of collective bargaining in unionized professional sports. Thus, the players union is empowered to protect the players' participation interests by negotiating the conduct subject to discipline, sanctions for violations, and grievance mechanisms. In most instances the union is able to limit the otherwise broad authority of a club or league commissioner to discipline players[168] through effective use of the collective bargaining process. There generally is a collectively bargained range of disciplinary sanctions for on-field or off-field player misconduct that violates league or club rules promulgated to: 1) maintain competitive balance (e.g., doping); 2) preserve the sport's integrity (e.g., gambling, doping); 3) maintain the sport's public image (e.g., criminal conduct, domestic violence, doping); 4) protect player health and safety (e.g., violence injuring opposing player, doping); and 5) team unity and appropriate decorum.

Currently, most disputes regarding player discipline imposed by the league or a member club are resolved by an impartial arbitrator mutually selected by the union and league representatives.[169] The union files a grievance on the player's behalf and represents him in the arbitration proceeding. It is not uncommon for an arbitrator to reduce the length of a player's disciplinary suspension for misconduct that initially was imposed by league or

---

[167] See notes 154–5 and accompanying text *supra*.

[168] Absent limits imposed by the collective bargaining agreement, courts generally provide a professional sports league and its clubs with substantial discretion to impose player discipline and are very deferential to their decisions. See, e.g., *Molinas* v. *NBA*, 190 F. Supp. 241 (S.D.N.Y. 1961) (upholding indefinite suspension of player for admittedly gambling on his team's games in violation of his contract and league rules).

[169] A notable exception is the NFL Conduct Policy, which was established in April 2007 after input from the National Football League Players Association's (the union that is the exclusive bargaining representative of NFL players) then Executive Director Gene Upshaw and the NFL Player Advisory Council, that gives NFL Commissioner Roger Goodell broad unilateral discretion to discipline NFL players for off-field violent and/or criminal conduct that is not subject to external review. NFLPA.org, Player Policies – Conduct Policy, http://www.nflplayers.com/user/template. spx?fmid=181&lmid=336&pid=0&type=n (last visited Aug. 13, 2008).

club officials.[170] Even if his disciplinary sanction is upheld by an arbitrator, a player has had a fair opportunity to be heard as well as the advantages of other procedural safeguards to protect his future opportunity to participate in the sport. The arbitrator's decision is final and binding, and it will be judicially invalidated only on very narrow grounds.[171]

B.　Individual Performer Sports

1.　Initial eligibility requirements

Those who participate in professional individual performer sports such as golfers, swimmers, and track and field athletes generally are independent contractors who must satisfy a governing body's eligibility criteria and performance standards in order to participate in a competition. Because these athletes are not employees, there is no union to bargain collectively on their behalf.[172] In most instances the sport's governing authority or the event organizer unilaterally establishes the conditions of participation. To maximize an individual performer sport's commercial appeal to fans and spectators, an independent sports governing authority has a strong economic incentive to encourage and permit participation by the most highly skilled athletes without discriminating based on non-performance-related factors.[173] Absent violation of an athlete's federal or state civil rights,[174] courts generally are reluctant to invalidate athlete eligibility rules established by

---

[170]　See *NBA Players Ass'n on Behalf of Player Latrell Sprewell and Warriors Basketball Club and NBA Arbitration Decision* in MITTEN ET AL., note 124 *supra*, at 638. See also *Major League Baseball Players Ass'n* v. *Comm'r (John Rocker)*, 638 PLI/PAT 765 (Feb. 2001) (Manfred, Arb.). But see *Terrell Owens* v. *Philadelphia Eagles* (Nov. 18, 2005) (Bloch, Arb.) available at http://sports. espn.go.com/espn/print?id=2234819&type=story (last visited Jan. 24, 2008) (finding club had authority to suspend player without pay for conduct detrimental to team for maximum of 4 weeks under CBA, but that coach had discretion not to permit him to play or practice thereafter due to his misconduct's destructive and continuing threat to team).

[171]　See, e.g., *Major League Baseball Players Ass'n* v. *Garvey*, 532 U.S. 504 (2001); *Sprewell* v. *Golden State Warriors*, 266 F.3d 979 (9th Cir. 2001).

[172]　As a result, minimum age requirements are potentially subject to antitrust challenge. For example, the Ladies Professional Golf Association's requires its players to be at least 18 years old, but underage players may apply for a waiver. See also Joe Menzer, *Feelings Mixed on Talk of Raising Age Requirement*, available at http://www.nascar.com/2008/news/headlines/cup/01/24/jgibbs.mini-mum.age/index.html (Jan. 24, 2008) (NASCAR is considering raising the minimum age require-ment from 18 to 21 for drivers in the Sprint Cup Series).

[173]　Nevertheless, in some instances such discrimination has occurred. For example, the Profes-sional Golfers Association formerly had a 'whites only' provision, which prevented minorities from participating in its golf tournaments. ARTHUR ASHE, A HARD ROAD TO GLORY: A HISTORY OF THE AFRICAN-AMERICAN ATHLETE 1919–1945 69 (1993) (commenting on PGA's informal policy of excluding blacks from tour stops); Stanley Mosk, *My Shot: The tour's fear of carts is the same form of bigotry that caused the Caucasian-only clause*, SI.COM, http://sportsillustrated.cnn.com/golf/news/2001/06/05/my_shot/ (last visited Feb. 9, 2008) (commenting on the same).

[174]　See, e.g., *PGA Tour, Inc.* v. *Martin*, 532 U.S. 661 (2001) (ADA requires PGA Tour to permit physically impaired professional golfer to use cart to enable him to compete in its tournaments); *Richards* v. *United States Tennis Ass'n*, 400 N.Y.S.2d 267 (N.Y. Sup. Ct. 1977) (issuing preliminary injunction to enable transsexual to qualify to participate in the United States Open Tennis Tournament based on plaintiff's likely success in proving that use of Barr body test as sole criterion of gender violates New York's human rights law).

an independent sports governing body or event organizer.[175] For example, it is permissible to adopt non-discriminatory, unbiased eligibility rules or methods for evaluating an individual performer sport athlete's playing ability and skills.[176]

2. Disciplinary sanctions affecting athlete eligibility and dispute resolution process

Because individual performer professional sports are not unionized, there is no collectively bargained disciplinary process and range of sanctions. Today, in most instances, player discipline for violations of the sport's rules, including suspension from competition, is imposed by an independent commissioner or governing authority. Under contract or private association law, courts will provide limited judicial review to ensure that an appropriate level of procedural process is provided, contract rights are respected, and that decisions are not made in bad faith.[177]

C. Analysis and Conclusions

Unlike the Amateur Sports Act, which safeguards the opportunity of all United States athletes (including professional individual and team sport athletes) to qualify for, and participate in, the Olympic Games and other protected international sports competitions, there is no comparable federal law that directly regulates professional sports leagues and governing bodies and protects professional athletes. But professional athletes are covered by the federal civil rights statutes, which prohibit discrimination based on 'race, color, or national origin.'[178] Federal labor law also provides the basis for collectively bargained contractual provisions (and eligibility dispute resolution procedures) that both define and protect unionized professional athletes' athletic participation opportunities.

Like Olympic sport athletes, professional athletes have no athletic participation 'rights' absent those established by contract or applicable federal civil or human rights laws. Through the collective bargaining process, unionized professional athletes have the ability to negotiate initial eligibility requirements, limits on league and club disciplinary authority, and a dispute resolution process that adequately protects their athletic participation interests. Except when collectively bargained initial eligibility rules temporarily preclude athletes such as Maurice Clarett from participating, professional team sport athletes have legal protections equivalent to, and in some instances, greater than those available to Olympic sport athletes.

---

[175]   See, e.g., *Toscano* v. *PGA Tour, Inc.*, 201 F. Supp.2d 1106, 1113 (E.D. Cal. 2002) (rejecting antitrust challenge to Senior PGA Tour's per-event limit of 78 golfers and its eligibility rules limiting the ability of new and non-exempt players to compete in its events because '[t]he Tour provides an entertainment product in which primarily well known and popular senior golfers may compete against one another.').

[176]   *Deesen* v. *Prof'l Golfers' Ass'n of America*, 358 F.2d 165 (9th Cir. 1966).

[177]   See, e.g., *Crouch* v. *NASCAR*, 845 F.2d 397 (2d Cir. 1988); *Koszela* v. *NASCAR*, 646 F.2d 749 (2d Cir. 1981). But see *Blalock* v. *Ladies Prof'l Golfers Ass'n*, 359 F. Supp. 1260 (N.D. Ga. 1973) (finding that golfer's one-year suspension imposed with 'completely unfettered, subjective discretion' by a group of her competitors violates the antitrust laws). In some situations (e.g., doping offenses), an individual sport athlete may have a contractual right to have an independent arbitrator review a decision by the sport's governing authority that adversely affects his eligibility to compete. See notes 65–6 *supra* and accompanying text.

[178]   42 U.S.C. § 2000(d) et seq. (2006); 42 U.S.C. § 2000(e) *et seq.* (2006).

By contrast, unlike unionized professional team sport athletes, individual performer sport athletes are unable to engage in arms-length negotiation of eligibility requirements. However, the sport's independent promoter or governing body has a strong profit motive to produce a commercially viable form of athletic competition attractive to sports fans, which provides an economic incentive not to restrict unduly athletic participation opportunities. Because of limited judicial precedent, it is unclear whether the federal antitrust laws adequately protect participation opportunities for individual performer sport athletes, although the threat of antitrust litigation by an excluded athlete creates a similar incentive. Courts appropriately recognize the legitimate regulatory and disciplinary authority of independent sport governing bodies and promoters, but should ensure that athlete eligibility rules and their application in specific situations further legitimate objectives without unnecessarily excluding or limiting athletic participation opportunities.

IV.   INTERSCHOLASTIC AND INTERCOLLEGIATE ATHLETIC COMPETITION: JUDICIAL DEFERENCE TO THE 'GOLDEN RULE'

A.   Individual and Societal Benefits of Participation in High School and College Sports

Competing in athletics in interscholastic and/or intercollegiate athletics provides a unique educational experience with a significant potential to shape positively several aspects of a student-athlete's academic, personal, and professional life. Some of the most important traits and skills developed from competing in athletics are motivation, self-esteem, a strong work ethic, discipline, and the ability to work in a team environment, all of which are important factors in determining one's academic and career success. Former United States Supreme Court Justice Byron White, who played college football as a student at the University of Colorado and finished second in the 1937 Heisman Trophy voting, said that:

> [s]ports and other forms of vigorous physical activity provide educational experiences which cannot be duplicated in the classroom. They are an uncompromising laboratory in which we must think and act quickly and efficiently under pressure and then force us to meet our own inadequacies face-to-face and to do something about them, as nothing else does ... Sports resemble life in capsule form and the participant quickly learns that his performance depends upon the development of strength, stamina, self-discipline and a sure and steady judgment.[179]

Others have similar views. The Duke of Wellington claimed that, 'The Battle of Waterloo was won on the playing fields of Eaton.'[180] Sarah Palin, Alaska's first female governor and the 2008 Republican candidate for vice president, asserts that, 'Everything I need to know, I learned on the basketball court.'[181] Extensive empirical evidence demonstrates that

---

[179]   John M. Barron et. al., *The Effects of High School Athletic Participation on Education and Labor Market Outcomes*, 82 THE REVIEW OF ECONOMICS AND STATISTICS 409, 409 (Aug. 2000).

[180]   BARTLETT'S FAMILIAR QUOTATIONS 421 (15 ed. 1980).

[181]   Kathy Kiely, *Alaska's New-style Governor Already Shaking Things Up*, USA TODAY, Jan. 4, 2007, at 6A.

participants in interscholastic or intercollegiate sports competition more enjoy post-graduate success compared with non-athlete peers.[182]

B.   The 'Golden Rule' and the Limited Applicability and Effectiveness of Public Laws

At both the high school and college levels, athlete eligibility rules are adopted, interpreted, and enforced by a state governing body for interscholastic athletics or a national association for intercollegiate athletics (e.g., National Collegiate Athletic Association (NCAA)), which is comprised of their respective member educational institutions. A state or national governing body often has monolithic power, and each high school and university also frequently has its own athlete eligibility rules and requirements. In contrast to athletes who participate in Olympic sports, high school and college athletes do not have direct representation on these governing bodies or a vote regarding athlete eligibility rules.[183] Unlike professional sport athletes, no union represents the interests of high school or college athletes[184] or collectively bargains for eligibility rules or an eligibility dispute resolution process (e.g., arbitration) on their behalf. Similar to the well-known 'golden rule' in business and politics, high school and college sports governing bodies have the 'gold,' which provides broad and exclusive authority to adopt, interpret, and enforce athlete eligibility 'rules' subject only to applicable legal constraints.

---

[182]   See, e.g., Jacquelynne S. Eccles and Bonnie L. Barber, *Student Council, Volunteering, Basketball, or Marching Band: What Kind of Extracurricular Involvement Matters?*, 14 J. ADOLESCENT RESEARCH 10 (1999) (athletic participation increases high school grades and likelihood of college enrollment); WOMEN'S SPORTS FOUNDATION, *The Women's Sports Foundation Report: Her Life Depends On It: Sport, Physical Activity and the Health and Well-Being of American Girls*, 2004 at 30–31, available at http://www.womenssportsfoundation.org/binary-data/WSF_ARTICLE/pdf_file/990.pdf (last visited Dec. 20, 2007) (girls' participation in high school sports results in better health and grades and increased interest in college attendance and fewer problems with truancy, dropping out, and disciplinary problems); Andrew Postlewaite and Dan Silverman, *Social Isolation and Inequality*, 3 J. ECONOMIC INEQUALITY 243 (2005), Eric R. Eide und Nick Ronan, *Is Participation in High School Athletics an Investment or a Consumption Good? Evidence From High School and Beyond*, 20 ECON. EDUC. REV. 431 (2001); Barron, note 179 *supra*; B. Ewing, *High School Athletics and the Wages of Black Males*, 24 REV. BLACK POL. ECON. 67 (Summer 1995) (African-American and white males participating in high school athletics earn more than non-athletes); Postlewaite and Silverman, *supra* at 7 (male high school athletes less likely to skip school, have unprotected sex, use drugs or tobacco, or be charged with a crime).

[183]   As one court observed: 'as a student, Carlberg has not voluntarily subjected himself to the rules of the [state high school athletic association]; he has no voice in its rules or leadership. We note as well the relatively short span of time a student spends in high school compared to the amount of time often required for institutional policies to change. These factors all point to the propriety of judicial scrutiny of [state high school athletic association] decisions with respect to student challenges.' *Indiana High Sch. Athletic Ass'n v. Carlberg*, 694 N.E.2d 222, 230 (Ind. 1997). The same is essentially true for college athletes. *Gulf S. Conference v. Boyd*, 369 So.2d 553, 558 (Ala. 1979) ('The individual athlete has no voice or participation in the formulation or interpretation of these rules and regulations governing his scholarship, even though these materially control his conduct on and off the field. Thus in some circumstances the college athlete may be placed in an *unequal bargaining position*.').

[184]   Robert A. McCormick and Amy Christian McCormick, *The Myth of the Student-Athlete: The College Athlete as Employee*, 81 WASH. L. REV. 71 (2006) (arguing that NCAA athletes are employees who should have right to unionize and collectively bargain).

After exhausting all available internal avenues of relief,[185] a student-athlete's only option is to pursue litigation if he or she is dissatisfied with a rule or decision of a high school or college governing body (or educational institution) that adversely affects his or her eligibility to participate in an interscholastic or intercollegiate sport. Unlike Olympic sports that are governed by the Amateur Sports Act, no federal law provides a framework for directly regulating high school or college sports or establishes an independent governing body charged with a legal duty to protect student-athletes' sports participation opportunities. There is no federal (or state) constitutional law right to participate in either interscholastic or intercollegiate athletics,[186] and courts rarely find that athlete eligibility rules or their application in individual cases violate the United States Constitution or any state constitution.[187] Courts also have uniformly rejected antitrust challenges to NCAA student-athlete eligibility rules, thereby creating a body of federal antitrust law jurisprudence holding that these rules are essentially per se legal.[188]

Although high school and college sports are offered because of their inherent educational benefits to participants, United States courts almost uniformly refuse to recognize a legally protected interest in interscholastic or intercollegiate athletic participation (which is the means to the end of achieving these benefits) absent a valid contractual right to play a sport. Unless a governing body or educational institution violates federal or state civil rights laws by promulgating and/or applying eligibility rules that deny a high school or college student-athlete an opportunity to participate in sports based on race, color, national origin, gender, or learning or physical disability[189] courts refuse to apply *de novo* review or anything more than very limited rational basis scrutiny.[190]

---

[185]   See e.g. *Florida High Sch. Athletic Ass'n* v. *Melbourne Cent. Catholic High Sch.*, 867 So.2d 1281, 1287 (Fla. Ct. App. 2004); *Bloom* v. *NCAA*, 93 P.3d 621 (Colo. App. 2004).

[186]   See, e.g., *In re United States ex rel. Missouri High Sch. Ath. Ass'n*, 682 F.2d 147 (8th Cir. 1982); *Walsh* v. *Louisiana High Sch. Athletic Ass'n*, 616 F.2d 152 (5th Cir. 1980); *Hysaw* v. *Washburn Univ.*, 690 F. Supp. 940 (D. Kan. 1987); *Yeo* v. *NCAA*, 171 S.W.2d 863 (2005); *Hart* v. *NCAA*, 550 S.E.2d 79 (W. Va. 2001).

[187]   See generally Scott C. Idleman, *Religious Freedom and the Interscholastic Athlete*, 12 MARQ. SPORTS L. REV. 295 (2001). Courts will intervene, however, to protect student-athletes' substantive rights premised on federal or state constitutional law and statutes. See, e.g., *Pryor* v. *NCAA*, 288 F.2d 548 (3rd Cir. 2002) (holding that student-athletes' complaint alleged intentional racial discrimination in violation of federal statutes); *Hill* v. *NCAA*, 865 P.2d 633 (Cal. 1994) (although ultimately rejecting student-athletes' claim against the NCAA, the court acknowledged the existence of a state constitutional right of privacy).

[188]   See, e.g., *Smith* v. *NCAA*, 139 F.3d 180, 185–6 (3rd Cir. 1998) (finding NCAA eligibility rules are not related to the NCAA's commercial or business activities and therefore are not subject to Sherman Act scrutiny); *Banks* v. *NCAA*, 977 F.2d 1081 (7th Cir. 1992) (NCAA student-athlete amateur eligibility rules have no anticompetitive effects); *McCormack* v. *NCAA*, 845 F.2d 1338 (5th Cir. 1988) (eligibility rules have predominately pro-competitive effects and do not violate antitrust laws).

[189]   See, e.g., *Garvey* v. *Unified Sch. Dist. 262*, 2005 WL 2548332 (D. Kan.) (Title VI provides college athlete with private cause of action for claims of intentional discrimination); *Mercer* v. *Duke Univ.*, 401 F.3d 199 (4th Cir. 2005) (finding the same for gender discrimination); *Cole* v. *NCAA*, 120 F. Supp.2d 1060 (N.D. Ga. 2000) (finding the same with respect to discrimination based on a participant's disability).

[190]   *Carlberg*, 694 N.E.2d at 230–31.

C. Analysis and Conclusions

The important individual and social benefits of athletic participation at the high school and college levels justify legal recognition and more significant protection of a student-athlete's opportunity to participate in sports competition offered by public or private educational institutions.[191] It is ironic that participation in intercollegiate and interscholastic sports is a sufficiently important interest for purposes of applying federal anti-discrimination laws such as Title IX,[192] invalidating an exculpatory waiver of negligence claims as condition of participating in high school sports,[193] and rejecting a public university's claimed sovereign immunity from tort liability for injury to college athletes,[194] but generally not otherwise. Although we agree that participation in high school or college sports in itself should not be characterized as a 'property right' or 'liberty interest' (much less a 'fundamental right') under the Constitution, the opportunity to do so currently lacks adequate statutory or common law protection. Legislative recognition and protection of this opportunity (e.g., giving home-schooled students a conditional right to participate in sports) would be preferred, but we recognize the traditional reluctance of Congress or state legislatures to enact sport-specific legislation that benefits student-athletes.

We acknowledge it is not feasible or appropriate for student-athletes to participate in the making, interpretation, and application of eligibility rules for sports competitions offered as part of high school or college education. It also is important that appropriate deference be given to educational institutions and athletic governing bodies to avoid judicial micro-management of and intrusion into athlete eligibility disputes. Although arbitration is an efficient process that works well for resolving athletic eligibility disputes for the few thousand United States professional and Olympic sport athletes, it may not be a feasible alternative for resolving eligibility disputes affecting the nation's more than 7 million high school athletes or 400 000 NCAA student-athletes. Moreover, given the current deferential scope of judicial review, the NCAA, state high school governing bodies, and their respective educational institutions have little incentive to agree to submit athlete eligibility disputes to final and binding arbitration. In addition, arbitration may not lead to the development of a body of uniform precedent that provides clear legal guidance to university and high school athletics governing bodies and administrators. Other potential drawbacks to the development of an effective arbitration system may be a scarcity of arbitrators who possess the requisite expertise to adjudicate college and high school sports athletic eligibility disputes as well as an arbitrator's more limited scope of authority to fashion effective relief vis-à-vis a federal or state judge.

To ensure that student-athletes are not denied the lifetime educational benefits of athletic participation opportunities without an adequate justification, courts should apply a higher level of judicial scrutiny than the traditional common law rational basis or

---

[191] We do not assert that elimination of athletic participation opportunities due to budget constraints or to comply with Title IX is illegal conduct that violates student-athletes' legally protected rights. However, our strong preference would be to create, rather than eliminate or reduce, sports participation opportunities for all student-athletes.

[192] See, e.g., *Pederson* v. *Louisiana St. Univ.*, 213 F.3d 858 (5th Cir. 2000).

[193] *Wagenblast* v. *Odessa Sch. Dist.*, 758 P.2d 968 (Wash. 1988).

[194] *Avila* v. *Citrus Cmty. Coll. Dist.*, 131 P.3d 383 (Cal. 2006).

arbitrary and capricious standards. We do not advocate *de novo* or strict judicial review, but the significant educational and potential economic benefits of athletic participation (e.g., a scholarship or professional sports career) warrant more than courts merely asking the very deferential and frequently outcome determinative question of whether an eligibility rule or its application is merely rational or arbitrary and capricious. We propose a uniform heightened level of judicial scrutiny that allows a student athlete to prove, by clear and convincing evidence, that his or her exclusion from athletic participation does not substantially further an important and legitimate interest of an interscholastic or intercollegiate sports governing body or educational institution.[195]

This standard would better balance the parties' respective interests in an athletic eligibility dispute, but it poses the risk of unwarranted judicial micro-management of high school and college athletics and potentially more litigation. On the other hand, because a student-athlete has a significant burden of persuasion to satisfy, an adverse eligibility determination will be judicially vacated in relatively few cases. This standard, however, may provide a means of legal redress that enables athletic participation in the following examples of cases that we believe were inappropriately decided against student-athletes: 1) categorical exclusion of home-schooled students from athletic participation opportunities[196] (although conditioning participation on appropriate academic requirements and the

---

[195]   In effect, we are advocating that athletic eligibility rules be judicially evaluated in light of their teleological or purposive nature. See Jonathan Yovel, *Correctness, Not Fairness: Formalism and Institutional Norms* in *NBA Disciplinary Rulings*, 8 VA. SPORTS & ENTERTAINMENT L.J. 33, 44–5 (2008) (summarizing and advocating 'purposive interpretation' of sports governing body rules that affect player eligibility to participate). For example, as Justice Dickson explained: 'The IHSAA's action against Jason is blatantly contrary to the expressed purpose of the IHSAA Transfer Rule. The IHSAA rules provide that, 'Standards governing residence and transfer are a necessary prerequisite to participation in interschool activities because: ... (5) *they keep the focus of students* and educators *on the fact that they attend school to receive an education first* and participate in athletics second.' Record at 170 (citing Indiana High School Athletic Association (the voluntary not-for-profit organization that regulates interscholastic athletic activities of its member schools in the state of Indiana) IHSAA Rule 19(c)(5)) (emphasis added). The trial court found that the Carlbergs have always put Jason's education first and the IHSAA officials 'indicated they had no reason to believe Jason Carlberg's transfer was athletically motivated.' Record at 11. Thus, the arbitrariness of the IHSAA's application of its rule becomes apparent in the present case: A rule purporting to limit athletically-motivated transfers and promote education as the primary value of school in fact punishes a student whom the IHSAA found did *not* transfer for an athletic reason and where the uncontradicted evidence points only to academic reasons for the transfer. Common sense instructs that application of the Transfer Rule to limit Jason's opportunities for participation would be blatantly arbitrary and capricious. The trial court was correct in making such a finding.' *IHSAA* v. *Carlberg*, 694 N.E.2d 222, 245 (Ind. 1997) (Dickson, J., concurring and dissenting).

Regarding student-athlete eligibility disputes with the NCAA, it is important to ensure national uniformity and consistency as well as to avoid a potential dormant Commerce Clause violation if multiple, differing state law standards are applied. Therefore, if the Indiana supreme court or legislature adopts our proposed heightened legal standard, we suggest that the NCAA (which is based in Indianapolis, Indiana), its member institutions, and student-athletes contract to have Indiana state law govern the resolution of eligibility disputes. Establishing a uniform national substantive law for resolving intercollegiate athletic eligibility disputes would be consistent with the CAS objective of establishing a worldwide, uniform *lex sportiva* for Olympic and international sports. See notes 42–4 and accompanying text *supra*.

[196]   See, e.g., *Jones* v. *W. Va. State Bd. of Educ.*, 622 S.E.2d 289 (W. Va. 2005) (categorically excluding home-schooled children from athletic participation).

ems appropriate); 2) ineligibility because a mistake by an educa-
cause of a student-athlete's failure to comply with a governing
equirements;[197] 3) NCAA refusal to grant a waiver of its post-
to a student-athlete who graduated in 2½ years and was unable to
ee in a chosen field at her undergraduate institution;[198] and 4) an
einstate a student-athlete's eligibility after he was removed from a
ion for successfully appealing a coach's recommendation that his
scholarship not be renewed.[199] Under this new heightened legal standard, the NCAA
would have a higher burden, to justify, for example, its 'advertisement and endorsement,'
rules[200] as well as its 'no draft' and 'no agent' rules,[201] although these 'amateurism' rules
ultimately may be upheld under more exacting judicial scrutiny. At a minimum, a greater
scope of legal protection of student-athletes' athletic participation opportunities would
provide a legal incentive for interscholastic and intercollegiate sports governing bodies and
educational institutions to be more liberal in applying their eligibility rules and not restrict
athletic participation opportunities unless necessary to further legitimate objectives.[202]
Doing so also will provide a necessary legal check on the exercise of monolithic power by
these organizations to the detriment of student-athletes.

---

[197]   See, e.g., *Yeo,* v. *NCAA,* 171 S.W.3d 863 (Tex. 2005); *Hendricks* v. *Clemson Univ.*, 578 S.E.2d
711(S.C. 2003); *Perry* v. *Ohio High Sch. Athletic Ass'n,* No. 05-cv-937, 2006 WL 2927260 (S.D. Ohio
2006). See also Rick Reilly, *The Punishment Is the Crime,* Sports Illus., Nov. 26, 2007 at 88
(Washington Interscholastic Athletic Association requires high school football team to forfeit
games and not participate in state playoffs because school officials failed to ensure that one player's
physical fitness exam was updated within the required time).

[198]   *Smith* v. *NCAA,* 139 F.3d 180 (3d Cir. 1998)

[199]   *Richard* v. *Perkins,* 373 F.Supp.2d 1211 (D. Kan. 2005)

[200]   See e.g., *Bloom* v. *NCAA,* 93 P.3d 621, 624 (Colo. App. 2004).

[201]   See *Banks* v. *NCAA,* 977 F.2d 1081 (7th Cir. 1992).

[202]   We also advocate that courts scrutinize and perhaps invalidate on public policy grounds
rules of restitution promulgated by the NCAA and state athletic associations. A rule of restitution
permits athletic associations to impose particular types of penalties (e.g., forfeiture of games and
vacatur of individual and team records and performances) if an institution is deemed to have
violated an association's rules prohibiting ineligible student-athletes from engaging in interscholastic or intercollegiate athletic competition. See *NCAA* v. *Lasege,* 53 S.W.2d 77, 87 (Ky. 2001)
(describing and upholding the NCAA's rule of restitution; National Collegiate Athletic Association, 2010–11 NCAA DIVISION I MANUAL, 326, art. 19.7 (describing penalties that may be imposed
pursuant to NCAA's rule of restitution). The actual or threatened application of rules of restitution
provides a strong disincentive for schools to allow student-athletes to participate in athletic
competition even when athletes have prevailed in litigation against a sports governing body at the
trial court level. Schools fear that appellate court reversal of a lower court ruling in favor of a
student-athlete will lead to application of a rule of restitution, which creates a strong disincentive to
allow him or her to participate in athletic competition until the litigation is finally resolved.

10 Anti-discrimination law and policy*

Klaus Vieweg and Saskia Lettmaier

I. INTRODUCTION: SPORT, EQUALITY, DIFFERENCE, AND THE ELUSIVE LEVEL PLAYING FIELD

Sport is a common denominator of most cultures. It is a universally popular pastime, a globe-spanning institution. Sports transcend national, racial, religious, gender, and class lines. Sports are what people love, what unite them, and, perhaps, help define them. As Nelson Mandela put it, 'Sport has the power to change the world. It has the power to inspire. It has the power to unite people in a way that little else does.'[1] As Number 5 of the Fundamental Principles of Olympism declares: 'Any form of discrimination with regard to country or a person on grounds of race, religion, politics, gender or otherwise is incompatible with belonging to the Olympic movement.'[2] At the same time, divisions in sport are widespread. We distinguish according to nationality, sex, weight, and age, between the able-bodied and the disabled: national teams exclude foreigners; men and women play and compete separately; there are weight classes in boxing and wrestling; senior competitions protect older participants from younger adversaries; much energy has been quietly and successfully invested in creating sporting activities expressly for people with disabilities (such as the Paralympics, the Special Olympics, and wheelchair basketball). In sports, as elsewhere in society, we seem to be both united and divided, and the reasons for the divisions are not difficult to uncover: differentiation in sport is often justified in order to ensure fairness and a level playing field in competition. Competitors are divided into various groups so that they can compete against those of similar or presumptively similar ability. For example, sex-based and age-based divisions are assumed to reflect actual physical differences and to be appropriate, perhaps better, for the presumptively less capable class.

Discrimination, on the other hand – a drawing of distinctions for which there is no 'level playing field' justification – is considered as pernicious in the sporting context as it is in any other. Still, major components of sports and the sports industry have historically been closed off to large segments of society. In some cases, the exclusion has been obvious and intentional (the anti-Semitism that pervaded German sports during the Third Reich, apartheid in South Africa, and the longstanding color bar in Major League Baseball provide conspicuous examples[3]); in others, exclusion has been harder to trace, emanating

---

*   This chapter was completed in February 2010.
[1]   Laureus Foundation Switzerland, Nelson Mandela, Patron of Laureus, Meets Members of Laureus World Sport Academy (November 9, 2006), available at http://www.aipsmedia.com/index/php?page=news&cod=523&tp=n (last accessed October 28, 2009).
[2]   Olympic Charter (July 7, 2007).
[3]   Bernett, Hajo (1978), *Der jüdische Sport im nationalsozialistischen Deutschland 1933–1938*; Vieweg, Klaus (1985), 'Gleichschaltung und Führerprinzip – Zum rechtlichen Instrumentarium der

from apparently neutral practices, which in fact have a disproportionate impact on certain historically disadvantaged groups and thus serve to perpetuate earlier discriminatory structures. For example, several of the rules promulgated by the National Collegiate Athletic Association (NCAA) – a non-profit voluntary association governing the athletics participation of student-athletes in the United States – were once alleged to reflect racial bias, in particular the initial academic eligibility standards.[4]

Since the 1960s and 1970s,[5] there have been increasingly concerted efforts at national and supranational levels to stamp out discrimination in a variety of areas in society. The purpose of the present chapter is to enlighten the reader as to the extent and the shortcomings of the existing anti-discrimination framework and its application within the sports context. The chapter examines various grounds of discrimination, namely sex (including the emerging issues of sexual orientation and gender identity), disability, nationality, religion, race and ethnic origin, and age (see section II). While it is hoped that the list covers the majority of grounds of discrimination that might be of relevance in the sports context, it is not intended as exhaustive. Furthermore, different grounds of discrimination are not afforded equal attention, with the most in-depth treatment being accorded to sex, disability, and nationality discrimination. This is not to suggest that discrimination, whatever its basis, is not always equally insupportable. Rather, the focus reflects the greater legal and popular attention that the problem of ensuring equal access to sporting opportunities irrespective of sex, disability, and nationality has attracted in the recent past. As this is an international and comparative account, the materials referred to come from a variety of jurisdictions. Once again, constraints of space have enjoined selective rather than comprehensive treatment. Thus, the discussion will largely focus on United States and German anti-discrimination law and policy, for the practical reason that the United States and Germany are the legal systems with which the authors are most familiar. As equality law in Germany, as in all European Union countries, is chiefly of European Union origin and follows the supranational framework developed as a result of Article 19 of the Treaty on the Functioning of the European Union (TFEU) (ex: Article 13 EC), which allows the European Union to take measures combating discrimination based on sex, racial or ethnic origin, religion or belief, disability, age, or sexual orientation, the German approach is usually reflective of the stance taken by European Union countries more generally. Where appropriate, reference will be made to the protective framework in European Union countries other than Germany. The chapter concludes with an evaluative summary of the existing protective frameworks (see section III).

Organisation des Sports im Dritten Reich', in: P. Salje (ed.), *Recht und Unrecht im Nationalsozialismus*, pp. 244, 251 *et seq.*; Margolies, Jacob (1993), *The Negro Leagues, The Story of Black Baseball.*

[4] NCAA Proposition 16, requiring minimum SAT scores for athletic eligibility, has been challenged for relying too heavily on what are believed to be culturally and racially biased standardized tests. Davis, T. (1996), 'African-American Student-Athletes: Marginalizing the NCAA Regulatory Structure?', *6 Marq. Sports L.J.* 199, 208.

[5] The United States and the United Kingdom were front-runners in passing specific anti-discrimination legislation in the form of the Civil Rights Act 1964, Pub. L. 88–352, 78 Stat. 241 (United States) and the Sex and Race Discrimination Acts 1975 and 1976 (United Kingdom) respectively.

II. GROUNDS OF DISCRIMINATION IN THE CONTEXT OF SPORT

a.   Sex, Sexual Orientation, and Gender Identity

(1)   Sex discrimination and sports

Women's historical exclusion from sports is well documented: when modern sports evolved during the period of industrialization in the late 1800s, sports were believed to harm female reproductive health. Accordingly, women were discouraged from engaging in sports and advised that if they participated in sports at all, the sports in question should be gentle exercises, conducted out of the public eye.[6] Women's participation in sports increased during the 1920s and 1930s, due in part to the admission of women into the Olympic Games (1928).[7] Legislative measures introduced in the second half of the twentieth century have further enhanced women's access to sporting opportunities at both the amateur and the professional level.

Sexism can occur in almost every aspect of sports. Restrictions on women's athletic opportunities run the gamut from rules excluding women from participation in certain sports events or teams – an example is provided by the longstanding failure of the International Olympic Committee (IOC) to introduce 5000-meter and 10 000-meter running events for women in the summer Olympic Games while including them for men[8] and by the fact that women's boxing was not admitted until 2009, making ski jumping the last remaining sport in the Olympics which is open only to men – to applying different game rules to women's sports contests (e.g. a half-court rule in high school girls' basketball when a full-court rule operates for boys[9]). Another form discrimination may take is the failure to provide equal funding, prize money, locker rooms, practice times, competitive facilities, and sports equipment for female athletes.

Discriminatory measures may not be based on the athletes' sex *per se*, but rather on their sexual orientation or their gender identity. Gay, lesbian, and transgender athletes often face significant targeting, baiting, and discrimination. Where there are no specific provisions outlawing discrimination on the grounds of sexual orientation and gender identity, the question arises as to whether protection can be afforded by anti-sex-discrimination laws. Some of the challenges posed by homosexuality and transgenderism for competitive sports will be discussed under (4) *infra*.

---

⁶   Kosofsky, S. (1993), 'Toward Gender Equality in Professional Sports', *4 Hastings Women's L.J.* 209, 217–18.

⁷   *Ibid.* 218.

⁸   This practice sparked off a lawsuit in 1984, when a group of women runners sued the IOC, the United States Olympic Committee (USOC), and the International Amateur Athletics Federation (IAAF), basing their claim on a violation of their constitutional right to equal protection. See *Martin* v. *International Olympic Committee*, 740 F.2d 670 (9ᵗʰ Cir. 1984). The bid to force the 1984 Olympic organizers to immediately include these two women's track events failed. It was not till Barcelona in 1992 that these events were added to the Olympic menu. See Little, J. (2008), 'Running Against the Wind: Sex Discrimination in High School Girl's Cross Country', *76 UMKC L. Rev.* 711, 711.

⁹   In *Dodson* v. *Arkansas Activities Ass'n*, 468 F.Supp. 394 (D.C. Ark. 1979), the court struck down this rule, reasoning that paternalistic tradition alone was insufficient justification for the different rules.

(2) Possible approaches to sex discrimination

In an attempt to solve or at least ameliorate these problems, there are three basic types of approaches an anti-discrimination framework may adopt: it may opt for (1) a special treatment approach (with a concomitant preference for the establishment of separate but equal athletic opportunities for women because of a fear that women will be crowded out by men if denied exclusive participation rights); (2) a formal equal treatment model, where the only criterion for participation is the individual person's ability to play (leading, *inter alia*, to the adoption of mixed-sex teams and competitions); or (3) an amalgam approach that combines features of the other two approaches.

While the doctrine of separate but equal as applied to racial disparity has been utterly discredited – in the United States it was resoundingly thrown out by the landmark case of *Brown* v. *Board of Education*[10] – separation still seems to represent the dominant solution to the problem of sex discrimination in the sports context.[11] In terms of United States law, the governing instrument for amateur – in particular collegiate – sports is Title IX of the 1972 Education Amendments, which prohibits discrimination, on the basis of sex, 'under any education program or activity receiving Federal financial assistance.'[12] Although the wording of Title IX does not include any specific reference to athletics, the use of the words 'any education program or activity' has been interpreted to encompass collegiate athletics.[13] Discrimination is understood expansively, with direct as well as indirect discrimination,[14] sexual harassment,[15] and even retaliation – i.e. adverse treatment in response to an allegation of sex discrimination[16] – all constituting forms of sex discrimination prohibited by Title IX. One of the most controversial types of claim to have arisen under Title IX concerns attempts by female (and occasionally male) athletes to gain access to teams that the educational institution has chosen to confine to one sex ('sex-segregated teams'). Regulations that have been promulgated to assist in the application of Title IX provide that separate teams for each sex are permissible in contact sports and where selection for teams is based on competitive skill provided the institution is offering teams in the sport in question for both sexes.[17] The regulations go on to provide that whenever a school has a team in a given sport for one sex only, and the athletic opportunities for the

---

[10] 347 U.S. 483 (1954).

[11] For the United States, Mark A. Kadzielski concludes that 'the concept of separate but equal is very much with us in the realm of gender-based classifications.' Kadzielski, Mark A. (1982), 'Legal Approaches to Sex Discrimination in Amateur Athletics: The First Decade', in: Ronald J. Waicukauski (ed.), *Law and Amateur Sports*, p. 95, at p. 98 *et seq.*

[12] 20 U.S.C. § 1681(a).

[13] *Haffer* v. *Temple University of Com. System of Higher Ed.*, 688 F.2d. 514, 541 (C.A. Pa. 1982).

[14] Direct discrimination refers to basing a decision or practice on the ground in question, e.g. refusing to hire a woman coach due to her gender. The concept of indirect discrimination allows challenges of facially neutral practices and structures, which in fact have a disproportionate impact on those belonging to the protected class.

[15] Hogan, H. (2006), 'What Athletic Departments Must Know About Title IX and Sexual Harassment', *16 Marq. Sports L. Rev.* 317.

[16] A coach who claims sexual discrimination on behalf of others and is retaliated against in consequence is protected under Title IX. *Jackson* v. *Birmingham Bd. of Ed.*, 544 U.S. 167, 125 S. Ct. 1497 (U.S. 2005). This decision expands the scope of Title IX to protect whistleblowers as well as direct victims.

[17] See 34 C.F.R. §106.41(b).

other sex have previously been limited, members of the excluded sex must be allowed to try out for the team offered unless the sport involved is a contact sport.

While the contact sports exception is confined to sports the major activity of which involves bodily contact (like rugby, boxing, ice hockey, or basketball) and therefore reasonably narrow, a competitive skill exception is considerably broader and may in fact be invoked for almost any sport because athletics, by its very nature, is based on competitive skill. It follows that sex-segregated teams are permissible for most sports. The position is similar in England, where s. 44 of the Sex Discrimination Act 1975 sanctions sex segregation in any sport, game, or other activity of a competitive nature if 'the physical strength, stamina or physique of the average woman puts her at a disadvantage to the average man.'[18] It is only once an institution has – of its own accord – allowed a woman to try out for an all-male team that the institution in question becomes subject to a duty not to treat the woman any differently on account of her sex. Thus, in *Mercer* v. *Duke University*, Duke had allowed Heather Sue Mercer to try out for the all-male football team as a placekicker. Mercer was listed on the spring roster, but was not allowed to attend a summer training camp or dress for the games. When she was later cut from the team, Mercer brought suit, alleging that once she was allowed on the team, treating her differently constituted a form of sex discrimination under Title IX, even with the recognition of the contact sports exception. In 2000, a federal jury agreed, ordering Duke University to pay Mercer $1 in actual and $2 million in punitive damages.[19]

Constitutional guarantees provide yet another means of protecting women athletes against discrimination on the basis of sex. Specifically, the Fourteenth Amendment to the United States Constitution provides that 'no State shall make or enforce any law which shall ... deny to any person ... the equal protection of the laws.'[20] Once again, the predominant equal protection claim to have arisen in the sports context involves women who challenge their exclusion from all-male teams.[21] When bringing an action founded on the Equal Protection Clause of the Fourteenth Amendment, there must first be a finding that some 'state action' is involved. If state action is found, the appropriate standard of review must be determined. Courts apply different standards depending on the class of individuals alleging a violation and the interest affected by the classification.[22] For instance, the United States Supreme Court has ruled that all government classifications based on race and national origin are inherently 'suspect' requiring 'strict scrutiny.' By this, the court means that the classification must be necessary to achieve a compelling state interest.[23] The 'strict scrutiny' test also applies whenever a fundamental right is at stake, but so far the courts have failed to regard participation in any sports activity as a

---

[18]   (1975) c. 65. This may not apply to girls in the pre-puberty state, where differences in the physical capacity of the sexes are marginal. See 'Theresa Wins £250 and the Right to Tackle the Boys', *The Daily Mail* (June 16, 1978), p. 15.

[19]   190 F.3d 643 (4th Cir. 1999).

[20]   U.S. Const. amend. XIV.

[21]   Jones, Michael E. (1999), *Sports Law*, p. 53.

[22]   In general, the U.S. Supreme Court uses three levels of scrutiny when applying judicial review to a state actor that has distinguished between certain classes: strict scrutiny, intermediate scrutiny, and rational relationship review. Anderson, Paul M. (1999), *Sports Law: A Desktop Handbook*, p. 37.

[23]   See, e.g., *Loving* v. *Virginia*, 388 U.S. 1, 11 (1967).

'fundamental right.'[24] For sex-based classifications, the courts have not endorsed the 'strict scrutiny' standard. Instead, the case law suggests that if a state actor wishes to classify a particular team as male only, it has to demonstrate that the classification serves an 'important government interest' and that it is 'substantially related' to meeting this government objective ('intermediate scrutiny').[25] Where a separate women's team exists, the courts have in the main allowed a separate-but-equal policy under the intermediate scrutiny standard, citing an important state interest in the health and safety of female athletes as well as in the prevention of male domination of women's teams.[26] For instance, the United States Supreme Court let stand a lower court's ruling permitting separate but substantially equal men's and women's teams in contact sports. The court rejected the argument of an outstanding 11-year-old female athlete that allowing her to play on the boys' rather than the girls' basketball team would help her to advance her skills more rapidly.[27] For non-contact sports, where separate-but-equal teams exist, the health and safety rationale for keeping teams single sex is not as compelling, and many schools are in fact electing to provide mixed-sex teams. Track-and-field, cycling, cross country running, skiing, and swimming are among the more common mixed-gender sports.[28] Where there is no separate women's team, the courts are divided. Some courts have held that a total ban on women is overly inclusive since it rests on the paternalistic generalization that all females are relationally fragile.[29] In particular in non-contact sports, where there are no health and safety risks and no separate women's team, the courts tend to hold that total exclusion violates equal protection.[30] In German law, the claim to admission or participation is assessed on an individual basis. Such a claim may derive from s. 20 sub-s. 1 of the Act against Restraints of Competition or from ss. 826, 249 of the German Civil Code in conjunction with s. 19 sub-s.4 of the Act against Restraints of Competition.[31] Its basis in

---

[24] Jones, note 21 *supra*, p. 52.

[25] *Reed* v. *Reed*, 404 U.S. 71 (1971); *Craig* v. *Boren*, 429 U.S. 190 (1976).

[26] Champion, Walter T. Jr. (2005), *Sports Law in a Nutshell*, p. 316.

[27] *O'Connor* v. *Bd. of Ed. of School Dist. No. 23*, 449 U.S. 1301, 1307 (U.S. Ill. 1980), cert. denied, 451 U.S. 1004 (1981). For a contrasting decision, see *Fortin* v. *Darlington Little League, Inc.*, 514 F.2d 344 (1st Cir. 1975).

[28] Jones, note 21 *supra*, p. 55.

[29] *Hoover* v. *Meiklejohn*, 430 F.Supp. 164 (D. Colorado 1977), requiring a case-by-case assessment when determining female access to all-male teams in contact sports where no separate female teams exist; see also *Israel* v. *West Virginia Secondary Schools Activities Com'n*, 388 S.E.2d 480 (W. Va. 1989), allowing a skilled female baseball player to at least try out for the (boys') high school team on the grounds that the softball option for girls was not a substantial equivalent.

[30] In *Haas* v. *South Bend Community School Corp.*, 259 Ind. 515, 522; 289 N.E.2d 495, 499 (Ind. 1972), the Indiana Supreme Court ruled 3:2 in favor of the plaintiff where only one (all-male) team existed in a non-contact sport. Significantly, however, four of the judges indicated that if a comparable athletic program for females had existed, they would have found the regulation valid under equal protection standards. See also *Brenden* v. *Independent School Dist. 742*, 477 F.2d 1292 (8th Cir. 1973), allowing female students access to men's tennis, running, and skiing teams in the absence of comparable female teams. For a summary account see Champion, note 26 *supra*, p. 316.

[31] Zinger, Susanne (2003), 'Gleichbehandlung im Sport – Unter besonderer Berücksichtigung US-amerikanischer Rechtsprechung', in: K. Vieweg (ed.), *Spektrum des Sportrechts*, pp. 1, 26 note 95; Vieweg, Klaus (1993), 'Teilnahmerechte und –pflichten der Vereine und Verbände', in: E. Deutsch (ed.), *Teilnahme am Sport als Rechtsproblem*, pp. 23, 34 *et seq.*

the Constitution is the doctrine of the third-party effect of constitutional rights.[32] According to this doctrine, the conflicting constitutional rights – in this instance, freedom of association (Article 9 s. 1 of the German Constitution) and the right to equal treatment irrespective of sex (Article 3 s. 1 sub-s.1, s. 3 sub-s. 1) – must also be taken account of in horizontal relationships between private parties, and not just in vertical relationships between a private individual and the state. The conflict must be resolved according to the principle of proportionality, with both rights being given maximum effect.[33] The current situation in the European Union is similar. Article 19 TFEU (ex: Article 13 EC) authorizes the Council to take measures to fight discrimination, and the European Court of Justice (ECJ) has declared the principles of equality of opportunity and non-discrimination according to sex to be grounded in the common constitutional principles of the EU Member States (cf. Article 6 s. 2 TEU).[34] But the ECJ also regards freedom of association as a fundamental Community right arising from Article 11 of the European Convention on Human Rights (ECHR) and the common constitutional principles of Member States.[35] Therefore the principle of proportionality must be considered in balancing freedom of association against the fundamental freedoms and non-discrimination rules.[36] Pursuant to the *Meca-Medina* ruling[37] by the ECJ sport activities are, as far as they are professionalized and commercialized, subject to the TFEU, especially the fundamental freedoms, the non-discrimination rule, the prohibition of restraints of competition, and the misuse of a monopoly. It follows that a process of fair balancing that considers the affected interests and the specific conventions of sport – especially the central principle of equal competitive opportunities and fairness[38] – is characteristic of the European as well as of the German approach. Questions such as whether or not the respective sport is considerably affected by sex-related differences and whether or not there is an inequality in performance between males and females due to their different and incommensurable physiques, techniques, or style are of the utmost importance. After balancing these interests, the courts would likely decide in favor of the sport associations, relying on arguments such as the monopolistic structure; the health of female athletes; the number of athletes; the interest in a limitation of the program and the competition; marketing opportunities; and the public interest in a complete and binding definition of a sport (e.g. synchronized swimming as an exclusive event for women). The reason there have been few court rulings[39] on sex discrimination in sports, at least in Germany, may reside in the considerable clout of the associations. Attempts at achieving

---

   [32]   Established case law of the Federal Constitutional Court, e.g. BVerfG E 7, 198, 205 *et seq.*; 112, 332, 358.

   [33]   Vieweg, Klaus (1990), *Normsetzung und -anwendung deutscher und internationaler Verbände*, p. 192.

   [34]   Streinz, Rudolf (2008), *Europarecht*, p. 291.

   [35]   Vieweg, K. and A. Röthel (2002), 'Verbandsautonomie und Grundfreiheiten', *ZHR* 166, pp. 6, 14.

   [36]   *Ibid.* 34.

   [37]   *Meca-Medina and Majcen* v. *Commission* (2006) E.C.R. I-6991.

   [38]   Vieweg, Klaus (2005), 'Verbandsrechtliche Diskriminierungsverbote und Differenzierungsgebote', in: Württembergischer Fußball-Verband e. V. (ed.), *Minderheitenrechte im Sport*, pp. 71 *et seq.*

   [39]   The Newark County Court ruled in favor of a 12-year-old girl, who wanted to play on a boys' football team: *The Guardian* (June 15, 1978), p. 1; *The Daily Mail* (June 16, 1978), p. 15.

inclusion are more likely to succeed at the association level (e.g. mixed-sex teams in football until adolescence).[40]

The separate-but-equal approach favored in United States and European anti-discrimination law and policy may, at first sight, appear to provide the perfect solution to the problem of sex discrimination in sports. The courts are clearly animated by the concern that adopting a formal equal treatment model and allowing mixed-sex teams and competitions might, because of physiological differences between the sexes which tend to give the average male a competitive advantage over the average female,[41] result in male domination of women's events to the detriment of female participation.[42] However, the assumption underlying this concern – i.e. the belief that allowing women access to men's team necessarily entails opening women's teams to men, with the resultant risk of a male 'takeover' of women's teams – may not, in fact, be well founded. There has long existed a strong sentiment in anti-discrimination jurisprudence that discrimination in favor of a traditionally underrepresented group ('reverse discrimination') is not discrimination in a prohibited sense, in that it is not the kind of discrimination the anti-discrimination provision in question was intended to prevent. Thus, claims by men to compete on women's teams have met with little success under Title IX, the courts tending to take the view that the statute's requirement of 'previously ... limited' athletic opportunities meant a history of exclusion from athletic opportunities generally, rather than a history of exclusion from a particular sport. While men may well have had limited opportunities in specific sports – such as rhythmic gymnastics, softball, and synchronized swimming – it is difficult to argue that their *general* athletic opportunities have previously been limited. Because of the specificity of the inquiry conducted by the courts, the majority of reported cases have rejected Title IX challenges to the exclusion of men from women's teams.[43] Similarly, equal protection challenges by men seeking access to female teams have usually failed because securing equal opportunities to women and redressing past discrimination have been judged important government interests sufficient to legitimate the discriminatory practice.[44] But if no risk of cross-infiltration exists, there seems to be no good reason for denying individual members of the 'weaker' group the right to waive their special protection, at least where the persons in question do not thereby expose themselves to

---

[40] E.g. female hockey was first included by the IOC in the Olympic program after the international associations' Federation International de Hockey (FIH) and International Federation of Women's Hockey Associations (IFWH), which had been competing since the 1920s, had merged; Vieweg, note 33 supra, p. 63 note 93.

[41] On average, men are taller and heavier. The average adult female body contains only about half the muscle mass of the adult male body, and the average female body is considerably fatter. See Gerber, Ellen W., Pearl Berlin, and Waneen Wyrick (1974), *The American Woman in Sport*, p. 448 *et seq*. However, these sex differences are average rather than absolute, with some females outperforming some males. Also, some competitions might give a competitive edge to females, in particular those stressing grace over power, like figure skating, gymnastics, or synchronized swimming.

[42] This rationale was specifically advanced in *Bucha* v. *Illininois High School Ass'n*, 351 F.Supp. 69, 75 (D.C. Ill. 1972); *Hoover and Meiklejohn*, 430 F.Supp. 164, 170 (D. Colorado 1977); *O'Connor* v. *Bd. of Ed. of School Dist. No. 23*, 449 U.S. 1301, 1306–07 (U.S. Ill. 1980).

[43] For a summary of the case law, see Cozzillio, Michael J. and Robert L. Hayman, Jr. (2004), *Sports and Inequality*, p. 495.

[44] See, e.g., *Clark* v. *Arizona Interscholastic Ass'n*, 695 F.2d 1126 (9th Cir. 1982), upholding the exclusion of males from all-female teams despite the lack of a separate all-male team.

greatly increased health and safety risks.[45] Granting women the right to 'play up' to the men's team would solve the dilemma of the superior female athlete who outperforms her female competitors.[46] As the law stands, on the other hand, the superior sportswoman is effectively prevented by the separate-but-equal standard from competing against the most able athletes (irrespective of sex) in her field and thus deprived of the opportunity fully to develop her athletic potential.[47]

Given that both the special treatment and the formal equal treatment models have something to offer that could be beneficial to the interests of female athletes, an amalgam approach that combines the best features of each model might well be the ideal system. In the United States, such an amalgam approach was recently introduced to address the problem of pregnant student athletes. The plight of college athletes who become pregnant had been entirely absent from the United States discourse regarding sex equality in sports until relatively recently.[48] It was only in 2007 that a widely viewed ESPN episode entitled *Pregnant Pause* exposed the hardships confronting pregnant student athletes.[49] Discriminatory practices were found to range from the outright withdrawal of athletic scholarships, over the requirement that the athlete earn back her scholarship by proving that she can return to competition after having her child, to the stipulation that the athlete sign a contract on joining the team, promising not to get pregnant and agreeing to forfeit her athletic scholarship if she does.[50] The television program provoked a firestorm of publicity and a remarkably strong response by the Department of Education's Office for Civil Rights (OCR), the primary federal agency charged with enforcing Title IX.[51] The OCR issued a 'Dear Colleague' letter to federal funding recipients, which melds a comparative equal treatment standard with an accommodation/special treatment mandate.[52] In addition to forbidding institutions from treating pregnant athletes any worse than athletes with other medical conditions (equal treatment),[53] the letter requires funding recipients to accommodate a college athlete's pregnancy irrespective of how other conditions are treated (special treatment). For example, the letter's forceful statement that an institution may not terminate or reduce an athletic scholarship because of an athlete's pregnancy sets an absolute standard rather than one that is contingent on the institution's

---

[45]   *Fortin* v. *Darlington Little League, Inc.*, 514 F.2d 344 (1st Cir. 1975), allowing a girl to participate in boys' contact sport because physical abilities of girls aged between eight and 12 were found to be similar to those of boys, removing a health and safety hazard. On the permissibility of paternalistic restrictions, see section (b)(2) *infra*.

[46]   For a similar argument see Greely, H.T. (2004), 'Disabilities, Enhancements, and the Meanings of Sports', *15 Stan. L. & Pol'y Rev.* 99, 124.

[47]   On the quandary faced by the superior female athlete see Kadzielski, note 11 *supra*, p. 101; Cozzillio and Hayman, note 43 *supra*, p. 564; see also Robinson, D. (1998), 'A League of Their Own: Do Women Want Sex-Segregated Sports?', *9 J. Contemp. Legal Issues* 321.

[48]   Brake, D.L. (2008), 'The Invisible Pregnant Athlete and the Promise of Title IX', *31 Harv. J.L. & Gender* 323, 324.

[49]   *Outside the Lines: Pregnant Pause* (ESPN television broadcast May 13, 2007).

[50]   Brake, note 48 *supra*, 327.

[51]   *Ibid.* 330.

[52]   *Ibid.* 331.

[53]   E.g., pregnant students are entitled to receive the same level of privacy and the same level of assistance and rehabilitation to return to game-shape as other athletes on the team for their medical conditions more generally.

trcatment of athletes with other medical problems.[54] In recognition of the fact that pregnancy constitutes the quintessential 'dilemma of difference,'[55] Title IX straddles the equal treatment/special treatment divide. The resulting amalgam provides strong protection for pregnant student athletes.

(3) The reach of (sex) discrimination law

One of the first issues the courts must decide when hearing a (sex) discrimination challenge is whether the entity being sued for discrimination is subject to the anti-discrimination provision in question. The problem usually presents itself in the form of discrimination by – usually private – sports clubs and associations, which operate a policy of gender exclusivity. A similar problem arises, *mutatis mutandis*, where the entity in question discriminates on other grounds, for example, race or disability. In the United States, much of the litigation that has arisen in this context has revolved around the all-male membership policies of one of the last bastions of male privilege: private golf clubs.[56] Determining the proper reach of anti-discrimination law is problematic because it calls for a compromise between two substantial and potentially conflicting interests: the association's right to pick and choose its members and to regulate its internal affairs (in short, its right to freedom of association) and the individual athlete's right to move in society freely and equally without discrimination (i.e. the athlete's right to equal treatment). Both are important concerns and must be reconciled. As a general rule, constitutional equal protection guarantees do not provide a remedy for discrimination at private sports clubs. The Fourteenth Amendment's Equal Protection Clause, for example, is premised on a finding of 'state action,' and does not extend to private parties.[57] The situation is somewhat different in Germany, where, as we saw above, constitutional equal treatment guarantees enter into the equation in claims against private entities under the principle of the third-party effect of fundamental rights.[58] The German courts have the power to review the rules and regulations of at least those private sports bodies that wield

---

[54]   See Dear Colleague Letter from Stephanie Monroe, Office of the Assistant Sec'y, Office for Civil Rights, Dep't of Educ. (June 25, 2007), available at http://www.ed.gov/about/offices/list/ocr/letters/colleague-20070625.html (last accessed October 23, 2009).

[55]   See Brake, note 48 *supra*, 344. As pregnancy constitutes an undeniable sex difference, it presents difficulties for a formal equal treatment approach, which is premised upon the similarities between men and women.

[56]   See, e.g., Garrity, J., 'Willing to Go it Alone: Women Are Often Forced to Pay a Painful Price for Demanding Equality at Their Country Clubs', *Sports Illustrated* (March 2, 1998); Frank, S. (1994), 'The Key to Unlocking the Clubhouse Door: The Application of Antidiscrimination Laws to Quasi-Private Clubs', *2 Mich. J. Gender & L.* 27; Kamp, N. (1998), 'Gender Discrimination at Private Golf Clubs', *5 Sports Law. J.* 89.

[57]   Kamp, note 56 *supra*, 92. There are three narrow bases for deeming apparently private action as state action for purposes of the Equal Protection Clause: (1) the public function test, where a private concern provides goods and services traditionally performed as a government function; (2) the state compulsion theory, where a government becomes so involved in a private entity that it encourages or requires the conduct; and (3) the joint action or nexus theory, where a government judicially enforces a private party's right to discriminate. None of these theories would include a private sports club under the state action doctrine. See Kamp, note 56 *supra*, 92–3.

[58]   Vieweg, Klaus and Anne Müller (2009), 'Gleichbehandlung im Sport', in: Gerrit Manssen, Monika Jachmann, and Christoph Gröpl (eds.), *Festschrift für Udo Steiner*, p. 907.

considerable socio-economic influence.[59] However, in balancing the competing rights, the courts generally come out in favor of a private body's freedom of association.

United States laws barring discrimination in public accommodations[60] generally do not extend to the membership policies of private clubs and associations, although they may outlaw discriminatory practices in a private club's activities to which non-members are admitted.[61] In fact, 'private' and 'distinctly private' clubs are specifically exempted from the scope of many anti-discrimination laws.[62] Moreover, where an anti-discrimination provision purports to reach private clubs, it may run afoul of constitutional guarantees. The constitutional rights at issue for the clubs' defense are based on freedom of association. The Supreme Court has divided freedom of association into freedom of expressive association (grounded in the First Amendment right to free speech and freedom of assembly) and freedom of intimate association (derived from the right of privacy).[63] Neither right is absolute, but can be infringed upon by a compelling state interest achieved by the least restrictive means.[64] Conflicts between a state's compelling interest in preventing discrimination and a private membership organization's associational rights must be resolved on a case-by-case basis. To merit expressive association protection, the club must show a strong nexus between its membership exclusion and its expressive interest.[65] In the case of an all-male sports club, it is difficult to see how the inclusion of women could contravene the club's main purpose as long as that purpose is defined as 'playing a particular sport' rather than as 'male bonding.' It is submitted that – at least in the case of *sports* clubs – any suggestion that the club's primary expressive aim is to raise male consciousness should be rejected as pre-textual. The Supreme Court has not yet decided a case in which a sports club was able to establish a genuine connection between its discrimination and its expressive activities.[66] The Supreme Court's guidelines for intimate association protection tend to permit discrimination only in small, selective, and purely social entities. If a club fails to meet any of these criteria, the state's compelling interest in ensuring equal access free of discrimination is generally held to override the club's associational rights.[67]

---

[59]   *Ibid.* 908.

[60]   The term 'public accommodation,' whether used in Title II of the Federal Civil Rights Act of 1964, Title III of the Americans with Disabilities Act of 1990 (ADA), or state and municipal anti-discrimination laws, is most commonly defined in terms of the entity's openness to the general public. There is, however, considerable interstate variation, with some states defining it in terms of the business aspects of the organization, others in terms of its public use. On the various interpretations of the term, see Frank, note 56 *supra*, 44 *et seq.*

[61]   Frank, note 56 *supra*, 53 *et seq.*

[62]   See, e.g., Title II of the Civil Rights Act of 1964, 42 U.S.C. A. §2000a(e) (1994). In considering whether a club is (distinctly) private, the court will take account of factors like genuine selectivity of membership; limitation of use of facilities to members; membership control; non-profit character; and club publicity. Frank, note 56 *supra*, 51, 64.

[63]   *Roberts* v. *United States Jaycees*, 468 U.S. 609, 617–18 (1984).

[64]   Cozzillio and Hayman, note 43 *supra*, p. 728.

[65]   Johnson, R.N. (1988), '*Board of Directors of Rotary International* v. *Rotary Club of Duarte*: Redefining Associational Rights', *1988 B.Y.U. L. Rev.* 141, 158.

[66]   Frank, note 56 *supra*, 59.

[67]   *Ibid.* 79.

(4) Sexual orientation and gender identity

Anti-discrimination protection for gay, lesbian, and transsexual athletes remains the exception rather than the rule.[68] In the European Union and in Germany, the situation is the same as for sex discrimination. The ECHR, for instance, explicitly prohibits sexual-orientation-based discrimination. In addition, Article 3 s. 1 of the German Constitution requires that like things be treated alike. This problem might arise, for example, if a same-sex couple wanted to participate in competitions which are traditionally mixed, such as pairs skating or ice dancing, or if a couple insisted on having separate same-sex competitions. Under the balancing of interests approach discussed above, these claims would likely fail.[69] In the United States, there currently are no federal laws expressly protecting athletes from sexual-orientation- or gender-identity-related discrimination or harassment.[70] The Employment Non-Discrimination Act (ENDA), a proposed federal statute, would prohibit discrimination on the grounds of sexual orientation and gender identity in employment relationships. Although introduced in virtually every Congress since 1994, it has as yet failed to pass both the House and the Senate. Protection at the state-level is patchy, with only some states having chosen to extend their sex-based civil rights protections to sexual orientation and even fewer to gender identity.[71] The existing case law has tended to focus on the Equal Protection Clause, Title VII of the Civil Rights Act, and Title IX of the Education Amendments as possible bases for protecting homosexual and transgender athletes against at least some kinds of sexual-orientation- or gender-identity-based discrimination.

Equal protection claims have had little success as courts apply a tiered-scrutiny approach dependent upon the issue being addressed. As sexual orientation and gender identity have not been held to constitute either suspect or quasi-suspect classifications, they attract the lowest level of scrutiny ('rational basis review'). A discriminatory law will be upheld if it is reasonably related to a legitimate government interest.[72] Title VII and Title IX have been interpreted as limited to discrimination based on sex and not to cover sexual orientation or gender identity.[73] Judicial interpretation has somewhat broadened their scope, with Title VII held to protect against sexual harassment due to non-conformity to gender stereotypes.[74] Thus, a 'butch' lesbian athlete might have a cause of action under Title VII if directed by her coach to dress in more feminine clothing or to wear her hair in a more feminine style. While this 'gender non-conformity equals sex discrimination' approach might help in some sexual orientation discrimination cases, it

---

[68] Cozzillio and Hayman, note 43 *supra*, p. 845.

[69] See Vieweg, note 38 *supra*, pp. 71, 88.

[70] Title VII of the Civil Rights Act of 1964, e.g., only applies to race, color, religion, sex, or national origin (42 U.S.C. § 2000e-2), with the term 'sex' held to refer only to membership in a class delineated by gender, not by sexual affiliations. *Simonton* v. *Runyon*, 232 F.3d 33, 36 (2nd Cir. 2000).

[71] Pilgrim, J., D. Martin, and W. Binder (2003), 'Far from the Finish Line: Transsexualism and Athletic Competition', *13 Fordham Intell. Prop. Media & Ent. L.J.* 495, 544 *et seq.*

[72] Osborne, B. (2007), 'No Drinking, No Drugs, No Lesbians: Sexual Orientation Discrimination in Intercollegiate Athletics', *17 Marq. Sports L. Rev.* 481, 487.

[73] Hébert, L.C. (2009), 'Transforming Transsexual and Transgender Rights', *15 Wm. & Mary J. Women & L.* 535, 578.

[74] *Price Waterhouse* v. *Hopkins*, 490 U.S. 228, 251 (1989). Title VII case law has served as a model for Title IX interpretation. See Osborne, note 72 *supra*, 493.

leaves many potential claimants uncovered. As Julie Baird has pointed out, the 'funda-mental flaw is that the argument assumes that every gay or lesbian plaintiff acts in a stereotypical way. In other words, the assumption that every lesbian plaintiff walks, talks, and appears masculine, while every gay male plaintiff walks, talks, and acts feminine, leaves out feminine lesbians and masculine gay men.'[75] Unless the courts go one step further and treat homosexuality and transgenderism themselves as failures to conform to gender stereotypes, thus bringing all sexual orientation and gender identity discrimina-tion within the reach of sex discrimination law, or sexual orientation and gender identity are themselves made illicit grounds of discrimination, the United States protective framework for homosexual and transgender athletes will remain incomplete.

In the realm of competitive sports, transgender athletes pose a dilemma in some contexts. In gender-affected sports, where sex-related differences in strength, oxygen transport in the blood, and power-to-weight ratio can affect performance, the sexes usually compete separately to ensure fair play. To enforce this separation and to prevent men from passing themselves off as women, the IOC once required a mandatory sex verification test, using various strategies ranging from visual inspection of genitalia to chromosomal analysis for all females competing in the Olympics.[76] The existence of separate men's and women's divisions in gender-affected sports poses a dilemma for post-operative male-to-female and female-to-male transsexuals who wish to participate. In the case of male-to-female transsexuals (especially those whose reassignment surgery took place after puberty), there is concern about a potential competitive advantage as these athletes have been influenced by performance-enhancing hormones under their pre-operative sex. The popular belief is that transsexuals retain the athletically advanta-geous male physical characteristics. Castration (removing the gonadal source of testoster-one) and estrogen therapy cause a reduction in skeletal muscle mass and in blood hemoglobin. While the larger male skeletal bone mass remains, it is now being powered by a smaller skeletal muscle mass, which decreases power-to-weight ratio and results in an undeniable disadvantage vis-à-vis unaltered males[77] – a competitive advantage vis-à-vis unaltered *females* might, however, remain. Female-to-male transsexuals undergoing tes-tosterone therapy risk exclusion by the prevailing anti-doping rules, although some sports may permit the athlete to obtain a medical waiver.[78]

There are various ways one might deal with the transgender problem. Total exclusion, rigid assignment to birth sex, and the establishment of separate transsexual divisions and competitions are all equally unpalatable options. A more meaningful route might be to use body-based classification schemes – like weight, height, body mass, etc. – as in boxing to match competitors fairly.[79] The policy of choice, in recent years, has been to permit transgender athletes to compete as their 'corrected' (rather than their birth) sex. In 2004, for instance, the IOC announced that it would permit transsexual athletes to compete in

---

[75] Baird, J.A. (2002), 'Playing It Straight: An Analysis of Current Legal Protections to Combat Homophobia and Sexual Orientation Discrimination in Intercollegiate Athletics', *17 Berkeley Women's L.J.* 31, 60.

[76] Pilgrim, Martin, and Binder, note 71 *supra*, 499.

[77] *Ibid.* 530.

[78] *Ibid.* 531.

[79] Shy, Y.L.A. (2007), ' "Like Any Other Girl": Male-to-Female Transsexuals in Professional Sports', *Sports Law. J.* 95, 105.

their acquired gender if the athlete's reassignment surgery took place before puberty or (where after puberty) if hormone therapy has been given long enough to minimize any gender-related advantages.[80] The same year, the British Parliament passed the Gender Recognition Act prohibiting discrimination based on transsexual status but allowing prohibitions and restrictions in gender-affected sports where these are necessary to secure fair competition or the safety of competitors.[81] A recent example which clearly highlights the problem of intersexuality in sport and which is causing quite a stir politically is the case of the South African runner, Caster Semenya. As world champion in the 800-meter running event at the 2009 World Athletics Championships in Berlin, 18-year-old Semenya was the clearly head and shoulders above her fellow competitors.[82] Semenya's unusual appearance and a significant improvement in performance of over 8 seconds within one year, however, led to doubt being cast upon her gender. As a result, the IAAF ordered a medical examination during the World Championships in order to clarify her sex. Although similar cases had already arisen, the athletes concerned were given the opportunity to end their careers out of the public eye. In Semenya's case, though, her gender was questioned by the General Secretary of the IAAF at a press conference after the final of the 800-meter race.[83] In order to clarify gender, a laborious series of examinations is necessary. In South Africa, in particular, the gender test ordered by the IAAF – which was apparently performed unbeknownst to the athlete in question[84] – was heavily criticized and accusations of discrimination, racism, and neocolonial behavior were leveled at the IAAF.[85] After the World Championships, it emerged that the South African Athletics Association (Athletics South Africa – ASA) had already cast doubt upon Semenya's gender and had carried out a gender test.[86] The results of the examination have not yet been published in order to avoid an invasion of the athlete's privacy.[87] Within the context of sports law, we are confronted with the problem of what consequences intersexuality, once established, may legitimately have. In answering this question, however, regard must be had to the basic principle of equal treatment of intersexed individuals, which is, for instance, laid down in Article 21 I of the European Union's Charter of Fundamental Rights.

h. Disability

Traditionally, the principle of equal opportunities in sports led to a distinction between the able-bodied, on the one hand, and handicapped persons, on the other. In time, the concept of competition gained acceptance in disabled sports and caused the evolution of new types of competition (e.g. wheelchair-basketball) as well as the definition of disability categories. At an international level, certain competitions are pointing the way to the future – in particular, the Paralympics which have been taking place since 1992. Some

---

[80]   *Ibid.* 108–9.
[81]   (2004) c. 7, s. 19.
[82]   *Frankfurter Allgemeine Zeitung* (August 21, 2009), p. 30.
[83]   *Frankfurter Allgemeine Sonntagszeitung* (September 27, 2009), p. 20.
[84]   *Frankfurter Allgemeine Zeitung* (August 25, 2009), p. 26.
[85]   *Frankfurter Allgemeine Zeitung* (September 21, 2009), p. 22.
[86]   *Frankfurter Allgemeine Zeitung* (September 27, 2009), p. 20.
[87]   *Frankfurter Allgemeine Zeitung* (September 12, 2009), p. 28.

spectacular cases (Casey Martin, Oscar Pistorius) have drawn the attention of sports law to this difficulty. These cases will be examined in more detail below. In particular, problems relate to the participation of handicapped persons using technological aids in able-bodied competitions (section II.b.(1) *infra*); the exclusion of athletes because of a risk of self-injury (section II.b.(2)); the participation of the able-bodied in contests for the disabled (section II.a.3); and the classification of disabled sports by type and degree of disability (section II.b.(4)).

(1) Ensuring access through special accommodations

Until relatively recently, there had been little litigation involving persons with disabilities and sports. The most highly publicized case on the issue arose in 2001, when Casey Martin, a professional golfer afflicted with Klippel-Trenaunay-Weber syndrome, a degenerative circulatory disorder that obstructs the flow of blood from Martin's right leg back to his heart, fought all the way to the United States Supreme Court to obtain a reasonable accommodation for his disability in the form of the use of a golf cart in professional golf tournaments.[88] The *Martin* case marked the first stage in a growing controversy surrounding the integration of disabled athletes into mainstream competitive athletics. Most recently, the focus of this debate has been on the South African sprinter Oscar Pistorius, who was aiming to run at the Beijing Olympics in the summer of 2008, either in the 200 meter or the 400 meter or as a member of the South African relay team, despite the fact that – born without fibula bones – he had had both legs amputated below the knee before his first birthday.[89] The question was whether Oscar Pistorius should be allowed to compete in the Olympics using a pair of J-shaped carbon fiber blades known as 'Cheetahs' attached to his legs.[90]

Requests like those by Martin and Pistorius – for special accommodations or a change in the rules of the game on account of their physical shortcomings – present the tension between equality and the competitive ethos of sport in unusually stark relief. Thus, one might argue that the very idea of special accommodations is inappropriate for sports competitions because these competitions, by their very nature, are intended to identify and reward the very best. As Justice Scalia of the United States Supreme Court remarked in his forceful *Martin* dissent:

> [T]he very *nature* of competitive sport is the measurement, by uniform rules, of unevenly distributed excellence. This unequal distribution is precisely what determines the winners and losers – and artificially to 'even out' that distribution, by giving one or another player exemption from a rule that emphasizes his particular weakness, is to destroy the game.[91]

---

88   *PGA Tour, Inc.* v. *Martin*, 532 U.S. 661 (2001). For an in-depth discussion, see Zinger, Susanne (2003), *Diskriminierungsverbote und Sportautonomie*, p. 192 *et seq.*

89   Pistorius was the gold medalist in the 200 meter as well as the bronze medalist in the 100 meter at the 2004 Summer Paralympics in Athens. In addition, he is the double amputee world record-holder in the 100-, 200- and 400-meter events. See, e.g., Charlish, P. and S. Riley (2008), 'Should Oscar Run?', *18 Fordham Intell. Prop., Media and Ent. L.J.* 929.

90   Pryor, M., 'Oscar Pistorius is Put through his Paces to Justify his Right to Run', *The Times* (London) (November 20, 2007), available at http://www.timesonline.co.uk/tol/sport/more_sport/athletics/article2903673.ece (last accessed October 24, 2009).

91   *PGA Tour, Inc.* v. *Martin*, 532 U.S. 661, 703–04 (2001) (emphasis in original). Justice Thomas joined in the dissent.

However, unlike in the sex discrimination context, where, as we saw above, a separate-but-equal model still seems to represent the dominant approach, one of the key principles of anti-disability discrimination law is the concept of mainstreaming. The policy is that individuals with disabilities should be allowed to participate in programs in the least restrictive environment.[92] Thus, the main anti-disability discrimination statute in the United States – the Americans with Disabilities Act (ADA) of 1990[93] – requires that 'reasonable modifications' be made for a qualified person with a disability.[94] The relevant legislation in England and Wales is similar. Under the Disability Discrimination Act (DDA) 1995, as amended in 2005,[95] a duty exists to make reasonable adjustments to accommodate the disabled individual to whom the act may apply.[96] In fact, a positive duty to make reasonable accommodation for disabled persons exists throughout the European Union: Article 5 of Council Directive 2000/78/EC, which is binding on Member States as to the object to be achieved, provides that in order 'to guarantee ... equal treatment in relation to persons with disabilities, reasonable accommodation shall be provided ... unless such measures would impose a disproportionate burden on the employer.'[97]

Once it has been determined that the relevant anti-disability discrimination provision is in principle applicable – and, as we saw above, there may be some difficulty in enforcing the legislation against private entities[98] – much will depend on the reach of the statute's exempting provisions, i.e. on the recognized limits to integration. Broadly speaking, defenses to a claim of disability discrimination in the sports context can arise in two kinds of case.

(i)   Fundamental alterations   In *PGA Tour, Inc.* v. *Martin*, a case which continues to define the legal issues surrounding disability and mainstreaming in sports, the PGA Tour did not actually dispute that Martin had a disability for which the use of a golf cart was both a reasonable and a necessary accommodation. Rather, it defended its actions based

---

92   See, e.g., the provisions of the Americans with Disabilities Act, 42 U.S.C.A. § 12182(b)(1)(B) ('accommodations shall be afforded to an individual with a disability in the most integrated setting') and (C) ('Notwithstanding the existence of separate ... programs ... an individual with a disability shall not be denied the opportunity to participate in such programs ... that are not separate').

93   42 U.S.C.A. §§ 12101–213. The ADA expanded upon the provisions of the Federal Rehabilitation Act (RA) of 1973, 29 U.S.C.A. §§701–96, which was limited to the federal government, its contractors and grantees. The ADA prohibits discrimination against people with disabilities by employers (Title I), public entities (Title II), and privately owned businesses and services that provide public accommodations (Title III).

94   42 U.S.C.A. § 12182(b)(2)(A)(ii) and (iii).

95   Public Acts 1995 c. 50.

96   See, e.g., Part III (Discrimination in Other Areas) s. 21.

97   Official Journal L 303, 02/12/2000 P. 0016–0022.

98   See section II.(a)(3) *supra*. The Supreme Court expressly considered the reach of the ADA in *PGA Tour, Inc.* v. *Martin*. The PGA is a private tour that does not employ professional golfers and receives no funds from the state or federal governments. It argued that it was a public accommodation only with respect to the spectators, not the competitors. The Supreme Court agreed with the lower courts that the tournaments held by the PGA were, in fact, public accommodations for the competitors as well as the spectators, making Title III of the Act applicable (532 U.S. 661, 678–80). The case sends the broader message that courts should construe the ADA's coverage liberally. It is likely that only a few events, held at legitimately private clubs that own their own facilities, will avoid ADA coverage.

on the language of § 12182(b)(2)(A)(ii) of the ADA, which provides an exemption from the modification requirement if 'the entity can demonstrate that making such modifications would fundamentally alter the nature of such goods, services, facilities ... or accommodations.' The case was then argued on the basis of whether waiving the PGA Tour rule requiring golfers to walk the course without the use of a cart in Martin's case would fundamentally alter the nature of the PGA Tour event.

The United States Supreme Court held that there were two ways in which a rule change might fundamentally alter the activity in question: by changing 'such an essential aspect of the game of golf that it would be unacceptable even if it affected all competitors equally,' or by giving the disabled person not only equal access but 'an advantage' over other competitors.[99] As regards the first part of the inquiry, the Court concluded that allowing the use of a cart would not change an essential aspect of the game of golf because 'the essence of the game has been shot-making.'[100] The court also noted that the ban on carts is not required by golf's general rules and that carts are indeed strongly encouraged in much of golf.[101] By contrast, allowing a wheelchair user to return the ball after its second bounce in racquetball has been held to alter such an essential aspect of the game that it would be unacceptable even if the modification affected all competitors equally. The Supreme Judicial Court of Massachusetts reasoned that the essence of the game of racquetball, as expressly articulated in the official rules, was the hitting of a moving ball before the second bounce and that giving a wheelchair player two bounces and a footed player one bounce in head-to-head competition would create a new game, calling for new strategies, positioning, and movement of players.[102] The second leg of the Supreme Court's inquiry in *Martin* concerned whether the modification in question – the use of a cart – would give Martin a competitive advantage. The court held that the ADA required the PGA to make an individualized assessment of Martin's claim. Relying on the trial court's findings that Martin 'easily endures greater fatigue even with a cart than his able-bodied competitors do by walking,'[103] the court found that using a cart did not give Martin an advantage and that it was the PGA's duty under the ADA to provide him with one.

While *Martin* opened the door for suits by athletes seeking accommodations or rule modifications for their disabilities, it does not make every modifications suit a winner. The more recent Pistorius controversy is illustrative in this regard. Pistorius's bid for entry into the 2008 Summer Olympic Games ran up against a March 2007 amendment to its competition rules by the IAAF.[104] The amendment banned the 'use of any technical device that incorporates springs, wheels or any other element that provides the user with an advantage over another athlete not using such a device.'[105] Undoubtedly, the artificial limbs used by Pistorius were technical devices, and, equally undoubtedly, they afforded Pistorius a performance advantage over and above anything he could have achieved

---

99   532 U.S. 661, 682.
100   *Ibid.* 683.
101   *Ibid.* 685–6. Even the PGA does not ban carts in some of its tours.
102   *Kuketz* v. *Petronelli*, 433 Mass. 355, 821 N.E.2d 473 (2005).
103   *Ibid.* 690 (quoting *Martin* v. *PGA Tour, Inc.*, 994 F.Supp. 1242, 1252 (D. Or. 1998)).
104   Some have suggested that this rule was introduced specifically to deal with the threat posed by Pistorius, an allegation vehemently denied by IAAF council member Robert Hersh. Charlish and Riley, note 89 *supra*, 930.
105   IAAF Competition Rule 144.2(e) (2008).

without such limbs. The crucial question, however, was whether the artificial limbs overshot their (permissible) aim of compensating for Pistorius's lack of lower legs and instead constituted an (impermissible) enhancement – what some have called 'techno-doping.'[106] A 2007 study conducted by German professor Gert-Peter Brüggemann for the IAAF found that Pistorius's limbs used 25% less energy than able-bodied runners to run at the same speed and that they led to less vertical motion combined with 30% less mechanical work for lifting the body.[107] Brüggemann concluded that Pistorius had considerable advantages over athletes without prosthetic limbs.[108] Based on these findings, the IAAF ruled Pistorius's prostheses ineligible for use in competitions conducted under the IAAF rules, including the 2008 Summer Olympics.[109]

In May 2008, however, the Court of Arbitration for Sport (CAS) reversed the ban, clearing the way for Pistorius to pursue his dream, although the athlete ultimately failed to qualify for the Olympics. A major component of the court's decision was that there was insufficient evidence that the prosthetics provided an *overall* advantage to Pistorius when their disadvantages were taken into account.[110] In other words, the court held that what mattered was the whole package of benefit and detriment over the entire course of the race – the net status of performance – rather than the impact of the prosthetic limbs in isolation.[111] For instance, while Pistorius's prosthetics may return more impact energy than the human foot, as the Brüggemann study found,[112] this benefit might be offset by their also causing slower starts,[113] being ill adapted to rainy and windy conditions, and difficult to handle in navigating bends. Similarly, just as Pistorius has the advantage of

---

[106] For the term, Longman, J., 'An Amputee Sprinter: Is He Disabled or Too-Abled?', *The New York Times* (May 15, 2007), available at http://www.nytimes. com/2007/05/15/sports/othersports/15runner.html?_r=1&oref=slogin (last accessed October 24, 2009).

[107] For further information, Brüggemann, G-P., A. Arampatzis, F. Emrich, *et al.* (2008), 'Biomechanics of Double Transtibial Amputee Sprinting Using Dedicated Sprinting Prostheses', *Sports Technol.*, 1, No. 4–5, 220, 226 *et seq.*; 'Blade Runner Handed Olympic Ban', *BBC Sport* (January 14, 2008), available at http://news.bbc.co.uk/sport2/hi/olympics/athletics/7141302.stm (last accessed October 24, 2009).

[108] 'Studie beendet Olympiatraum von Pistorius', *Welt Online* (December 19, 2007) available at www.welt.de/welt_print/article1475643/Studie_beendet_Olympiatraum_von_Pistorius.html (last accessed October 24, 2009).

[109] 'IAAF Call Time on Oscar Pistorius' Dream', *The Daily Telegraph* (January 10, 2008), available at www.telegraph.co.uk/sport/othersports/athletics/2288489/IAAF-call-time-on-Oscar-Pistorius-dream.html (last accessed October 24, 2009).

[110] The evidential burden of proving the 'advantage' in terms of IAAF rule 144.2.(e) is on the sports association which imposed the suspension. The applicable standard the association must apply to prove that the user of the prosthesis has an overall net advantage over other athletes not using such devices is the 'balance of probability.' CAS 2008/A/1480, *Pistorius* v. *IAAF*, para. 92.

[111] The IAAF did not ask Professor Brüggemann to determine whether the use of the prosthesis provides an overall net advantage or disadvantage. CAS 2008/A/1480, *Pistorius* v. *IAAF*, paras. 85, 93 = *SpuRt 2008*, 152, 154. The only purpose of the determination was the question whether Pistorius's use of the prosthesis provided him with any kind of advantage.

[112] 'Studie beendet Olympiatraum von Pistorius', *Welt Online* (December 19, 2007), available at www.welt.de/welt_print/article1475643/Studie_beendet_Olympiatraum_von_Pistorius.html (last accessed October 24, 2009).

[113] Observing Pistorius's run, one can see that he was slower than other able-bodied runners off the starting blocks and during the acceleration phase, but faster during the second and third 100 meter; CAS 2008/A/1480, *Pistorius* v. *IAAF*, 41= *SpuRt 2008*, 152, 153.

suffering no fatigue in his legs below his knees, so also is he subject to the disadvantage of only being able to produce propulsive effects via muscles above his knees.[114]

Of course, the net effect of technical aids on a disabled athlete's overall performance must be difficult, if not impossible, to quantify accurately (and any attempt to do so is bound to have significant resource implications[115]). One suspects that one reason why *Martin* has not set off a barrage of suits by disabled athletes seeking an accommodation to participate in mainstream sports[116] is that, because of the ethos of competition, most disabled athletes do not want, or accept, any actual or perceived favors. To receive or to be suspected of receiving special aid devalues the athletic achievement. As Pistorius told reporters, 'If they [the IAAF] ever found evidence that I was gaining an advantage, then I would stop running because I would not want to compete at a top level if I knew I had an unfair advantage.'[117]

What if the tests carried out on Pistorius had been conclusive that the prosthetic limbs did in fact go further than merely redressing his overall performance balance? Indeed, in some cases, it might not be possible to accommodate a disabled athlete without at the same time improving his situation beyond that of the average competitor. This need not necessarily preclude participation. One solution to the dilemma might be to impose a scoring handicap equivalent to the (illicit) advantage on the athlete concerned.[118] Sports have developed a sophisticated machinery to set various forms of handicaps: occasionally, better competitors are physically hindered;[119] in team sports, weaker teams are sometimes given special advantages;[120] and in a few sports, the actual scoring is adjusted to help inferior competitors.[121] Perhaps we should consider using these various handicapping methods to further the integration of disabled athletes into mainstream sports.

---

[114]   Charlish and Riley, note 89 *supra*, 936. Another advantage the use of a prosthesis may provide is the mental impact on the other athletes who have to start next to an amputee. It is an open question whether this is the case and whether a possible psychological obstacle of the able-bodied athletes may be considered given the non-discrimination rule.

[115]   The tests conducted on Pistorius cost in the range of €30 000. See Charlish/Riley Charlish and Riley, note 89 *supra*, 939. If funding such tests is left to the individual athlete, challenges are unlikely to be brought. If sports governing bodies are left to pick up the tab, on the other hand, the financial burden on these might also be immense. The respective sports association should, however, regulate the process by which a disabled sportsperson who uses a prosthetic can take part in competitions for able-bodied sportspeople in a way that guarantees safety and saves money. Thus, the sports association should compile a list of all institutions to be considered in the necessary studies, enumerate all factors to be investigated, and set out the procedure to be followed in the event that a disabled sportsperson makes an administrative appeal. Chappel, A. (2008), 'Running Down a Dream: Oscar Pistorius, Prosthetic Devices, and the Unknown Future of Athletes with Disabilities in the Olympic Games', *10 NC JOLT On line Ed. 1*, 16, 26.

[116]   On the limited impact of *Martin* in terms of similar cases brought, Greely, note 46 *supra*, 111.

[117]   'Pistorius Is No Novelty Sprinter', *The Daily Telegraph* (Sport) (July 11, 2007), available at http://www.telegraph.co.uk/sport/othersports/athletics/2316794/pistorius-is-no-novelty-sprinter.html (last accessed October 24, 2009).

[118]   For a similar proposal see Greely, note 46 *supra*, 122 *et seq.*

[119]   In most thoroughbred horseracing, e.g., weight is added to some of the horses to balance out the different weights of the jockeys.

[120]   In many professional leagues in the United States, the worst teams get the first choice of players who enter the draft, presumably allowing them to equalize ability in the league over time.

[121]   Amateur golf and bowling, e.g., give special scoring advantages to weaker competitors based on their previous results.

(ii)   Risk of injury to others   Allowing a disabled individual to compete with the help of an accommodation may present substantial injury problems with other competitors. For instance, if Pistorius had qualified for the Olympics and been allowed to run in the main pack of the race, his running blades might have posed a safety hazard for fellow athletes.[122] Under the ADA, the employment qualification standards under Title I may include 'a requirement that an individual shall not pose a direct threat to the health and safety of other individuals in the workplace,'[123] while Title III declares that public accommodations are not obliged 'to permit an individual to participate ... where such individual poses a direct threat to the health and safety of others ... that cannot be eliminated by a modification of policies, practices, or procedures or by the provision of auxiliary aids or services.'[124] In *Badgett* v. *Alabama High School Athletic Ass'n*,[125] Mallerie Badgett, a minor wheelchair-bound track-and-field athlete with cerebral palsy, brought a claim against the Alabama High School Athletic Association (AHSAA) under the ADA because she wished to compete in the able-bodied track-and-field competition. The court denied her claim, finding that the AHSAA had made reasonable modifications by establishing a separate wheelchair division. The court held that in deciding what was reasonable both competitive and safety considerations had to be taken into account and that there were legitimate safety concerns about having able-bodied and wheelchair-bound athletes compete in mixed heats.

(2)   Excluding athletes because of a risk of self-injury
Quite apart from the question of whether there is a duty to ensure access for disabled individuals through special accommodations, there is the issue of whether a disabled athlete can be excluded on the (paternalistic) ground that participation carries a high risk of self-injury.[126] An example is the person who has only one kidney but still wants to participate in a contact sport such as interscholastic wrestling.[127] In the United States, the focus of the inquiry is on whether the disabled athlete is an otherwise 'qualified individual,'[128] i.e. whether he is able to meet all of the program's requirements in spite of his handicap.[129]

---

[122]   IAAF general secretary Pierre Weiss in fact voiced this concern, expressing a wish that the South African Olympic Committee not select Pistorius for its relay team 'for reasons of safety'. See 'Relay Safety Fears Over Pistorius', *BBC Sport* (July 15, 2008), available at http://news-bbc.co.uk/sport2/hi/olympics/athletics/7508399.stm (last accessed October 25, 2009). The CAS did not, however, address the question whether the use of prosthetics could lead to an increased risk of stumbling, thereby creating a greater risk of injuring other athletes.
[123]   42 U.S.C.A. § 12113(b).
[124]   42 U.S.C.A. § 12182(b)(3).
[125]   2007 WL 2461928 (N.D. Ala. May 3, 2007).
[126]   For discussion, see Anderson, note 22 *supra*, p. 52 *et seq.* and Zinger, note 31 *supra*, p. 13 *et seq.*
[127]   *Poole* v. *South Plainfield Bd. of Ed.*, 490 F.Supp. 948 (D.C.N.J. 1980).
[128]   Many of the cases predated the ADA and were decided under § 504 of the Rehabilitation Act of 1973 (RA), which prohibits discrimination against 'otherwise qualified' individuals, in federally funded programs, solely because of their handicap (29 U.S.C. § 794).
[129]   *Southeastern Community College* v. *Davis*, 442 U.S. 397, 398 (1979).

In *Pahulu* v. *University of Kansas*,[130] the plaintiff was injured during football practice and later diagnosed with a very narrow cervical canal, leading team doctors to believe that he was at very high risk of serious neurological injury. As a result, Pahulu was suspended from football. He sued, claiming the university discriminated against him by disqualifying him only on account of his disability. The court denied Pahulu's injunction, holding that he failed to meet the 'otherwise qualified' standard because he did not fulfill the team's medical requirements. The court found that the team doctors' risk assessment provided a reasonable and rational basis for the disqualification, precluding further judicial scrutiny.[131]

Where a disabled athlete is aware of and willing to incur the dangers involved in continued athletic participation, allowing a third party to interpose its 'benevolent paternalism,'[132] as the *Pahulu* court did, requires some strong justification. Citing a sport organization's 'inherent right to protect an athlete's health'[133] – from himself (!) – should not be regarded as sufficient as this amounts to justifying paternalism for paternalism's sake. Whether protecting the organization's reputation, which might be tarnished by a competitor being severely injured or killed in competition,[134] or averting a liability risk should trump the athlete's right to decide is questionable, especially where the athlete is prepared to sign a waiver that would release the organization from all liability.[135] While paternalism might be appropriate in amateur, in particular in high school and collegiate sports (where the persons protected are usually minors), it seems very hard to justify in the case of *professional* (adult) athletics. Where a competent athlete's livelihood is threatened if made to abstain from sports participation, his right to decide what is in his own best interests should be regarded as paramount.[136]

(3)   Participation of the able-bodied in competitions for the disabled

Another facet to the participation problem presents itself where able-bodied athletes wish to take part in competitions for the disabled. In wheelchair-basketball, for example, up to two non-disabled athletes may be included on a team. Also, an able-bodied athlete could take the view that he has no advantages in sports intended for the disabled, giving him a

---

130   897 F.Supp. 1387 (D. Kansas 1995).

131   *Ibid.* 1394. For a similar decision, see *Knapp* v. *Northeastern University*, 101 F.3d 473 (7th Cir. 1996) (holding that requiring medical qualification did not violate the RA, provided the school had significant medical evidence indicating a serious risk of injury). For a decision that went in the opposite direction, see *Poole* v. *South Plain Field Bd. of Ed.*, 490 F.Supp. 948 (D.C.N.J. 1980) (holding school had neither duty nor right under RA to exclude student who knew of dangers and – with parents' consent – still chose to compete).

132   For this term, see Tucker, B. P. (1996), 'Application of the Americans with Disabilities Act (ADA) and Section 504 to Colleges and Universities: An Overview and Discussion of Special Issues Relating to Students', *23 J.C. & U.L.* 1, 33.

133   For this argument, see Mitten, M. J. (1998), 'Enhanced Risk of Harm to One's Self as a Justification for Exclusion from Athletics', *8 Marq. Sports L.J.* 189, 192.

134   *Knapp* v. *Northwestern University*, 942 F.Supp. 1191, 1199 (N.D. Ill. 1996); Mitten, note 133 *supra*, 192.

135   On the legal validity of waivers, see Church, T.G. and J.R. Neumeister (1998), 'University Control of Student-Athletes with Disabilities under the Americans with Disabilities Act', *25 J.C. & U.L.* 105, 180 *et seq.*

136   For the argument that a distinction be drawn between professional and amateur sports, Mitten, note 133 *supra*, 221 *et seq.*

right to participate. Similarly, an able-bodied person might wish to take part in a marathon for persons using wheelchairs. This particular problem may be approached in the following way: the relevant association rules and their application are subject to judicial scrutiny. The facts of the individual case and the principle of proportionality are the decisive criteria. The question of whether participation may be confined to disabled persons, as intended by the association, has to be addressed by balancing the interests at stake.

(4)   Classifications by type and degree of disability
In disabled sports, there are various classifications to ensure equal opportunities. The need for classification arises from the existence of different types of disabilities and their varying severity. There is a distinction, for example, between physical and intellectual disability. Persons who are physically disabled are further categorized into subgroups, such as athletes with a visual impairment or athletes using wheelchairs. These groups are again subdivided according to the severity of the disability, in particular according to the individual's mobility impairment due to the disability. This classification, however, may run into difficulties. On the one hand, the various categories should not be overly strict, given that, otherwise, there would not be a sufficient starting field. On the other hand, they should only cover athletes who have similar physical conditions in order to comply with the principle of equal opportunities. Finding a solution to such a conflict of objectives is difficult and can lead to judicial review if an athlete feels discriminated against by the definition of the categories or by his or her classification. In discus throwing, for example, various grades of disability are united in one competition to provide a sufficient starting field. To offset this, however, a points system based on the grade of the disability is introduced: the more severe the impairment, the less the distance required in order to gain an accordant score. To ensure equal opportunities in discus throwing, it is of the utmost importance that the conversion factor which determines the score be non-discriminatory with regard to the grade of disability.[137]

Up until now, these questions have not been subject to judicial review. For this reason, questions of proof which would be much more relevant in this context than in the *Martin* and *Pistorius* cases have not played a role so far.

c.   Nationality

Throughout the history of sport, the idea of competition – one of the guiding principles of modern sport besides those of equality, fairness, and performance – has used the nationality of the athletes as a criterion for differentiation. Furthermore, the creation of national and international organizations through the foundation of national and international sport associations is based upon the nationality of members, however defined. Particular milestones were the foundation of the IOC in 1894 and the staging of the first Olympic Games in Athens in 1896. The foundation of the first international sport

---

[137]   Marianne Bruchhagen, e.g., a paraplegic discus thrower, abandoned her career because she found the points system to be unfair. The system is based exclusively on the respective world record of one grade of disability: see *Frankfurter Allgemeine Zeitung* (July 7, 2008), p. 31.

associations also took place in this era: the International Gymnastics Federation (Fédération Internacionale Gymnastique, FIG) (1881), International Rowing Federation (Fédération Internationale des Sociétés d'Aviron, FISA) (1892), International Organization for Standardization (ISO) (1892), International Cycling Union (Union Cycliste Internationale, UCI) (1900), IAAF (1912). The number of participating nations was still comparatively small, compared with the number of National Olympic Committees accepted by the IOC in 2009 (205): only 5 nations took part in founding the FISA (17 in the case of the IAAF and 18 in that of the International Equestrian Foundation (FEI), respectively). The staging of world championships started in the 1890s (UCI in Chicago in 1893, 1895 for professionals in Cologne on the occasion of the 25-year celebration of the defeat of France). The first football World Cup took place in 1930. International football matches had already started by 1872.

On a national level, sport associations had been founded even earlier (e.g. the German Gymnast Association in 1860, the Football Association (FA) in 1863, the German Football Federation in 1900). The growing popularity of sporting events, their worldwide broadcasting through the media, and also the comparison of different political systems increasingly drew attention to the criterion of nationality. It was used as an instrument of propaganda in the 1936 Olympic Games. This same comparison of nations and systems finds clear expression in the unofficial medal table of the Olympic Games.

Irrespective of this basic conformity, there are many problems linked to differentiation by nationality. For one thing, the terms 'nation' and 'state' are not synonymous. One state can incorporate several nations (e.g. USSR, Yugoslavia) or the other way round (e.g. Germany, China, Korea). Separatism (e.g. Catalonia)[138] and partial political autonomy (e.g. Puerto Rico) must also be considered. This has practical consequences for the IOC or the international sports associations when admitting national teams. Acceptance by the law of nations and admittance by an independent National Olympic Committee or another sports association can differ in individual cases. Thus, the IOC has acknowledged 205 National Olympic Committees. The IAAF counts 213 national track and field associations. By comparison, the United Nations has 192 member states.

A further problem is posed by the admission of individual athletes into international competitions if these individuals are either stateless or of multiple nationality – i.e. persons with double or multiple citizenship – or, further, where an individual changes his or her nationality – for example, as a result of marriage or naturalization. The international sports associations have drawn up regulations, the purpose of which is, on the one hand, to solve the conflict of aims arising particularly out of the generous practice of naturalization in one state which can affect equality of opportunity between national teams and, on the other hand, to ensure that athletes may reach personal decisions without having their participation in international sporting events inhibited in a discriminatory manner. In particular, they encompass binding agreements on the part of athletes, waiting periods for changing one's citizenship, and certificates of release from the national sports associations to which the athletes previously belonged.

---

[138]   See the proceedings of the congrés internacional del dret il'esport, Barcelona, 26, 27 i 28 de marc de 1992, edited by Generalitat de Catalunya, Secretaria General de l'Esport.

Although sometimes intersecting with discrimination on the basis of race and ethnic origin,[139] the issue of nationality discrimination – in the European Union context – merits separate consideration. Articles 45 *et seq.* and 56 *et seq.* of the TFEU (ex: Articles 39 *et seq.* and 49 *et seq.* EC) address freedom of movement for workers and freedom to provide services, respectively, and prohibit any form of – direct or indirect – discrimination[140] based on nationality. The ECJ has made clear that nationality restrictions in professional sport are not beyond the scope of the TFEU (ex: EC Treaty)[141] and that professional and semi-professional athletes can invoke the anti-discrimination provisions.[142] Moreover, the reach of European Union anti-discrimination law is not limited to states or bodies exercising public law functions, but also applies to rules laid down by (private) sporting associations, such as the Fédération International de Football Association (FIFA) or the Union of European Football Associations (UEFA), which determine the terms on which professional sportsmen can engage in gainful employment.[143] The Treaty's guarantee of free movement would be compromised if organizations could justify barriers to free movement merely by pointing to their exemption from public law.[144]

The ECJ case that laid down the ground rules on the permissibility of nationality restrictions in European sports is *Union Royale Belge des Sociétés de Football Association* v. *Bosman*,[145] which concerned UEFA's '3+2' rule. Under the '3+2' rule, each UEFA club team could field at most three players who were nationals of other European Member States plus two 'assimilated foreigners' who had played in the host Member State for an uninterrupted period of five years.[146] These restrictions, according to the ECJ, constituted

---

[139]   On this, see section II.e *infra*.

[140]   On the distinction between direct and indirect discrimination see note 14 *supra*. In addition to applying to directly as well as to indirectly discriminatory measures, Articles 45 *et seq.* and 56 *et seq.* TFEU (ex: Articles 39 *et seq.* and 49 *et seq.* EC) also prohibit non-discriminatory obstacles to free movement (so-called mere restrictions) unless these can be justified. See Fritzweiler, Jochen, Bernhard Pfister and Thomas Summerer (2007), *Praxishandbuch Sportrecht*, p. 613.

[141]   In *Walrave and Koch* v. *Association Union Cycliste Internationale* (1974) E.C.R. 1405, the ECJ had held that sport was subject to Community law only in so far as it constituted economic activity (para. 4), encouraging some sports governing bodies to propose that the entirety of their regulation fell within this 'sporting exception' and thus outside the scope of the Treaty. However, following the ECJ's clarification in *Meca-Medina and Majcen* v. *Commission* (2006) E.C.R. I-6991, if the rule has even the slightest economic effect, a sporting rule other than a nationality restriction applicable to national teams playing on behalf of a Member State cannot be considered *a priori* exempt but must be justified (para. 27 *et seq.*). The process thus involves objective justification rather than wholesale exclusion of sports regulations from the scope of the Treaty.

[142]   For athletes engaged in professional team sports, Article 45 *et seq.* TFEU (ex: Article 39 *et seq.* EC) apply. Other professional athletes, e.g. tennis players, would be classed as independent contractors and be protected by Article 56 *et seq.* TFEU (ex: Article 49 *et seq.* EC). Fritzweiler, Pfister, and Summerer, note 140 *supra*, p. 612. Where an athlete is not undertaking genuine economic activity, as in amateur sports, he may rely on the broader, citizenship-based rule of non-discrimination found in Article 18 TFEU (ex: Article 12 EC).

[143]   *Walrave and Koch* v. *Association Union Cycliste Internationale* (1974) E.C.R. 1405, 1417, para. 15 *et seq.*; *Union Royale Belge des Sociétés de Football Association ASBL* v. *Jean-Marc Bosman* (1995) E.C.R. I-4921, para. 87.

[144]   *Walrave and Koch* v. *Association Union Cycliste Internationale* (1974) E.C.R. 1405, 1418, para 18.

[145]   (1995) E.C.R. I-4921.

[146]   *Ibid.* at para. 27.

unlawful direct nationality discrimination under Article 45 TFEU (ex: Article 39 EC).[147] The ECJ rejected the proposition that restrictive nationality clauses taking the form of fixed quotas were justifiable on non-economic grounds.[148] Specifically, UEFA had argued that nationality quotas were needed (1) to preserve links between each club and its country in order to enable fans better to identify with their teams, (2) to secure a pool of high-class national players for national team recruitment, and (3) to maintain a competitive balance between clubs by preventing the richest clubs from monopolizing the best players.[149] The court observed that the asserted attempt to solidify 'fan identification' ignored the fact that no comparable restrictions existed to require even minimal representation from a team's own locality, region, or territory,[150] that national teams were not restricted to players registered to play for clubs in their home country and that clubs were already bound to release foreign players for national teams;[151] and that the '3+2' rule did not really address the problem of competitive imbalance because rich clubs routinely recruited the best players within the boundaries of existing rules.[152]

Although *Bosman* clearly applied to all sports and not just to football, the decision left open whether the rationale also extended to non-European Union nationals whose home countries had entered into association or cooperation agreements with the European Union. Many of these agreements contained non-discrimination provisions regarding employment conditions for third-party nationals legally employed within the European Union.[153] The post-*Bosman* case law has extended *Bosman*'s anti-discrimination principles to Eastern and Central European countries that have signed association or cooperation agreements, including Russia, as well as a number of North African countries that have signed special cooperation agreements with the European Union.[154] However, the scope of these decisions is limited by the fact that *Bosman*'s anti-discrimination principles only apply via association and cooperation agreements to non- European Union athletes already lawfully employed within a Member State. There is nothing in the decisions that would provide non- European Union nationals with a general right of access to Member States' internal labor markets.[155]

With the impact of athlete migration on the economic and socio-cultural dynamics of European sport still a controversial topic, professional European sports organizations persist in their attempts to stem the influx of foreign players. *Bosman* and its progeny defined the outer limits of (im)permissibility, outlawing fixed nationality-based quotas and sanctioning nationality restrictions in one tightly circumscribed set of circumstances

---

[147]   *Ibid.* at para. 137.

[148]   *Ibid.* at paras. 122–5, 130.

[149]   *Ibid.* at paras. 123–5.

[150]   *Ibid.* at para. 131.

[151]   *Ibid.* at para. 133.

[152]   *Ibid.* at para. 135.

[153]   Penn, D. W. (2006), 'From *Bosman* to *Simutenkov*: The Application of Non-Discrimination Principles to Non-EU Nationals in European Sports', *30 Suffolk Transnat'l L. Rev.* 203, 217 *et seq.*

[154]   See Case C-438/00, *Deutsher Handballbund eV* v. *Maros Kolpak* (2003) ECR I-4135, discussed in *International Sports Law Journal*, 2003/2: Case 265/03, *Igor Simutenkov* v. *Ministerio de Educación y Cultura and Real Federación Española de Fútbol*; Tams, C.J. (2005), 'Nichtdiskriminierung im europäischen Profi-Sport', *EuR 2005*, 777, 783; Penn, note 153 *supra*, 217 *et seq.*; Fritzweiler, Pfister, and Summerer, note 140 *supra*, p. 621 *et seq.*

[155]   Penn, note 153 *supra*, 224; Fritzweiler, Pfister, and Summerer, note 140 *supra*, p. 619 *et seq.*

only: recruitment of national teams playing on behalf of a Member State. However, the decisions left uncharted middle ground. The 'Home-Grown Player Rule,' which limits European club play according to the facially neutral criterion of training program participation rather than a directly discriminatory nationality-based requirement like *Bosman*'s '3+2' rule, represents UEFA's most recent attempt to plumb the depths of the *Bosman* ruling.[156] Under the 'Home-Grown Rule,' as of the 2009 season, 'A' clubs must include on their maximum 25-man roster at least eight 'locally trained' players. Locally trained players can be either 'club-trained' or 'association-trained.' To qualify as 'club-trained' or 'association-trained,' a player must be registered for at least three entire seasons with his club or within the same national organization when he is between the ages of 15 and 21.[157] UEFA has sought to justify this rule as a means to restore local identity to clubs, redress competitive imbalance, encourage the training of local youngsters, and reinvigorate national teams[158] – arguments that sound uncomfortably similar to the ones the ECJ rejected in *Bosman* and its progeny. However, while the 'Home-Grown Rule' has similar aims to the '3+2' rule, it is legally distinguishable in that it is not structured around nationality *per se*, but residence and club affiliation (criteria that more nationals than non-nationals are likely to fulfill). Thus, the method employed is not one of direct discrimination, but of indirect discrimination.[159] Since the rule is indirectly rather than directly discriminatory, categories of objective justification beyond the express Treaty derogations are available.[160] The test involves scrutiny of whether a rule with indirectly discriminatory effects is justified by imperative requirements in the general interest, fit for the purpose it claims to serve, and proportionate to those aims. Whilst the objectives of maintaining competitive balance, fostering the young, and protecting national teams have been recognized as legitimate requirements in the general interest by the ECJ,[161] there are doubts over whether the 'Home-Grown Rule' is a *proportionate* means of achieving those

---

[156]   See Streinz, R. (2008), ' "6+5' Regel oder Homegrown-Regel – was ist mit dem EG-Recht vereinbar', *SpuRt 2008*, 224 *et seq.*

[157]   Regulations of the UEFA Champions League 2008/09 Competition, Player Eligibility, p. 22 *et seq.*, available at http://www.uefa.com/multimediafiles/download/regulations/uefa/others/70/22/60/702260-download.pdf (last accessed October 25, 2009).

[158]   Penn, note 153 *supra*, 227. For an extended consideration, see Miettinen, S. and R. Parrish (2007), 'Nationality Discrimination in Community Law: An Assessment of UEFA Regulations Governing Player Eligibility for European Club Competitions (The Home-Grown Player Rule)', 5 *E.S.L.J.*, paras. 17–34.

[159]   Streinz, note 156 *supra*, 228. Under the 6+5 rule, each club must field at least six players eligible to play for the national team of the country of the club at the beginning of the match. However, there is no restriction on the number of non-eligible players under contract with the club, nor on substitutes to avoid non-sportive constraints on the coaches. The 6+5 rule in club football was accepted as a resolution by FIFA at its meeting in Sydney on 29 and 30 May 2008.

[160]   A finding of direct discrimination can be justified only if it can be covered by an express derogating provision in the TFEU. These are substantially identical for all fundamental freedoms, namely public policy, public security, and public health. Indirectly discriminatory rules may be justified with reference to Treaty grounds and broader categories of objective justification based on public interest requirements.

[161]   *Union Royale Belge des Sociétés de Football Association ASBL* v. *Jean-Marc Bosman* (1995) E.C.R. I-4921, para. 106; *Walrave and Koch* v. *Association Union Cycliste Internationale* (1974) E.C.R. 1405, para. 8.

objectives. It would seem that a number of less restrictive alternatives exist: a redistribution of income from richer to poorer clubs through solidarity payments may aid competitive imbalance, while a club licensing scheme requiring applicant clubs to run approved development programs might meet UEFA's youth training objectives.[162] It is not certain, therefore, whether UEFA's 'Home-Grown Player Rule' would survive a challenge in the European courts.[163]

The only remaining avenue of redress for sports organizations seeking to minimize the influx of non-European Union athletes seems to lie with the domestic immigration and labor laws of individual Member States. Each Member State, in exercising its power to regulate labor and immigration within its borders, may determine the number of residence and work permits granted to non-European Union nationals on teams within that state. Sports organizations could lobby and cooperate with national governments to modify existing regulations and restrict the issue of residence and work permits for non-European Union athletes.[164]

d. Religion

The attitudes of the various world religions towards sport differ. It is true that none of the major religions impose a blanket ban on (competitive) sports. Nor do the regulations of the main sporting organizations exclude any particular religions from participating in sporting events. Indeed, the articles of association of the major national and international sporting organizations emphasize their neutrality in religious matters. The IOC even regards discrimination on the basis of religion as an infringement of the fundamental principles of the Olympics.[165]

Religious obligations, however, can conflict with the exercise of sport – particularly in the competitive and professional arenas. The overview which follows aims to provide an insight into the problems arising in this area, having particular regard to discrimination. There are clear parallels, or rather overlaps with discrimination for reasons of race[166] and discrimination against women.[167]

An early example of discrimination for religious reasons is provided by the 1960 Olympic boxing champion, Cassius Clay, who in 1964 converted to Islam and who, during the Vietnam War, refused to comply with his draft into the United States army. As a priest of the religious society, 'Nation of Islam', he felt that he was entitled to refuse to perform military service.[168] As a result, Clay, who in the meantime had changed his name to Muhammad Ali, was stripped of his title of world champion in 1967. His boxing license was revoked and was reissued to him only in 1970. A further case which demonstrates the conflict between sport and religion but which did not lead to discrimination is that of the

---

    162   On these and other less restrictive alternatives, see Miettinen and Parrish, note 158 *supra*, paras. 27–34. Seriously discussed alternatives are the adoption of a salary cap and an effective licensing procedure, which limits the level of debt of the clubs: see Streinz, note 156 *supra*, 229.
    163   For the same assessment, see Penn, note 153 *supra*, 231.
    164   Penn, note 153 *supra*, 230–31.
    165   See note 2 *supra*.
    166   See section II.e *infra* on the *Gretel Bergmann* case.
    167   See section II.a *supra*.
    168   Krämer, Harald and Fritz K. Heering (2001), *Muhammad Ali*, pp. 52 *et seq.*

Indian gymnast, Daldschit Singh, who participated in the 1970 World Championships. As a Sikh, Singh was forbidden from cutting his hair. Due to the regulations of the international association, the FIG, which provided that points must be deducted should a competitor have longer hair, Singh had no other option but to compete with his hair covered by a turban.[169]

Particularly topical in recent years has been the conflict caused by the religious obligations and proscriptions which apply to Muslim athletes and which can interfere with their sporting performance or even result in their being unable to compete in their chosen field.[170] In the area of professional sport in particular, the observance of religious obligations such as regular prayer and fasting during Ramadan can lead to the athlete being unable to carry out the obligations outlined in his contract of employment,[171] a possible consequence of which is discrimination. Sports associations and teams may, for instance, avoid concluding contracts with Muslim athletes in order to avoid hassle or athletes may be sanctioned or, possibly, even have their contracts terminated if they abide by their religious duties, thereby violating their professional duties. The matter of whether the contract of employment could give rise to a duty on the part of Muslim athletes to provide information to their clubs as to whether they must observe certain religious obligations – in particular the duty to fast – is contentious.[172]

A second area in which conflict can occur is that of the regulation of clothing by sports associations. These regulations generally provide that the athletes' attire should facilitate the specific type of movement necessitated by the sport in question and that it should convey a uniform image. Keeping in mind the adage of 'sex sells,' the sport should also be made attractive to some extent for spectators and sponsors. A good example of this is the regulation of clothing for beach volleyball.[173] By contrast, according to the precepts of Islam, female Muslims should cover their hair and bodies in public, excluding face and hands and, in some cases, forearms.[174] This explains why Muslim women seldom participate in international competitions in which the required clothing does not correspond with the precepts of the religion, be this for reasons of practicality or for reasons arising out of binding association rules.[175] A further reason is that the exercise of sport in the presence of men[176] – for example, spectators, trainers, or referees – even in clothing which is unobjectionable on a religious basis, is forbidden if these men could possibly come into physical contact with the female athlete.[177] There is no discrimination in this case. On the

[169]   *Der Spiegel*, issue 22/1971, p. 129.
[170]   See Hoevels, Niloufar (2005), 'Rechtsprobleme muslimischer Sportler in Deutschland', in: K. Vieweg (ed.), *Perspektiven des Sportrechts*, pp. 63, 67 *et seq.*
[171]   For an instructive overview, Hoevels, Niloufar (2003), *Islam und Arbeitsrecht*, p. 248 *et seq.*
[172]   *Frankfurter Allgemeine Zeitung* (October 15, 2009), p. 32 (FSV Frankfurt).
[173]   No. 5.1 Official Beach Volleyball Rules available at http://www.fivb.ch/en/beachvolleyball/Rules/bvrb0912_forweb_EN.pdf (last accessed February 8, 2010).
[174]   Hoevels, note 170 *supra*, p. 74 *et seq.*
[175]   A striking example was provided by the track and field athlete Rakia Al Gassra of Bahrain who, in the heats of the 100 meter in the Sydney Olympic Games, wore a long-sleeved shirt, long trousers and a headscarf. Photographs of female Muslim athletes are printed in Hoevels, note 171 *supra*, p. 263 *et seq.*
[176]   Hoevels, note 170 *supra*, p. 76 with further references.
[177]   The vice-president of the Iranian National Olympic Committee, Abdolreza Sayar, provided as an example the Olympic combat sport, Taek Won Do. In one match, the referee grabbed and

contrary, the imposition of Muslim clothing requirements – for example, the wearing of so-called 'burkinis' – on non-Muslims would discriminate against these athletes. However, a different standard could apply to the wearing of the Islamic headscarf which is, in some cases, considered as a violation of neutrality in respect of religion. For the same reason, FIFA forbids the display of religious symbols during football matches.[178] The Federation of Olympic Committees of Asia imposes sanctions upon athletes who use their clothing for the purpose of disseminating religious beliefs.[179] However, there are also attempts to row against the trend of banning religious symbols on the playing field; the German Football Association, for example, is trying to water down FIFA's ban on religious symbols in order to render it possible for young Muslim girls to play football.[180] The football association of the Australian state of Victoria has also anchored in its rules of competition the right of female Muslim footballers to wear the headscarf.[181]

A third area of conflict is the prohibition of demonstrations of faith on the playing field, in particular, of prayers. Thus, the Brazilian football team was cautioned by FIFA because they prayed as a group on the soccer pitch – also at the Confederation Cup in South Africa. The Egyptian team, on the other hand, was not sanctioned when, in accordance with Muslim tradition, the players turned towards Mecca to pray in the middle of the football field.[182] In this vein, it will be interesting to observe how football associations react to David Beckham's newest tattoo, which appears on the right side of his body and portrays a grief-stricken Jesus Christ, when he removes his shirt during play.[183]

This area also encompasses the converse situation – as demonstrated by the *Akiyama*[184] case. In judo, a sport which has its roots in Shintoism, bowing is customary and, according to the rules, compulsory for all participants. The bowing takes place before stepping into the competition area and before stepping onto the mat. Before competing, all contestants must bow *en masse*. In two cases taken by the same plaintiffs, courts in the United States and Canada had to decide whether judoka who refused to perform the bowing ritual could take part in competition. The plaintiffs, James and Leilani Akiyama and Jay Drangeid, were members of a club which did not practice bowing. When a Seattle tournament refused to allow the plaintiffs' team to participate without bowing, however, they filed a suit in the United States Federal Court and, arising out of this, in 1997 obtained a preliminary injunction which prohibited the International Judo Federation

---

raised the arm of an Iranian athlete as a sign of her victory: see *Frankfurter Allgemeine Zeitung* (January 3, 2008), p. 27.

[178]   No. 10.2, FIFA Equipment Regulations. See also the decision of the International Football Association Board: 'The team of any player whose compulsory basic equipment displays political, religious or personal messages will be penalized by the host of the competition in question or by FIFA.' http://www.ubbo-voss-sr-lehrarbeit.de/fussballregeln-2009–2010/fussballregeln-aus ruestung.html (last accessed February 8, 2010).

[179]   *Frankfurter Allgemeine Zeitung* (December 12, 2006), p. 37.

[180]   *Frankfurter Allgemeine Zeitung* (March 5, 2008), p. 32.

[181]   Hoevels, Niloufar (2005), 'Muslimische Sportler in Deutschland', in: Württembergischer Fußballverband e.V. (ed.), *Minderheitenrechte im Sport*, pp. 59, 68 with further references.

[182]   http://www.livenet.ch/www/index.php/D/article/195/47420/ (last accessed February 8, 2010).

[183]   See *Frankfurter Allgemeine Zeitung* (January 1, 2010), p. 26.

[184]   *Black Belt magazine*, Oct. 1999, Vol. 37, No. 10, p. 140.

and the United States Judo, Inc. (USJI) from requiring them to bow.[185] The injunction being specific to the United States, the Akiyamas also sought relief in other countries and a hearing took place before the British Columbia Human Rights Tribunal in which the Akiyamas objected to the claims of Judo B.C. that contestants should bow to various areas and persons. The tribunal found that, contrary to the plaintiffs' claims, bowing in judo was a cultural ritual and not a religious gesture. Furthermore, bowing to one's opponent was a gesture of courtesy and respect arising out of the philosophy of the sport. As such, it was a bona fide sporting requirement. For these reasons, requiring the plaintiffs to bow was not an act of religious discrimination and because of the non-religious nature of the requirement, there was no need for Judo B.C. to accommodate the plaintiffs on grounds of religion.[186] In the 2002 hearing before the United States District Court, Judge Robert S. Lasnik ruled that the claimants must observe the ritual while participating in competitions.[187] In dismissing the 1997 injunction, he wrote that 'virtually any restriction or regulation imposed by a public accommodation could impinge on a person's religious beliefs.'[188]

e. Race and Ethnic Origin

In the past, discrimination due to race and ethnic origin in sports received considerable attention. The fate of Jewish sports in Germany after Hitler's *Machtübernahme* in 1933 mirrored the fate of the Jewish people in the Third Reich.[189] Two Jewish sports umbrella associations with their affiliated sports clubs and associations served as a rallying point for 20 000 athletes who were excluded from other societies or forced to leave due to certain laws ('*Arier-Paragraph*'). Jewish sports clubs and associations were subject to fluctuating political interference. In this connection, the imminent boycott of the 1936 Olympic Games in Berlin by the United States[190] played a major role. Jewish sports clubs were discriminated against in their use of sports areas: they were forced to register sports events at the local police station 48 hours before they began. Due to emigration, the number of sports club members declined – with the so-called *Reichspogromnacht* of 1938, Jewish sports in Germany ceased. After 73 years, the case of Gretel Bergmann[191] has resurfaced and her story is now the subject of a feature film.[192] In 1930, the United States Olympic Committee threatened to boycott the Berlin Olympics if Jewish athletes were not included in the German pool of participants. It was for this reason that the Jewish high jumper

---

[185] *Ibid.*

[186] http://www.queensu.ca/humanrights/hreb/Religion2/Akiyamacase.htm (last accessed February 8, 2010).

[187] *Akiyama* v. *U.S. Judo Inc.*, 181 F.Supp.2d 1179 (W.D. 2002).

[188] http://www.beliefnet.com/Faiths/Shinto/Judo-Bow-Not-Religious-Judge-Rules.aspx (last accessed February 8, 2010).

[189] For discussion, see Vieweg, Klaus (1985), 'Gleichschaltung und Führerprinzip – Zum rechtlichen Instrumentarium der Organsiation des Sports im Dritten Reich', in: P. Salje (ed.), *Recht und Unrecht im Nationalsozialismus*, pp. 244, 252.

[190] http://en.wikipedia.org/wiki/1936_Summer_Olympics#Boycott_debate_in_the_United_States_of_America (last accessed February 8, 2010).

[191] Today Gretel Bergmann, now Margaret Lambert, lives in New York, aged 94.

[192] *Frankfurter Allgemeine Zeitung* (September 10, 2009), p. 34; (November 28, 2009), p. 31; *Der Spiegel*, issue 35/2009, 'The German Mädel', p. 112 et *seq.*

Gretel Bergmann was invited to take part in the German training camp. However, Bergmann was not permitted to take part in the Games. Seventy-three years later, the German Amateur Athletics Federation recognized her high jump record. The National Socialist sports body had refused to do so at the time.

In the United States, minority athletes had a similar experience of discrimination and exclusion:[193] during the early years of professional and collegiate sports, a period extending from the Civil War to the early 1900s, blacks were allowed to participate, but subject to the indignities (e.g. taunts and physical attacks) that flowed from racial discrimination. These early years of inclusion were followed by a period of segregation during which formal and informal rules excluded blacks from participating in sports alongside whites at the amateur and professional levels. It was not until the 1950s and 1960s that professional leagues and college sports were finally desegregated,[194] although other forms of race discrimination persisted. Protests and boycotts were used to draw attention to this type of discrimination and to provoke political action: at the 200-meter presentation ceremony at the 1968 Olympics in Mexico City, for instance, Tommie Smith and John Carlos, their clenched fists encased in black gloves, publicized the Black Power Movement, directed against racial discrimination in the United States. The same two athletes co-founded the 'Olympia Project for Human Rights' at San José University. In the aftermath of their protest, they were excluded from the Olympic Games by the USOC.

Race discrimination in Germany and in the United States did not lead to sanctions by international sports bodies or the international community. However, international sports organizations and the United Nations fought apartheid in South-African sports with various measures.

The situation in South-African sports during the apartheid era can be characterized as follows:[195] in contrast to other areas of life, apartheid in South-African sports was not based on specific laws but on tradition and general rules of apartheid. In any event, white and non-white athletes did not participate in sporting competitions together or to compete against one another. Other countries were expected to respect this practice, and on this basis non-white athletes from abroad were also prohibited from competing against white athletes in South Africa. Invitations from abroad directed at non-white South-African athletes were ignored. Thus, it was impossible for non-whites to represent South Africa on the sporting field, irrespective of their achievements.

The international sports organizations responded with any measures at their disposal, including suspension and exclusion of South African teams, and therefore can claim to have played their part in the abolition of apartheid. In particular, the exclusion of the South-African Table Tennis association from the International Table Tennis Federation (ITTF) in 1956, the suspension (1961) and finally the exclusion (1976) of the whites-only Football Association of South Africa (FASA) by the FIFA and, above all, the exclusion of

---

193   See Zinger, note 31 *supra*, p. 28 *et seq.*

194   Davis, T. (1997), 'Who's In and Who's Out: Racial Discrimination in Sports', *28 Pac. L.J.* 341, 346 *et seq.*, reviewing Shropshire, Kenneth L. (1996), *In Black and White: Race and Sports in America.*

195   See in detail Wax, Andreas (2009), *Internationales Sportrecht – Unter besonderer Berücksichtigung des Sportvölkerrechts*, pp. 200 *et seq.* as well as Krumpholz, Andreas (1991), *Apartheid und Sport – Rassentrennung und Rassendiskriminierung im südafrikanischen Sport sowie Sportboykott Südafrikas*, passim.

the South African Olympic Committee from participation in the Olympic Games in 1970 should be noted. This was in line with one of the fundamental principles enshrined in the Olympic Charter, namely that 'any form of discrimination with regard to a country or person on grounds of race ... is incompatible with belonging to the Olympic Movement.' By 1964, the invitation of South Africa to the Olympic Games in Tokyo had been withdrawn and participation in the Olympic Games of 1968 was denied due to numerous boycott threats. In 1976, many African countries boycotted the Olympic Games after the New Zealand national rugby team lined out in South Africa.

The United Nations was instrumental in fighting apartheid in South Africa. From 1968 to 1984, the UN General Assembly passed several resolutions, which appealed to other states to cancel any sporting relations with the apartheid regime and with South-African sports associations practicing apartheid. From 1971, this request was addressed not only to countries and sports associations but also to individual athletes. Countries were requested in particular to exert influence on the national sports associations in order to achieve the exclusion of South African sports associations from international sports organizations. In their annual resolutions from 1979 to 1984, the UN General Assembly called on countries and sports organizations to transpose the international declaration against apartheid[196] agreed upon in 1977 into the sports arena. The media were also called upon to refuse to provide a platform for sports in South Africa. The names of the athletes who maintained sporting relations with South Africa were published on a so-called 'Blacklist' (secondary boycott). Furthermore, between 1986 and 1993, the UN General Assembly passed annual resolutions with the purpose of fighting apartheid in sports. In 1994, the United Nations declared that apartheid in South Africa was over.

In addition to numerous non-binding resolutions, the international agreement against apartheid in sports is worth mentioning.[197] It was passed in 1985 and came into force in 1988. However, no Western country signed the agreement. The obligations of the parties to the agreement included, amongst other things, that sporting relations between associations, teams, and single athletes with apartheid states be prohibited; that entry be denied to South African teams and athletes; that apartheid sports associations be excluded from international sports organizations; and that entry be denied to associations, teams, and athletes that participated in competitions in South Africa, insofar as this was compatible with the statutes of the international sports organizations (secondary boycott). The various worldwide boycott measures led to South Africa's isolation in international sports and constituted a considerable source of mental pressure. This finally proved an effective means to achieve the abolition of race discrimination in sports – in a peaceful manner for the most part. Consequently, from 1986 onwards, South Africa allowed an increase in the number of mixed-color teams and spectators ('multinational sport'). After the abolition of apartheid, the return of South Africa to international sports was possible. The South African National Olympic Committee was readmitted to the Olympic Games in 1992.

In the United States, a robust anti-race discrimination framework has been put in place composed, *inter alia*, of strict scrutiny review under the Fourteenth Amendment as well as federal statutes outlawing race discrimination in employment, federally funded programs,

---

196 See in detail Wax, note 195 *supra*, p. 206 *et seq.*; Krumpholz, note 195 *supra*, p. 94 *et seq.*
197 See in detail Wax, note 195 *supra*, p. 210 *et seq.*; Krumpholz, note 195 *supra*, p. 97 *et seq.*

and, in general, contracting.[198] In the European context, Article 19 TFEU (ex: Article 13 EC) – as implemented through Council Directive 2000/43/EC[199] and transposing legislation in the various Member States – provides robust protection against discrimination based on racial or ethnic origin.

Although great strides have been made in combating racism in sports, Europe is still far from the finish line. For example, unlike the United States, where there has been a decrease in the incidence of fan racism at sporting events (there was, in any case, never very much), spectator racist abuse remains a serious problem in European soccer;[200] and even though today African-American athletes may be disproportionately represented on the playing field in major sports such as football and basketball, it is alleged that (unconscious) racial discrimination continues to circumscribe managerial and ownership opportunities for African-Americans in professional sports.[201]

Reverse discrimination has found little favor as a strategy to enhance racial diversity in sports. For example, in the course of the abolition of apartheid in South Africa, quotas were introduced, regulating the racial composition of national teams. These quotas were based on the overall racial composition of the South-African population. Due to a resulting loss of quality, however, the quota rule was abolished for cricket in 2002 after some frustrated white top players had emigrated because of the quotas. The South African government also abolished the quota regime for rugby after the 'Springboks' won the World Championship with 13 whites on a team of 15.[202] Similarly, in the United States, the Court of Appeals for the Fifth Circuit has stated that all racial classifications, including those characterized as remedial, have to pass the strict scrutiny test,[203] casting some doubt on the constitutionality of race-conscious affirmative action initiatives premised on promoting racial diversity in the sports arena.

f. Age

Incredible achievements by younger and younger athletes, on the one hand, as well as the prowess of athletes competing well into their forties (e.g. Henry Maske's victorious return to the ring at age 43), on the other, have launched discussion about age discrimination in the sports setting.[204] However, there is little legislation and case law addressing this issue in either the United States or in Europe.

In the United States, the only applicable federal statute dealing with age discrimination is the Age Discrimination in Employment Act of 1967 (ADEA),[205] which covers only employees (of employers employing a minimum of 20 people) over the age of 40.[206] It follows that the Act is usually only implicated by discrimination against an athlete because

---

[198]   Titles VI (federally funded programs) and VII (employment) of the Civil Rights Act of 1964, 42 U.S.C. §§ 2000d, 2000e-2(a); 42 U.S.C. § 1981 (contracting).

[199]   Official Journal L 180, 19/07/2000 P. 0022–0026.

[200]   On this issue and how to resolve it, see Ryan, M. (2008), 'The European Union and Fan Racism in European Soccer Stadiums: The Time Has Come for Action', *20 Fla. J. Int'l L.* 245.

[201]   Davis, note194 *supra*, p. 345.

[202]   *Frankfurter Allgemeine Zeitung* (November 10, 2007), p. 33.

[203]   *Hopwood* v. *Tex.*, 78 F.3d 932, 940 (5th Cir. 1996), cert. denied, 533 U.S. 929 (2001).

[204]   For discussion, see Vieweg and Müller, note 58 *supra*, p. 904 *et seq.*

[205]   29 U.S.C. §§ 621–34 (2005).

[206]   29 U.S.C. § 631(a).

he is too old (e.g. by fixing a maximum age) rather than because he is too young and fails to meet a certain minimum age. The Act's reach is further limited to team sports, as athletes engaged in individual performer sports are classed as independent contractors rather than employees. In addition, minimum and maximum age limits set by professional sports leagues and governing bodies as part of their eligibility requirements have been held to fall within the non-statutory labor exemption and thus to be immune from antitrust scrutiny, if they are the product of a lawful collective bargaining process between the sports organization and the players' union.[207] Moreover, the breadth of the defenses available would likely shield the employing sports organization from liability. Age differentiation is not unlawful, for example, where it is based on reasonable factors other than age (such as an aging athlete's diminishing speed, strength, and stamina)[208] or where age is a bona fide occupational qualification reasonably necessary to the sport in question.[209] Not surprisingly given these limitations, most ADEA cases involve claims by coaches, support staff, and administrators rather than by professional athletes.[210]

The situation is similar in Europe. The ECJ considers the right to equal treatment to be a fundamental right of all European Union citizens.[211] Furthermore, in its controversial *Mangold* decision,[212] it interpreted the 'general framework for equal treatment' established by Council Directive 2000/78/EC[213] as encompassing the prohibition of age discrimination, which allegedly existed irrespective of the directive as a principle of European Union law.[214] In Germany, the transposition of the directive into national law through the General Equal Treatment Act[215] made clear that the traditional division into classes according to age might not be in conformity with the law.[216] As there is no special legislation for sports and, as yet, no case law, the following remarks confine themselves to the presentation of the problem that would have to be resolved according to the above-mentioned principles of a balancing of interests and proportionality.

Both maximum and minimum age limits are common in sports as is the merging of several age groups into one peer group – largely for good reason. The fixing of a minimum age for participation in sports competitions and in competitive sports is mainly motivated by concern for the protection of children and young people. The physical and psychological impact of a competitive sport upon an underage competitor is regarded as unacceptable.[217]

---

[207] *Clarett* v. *Nat'l Football League*, 369 F.3d 124 (2nd Cir. 2004), cert. denied, 544 U.S. 961 (2005). Even where the governing authority establishes the age limit unilaterally, the courts are generally reluctant to apply more than a very limited rational basis review absent violation of an athlete's federal or state civil rights.

[208] 29 U.S.C. § 623(f)(1).

[209] *Ibid.*

[210] Epstein, A. (2006), 'The ADEA and Sports Law', *16 J. Legal Aspects of Sports* 177.

[211] Streinz, note 34 *supra*, p. 291.

[212] EuGH, Rs. C-144/04 Mangold /.Helm Slg. 2005, I-9981.

[213] OJ L 303/16.

[214] Streinz, note 34 *supra*, p. 445.

[215] In force since August 18, 2006.

[216] See Gutzeit, Martin (2009), 'Auswirkungen des Allgemeinen Gleichbehandlungsgesetzes auf das Sportrecht', in: K. Vieweg (ed.), *Facetten des Sportrechts*, p. 64 *et seq.*

[217] The argument in favor of a minimum age that, especially in gymnastics, pre-pubertal physical conditions are better and, thus, that this age group should not be allowed to participate in order to establish equal opportunities, is not made.

Such regulations, though they may appear enlightened, raise many questions. Is the minimum age scientifically grounded or is it based upon tradition? Is it not contradictory that there is no minimum age for participation in training regimes, although these are frequently more punishing than the competitions themselves? And how does the minimum age in the sports setting compare with general labor protection laws for children and young people in the workplace?

As regards the problem of equal treatment, fixing a certain minimum age for reasons of health protection is in itself problematic. For example, a minimum age of 16 for participation in girls'/women's gymnastics would seem to little more than an arbitrary point on a gliding scale of age. Moreover, 'calendar' age and biological age are by no means always identical. For reasons of practicality, however, only the calendar age can be decisive. Does such an age limit discriminate against those athletes who, biologically, have already reached the minimum (or, conversely, not yet exceeded the maximum) age and could, accordingly, be entitled to compete? In their cases, health protection does not seem warranted. Finally, enforcement problems should not be discounted. The principle of equal treatment calls for strict and precise enforcement. Whether official documents should be regarded as more reliable than journalistic research – cases involving several Chinese gymnasts in the Olympic Games in Beijing come to mind[218] – remains to be seen.

Udo Steiner,[219] formerly a judge of the German Constitutional Court, has dealt with the duty of the state to protect the life and bodily integrity of children in competitive sports. His conclusion – which seems sound – is as follows:

> For the time being, children's high-level sports are constitutionally permissible. Under Article 2 s. 2 of the German Constitution, the state should concentrate its efforts on promoting the physical and mental development of our children, particularly in the area of school sports. This active duty to protect the health of future generations takes precedence over the frequently desired watchdog role of the state in children's high-level sports which are not central to society.

There have been repeated calls to introduce a maximum age limit for boxers for reasons of health protection. Comparable restrictions have already been put in place for football referees and for certain officials in several associations. Ensuring the athlete's and officials' fitness to carry out the assigned duties could be a sufficient justification for this unequal treatment, given the difficulty of setting the 'correct' age limit and the problematic divergence between calendar and biological age arising in this context.

In the case of many competitive sports in both youth and senior categories as well as in that of the attainment of a sports badge (*Sportabzeichen*[220]), several age groups are merged into one peer group. This is often necessary to ensure a sufficient number of competitors, and should, in any event, be covered by the association's freedom of

---

[218]   International gymnastics officials have since pronounced themselves satisfied that China's female gymnasts met minimum-age requirements during the 2008 Beijing Olympics. See http://voices.washingtonpost.com/olympics/2008/10/fig_2008_gymnasts_were_of_age_2.html (last accessed February 8, 2010).

[219]   Udo Steiner is one of Germany's leading sports lawyers. For selected works, see Tettinger, Peter J. and Klaus Vieweg (2004), *Gegenwartsfragen des Sportrechts*. Quote is taken from the article 'Kinderhochleistungssport in Deutschland – Thesen zur Verfassungslage', *ibid.* pp. 154, 176.

[220]   A *Sportabzeichen* is a badge awarded for certain sporting achievements by the German Olympic Sport Association.

self-regulation. It is true that there might be a less restrictive alternative to the forming of age groups, namely to consider the athlete's age in evaluating his or her achievement. For example, in the high- or long-jump, the height or distance respectively could be staggered according to age group. A proportional points system, based upon the average potential of a certain age group, could be put in place in order to differentiate among age groups. Such a procedure would, however, not just run into the calendar/biological age predicament discussed above; it would also face the problem of almost incalculable expense and lead to a pseudo-precision which is not required by the principle of equal treatment.

III. CONCLUSION

Turning the spotlight on sports and discrimination reveals a mixed history: many sports have an unfortunate past of racist, sexual, and other insult and injury, both internally and in their spectators' conduct; at the same time, participation in sports has long provided an opportunity for the disenfranchised to win acceptance in society and been a way to build bridges between people who might not think that they have much in common. Anti-discrimination law and policy within the European Union and the United States have developed in stages and have undoubtedly improved over the years in coherence and effectiveness. Thanks to the input of the European Union, anti-discrimination law has been given a new, dense, and unified treatment within the various Member States. In addition, anti-discrimination law has developed a sophisticated concept of indirect discrimination, which allows challenges to be brought to apparently neutral practices and structures, and harassment is now acknowledged as a form of discriminatory conduct. As well as legislative developments, there has been an (equally important) move towards tackling discrimination in other ways, as evidenced by the successful fight against apartheid by the United Nations, national and international sports organizations and individual athletes. However, there is still no unified anti-discrimination framework in either the European Union or the United States. Rather, protection is afforded in a piecemeal fashion, with state or federal laws only targeting specific aspects of social life and select grounds of discrimination. Unsurprisingly, discrimination has been stamped out more successfully in some areas (e.g. race) than in others. It is therefore imperative that anti-discrimination law and policy continue to move forward, past the standard that has been attained. Achieving a discrimination-free playing field takes time and sometimes unusual measures, but it is well worth the effort.

11 Protection of young athletes

Steve Cornelius and Paul Singh

1. INTRODUCTION

Sport has become a major global industry in which billions of dollars are turned over annually. Major championships attract vast numbers of television viewers globally with the result that television networks are willing to part with astronomic amounts of money to secure the broadcasting rights for major sports events. Television attracts sponsors who invest even more money into events and star athletes. The result is that winning and success overshadow other values, such as physical and mental well-being, education and sportsmanship.

Ironically, the sustainability of professional sport is in the hands of children. The future of sport as an industry is heavily dependent not only on the participation of children from a young age, but also on keeping the largest possible number of talented young athletes involved in sport, both as participants and as spectators. The children of today will be the stars and fans of tomorrow. Without stars or fans, professional sport will collapse.

As professionalism swept across the sports world during the second half of the twentieth century, it was inevitable that children would also be swept up in the frenzy to achieve success and earn vast amounts of money. Coaches saw talented youngsters as mere commodities which could be cultivated to improve the coaches' success ratings. Parents began to see their talented children as a means to generate an income which could sustain both parents and children. Parents and coaches placed more and more pressure on children to perform, with little regard to the best interests of the children:

> When the child is not properly guided by adults in his/her sporting activity, sports can enter the realm of abuse and exploitation. Is four hours of daily training for a 5-year-old child truly beneficial? How much stress can a child take? Should a young adolescent be traded between teams for thousands of dollars? Is it good for a 15-year-old swimmer to have turned his shoulder 1.5 million times? Is it normal for a 16-year-old gymnast, who trains 7 hours a day, to be only 130 cm and weigh less than 30 kilograms? Is it real support when a 12-year-old boxer's parents urge him to knock-out his opponent … ? In other words, is the reality of competitive sports always following the best interests of children? Or are some narrow-minded and over-ambitious adults putting [children] … into jeopardy through competitive sports?[1]

The misdirected ambitions of adults are not the only threats faced by children in sport however. If left unchecked, youth sport also provides a fertile hunting ground for predators who prey on children. Sport is particularly vulnerable in this regard because it often involves close relationships between adults and children and usually these adults are in a position of trust and authority. The relative social and legal freedom afforded to

---

[1] P. David, 'Children's Rights and Sports' 7 *International Journal of Children's Rights* (1999) p. 53.

voluntary sport allows large numbers of young athletes to be entrusted to adults about whom parents know very little, other than their credentials as coaches. With coaches capable of exercising great power and authority over young people desperate to achieve success, the ingredients of the coaching situation lead to a potentially risky mix where children are susceptible to abuses of power by unscrupulous adults.

Furthermore, not all sports organisations understand the legal and ethical ramifications of ignoring harassment and abuse. Sports federations increasingly deny that children may be subjected to abuse in their sport either because they do not know how to deal with it, or they believe that if they openly address harassment, it may generate negative publicity for them.

The Universal Declaration on Human Rights,[2] the Convention on the Rights of the Child[3] and the Charter of Physical Education and Sport[4] recognise the right of children to have the full opportunity for play which promotes their general culture and well-being, and to have equal opportunities provided for cultural, artistic and recreational activities.[5] Children have a right to appropriate care and to be protected from abuse. These rights of children, when applied to sport, recognise that participation increases the potential for the child to develop skills and abilities not only in sport, but also in the dimension of life-skills such as teamwork, co-operation and strategy development that will assist them to function better in larger society.

When parents send their children to a sport club, they expect the club to provide a safe, nurturing and enjoyable environment. They expect their children to be educated about sport, and through sport. They expect them to be encouraged to learn and to play, not to be abused in any way. Parents place their ultimate trust in sport organisations, their coaches and administrators. But what happens when that trust is breached? From the social to the elite levels, sport can provide a breeding ground for those who like to prey on children.[6]

Child abuse (as defined in the following section) is a serious social and legal concern that is centuries old. It crosses all social and economic boundaries. The prevention of violence against women and children is a high political priority in many countries in the world. However, until recently, this issue has not received sufficient attention in the sphere of sport, probably because most people associate sport with fair play, ethical values and high moral standards. The reporting of abuse against children has increased significantly over recent years. This is due in part to young people today becoming less inclined to have blind faith in those who exercise authority. They are increasingly more assertive and aware of their human rights, and the recourse they have to address their transgressions. Further,

---

2   United Nations, *Universal Declaration on Human Rights* General Assembly Resolution 217A (III), U.N. Doc. A/810 at 71 (1948).
3   United Nations, *Convention on the Rights of the Child* (New York, 20 November 1989).
4   United Nations Educational Scientific and Cultural Organisation, *International Charter of Physical Education and Sport* (Paris, 21 November 1978).
5   P. Stirbys, 'Child's Play: In The Best Interests Of The Child', paper presented at the Conference on Sport and Human Rights, Australia, 1–3 September 1999, p. 1. See also P.C. Singh, 'Human Rights in Sport' 24(2) *South African Journal for Research in Sport, Physical Education and Recreation* (2002) pp. 67–8.
6   T. Leahy 'Preventing the Sexual Abuse of Young People in Australian Sport' (2002) Australian Sports Commission, available at: http://www.activeaustralia.org/hfs/research_sexualabuse.htm.

programmes have been established to educate children and youth to report incidents of suspected abuse. There is greater community awareness with organisations implementing tighter checking procedures, and the introduction of new child protection legislation.[7]

2.   ABUSE AND HARASSMENT IN SPORT

2.1   Defining Abuse and Harassment

Child abuse is a term that is used to describe the ways in which children are harmed, usually by adults and often by those they know and trust. It includes behaviours that individuals or sport organisations commit, or omit, that directly or indirectly harm children or ruin their prospects of a safe and healthy development. It may include any one or a combination of the following:

- Physical abuse – which results in non-accidental injuries or harm.
- Emotional abuse – which causes psychological or emotional harm.
- Sexual abuse – which includes a range of sexual activity and exploitation of children that can result in physical and/or psychological harm.
- Neglect – which results in ill-health and stunts development.
- Child labour – where children are employed to work in conditions that are not conducive to their development and well-being.
- Child trafficking – where children are illegally moved across borders, often ending up in a state of slavery or neglect.

All people looking after children and young people have a responsibility to provide a safe environment for them, including those in the sport and recreation industry. Abuse upon children can have long-term, harmful effects on personal development, self-esteem and relationships. Its initial traumatic and long-term consequences impact on the individual, team, family, sport and community.[8]

2.2   Neglect

Neglect is the persistent failure to meet a child's physical and/or psychological needs and is likely to result in significant harm. It may involve a parent or care-giver failing to provide adequate food, shelter and clothing, failing to protect a child from physical harm or danger, failing to ensure access to appropriate medical care or treatment, lack of stimulation or lack of supervision. It may also include neglect of or not responding to a child's basic emotional needs.

Institutionalised neglect raised its head in professional sport during the 1990s when it was revealed that talent scouts and professional football clubs in Europe were luring young players, some younger than 15 years of age, from Africa and Latin America to training centres where they would be 'tested', with some remote promise of being

---

[7]   D. Simms, 'Child Protection and Sport, An Overview of Legislation and Sports' Obligations' (2001), Australian Sports Commission, available at: http://www.activeaustralia.org/adults/hfs.htm.

[8]   Leahy, note 6 *supra*, p.1.

recruited if they were found to have the necessary talent and skills. The overwhelming majority of these players found themselves all alone and far from home in a strange land and in an unforgiving and unrelenting environment. Invariably the majority of these young players lacked the ability to become professional players in a highly competitive market. In most instances, unsuccessful players were left to their own devices, without any support structures or financial backing to ensure that they were taken care of or able to return home.[9]

In response to the problem and with some pressure from the European Commission to act, the International Federation of Football Associations (FIFA) restricted the international transfer of players under the age of 18 years. Article 19 of the Laws of Football permits the international transfer of a younger player in only three situations. If the parents of the player have moved from one country to another for reasons not associated with football, the younger player may be registered to play in the new country. Similarly, if a player between the ages of 16 and 18 years wishes to move within the European Union, international transfer is allowed provided that the new club makes adequate provision for the player's education, training and well-being. Lastly, international transfer is also allowed where the player's home and the transferee club are both within 50 km of the national border between them and are no more than 100 km apart.

Professional baseball has also had it share of institutionalised neglect. Scouts recruit hundreds of young baseball players from Latin American countries to play in the United States. Most of these players never make it into a professional franchise and many are left without any legal residence permit or the means to provide for themselves.[10] Major League Baseball (MLB) has attempted to deal with this problem by imposing an age limit of 17 years for the signing of players, but this rule has been repeatedly violated by teams.[11]

2.3 Physical Abuse

Physical abuse is the deliberate physical injury to a child or the wilful or neglectful failure to prevent physical injury or suffering. This may involve hitting, shaking, throwing, poisoning, burning or scalding, drowning, suffocating, confinement or inappropriately giving drugs to a child.

Participation in sport can itself become a form of physical abuse when young athletes are pushed to train excessively for hours on end, day after day, with insufficient rest to allow for proper recovery or where young athletes are encouraged to participate despite being injured. Some leagues for children as young as 9 years old play as many as 70 games per season and involve extensive travelling to and from the various games. The result is a dramatic increase in stress fractures, tendonitis, bursitis, joint disorders and other overuse injuries.[12]

---

[9] P. David, *Human Rights in Youth Sport – A Critical Review of Children's Rights in Competitive Sports* (London: Routledge Taylor & Francis Group, 2005) p. 163 *et seq.*

[10] David, note 9 *supra*, p. 166 *et seq.*

[11] *Ibid.* p. 167.

[12] D.E. Abrahams, 'The Challenge Facing Parents and Coaches in Youth Sports: Assuring Children Find an Equal Opportunity' 8 *Villanova Sports and Entertainment Law Journal* (2001–02) p. 253 at p. 266.

Physical abuse can also occur whenever peer violence is not adequately controlled, or even condoned. This may involve excessive aggression on the field of play or induction rituals such as 'hazing'.

2.4   Emotional Abuse

Emotional abuse is the persistent ill-treatment of a child that causes severe adverse effects on the child's emotional development. Some level of emotional abuse is involved in all types of ill-treatment of a child, although it may occur on its own. Emotional abuse may involve conveying to children that they are worthless or unloved, inadequate or valued only insofar as they meet the needs of another person. It may involve causing children frequently to feel frightened or in danger, or lead to the exploitation or corruption of children. Smothering a child's development through over-protection can also be a form of abuse.

Parents' reactions on the sidelines may also result in emotional distress for a young athlete. The biggest danger in this regard is what psychologists call 'achievement by proxy' where parents or coaches place undue pressure on children to perform because the parents or coaches did not have much success when they were young or have not enjoyed much success or prestige in their adult life:[13]

> Psychologists have begun speaking about 'youth sports rage' as fistfights and other physical and verbal confrontations involving parents and coaches have disrupted youth leagues, frequently brought under control only by police intervention and actual or threatened criminal prosecution. Brawling parents have even disrupted preschoolers' … games. In one such brawl precipitated by a dispute about an umpire's call, more than twenty parent and coaches spilled onto the field, swinging punches and tackling each other while bewildered children looked on … After an informal Massachusetts youth hockey scrimmage in July of 2002 … one player's father beat an opposing player's father senseless while the ten-year-olds watched in horror …[14]
>
> Children have four basic emotional needs in organized sports, and they will not have fun unless the adults meet each one: 1) child athletes need to play without unhealthy pressure to win imposed by parents and coaches; 2) child athletes need to be treated like children, and not like miniature professionals; 3) child athletes need adult role models whose sportsmanlike behavior helps make participation fun; and 4) child athletes need to play without adult-imposed pressure for financial gain inspired by professional or big-time collegiate sports.[15]

The challenge for sports organisations is to ensure that these needs are met.

2.5   Sexual Abuse

Sexual abuse is considered to be any sexual activity with a child or an adult where informed consent is not or cannot be given. These acts constitute a criminal offence and may include non-contact, such as exposure or exhibitionism; contact, such as sexual touching; and penetrative sexual acts.

The world of sport is not immune from this social phenomenon. Research has shown that those who exploit children sexually may be school heads, care workers, instructors,

---

13   *Ibid.* p. 270.
14   *Ibid.* p. 258.
15   *Ibid.* p. 266.

chaperones, parent-helpers, bus drivers, peers or anyone with access to young or vulnerable people.[16] Consequently, one cannot assume that any individual or group is immune from blame by virtue of their status. Further research into the roles of all stakeholders should seek to provide sound information to those with responsibility for promoting safety in sport.[17]

It is only since the 1980s that research has been conducted on the range of ways that people experience sexual exploitation, its effects on their lives and its costs to society. Internationally, almost all research on sexual exploitation has taken place in the workplace and within the educational system. Very little is known about the causes or characteristics of sexual harassment and abuse in sport. By contrast, most research on sexual abuse has focussed within the family. Research about sexual harassment in the workplace and educational settings indicate that sport organisations may also represent an environment or culture where sexual exploitation can easily occur.[18] However, supportive evidence is largely anecdotal. Specific information about the extent and types of violations of personal and sexual security in sport is chronically short because of the lack of systematic research. Mainstream literature on sexual aggression and child abuse has ignored sport as a specific discipline of research or practical interest.

2.6   Child Labour

As the last vestiges of amateur sports disappeared during the 1990s, the participation of young athletes in professional sport raised the issue of child labour and the question relating to the appropriate age for young athletes to join the professional stage. These issues were highlighted by the meteoric rise and fall of Jennifer Capriati, who became a professional tennis player at the age of 13, only to succumb to the pressures of life as a professional athlete before her eighteenth birthday,[19] succumbing to substance abuse, injury and burnout.[20] Other top athletes have bemoaned the fact that their childhood was taken from them too soon.[21]

Article 2 of the International Labour Organization's (ILO) Convention No. 138 provides that work is prohibited for children under the age of 15 years (or 14 years in the case of developing countries), with the exception of 'light work' that might be carried out by children aged 13 (or 12 years in the case of developing countries) in accordance with Article 7 of the Convention.

Involvement of children in professional sports may thus be seen as a questionable form of child labour in violation of international law. Children who participate in professional sport train in a work-like environment, compete regularly and generate revenue. Adults

---

[16]   C.H. Brackenridge, *Spoilsports: Understanding and Preventing Sexual Exploitation in Sport* (London: Routledge, 2001).
[17]   *Ibid.*
[18]   *Ibid.* p. 45.
[19]   E. Siegel, 'When Parental Interference Goes Too Far: The Need for Adequate Protection of Child Entertainers and Athletes' 18 *Cardozo Journal of Arts and Entertainment* (2000) p. 427 at p. 460 *et seq.* See also G. Couch, 'The Rise and Fall and Rise of Jennifer Capriati', *Chicago Sun-Times*, 26 January 2001.
[20]   D.L. Andrews and S.J. Jackson, *Sport Stars: The Cultural Politics of Sporting Celebrity* (London: Routledge, 2002) p. 94.
[21]   David, note 9 *supra*, p. 60.

often depend on the 'work' of such children for their own employment as coaches or maintenance of parents.[22]

In response to the legal issues under the ILO Convention and otherwise, some sports federations have attempted with various degrees of success to impose minimum age requirements. The International Tennis Federation imposed a minimum age of 15 years but allowed players aged 14 to enter no more than four minor professional tournaments in a year. The ITF eventually succumbed to threats of litigation and allowed 14-year-olds to participate in seven tournaments. Similarly, in the United States, the National Football League's rule that a player could only join the professional league 3 years after graduating from high school was challenged.[23]

Young athletes who participate in amateur sports do not earn an income from sport and are therefore not protected by measures dealing with child labour. Even though the top young athletes may spend many hours, day in and day out, training for their particular sport, there is no legislation that deals with the rights of these young athletes.[24]

2.7 Child Trafficking

Professionalism also brought sport into the firing line of child traffickers. Organised crime relies on young athletes' passion for sport to lure them with promises of careers in professional leagues. For example, hundreds of young baseball players are brought from Latin America into the United States annually. In spite of the MLB rule that requires players to be 17 years of age when they are signed, some teams have violated this rule by importing players as young as 14. The result is that unofficial scouts, known colloquially as *Buscones*, lure young players to the United States, often illegally; when the players fail to secure a contract with a professional team, they are left in state of neglect or virtual slavery as these 'scouts' turn human traffickers.[25]

There is also a lucrative trade in young football players from Africa and Latin America in various European football leagues. Reports suggest that thousands of young hopefuls are imported from outside the European Union into various European countries, most illegally, while less than one in ten manages to secure contracts that are properly registered.[26]

3. CONDITIONS CONDUCIVE TO ABUSE IN SPORT

Sport is a particularly vulnerable activity because it often involves close relationships between adults and children, and usually these adults are in a position of trust and authority. The relative social and legal freedom afforded to voluntary sport allows large numbers of youth to be entrusted to adults about whom parents know very little, other

---

[22] S. Farstad, 'Protecting Children's Rights in Sport: The Use of Minimum Age', available at: http://www.nottingham.ac.uk/shared/shared_hrlcpub/Farstad.pdf (accessed 30 September 2008).

[23] *Clarett* v. *National Football League* 369 F.3d 124 (2004). See also David, note 9 *supra*, p. 43 *et seq.*

[24] Siegel, note 19 *supra*, p. 457 *et seq.*

[25] David, note 9 *supra*, p. 163 *et seq.*

[26] *Ibid.* p. 164 *et seq.*

than their coaching credentials perhaps. With coaches capable of exercising great power and authority over young people desperate to achieve success, the ingredients of the coaching situation lead to a potentially risky mix where children are susceptible to abuses of power by unscrupulous coaches.[27] Additionally, not all sports organisations understand the legal and ethical ramifications of ignoring harassment and abuse while others deny that children may be subjected to abuse in their sport due to ignorance or to avoid negative publicity.[28]

If a sports club has no policy for preventing exploitation, it is unlikely that there will be cultural support for athletes who come forward with complaints. Before athletes can make a formal complaint, they must have some confidence that the authorities will treat it fairly and confidentially.[29]

Outside of sport, the potential for exploitative relationships is recognised and addressed by professional codes of conduct, as in the case of lawyers and medical doctors. Within sport it is regulated by the codes of conduct for coaches, sport officials and administrators that are administered by international and national federations. Additionally, specific codes of conduct regulate the behaviour of those, such as sport psychologists, sport scientists, sport medicine practitioners and others, who render support services to sport. These codes prohibit sexual relationships between the pertinent professionals and their students/patients/athletes.

The issue of sexual relationships between child (as well as adult) sport participants in unequal power relationships should be analysed in the context of creating a safer sport environment. In the case of children, there is no doubt that such relationships are exploitative. Even if both parties are legally adult, such relationships can be exploitative because there is usually a disparity between the parties in terms of authority, maturity, status and dependence. Examples of this are employer–employee relationships, where employers have the power to hire and fire, or coach–athlete relationships, where coaches can influence the career opportunities of athletes, or athletes' sense of self-esteem.

Although exploitative relationships between adults in sport may not necessarily be unlawful, and therefore may not carry the risk of vicarious liability for a sport organisation, administrators have a moral obligation to discourage such relationships because of the damage that they can do to a more vulnerable party. Such damage can affect sport performance and the future involvement of an athlete. There is also the possibility that if coercion is a factor, such relationships can amount to unlawful harassment, thus having consequences for the liability of the organisation. Sex with a minor, whether involving a minor of the same or opposite sex, constitutes a criminal offence, which must be reported to the police.

Many distressing situations can arise when coaches unwittingly get caught in the unclear delineation between the power and authority inherent in the coach–athlete relationship. When that happens, the result is unhappy athletes and compromised coaches. Power legitimately follows any position requiring expertise and the ability to

---

[27]   C.H. Brackenridge, 'Harassment, Sexual Abuse, and Safety of the Female Athlete' 19(2) *Clinics in Sports Medicine* (2000) pp. 187–98.
[28]   Australian Sports Commission, 'Protecting Children from Abuse in Sport; Fact Sheet', available at: http://www.activeaustralia.org/hfs/child_protect.htm (accessed 30 September 2008).
[29]   Brackenridge, note 27 *supra*, p.116.

make decisions. A coach's legitimate power is based on experience, education and knowledge brought to the job. That is what makes athletes go to them; they are hired for their expertise. The challenge to the coach is to recognise this power and learn how to use it judiciously.[30]

4.　PREVALENCE OF ABUSE IN SPORT

It is generally acknowledged that there is considerable under-reporting of instances of child abuse, including rape, both to the criminal justice and social welfare authorities and to researchers.[31]

Internationally, research has increasingly focussed on exploitation and harassment in sport. An Australian study assessed a range of factors related to the occurrence and long-term traumatic impact of sexual abuse in athletes' lives.[32] From a group of 370 elite and club male and female athletes, 31 per cent of female athletes and 21.3 per cent of male athletes reported that they had experienced sexual abuse at some point in their lives. Almost half (46.4 per cent) of the elite group that reported sexual abuse had been sexually abused by sports personnel. In the club group, this figure was 25.6 per cent. The data reveal that for athletes who report being sexually abused and who are involved in competitive sport at the elite level, the chances are almost even that someone associated with that environment will have abused them. At the club level, there is a 25 per cent chance that an athlete reporting sexual abuse will have been abused by someone associated with that environment.[33]

Those in positions of authority or trust with the athletes mainly perpetrated the sport-related abuse. Primarily, they included coaches and, less frequently, support staff and other athletes. Over 96 per cent of the perpetrators were males. The Australian study reported two key findings:[34] first, the most harmful and far-reaching effects of sexual abuse were related to the perpetrators' strategies to engage in emotional manipulation and emotional abuse. The perpetrators' *modus operandi* targeted the individual's emotional life as a method of keeping that person in a state of emotional confusion, fear and entrapment. The acceptance of emotionally abusive practices is one of the singularly most dangerous systemic risk factors in organised competitive sport. It not only effectively masks but also actively facilitates the perpetrator's *modus operandi*. Second, the prevalence of the 'bystander effect' compounded the long-term psychological harm for sexually abused athletes. The bystander effect refers to the non-intervention by others who knew about or suspected the sexual abuse.[35]

Following Ben Jonson's positive drug test at the 1988 Seoul Olympic Games, Canadian sport was torn apart for the second time in the mid-1990s with revelations of widespread sexual abuse in ice hockey. Coach Graham James was convicted of sexual offences against

---

[30]　See http://www.harassmentinsport.com/e/coaches/Copower.html (accessed 30 September 2008).

[31]　Brackenridge, note 27 *supra*, p.54.

[32]　Leahy, note 7 *supra*.

[33]　*Ibid.* p. 2.

[34]　*Ibid.* pp. 2–3.

[35]　*Ibid.*

the respected professional player, Sheldon Kennedy.[36] He was one of a large number of National Hockey League players coached by James, who had played for James for four seasons and was sexually abused more than 300 times from 1984 through to 1994. James received a 3.5-year prison sentence in January 1997.[37]

The Supreme Court of Canada ruled in May 2001 that a 22-year-old teacher having sexual relations with a student automatically breached his responsibilities as an authority figure.[38] This decision dispelled the last traces of confusion around Section 153 of the Canadian Criminal Code. Although the case before the court involved a teacher, experts agreed that the implications for coaches are clear. The ruling reinforced clear wording of Section 153 that consent is in no way a mitigating element of the offence.

In the United Kingdom, the most notable criminal trial was held in 1993 when Olympic swimming coach Paul Hickson was charged with sexually assaulting his teenage swimmers. Hickson was convicted of 15 sexual offences, including two rapes.[39] His prison sentence of 17 years was the longest-ever rape sentence imposed by an English court. He was also cleared of two other indecent assaults. He denied all charges, claiming that he was the victim of teenage girls' fantasies.[40] Until this case, sexual abuse in sport was not even on the national research or policy agenda in the United Kingdom. By contrast, swimming coach Eric Henderson won an unfair dismissal action. Two pool attendants charged that he had 'patted girl's bottoms and looked into their changing rooms' resulting in his suspension from the Amateur Swimming Association and dismissal by the Bristol City Council as coach after 13 years of working with the City of Bristol swimming squad. He was awarded £27 000 compensation.[41]

In 1996 the British Amateur Swimming Association (ASA) published its first document on procedures for child protection as a result of another public court case. The ASA has a membership of approximately 250 000 swimmers, of whom 90 per cent are under 16 years old. Further, 58 per cent of reported and registered cases of abuse were in the 5–15-year age group. Given these statistics the ASA recognised and accepted greater responsibility for promoting the welfare of children within swimming.[42]

5. APPROACHES AND LEGISLATION OF LEADING COUNTRIES

There are no examples of sport-specific legislation that regulate the treatment and provide for the protection of young athletes. Instead, legal systems rely on the general principles of

---

[36]   L. Robinson, *Crossing the Line: Sexual Harassment and Abuse in Canada's National Sport'* (Toronto: McClelland and Stewart Inc., 1998).

[37]   D. Deak, 'Out of Bounds: How sexual abuse of athletes at the hands of their coaches is costing the world of sports millions' 9 *Seton Hall Journal of Sport Law* (1999) p. 174.

[38]   See http://www.harassmentinsport.com/e/coaches/Cotrust.html (accessed 30 September 2008).

[39]   *R* v. *Hickson* [1997] Crim. L.R. 494 (C.A.).

[40]   S.J. Gardiner, M. James. J. O'Leary, *et al.*, *Sports Law*, 3rd ed. (London: Cavendish Publishing, 2006).

[41]   1(1) *Sports Law Bulletin* (January/February 1998) p. 4. Dismissal: *Henderson* v. *Bristol City Council* (1997, unreported 14 November), IT Case No 1400195/97.

[42]   Gardiner, James, O'Leary, *et al.*, note 40 *supra*, p. 143 *et seq.*

tort and criminal prosecution to redress any improper conduct. In addition, most countries have passed legislation dealing with issues relating to children, mostly as a result of ratifying the Convention on the Rights of the Child,[43] the Hague Convention on the Civil Aspects of International Child Abduction[44] and the European Convention on the Exercise of Children's Rights.[45]

In the International Charter of Physical Education and Sport the only reference to the protection of children is found in Article 7.3, which provides that:

> [i]t is important that all sports authorities and sportsmen and women be conscious of the risks to athletes, and more especially to children, of precocious and inappropriate training and psychological pressures of every kind.

The Charter not only falls short in respect of child abuse in sport, but also has no legally binding effect and can therefore only have a limited influence in practice.

Many strategies have been developed in the United States to expose and prevent exploitation of child athletes. These include criminal and civil law remedies, organisational awareness, development of preventive measures, specific codes of conduct and the screening of potential coaches.[46]

In the United Kingdom *Hickson*[47] led to the development of greater awareness and recognition of child abuse and the promotion of best practices for those working with children also became a priority. The ASA has been at the forefront of addressing the issue. It published the first 'Child Protection Guidelines' in 1996.[48] In 1998, it launched 'Swimline' in conjunction with the National Society for the Prevention of Cruelty to Children (NSPCC). Swimline is a 'hot line' manned by skilled counsellors who offer telephonic assistance to children and parents of children who have suffered child abuse, and to coaches and teachers who may be concerned about how they should be acting. It complements Childline and other agencies by providing sport specific advice. Anyone telephoning Swimline has the option of being automatically transferred to the NSPCC Childline for emergency assistance. To date, the ASA has handled more than 200 cases of child abuse. It has succeeded in establishing a 'Culture of Vigilance' in sport, which promoted 'whistleblowing' and heightened expectations of all people working with children. It has established a database of coaches and helpers. The ASA has also developed specific guidelines dealing with photography and videos of young swimmers. It has introduced specific changes to ASA Laws. ASA Law 305 specifically deals with procedures regulating child protection. The ASA has also appointed its own 'Child Protection Officer'.[49]

---

[43]   United Nations, *Convention on the Rights of the Child* (New York, 20 November 1989).

[44]   Hague Conference on Private International Law, *Hague Convention on the Civil Aspects of International Child Abduction*, 25 October 1980, Hague XXVIII.

[45]   Council of Europe, *European Convention on the Exercise of Children's Rights*, 25 January 1996, ETS 160.

[46]   G.B. Fried, 'Unsportsmanlike Contact: strategies for reducing sexual assaults in youth sports' 6(3) *Journal of Legal Aspects of Sport* (1996) p. 155.

[47]   Note 39 *supra*.

[48]   See National Coaching Foundation/NSPCC, *Protecting Children From Abuse: A Guide For Everyone Involved in Children's Sport* (Leeds: NCF, 1996).

[49]   Gardiner, James, O'Leary, *et al.*, note 40 *supra*, p. 143 *et seq.*

The Australian Sports Commission has a 'Harassment-Free Sport' programme that forms part of the 'Active Australia' initiative. As part of this programme, it makes available information on resources for child protection, training opportunities and website links to agencies that could assist the various stakeholders. Australian law also provides for the screening of those who care of or supervise children. For example, Surf Life Saving Australia has taken a proactive approach. It has a 'Member Protection Policy' which is very definite and spells out exactly what team managers should and should not do in particular situations. This policy has cleared up many grey areas, and it protects both children and the officials, who will not be subject to unfounded accusations.[50] Many sports organisations are also putting their own policies and procedures in place.

Canada has been one of the leading countries in the development of legislation that addresses basic human rights. As all sport organisations provide services to the public, they fall within the jurisdiction of federal, provincial and territorial human rights legislation. Canada has progressed beyond the human rights approach in dealing specifically with the issue of harassment and abuse. Every province and territory has legislation aimed at protecting children from abuse and neglect. In terms of this legislation, authorities may investigate a reasonable belief that a child is being harmed. The police may then lay charges, in terms of the Criminal Code of Canada, against such individual(s) who abused the child. Further, any person who has a reasonable belief that a child is in need of protection is legally obliged to report such belief to the authorities. This responsibility applies to coaches, parents, athletes and others within the sport environment.[51]

All individuals and organisations in Canada are subject to the Criminal Code. A breach of the Code can result in criminal prosecution and criminal sanctions, including imprisonment. Harassment and abuse in their most extreme forms may be criminal offences although the Criminal Code does not identify the term 'abuse' directly. With regard to the internal laws of sport organisations, they have an obligation to provide a safe environment and to protect participants from harm, including physical and emotional harm that may emanate from harassment or abuse. Even though such harm might be inflicted by individuals who may be acting only in their own interests and not for the sport organisation, the law has clearly established that the organisation has a duty to act prudently to prevent such harm. If an individual from an organisation commits a crime, the sport organisation may be vicariously liable for failing to be diligent.[52]

In South Africa section 28 of the Bill of Rights[53] deals specifically with the rights of children. It provides that every child has the right to family care or parental care, or to appropriate alternative care when removed from the family, and to be protected from maltreatment, neglect, abuse or degradation. It further provides that a child's best interests are of paramount importance in every matter concerning the child. Children thus have a constitutional right to appropriate care and to be protected from abuse. The provisions of section 28 receive added significance in view of section 8 (2) of the Bill of

---

[50] See http://www.activeaustralia.org/hfs/protect.htm.
[51] H. Findlay and R. Corbett, 'Developing Policies and Procedures' (2002), available at: http://www.harassmentinsport.com/e/Handbook/Sec1ch1.html.
[52] *Ibid.*, pp. 2–4.
[53] Chapter 2 of the Constitution of the Republic of South Africa 1996.

Rights,[54] which provides that it binds a natural or a juristic person to the extent that it may be applicable. The effect is that constitutional rights may be enforced even in private disputes involving individuals where no state action is alleged. The issue of child abuse is further dealt with generally in terms of the Children's Act 38 of 2005 and Roman–Dutch common law, which, at the risk of oversimplification, provides a general civil remedy in any situation where one person suffers loss, damage or physical or psychological injury due to the unlawful culpable conduct of another person.

While these and other measures around the world may go a long way in protecting children from abuse in general, the failure to recognise the unique nature of sport and the opportunities for various forms of abuse which sport provide, limits the effectiveness of the measures.

Most sport organisations develop codes of conduct in order to address their legal responsibility to provide a safe environment. While they describe what ethical and unethical practices are, they provide only a limited view of ethical practice, namely a contractual one. This could devalue the idea of individual virtue and responsibility in sport. '[A] code of practice should be seen as only *one*, limited step towards the prevention or eradication of … exploitation … [S]ports managers therefore need to acknowledge the limitations of codes, without a comprehensive implementation strategy, they are often meaningless in practice.'[55]

6. CONCLUSION

It is clear that sport provides unique challenges for the protection of children against all forms of abuse. Whenever laws fail to address the problem specifically in the context of sport, it remains for sports organisations themselves to address the problem of abuse.

The following agenda could be used by sport organisations as initial guidelines to protect children from abuse in sport:

- Adopt a child protection policy. Make a clear statement that child abuse is criminal behaviour and is not acceptable.
- Develop a code of conduct for all personnel, with specific instructions on how to behave when dealing with children.
- Implement an education and training programme to raise awareness of abuse in sport, and acceptable treatment of children.
- Only utilise accredited coaches and officials.
- Use a screening procedure whereby the backgrounds of all personnel are checked, including a police screening where circumstances warrant it.
- Designate an abuse contact officer, and develop procedures to ensure that allegations of child abuse are dealt with appropriately and effectively.
- Adopt thorough recruitment practices, such as creating job descriptions, interviewing candidates for positions carefully and checking personal references.

---

54 *Ibid.*
55 Brackenridge, note 27 *supra*, p.189.

A safe playing environment undoubtedly has to be guaranteed to children in sport. Any singular approach or organisation will meet with limited success to achieving this end. A multi-faceted and multi-level approach involving proactive measures by national governments and sport federations to local authorities and clubs, together with child athletes and their parents, will certainly assist in eradicating harassment and abuse in sport.

PART III

COMMERCIAL ISSUES

12 Competition law and labor markets
Stephen F. Ross

1. INTRODUCTION

Shortly after the first professional sports league (Baseball's National League) was created in 1876, and years before enactment of the Sherman Antitrust Act, baseball's founders openly admitted that the principal justification for agreements among clubs to restrain competition for players was the desire to hold down salaries and increase profits. After the enactment of federal legislation subjecting antitrust violators to liability for treble damages, baseball officials changed their tune, arguing that labor restraints were essential to promote competitive balance among the teams.[1] Since then, there has been an ongoing debate about the proper application of competition law to labor market restraints.[2]

Competition law can constrain the ability of sports leagues to restrain trade in the market for player services. Many sports leagues have market power in both labor and output markets. Where such power exists, restraining competition *inter sese* is likely to yield monopsony profits. Imposing contract terms that limit the ability of players to be employed elsewhere has the potential to exclude a sports league's potential rivals. Even if these schemes harm the consumer attractiveness of their product, the lack of reasonable substitutes for sports fans means that 'market retribution will [not] be swift.'[3]

At the same time, well-organized sports competitions may find that imposing some fetters on a wholly competitive labor market improves the quality and public appeal of their product. Courts have accepted the potential need to restrain trade to promote competitive balance as one such justification, have given mixed reaction to assuring a return on a club's investment in training a player, and have yet specifically to address claims that restraints are needed to promote fiscal solvency or the strategic expansion of a sport in broader inter-sport competition. This chapter will discuss how courts applying

---

[1] Dean A. Sullivan (ed.), *Early Innings: A Documentary History of Baseball, 1825–1908* (Lincoln: University of Nebraska Press, 1995), at 114.

[2] This chapter's discussion is limited to elite professional sports leagues. The legality of rules of minor or second-tier leagues, in particular rules to limit competition to players of more limited ability or age, is beyond its scope. Cf. *M & H Tire Co.* v. *Hoosier Racing Tire Corp.*, 733 F.2d 973, 985 (1st Cir. 1984) (upholding legality of rule limiting auto competition to cars with a single tire). Also, beyond the scope of this chapter is consideration of how statutes regulating relations between employers and employees might constrain employers. Although labor law statutes may serve the ultimate public interest in industrial stability and macroeconomic benefits to workers, their principal focus is on fairness between management and labor.

[3] *Valley Liquors, Inc.* v. *Renfield Importers., Ltd.*, 678 F.2d 742, 745 (7th Cir. 1982) (Posner J.). See also *Brookins* v. *Int'l Motor Contest Ass'n,* 219 F.3d 849 (8th Cir. 2000) (absent showing of market power, 'Irrational decisions and unfair treatment of suppliers will result in an unpopular game, and players and spectators will take their entertainment dollars elsewhere').

competition law – either statutory or the common law of restraint of trade – have evaluated labor market restraints where these sorts of justifications are plausible.

Synthesizing existing case law from common law and European courts, this chapter concludes that courts apply similar standards whether applying the common law or interpreting statutory text. With regard to inter-club agreements, once the claimant has shown that the league has market power (that is, there are no reasonable substitute employers competing for players' services[4]), courts tend to uphold restraints when reasonably tailored to achieve a legitimate goal, but find them illegal when no legitimate justification is accepted or where the challenged restraint is found to be overly restrictive. With regard to agreements with players that impair the ability of a rival to enter the marketplace, the more limited case law suggests that long-term contracts that effectively bar competitors are likely to be held illegal unless justified.

Because both these tests require a fairly intensive case-by-case inquiry into the pro- and anti-competitive effects of particular rules, courts look for short-cuts where possible. A common one is the market power requirement: if leagues vigorously compete in product or labor markets, inefficient and anti-consumer rules are less likely to survive, and judicial intervention is not necessary. Thus, a court summarily dismissed a challenge to an agreement among US college football programs to limit the size of commercial logos on uniforms, because the plaintiffs did not allege any harm in the relevant market for commercial advertising.[5] Although the judge did not expand on the point, the logic of this holding is that, absent market power or specific proof of competitive harm, the challenged rule is either designed to pursue some non-commercial end or to maximize the appeal of college sports. In contrast, regulations of dominant leagues warrant careful judicial scrutiny. As Lord Denning noted in permitting a third-party challenge under the common law of restraint of trade, 'we are not considering a social club, we are considering an association which exercises a virtual monopoly in an important field of human activity.'[6] At the same time, US courts have refused to invalidate summarily, as 'group boycotts' or 'price fixing,' a variety of sports league rules that might in other industries be condemned as 'illegal per se.'[7] This flexibility contrasts with antitrust treatment of

---

[4]   The test of 'reasonable substitutability' comes from the US Supreme Court decision in *United States* v. *E. I. Du Pont de Nemours & Co.,* 351 U.S. 377, 395 (1956) ('No more definite rule can be declared than that commodities reasonably interchangeable by consumers for the same purposes' are included in the relevant market). US courts have generally found no substitutes for each major league sport. See, e.g., *International Boxing Club* v. *United States,* 358 U.S. 242 (1959). European courts take the same approach. See, e.g., *United Brands Co* v. *Commission* (Case 27/76) [1978] E.C.R. 207, [1978] 3 C.M.L.R. 83 (ECJ) (dominant position determined by whether product was reasonably interchangeable for consumers); 'Commission opens formal proceedings into Formula One and other international motor racing series,' IP/99/434, June 30 1999, available at: http://europa.eu/rapid/pressReleasesAction.do?reference=IP/99/434&format=HTML&aged=0& language=EN&guiLanguage=en.

[5]   *Adidas* v. *NCAA,* 64 F. Supp. 2d 1275 (D. Kan. 1999).

[6]   *Nagle* v. *Feilden* [1966] 2 Q.B. 633 at 644 (C.A.) (invalidating Jockey Club refusal to grant a license to a female jockey).

[7]   *Justice* v. *NCAA,* 577 F. Supp. 356 (D. Ariz. 1983) (no showing that association of colleges penalized University of Arizona football team to protect themselves from competition from the Wildcats); *Gunter Harz Sports* v. *United States Tennis Ass'n,* 511 F. Supp. 1103, 1116 (D. Neb. 1981), *aff'd,* 665 F.2d 222 (8th Cir. 1981) (tennis association rule prohibiting use of certain tennis rackets

ordinary businesses; unlike typical firms, sports clubs may have legitimate reasons to limit unfettered competition.

Courts have difficulty evaluating labor market restraints in the sports industry. These restraints might improve the efficient operation of the sport and maximize fan appeal; or, clubs might agree to restrain trade to hold down labor costs and exclude rival leagues. Absent an objective evaluation of the precise facts of each case, it is hard to reach a conclusion, because the rules are often adopted by self-interested clubs more interested in maximizing their own profits (by holding down labor costs or excluding rivals) than fostering an optimal sporting competition.

After detailing the need for competition law to take a nuanced approach to sports league restraints, upholding efficient ones while protecting consumers and others from anti-competitive agreements, the chapter explains how the common law and the statutory competition regimes applicable in major Western countries converge, all finding that dominant sports league rules are lawful if reasonably tailored to achieve a legitimate goal. The next section of the chapter identifies the contours of legitimate goals that justify labor restraints, and the following section discusses objectives rejected by courts as illegitimate. After a brief discussion of the abuse of dominance through labor restraints that exclude rivals, the chapter finally turns to its central thesis: that – like the business judgment rule in corporate/company law – competition law analysis ought to turn primarily on whether the rule was established by a self-interested or independent source. Careful analysis is warranted in the case of the former (now typical for most sports leagues) but not necessarily the latter.

2. THE NEED FOR A NUANCED COMPETITION LAW TO PREVENT ANTI-COMPETITIVE RESTRAINTS OF TRADE

Competition allows us to trust the marketplace to self-correct. To illustrate, several years ago Italian soccer authorities considered imposing a salary cap on Serie A clubs, given the parlous financial condition many faced, such a proposal was never close to implementation, as stakeholders quickly realized that the only effect would be to cause all leading players to desert the league in favor of English, German, or Spanish clubs.[8] With market power, however, clubs have an incentive to agree among themselves to reduce competition in bidding for player services. Likewise, sports employers with market power have an incentive to adopt otherwise costly or inefficient restrictions in order to exclude rival leagues, a strategy unlikely to be effective if vigorous competition existed. Thus, while cricket authorities sought to ban participants in a rival competition from playing for the

---

was not subject to per se rule where it served to protect fair competition in sport and did not involve agreement between business competitors in traditional sense).

[8] See Paolo Menicucci, *Salary Cap Fits Serie B*, Uefa.com website, 27 April 2006, available at: http://www.uefa.com/magazine/news/Kind=128/newsId=417259.html (discussing viable cap for Italian 'minor league' soccer but acknowledging no plans to implement caps for the major league Serie A, because 'in general salary caps have only really been applied in sports where there is no true global player market').

Australian and England national teams,[9] no one would seriously suggest that a Spaniard who left Sevilla for Liverpool would be banned from Spain's national soccer team.

Anti-competitive restraints not only harm players who might receive lower wages, but harm fans as well. When clubs limit labor market competition simply to hold down salaries, the result is that otherwise desirable player movement is foreclosed, often by preventing inferior teams from improving.[10] The anti-fan consequences when talented players are blacklisted by a dominant league for participation in a rival competition are even more apparent.

Although the unfettered exercise of power therefore needs to be subject to some legal constraint, there are circumstances when dominant sports leagues can improve sporting competition by limiting their member clubs' ability to compete in labor markets.[11] The most commonly offered and accepted justification is that labor restraints help promote a level of outcome uncertainty or competitive balance that is more attractive to fans. Another oft-used justification, particularly in leagues composed of not-for-profit clubs, is the particular need to avoid insolvency among clubs participating in the sports league. As will be discussed below, different goals will call for different restraints. For now, the key point is that some types of labor market restraints may be justifiable and need to be accounted for under a competition law regime.

3.   INTERNATIONAL CONVERGENCE – AGREEMENTS LESSENING COMPETITION AMONG CLUBS ARE LEGAL IF REASONABLY TAILORED TO ACHIEVE A LEGITIMATE GOAL

This section discusses the applicable legal standard used to judge the legality of sports league restraints on competition for player services under a variety of legal regimes: the common law, the US Sherman Act, the EU Treaty, and the Canadian Competition Act. Although the law is not conclusively settled on every point in each jurisdiction, these legal regimes all allow even dominant sports leagues to restrain trade when the leagues can persuade judges that their restraint is reasonably tailored to achieve a legitimate goal. (What constitutes a legitimate goal is considered in detail in Section 4, below.)

The landmark decision of *Mitchel* v. *Reynolds*[12] established the foundation for professional sports league trade restraints: some voluntary restraints are lawful, but restraints broader than necessary to protect legitimate interests are invalid. This principle was restated in 'black letter' form in the leading common law restraint of trade case, *Nordenfelt* v. *Maxim Nordenfelt Gun & Ammunication Co.*, where Lord Macnaghten defined the reasonableness standard as:

---

[9]   *Greig* v. *Insole* (1978) 1 W.L.R. 302 (Ch.).

[10]   Stephen F. Ross and Robert B. Lucke, 'Why Highly Paid Athletes Deserve More Antitrust Protection than Unionized Factory Workers' (1997) 33 *Antitrust Bulletin* 641.

[11]   Per Lord Wilberforce: 'Regard must be had to the special character of the area in which the restraints operate – different from that of industrial employment – and to the special interests of those concerned with the organisation of professional football.' *Eastham* v. *Newcastle United Football Club Ltd.* (1964) Ch. 418 at 432.

[12]   24 Eng. Rep. 347, 349–50 (Q.B. 1711).

... in reference to the interests of the parties concerned and reasonable in reference to the interests of the public, so framed and so guarded as to afford adequate protection to the party in whose favour it is imposed, while at the same time it is in no way injurious to the public.[13]

English courts have refined the test further, making it clear that labor restraints required a *legitimate* justification,[14] and that the public interest determined whether asserted employer interests were legitimate.[15] The New Zealand Court of Appeal set forth these tests in the context of sports league restraints, declaring that, in determining legitimate goals, courts must take into consideration consumer interests and individual freedom for players.[16]

The path-marking case applying these principles to sports leagues is *Eastham v. Newcastle United Football Club*, a challenge to the English 'retain and transfer' rule, similar to baseball's 'reserve clause,' which bound a player to his former club, even if the contract had expired and the club was not paying him. Finding a real inequality in bargaining power, Lord Wilberforce stated that the pervasive use of this system by sports league employers justified careful judicial consideration of whether the rules went 'further than is reasonably necessary to protect their legitimate interests.'[17] Significantly, although he recognized that the Football League had a special and legitimate interest in maintaining the overall quality of the sport through competitive balance, Lord Wilberforce placed a significant burden on owners and leagues to justify restraints on this ground. His opinion demands proof that (1) the challenged restraints would actually achieve balance, and (2) that the restraints were necessary to achieve the goal. Ultimately, he concluded (for reasons detailed *infra*) that the league failed to demonstrate the need for these restrictions. *Eastham*'s approach has been followed in other common law countries as well.[18]

The US Sherman Act broadly proclaims that 'every contract, combination in the form of trust or otherwise, or conspiracy, in restraint of trade or commerce among the several States, or with foreign nations, is declared to be illegal.'[19] Although the Supreme Court at one point suggested that it would apply the statute literally to ban any restraint, no matter

---

[13]   [1894] A.C. 535, 565 (H.L.)

[14]   *Kores Mfg Co* v. *Kolok Mfg Co* [1959] Ch. 108, [1958] 2 All E.R. 65 (C.A.).

[15]   *Petrofina (Great Britain) Ltd.* v. *Martin* [1966] Ch. 146, [1966] 1 All E.R. 126 (C.A.) (Lord Diplock).

[16]   *Blackler* v. *New Zealand Rugby Football League* [1968] N.Z.L.R. 547 (N.Z.).

[17]   *Eastham,* note 11 *supra*, at 438.

[18]   See also *Adamson* v. *New South Wales Rugby League Ltd.* (1991) 31 F.C.R. 242 (Australian rugby league draft overbroad in applying to all players rather than stars who might actually affect competitive balance). The development of the common law of restraint of trade occurred primarily in litigation over the enforceability of agreements between the litigating parties. The right of injured parties to challenge cartel agreements among rivals that eliminated competition, although originally was not recognized during the *laissez faire* era of the common law (see *Mogul Steamship Co.* v. *McGregor, Gow & Co.* [1892] A.C. 25 at 45–46 (H.L.)), has been replaced by precedents granting injunctive relief in aid of a cause of action for a declaratory judgment. See *Eastham*, at 415. *Accord, Buckley* v. *Tutty* (1972) 125 C.L.R. 353 (Austl.); *Blackler* v. *New Zealand Rugby Football League,* (1968) N.Z.L.R. 547; *Newport Association Football Club Ltd* v. *Football Association of Wales Ltd* (1994) 144 N.L.J. 1351 (Ch.); *Johnston* v. *Cliftonville Football and Athletic Club Ltd.* (1984) N.I. 9. See generally Stephen F. Ross, 'The Evolving Tort of Conspiracy to Restrain Trade Under Canadian Common Law' (1996) 75 *Can. Bar Rev.* 1193.

[19]   15 USC §1.

how reasonable,[20] the landmark decision in *United States* v. *Addyston Pipe & Steel Co.* held that the statute was to be interpreted as intended by Congress: to make criminal and tortious those contracts that were void as unreasonable restraints of trade under the common law.[21] Judge (later President and Chief Justice) William Howard Taft concluded that the common law tolerated restraints among competitors only when 'ancillary to the main purpose of a lawful contract, and necessary to protect the covenantee in the enjoyment of the legitimate fruits of the contract.'[22]

This general principle was applied to sports by the Supreme Court in *National Collegiate Athletic Association* v. *Board of Regents*.[23] The court observed that the antitrust laws traditionally presume that certain types of agreements among competitors are unreasonable, but the court recognized that competing sports teams must agree among themselves on a host of issues in order for the product to exist at all. Thus, sports league rules are not 'per se illegal,' but are subject to antitrust scrutiny under a 'rule of reason.'[24] Where, however, the plaintiffs had demonstrated that the restraints had raised price, reduced output, or rendered output 'unresponsive to consumer preference,' the defendants have a 'heavy burden' to justify the restraints. Thus, the court invalidated broadcast restraints which were not 'arguably tailored' to promote competitive balance.[25]

Lower courts have made clear that more plausibly justified restraints are still invalid when broader than necessary to achieve legitimate goals. Thus, in *Mackey* v. *National Football League*, the NFL failed to justify on competitive balance grounds a rule limiting free movement of players. The appellate court noted that the rule applied to all players, while the trial record indicated that competitive balance concerns only came into play with the movement of the better athletes.[26] Significantly, where revenue sharing or other alternatives can achieve the goals sought to be achieved by trade restraints among clubs, the latter will also be found invalid. This principle is illustrated in a non-labor case, *Chicago Professional Sports Ltd. Partnership* v. *National Basketball Association*, where the NBA's limit on the number of Chicago Bulls games featuring Michael Jordan shown on cable television outside of the Chicagoland area was not justified to prevent 'free riding' by the Bulls on the promotional efforts of other clubs or the league as a whole. The appellate court wrote:

---

[20]   *United States* v. *Trans-Missouri Freight Ass'n,* 166 US 290 (1897).
[21]   85 Fed 217 (6th Cir. 1898), *aff'd*, 175 US 211 (1899).
[22]   *Ibid.* at 282.
[23]   468 U.S. 85 (1984).
[24]   *Ibid.* at 100–103.
[25]   Ibid. at 107, 113.
[26]   *Mackey* v. *National Football League*, 543 F.2d 606, 622 (8th Cir. 1976). See also *McNeil* v. *National Football League*, 1992-2 Trade Cas. (CCH) ¶ 69, 982 (D. Minn. 1992); *McCourt* v. *California Sports, Inc*, 460 F. Supp. 904, 909–10 (E.D. Mich. 1978), *vacated on other grounds,* 600 F.2d 1193 (6th Cir. 1979) (unreasonable rule lawful under labor exemption because included in collective bargaining agreement); *Boris* v. *USFL,* 1984-1 Trade Cas. (CCH) ¶ 66,012, at 68, 462 (C.D. Cal. 1984) (finding that USFL's myriad justifications for refusing to sign college football players with remaining years of collegiate eligibility, one of which was competitive balance, had 'varying degrees of merit,' but concluding that the practice was unreasonable because it was principally based on a desire to comply with the demands of college football coaches).

What gives this the name free-riding is the lack of charge ... When payment is possible, free-riding is not a problem because the 'ride' is not free. Here lies the flaw in the NBA's story. It may (and does) charge members for value delivered. As the NBA itself emphasizes, there are substantial revenue transfers, propping up the weaker clubs in order to promote vigorous competition on the court. Without skipping a beat the NBA may change these payments to charge for the Bulls' ride.[27]

The Treaty of the European Union contains several provisions of relevance to sports league restraints. Article 39 prohibits restrictions on the free movement of workers, while Article 101 prohibits 'concerted practices which may affect trade between Member States and which have as their object or effect the prevention, restriction or distortion of competition within the common market,' and Article 102 prevents the abuse of a dominant position. In *Union Royale Belge des Societes de Football Association* v. *Bosman*,[28] the European Court of Justice found that Article 39 prohibited rules, promulgated by the Union of European Football Associations (UEFA) and adhered to by all European professional football clubs, that required compensation for players signing with new clubs after the expiration of their contract. It did not reach, but by implication its reasoning is consistent with, the prior conclusion of the Advocat General that the rules violated both articles 39 and 101.

In recognizing that the EU Treaty limits the ability of dominant leagues and clubs to restrain trade, *Bosman* acknowledged that restrictions would be compatible with the Treaty if they pursued a 'legitimate aim' and were reasonably necessary to achieve the public interest.[29] However, as the Court emphasized in *Lehtonen* v. *Federation Royale Belge des Societes de Basket-ball*, 'measures taken by sports federations with a view to ensuring the proper functioning of competitions may not go beyond what is necessary for achieving the aim pursued.'[30]

Sports restraints in Canada have been primarily litigated under the common law.[31] However, the Competition Act contains a specific provision governing sports league restraints. When the Canadian statute was amended in 1976 to cover conspiracies to restrain trade in services as well as goods, sports leagues were concerned that the broad provisions of the general conspiracy section could proscribe virtually all agreements among sports league owners. Parliament responded by enacting a specific provision

---

27   961 F.2d 667, 674 (3rd Cir. 1992).

28   (1996) 1 C.M.L.R. 645.

29   *Ibid.* at ¶ 104.

30   (2000) 3 C.M.L.R. 409 at ¶ 56. In his preliminary decision in *Lehtonen*, the Advocat General was more explicit: 'Competition-restricting rules such as in the present case which have the effect of promoting the establishment of competition on the market in question may therefore be compatible with [Article 101] if they are necessary and reasonable for achieving that objective.' *Ibid. at* ¶ 107.

31   This is also true in Australia. Although Australia has a statutory ban on anticompetitive restraints, the Trade Practices Act expressly excludes 'the performance of work under a contract of service.' Trade Practices Act 1974 (Cth.) s. 4. But see *Adamson,* note 18 *supra,* 31 F.C.R. 242 at 245, suggesting that if players demanded to provide their services as independent contractors who would be subject to competition legislation, it would be unlawful for the clubs to agree among themselves to refuse to employ players in that manner. See also *Hughes* v. *Western Australia Cricket Ass'n* (1986) 19 F.C.R. 10 (agreement between Western Australia Cricket Association and its constituent clubs was not subject to s. 45(2)'s ban on competition-lessening agreements, because the clubs who directed the amateur game were not trading corporations for purposes of the statute).

making it illegal for sports owners to 'limit unreasonably the opportunity for any other person to negotiate with and, if agreement is reached, to play for the team or club of his choice in a professional league.'[32] In evaluating restraints, courts are specifically directed to consider 'the desirability of maintaining a reasonable balance among the teams or clubs participating in the same league.'[33] Although Canadian courts have yet to interpret the statute definitively, it would appear that the statute was designed to incorporate the common law standards of reasonableness discussed above.[34]

The broad 'black letter' standards of various competition laws expressly contemplate a balancing of interests in determining the reasonableness of a challenged restraint.[35] This has led some judges to suggest that a similar balancing of interests ought to be applied in challenging sports league labor restraints.[36] Closer analysis reveals that this step of the analysis should almost always be superfluous. It is difficult to envision a case where the league is able to demonstrate that a challenged rule is necessary to accomplish a legitimate goal, yet the judge would find that the harm to the claimant's interests nonetheless render the rule unreasonable. Likewise, it would seem that the interests of unrestrained trade would always triumph if the challenged rule is overbroad or unnecessary.

4. LEGITIMATE GOALS THAT JUSTIFY LABOR MARKET RESTRAINTS

4.1. Competitive Balance

Almost all courts which have considered the issue have found that the promotion of competitive balance is a legitimate goal of sports leagues.[37] An early and sophisticated analysis in a non-labor context observed that sports is an unusual business in that, while

---

[32]   Competition Act, s. 48 (1)(b), R.S.C. 1985 (2d Supp.), c. 19, c. 34.

[33]   *Ibid.*, s. 48 (2).

[34]   See Stephen F. Ross, 'The NHL Labour Dispute and the Common Law, the *Competition Act* and Public Policy' (2004) *U.B.C. Law Rev.* 37, 370–8. Unlike the Sherman Act, the general conspiracy section of the Competition Act, s. 45, prohibits agreements that restrain trade 'unduly,' which Canadian courts have interpreted to exclude 'a full-blown discussion of the economic advantages and disadvantages of the agreement, like a rule of reason would.' *R* v. *Nova Scotia Pharmaceutical Soc'y* [1992] 2 S.C.R. 606, 650 (Can. Sup. Ct.). As a result, any restrictive agreements among those controlling a monopoly share of the market, like National Hockey League (NHL) owners agreeing on a labor restraint, would appear to be precluded by that section. The government thus agreed with NHL complaints and supported the 'reasonableness' standard in s. 48.

[35]   See *Nordenfelt,* note 13 *supra; Chicago Board of Trade* v. *United States,* 246 U.S. 231 (1918).

[36]   See, e.g., *Adamson* (Gummow J), note 18 *supra,* at 284.

[37]   In addition to cases cited in text, see *Mackey, NCAA* v. *Board of Regents,* and *Bosman,* notes 26, 23, and 28 *supra.* There are two US precedents to the contrary, but neither likely reflects sound law today, especially in light of the clear endorsement of output-increasing competitive balance in the *NCAA* case, *supra,* 468 U.S. 85 at 117. In *Smith* v. *Pro Football, Inc.,* 593 F.2d 1173, 1186 (D.C. Cir. 1978), the court held that the NFL's reverse-order amateur draft was illegal because it was pro-competitive 'in a very different sense than in which it is anticompetitive.' The harm was to players, but the alleged benefit was 'on the playing field.' The court found that although the draft may 'improve the entertainment product open to the public,' this was not a justification because it neither lowered cost or increased entry of rivals. As the Supreme Court recognized in *NCAA*, the hallmarks of the rule of reason under antitrust law include both the quantity of price and output

'the ordinary businessman [this was written in 1953] is not troubled by the knowledge that he is doing so well that his competitors are being driven out of business,' in sports, 'not only would the weaker teams fail, but eventually the whole league [would as well].'[38]

This truism, however, has led some courts to leap to a *factual* conclusion that parity among teams is always good for the sport, and therefore justified under competition law. For example, the Australian High Court declared that leagues had a legitimate interest in ensuring that 'teams fielded in the competitions are as strong and well matched as possible, for in that way the support of the public will be attracted and maintained, and players will be afforded the best opportunity of developing and displaying their skill.'[39] However, the claim that public support is maximized when teams are as 'well matched as possible' has yet to be empirically verified – many social scientists have rigorously sought to review data measuring public support, in terms of attendance and television ratings, without any reliable proof that any particular level of competitive balance systematically improves such support.[40] (Anecdotally, the current popularity of the English Premier League and the popularity of the National Basketball Association during the dynastic reign of the Michael Jordan-led Chicago Bulls suggests that parity is not essential. Nor, in the context of multiple leagues, as exist in European football, is it clear that balancing domestic competitions by restraining the top teams' ability to compete in trans-European football would enhance football's appeal.) Thus, one US court has found that a league's interest was promoted not by strict parity but where 'each team has the opportunity of becoming a contender over a reasonable cycle of years.'[41] The US Supreme Court, which has also recognized competitive balance as 'legitimate and important,' has suggested that leagues need to actually prove the underlying hypothesis that 'equal competition will maximize consumer demand for the product.'[42]

Even if we presume that increased parity legitimately justifies a labor restraint, courts impose significant limits on leagues' ability to legally justify particular restraints. *Eastham* demands leagues prove that (1) absent the challenged restraint, richer teams would indeed be more active in signing free agents than financially poorer clubs, and (2) the free agents signed would be better, thus directly exacerbating competitive imbalance. There are, to be sure, some restraints that would appear to directly weaken superior teams and assist inferior teams. For example, most US sports leagues have roster limits and a 'waiver rule'

---

but also whether 'output is responsive to consumer preference.' 468 U.S. 85 at 107. Agreements among rivals that improve quality without increasing the price of the product are thus valid. Likewise, an earlier court failed to appreciate that agreements necessary to provide the desired quality of a product to consumers are lawful. *Gardella* v. *Chandler*, 172 F.2d 402, 415 (2nd Cir. 1949) (Frank J., concurring) (rejecting justification for baseball's Reserve Clause because 'the public's pleasure does not authorize the courts to condone illegality').

[38]   *United States* v. *National Football League*, 116 F. Supp. 319, 323 (E.D. Pa. 1953).
[39]   *Buckley* v. *Tutty*, note 18 *supra*, at 377.
[40]   Stefan Szymanski, 'The Economic Design of Sporting Contests' (2003) 41 *J. Econ. Lit.* 1137.
[41]   See *Philadelphia World Hockey Club, Inc.* v. *Philadelphia Hockey Club,* 351 F. Supp. 462, 486 (E.D. Pa. 1972). A similar approach was proposed by a Blue Ribbon panel of experts retained by Major League Baseball. Richard C. Levin *et al.*, *The Report of the Independent Members of the Commissioner's Blue Ribbon Panel on Baseball Economics* 8 (2000), available at: http://www.mlb.com/mlb/downloads/blue<uscore>ribbon.pdf (MLB should ensure that each team has 'a regularly recurring reasonable hope of reaching post-season play').
[42]   *NCAA* v. *Board of Regents,* note 23 *supra*, at 117, 120.

that requires teams, when discharging a player from their limited roster, to assign his contract for a nominal fee to another club in the league willing to put the player on their roster, with the lowest-ranked team having priority in case of multiple claims. Likewise, for one year the NFL experimented with a rule that imposed graduated payroll caps on superior teams which had advanced in the post-season playoffs, freeing inferior teams to compete freely. These rules, however, stand in contrast to most labor restraints challenged under competition laws, which impose 'blanket restraints' that limit competition for services for good and bad teams alike.

Eastham cited a number of reasons why barring 'rich' teams from to actively competing in a labor market might not improve competitive balance. First, clubs commonly transferred rights to players to other clubs for a fee, and thus richer clubs already used their superior resources to buy players. Second, clubs with good employee relations could draw upon the natural reluctance of a player to betray feelings of loyalty as well as to disrupt his family. Third, '[n]o club desires more than so many centre forwards,' so that players are unlikely to switch to talent-laden teams where they might not make the first 11.[43] Several US courts have likewise struck down restraints where there was no showing of how they actually improved competitive balance.[44]

Lord Wilberforce's third point deserves additional note. All things being equal, a player is more likely to be more highly valued by an *inferior* team, and so the free market naturally tends to *improve* competitive balance. A championship team will find it very difficult to sustain the salary demands of all its players; a team with a disappointing record will have a greater incentive to demonstrate improvement next year, and is more likely to find players with subordinate roles on top teams who can become stars on their own rosters. Both US and Australian commentators have observed that unrestrained labor markets permit players to move from superior to inferior teams and restrained markets often rigidify the dominance of a few teams.[45]

The judicial consensus that limitations on labor market competition be no more restrictive than necessary to attain the league's legitimate competitive balance objectives is

---

[43]   *Eastham*, note 11 *supra*, at 434. As an Australian court noted, a 'player of skills and physical characteristics of a particular kind may well have a far better opportunity of being selected to play and of becoming a footballer of high repute if he is able to join a club which has not any other or few other players of that kind than if he joins a club which has a number of them.' *Hall* v. *Victorian Football League* [1982] V.R. 64 at 70 (Vic. Sup. Ct.) (striking down restraint assigning players to clubs based on residence, where player assigned to dominant Collingwood club preferred to play for also-ran South Melbourne). See also *Adamson* v. *New South Wales Rugby League* (1991) 103 A.L.R. 319, 500 (Fed. Ct.) (one reason for players to choose to change clubs was to improve player's chance to play in the top league 'which might be poor if the player were required to play with a team already well catered for in the position of his choice'); *Johnston* v. *Cliftonville Football and Athletic Club Ltd.* [1984] N.I. 9 at 21 (Ch.) (in light of roster maxima, fear that top two clubs in Northern Ireland would sign all the best players 'does not bear examination'); Stephen F. Ross, 'The Misunderstood Alliance Between Sports Fans, Players, and the Antitrust Laws' (1997) *Univ. of Illinois L. Rev.* 519, 565 (describing how champion New York Yankees did not seriously bid on a key relief pitcher because they had a younger player at the same position and the veteran's skills were more valued by other team).

[44]   *NCAA* v. *Board of Regents,* note 23 *supra* (television restraints); *Law* v. *NCAA*, 134 F.3d 1010 (10th Cir. 1998) (salary cap on fourth assistant basketball coach).

[45]   Brian Ward, 'Fair Play: Professional Sports and Restraint of Trade' (1985) 59 *L. Inst. J.* 545; Ross and Lucke, note 10 *supra*.

another significant obstacle to the validity of many labor restraints. Instructive is the logic of *Adamson* v. *New South Wales Rugby League Ltd*.[46] The court found that a draft for out-of-contract players was an unreasonable restraint of trade. Rejecting the league's competitive balance argument, the court noted that the plaintiffs had not challenged another league rule imposing an A$1.5 million salary cap on each club, and that the cap prevented the sort of imbalancing 'cheque book warfare' that the league feared would occur if labor market competition were unfettered.[47] In addition to salary caps (which have their own problems), there are a variety of other tools a league might employ to promote competitive balance other than blanket labor market restraints. Revenue redistribution schemes can lessen the competitive advantage that 'rich' teams might have, where a club's wealth is based on factors other than on-field competitive success (such as location in a larger or wealthier city in the US, or access to financial support from gambling-supported member clubs in Australia). Local revenue sources can also be taxed, to limit club incentives to wildly spend to achieve competitive success.

4.2.   Integrity of the Competition

Since the founding of the National League in 1876, sports competition organizers have recognized that the perception of a competition played under the rules is essential to maximizing fan appeal. The one major change in the structure of US sports leagues since that time – the introduction of a powerful League Commissioner to rule on match-fixing and other integrity issues – came in the face of a gambling scandal.

Courts have also recognized that preservation of integrity of the competition is a legitimate justification for engaging in what would otherwise be an unlawful trade restraint. Thus, even at a time when case law suggested that any concerted refusal to deal among competitors was illegal per se, a court upheld the NBA's lifetime ban on a player who admittedly had gambled on a game in which he was playing.[48] The court observed that the NBA 'could reasonably conclude that in order to effectuate its important and legitimate policies against gambling, and to restore and maintain the confidence of the public vital to its existence, it was necessary to enforce its rules strictly, and to apply the most stringent sanctions.'[49] Similarly, considering a challenge to strict anti-doping rules that penalized horse racing trainers when after race tests demonstrated illegal drug use, absent 'substantial evidence' refuting the presumption that the trainer was responsible, the court held that the 'procompetitive benefits of the rule clearly predominate.'[50]

Applying similar principles under European competition law, the ECJ likewise found that anti-doping rules did not distort or restrain trade in violation of Article 101 of the European Treaty because they were necessary to ensure fair sporting competitions.[51]

---

46   Note 18 *supra*.
47   *Ibid.* at 249.
48   *Molinas* v. *National Basketball Ass'n*, 190 F. Supp. 241 (S.D.N.Y. 1961).
49   *Ibid.* at 244.
50   *Cooney* v. *American Horse Shows Ass'n*, 495 F. Supp. 424, 431 (S.D.N.Y. 1980).
51   *Meca-Medina & Macjen* v. *Commission* (Case 519/04) ECR 2006 1–6991.

4.3.   Maintenance of Fiscal Solvency

Because of the interdependence of clubs on others to maintain a viable competition, free-wheeling spending on players could lead a club into insolvency, jeopardizing not only their own organization and supporters but those of the entire league. Although this goal has been held to be legitimate in theory,[52] there are no cases that support the typical sort of labor market restraints – limits on competition for out-of-contract players, salary caps, and the like – as a means of ensuring fiscal solvency. In a successful challenge to a (Northern) Ireland Football Association salary cap, the court rejected testimony that removing the cap would lead to financial ruin. The judge noted that:

> ... this is an argument to the effect that football boards need to be protected from their own financial folly ... I could not find that it is reasonable for the League to retain the maximum wage regulation for players in order to save the clubs from financial disaster unless I had had before me a general survey of the finances of the clubs in the League and an expert opinion based on that survey to the effect that such a disaster is at least a real risk.[53]

As a matter of economics, it is difficult to see how a general labor restraint could be shown necessary to promote this goal. However, given the external effect of club profligacy, it would likely be reasonable to impose a focused and indirect labor restraint – such as that adopted in French soccer – whereby a league assures club viability by a combination of revenue-sharing and limits on payroll in terms of each individual club's revenues or debts.[54] At the same time, a case-by-case analysis may be required, as with other justifications, to assure that the debt limitations are not primarily designed to reduce payroll rather than assure solvency.[55]

4.4.   Protecting the 'Organization and Administration of the Game'

In the US, the elite professional competitions are run by the for-profit clubs comprising the major professional sports leagues. In the rest of the world, these leagues are subject to further governance, and are sometimes operated directly, by non-profit federations that control both professional and amateur aspects of the game. This perhaps explains the more cynical approach of US courts to non-economic justifications. As Judge Higginbotham wrote: 'Despite the thousands of words uttered on this record by all parties about the glory of the sport of hockey and the grandeur of its superstars, the basic factors here are not the sheer exhilaration from observing the speeding puck, but rather the desire to

---

[52]   *Stevenage Borough Football Club Ltd* v. *Football League Ltd* [1996] E.W.C.A. Civ. 569 (Ch. D.) (although 'the Football League has a legitimate interest in the financial stability of its members, since failure by a club during the season will have an adverse effect not only on its ability to complete its existing programme, but also on the image of the League generally,' particular criteria used to deny promotion to the plaintiff club, which did not apply to existing clubs in the league to which the plaintiff sought promotion, was unreasonable).

[53]   *Johnston*, note 43 *supra*.

[54]   The French system is described in Jean-Jacques Gouget and Didier Primault 'The French Exception' (2007) 7 *J. Sports Econ.* 47 at 56–7.

[55]   Indeed, the NFL withdrew proposed debt limits in the face of a complaint by the players' association that such a rule violated terms of their collective bargaining agreement that bars clubs from colluding with each other with regard to signing of out-of-contract players. Daniel Kaplan and Liz Mullen, 'NFL Halts Plan to Reduce Debt' (2008) *Sports Bus. J.*, Apr. 7, at p. 1.

maximize the available buck.'[56] In a similar vein, the US Supreme Court summarily invalidated an NFL owners' blacklist of players who had participated in rival leagues.

In contrast, in *Greig* v. *Insole,* an English judge, hearing a challenge to cricket authorities' efforts to ban from international test matches players who had participated in a rival competition, seriously considered (before ultimately rejecting as unnecessary) the claim that the ban was 'no more than is reasonably necessary for the protection of the organisation and administration of the game.'[57] Favorably citing Lord Wilberforce, the opinion recognizes that sporting associations 'were in a sense custodians of the public interest.'[58]

The precise contours of this justification remain unclear from the exhaustive *Greig* opinion (an edited version in the All England Law Reports exceeds 40 000 words). Justice Slade candidly observed that there is no 'comprehensive judicial statement of the principles defining which interests are and which are not entitled to protection by the law' and that he did not 'propose to attempt to formulate any such statement.'[59] For him, the conclusion of unreasonable restraint was made easier by the retroactive boycott of players participating in the rival series.

There are portions of the opinion that are quite favorable to dominant federations. The court expressed 'considerable sympathy' with the Board's argument that a rival series would diminish interest, prestige, and attraction of touring and test matches in and between various countries, the income to be derived from their promotion and attendance and the benefit in terms of experience, fame and improvement of skills to be enjoyed by their participants. Diminution of income from touring and test matches, it was pleaded, will adversely affect the playing and provision of cricket at all levels.[60]

Later, Justice Slade wrote:

> There would, I think, have been much to be said for the reasonableness and thus for the validity of a resolution ... of which the effect had been merely to inform cricketers in clear terms that any of them who thereafter contracted with and elected to play cricket for a private promoter, such as World Series Cricket, could not subsequently expect to be engaged to play in official test matches by any of the cricketing authorities of the test-playing countries.[61]

---

[56]   *Philadelphia World Hockey Club, Inc.* v. *Philadelphia Hockey Club*, 351 F. Supp. 462, 466 (E.D. Pa. 1972).

[57]   (1978) 1 W.L.R. at 347. See also *Newport Association Football Club Ltd* v. *Football Ass'n of Wales Ltd.* [1995] 2 All E.R. 87 (Ch. 1994) (triable issue whether restraint was justified as 'good for Welsh football as a whole').

[58]   *Ibid.*

[59]   *Ibid.* at 346. This is common in British legal reasoning. See *Esso Petroleum Ltd.* v. *Harper's Garage (Stourport) Ltd.* [1968] A.C. 269 at 300, 331, where Lord Wilberforce wrote: 'The common law has often (if sometimes unconsciously) thrived on ambiguity and it would be mistaken, even if it were possible, to try to crystallise the rules of this, or any, aspect of public policy into neat propositions. A doctrine of restraint of trade is one applied to factual situations with a broad and flexible rule of reason.'

[60]   *Greig*, note 9 *supra*, at 348.

[61]   *Ibid.* at 352.

Elsewhere, however, the court carefully reviewed the precise economic harm from the rival series, minimizing the actual economic injury to various Test cricket countries.[62] This suggests a heavier burden on federations to show how labor restraints were necessary to protect the organization and administration of the game. Indeed, if federations' legitimate interests in obtaining revenue (historically derived solely from Test matches) for other worthy purposes is that strong, a less restrictive alternative would be to impose a fee on the revenues of all professional competitions so that these legitimate functions can go forward regardless of the form of professional sport.

Most significantly, the claim that labor restraints are justified in order to protect the federations' revenue derived from Test matches would logically lead to the conclusion that even the boycott at issue in *Grieg* was justified on deterrence grounds. Indeed, this was precisely the argument made by counsel. While again emphasizing his concerns with the retroactive aspect of the challenged boycott, Justice Slade expressly noted another important consideration that led him to reject the justification: 'the public will be deprived of a great deal of pleasure, if it is to be deprived of the opportunity of watching those talented cricketers play in those many official test matches which do not clash with World Series Cricket matches, and for which they would otherwise be available.'[63] This further suggests that the balancing of the legitimate private interests of the parties with the public interest, required under the common law for over 150 years, should rarely tolerate the use of boycotts to promote the administration of the game.

Still, *Grieg*'s ambiguities suggest that common law courts may go farther that those operating under competition statutes. Consider *Linseman* v. *World Hockey Association*,[64] where the court struck down a league rule barring teams from signing players under 20 years of age. (Ironically, this decision led the league's Indianapolis Racers to sign 17-year-old Wayne Gretzky and helped establish the rival league's viability.) Responding to the league's claim that it had been coerced into adopting the rule by Canadian national hockey authorities, the court rejected the argument that the ban was necessary to preserve Canadian junior league teams, who allegedly would fail if the most talented teenagers were signed by professional teams. If the Canadian junior leagues provided essential training for prospective players, the court observed, the WHA could devise a means, at its own cost, for setting up that training. Although the court did not expound upon this point, if the Canadian junior league teams would not be financially viable without teenagers talented enough to play major professional hockey, then the WHA and its rival, the NHL, could provide financial subsidies to keep the junior leagues afloat. But, as the court noted, 'the Sherman Act does not permit a failing enterprise to be buoyed up with an illegal agreement to restrain trade.'[65]

One of the arguments that the English court seemed to accept in *Grieg* was that private parties could potentially be allowed to restrain trade, if necessary to raise money for worthy causes that cannot be supported by the free market. The Sherman Act reflects the public policy that competition is in the public interest, and that activities that the market

---

[62]   In addition to noting that some of the adversely affected Tests were not profitable, the court observed that in some cases, the loss of star players from the Australian team might make the Tests more exciting. *Ibid.* at 341.

[63]   *Ibid.* at 354.

[64]   439 F. Supp. 1315 (D. Conn. 1977).

[65]   *Ibid.* at 1322.

cannot support should be provided through public subsidy or, if by private parties, through an express legislative exemption.[66]

The US approach is reflected not only in professional sports cases but, perhaps more closely analogous to European and Australian sports, to major college football programs. Just as Test cricket's proceeds subsidize many worthy amateur cricket programs, proceeds from the most profitable major college football programs subsidize 'non-revenue' sports, such as swimming, tennis, lacrosse, etc., which are engaged in without significant spectator support. In *National Collegiate Athletic Association* v. *Board of Regents*,[67] the US Supreme Court made it clear that broadcast restraints on major programs could not be justified in order to protect the market for less attractive programs. NCAA's counsel did not even seek to argue that the NCAA should be able to restrict output and increase price in order to use the proceeds to support sports that could not generate sufficient revenues to cover their own expenses.

Rejecting the dissenting views of two justices (including Justice Byron White, a former college and professional football star), the majority held that the only justifications that college football programs could use to restrain trade were commercial ones: those necessary for differentiating college football from professional football in a manner that maximized output or output responsive to consumer demand. On this basis, however, the majority suggested that labor market restraints (NCAA rules bar players from receiving compensation other than the equivalent of educational expenses such as tuition, room and board, and books) would be lawful:

> ... the NCAA seeks to market a particular brand of football – college football. The identification of this 'product' with an academic tradition differentiates college football from and makes it more popular than professional sports to which it might otherwise be comparable, such as, for example, minor league baseball. In order to preserve the character and quality of the 'product', athletes must not be paid, must be required to attend class, and the like. And the integrity of the 'product' cannot be preserved except by mutual agreement; its effectiveness as a competitor on the playing field might soon be destroyed.[68]

Thus, the US Supreme Court seems to have somewhat narrowly defined the English justification of protecting the 'organization of administration of the game' to focus on ways to preserve and maximize public appeal of 'the game': its rules 'widen consumer choice – not only the choices available to sports fans but also those available to athletes – and hence can be viewed as procompetitive.'[69]

Although there is no empirical evidence to support the court's claim that athletes must not be paid in order to preserve the character of college football, this concept is the basis for several lower courts to reject antitrust challenges to agreements among colleges barring

---

[66] Indeed, one reason why Congress has not repealed the judicially created antitrust exemption for baseball is that Major League Baseball uses its profits to support minor league baseball teams throughout the nation.

[67] Note 23 *supra*.

[68] *Ibid.* at 100–101.

[69] *Ibid.* at 102.

compensation in excess of scholastic aid.[70] Still, the court's insistence on commercial justifications for commercial restrictions provides a useful lesson.

At the same time, the US Supreme Court has given far more leeway to non-profit governing federations to adopt *non-commercial restrictions*, where the member schools do not stand to profit from the restraint. Thus, an antitrust challenge to a rule barring graduate students from participating in intercollegiate athletics competition, unless they played for the same school at which they earned their undergraduate degree, was rejected: the court determined that these rules were not subject to antitrust review because they 'are not related to the NCAA's commercial or business activities.'[71] This finding is consistent with empirical evidence that NCAA members schools vote on commercial policies in a manner consistent with each institution's economic self-interest, but their votes on non-commercial rules do not follow such a pattern.[72]

4.5.   Recoupment of Clubs' Investment in Training and Developing Young Players

Opinions applying the Sherman Act have refused to accept claims by professional sports leagues that the need to secure clubs' investment in training and developing young players justifies labor restraints. As the appellate court explained in *Mackey,* recouping costs for training employees is 'an ordinary cost of doing business and is not peculiar to professional football.'[73] As in other industries, either employers provide uncompensated training and development in order to attract top workers, or, where training and development are particularly expensive, provisions for repayment can be negotiated by each club in its individual contracts with players. (Large US accountancy firms routinely subsidize young employees' training in obtaining an MBA degree, with the proviso that the funds must be repaid if the employee does not remain at the firm for a substantial period of time after obtaining the degree, but there is no agreement among firms to do so.)

The common law is less clear in this regard. A venerable precedent of general application explicitly rejected a claim that employers were justified in agreeing among themselves to restrain trade to ensure that they receive an adequate return on their human resource investments.[74] Most significantly, Lord Wilberforce observed that clubs could adequately protect themselves by individually negotiated agreements with younger players to ensure that the club could recoup its investment.[75]

---

70   *Banks* v. *NCAA*, 977 F.2d 1081, 1092 (7th Cir. 1992) (rule barring players who submit to the NFL draft from continued participation in college football upheld as part of NCAA's effort to 'preserve bright line of demarcation between college and "play for pay" football'); *Justice* v. *NCAA,* note 7 *supra.*

71   *Smith* v. *NCAA*, 139 F.3d 180, 184–87 (3rd Cir. 1998).

72   Lawrence DeBrock and Wallace Hendricks, 'Roll Call Voting in the NCAA' (1996) 12 *J. L. Econ. Org.* 497.

73   *Mackey*, note 26 *supra*, at 621. There is one contrary US precedent, a district court opinion in *Nassau Sports* v. *Peters*, 352 F. Supp. 870 (E.D.N.Y. 1972). This decision, hastily written in response to a motion for a preliminary injunction, is inconsistent with the express holding of the court of appeals in *Mackey.*

74   *Mineral Water Bottle Exchange and Trade Protection Soc'y* v. *Booth* (1887) 36 Ch. 465 (Ch.).

75   *Eastham,* note 11 *supra*, at 435–436. Language in *Detroit Football Co.* v. *Dublinski* [1957] O.R. 58, 7 D.L.R. (2d) 9, 14–15 (C.A.), is not to the contrary. There, the court found merit in the Detroit Lions' claim that among the injuries it suffered by Dublinski's breach of an option to play for the

Those common law opinions with contrary conclusions can be distinguished on the basis suggested by Lord Wilberforce's reasoning: in those cases, individual negotiation was not available to protect clubs' investment in training young players adequately. Thus, the New Zealand Court of Appeal recognized the legitimate need of the New Zealand Rugby Football League to have some means of recouping its investment, in light of the specific transitional context of the sport at the time, which was an amateur sport in New Zealand but a professional sport in Australia and England.[76] Similarly, although *Greig* v. *Insole* recognized an interest in preventing a rival league from 'creaming off ... the star players who it has itself incurred no expense in training and preparing for stardom,'[77] *Greig* may also be unusual in that the need to negotiate investment–recoupment provisions in individual contracts may not have been reasonably foreseen by national cricket authorities, in light of the unprecedented rival competition being organized by Australian media magnate Kerry Packer.[78]

Nor are agreements *among teams* to restrict competition for players' services necessary to promote player development by lower-tier clubs. Leagues are free to raise and redistribute revenue for this goal. For example, a straight 5 percent tax on all club payrolls would not likely cause a significant restraint on bidding for player services.

In contrast with US and common law precedents, EU competition officials appear to approve of properly tailored rules that justify trade restraints to assure investment recoupment by professional clubs. In *Bosman*, the European Court of Justice found that the challenged rule – an open-ended requirement that the prior employer consent to the re-registration of a player with a new club – was overbroad, because the sporting future of players is so uncertain that the prospect of transfer fees for out-of-contract players, especially for smaller clubs, is unlikely to be decisive in their incentives. To be sure, the Advocat General did acknowledge that in some cases it might be reasonable for clubs to

---

Lions in 1955 (he signed instead with the Toronto Argonauts) was its inability to recoup its investment in training him. The issue in the case, however, was the validity of a one-year option agreement in Dublinski's contract, not a perpetual refusal of other NFL teams to bid on Dublinski's services. Prior to 1963, there were no restraints on an NFL team's ability to sign a contract with a player whose contractual obligations with another team had expired. See *Mackey* v. *National Football League*, 503 F.2d 606, 610 (8th Cir. 1976).

[76]   *Blackler* v. *New Zealand Rugby Football League* [1968] N.Z.L.R. 547 (N.Z.). *Cf. Wickham* v. *Canberra District Rugby League Football Club Ltd.* (1998) A.T.P.R. 41–664, 1998 AUST ACTSC LEXIS 24 (Sup. C.A.C.T. Sept. 10, 1998) (upholding rule that effectively tied a junior player to the club with which he was initially registered for 3 or 4 years, concluding that the modest remuneration for junior players did not make them professionals). Implicit in *Wickham*'s analysis is that, at a junior amateur level, individual contracting is not an economically viable alternative. There are dicta in *Buckley* v. *Tutty*, note 18 *supra*, at 378, that could be read to validate a league rule imposing a transfer fee that attempted to recoup the benefit a player received 'from his membership of or association with' his former club. This issue was not before the Australian High Court and, in light of the court's recognition that team stability could be achieved by provisions in individually negotiated contracts, see *ibid.* at 377, there is no reason to suppose that the same alternative would not suffice even if a court were to conclude, contrary to *Eastham* and *Blackler*, that clubs had a legitimate interest in recouping their 'investment' in a player.

[77]   *Greig*, note 9 *supra*, at 499.

[78]   See Gideon Haigh, *The Cricket War: The Inside Story of Kerry Packer's World Series Cricket* (Melbourne: Text Publishing Co., 1993).

agree on compensation for actual work done by a club initially training the player.[79] A key focus of the Advocat General's analysis was expenses incurred by a low-tier amateur or semi-professional club. More recently, FIFA rules regarding mandatory compensation for players, even when transferring after the expiration of their contract, have been approved by EC Competition Commissioner Mario Monti.[80]

In light of the general convergence between EU competition law, US antitrust law, and the common law of restraint of trade, the European approach is best understood in the particularized context of a pan-European labor market where domestic contract law may not allow individual clubs to adequately protect themselves in contracts with individual players (the alternative suggested by Lord Wilberforce in *Eastham*). Although the common law and most civil codes assure the enforcement of freely negotiated long-term contracts,[81] some continental jurisdictions have superseding statutory provisions specifying that workers may breach employment contracts with minimal penalty.[82] As a result, for example, Ajax Amsterdam may have no remedy from Dutch courts if Manchester United lured one of its stars in mid-contract, while PSV Eindhoven would likely face liability from a British judge if it tried to induce a Liverpool player from jumping across the North Sea.[83]

The economic approach to protecting a club's interest in recouping its investment in player development presupposes unfettered freedom of contract: clubs and players agree on an appropriate levels of risk sharing, so that clubs are willing to commit substantial money and effort into developing players, and players agree that if they are good and fortunate enough to become highly successful, the training club will share the wealth. There are hints in European jurisprudence that this sort of free-market approach may be inconsistent with Article 39's protection of the free movement of workers. Consider the

---

[79] *Bosman*, note 28 *supra*, at 654 (¶ 239).

[80] See 'Commission closes investigations into FIFA regulations on international football transfers' available at: http://europa.eu/rapid/pressReleasesAction.do?reference=IP/02/824&format=HTML&aged=1&language=EN&guiLanguage=en.

[81] See, e.g., *Lemat Corp* v. *Barry*, 80 Cal, Rptr, 240 (Cal, Ct, App, 1969) (enjoining Barry, named one of the 50 greatest players in history by the NBA in 1996, and the only player to lead the NCAA, ABA, and NBA in scoring for an individual season, from jumping to a team in a rival league under he had discharged his contract with the NBA's Golden State Warriors); *Philadelphia Ball Club Ltd.* v. *Lajoie,* 202 Pa. 210 (1902) (enjoining Hall of Fame infielder from breaching contract with National League Phillies to play for new American League rival Philadelphia Athletics).

[82] For a critique of the US approach and an explanation of the difficulty that clubs would have enforcing long-term promises under Danish law, see Lars Halgreen, *European Sports Law* (Forlaget: Thomson, 2004) at pp. 258–61. Chapter 54–1 of the Labor Code of the Russian Federation was recently amended in February 2008 to permit enforceability of long-term contracts, in response to several notable cases of Russian players terminating contracts with Russian clubs and signing with NHL clubs. See too William E. Butler, *Russia & the Republics: Legal Materials* (Huntington, NY: Juris Publishing, 2008).

[83] Earlier English non-sports cases were the foundations for the US precedents. See, e.g., *Lumley* v. *Wagner* (1852) 1 De G.M. & G. 604. These have been called into question by more recent cases, although one reported decision refusing to grant injunctive relief, *Nichols Advanced Vehicle Systems Inc* v. *de Angelis* [1989] 1 W.L.R. 853, emphasized the problem with effectively forcing a Formula One driver to race with those in whom he lacked confidence. Common law claims for the tort of unlawful interference would also be available for damages, including exemplary damages, for inducing a breach. See, e.g., *RBC Dominion Securities Inc.* v. *Merrill Lynch Canada Inc.*, 2008 SCC 54 (S. Ct. Can. Oct. 9, 2008) (upholding multi-million dollar award for inducing rival's employees to breach contract).

recent controversial arbitral decision in *Wigan Athletic FC* v. *Heart of Midlothian*, which rejected an interpretation of the EU-approved FIFA Status Regulations that would have allowed Hearts (one of two Edinburgh-based Scottish Premier League teams) to reap a substantial capital gain from its investment in a Scotland national soccer player.[84] In 2001, Hearts paid £75 000 to a small, lower-tier club to acquire 19-year-old Andrew Webster. In 2003, he signed a 4-year contract, and rose to domestic and international success. When negotiations to extend the contract failed in 2006, Webster notified Hearts that he was terminating the contract, and a few months later signed a 3-year contract with Wigan, a mid-table English Premier League club.

Hearts' claim for damages for breach of contract was resolved by a panel of distinguished sports lawyers appointed by the Court of Arbitration for Sport in Switzerland. The question was to be resolved based on Article 17(1) of the EU-approved FIFA Status of Players regulation, which provides that 'compensation for the breach shall be calculated with due consideration for the law of the country concerned, the specificity of sport, and any other objective criteria.' The panel awarded Hearts £150 000, rejecting Hearts' claim of an additional £4 million, based either on Webster's replacement value or Webster's 'market value' to which Hearts was entitled by virtue of its investment in training and development. These claims failed, the panel reasoned, by striking 'a reasonable balance between the needs of contractual stability, on the one hand, and the needs of free movement of players, on the other hand.'[85] Although the panel hinted that clubs could in the future enter into the sort of risk-sharing contracts suggested by Lord Wilberforce by express contractual language,[86] the reference to the EU commitment to free movement, and the regulation's limitation on contracts to 5 years maximum, point to unique factors not present outside of Europe.

In sum, it would appear that tribunals generally regard individual contracting as a superior alternative to collective agreement as a means to permit clubs to recoup its investment in player development. When an investing club is an amateur club or dealing with very young players, or where domestic law or preemptive European rules prevent free contracting, a limited and reasonable agreement among clubs may be justifiably sustained.[87]

4.6.   Restraints in Collective Bargaining Agreements

The US National Labor Relations Act provides that, when chosen by a majority of workers in a bargaining unit (a term of art defined by an administrative agency), a union

---

[84]   CAS 2007/A/1299, available at: http://www.apdd.pt/admin/manage/files/files/jurisprudencia/eng/webster.pdf.

[85]   *Ibid.* at ¶ 132.

[86]   *Ibid.* at ¶ 139 (lost profits or replacement value claim rejected 'because any form of compensation was not clearly agreed upon contractually' and thus would constitute unjust enrichment of the club); *ibid.* at ¶ 149 (additional club protection 'cannot be implied – there should be a negotiation and a meeting of the minds on the subject').

[87]   The EU's commitment to free worker movement has led European competition authorities to limit restraints on *within-contract* bidding for services as well as bidding for those, like Bosman himself, whose contractual relationship with his team had expired. Recognizing the legitimate interests involved, FIFA rules approved by European competition authorities permit restraints that serve to enforce multi-year contracts, but only for 3 years' time.

becomes the exclusive representative of all current and potential workers in that unit.[88] The Clayton Act, another US antitrust statute, provides that labor is not a 'commodity or article of commerce' and exempts trade union activity from the antitrust laws.[89] Although typical industrial unions seek to *reduce* competition among workers (by negotiating fixed pay scales, for example), a major priority for players' unions in the 1970s was to negotiate rules permitting *increased* competition for player services. Courts have held that labor market restrictions agreed to through arms length bargaining, such as limits on competition for veteran players or a cap on total payroll would be immune from antitrust scrutiny.[90] This approach sensibly accounts for the public interest in permitting unions and management to reach compromise agreements that insure industrial stability. In the sports context, fan appeal is certainly maximized by ensuring that competitive seasons are not interrupted by industrial action. However, the US Supreme Court unfortunately extended this exemption, in *Brown* v. *Pro-Football Inc.*,[91] to restrictions not agreed to by the union, thus putting players to the choice of collectively bargaining or asserting antitrust rights.[92]

*****

In sum, there are several reasons why labor restraints might be justified under competition law regimes. Because of club owners' incentive to restrain trade for anti-competitive reasons, the precedents require the leagues to show that labor restraints are necessary for legitimate goals, and observers are properly skeptical of these claims. It is noteworthy that in the one major US sport (stock car racing) where rules are not set by the clubs but an independent competition organizer (NASCAR) – there are hundreds of intricate engineering rules designed to promote competitive balance and fiscal prudence but absolutely no restrictions on competition for services of skilled drivers, crew chiefs, or engineers.[93]

5. OBJECTIVES REJECTED BY COURTS AS JUSTIFICATIONS FOR LABOR MARKET RESTRAINTS

Courts have rejected a variety of other justifications proffered by leagues in defense of labor market restraints. Several courts have rejected *long-term roster stability* as a legitimate goal. These courts have recognized that a club's interest in preserving roster

---

[88]   29 USC § 159(a).
[89]   15 USC § 17.
[90]   *McCourt*, note 26 *supra*; *Wood* v. *National Basketball Association*, 809 F.2d 945 (2nd Cir. 1987).
[91]   518 U.S. 231 (1996).
[92]   As detailed elsewhere, Ross and Lucke, note 10 *supra*, because labor market restraints can also significantly affect product quality – through the inefficient allocation of players among teams, particularly via restraints that harm competitive balance by making it more difficult for inferior teams to improve – the public interest in competition ought only be sacrificed only when the benefits of labor peace are likely to be achieved.
[93]   Stephen F. Ross and Stefan Szymanski, *Fans of the World, Unite!* (Stanford, Calif.: Stanford University Press, 2008), at pp. 100–102.

stability can be achieved through individual contact negotiation.[94] As a matter of economics, this justification has little to offer. A pro-competitive efficiency justification for roster stability presumes that a player is more valuable as a veteran of the same team, rather than plying his services with a new set of teammates. If this is so, then in an unrestrained market his current club would outbid rivals for his services.

The justification of *cost certainty*, used recently in the National Basketball Association (NBA) and the National Hockey League (NHL), is simply not a legitimate, pro-competitive goal for an established league. The rhetoric may have originated in 1982 when the NBA's commissioner persuaded the players' union to agree to a salary cap (thus exempting the cap from antitrust challenge), in part based on the need to attract additional investment into a game that was faltering. Absent viability-threatening circumstances, the desire of owners to be certain of future costs is completely antithetical to competition. Owners *should* be uncertain about their costs. In other industries, firms whose poor business acumen results in an inferior product are obliged to spend more than their rivals to bring their goods or services up to par. In sports, when front-office managers make poor personnel or coaching decisions that result in an inferior team on the field, they too should be required to increase spending. There is no legal authority for the claim that cost certainty is a legitimate justification for a trade restraint.[95] Likewise, *cost-reduction* is not a legitimate justification. If it were, any buyer-side antitrust defendant could invoke it as a means of price fixing.[96]

6. ABUSING DOMINANCE BY LABOR RESTRAINTS THAT EXCLUDE RIVALS

The foregoing demonstrates how clubs that set labor rules for their sport have conflicting incentives to adopt policies that (1) increase fan appeal and promote the sport, or (2) impose unnecessary or even harmful policies simply to reduce labor costs. In similar fashion, leagues that profit from the absence of real competition have conflicting incentives to adopt labor rules that (1) increase fan appeal or (2) harm fans through policies designed principally to improperly exclude rivals. Specifically, clubs in dominant leagues could draft player contracts in a way that prevents rival leagues from obtaining the necessary player talent to viably compete. Although the law is less certain in this regard,

---

[94]   In *Eastham*, note 11 *supra*, at 435, Lord Wilberforce reasoned that clubs could reduce turnover by signing players to staggered long-term contracts. See also *Adamson*, note 18 *supra* (interest in preventing mid-season 'poaching' achievable by early negotiations with players as well as rules setting reasonable dates for negotiating with other clubs). Likewise, Marks J. of the Victoria Supreme Court struck down a rule limiting the ability of cricket players to move among Australian states, finding that the stability of state all-star teams participating in interstate cricket competitions could be achieved by signing contracts with players prior to the competition's start. *Nobes* v. *Australian Cricket Board* (16 December 1991, unreported).

[95]   *Cf. Weidman* v. *Shragge* (1912) 46 S.C.R. 1 at 28 (S. Ct. Can.) (Idington J.) ('To apply the standard of profit that might enable the stupid, the slothful, the ignorant, the over-capitalized man ... to compete with the standard that may be fairly reached by the men of brains, of energy, of sleepless vigilance, with only adequate capital to earn dividends for ... would be a sorry one indeed for society.').

[96]   *Law* v. *NCAA*, 134 F.3d 1010, 1022 (8th Cir. 1988).

when this sort of 'foreclosure' can be shown, the common law or competition law may operate to find that otherwise reasonable 'vertical' agreements between clubs and players become unreasonable.

The one clear precedent on point is *Philadelphia World Hockey Club, Inc.* v. *Philadelphia Hockey Club.*[97] For years, like other sports leagues, the National Hockey League's standard player contract contained a 'reserve clause' whereby the club had the right to renew the player's contract at expiration on the same terms other than salary; in effect, this precluded any other club for bidding for the player's services, at least for a 3-year period (the length of the governing collective bargaining agreement with the players' union). The NHL asserted that the contract also operated to prevent a club in a rival league, the World Hockey Association (WHA), from signing a player at the expiration of his existing contract. The WHA claimed that the contract violated the Sherman Act. The court found that enforcement of the reserve clause would 'destroy the economic viability of the new league and to return to the NHL their monopoly over major league professional hockey.'[98] Thus, the clause constituted unlawful monopolization under section 2 of the Sherman Act.[99]

The key factual finding that labor contract terms had to be voided in order to prevent a monopoly makes this finding rare. The employees need to be especially skilled and few in number, and the opportunities for competition from existing firms or new ones must be limited. The terms also must be somewhat lengthy: thus *Philadelphia Hockey* was distinguished in a case involving a dominant tennis organization signing all the top players for a 36-week term.[100]

Although there appears to be no European sports cases directly on point, analogy may be had from several judicial and administrative declarations outside the sports industry. Under EU law, agreements that public houses will exclusively trade in beer from a single supplier (analogous to agreements that players will perform only as authorized by a dominant league) constitute restraints of trade in violation of Article 101 of the Treaty when they significantly contribute to market foreclosure.[101] The European Commission's Guidelines on Vertical Restraints declare that dominant firms may not impose non-compete obligations on buyers 'unless they can objectively justify such commercial practice within the context of Article [102].'[102] The Court of First Instance found that a dominant ice cream manufacturer violated Article 102 in providing freezer cabinets to small stores with a condition barring the stocking of rival brands. The court expressly noted that conduct that 'contributes to an improvement in production or distribution of goods and which has a beneficial effect on competition in a balanced market may restrict

---

97   351 F. Supp. 462, 466 (E.D. Pa. 1972).

98   *Ibid.* at 496.

99   The opinion was based on a preliminary record (on application for injunction *pendente lite*); based on that record, the judge was unable to find that the restraint on competition among NHL teams was unreasonable under § 1 of the Sherman Act, because of the justification of promoting competitive balance within the league.

100   *Volvo North America Corp.* v. *Men's Int'l Professional Tennis Council*, 678 F. Supp. 1035 (S.D.N.Y. 1987).

101   *Delimitis* v. *Henninger Br u AG* (Case C-234/89) [1991] ECR I-935.

102   Guidelines on Vertical Restraints, COM(2000/C 291/01), available at: http://europa.eu/scadplus/leg/en/lvb/l26061.htm.

such competition' when done by a dominant firm.[103] European tribunals have generally condemned the insistence by a dominant firm that non-dominant products be acquired as a condition of purchasing products for which there were few substitutes.[104] These authorities suggest that unjustified contract terms by dominant leagues that effectively preclude rival competitions may be found contrary with European competition law.

Under common law restraint of trade doctrines, exclusionary contracts would be invalidated under the 'public interest' prong of the traditional *Nordenfelt* test. In several unusual instances, courts have refused to enforce post-employment restrictions because of the ensuing harm to competition.[105] Although not explicit on this point, a number of decisions finding long-term exclusive contracts between petroleum companies and retail gas stations to unreasonably restrain trade use language supporting a conclusion that contracts of relatively long duration that foreclose new sports leagues from forming would be found in restraint of trade.[106]

This issue has arisen in the sporting context primarily in the context of dominant sporting federations refusing to permit star players to participate in representative competitions (on behalf of country, state, or region) because of the players had contracted with a rival league for other purposes. In two cases, the courts found the refusal to be unreasonable;[107] however, in both cases the additional factor of unannounced, retroactive effect was present. Still, both judges relied on the public's interest in seeing the best stars play in representative competition as well as the unfairness of retroactivity, as well as the failure of the dominant federation adequately to explain why its interests in the sound organization of the game required them to ban participants in rival competitions from international test play. Although there is language in the landmark *Greig* v. *Insole* opinion suggesting it would have been reasonable for the dominant cricket authorities in each country to have contracted in advance with all the best cricket players as a way of precluding a rival competition from getting started,[108] this dictum is inconsistent both with the non-sports precedents about exclusionary contracts as well as the court's own findings about the public interest in viewing the best players in international competition and the inadequacy of justification for the need for this harsh action by the dominant federations. In applying common law doctrines, another Australian court was particularly

---

103   *Van den Bergh Foods Ltd* v. *Commission* [2004] 4 C.M.L.R. 1 at 66.

104   See, e.g., *Tetra Pak* v. *Commission* [1997] 4 CMLR 662, [1997] All E.R. (E.C.) 4.

105   See, e.g., *Sherk* v. *Horwitz* [1972] 2 O.R. 451 (Ont. C.A.) (shortage of obstetricians in area); *Thomas Cowan & Co Ltd* v. *Orme* (1960) 27 M.L.J. 41 (H.C. Singapore) (defendant and plaintiff only two persons licensed to use particular fumigation chemicals); *Lindner* v. *Murdock's Garage* (1950) 83 C.L.R. 628 (H.C. Aus.) (severe post-war labor shortage).

106   See, e.g., *Amoco Australia Pty Ltd* v. *Rocca Bros. Motor Engineering Co Ltd.* (1973), 133 C.L.R. 288 at 325, 1 A.L.R. 385 (H.C.) (Stephen J.) (noting 'virtually all' South Australian retail outlets tied to particular oil companies); *Esso Petroleum*, note 58 *supra*, at 301 (Lord Reid noted that over 90 percent of existing retail outlets tied); *Stephens* v. *Gulf Oil* (1975), 11 O.R. 2d 129, 65 D.L.R. (3d) 193, ¶ 47 (Ont. C.A.) (finding exclusive dealing 'common' throughout the Canadian petroleum industry).

107   *Greig* v. *Insole*, note 9 *supra*; *Daley* v. *New South Wales Rugby League Ltd & Ors* (1995) 78 I.R. 247 (Indus. Ct. N.S.W.). In the latter case, the court's jurisdiction was based on a statute that invalidates employment contract provisions that are 'unfair' or 'against the public interest' and the judge held that contracts in restraint of trade met the statutory criteria.

108   *Greig*, note 9 *supra*, 1 W.L.R. 302 at 352.

critical of cricket authorities' generalized ban on players participating in 'unauthorized' competitions that did not interfere with the player's ability to participate in international tests.[109]

Sound application of the common law's public interest test would find contracts to be unreasonable where found to be exclusionary and unnecessarily lengthy or unnecessarily restrictive. In international sports such as cricket and rugby, where stars' principal remuneration is for participating in international contests, if their contracts bar them from playing in 'unauthorized competitions' but allow them to negotiate separately to play in 'authorized competitions,' the public interest doctrine of restraint of trade may come into play.

7. COPING WITH THE OPEN-ENDED ANALYSIS REQUIRED

Like Churchill's view of democracy as the worst form of government except for all the alternatives, case-by-case judicial review of trade restraints may be a necessary evil. The nature of dominant sports leagues precludes reliance on the competitive marketplace to produce goods, services, and prices that are responsive to consumer demand. At the same time, giving dominant sporting organizations leeway to restrain trade if 'reasonably necessary for the protection of the game' may require opening the 'floodgates' to 'an enormous volume of evidence' regarding the structure and finances of organizing bodies.[110] In the view of a leading commentator, if the public interest test reflected in both the common law and most competition statutes is to be meaningful, it is difficult to see how such a broad inquiry can be avoided.[111] At the same time, learned commentators have expressed skepticism that generalist judges and locally biased juries can properly weigh these myriad facts to determine whether a particular sports rule is reasonable.[112]

In the area of corporate law, a similar problem arises with challenges to decisions by company directors from shareholders who claim that the decisions did not maximize profits or shareholder value. (Many US students learn this in the context of a famous suit by a minority shareholder challenging the refusal of the majority owner of the Chicago Cubs baseball team to install lights for night baseball at Wrigley Field.[113]) The general rule is that courts presume that the directors acted properly unless the relevant corporate decision makers face significant conflicts of interest (for example, a sale of corporate property to another entity owned by individual directors).[114]

This sound approach can be meaningfully applied in the area of competition law and sports as well. The current 'hands on' approach judges usually take to labor market

---

[109]   *Hughes* v. *Western Australian Cricket Ass'n* (1986) 69 A.L.R. 660 at 703 (Fed. Ct.).

[110]   *Greig*, note 9 *supra*, at 497.

[111]   Michael Trebilcock, *The Common Law of Restraint of Trade* (Toronto: Carswell, 1986), at p. 220.

[112]   See, e.g., Gary R. Roberts, 'The Case for Baseball's Special Antitrust Immunity' (2003) 4 *J. Sports Econ.* 302. But see *McNeil* v. *NFL*, note 26 *supra* (special jury verdict for plaintiff after careful instruction found that NFL had legitimate interest in competitive balance but particular restraint was overbroad).

[113]   *Shlensky* v. *Wrigley*, 237 N.E.2d 776 (Ill. App. 1968).

[114]   Linda O. Smiddy and Lawrence A. Cunningham, *Soderquist on Corporate Law and Practice* (3rd ed., New York: Practicing Law Institute, 2008), at § 8:3.

restraints is justified because those who are making the decisions – either clubs or federations significantly influenced by the clubs – have a conflict of interest. Although charged with maximizing fan appeal, most of the current rules are made by those who also have an interest in limiting payroll and other motivations that could lead them to adopt overbroad and unjustified restraints. Whatever the merits of justifications for today's labor restraints, few seriously claim that the total ban on competition for player services the prevailed for most of the twentieth century in soccer and baseball was really necessary to promote appeal-enhancing competitive balance or serve any other legitimate need. Rather, clubs agreed to these invalid restraints because they served the illegitimate interests of clubs and others in holding down payroll. Thus, while competitive balance in Major League Baseball increased immediately after elimination of the Reserve Clause, and attendance increased 57 percent over the following 7 years, we can see why owners agreed to the Reserve Clause in the first place, because salaries increased 316 percent![115]

This analysis demonstrates why US courts have rejected efforts to characterize sports leagues as 'single entities' analogous to a single corporation, whose decisions cannot be challenged as agreements under the Sherman Act or restraints of trade under the common law.[116] A single corporation is governed by management and a board of directors whose sole fiduciary duty is the good of the corporation as a whole, not some constituent parts.

At the same time, US antitrust doctrine has drawn a distinction between decisions reached as a result of agreements among independent parties and those who are competitors with the claimant. For example, a plaintiff alleged that he was wrongfully excluded from racing horses at a number of tracks based on false accusations of wrongdoing; his antitrust suit was dismissed on the pleadings because the defendants did not have any economic interest in excluding him from racing nor did his exclusion increase their market power in any way.[117] In a similar vein, a NHL rule barring players with only one eye was

---

[115] Stephen F. Ross 'Monopoly Sports Leagues' (1989) 73 *Minn. L. Rev.* 643, 676.

[116] *American Needle, Inc. v. National Football League*, 130 S. Ct. 2201 (2010).

[117] *Currone v. Ogden Suffolk Downs, Inc.*, 683 F. Supp. 302, 307 (D. Mass. 1988). See also *Brookins v. Int l Motor Contest Ass'n*, 219 F.3d 849, 855 (8th Cir. 2000) (upholding rule excluding plaintiff's transmission from auto racing because of lack of self-interest of defendants in helping rival transmission manufacturers); *Justice v. National Collegiate Athletic Ass'n*, 577 F. Supp. 356 (D. Ariz. 1983) (sanctions against Arizona Wildcats college football program for violating NCAA rules not shown unreasonable, court noting no evidence that NCAA or its officials 'had any purpose to insulate themselves from competition by imposing sanctions on the University of Arizona or any of the other universities currently on probation'); *United States Trotting Ass'n v. Chicago Downs Ass'n, Inc.*, 665 F.2d 781, 789 (7th Cir. 1981) (per se rule inapplicable to trotting association's prohibition against members' participation in races on non-member tracks, where rule's purpose was not to exclude competition and there was no showing that groups of drivers used association as a means to eliminate other drivers from competition); *Neeld v. National Hockey League*, 594 F.2d 1297, 1299–1300 (9th Cir.1979) (bylaw of professional hockey league precluding player with one eye from participating properly reviewed under rule of reason where rule had safety purpose and at most an incidental anticompetitive effect); *Bridge Corp. of America v. The American Contract Bridge League, Inc.*, 428 F.2d 1365, 1370 (9th Cir.1970), (refusal of bridge league to sanction local tournament if plaintiffs' computer was used, where motivated by desire to preserve integrity of scoring system, did not warrant application of per se rule); *Cooney v. American Horse Shows Ass'n*, 495 F. Supp. 424, 430 (S.D.N.Y.1980) (suspension of horse trainer under association drug rule creating rebuttable presumption of trainer responsibility for horse's condition could not be

upheld as motivated by safety, absent any plausible theory that the intent or effect of the rule was to restrict labor market competition.[118] The appropriate doctrinal analysis, following the Supreme Court's reaffirmance of its focus on whether the agreement deprives the market of independent sources of competition[119] – ought to be whether the entity that enacted the challenged rule is governed by those with a fiduciary duty to the whole, as characterizes genuinely single economic entities. Because modern sports leagues are not governed in this manner, they should not be so considered. In the case *sub judice*, the collective sale of intellectual property might be efficient and pro-competitive, or it might have been agreed to by league owners to frustrate particularly innovative teams' desire to obtain an advantage due to their own marketing skill, just (as discussed earlier) labor restraints could be designed to maximize fan appeal or simply hold down labor costs. Close inquiry remains necessary unless the decision to license centrally were made by an entity divorced from the clubs.[120]

Similar concerns should be relevant in countries where sports are governed by dominant not-for-profit federations. For example, *Grieg* v. *Insole* reported that the mandate of the Test and County Cricket Board (now the England and Wales Cricket Board) included (1) the organization and administration of test matches in the United Kingdom and MCC overseas tours, (2) the administration and promotion of the first-class County Championship, (3) the rules governing the registration and qualification of cricketers in county cricket, (4) the sponsorship of one day matches between the test-playing countries, (5) other sponsored competitions involving the first-class counties,[121] not to mention the entire operation of the grass roots promotion and maintenance of a thriving amateur game. The decision revealed the clear conflict of interest involved in the Board's decision to bar attractive and popular cricketers from county cricket because their conduct had injured the Australian Cricket Board.

In contrast, if sports leagues were restructured so that rules were implemented by organizers whose own financial interest lay in maximizing revenues (rather than club profits), courts could be more confident that restraints were indeed imposed for legitimate reasons. As noted earlier, NASCAR does not impose any labor market rules. The one other major league that follows a structure independent of clubs is the new Indian Premier (Cricket) League. The board of directors is appointed by India's governing cricket federation, and for-profit franchises participate in their competition. Labor market rules are set by the directors, not the clubs; the federation receives a fixed share of TV revenue,

---

characterized as group boycott per se illegal, given rule's purpose to foster fair competition); *Jones* v. *NCAA*, 392 F. Supp. 295, 304 (D. Mass.1975) (per se rule not applicable to NCAA rule barring student who had previously received compensation for playing hockey from playing intercollegiate hockey, where NCAA's purpose was not to exclude plaintiff from market but to promote principles of amateurism).

[118]   *Neeld* v. *National Hockey League*, 594 F.2d 1297 (9th Cir. 1979).

[119]   *Copperweld Corp.* v. *Independence Tube Corp.*, 467 U.S. 752, 769–71 (1984), cited with approval in *American Needle*, 130 S. Ct. 220 at 2209.

[120]   Cf. *Sullivan* v. *NFL*, 34 F.3d 1091 (1st Cir. 1994) (rule barring club ownership by publicly traded corporations could have been adopted by owner-run league in order to shield inefficient owners from more efficient competition).

[121]   *Grieg*, note 9 *supra*, at 308–309.

thus providing it with an incentive to maximize fan appeal rather than increase club profitability by holding down labor costs.[122]

Where labor restraints are imposed by an entity independent of clubs, whose economic incentives and legal obligations are to the league as a whole, courts should review challenges with a far greater presumption in favor of the challenged rule. In addition to the law's current requirement that the claimant show an actual restraint of trade, and that the restraint is not reasonably necessary to achieve a legitimate goal, claimants challenging rules implemented by independent organizers should have to demonstrate why these organizers would enact an anti-competitive rule. Such a burden is properly a heavy one.

8. CONCLUSION

Sports leagues around the world often enact regulations that limit off-field competition among rival clubs for the services of highly-skilled players. In many of these labor markets, there are no reasonable substitute employers, so the leagues have market power; in many others, potentially competing leagues agree, through international federations, on these restraints. Player restraints can serve legitimate goals that enhance the viability and attractiveness of the sporting competition. They can also be enacted with the purpose or effect of suppressing salaries without achieving legitimate goals. Indeed, clubs have the incentive to restrain trade where the benefits in saved labor costs may exceed the costs of reduced revenue from lowering the quality of the contest. Thus, competition law needs a nuanced approach that will validate 'reasonable' rules that are tailored to promote legitimate goals while prohibiting 'unreasonable' rules that either serve no legitimate purpose or are demonstrably overbroad.

The competition statutes and the common law of restraint of trade have approached international convergence on the following standard: agreements lessening competition are legal if reasonably tailored to achieve a legitimate goal. Legitimate goals may include promoting competitive balance, maintaining the integrity of the competition, ensuring fiscal solvency, and, in some circumstances, protecting the administration of the game, recouping investment in young players, and immunizing collective bargaining agreements with players' unions. There is no judicial support for justifying restraints to achieve roster stability, cost certainty, or cost reductions.

Competition law also prevents dominant firms from engaging in unreasonable restrictions with players that have the effect of excluding rival competitions. Even rules that may be legitimate if adopted by one league in a competitive market may be unreasonable if imposed by a dominant league.

These doctrines inevitably require courts to engage in the somewhat messy business of carefully reviewing sports league rules for their reasonableness. Like the business judgment rule, this 'hands on' approach could be limited if labor rules were set by an entity separate from the clubs competing in the competitions. Sports leagues such as NASCAR

---

[122]   For the initial season, clubs were limited in overall payroll by a salary cap and by specific rules designed to enhance both league and localized appeal: a limit of four international players, and four India national team players and a requirement that at least four players be from the local area and four be younger players. The league was a huge success. *Caveat*: I acted as a consultant for the sports management firm that assisted the Indian Premier League.

and the Indian Premier League exemplify this independent approach, and courts can appropriately adopt a more deferential approach when rules are not imposed by the clubs that would benefit from the anti-competitive suppression of competition in the labor market.

13 The tampering prohibition, antitrust, and agreements between American and foreign sports leagues

Lewis Kurlantzick[1]

Practices that are commonplace and viewed as unremarkable in professional athletics would be regarded as unusual, if not bizarre, in more conventional commercial settings. Imagine, for example, graduates of medical and law schools being drafted by practices throughout a country so that for a period of time these doctors and lawyers would be limited to working for the one practice that drafted them (and be forced to seek employment abroad if they did not approve of the domestic employer by which they had been selected). Similarly, think of an employee of one company being 'traded' to another company, for which he would now be obliged to render his services.

Among the more peculiar of these practices is the prohibition against 'tampering.' To recognize its unusualness consider the following highly typical scenario:

> A works for company X under a three-year employment agreement that will expire in three months. Company Y contacts A to discuss the possibility of future employment. A meets with a representative of Y over dinner. After a period of negotiation A agrees to come to work for Y when his obligation to X ends.

Needless to say, this kind of interaction, which facilitates employment transition, is an everyday occurrence. And A regards it as advisable to have a new job before he departs his old job.

But in much of the world of professional athletics, this interaction is banned! Under typical rules of professional sports leagues, a team – without special permission from the current employing club – may not have contact with a player (or coach) of another team while that employee is still under contract.

Thus, the Major League Baseball Rule, which is representative, states:

> To preserve discipline and competition, and to prevent the enticement of players, coaches [and] managers …, there shall be no negotiations or dealings respecting employment, either present or prospective, between any player, coach or manager and any Major … League Club other than the Club with which the player is under contract … unless the Club … with which the person is connected shall have, in writing, expressly authorized such negotiations or dealings prior to their commencement.[2]

---

[1]   A somewhat different version of this chapter appeared in article form, *The Tampering Prohibition and Agreements Between American and Foreign Sports Leagues*, 32 COLUM. J.L. & ARTS 271 (2009).

[2]   Major League Baseball Official Rules § 3(k) (2005). In fact, leagues interpret the prohibition expansively so as to include even team expression of interest in a player (or player expression of interest in a team). See text accompanying notes 47–53 *infra*; *CFL Fines Stamps' Rooke*, CBC.CA, Nov. 27, 2004, http://www.cbc.ca/sports/story/2004/11/26/rooke041126.html (last visited Apr. 12, 2008). For other examples of the proscription, see National Hockey League Standard Player's

What explains this distinctive prohibition? And is its justification persuasive?

In this chapter I will explore the justifications offered for the tampering proscription and analyze the legality of the practice under the Sherman Act in light of these rationales. With this analysis as background I will then examine some of the agreements between American and foreign sports leagues governing movement of players and assess the status of these agreements under United States antitrust law.

EMPLOYMENT POLICY AND EMPLOYEE MOBILITY: THE UNUSUALNESS OF THE RESTRICTION

The legal conclusion that Y's conversation and negotiation with A produces no liability – neither breach of contract by A nor inducement of breach of contract by Y – rests on a policy judgment about the existence and plan of competitive enterprise, more particularly about where the line is properly drawn between constraint and freedom to pursue employment opportunities. The social interest in competition, it is thought, would be unduly hampered if one were prohibited from in any manner persuading a competitor's prospective employees (and customers) not to deal with him. Thus, the legal assessment rests not only on a concern about A's interest in efficient pursuit of employment options but also on Y's interest in pursuit of advancement by being able to offer superior terms.[3] Moreover, if A were unable to attend to future use of his services until his agreement with X had expired, he would face the prospect of a period of unemployment until a new agreement was consummated. Accordingly, our legal system, for good reason, does not ordinarily condemn the interaction between A and Y (and X is aware of this posture).[4]

Giving outsiders freedom to bargain for the services of an employee who is presently under contract to another, then, is firmly rooted in a strong public policy favoring open

---

Contract § 10, NHL/NHLPA Collective Bargaining Agreement, Exhibit 1 (2005 Form); National Basketball Association Uniform Player Contract § 5(f), NBA-NBPA Collective Bargaining Agreement 2005–2011, Exhibit A; National Football League Constitution & By-laws, art. 9.1(C)(11). The tampering restriction is not limited to United States sports leagues. For example, a similar ban exists in the world of British soccer. See note 12 *infra*.

Sanctions for violation of the tampering proscription may be severe. Punishment could include a fine and loss of draft choices. See, e.g., text accompanying notes 47–49 and note 49 *infra*; National Basketball Association Constitution, art. 35(f); National Football League Constitution & By-laws, art. 9.2.

Though it does not involve a core application of the proscription, apparently in one setting the anti-tampering rule is more honored in the breach in the NFL. Before free agency begins in March, contact between teams and potential free agents is prohibited. However, this directive is routinely ignored. See Peter King, *The NFL's Mob Mentality*, SPORTS ILLUSTRATED, Sept. 24, 2007, at 19; Peter King, *Sanders Stars for Colts; Readers React to Week 2, More*, SPORTS ILLUSTRATED, Sept. 18, 2007, http://sportsillustrated.cnn.com/2007/writers/peter_king/09/17/week.2/index/html. See also Peter King, *Goodell Comes Down Hard on Tampering*, http://sportsilllustrated.cnn.com/2008/writers/peter_king/03/25/tampering/index.html (last visited Mar. 25, 2008) (first time in 13 years that Commissioner has found NFL team guilty of tampering with another team's employee).

[3]   See RESTATEMENT (SECOND) OF TORTS § 767, cmt. g (1979); *id.* § 768, cmts. b, e, i (1979).

[4]   See RESTATEMENT (SECOND) OF TORTS § 768 & cmt. i (1979); *id.* § 767, cmt g. With respect to the situation where X can lawfully hold A to a post-employment non-compete clause, see notes 37–38 and accompanying text *infra*.

competition in the labor marketplace. The presence of competition serves as a check on harsh contract terms and facilitates establishment of terms that reflect the value of the employee's services. This policy choice favoring inter-employer competition and its implementation reflects proper concern for the interests of the employee, competing enterprises, and the public in general.

The present employer, of course, would prefer not to permit negotiation during the term of the existing contract as such a restriction would greatly enhance his bargaining position. An employee, then, would be less willing to sever the relationship and lose goodwill without the assurance of another employment opportunity.[5]

The qualification to this proposition that negotiation between an employee and a prospective employer is permissible is that the interaction cannot improperly interfere with performance of a contract – i.e. one (Y) cannot induce another (A) not to perform an existing contract.[6] The question becomes: to what is the present employer due? And a related question is: what practices used in the recruitment of employees are to be deemed improper interference with the existing contractual relationship? The balance sought is between the employer's interest in stability in his relationship with his employees and the other employer's interest in competing with the first employer for the service of those same employees. No greater intrusion into an existing employment relationship than necessary to achieve the desired competition for employee services will be deemed legitimate. A clearly tortious interference would be the entrance into a new contract that calls for performance to begin at a point in time when the employee is still under contract to the original employer.[7]

A borderline issue is whether the new employer may properly offer financial inducements to an employee while he is still under contract with the existing employer. For example, may a team pay a signing bonus to a player while he is contractually bound to the original club?[8] Promises of rewards that may affect the athlete's on-field performance while still tied to the original team – e.g., a bonus for scoring a set number of points – should be deemed unacceptable.[9] A related issue is the propriety of a player's promotional

---

[5]   JOHN C. WEISTART AND GYM H. LOWELL, THE LAW OF SPORTS 385–86 (1979).

[6]   RESTATEMENT (SECOND) OF TORTS § 766 (1979). However, a seller of goods (or an employer of services) may still advertise his goods and celebrate their quality to one who is presently a customer (or employee) of a competitor. *Ibid.* at cmt. m.

[7]   Of course, to be liable a person must have knowledge of the contract with which he is interfering and of the fact that he is interfering with its performance. See RESTATEMENT (SECOND) OF TORTS § 766, cmt. i (1979).

This question of whether activity constitutes greater-than-necessary intrusion and fails to exhibit proper respect for an employee's previous commitments arises doctrinally with claims of tortious interference with contract and 'unclean hands.' Typically, in the tort action the former team files suit against the signing team, alleging improper interference with a valid business relationship. The unclean hands allegation arises in a scenario where a player signs with a new team, reconsiders, returns to the old team, the new team sues, and the defendant pleads that the unclean hands of the new team preclude the award of equitable relief.

[8]   A tampering rule, of course, aims to prevent this question from even arising since it prohibits the parties from talking at all.

[9]   WEISTART AND LOWELL, note 5 *supra*, at 388 n. 288. Though the future employer has an interest in the maintenance of the athlete's star status while he is completing his present contract, promised rewards tied to on-field performance by the future employer infringe on the existing employer's right to define the player's role as a member of the team, including designing plays which

activities for the future employer while he is presently bound to the old club. Courts have indicated that the publicity that necessarily flows from signing with a new team is unavoidable and not tortious. It is likely, however, that publicity engagements by the player beyond that point are improper and will be regarded as tortious interference with the existing contractual relations of the old team.[10]

THE JUSTIFICATIONS PROFFERED FOR THE TAMPERING RULE

A no-tampering rule, thus, stands at odds with employment practices and policies common outside the sports industry.[11] The rule can be seen as illustrative of the central conflict between teams' interest in protecting themselves from raids of their personnel and the interest of individual players in maximum mobility.[12] And it can be conceived as part

---

may limit the player's scoring chances. Concern about such conflicts is not limited to the athletic arena as an employer generally can insist that his employees remain free from the influence of payments offered by outsiders. *Ibid.*

[10]   See *World Football League* v. *Dallas Cowboys Football Club*, 513 S.W.2d 102, 105 (1974); WEISTART AND LOWELL, note 5 *supra*, at 402–3.

A tampering rule might be seen as connected to this general question of what is due the present employer – to what is X entitled? But in a sense the tampering prohibition goes beyond satisfaction of the entitlement concern. That is, a player who has signed with another team for his future services can still offer his best efforts to his present employer and thereby not deprive that employer of his services. See *Cincinnati Bengals, Inc.* v. *Bergey*, 453 F. Supp. 129 (S.D. Ohio 1974). However, the tampering rule, which prohibits such signing, says that the commitment of such efforts is insufficient. See text accompanying notes 24–30 *infra* (conflict of interest; consumer perception).

[11]   As one advocate for a noted British footballer put it, 'Soccer players, alone … are forbidden to speak to prospective employers.' Rob Hughes, *Soccer: Lawyers Smell Blood as Star Is Punished*, INT'L HERALD TRIB., June 3, 2005, at 21. The tampering rule limits a player's ability to determine when he will negotiate with another team and therefore may affect his ability to determine with which league team he will play.

[12]   This mobility is especially significant to athletes with short high-earning periods. In contrast to more conventional employment settings, the tampering rule shifts, in a way detrimental to players, the line implicitly drawn by existing contract (and tort) law between constraint and freedom to pursue employment opportunities. The rules of the British Football Association Premier League (FAPL) also contain a no-tampering proscription that restricts a player's ability to safeguard his future employment. Rule C1 prohibits a player from speaking to another club while under contract, thereby preventing him from identifying clubs that might be interested in employing him and ascertaining salary levels that he could expect to achieve. See Rules of the Football Association Premier League § C(1)(n)(ii)(B) (2008) (covering approaches to and by players). The operation of this restriction is particularly harsh with respect to players who are nearing the end of their playing careers. Alison Green and Graham Shear, *Premier League Transfer Rules and EC Law*, WORLD SPORTS L. REP., Sept. 2006, at 3–5. But see Jack Bell, *Unwillingness To Break Contract Seen as Oddity in Europe*, N.Y. TIMES, July 29, 2008, at D2 (contact between player representative and another team common in Europe).

Apparently, in the world of British soccer this rule has regularly been circumvented. 'Tapping-up' is the slang phrase for direct violation of the tampering rule. It refers to an approach by one soccer club to a player under contract to another club without that club's knowledge or permission. Such direct violations occur with some frequency, often via unauthorized contact by player agents. See, e.g., Tom Fordyce, *Transfer Corruption 'Rife'*, Jan. 30, 2004, available at http://news.bbc.co.uk/sport2/hi/football/3444871.stm; Paul Fletcher, *The Truth About 'Tapping Up'*, BBC Sport, June 1,

of the larger question of the ability of organized sports to improve their status beyond that provided by contract and tort law.[13] What, then, are the justifications for the tampering rule?

One justification points to the disruption that a player signing with another team will produce.[14] There is a legitimate team concern about the potential disruptive effect of allowing an athlete to become contractually involved with another team. And that concern exists whether the other team is within the same league or not, though it is stronger if the team is within the same league. Accordingly, this objection would not only ground a rule against intra-league tampering but would also support a restriction against a player dealing with another league.[15]

But in the rest of the commercial world this concern about disruption (and lack of loyalty) does not outweigh the employee's interest in seeking other employment. The club may understandably be concerned about the effects of a signing upon team cohesiveness, but the player and new employer cannot be held responsible for the reactions that others have to the signing.[16] And these reactions may be irrational or based on sentiments such as professional jealousy.[17]

2005, available at http://news.bbc.co.uk/sport2/hi/football/4599103.stm. A milder form of 'tapping-up' and rule circumvention involves a team letting its admiration for a player on another team become known. Against a background where cash sales are common, if club Y is interested in player A, the club does not contact A but rather announces publicly that it is going to try to negotiate with club X to purchase the player's contract. See *UK Corrupt Sports Press Slang Concealing Corruption 593*, Oct. 2, 2006, http://www.barossa-region.org/football_soccer/index0010.html. The economic effect is that A knows who is interested in his services and for how much. This form of evasion is precluded in American sports leagues, which construe the tampering prohibition broadly so as to encompass team expression of interest in a player. See text accompanying notes 46–50 *infra*.

[13]   To employ a phrase from industrial relations, what is involved is an effort to shift the 'frontier of control' by management over players. See CARTER L. GOODRICH, THE FRONTIER OF CONTROL: A STUDY OF BRITISH WORKSHOP POLITICS 56–62 (1920).

[14]   See, e.g., Peter Vecsey, *Breaking the Rules*, N.Y. POST, Feb. 1, 2005 (coaches and players speaking publicly about coaching and playing elsewhere disrupts and infuriates their teams), *World Football League* v. *Dallas Cowboys Football Club*, 513 S.W.2d 102, 105 (Tex. Civ. App. 1974) (morale of team), *Cincinnati Bengals, Inc.* v. *Bergey*, 453 F. Supp. 129, 136–37 (S.D. Ohio 1974) (divisive influence on teammates; football uniquely requires emotional commitment as member of cohesive unit; coach's control undermined).

[15]   An example would be an NFL player negotiating with a team in a new league, such as the USFL, about joining the team in the new league after he completes his obligation to his NFL employer.

[16]   Of course, a tampering rule does not just say that the player cannot sign with another team; it says that he cannot even talk with another team while under contract.

If an employer was concerned about the effect of a signing upon workforce cohesion and customer loyalty, he could include a provision in the employment agreement that barred any negotiation during the period of the contract. Indeed, the availability of this instrument for the individual employer undercuts any argument that an industry-wide tampering rule is necessary to meet the disruption concern.

Justifications for prohibition on communication that are plausible in other settings have no application here. For example, an anti-recruiting rule that prohibits high school coaches from pursuing middle school athletes rests on the proposition that hard-sell tactics aimed at middle school students could lead to exploitation, distortion of competition between high school teams, and an environment in which athletics are prized more highly than academic achievement. These concerns are not operative in the context of professional athlete negotiations with a team, or more

Is the disruption likely to be greater in the sports setting than in other employment contexts?[18] An effect on team performance is plausible. However, that effect appears no different than the potential impact on corporate performance when an employee signs with a new employer. Perhaps a sports team is distinctive in that it involves a small, intimate group whose functioning requires a high level of trust. But that characterization could apply to at least some other forms of employment.

Rather than a reflection of club concern about the effects of a signing upon others, the rule may bespeak concern about the impact of a signing on the performance of the player himself.[19] (Of course, the tampering proscription does not only prohibit signing with another team, it prohibits any communication with that team.) How realistic is an apprehension about impaired incentives? It is quite unlikely that a star athlete would make a calculated effort to reduce his performance below an acceptable level. Not only have professional athletes internalized norms of competitiveness but also extra-legal forces operate to insure their effort. Sub-par performance would engender conflict with team-mates and fans and would yield statistics that would be unhelpful in future salary and endorsement negotiations.[20] Again, it is difficult to see how the position of the athlete and

---

generally with an adult employee dealing with a prospective employer. See generally *Tennessee Secondary Sch. Athletic Ass'n v. Brentwood Acad.*, 551 U.S. 291 (2007) (rule barring high school coaches from recruiting middle school athletes does not violate the First Amendment).

[17]As the player and prospective employer cannot control possible divisive reactions by team-mates, the only way to avoid such reactions is to refrain from dealing with each other, a response that would unduly restrict the player's interest in realizing the maximum value of his services.

[18]   Of course, talk about disruption raises the question, disruption to whom? Fans? Teammates?

[19]   Again, this rationale would support a restriction on signing with a team in another league as well as signing with a team in the player's present league. A restriction that affects another league implicates additional considerations, as the rule may act as a barrier to the formation of a competitor to the existing league. Permitting established teams to insulate their players from competing offers for their future services runs counter to the policy in favor of economic competition between business entities and minimization of the difficulties of new entrants.

[20]   See STEFAN SZYMANSKI, PLAYBOOKS AND CHECKBOOKS 116–17 (2009) (shirking by athletes unlikely). In *Cincinnati Bengals v. Bergey*, 453 F. Supp. 129 (S.D. Ohio 1974), the National Football League (NFL) Bengals requested an injunction to void star linebacker Bill Bergey's contract to join the Virginia Ambassadors of the new World Football League (WFL). Under the agreement Bergey was to begin play with Virginia in the future after his obligation to the Bengals had ended. The Bengals argued that the new agreement would reduce his effectiveness with Cincinnati during his existing contract. The court rejected the argument, reasoning that a future obligation would be highly unlikely to affect Bergey's performance under his current Bengals contract in light of his pride and desire to maintain his reputation as an outstanding player. See Geoffrey Christopher Rapp, *Affirmative Injunctions in Athletic Employment Contracts: Rethinking the Place of the Lumley Rule in American Sports Law*, 16 MARQ. SPORTS L. REV. 261, 271–73 (2006). See also *World Football League, Inc. v. Dallas Cowboys Football Club, Inc.*, 513 S.W.2d 102 (Tex. Civ. App. 1974) (at least in case of negotiation with new league, concerns about reduced effort and effect on team morale are outweighed by the desirability of protecting player's and prospective employer's freedom to contract).

The large salaries of most contemporary professional athletes limit, to some extent, the concern about the athlete 'tanking' his performance due to a conflict of interest. Just as a highly compensated player is unlikely to 'fix' a game in service to gamblers in light of what he stands to lose, so, for the same reason, he is unlikely to diminish his performance in service to a potential or actual future employer. Indeed, though not often noted, the generous compensation of athletes provides a major assurance against players altering outcomes other than on the merits of the contest. And it is those

team differs from that of the employer and employee in a more conventional industrial setting. Indeed, this claim about impaired incentives may be too sweeping, as it can be made in any case and therefore could be the basis for limiting a player's movement from his original team for the remainder of his career.[21]

Justifications for the tampering rule based on effect of signing on player performance or impact on others, then, are of little weight.[22] Can more convincing arguments be made in support of the rule?[23] A more promising rationale for limiting player (and team) opportunity for bargaining focuses on the effects of player communication and/or signing with another team on the marketability of the product that the teams and league are selling. Here the focus is on the potential impression of the prohibited behavior on the consumer, rather than on the player or his teammates. This account, which rests the legitimacy of the ban on its necessity for the creation and marketing of the group's product, supports a restriction that is limited to intra-league communication. In other words the rationale that is grounded in a concern about conflict of interest and the appearance of conflict of interest would not justify a restriction on a player dealing with a team in another league about his future services.

Imagine that in the middle of a season a basketball (or baseball) player, or a coach or manager, who will become a free agent at the end of the season enters negotiations and signs a contract with another team in the same league to commence employment with that team at the end of the season. What will the perception of fans be when the team that presently employs the player plays his future team? Surely, it would not be unreasonable for fans to wonder whether the player's performance – or the coach's decisions – are affected by his future commitments.[24]

Indeed, this potential conflict is not limited to games between the present and future organizations. Since the result of any game in a league affects the fortunes of all other

---

without such compensation, such as college players and referees, who are the more likely targets for gamblers and the more likely agents for fixing of games. See SZYMANSKI, *supra*, at 119–21; Justin Wolfers, *Point Shaving: Corruption in NCAA Basketball*, AMER. ECON. REV, May 2006, at 279 (AEA papers and proceedings). See generally Yang-Ming Chang and Shane Sanders, *Corruption on the Court: The Causes and Social Consequences of Point Shaving in NCAA Basketball*, 5 REV. L. & ECON. 269 (2009).

[21]   See WEISTART AND LOWELL, note 5 *supra*, at 400–1.

[22]   A number of additional, related reasons have been offered in support of the anti-tampering prohibition – preservation of the sport's public image, maintenance of harmonious relations among teams, player awareness of limitations on teams' recruitment practices. See MARTIN J. GREENBERG, *ET AL.*, 1 SPORTS LAW PRACTICE 2–63 (3rd ed. 2009). None of these reasons are persuasive. Much, if not all, of the claimed benefits can be achieved by provision of clear notice of a rule, whatever the rule is.

[23]   Of course, one could argue that a no-tampering rule reinforces protection of the employer's trade secrets and other economically valuable information. That is, if an employee cannot speak with competitors at all, not only can he not discuss future employment but he cannot, during the term of employment, reveal proprietary information. However, that argument would apply to the conventional, non-sports setting as well. Yet a no-tampering regime is not accepted there, and instead employers are left to rely on trade secret law and other post-employment restrictions for protection of information. See text accompanying notes 36–38 *infra*.

[24]   '[I]s a striker going to go all out against a club making significant advances for him?', *Should You Be Allowed To 'Tap Up'?*, BBC RADIO 1XTRA , http://www.bbc.co.uk/1xtra/tx/tappingup.shtml (last visited Feb. 18, 2009).

league teams, this concern would exist in games between the athlete's present team and any other team. As a result, the integrity of the contest – what, at bottom, all sports leagues sell – is compromised by this conflict of interest.[25] The fan's interest is in seeing an honest effort by both teams to do their best to win a contest in which the outcome is unknown beforehand. The outcome of that contest should be determined by sporting skill or ability, not extraneous factors such as the conflicted performance of a player or coach. As with prohibitions on gambling,[26] the tampering rule may thus be necessary to maintain public confidence in the probity of the enterprise that is vital to the leagues' existence.

Under this rationale, then, the concern is with the possibility of a conflict of interest arising between a player (or coach) and his current team. The line of thought is that if the player knows another team is interested in or has engaged his future services, he will not exert the same effort as he otherwise would for his current team. Particularly, but not exclusively, if a player was negotiating with or was contractually obligated to another team, there may be some chance that his play against that team would not be as aggressive as it otherwise would be.[27] Moreover, and fundamentally, the league is concerned with image and perception. That is, even if a player has not actually withheld his best effort, there is a risk that fans will perceive the situation in that way. Thus, a below-par performance by the player might be perceived to have been prompted by his interest in improving the position of his potential (or future) employer. Since the belief that the outcome of games is determined by the merits of the competition is central to the attraction of a league's product, widespread perceptions of this sort by consumers would be seriously damaging to the league and its teams.[28] And a blanket, prophylactic rule – rather than an individualized, post hoc inquiry[29] – is needed to prevent that damage.[30]

---

[25]   See Ian Ayres, *Give Freakanomics a Chance,* ECONOMISTS' VOICE, Nov. 2007, at 1 (guilty plea by NBA referee calls into question integrity of entire league; NBA's product is fair competition; customers may stay away if they start worrying games are rigged).

[26]   See Lewis Kurlantzick, *Pete Rose: The Fundamental Conflict,* FOR THE RECORD: THE OFFICIAL NEWSLETTER OF THE NATIONAL SPORTS LAW INSTITUTE, Apr.–June 2004, at 6; see generally *Molinas* v. *Nat'l Basketball Ass'n,* 190 F. Supp. 241 (S.D.N.Y. 1961) (ban of basketball player for betting on games in which he played upheld against antitrust challenge; need for preservation of public confidence in the authenticity of the competition on the playing field); Alan Schwarz, *Referees' Limits on Betting Are Spelled Out by NBA,* N.Y. TIMES, July 24, 2007, at D1.

[27]   Cf. RESTATEMENT (SECOND) OF AGENCY § 387 (1958) (duty of loyalty). While the obvious case for conflict is a game between the player's current team and his possible future employer, the dual loyalty concern could exist as well in games against other teams when the outcome of those games might affect the fortunes of his prospective employer.

[28]   See Roger G. Noll, *The U.S. Team Sports Industry: An Introduction,* in GOVERNMENT AND THE SPORTS BUSINESS 4–5 (Roger G. Noll ed., 1974):

> The prohibition against tampering has two purposes. Obviously, it is designed to prevent interteam competition for players, but it is also said to maintain public confidence in the honesty of play. If a player were known to be negotiating with other teams and a misplay on his part led to a crucial defeat for his current team, the question could arise whether the player had intentionally committed the misplay or, at least, had been playing with something less than full dedication to victory. Sports entrepreneurs believe that there would be less public interest in professional sports if contests were regarded as 'exhibitions' rather than 'competitions' – that is, if the outcome were predetermined or not the paramount concern of the teams.

A concern for dual loyalties, and whether the current employer is receiving what is due him, exists

References to the tampering prohibition often speak of the need to obtain permission from the present employer before any contact with an employee can take place.[31] Thus, for example, if team A wants to approach the coach of team B about subsequent employment, it is said that team A must have team B's consent before any communication with

---

both where the prospective employer is a member of a new league and where it is a member of the present league. In cases involving efforts of an existing league to restrict a new league from negotiating with its players, the courts have been unsympathetic to the existing league's efforts and have given little credence to the dual loyalty concern. Rather, they have affirmed the general policy in favor of inter-employer competition. See *World Football League* v. *Dallas Cowboys Football Club, Inc.*, 513 S.W.2d 102 (Tex. Civ. App. 1974); *Cincinnati Bengals, Inc.* v. *Bergey*, 453 F. Supp. 129 (S.D. Ohio 1974); *Munchak Corp.* v. *Cunningham*, 457 F.2d 721 (4th Cir. 1972); *Washington Capitols Basketball Club, Inc.* v. *Barry*, 304 F. Supp. 1193 (N.D. Cal. 1969). However, the potential conflict of interest is stronger when a player negotiates with a team in his own league since he will face games against that team and be able to affect its fortunes in other contests as well. This distinction underlies the point that intra-league conflict of interest – and the fear of consequent erosion of fan interest – is the only weighty justification for the tampering rule. Indeed, there is no doubt that an accord between leagues under which teams in one league agree not to negotiate with or sign any player from the other league until that player has played his last game under his current contract would be a violation of section 1 of the Sherman Act.

The rules of the British FAPL do not distinguish between intra-league and interleague contact. Thus, unlike players from other European countries, Premier League players may not speak about future employment with clubs outside the FAPL. Green and Shear, note 12 *supra*, at 5. Failure by a sports league to recognize this distinction cannot be justified. See note 25 *supra* and accompanying text.

In fact, interleague competition for player services had disappeared from American professional sports by the 1990s, as only one established league emerged in each sport. The emergence of free agency, though, has stimulated considerable intra-league bidding for player talent. And it is here that the tampering rule, which precludes any discussions, let alone signings, between a player and a new team until the prior contract has expired on the specified date when free agency begins, has its contemporary bite.

[29]   A post hoc inquiry would be attended by complexities of proof and assessment in an effort to pass judgment on the quality of the athlete's performance. See RESTATEMENT (SECOND) OF CONTRACTS § 367 cmts. a b (1981).

[30]   In the case of a player who has signed with another team and has pledged his future services to that employer, the conflict of interest and possible deleterious consumer perception derived from that conflict are creditable as foundations for the tampering prohibition. But is a ban on contact with a possible future employer warranted as well? Though the connection is more attenuated, fan perception might well be affected by the knowledge that a player is negotiating with another team. Contact alone may generate suspicion, and therefore it may be prudent simply not to run that risk with respect to a matter that is so central to the definition of the product being offered. Moreover, in terms of enforcement, contact may be easier – or at least as easy – to detect than an agreement, which may be kept secret. And contact may reasonably be viewed as the first step to the disfavored agreement.

A prophylactic arrangement that is even more restrictive than the tampering rule and rooted in related concerns is the revolving door rules applicable to holders of public office and government employees. Aimed at the promotion of integrity in governmental processes, these ordinances limit the activities of officials after leaving office, typically prohibiting them from engaging with their prior agency for a period of time ('cooling-off period'). See, e.g., Conn. Gen. Stat. § 1–84b (2009); 18 U.S.C. § 207(a) (2000). *Compare* MODEL RULES OF PROF'L CONDUCT R. 1.11 (2002). In addition to responding to the concern about a government lawyer throwing a case in order to seek favor with a prospective private-sector employer, they are designed to insure that former employees derive no unfair advantage from the confidential information to which they previously had access or from their former association with government.

the coach of B.[32] A requirement of consent by team A makes sense as it has an obvious concern about the coach's undivided effort being devoted to its success. However, in light of the policy justifying the tampering rule – at least the only policy that may be persuasive – permission from team A seems an inadequate requirement. If team A were able to hire the coach of team B for the following year, the coach's conflict of interest would not be limited to contests between A and B. His behavior could affect other games (and off-field activity) that would bear on team A's fortunes. Yet no league appears to impose any additional requirement, such as a need for league office assent to contact. This structure may reflect an assumption that in-season contact and permission is unlikely – as it is improbable that a team would reasonably believe that its interests will not be affected because of the conflict – and that the requirement of team consent during the off-season will be adequate protection against conflicts of interest.[33]

---

   [31]   See, e.g., Major League Baseball Official Rules § 3(k) (2005): 'there shall be no negotiations or dealings respecting employment … between any player … and any Major … League Club other than the Club with which the player is under contract … unless the Club … with which the person is connected shall have, in writing, expressly authorized such negotiations or dealings prior to their commencement.'
   [32]   In 1995 the Miami Heat of the NBA violated this injunction by communicating with Pat Riley, the then coach of the New York Knickerbockers, about the possibility of coaching the Heat the following season without first seeking authorization from the Knicks. Similarly, Riley disregarded the proscription by initiating and/or participating in these employment discussions. At the time Riley still had one year remaining on his contract with the Knicks. It was not until after Riley resigned and the Knicks filed a tampering charge with the league that the Heat asked the Knicks for permission to negotiate with Riley, a request that was denied. See *Riley Sought Heat Contract Before Quitting Knicks*, N.Y. TIMES, Aug. 25, 1995 at B9; PHIL BREAUX, INTRODUCTION TO SPORTS LAW & BUSINESS 28–9 (2007).
   [33]   In the middle of February 2006 Bryan Colangelo, the general manager of the NBA's Phoenix Suns, left the team to become the general manager of the Toronto Raptors. When I first became aware of this move by the reigning NBA executive of the year, I noted no reference to tampering. Yet initially I also saw no mention of advance permission. I then wondered whether front office executives might not be among the addressees of the league's tampering constraint – an exclusion that would be odd, to say the least. It is true that, unlike players, GMs do not perform on the court, and, unlike coaches, do not direct practice and game activity. However, they exercise major influence over the personnel composition of the team and can also influence coaching behavior. Accordingly, their omission from the coverage of a prophylactic rule rooted in the prevention of conflicts of interest would make no sense. Further investigation revealed that the Suns' owner had, in fact, granted permission to Colangelo and the Raptors to discuss the Raptors' job. See Scott Bordow, *Strange Move by Suns*, EAST VALLEY TRIB. (Ariz.), Feb. 9, 2006, available at http://www.eastvalleytribune.com/index.php?sty=58775. Baseball's Major League Rules refer to the enticement of 'players, coaches, managers and umpires.' Major League Baseball Official Rules § 3(k) (2005) (tampering). The NBA Uniform Player Contract prohibits enticement of 'any player or coach who is under contract to any NBA team …' Uniform Player Contract, § 5(f), NBA-NBPA Collective Bargaining Agreement 2005–2011, Exhibit A. Surprisingly, the British Football Association Premier League's player tampering rule, see note 12 *supra*, does not apply to managers (coaches), who are free to approach other clubs during the term of their contract. Graham Shear and Alison Green, *Should a Football Association Premier League (FAPL) Footballer Be Treated Differently from Other Employees on Fixed Term Contracts?*, available at http://www.tsslaw.co.uk/documents/Premier%20League%20Football%20and%20the%20K5%20Rule.doc.
   This kind of in-season contact highlights the point that league interests that extend beyond the interest of the employing team may be involved when such an approach takes place.
   The prohibition of off-season contact raises the question of whether the time at which an

In fact, it is hard to imagine a league granting approval to an in-season arrangement under which team B, in exchange for money, permits team A to negotiate with and sign B's coach to a contract for future services. Though it is unlikely that B would, in fact, consent to this conflict of interest, even if it did, in exchange for ample consideration, it is virtually inconceivable that the league would validate the agreement.[34] The collective interest in fan perception of the presentation of authentic contests would be viewed as paramount and would outweigh the preference of an individual league member.[35]

HOW PECULIAR IS THE TAMPERING PROHIBITION?

As we have noted, the tampering prohibition is likely to strike one familiar with common employment relations as highly unusual. And that reaction is supported by accepted legal

---

approach is made affects the argument(s) for application of the prohibition. Thus, if contact occurs in the off-season, is the rationale weakened? The role of the person in the off-season would be relevant. For example, a coach may play an active role in the evaluation of talent and draft preparation. Also, if the coach (or player) is under contract for the coming season, the potential conflict of interest concern would apply to an approach to him, even if in the off-season, as it might affect his behavior in the following season and what was said to him would not be known. Moreover, if it were believed that it is difficult to prove exactly when an impermissible contact occurs, then it might make sense to design a rule that prohibits any contact and avoids difficult inquiries about timing.

[34] The NBA, on its website, indicates that the league takes tampering very seriously, but it will not investigate unless another team files tampering charges. See Larry Coon, *NBA Salary Cap FAQ*, http://www/cbafaq.com (last visited May 11, 2011) (question 95). However, it is highly unlikely that the league would permit the behavior described in the text, and it would likely act on its own initiative, if necessary, to stymie it. See generally Jim Thomas, *On Way to Super Bowl, Chiefs Shift into Reverse*, ST. LOUIS POST-DISPATCH, Jan. 8, 1995, at 9F (Pittsburgh Steelers fined for permitting Carolina Panthers to speak with Steelers' assistant coach during playoffs and before Steelers' season had concluded).

An additional way to view the sports league Commissioner's position in this situation is to see it as an expression of a skeptical (realistic?) view of human capacity. That is, it represents a judgment of no confidence that a coach or player can be reasonably expected to serve both teams well. Therefore, the rule does not permit the player or coach to speak with a second team about future employment, much less sign an agreement for such employment.

[35] Late in the composition of this chapter, one of the volume's editors suggested to me another plausible rationale for a tampering rule. That rationale focuses on the exclusive right conferred on a team to negotiate with a player for a contract extension. In other words, under the uniform player contract, among the set of rights a team acquires is the exclusive authority to negotiate with the player about a contract extension. That exclusivity is valuable to the team and supports roster stability. In addition, it also facilitates mid-contract trades of players to other teams, which often are as interested in obtaining exclusive negotiating rights as in securing the player's services for the rest of the contract term. This justification would appear to have merit, as the commercial value of exclusivity is well recognized. Indeed recognition of that value is apparent in another sports setting, that of agreements between sports leagues and television broadcasters. Thus, a common feature of these arrangements is that the league, e.g., the NFL, must first negotiate exclusively with its present broadcast partners before inquiring whether other networks have interest in the next football contract. See, e.g., Jarrett Bell, *Prime-time Negotiations Stalled*, USA TODAY, March 21, 2005, at 14C (ABC exclusive negotiating period with NFL re 'Monday Night Football'); *Sports Shorts*, ST. LOUIS POST-DISPATCH, Sept. 9, 1999, at D2 (CBS exclusive negotiating period with NCAA re men's basketball tournament); Richard Sandomir, *Waiting on Deck in the Lineup for Rights*, N.Y. TIMES, March 24, 2006, at D7 (Fox exclusive negotiating period with Major League Baseball).

doctrine which generally regards contact between an employee and a prospective future employer as neither a breach of contract nor a tortious act.

But are there practices in employment settings other than sports that offer some support for the tampering rule? For example, does trade secret law provide backing for a tampering rule? Trade secret law imposes a limitation on the content of communication between an employee and individuals outside the company both during and post employment. In that respect the law puts a constraint on employee contact with a prospective employer. And the doctrine does result in some clash between employee freedom to switch jobs (and make use of the skills he has developed) and company control over intellectual property. However, trade secret law and its accompanying restraints are not rooted in a concern about conflict of interest. Rather they reflect an interest in protection of a firm's investment and a distaste for disloyal behavior; and only protect trade secrets against being unmasked by methods that are thought to reduce efficiency, such as theft or contract breach. Accordingly, they do not proscribe communication about possible future employment. Rather, they demand that any such communication, and any post-employment communication, not include revelation of any trade secrets.[36]

Another common arrangement in the employment context, the covenant not to compete, also restricts the labor market. But this provision is directed to behavior after the termination of the existing employment relationship and is rooted in a different set of concerns. Thus, typically an employee is asked to sign a noncompetition agreement upon entering employment. The agreement restrains him from going to work for a rival or entering business in competition with the employer for a set period of time after the employment relationship ends. Accordingly, the covenant operates to restrain potential competitors.[37]

However, the covenant not to compete, unlike the tampering proscription, does not aim to influence behavior during the term of the employment relationship. And its animating rationale is quite different. The provision is not a reaction to a concern about the existence or appearance of conflict of interest but rather is usually a response to one of two other kinds of employer concerns. One, the employer may expend major resources on the training of an employee, but his training could be easily misappropriated by another

---

[36]   The notion of trade secret fits uncomfortably in the world of professional sports. The contests are performed publicly and are typically preserved on videotape. Thus, little of the activity is 'secret.' There have, though, been a few disputes involving playbooks in the possession of a football player who has been traded to another team. Moreover, 'stealing' an opposing team's signals, particularly in baseball, is viewed as part of the craft of competition in sports. See JOSHUA PRAGER, THE ECHOING GREEN: THE UNTOLD STORY OF BOBBY THOMSON, RALPH BRANCA AND THE SHOT HEARD ROUND THE WORLD (2006); Erik Matuszewski, *Spy Games*, N.Y. POST, Dec. 16, 2006, at 50. But see Judy Battista, *Sideline Spying: NFL Punishes Patriots' Taping*, N.Y. TIMES, Sept. 14, 2007, at A1 (team and coach disciplined for videotaping signals by opponent's coaches).

In fact, the treatment of 'trade secrets' by different sports varies greatly. Thus, NFL players are prohibited from taking playbooks with them when they depart, but are free to disclose anything they can from memory to their new team. In contrast Formula 1 racing employees are significantly restrained, perhaps owing to the large investment in unique cars. Baseball players and scouts, though, are free to share 'trade secrets' with their new employer.

[37]   In fact, noncompetition covenants have two effects on competition. By protecting the employer's investment, they make new entry more profitable. At the same time, they tend to make entry by new companies more arduous because of the greater difficulty in recruiting suitable employees.

employer, who could afford to pay more because the cost of training has already been paid. To meet this free-riding possibility the first employer may insist on an agreement that after training is finished the employee may not work for a rival for a significant period of time. Two, during the period of employment an employee may acquire information that would be valuable to a rival but is not adequately protected by the law of copyright or trade secret. Accordingly, concerned to prevent the misuse of confidential information, the employer may provide that its employee not work for a rival during a period of time sufficient for the protected information to become out of date or less valuable to the rival.[38]

Closer to the mark (perhaps) the Association of American Law Schools (AALS), interestingly, has a policy that limits employment mobility that might be viewed as inconsistent with the interests in employee liberty and competition for employee services. The AALS Statement of Good Practices for the Recruitment of Full-Time Faculty Members provides that a law school should make an offer of an indefinite appointment as a teacher during the following academic year no later than March 1.[39]

What concerns animate this policy, are they more persuasive than those we have previously examined, and how does the practice compare with the tampering proscription? The restriction is less extensive than the tampering rule because it prohibits neither contact nor contracting during the period of present employment. Rather, it specifies a date by which an offer is to be made. The interest to be served is not prevention of conflict of interest but rather facilitation of administrative order. The concern is that unless the law school is given sufficient time to make arrangements to find someone to offer the courses taught by the departing teacher, the reasonable expectations of students will be frustrated and the school's educational program otherwise disrupted.[40]

---

[38]   See 13 HERBERT HOVENKAMP, ANTITRUST LAW 210–12 (2ⁿᵈ ed. 2005). Employee covenants not to compete are generally lawful under the antitrust laws simply because the employment market is highly competitive. However, many of these agreements are unenforceable under state law, which requires that the arrangement be 'reasonable' in time and geographical scope. *Ibid.* at 212. See also David K. Haase and Darren M. Mungerson, *Agreements Between Employers Not To Hire Each Other's Employees: When Are They Enforceable?*, 21 LAB. LAW. 277 (2006).

On restrictions on post-employment opportunities for government employees, see note 30 *supra*.

[39]   ASS'N AM. L. SCHOOLS, STATEMENTS OF GOOD PRACTICES FOR THE RECRUITMENT OF AND RESIGNATION BY FULL-TIME FACULTY MEMBERS (1986), http://www.aals.org/about_handbook_sgp_rec.php. Similarly, the Statement provides that a full-time faculty member should not resign later than March 15 to accept an indefinite appointment as a teacher at another law school during the next academic year. These time limits may be extended up to two months by acquiescence of the dean of the law school on whose faculty the person serves. The Statement does not apply to the recruitment of a teacher who is on terminal appointment.

[40]   Does this desire to avoid disruption reflect weightier concerns than those we have previously analyzed in the sports setting? One factual difference between the two settings that affects party expectations is that the professor's employment is pursuant to an indefinite appointment unlike the situation where the person is employed for a definite term that is expiring.

In view of the most plausible rationale for the tampering rule, examination of the treatment of conflicts of interest in the legal profession, in particular when a lawyer moves from one firm to another, may well be instructive. See Lewis Kurlantzick, *The Tampering Prohibition and Agreements Between American and Foreign Sports Leagues*, 32 COLUM. J.L. & ARTS 271, 282–7 (2009).

PROTECTION BEYOND CONTRACT AND TORT LAW

The tampering rule can be viewed as part of the larger issue of the ability of a sports league, and its members, to improve their status beyond that provided by contract and tort law. In fact, the history of baseball provides a prime episode that illuminates this issue and demonstrates a response that goes beyond what is permissible. This affair, which involved the short-lived Mexican League, the Commissioner of Baseball, and the federal courts, highlights the conflict between teams' interest in protecting themselves from personnel raids and players' interest in mobility and clearly posed the question of what steps a league can, and cannot, take to shift the line implicitly drawn by existing contract law between constraint and freedom to pursue employment opportunities.

In 1946 Jorge Pasquel, the wealthy head of the Mexican League, began making offers to established major league players, principally from the Cardinals, Dodgers, and Giants. Pasquel's dream was to upgrade the Mexican League to major league status (and to create a racially integrated league). Offering double and triple the salaries paid by United States owners, Pasquel and his brothers signed a set of players, including such stars as Giant pitcher Sal Maglie, Dodger catcher Mickey Owen, and Cardinal pitcher Max Lanier.[41]

In response to this development, Albert B. (Happy) Chandler, the Commissioner of Baseball, announced in June 1946 that any player who had participated in a Mexican League game would be banned from the big leagues (and the minor leagues) for five years. Moreover, in addition to this ban from return to the majors, Chandler also decreed that any player caught on the same diamond with any of the Mexican League outcasts – for example, during an exhibition or barnstorming contest – could forget about ever playing in the big leagues.[42]

Chandler's disciplinary response, designed to strengthen the security of player contracts, however, is an example of an impermissible attempt to fashion a remedy beyond what contract law would provide. Since the players were under contract to a major league team, their move to Mexico constituted a breach of contract. Standard monetary and

---

[41]   See JOHN PHILLIPS, THE MEXICAN JUMPING BEANS: THE STORY OF THE BASEBALL WAR OF 1946 (1997); JAMES D. SZALONTAI, CLOSE SHAVE: THE LIFE AND TIMES OF BASEBALL'S SAL MAGLIE 50–73 (2002). Some of the defecting players were signed for the 1946 season. Others, though they had not yet entered an agreement with respect to the 1946 season, were still contractually bound to their teams by the reserve clause, which, *inter alia*, provided the team an option to sign a player for the following season and prohibited playing for any other team without the permission of the present team. The exact number of players who went south is unclear. The total appears to be approximately two dozen. See WILLIAM MARSHALL, BASEBALL'S PIVOTAL ERA 1945–1951 45–63 (1999) ('The Mexican Baseball Revolution'). The reserve clause, standard in all baseball contracts, bound a player indefinitely to the team that owned his services. It, thus, prevented players from transferring to other teams and averted bidding wars that favored the wealthier clubs.

[42]   See Simon Rottenberg, *The Baseball Players' Labor Market,* 64 J. POL. ECON. 242, 245–6 (1956). The Mexican League posed the first serious challenge to Major League Baseball since the collapse of the Federal League decades earlier. Although the caliber of many of the players who moved to Mexico was such that they would not be missed in the major leagues, the owners feared that the Mexican League's higher salaries could eventually attract better players and more of them. Moreover, competition from Mexico might well force up player salaries and cut into profits. Hence, Chandler's severe suspension action. Similarly, any league agreement with foreign teams that 1) they will not bid for a player while he is under contract or 2) they will restrict themselves in some way from bidding for a player when he is a free agent affects the market for baseball players here.

injunctive remedies were available to provide relief. In addition, presumably the Mexican League teams had committed the tort of inducing breach of contract with attendant liability. Major League Baseball, though, framed an additional, harsh response, an industry-wide ban on employment. It barred any employer in the industry from hiring a returning player, and it acted to deter players and competitors (and potential competitors) from bidding in this labor market. This anti-competitive boycott of players' services cannot be defended on policy grounds and, not surprisingly, would constitute an antitrust violation. No legitimate collective interest – for example, in the integrity of the product being offered to consumers – supports the restrictive practice.[43] Rather, the blacklisting is designed to protect the position of the existing league and to drive out competition by prohibiting employment of players who have once played in rival leagues.[44]

---

[43] See *Molinas* v. *Nat'l Basketball Ass'n*, 190 F. Supp. 241 (S.D.N.Y. 1961) (ban of basketball player for betting on games in which he played upheld against antitrust challenge; need for preservation of public confidence in the competition on the playing field). A collective decision by all members of an industry to exclude a person from work in that business is necessarily troubling. Such behavior implicates not only the values of market efficiency, expressed in the antitrust laws, and employee economic liberty but also a concern about concentration of power, the establishment of a kind of private government with no constitutional constraints and no input from those who are significantly affected by its decisions. A conspicuous union function, in protecting its members, is creation of mechanisms designed to curb arbitrary employer action. Thus, in baseball the Commissioner's disciplinary authority is significantly circumscribed by the just cause provision of the collective bargaining agreement with the players' union and the connected grievance process. See 2007–2011 Basic Agreement, art. XII(A) (Discipline: Just Cause). That just cause assessment involves two related questions. First, what sort of behavior warrants discipline, i.e. is the conduct legitimately a concern of the employer? Second, what form and level of sanction are apt, i.e. is the discipline excessive?

Caution in the construction and implementation of a disciplinary regime is especially appropriate in the setting of professional sports where the employment effect of a Commissioner's ruling, due to its industry-wide character, is more sweeping than an act of management discipline in a more conventional industry. For example, imagine an experienced Travelers Insurance Company employee who is well-paid but has limited competence outside insurance. Fortunately for him, market forces tend to limit the potential for abusive treatment by his employer and provide him with options if he is maltreated. Employment opportunities at other insurance companies affect Travelers' handling of the employee, and they offer comparable job possibilities if Travelers dismisses him. This market constraint, though, does not operate in professional sports because a Commissioner suspension amounts to a ban on hiring by all employers in the industry.

[44] The Mexican League episode did, indeed, give rise to antitrust litigation. Danny Gardella, an outfielder for the New York Giants, was one of the players who exited for the Mexican League before the 1946 season. Gardella played one year in Mexico, but in the spring of 1947 he sought to rejoin the Giants. He also approached a number of other major and minor league teams. He was uniformly rejected. Max Lanier and Fred Martin, who had left the Cardinals in 1946, received similar treatment. As a result, Gardella, Lanier, and Martin brought suit against their former major league teams, the American and National Leagues, Commissioner Chandler, and George Trautman, the president of the minor leagues, asserting that the blacklisting practices constituted a monopoly and a conspiracy in restraint of trade in violation of the Sherman and Clayton Acts. Gardella's suit was viewed as the leading challenge. The trial court, following *Federal Baseball Club of Baltimore, Inc.* v. *Nat'l League of Professional Baseball Clubs*, 259 U.S. 200 (1922), dismissed the suit for lack of jurisdiction, reaffirming Justice Holmes's holding that baseball was neither a subject of commerce nor an interstate activity. *Gardella* v. *Chandler*, 79 F. Supp. 260 (S.D.N.Y. 1948). However, on appeal the Second Circuit, in a 2–1 decision, held that the trial court did have jurisdiction and that *Federal Baseball* did not preclude further proceedings. *Gardella* v. *Chandler*,

Unlike the tampering rule, the blacklist of players who have chosen employment with a competing league[45] cannot be justified by reference to conflict-of-interest concerns. Recognition of the lack of this kind of justification[46] for this effort to supplement traditional contract and tort law provides a framework for assessment of the permissibility of the agreements in existence between American and foreign professional sports leagues with respect to player movement.

---

172 F.2d 402 (2d Cir. 1949). The majority consisted of Judges Learned Hand and Jerome Frank, each of whom wrote a separate opinion. Hand observed that in the years since *Federal Baseball* radio and television broadcasts of games had become common and Congress and the courts had agreed that radio and television were subjects of interstate commerce. He declined to pass on the legality of the reserve clause and remanded the case to the trial court for a specific determination of whether the expanded interstate activities were of such significance to the baseball industry that the interstate aspects of the sport could no longer be viewed as incidental, as they had been in *Federal Baseball*. Judge Frank was willing to go further. He noted that the precedents that gave a narrow reading of 'interstate commerce' for antitrust purposes, precedents on which Justice Holmes had relied in *Federal Baseball*, had been overturned by later decisions. Frank concluded not only that sufficient interstate involvement had been shown to distinguish the case from *Federal Baseball* but also that if plaintiff's allegations were proven, the reserve clause and associated blacklisting arrangements were illegal and made baseball 'a monopoly which, in its effect on ballplayers like the plaintiff, possesses characteristics shockingly repugnant to moral principles that … have been basic in America.' *Ibid.* at 409. Though the Second Circuit's decision suggested that *Gardella* was to become a landmark case, both sides had an interest in the matter not continuing in the courts. Accordingly, an out-of-court settlement of all three cases was reached in 1949, under which the players were reinstated and paid a sum in damages. In June of that year Chandler granted an amnesty to the Mexican League defectors. See MARSHALL, note 41 *supra*, at 231–49 ('Gardella's Folly'); David Mandell, *Danny Gardella and the Reserve Clause*, in SOCIETY FOR AMERICAN BASEBALL RESEARCH, THE NATIONAL PASTIME: A REVIEW OF BASEBALL HISTORY 41 (May 2006). See also, Comment, *The Super Bowl and The Sherman Act: Professional Team Sports and the Antitrust Laws,* 81 HARV. L. REV. 418, 426 (1967).

In two subsequent cases involving challenges to the legality of the reserve system, *Toolson* v. *New York Yankees*, 346 U.S. 356 (1953) and *Flood* v. *Kuhn*, 407 U.S. 258 (1972), the Supreme Court reaffirmed the proposition that 'the business of baseball' does not come within the scope of the antitrust laws. The anomalous result is that all professional sports with the exception of baseball are governed by the antitrust laws. In 1998 the passage of the Curt Flood Act limited baseball's exemption by providing that conduct relating to the employment of major league players is subject to the antitrust laws. 15 U.S.C. § 26b (2000). Accordingly, were any other American sports league to engage in the kind of blacklisting behavior present in the Mexican League episode, it would be exposed to antitrust liability. Major League Baseball, on the other hand, prior to the Flood Act, as the beneficiary of the idiosyncratic judicially created exemption, was subject to neither federal nor state antitrust norms.

45   The Mexican League experience has contemporary relevance in forcing attention to an anti-tampering policy from the perspective not just of the employee but of a new league as potential competitor of an existing league. The tampering rule operates as a barrier to formation of new leagues in that established teams are permitted to insulate their players from competing offers for their future services. The result runs counter to the policy in favor of economic competition between business entities and the minimization of barriers to new entrants.

46   The lack of a conflict-of-interest justification would likely condemn a straightforward international tampering rule agreed to between separate leagues as an antitrust violation. See note 79 *infra*.

THE JUSTIFICATIONS OFFERED FOR THE TAMPERING RULE AND ITS ANTITRUST STATUS

Multiple Uses of the Term 'Tampering'

The term 'tampering' is used with several somewhat different meanings in the sports setting, and awareness of this variation is important because while some of the denoted behavior may justifiably be condemned for other reasons, that proscribed behavior does not implicate the core value that differentiates the professional athletic employment setting from more conventional work. For example, 'tampering' was used to characterize the behavior of Atlanta Braves' owner, Ted Turner, in 1976 that led to his discipline by Commissioner Bowie Kuhn.[47] Turner was fined for tampering with Giants' outfielder, Gary Matthews. Matthews was to become a free agent at the end of the 1976 season. At that time a structure – the re-entry draft – was in place which governed the manner in which free agents were to be pursued. Under that structure the team to which the player had most recently been under contract had a period of time during which it exclusively could negotiate with the player.[48] On October 20, 1976 Turner commented to Giants' owner, Bob Lurie, that he would pay anything to obtain Matthews for the coming year. These comments were overheard by several reporters and appeared in newspapers the next day. On December 30 Commissioner Bowie Kuhn, in response to a complaint by Lurie, found that Turner's comments 'subverted the collective bargaining agreement and the re-entry draft procedures adopted pursuant to it.' As a result, Kuhn suspended Turner from baseball for one year.[49]

Baseball's anti-tampering rule then read:

> To preserve discipline and competition, and to prevent the enticement of players, coaches, managers and umpires, there shall be no negotiations or dealings respecting employment, either present or prospective, between any player, coach or manager and any club other than the club

---

[47] The term 'tampering' is also used in a number of state criminal statutes to condemn efforts to influence the outcome of a sports contest by illegitimate means, such as bribing a participant. *See, e.g.,* Ala. Code sec. 13A-11-143 (2005) (tampering with sports contest); Kan. Stat. Ann. sec. 21-4408 (2003) (tampering with a sports contest). Another common use is in connection with a professional sports league's rookie draft. A league will typically have in place a 'no-tampering' rule under which no team is permitted to negotiate prior to the draft with any player eligible to be drafted and no team can negotiate with, or sign, any player chosen by another team in the draft. See *Smith* v. *Pro Football, Inc.*, 593 F.2d 1173 (D.C. Cir. 1978).

[48] In July 1976 the owners and the players' union had negotiated an elaborate free agency system. Under this system, before the end of October players with six years of service in the major leagues could declare their intention to become free agents. In early November a draft would be conducted for these declared free agents, under which up to 12 clubs could choose to bid for any one player. Thereafter, only those teams that drafted a player's negotiation rights could enter into contract talks with the player. Prior to the draft, though, only the player's prior club (the 'team of record') had the right to negotiate terms with that player.

[49] Kuhn imposed an additional sanction as well. He deprived the Braves of its first round pick in the next summer's amateur draft. (If an amateur baseball player is from the United States or Canada, he can only sign with a Major League organization if he first enters the MLB draft and has graduated from high school.) However, this sanction was eliminated when a court ruled that its imposition went beyond the scope of Kuhn's authority under the Major League Agreement. See *Atlanta Nat'l League Baseball Club, Inc.* v. *Kuhn*, 432 F. Supp. 1213 (N.D. Ga. 1977).

with which he is under contract ... unless the club ... with which he is connected shall have, in writing, expressly authorized such negotiations or dealings prior to their commencement.[50]

Turner's conduct did not violate the clear language of Rule 3(g); after all, he did not negotiate directly with Matthews and the rule is silent as to whether a team may express its desire to obtain a player through means other than direct contact with that player. His actions, rather, were prohibited by a combination of Commissioner Kuhn's interpretation of the tampering rule and his authority to act in the best interests of baseball. The Commissioner's expansive view of the tampering rule, in particular his understanding of the meaning of the terms 'dealings' and 'negotiation,' was evidenced by three directives sent to teams in 1976, in which Kuhn explained the rule's provisions and warned would-be violators of potential discipline. The second directive most bore on Turner's situation:

> There should be no direct contacts of any kind with potential free agent players on another club ... The indirect contacts which are prohibited include (A) conversations between a club and the player through his representative or other third party intermediary; and (B) public comments which would indicate an interest in signing any such player.[51]

Kuhn, implementing the collective bargaining agreement's terms, also extended the restriction on negotiation of terms between player and club to include the period between the end of the post-season and the free agent re-entry draft:

> A player who has completed his option year without signing a new contract will be free to talk with any club and discuss the merits of his contracting with such club when and if he becomes eligible to do so. But the club and the player must not negotiate terms or enter into a contract unless or until the club has acquired negotiation rights with regard to the player as provided in the new basic agreement.[52]

Accordingly, Kuhn concluded that Ted Turner's comments regarding his intent to pursue Matthews violated Kuhn's warnings and his interpretation of the tampering rule.

While Turner's behavior was deemed 'tampering' by Commissioner Kuhn, it essentially amounted to a violation of a set of rules put in place to create an orderly process for the pursuit of free agents. The point is that this administrative arrangement, and its reinforcement, had nothing to do with a concern about conflict of interest. Indeed, Turner's approach to Matthews occurred after the conclusion of the season when Matthews was already a free agent and had no remaining contractual responsibilities to the Braves.[53]

Had the baseball owners, in the absence of any re-entry draft, unilaterally agreed not to pursue free agent players for a significant period of time after the conclusion of the season and to grant the player's prior club exclusive negotiating rights during that period – in effect, to establish a very limited reserve system – such an arrangement could be justified

---

[50]   Major League Baseball Official Rules § 3(g) (1976). The language of the present proscription on tampering is essentially the same. See Major League Baseball Official Rules § 3(k) (2005).

[51]   *Atlanta Nat'l League Baseball Club* v. *Kuhn*, 432 F. Supp. 1213, 1216 (N.D. Ga. 1977).

[52]   *Ibid.*

[53]   Earlier, in August or September 1976, the Braves' general manager had twice communicated with Matthews about playing for the Braves the following season. This in-season contact clearly constituted tampering under Rule 3(g), as it involved direct contact with Matthews by a team representative at a time when Matthews was still under contract with the Giants. This episode led Commissioner Kuhn to impose a $10,000 fine.

neither in terms of prevention of conflict of interest and preservation of the integrity of the product nor in terms of support of a necessary non-disruptive process for dealing with free agents. Accordingly, there is reason to think that such an arrangement, which tampers with the employment market and impairs the opportunities of those selling their services, would raise a serious issue of legality under the antitrust laws.[54]

Judicial assessment of the status of the arrangement under the Sherman Act would be conducted under the 'rule of reason'. That evaluation requires the court to consider both the anti-competitive effects and the pro-competitive benefits of the challenged practice, including the justifications offered for the collective action and the fit between these ends and the method chosen to accomplish them. The likely defense of the arrangement would be that it is a reasonable timing rule, limited in its duration and therefore in its possible market impact. While in certain circumstances a timing restriction may facilitate the creation and operation of a market characterized by informed buyers and seller and the minimization of buyer search costs,[55] the limitation here is not necessary to structure such an environment. Rather the rule, in conferring on only one team the authority to bid for a player's services and therefore leaving the player with no realistic alternatives for a period

---

[54] The rules which structured the free agency process in 1976 were the product of agreement between the players' union and management. As noted, had management unilaterally introduced a rule giving a team a substantial period of negotiating exclusivity, such a rule would be suspect as a matter of employment policy and antitrust law. Because the actual rule issued from the collective bargaining process, it was entitled to the protection of the non-statutory labor exemption and therefore not subject to antitrust scrutiny. In the wildly improbable scenario of a decertification of the union, joint employer action would be subject to antitrust scrutiny as a result of the Curt Flood Act, which eliminated MLB's exemption with respect to its dealings with its employees. 15 U.S.C. § 26b (2000).

Unlike players, coaches in the major professional sports are not unionized. They are, however, encompassed by the tampering restriction. Accordingly, an antitrust challenge to the rule with respect to coaches could not be repelled by invocation of the nonstatutory labor exemption. See PAUL C. WEILER AND GARY R. ROBERTS, SPORTS AND THE LAW 131–2 (3rd ed. 2004) (summary of tampering disputes arising from the movements of professional football coaches, Bill Parcells and Bill Belichick).

[55] The owners would look to *Chicago Board of Trade* v. *U.S.*, 246 U.S. 231 (1918) for support here. At issue in that case was the 'Call' rule adopted by the Board. Under that rule Board members were permitted to trade after the end of the regular session only at the session's closing price. The effect of the rule was to force all trades into an environment where relevant information was equally available to all participants and where consumer search costs were low. Though the court mentioned other factors, the key to its conclusion that the Board's restriction of members' hours of operation and prices while the exchange was closed was reasonable was the restriction's facilitation of the more effective working of the market. See HERBERT HOVENKAMP, FEDERAL ANTITRUST POLICY 211–13 (3rd ed. 2005).

A number of points, both primary and secondary, stressed by the court in *Chicago Board of Trade*, do not translate well to our hypothetical. In the case the timing restriction was quite brief, as a new price would be established competitively when the next day's session opened. In the hypothetical the assumption is that the period of time in which only one team will negotiate for the player's services is significant. Also, the court notes that the exchange rule affected only a portion of the daily grain shipped to Chicago and did not apply to grain shipped to other markets. But in professional sports in the United States players are faced with one established league in each sport; they cannot 'ship' themselves to another buyer. Finally, assuming it still has relevance today – a questionable assumption – the court's approval of the convenient shortening of the work day has no bearing on the hypothetical restriction.

of time, functions as a milder version of anti-competitive practices such as the historic reserve system and the rookie draft. As the contemporary practice of free agency makes clear, the restriction cannot be defended as a pro-competitive measure that is a necessary condition to a well-functioning market. The existence of a significant probability of anti-competitive effects depends on the length of the exclusive period and, more centrally, on whether (and to what extent) that exclusivity produces a significant first-mover advantage for the prior team. In the end, the resolution depends on the appropriate approach to take to the perhaps unusual situation defined by the lack of a pro-competitive justification and a potential anti-competitive effect with uncertainty about its magnitude.

The Tampering Rule: an Antitrust Assessment

A no-tampering rule, we have seen, stands at odds with employment practices and policies common outside the sports industry. The anti-competitive effect of the restriction is patent, as, via collective agreement, it interferes with the market in bidding for employees' (athletes') services. Are there persuasive justifications for the restriction that save it from a judgment of antitrust illegality?

No American court has evaluated the antitrust status of a no-tampering rule in an inquiry which focused on this practice alone.[56] One court, a federal district court, has given serious attention to the legality of a no-tampering rule, but it assessed the rule as part of the complex of restraints, including various restrictions on free agency, to which a professional football player then became subject once he signed a contract. The result of this assessment was a judgment that the regime of restraints was an unreasonable restriction that constituted a violation of section 1 of the Sherman Act.[57]

Joe Kapp was a quarterback for the Minnesota Vikings, who led the team to the 1970 Super Bowl. Kapp then agreed to play for the New England Patriots in the subsequent year but did not sign a standard player contract with the Patriots. When he refused to sign such a contract for the following year, he was not permitted to play. Kapp sued the NFL and its member clubs, alleging that he was denied the opportunity to play in the league because he refused to sign the standard player contact and seeking damages from the defendants for unlawfully terminating his playing career. Kapp contended that several clauses in the player contact, along with other league rules he would have been bound to follow, violated the Sherman Act. Among the alleged violations were the NFL's college player draft, the reserve clause and 'Rozelle Rule' which authorized the Commissioner to award compensation in the form of players and draft choices to teams that had lost a free agent player to another team,[58] the no-tampering rule, the option clause permitting a

---

56   There is no doubt about the market power of the employers who promulgate the tampering rules. Only one major league exists in the United States for professional baseball, football, basketball, and hockey. Thus, the rule has significant effects on the employment market for professional athletes. Accordingly, the only serious antitrust issue is the assessment of tampering rules under the rule of reason.

57   *Kapp* v. *Nat'l Football League*, 390 F. Supp. 73 (N.D. Cal. 1974), *aff'd in part on other grounds and vacated as moot in part*, 586 F.2d 644 (9ᵗʰ Cir. 1978), *cert. denied*, 441 U.S. 907 (1979). In the same vein, see *Mackey* v. *Nat'l Football League*, 407 F. Supp. 1000 (1975).

58   The Rozelle Rule restriction resembled the European soccer transfer fee system. There a player whose contractual obligation had expired could not move to another club unless that club

team to renew an expired player contract for a year beyond the stated term, and the rule requiring every player to sign a standard player contract approved by the league office.

While the reserve and option clauses prevented competition among teams for players already in the league, the draft prevented competition for new players. The complex of rules had one common objective – the elimination or minimization of free-agent status for players – and it effectively precluded a player from being able to play for the team that was willing to make him the best offer. The district court granted Kapp's partial summary judgment motion and held that 'league enforcement of most of the challenged rules is so patently unreasonable that there is no genuine issue for trial.'[59] More particularly, the court held the tampering rule to be 'patently unreasonable insofar as … [it is] used to enforce other NFL rules in that area.'[60] Kapp's victory was overturned on appeal but on grounds that did not involve review of the antitrust liability issue.[61]

Over the past few decades, the traditional restraints on player mobility have been dramatically reduced or eliminated as a result of antitrust litigation and collective bargaining. The open question, then, is whether a tampering rule, standing alone, is a violation of the antitrust laws. Of course, like many other practices historically common in professional sports – for example, baseball's memorable option clause – a 'tampering' proscription would be inconsequential if it simply appeared in an individually negotiated employment agreement. Thus, if an employer and employee agree that the employee will not communicate with a prospective employer during the term of the agreement, no antitrust question would be raised.[62] The problematic character of the tampering rule is a product of its industry-wide nature, the joint definition and enforcement of the restriction. The fact that all employers have agreed to the limitation, or, what is functionally the same, their authorized agent (the Commissioner) has imposed a league-wide rule, raises

---

paid a transfer fee stipulated by the selling club. That system was invalidated by the *Bosman* decision of the European Court of Justice. See note 192 *infra*. The court ruled that the transfer fee system constituted a barrier to freedom of movement for workers, a fundamental freedom guaranteed under Article 48 of the EC Treaty.

[59]   Kapp, note 57 *supra*, at 82.

[60]   *Ibid.*

[61]   Although the district court found that the draft, Rozelle Rule, and no-tampering rule violated section 1 of the Sherman Act, no interlocutory appeal of that decision was permitted. Accordingly, the case went to the jury, which found Kapp had not been injured by the antitrust violations, as he had quit football voluntarily; the case was then dismissed for lack of standing. On appeal the Ninth Circuit affirmed the jury's finding and therefore declined to hear the NFL's challenge to the rule of reason antitrust determination. The result was that there was no review of the liability decision.

[62]   And presumably the employee will have been compensated in some way for acceptance of the restriction.

Individually negotiated provisions that bar the employee from discussing other employment during the term of the agreement without first obtaining university permission appear in some college coaching contracts. See, e.g., *Northeastern Univ. v. Brown*, 17 Mass. L. Rptr. 443, at *2 (Super. Ct. 2004):

> Coach agrees to devote full time and effort to the University and agrees not to seek, discuss, negotiate for, or accept other employment during the term of this Agreement without first obtaining the written consent of the President of the University …

potential conflicts with systemic and individual interests expressed in the antitrust laws and the common law of contracts and torts.[63]

A determination of the tampering rule's antitrust status requires an assessment of the strength of a league's justifications for the restriction.[64] So, what reasons may be offered in

---

[63]   Similarly, option arrangements are commonplace and mutually beneficial. Imagine an employer who informs an applicant that he cannot offer a long-term commitment at the present time but that he can hire him for a year at $X with an option to extend the employment for a fixed period at $Y at the expiration of the year depending on the employee's performance. Thus, baseball's historic option clause, which permitted a team to renew a player's contract for a year at a percentage of his prior salary if team and player were unable to agree on a new contract, was offensive not because option arrangements are inherently undesirable but because the provision was collectively imposed, because it appeared in all employment agreements as part of a broader arrangement which 'reserved' players to a particular team for their entire careers.

[64]   Over the past few decades professional sports leagues have regularly responded to antitrust challenges to agreements between their members with the contention that they should be viewed as a single economic enterprise and therefore incapable of conspiring within the meaning of section 1 of the Sherman Act. This 'single entity' defense asserts that a league and its membership should be conceived as organizationally equivalent to a partnership with geographically scattered offices or a corporation and its subsidiaries. The contention is that although comprising separately owned teams, these clubs must cooperate as if they were a single economic undertaking for the league to operate effectively. In short, the argument is that the clubs are joint suppliers of a league product and they should be viewed as necessary collaborators that supply nothing alone. See SZYMANSKI, note 20 *supra*, at 51–3. The consequence of acceptance of this conception would be that the necessary 'contract, combination, or conspiracy' under section 1 of the Sherman Act would be absent. Rather the arrangements between league members would be regarded as the internal regulations of a single legal and economic body. Accordingly, league arrangements would be immune from scrutiny under section 1. This claim was decisively rejected by the Supreme Court in *American Needle, Inc.* v. *National Football League*, 130 S. Ct. 2201 (2010), a case involving a challenge to the joint management of the teams' intellectual property. Prior to *American Needle* the single entity defense was generally rejected by the lower federal courts. See, e.g., *Sullivan* v. *Nat'l Football League*, 34 F.3d 1091 (1st Cir. 1994); Philip J. Closius, *Professional Sports and Antitrust Law: The Ground Rules of Immunity, Exemption, and Liability*, in GOVERNMENT AND SPORT: THE PUBLIC POLICY ISSUES 140, 149–53 (Arthur T. Johnson and James H. Frey eds., 1985). Instead the predominant judicial response was to view a league as a form of joint venture with multiple firms and to apply the rule of reason in assessing the antitrust legality of agreements between league members. See, e.g., *Clarett* v. *Nat'l Football League*, 306 F. Supp. 2d 379 (S.D.N.Y. 2004), *rev'd on other grounds*, 369 F.3d 124 (2d Cir. 2004); Stephen F. Ross, *Competition Law as a Constraint on Monopolistic Exploitation by Sports Leagues and Clubs*, 19 OXFORD REV. ECON. POL'Y 569, 578 (2003) (view that leagues are analogous to corporations is severely flawed; courts have rejected argument based on formal organization of leagues as unincorporated associations of separately owned teams that do not share profits or losses, the independent management of each team, and active competition among teams that would occur but for challenged restraints). See also Stephen F. Ross, *An Antitrust Analysis of Sports League Contracts with Cable Networks*, 39 EMORY L. J. 463, 465–8 (1990); Stephen Weatherill, *Discrimination on Grounds of Nationality in Sport*, in 1989 YEARBOOK OF EUROPEAN LAW 55, 72 (1990) (Football (Soccer) League not properly described as 'single entity'; player restrictions are part of League governing structure but they are product of the independent input of each club and affect the independent business decision making of each club in player recruitment policy in wider labor market). See generally Roger G. Noll, *The Organization of Sports Leagues*, 19 OXFORD REV. ECON. POL'Y 530, 540–1 (2003) (historical experience indicates that joint venture structure is substantially more efficient than 'true' single-entity structure in which power is centralized in league office and teams are not independent organizations but rather operating divisions of the league; no single-entity league has ever been successful in any sport in North America or Europe). This approach was validated by the court's unanimous opinion in

support of the rule? As previously suggested, one rationale focuses on the disruption caused by the proscribed behavior.[65] The concern is with the disruptive effect of allowing an athlete to become contractually involved with another team. The premise is that the athlete's incentive to perform will be significantly reduced. But such an effect appears improbable. The situation in which an athlete would make an intentional effort to reduce his performance below an acceptable level is unlikely in light of the potential conflict with teammates and diminished standing with fans.[66] Undoubtedly, third party actions represent an intrusion on the employer's control of the athlete's loyalty, but that effect is true in non-sports settings as well and the consequence is regarded as necessary in order to vindicate the employee's right to market his services. Is there any reason to think that the impact on team performance generally will be more weighty than that on non-sports corporate performance? And, of course, the tampering rule does not say that an athlete cannot sign with another team; it says that he cannot even talk with that team.

Another, and related, club concern may be the effects of a signing upon others.[67] Beyond the possible impact on the individual player's performance, the cohesiveness of the team might be affected. But the player and the new employer should not be held responsible for reactions that others have to the signing, behavior over which they have no control. And, again, is there likely to be a different level of irrational feelings, such as jealousy, triggered in the non-sports employment setting? Accordingly, loss of employee loyalty and 'disruption' do not distinguish the sports setting so as to justify differential legal treatment.[68]

Apparently, maintenance of competitive balance and protection of teams' investment in player development have also been offered as supports for the no-tampering rule.[69] It is

---

American Needle, which characterized league arrangements such as collective licensing of teams' intellectual property as concerted, rather than independent, action and thus within the coverage of section 1.

[65]   See text accompanying notes 19–21 *supra*.

[66]   An athlete, concerned with his ability to command a high salary, has little incentive to reduce his effort. Indeed, at least before signing with a future team, a strong performance against a potential employer would make him more attractive to that team.

[67]   See text accompanying notes 14–18 and *supra*.

[68]   See generally Stephen F. Ross, *The NHL Labour Dispute and the Common Law, The Competition Act, and Public Policy*, 37 U.B.C. L. REV. 343, 359 (2004) (maintenance of stable labor force is illegitimate justification for employee restraints). More generally, a justification of labor market restrictions in terms of roster stability has little economic support. A pro-competitive efficiency rationale for roster stability presumes that a player is more valuable as a veteran of the same team, rather than offering his services to a new set of teammates. If that were so, then in an unrestrained market his current team would outbid rivals for his services – which is often not the case. *Ibid.*

[69]   See *Mackey* v. *Nat'l Football League*, 543 F.2d 606, 611 n.6 (8th Cir. 1976). These problematic justifications have been regularly offered in support of leagues' more direct limitations on player mobility, such as the college draft, reserve and option clauses, and restrictions on free agency. They are no more persuasive with respect to those restrictions. See, e.g., *ibid.* (Rozelle Rule limiting competition for player services unreasonable and Sherman Act violation); *Smith* v. *Pro Football, Inc.*, 593 F.2d 1173 (D.C. Cir. 1978) ('[b]ecause the NFL draft … had severe anticompetitive effects and no demonstrated procompetitive virtues, we hold that it unreasonably restrained trade in violation of § 1 of The Sherman Act'); Stephen Ross, *The Misunderstood Alliance Between Sports Fans, Players, and the Antitrust Laws*, 1997 U. ILL. L. REV. 519 (most of the controversial player restraints used by professional sports leagues would not be upheld under the Sherman Act).

difficult to see any serious connection between the tampering rule and the investment protection objective. However, in any case the rule – and related restrictions on mobility – are unnecessary to secure a team's investment in training and development of players. Individually negotiated contracts with young players can insure that the team has a reasonable opportunity to recoup its investment.[70] Since these mutually beneficial arrangements can be reached between individual teams and players, agreements among teams to restrict competition for player services are not needed to attain efficient risk allocation.[71]

Competitive balance, in the service of maximization of fan interest and the efficient allocation of player resources, is a legitimate joint objective.[72] But it is far fetched to argue

---

[70]   See Stephen F. Ross, *Restraints on Player Competition that Facilitate Competitive Balance and Player Development and Their Legality in the United States and in Europe,* in COMPETITION POLICY IN PROFESSIONAL SPORTS 91, 104–08 (Stefan Kesenne and Claude Jeanrenaud eds., 1999) (private contracting with young players can provide teams with incentive to invest in player development; to secure return on their investments teams can offer players multi-year or option contracts or agreements with buy-out provisions).

[71]   See *Eastham* v. *Newcastle United Football Club, Ltd* [1964] Ch. 413, (1963) 3 All E.R. 139; MICHAEL J. TREBILCOCK, THE COMMON LAW OF RESTRAINT OF TRADE 228 (1986) (one way to handle recoupment of player development costs, both with respect to players who succeed and those who do not, is through long-term contracts that pay successful players less than the value of their marginal product in later periods of their contracts); Ross, note 68 *supra*, at 359–60; Ross (2003), note 64 *supra*, at 574, 576, 579–80, 582 (difficult for intra-league sports restraint to be justified on free-rider grounds, as the obvious alternative of sharing revenue is almost always available). See generally Rottenberg, note 42 *supra*, at 256 (if it pays to invest in training and development in a monopsonistic market, it will also pay to do so in a free market). See also Stefan Kesenne, *The Bosman Case and European Football*, in HANDBOOK ON THE ECONOMICS OF SPORT 636, 638 (Wladimir Andreff and Stefan Szymanski eds., 2006) (research on clubs' investment decisions in training young talent found *Bosman* system superior to pre-*Bosman* system because it leads to higher investment in talent, a result that contradicts clubs' complaints that abolition of transfer system killed incentives to invest in talent).

In contrast to the distinctive interdependent interest of each league team in having other strong, competitive teams, insuring that an employer can recoup its investment in training young employees is not an issue unique to the sports setting. See *Mackey* v. *Nat'l Football League*, 543 F.2d 606, 621 (8th Cir. 1976) (development of skilled players in professional sports no different than development of skilled employees in other fields).

[72]   See, e.g., *Nat'l Collegiate Athletic Ass'n* v. *Board of Regents*, 468 U.S. 85, 117–120 (1984) (competitive balance is legitimate objective for sports leagues and can potentially justify otherwise unreasonable trade restraints); Ross (2003), note 64 *supra*, at 575–6. But see Salil K. Mehra and T. Joel Kuercher, *Striking Out 'Competitive Balance' in Sports, Antitrust, and Intellectual Property,* 21 BERKELEY TECH. L.J. 1499 (2006) (weaknesses in the competitive balance argument; argument seriously flawed). A distinctive aspect of sports leagues is that the output is a joint product where firms in the industry must compete and cooperate for the league to prosper. Teams compete to be successful, but if one team is 'too successful' and competitive balance within the industry is compromised, fans lose interest and the league fails. Thus, the competitive balance argument rests on the argument that in order for a league to be attractive to consumers, teams must be similar in quality so that game outcomes are uncertain and all teams are perceived as having a real chance to become champion. See, e.g., Walter C. Neale, *The Peculiar Economics of Professional Sports: A Contribution to the Theory of the Firm in Sporting Competition and in Market Competition,* 78 Q. J. ECON. 1–2, 4 (1964). In fact, competitive balance is multidimensional. See Rodney Fort, *Competitive Balance in North American Professional Sports*, in HANDBOOK OF SPORTS ECONOMICS RESEARCH 190 (John Fizel ed., 2006) (competitive balance assessed using three different measures –

that the tampering rule tends to spread good players evenly over the various teams and to thereby promote equally balanced teams. In fact, owners' efforts to suppress inter-club competition have harmed consumers and economic welfare.[73] In Major League Baseball the owners' wish to impose labor market rules that restrict competition has led to considerable disruptive industrial strife. In addition, because of the absence of a rival league owners can adopt rules that limit competition among themselves for players. The chance to pay players salaries less than the value that the players add to team revenues leads owners to embrace rules that inefficiently allocate players among teams, thereby decreasing the overall consumer appeal of Major League Baseball as a sporting competition.[74]

Is there another justification that is more likely to elicit judicial approval of this control? A more promising argument for limiting player (and team) opportunity for bargaining is that the limitation is necessary to preserve the image of league contests as involving honest, authentic athletic competition. This rationale asserts that the rule is needed to assure the integrity of the product being sold.[75] The concern is with the possibility of a conflict of interest arising between a player (or coach)[76] and his current team. The line of

---

game uncertainty, playoff uncertainty, consecutive-season uncertainty; where competitive balance is and how it has changed over time). See also Stefan Szymanski and Ron Smith, *Equality of Opportunity and Equality of Outcome: Static and Dynamic Competitive Balance in European and American Sports Leagues*, in TRANSATLANTIC SPORT: THE COMPARATIVE ECONOMICS OF NORTH AMERICAN AND EUROPEAN SPORTS 109 (2002); Jeffery Borland and Robert Macdonald, *Demand for Sport*, 19 OXFORD REV. ECON. POL'Y 478, 486–7, 491 (2003). But see Ross, note 70 *supra*, at 94–5 (not self evident that competitive balance within domestic soccer league will improve popularity of sport); SZYMANSKI, note 20 *supra*, at 47–50 (limited statistical evidence to support uncertainty-of-outcome hypothesis).

[73]   See Roger G. Noll, '*Buyer Power' and Economic Policy*, 72 ANTITRUST L.J. 589, 615–16 (2005) (virtually all economic studies of professional sport reject the claim that anticompetitive restrictions in the player market enhance efficiency by promoting competitive balance). See also *Eastham* v. *Newcastle United Football Club, Ltd*, note 71 *supra*; Ross (2003), note 64 *supra*, at 574–5.

[74]   Stephen F. Ross, *The Effect of Baseball's Status as a Legal Anomaly and Aberration*, in LEGAL ISSUES IN PROFESSIONAL BASEBALL 215, 220–27 (Lewis Kurlantzick ed., 2005). Competitive balance is enhanced when there is greater uncertainty about the outcome of games and uncertainty is increased when players move between seasons from superior rosters to inferior ones. If owners lacked monopsony power they would not look to introduce rules aimed primarily at reducing competition among themselves, rules that contribute to a sub-optimal allocation of players that inhibits the ability of low-quality teams to improve quickly. Such a sub-optimal scheme is attractive as long as the revenues lost from reduced fan appeal are offset by greater savings in labor costs that result from restraints on player wages. In fact, with the elimination of the reserve clause and the introduction of free agency, the number of teams that contended for a division title rose, as did the number of different teams winning titles while the occasions where no team finished within ten games of the division winner declined. See generally ANDREW ZIMBALIST, BASEBALL AND BILLIONS 95 (1992) (as of 1992 competitive balance has become noticeably more equal since free agency was introduced).

[75]   This rationale, which stresses the need to preserve public confidence in the authenticity of the contest, assimilates the justification for the tampering rule to that for anti-gambling proscriptions. See *Molinas* v. *Nat'l Basketball Ass'n*, 190 F. Supp. 241 (S.D.N.Y. 1961).

[76]   Interestingly, the National Collegiate Athletic Association (NCAA) does not have in place a tampering rule with respect to the hiring of college coaches. Its absence may be explained, in part, by a concern about antitrust liability. See Richard T. Karcher, *The Coaching Carousel in Big-Time Intercollegiate Athletics: Economic Implications and Legal Considerations*, 20 FORDHAM INTELL.

thought is that if the player knows another team is interested in his future services, he will not exert the same effort as he otherwise would for his current team. Particularly, but not exclusively, if a player were known to be negotiating with another team, there may be some chance that his play against that team would not be as aggressive as it otherwise would be.[77]

One might be skeptical about the premise underlying this concern – i.e. that an athlete will not exert his regular effort against a team he might (or will) play for in the future. The assumption is that a player's professionalism and competitiveness will not overcome the temptation. To the contrary, in *Cincinnati Bengals, Inc.* v. *Bergey* the defendant football player had signed a contract to play in the future with the World Football League, a new league. The Bengals, his present employer, argued that the signing, and the specific provisions of the contract, would potentially impair his ability to perform for the Bengals and would tempt Bergey to 'dog it.' The court rejected this argument, making particularized findings about whether Bergey's incentives would be weakened and concluding that he was personally committed to fulfilling his original contract.[78]

Yet, a league – without doubting the conclusion about the player's commitment in that case – might regard the approach of the *Bergey* court as unsatisfactory for several reasons. First, it calls for an individualized post hoc inquiry while the league's needs are arguably better served by a blanket, prophylactic rule. More fundamentally, and relatedly, the league is concerned with image and perception. That is, even if a player has not actually withheld his best effort, there is a risk that fans would perceive the situation in that way. Thus, a below-par performance by the player might be perceived to have been prompted by his interest in improving the position of his potential (or future) employer. Since the belief that the outcome of games is determined by the merits of the competition is central to the attraction of a league's product, widespread perceptions of this sort by consumers would be seriously damaging to the league and its teams.[79]

PROP. MEDIA & ENT. L.J. 1, 77 (2009). In contrast, the organization has promulgated such a rule with respect to the movement of athletes:

> An athletics staff member or other representative of the institution's athletics interests shall not make contact with the student-athlete of another NCAA or NAIA four-year collegiate institution, directly or indirectly, without first obtaining the written permission of the first institution's athletics director (or an athletics administrator designated by the athletics director) to do so, regardless of who makes the initial contact.

NCAA, 2008–09 NCAA DIVISION I MANUAL, bylaw 13.1.1.3.

[77]   See generally RESTATEMENT (SECOND) OF AGENCY § 387 (1958) (duty of loyalty). While the obvious case for conflict is a game between the player's current team and his possible future employer, the dual loyalty concern could exist as well in games against other teams when the outcome of those games might affect the fortunes of his prospective employer.

[78]   *Cincinnati Bengals, Inc.* v. *Bergey*, 453 F. Supp. 129, 136, 140 (S.D. Ohio 1974) (pride and desire to maintain reputation as outstanding player, *inter alia*, make impairment of effort unlikely). See also text accompanying notes 19–20 *supra*.

[79]   John C.Weistart, *Player Discipline in Professional Sports: The Antitrust Issues*, 18 WM & MARY L. REV. 703, 707 (1977):

> The success of most professional sports activities depends upon the fans' belief that games and matches represent honest competition … It is unlikely that the interest of fans would continue at present levels if they had reason to believe that the outcome of the competition was

Accordingly, since there is a legitimate joint interest in assuring customers of the authenticity of the league product, and a collective rule is necessary to serve that interest, the conflict-of-interest concern is the sole plausible rationale and a substantial justification for the tampering rule.

THE INTERNATIONAL DIMENSION: AGREEMENTS WITH FOREIGN LEAGUES

All of the major professional sports leagues in the United States have entered into agreements with foreign leagues or athletic organizations that regulate the international movement of players.[80] Thus, Major League Baseball has an agreement with Japanese Professional Baseball.[81] The National Basketball Association has an accord with FIBA,

---

controlled by factors other than the personal efforts of those participating and the pre-established rules of the game.

See HENRY G. DEMMERT, THE ECONOMICS OF PROFESSIONAL TEAM SPORTS 21 (1973). As previously noted (see note 28 *supra*), a concern for dual loyalties exists both where the prospective employer is a member of a new league and where it is a member of the present league. In cases involving attempts by an existing league to inhibit a new league from negotiating with its players, the courts have been unsympathetic to the existing league's efforts and have given little credence to the dual loyalty concern. They have, instead, affirmed the general policy in favor of inter-employer competition. The possible conflict of interest, though, is stronger when a player negotiates with a team in his own league since he will face games against that team and be able to affect its fortunes in other contests. This distinction underlies the point that intra-league conflict of interest – and the fear of consequent erosion of fan interest – is the only weighty justification for the tampering rule. Indeed, there is no doubt that an accord between leagues under which teams in one league agree not to negotiate with or sign any player from the other league until that player has played his last game under his current contract would be a violation of section 1 of the Sherman Act. See *Cincinnati Bengals* v. *Bergey*, 453 F. Supp. 129, 149 (S.D. Ohio 1974) (doubtful that parties could legally agree to a truce in their bidding war under which WFL teams would agree not to sign any Bengal player until he has played his last game in his option year; such an agreement would risk antitrust liability).

80   Migration of elite professional athletes has become an increasingly common phenomenon. Different patterns have emerged in specific sports and between geographical areas. See, e.g., Simon Gardiner and Roger Welch, '*Show Me the Money': Regulation of the Migration of Professional Sportsmen in Post-Bosman Europe*, in PROFESSIONAL SPORT IN THE EUROPEAN UNION: REGULATION AND RE-REGULATION 107, 108–11 (Andrew Caiger and Simon Gardiner eds., 2000) (soccer in Europe). Of course, immigration laws constitute a constraint on all forms of economic migration. See, e.g., 2 AARON N. WISE AND BRUCE S. MEYER, INTERNATIONAL SPORTS LAW AND BUSINESS 377–97 (1997) (United States visas for foreign athletes, their assistants and immediate family members); Tim Kerr, *Disciplinary Regulation of Sport: A Different Strand of Public Law?, in* THE REGULATION OF SPORT IN THE EUROPEAN UNION 97, 112 and n. 23 (2007) (tension between transnational sport labor market and national legal barriers in areas of naturalization and assimilation).

In addition to these international agreements, foreign leagues themselves also have internal rules that limit employment opportunities for American athletes. For example, the Japanese Professional Baseball League allows only four foreign players on the 25-man game roster. See note 149 and text accompanying note 192 *infra*.

81   United States–Japanese Player Contract Agreement (2000). The professional league in Japan is known as The Nippon Professional Baseball Organization of Japan (NPB). NPB is composed of

the international basketball federation.[82] The National Football League (NFL) has had an arrangement with the Canadian Football League (CFL).[83] And the National Hockey League (NHL) has an agreement with the International Ice Hockey Federation (IIHF) that regulates the transfer of players from European clubs.[84]

---

two leagues, Central and Pacific, each consisting of six teams. The Central League members are the Chunichi Dragons, Hanshin Tigers, Hiroshima Toyo Carp, Tokyo Yakult Swallows, Yokohoma BayStars, and Yomiuri Giants. The Pacific League clubs are the Chiba Lotte Marines, Fukuoka SoftBank Hawks, Hokkaido Nippon Ham Fighters, Orix Buffaloes, Saitama Seibu Lions, and Tohoku Rakuten Golden Eagles.

In contrast, amateur baseball players from countries that are not subject to the Major League Baseball draft (e.g., Venezuela) may be signed by any Major League organization and may be signed at age 16. As only residents of the United States, Puerto Rico, and Canada (and foreigners enrolled at United States universities) are subject to the reverse-order amateur draft, all other foreign ballplayers come to the United States as free agents. Foreign-born players today constitute more than one-fifth of all major leaguers. ANDREW ZIMBALIST, THE BOTTOM LINE: OBSERVATIONS AND ARGUMENTS ON THE SPORTS BUSINESS 77 (2006). Major League Baseball also has an accord with Korean Professional Baseball. United States–Korean Player Contract Agreement (2003). The terms of this pact closely parallel those of the United States–Japanese agreement. More recently, Major League Baseball has also entered an agreement with the China Baseball Association that permits major league teams to scout and sign Chinese players. *Sports Briefing*, N.Y. TIMES, Nov. 25, 2003, at D5. For a highly informative account of the history of baseball in Asia and the different approach to the game there, see JOSEPH A. REAVES, TAKING IN A GAME (2002).

82   Agreement By and Between National Basketball Association (NBA) and Federation Internationale de Basketball (FIBA) (1997) [hereinafter NBA–FIBA Agreement].

83   NFL/CFL Cooperative Relationship Agreement (2004–2006). There has been discussion about extension of this agreement, but a renewal has not yet been concluded. See Mike Wilkening, *Slim Pickings: CFL Short on NFL Prospects*, ProFootballWeekly.com, Oct. 25, 2007, http://www.profootballweekly.com/PFW/Features/NFLList/2007/nflist2216.htm.

The arrangements between the NFL and CFL reflect how the two leagues independently coexist as football organizations (and compete for market share in each other's sports markets) but at the same time also cooperate, to some extent, to control the movement of players and the quality and supply of professional football in North America and, in part, international markets. See FRANK P. JOZSA, JR., SPORTS CAPITALISM: THE FOREIGN BUSINESS OF AMERICAN PROFESSIONAL LEAGUES 80–2 (2004); NFL Canada, *The NFL-CFL Alliance: A Winning Team*, http://www.slam.canoe.ca/NFLCanadaPrograms/nflcflalliance.html (last visited June 25, 2009).

84   IIHF–NHL Player Transfer Agreement (2007–2011). The IIHF–NHL Agreement regulates transfers to the NHL from all non-North American IIHF-affiliated associations and leagues, except Russia. It defines the amount of money a NHL team signing a European player must pay as compensation, places an annual limit on transfers, and sets a transfer deadline. The IIHF distributes the compensation money among those national federations and clubs that lose players to the NHL, using a formula agreed upon by the IIHF and national federations. The NHL has a separate agreement with Hockey Canada and USA Hockey with respect to players signed from their developmental systems.

The IIHF–NHL Player Transfer Agreement was scheduled to remain in effect until 2011. However, in December 2007 the European nations involved, unhappy with the terms of the agreement particularly the size of compensation fees, exercised their right to re-open the agreement by giving the requisite notice and demanded that negotiations recommence. The NHL and IIHF were working to have a new agreement in place by spring 2009, but no accord has yet been reached. See *Transfer Agreement Between NHL and IIHF Expires*, CANADIAN PRESS, JUNE 16, 2008, available at http://www.tsn.ca/nhl/story/?id=240848; Press Release, Int'l Ice Hockey Fed'n, *Global Agreement Coming Closer: IIHF, NHL, and NHLPA to Work Towards an Agreement*, Jan. 10, 2008 (on file with author); Allan Hougaard, *IIHF Transfer Agreement Falls Apart After Czechs Opt Not*

These inter-league compacts regularize the interaction between leagues, teams and foreign players with respect to the export and/or import of teams' players. They contain rules about when a team can approach a player who is playing abroad and about when the team can sign such a player. Typically, they contain a private dispute resolution mechanism to deal with conflicts, such as disagreement about the contract status of a player. I want first to focus, descriptively and analytically, on the agreement between the National Basketball Association (NBA) and FIBA (Federation Internationale de Basketball) both because its provisions reflect care in composition and because those provisions raise key antitrust issues. I then want to compare the NBA–FIBA Agreement with that between Major League Baseball (MLB) and the Japanese Professional League (NPB) and to gauge the antitrust status of that agreement under United States antitrust law. I will also briefly describe and assess the antitrust legality of a few internal rules of foreign leagues that affect the employment of foreign athletes.[85]

NBA–FIBA AGREEMENT

The purpose of the agreement is to construct an arrangement under which each league (and its member teams) commits itself to honor existing and valid player contracts signed by the other league. Thus, if a player who had signed a contract to play with a team in a league affiliated with a federation that is a member of FIBA wishes to sign a contract with an NBA team, he must obtain a letter of clearance from the federation or FIBA. The only acceptable ground for denial of the letter is that the player is subject to an existing binding contract. In the absence of receipt of the clearance letter, the NBA will disapprove a proposed or signed NBA contract and the player will not be permitted to play in the NBA during the term of his existing contract.[86] The agreement, thus, defines which players can be approached. And league respect for each other's existing contractual commitments with players is implemented through a permission mechanism. If there is a disagreement about the validity of a contract, the agreement provides for resolution of that dispute by arbitration.[87]

The agreement, unlike NBA internal rules, contains no anti-tampering prohibition. That is, it does not proscribe communication between a team and a foreign player about

---

to Extend Deal, THE HOCKEY NEWS, May 1, 2008, http://thehockeynews.com/articles/15728-IIHF-transfer-agreement-falls-apart-after-Czechs-opt-not-to-extend-deal.html.

For a description of international alliances between teams in soccer, see Gardiner and Welch, note 80 *supra*, at 114–16.

[85] These restrictive rules are not the product of interleague agreement. See note 149 and text accompanying notes 192–203 *infra*.

[86] NBA–FIBA Agreement § 3. Essentially the same procedures govern the move of a player from an NBA team to a FIBA team. See *ibid.* at § 2. FIBA regulations require that clearance letters not be limiting or conditional. Accordingly, if the NBA is unable to grant an unconditional letter of clearance because a player is bound under a contract with an NBA team, FIBA rules will not permit the player to sign with a FIBA team – e.g., during a labor dispute resulting in a lockout of NBA players. The purpose of the FIBA rule is to prevent players from joining a FIBA team without being able to commit themselves to the remainder of the season. *Van Exel* v. *USA Basketball*, No. H-98–4306 (S.D. Tex. Dec. 31, 1998).

[87] NBA–FIBA Agreement § 2.3, 3.3.

future employment while that player is performing for another employer under an existing contract.[88] Presumably, that omission is deliberate and reflects the fact that the strongest justification for tampering rules – the prevention of the existence or appearance of a conflict of interest within a league – does not apply in the situation of an inter-league agreement. Indeed, it is doubtful that a persuasive rationale can be supplied for an international tampering rule, which inhibits negotiations during the tenure of a player's contract. And such a rule, which shifts, in a way detrimental to players, the line implicitly drawn by existing contract (and tort) law between constraint and freedom to pursue employment opportunities would likely constitute an antitrust violation.

While the agreement permits contact and communication about future employment – i.e. employment after an existing contract obligation expires – it allows interaction only with respect to future employment. Not surprisingly, it does not countenance behavior aimed at present employment. Thus, a team may not pursue a foreign player under contract to a foreign club with the objective of having him immediately join its roster.[89] Though this distinction in restriction may be understandable from the teams' perspective and initially appear sensible, the limitation on buyers is troubling from an antitrust perspective.[90] Is the arrangement that so restricts buyers' bidding for players an antitrust violation?

Determination of the legality of the basketball agreement involves consideration of the application of American antitrust law[91] to an international accord, specification of the relevant market, and assessment of the anti-competitive and pro-competitive effects of the arrangement on that market. There is little doubt that American antitrust law reaches cooperative arrangements with foreign leagues that limit competition for basketball

---

[88]   NBA–FIBA Agreement § 6.3 ('Agreement is not intended to prohibit negotiations concerning a new Player Contract, or the signing of a new Player Contract, so long as such new Player Contract is not to take effect until after the player is no longer subject to an existing and validly binding Player Contract').

[89]   More precisely, the NBA promises that it 'shall use its best efforts to discourage each and every NBA team from negotiating and/or signing an NBA Player Contract with a player … for a period during which the player is signed to a Player Contract with a FIBA team.' But the League's understanding of the arrangement is that teams cannot negotiate with players who are under contract. See Brian Schmitz, *Team in Spain Keeps Going after Kasun,* ORLANDO SENTINEL, Dec. 16, 2005, at D4. FIBA makes a similar commitment with respect to the pursuit of NBA players. NBA–FIBA Agreement § 6.1–6.2.

[90]   See Jean-Francois Pons, *Sport and European Competition Policy,* in INTERNATIONAL ANTI-TRUST LAW & POLICY 75, 84–5 (Fordham Corporate Law Institute, Barry E. Hawk, ed., 2000) (the blocking of player transfers where those players have unilaterally terminated their contracts and fulfilled relevant obligations under local employment law constitutes a violation of EC competition rules); Richard Parrish, *Football's Place in the Single European Market,* 3 SOCCER & SOC'Y 1, 7 (2002) (European Commission objection to international transfer system provision that prohibits players from transferring to another club following their unilateral termination of contract, even if player has complied with national law governing liability for contract breach).

[91]   As previously indicated, the chapter undertakes an assessment of the legality of the NBA (and MLB) accords under American antitrust law. Clearly the NBA–FIBA Agreement is also subject to scrutiny under the EC Treaty competition rules, in particular Article 81, whether by action of the European Commission or by private suit before a national court of a Member State. In a work in progress I evaluate the status under European Community competition law of quotas that European basketball leagues place on the number of 'foreigners' who can play for a team in the league.

players' services. In an interdependent world economy the central issue for policymakers is the identification of ways to distinguish international matters that affect United States commerce sufficiently to justify attention from our law. The core question in determining the applicability of the Sherman Act[92] is not the locus of conduct but rather whether the contested conduct has a substantial effect in the United States.[93] The NBA agreement inhibits player movement and affects both import commerce – importation of player services – and export commerce – exportation of player services.

The Foreign Trade Antitrust Improvements Act (FTAIA) of 1982[94] amended the Sherman Act to clarify the meaning of the statutory phrase: conduct involving 'trade or commerce ... with foreign nations.' While the statute's wording and organization are not models of stylistic grace, its terms do not alter the conclusion about the applicability of the Sherman Act to the basketball agreement. The Act basically creates two categories of 'foreign commerce' cases: those in which the effects of the challenged conduct are felt in domestic or import commerce; and those in which the conduct's effects are felt in the export trade of American exporters. Its effect is to exempt firms from attack under United States antitrust laws for activity in foreign commerce where the only injured parties are foreign firms or foreign consumers. With respect to the import aspect of the basketball agreement, import commerce is expressly excluded from the coverage of the FTAIA, and therefore the only question is whether the practice was meant to produce and does produce a substantial effect in the United States. The answer would appear to be 'yes.'[95] With respect to the export aspect of the basketball agreement, the Act permits jurisdiction in the case of conduct, wherever occurring, that restrains United States exports if the conduct has a direct, substantial, and reasonably foreseeable effect on exports of goods or services from the United States.[96] The basketball accord certainly meets this test.

In fact, the scenario that has proved troublesome historically with respect to jurisdictional limits is that of significant foreign anticompetitive conduct[97] – for example, an

---

[92] The Sherman Act prohibitions extend to restraint of 'commerce ... with foreign nations.' 15 U.S.C. § 1 (2000).

[93] See, e.g., *United States v. Aluminum Co. of America*, 148 F.2d 416 (2d Cir. 1945) (Hand J.); U.S. DEPARTMENT OF JUSTICE & FEDERAL TRADE COMMISSION, ANTITRUST ENFORCEMENT GUIDELINES FOR INTERNATIONAL OPERATIONS § 3.1 (1995) [hereinafter GUIDELINES]; see also RESTATEMENT (THIRD) OF THE FOREIGN RELATIONS LAW OF THE UNITED STATES § 402(1) (1987).

[94] 15 U.S.C. § 6a (2000):

This Act shall not apply to conduct involving trade or commerce (other than import trade or import commerce) with foreign nations unless –
(1) such conduct has a direct, substantial, and reasonably foreseeable effect –
(A) on trade or commerce which is not trade or commerce with foreign nations, or on import trade or import commerce with foreign nations; or
(B) on export trade or export commerce with foreign nations, of a person engaged in such trade or commerce in the United States ...

[95] The movement of players from FIBA to NBA teams is restricted, thereby depriving spectators of these players' performance.

[96] See GUIDELINES §§ 3.12, 3.122; ROBERT PITOFSKY, *ET AL.*, TRADE REGULATION 1231 (5th ed. 2003). As with the other restrictions analyzed in this chapter, the basketball agreement's effect is 'direct' in the sense that no intermediary is involved.

[97] See *F. Hoffman-La Roche Ltd.* v. *Empagran S.A.*, 542 U.S. 155 (2004).

agreement among foreign sellers to fix prices – that has an adverse domestic effect.[98] But that scenario is far from that of the basketball accord, where a major American actor is involved in the agreement and where an effect on American commerce is the objective of that agreement.

Application of American antitrust law to an international agreement such as the NBA–FIBA accord also raises issues of personal jurisdiction and remedy. Thus, when are foreign actors subject to the personal jurisdiction of American courts?[99] And are there significant difficulties in controlling foreign situations through a domestic decree?[100]

With respect to in personam jurisdiction, there are two possible authorizations of service of process that might be invoked. In the end, the utility of both depends on the extent of the defendant's contacts with the United States and whether these contacts meet the constitutional test for due process. First, the Clayton Act in section 12 contains a singular provision, applicable to corporations, which authorizes worldwide service of process:

> Any suit, action, or proceeding under the antitrust laws against a corporation may be brought not only in the judicial district whereof it is an inhabitant, but also in any district wherein it may be found or transacts business; and all process in such cases may be served in the district of which it is an inhabitant, *or wherever it may be found.*[101]

However, the provision presents the interpretive question of whether the two clauses are dependent or independent. That is, does the process provision, the extraterritorial service privilege, depend on first satisfying the requirements of venue under the initial clause?[102] The courts are split in their answer to that question.[103]

This split may not be all that consequential, though, because of the second possible source of authorization of service under the Federal Rules of Civil Procedure. Even if the clauses are viewed as dependent,[104] if a defendant is not subject to jurisdiction in any state

---

[98]   See, e.g., *Hartford Fire Insurance Co.* v. *California*, 509 U.S. 764 (1993); GUIDELINES § 3.121.

[99]   Federal courts have exclusive jurisdiction over Sherman Act claims. 15 U.S.C. § 4 (2000). See *General Investment Co.* v. *Lake Shore Ry.*, 260 U.S. 261 (1922).

[100]   See generally PHILLIP AREEDA AND LOUIS KAPLOW, ANTITRUST ANALYSIS 153–5 (4th ed. 1988). For discussion of remedial issues, see text accompanying notes 190–1 *infra*.

[101]   15 U.S.C. § 22 (2000) (emphasis added).

[102]   See 1A PHILLIP E. AREEDA AND HERBERT HOVENKAMP, ANTITRUST LAW 346–8 (2nd ed. 2000).

[103]   See *Daniel* v. *Am. Bd. of Emergency Med.*, 428 F.3d 408, 422–27 (2d Cir. 2005) (collecting the conflicting decisions). If the clauses are independent, then the service of process clause confers personal jurisdiction in any district court as long as the corporate party has minimum contacts with the United States. On the other hand, if the process clause depends on the venue clause, then the global service of process provision is only applicable if the case is brought in a district where the corporation is an inhabitant, may be found, or transacts business. EINER ELHAUGE AND DAMIEN GERADIN, GLOBAL ANTITRUST LAW AND ECONOMICS 24–25 (2007).

[104]   The view that the Clayton Act clauses are dependent would not preclude claimant recourse to the general venue statute, 28 U.S.C. § 1391 (2000), but in that case normal service of process limitations would apply and those limitations typically require a state long-arm statute and minimum contacts with the state in which the district court sits (rather than minimum contacts with the United States). See *Asahi Metal Industry Co.* v. *Superior Court of Cal.*, 480 U.S. 102 (1987). In the case of FIBA, though, the requisite contacts may exist with New York.

because it lacks sufficient contacts with any one state, then Rule 4(k)(2) permits worldwide service of process based on nationwide contacts for claims arising under federal law.[105] Moreover, the application of this rule, unlike the Clayton Act provision, is not limited to corporate parties and would reach noncorporate antitrust defendants as well.[106]

Assuming authorization for service of summons on the defendant, whether by statute or Rule, and satisfaction of the procedural requirement of service, the constitutional question remains of whether the court's exercise of jurisdiction would comport with due process under the Fifth Amendment.[107] The touchstone is whether the defendant has 'certain minimum contacts with [the forum] such that the maintenance of the suit does not offend "traditional notions of fair play and substantial justice".'[108] The analytic inquiry about contacts, though, is performed with reference to the United States as a whole, rather

---

[105] FED. R. CIV. P. 4(k)(2):

> For a claim that arises under federal law, serving a summons or filing a waiver of service establishes personal jurisdiction over a defendant if: (A) the defendant is not subject to jurisdiction in any state's courts of general jurisdiction; and (B) exercising jurisdiction is consistent with the United States Constitution and laws.

Thus, the rule authorizes worldwide service of process based on national contacts for suits in the federal courts generally, but only in circumstances where contact with no particular state is sufficient. Rule 4(k)(2) filled a gap in the enforcement of federal law. Under the previous rule, a problem existed when a foreign defendant had sufficient contacts with the United States to justify application of United States law but did not have sufficient contacts with any single state to support jurisdiction under state long-arm statutes or to meet Fourteenth Amendment due process limitations on state court territorial jurisdiction. In those cases a defendant was sheltered from federal law enforcement by the fortuity of a favorable limitation on the authority of state courts. Thus, the defendant could commit breaches without ever having enough contacts with one forum to give those injured a chance to pursue redress. With the Rule's enactment, service of a summons and complaint may confer personal jurisdiction over a defendant who is not subject to the jurisdiction of any particular state.

Though no case has yet tested the proposition and the lower federal courts have simply applied the Rule without ado, questions have been raised about the legitimacy of this rule under the Rules Enabling Act. The Act states that the Federal Rules 'shall not abridge, enlarge, or modify any substantive right.' 28 U.S.C. § 2072(b) (2000). Arguably, extension of jurisdiction in this manner 'enlarges' the scope of substantive federal law under which the defendant is being sued. See GEOFFREY C. HAZARD, JR., *ET AL.*, PLEADING AND PROCEDURE 243–4 (9th ed. 2005).

If service is only feasible in a foreign country, that service is only valid if it comports with foreign or international law or is authorized by some other federal law. In the case of FIBA or the Japanese Professional League, however, validity of service should not be problematic, as both Switzerland and Japan are members of the Hague Convention on the Service Abroad of Judicial and Extrajudicial Documents in Civil and Commercial Matters, Oct. 28, 1964, 20 U.S.T. 361, 658 U.N.T.S 163. See FED. R. CIV. P. 4(f). See generally *Brockmeyer* v. *May*, 383 F.3d 798 (9th Cir. 2004).

[106] In the absence of Rule 4(k)(2), an unincorporated defendant would need to be reached on the basis of sufficient minimum contacts with the forum state. See notes 104–105 *supra*.

[107] The constitutional limitations on the exercise of territorial jurisdiction by federal courts over foreign defendants arise here from the Fifth Amendment rather than from the Fourteenth Amendment, which limits state court reach. However, there is no reason to think that the central constitutional considerations will not be those of minimum contacts and reasonableness, as under Fourteenth Amendment due process jurisprudence.

[108] *International Shoe Co.* v. *Washington*, 326 U.S. 310, 316 (1945). In *International Shoe*, of course, the defendant was a United States corporation acting in a federal system in which other United States states would be compelled to enforce a judgment. In assessing whether, or how,

than with reference to a particular state. In other words, in assessing whether the requisite contacts exist, the court is to look to a nationwide aggregation of contacts between a foreign defendant and the United States.[109]

Are FIBA's contacts with the United States, then, sufficient to meet the requirements of fair play called for by due process? Yes. The nature and quantity of those contacts, the connection of the antitrust claim with those contacts, and the reasonable expectation that its behavior would have a significant effect on American markets provide a positive answer to the constitutional question.

FIBA has a substantial and continuing contractual relationship with the NBA – an unincorporated association headquartered in New York – that extends back to at least 1990.[110] Its actions under the agreement are not random or fortuitous and are purposefully directed to United States basketball teams and players.[111] Key also is that the contact with the forum – entry into the challenged agreement in New York and its ongoing partial performance in the United States – is related to the cause of action.[112] Indeed, impact on the American labor market is the intended, rather than an ancillary, effect of the agreement. In addition, the agreement contains a choice-of-law clause providing that all disputes will be governed by New York law.[113] Accordingly, FIBA, a sophisticated and experienced organization, has fair notice that the agreement, and course of dealing under it, may subject it to the jurisdiction.

---

foreign defendants should be treated differently than out-of-state defendants and, more particularly, whether the notion of 'minimum contacts,' as developed in the context of domestic litigation, is well suited to analyzing jurisdictional questions in international cases, attention must be given to a number of practical and policy differences between the two types of antitrust cases – the possible inconvenience to foreign defendants, the possible involvement of foreign courts and foreign governments, and the likely absence of an alternative forum for the claimant. AREEDA AND KAPLOW, note 100 *supra*, at 155.

[109]   See, e.g., *ISI Int'l, Inc.* v. *Borden Ladner Gervais*, 256 F.3d 548 (7th Cir. 2001) (Rule 4(k)(2)); *Centronics Data Computer Corp.* v. *Mannesmann*, 432 F. Supp. 659 (D.N.H. 1977) (Clayton Act); Note to Subdivision (k), Notes of Advisory Committee on Civil Rules on 1993 amendments.

[110]   The recitals in the NBA–FIBA Agreement indicate that the parties had previously entered an agreement for similar purposes in May 1990 and that they wished to continue that agreement with certain amendments.

[111]   FIBA has regular contacts with the United States in addition to those related to the agreement with the NBA. As the international basketball governing body, it operates through a set of national federations. In the United States that member national federation is USA Basketball, which is headquartered in Colorado Springs. FIBA also maintains relationships with major affiliates. In the United States those affiliates include the NCAA and the NBA, which are active members of USA Basketball.

[112]   '[W]hen contacts are related to the cause of action it can more readily be said that the lawsuit in question was foreseeable, for the defendant itself is responsible for any connection between the lawsuit and its contacts with the forum.' [AREEDA AND HOVENKAMP, note 102 *supra*, at 340. See ELHAUGE AND GERADIN, note 103 *supra*, at 1104 (creating any anti-competitive market effect suffices to create minimum contacts).

[113]   See *Burger King Corp.* v. *Rudzewicz*, 471 U.S. 462, 481–82 (1985) (choice of law provision reinforces defendant's deliberate affiliation with forum State and reasonable foreseeability of possible litigation there). In the same vein the NBA–FIBA Agreement § 2.3 provides that, with respect to players moving from an NBA team to a FIBA team, if there is a dispute about the validity of an existing player contract, that dispute will be resolved pursuant to the arbitration provisions of the NBA–NBPA collective bargaining agreement.

Moreover, having established the presence of the requisite minimum contacts, other factors do not dictate that the assertion of personal jurisdiction would be fundamentally unfair.[114] The United States has an obvious interest in providing a forum for its residents to obtain convenient and effective relief in accord with the public economic policy of the country. And litigation here poses no obvious serious burden for FIBA, a seasoned international association.[115] Thus, FIBA may be brought before an antitrust court here.[116]

NONSTATUTORY LABOR EXEMPTION

An initial question is whether the NBA–FIBA Agreement is immune from antitrust scrutiny[117] under the so-called 'non-statutory' labor exemption.[118] The federal courts have long recognized that:

> [A] proper accommodation between the congressional policy favoring collective bargaining under the NLRA and the congressional policy favoring free competition in business markets requires that some union-employer agreements be accorded a limited non-statutory exemption from antitrust sanctions.[119]

---

[114] Whether fairness is viewed as part of the minimum contacts inquiry or as an additional requirement of due process, see *Asahi Metal Industry Co.* v. *Superior Court of California*, 480 U.S. 102 (1987), fairness considerations do not support a conclusion that exercise of personal jurisdiction by a federal court would exceed the limits of due process. In *Asahi* the court noted that the burden on the defendant Japanese company was severe and that the forum state's interest in assertion of jurisdiction over the company was slight. Neither of these reasons is weighty with respect to FIBA.

[115] To the extent that litigation in a particular federal court is inconvenient, such concerns may be handled through a change of venue.

[116] The issue of adequate minimum contacts is more problematic in the case of the Japanese Professional Baseball League. See text accompanying notes 160–61 *infra*.

[117] The single entity defense would, of course, be irrelevant here since the challenged agreement is between an American and a foreign sports league, two separate bodies. See note 61 *supra*. However, an American league may choose to extend its international reach by the establishment of a subsidiary rather than by contractual arrangements with a foreign organization. One consequence of that choice would be that agreements between the league and the subsidiary would not be subject to antitrust scrutiny. See *Copperweld Corp.* v. *Independence Tube Corp.*, 467 U.S. 752 (1984). Apparently the NBA has chosen this approach in China. See Michael J. De la Merced, *Disney and 4 Chinese Investment Firms To Buy Stake in N.B.A.'s China Subsidiary*, N.Y. TIMES, Jan. 14, 2008, at C9.

[118] In fact, all labor exemptions are 'statutory' in that they depend on the meaning of the antitrust and labor statutes. At the same time, almost all such exemptions are judge-made in that the statutes seldom indicate precisely what conduct is and is not exempt from the antitrust laws. The 'nonstatutory' language, then, just refers to the fact that some labor-related arrangements are immunized because they are expressly described in the Norris-LaGuardia or Clayton Acts, while other arrangements are immunized by implication from the former immunity. Accordingly, the 'statutory'/'nonstatutory' language reminds us that some aspects of the labor exemption derive from explicit statutory provisions, while others are inferred more indirectly. AREEDA AND HOVEN-KAMP, note 102 *supra*, at 171–2.

[119] *Connell Construction Co.* v. *Plumbers Local 100*, 421 U.S. 616, 622 (1975). The exemption becomes relevant when the conduct would otherwise constitute an antitrust violation but antitrust disapproval would undermine federal labor policy. It reflects the policy judgment that the consumer interest in prevention of unreasonable labor market restrictions is outweighed by the consumer

A core example is a collective bargaining agreement that sets wages and hours of employment.[120] To direct employers and employee representatives that these terms of employment are to be determined collectively through good faith bargaining and to then subject the terms to review against a metric that assumes market determination free of collective decision would be to construct a schizoid legal structure.

Though this example of the intersection of labor law and antitrust law is unproblematic, the boundaries of the exemption have been uncertain.[121] That uncertainty applied not only to the specification of the conduct that is exempt. In addition, an unsettled question concerned the temporal dimension of the exemption. More particularly, the question was what happens to the exemption when the collective bargaining agreement expires. When, if at all, does the exemption terminate subsequent to expiration of the collective bargaining agreement? The position of the players' unions, not surprisingly, was that the exemption expires with the collective bargaining agreement and after the collective bargaining agreement's end the antitrust laws are again applicable.[122] The leagues' opposing view was that the exemption applied as long as a union, and a collective bargaining process, are in place. Lower federal courts gave various, conflicting answers to the question.[123]

In *Brown* v. *Pro Football, Inc.*,[124] its most recent pronouncement on the subject, the Supreme Court took an expansive view of the exemption and provided clarification of its reach. That case involved an agreement among NFL teams to restrict the salaries of developmental squad players. In 1987 the collective bargaining agreement between the NFL and the National Football League Players Association (NFLPA) expired. The parties then started bargaining for a new contract. During the lengthy negotiations the NFL teams agreed among themselves to a resolution that permitted each team to add a developmental squad of up to six rookies for purposes of practice and substitution for injured players. The NFL teams also agreed with each other to pay these players $1,000 per week. The union disagreed, insisting that these squad members have certain benefits equivalent to those of regular players and that their salaries be negotiated individually, as had always been the case for player salaries in the past.

---

interest in facilitation of strike-avoiding voluntary collective bargaining between the parties. See Ross, note 68 *supra*, at 382–3.

[120]   The existence of the exemption has led some professional sports unions to threaten or to commit a form of institutional suicide, decertification as bargaining representative – a process established with a very different set of circumstances in mind – in order to bring the antitrust laws into play. See, e.g., *McNeil* v. *Nat'l Football League*, 790 F. Supp. 871 (D. Minn. 1992).

[121]   Ultimately, the proper accommodation between the antitrust order of market determinations and the labor regime of collective bargaining rests on inferences from the several statues and, fundamentally, on one's understanding of federal labor policy. AREEDA AND HOVENKAMP, note 102 *supra*, at 174.

[122]   See, e.g., *Bridgeman* v. *Nat'l Basketball Ass'n*, 675 F. Supp. 960, 964 (D. N.J. 1987).

[123]   See *Nat'l Basketball Ass'n* v. *Williams*, 45 F.3d 684 (2d Cir. 1995) (exemption applies as long as collective bargaining relationship exists); *Powell* v. *Nat'l Football League*, 678 F. Supp. 777 (D. Minn. 1988) (exemption survives until parties reach an impasse), *rev'd*, 930 F.2d 1293 (8th Cir. 1989) (exemption applies beyond bargaining impasse but unclear how far beyond); *Bridgeman* v. *Nat'l Basketball Ass'n*, 675 Supp. 960 (D. N.J. 1987) (exemption for particular practice survives as long as employer continues to impose restriction unchanged and reasonably believes the practice or a close variant will be incorporated in the next collective bargaining agreement).

[124]   518 U.S. 231 (1996).

Negotiations on this issue reached an impasse.[125] The NFL then unilaterally implemented the plan. A group of developmental squad players sued, challenging the salary agreement under section 1 of the Sherman Act. Significantly, the NFL members were not merely agreeing to continue an arrangement that had existed under the old, expired collective bargaining agreement. Rather, the restraint was a new agreement among the NFL teams that had never been agreed to previously by the union and was being put into effect over its objections.

The Supreme Court majority found the nonstatutory labor exemption to be applicable. Looking to both history and logic, the court offered a decision that was considerably broader than previous applications of the exemption. Thus, the court extended the exemption to an employer agreement that did not involve an employee group as a participant; to the period of time after the collective bargaining agreement had expired; and to an agreement that was not contained in the expired collective bargaining agreement, provided that the contested agreement was sufficiently related to the collective bargaining process.[126] The touchstone for the court was whether the immunity was necessary to make the collective bargaining process work. Accordingly, it viewed the exemption as extending not only to agreements resulting from the collective bargaining process but also to other results of the process and to the process itself.

In the case of the NBA–FIBA Agreement the National Basketball Players Association (NBPA) was, and is, not a party to the compact. In fact, the union played no role in the creation of the agreement. The union was not involved in the negotiation of the agreement. Its participation was never solicited, and it never formally approved the pact.[127] In summarizing its decision in *Brown*, the Supreme Court said:

> [The challenged employer] conduct took place during and immediately after a collective-bargaining negotiation. It grew out of, and was directly related to, the lawful operation of the

---

[125] 'Impasse' in labor law refers to the situation where the parties have conducted exhaustive good faith negotiations but nonetheless face irreconcilable differences in their positions. The legal significance of an impasse under labor law is that when it is reached, the employer may introduce unilateral changes in working conditions, provided that these changes are not materially different from those proposed during negotiations and do not affect elements not discussed during collective bargaining. AREEDA AND HOVENKAMP, note 102 *supra*, at 232 n. 40.

[126] AREEDA AND HOVENKAMP, note 102 *supra*, at 233. Compare Ross, note 68 *supra*, at 379–84 (structure and history of Canadian Competition Act suggest that Canadian courts should not protect from antitrust challenge restraints imposed on unconsenting players by owners after expiration of collective bargaining agreement). As with other private challenges to sports league labor restraints, the *Brown* case was brought by a unionized player. It is possible that the result would be different if the government or a consumer alleging an adverse effect on the product market brought the challenge.

[127] Telephone interview with Jeffrey A. Mishkin, former General Counsel, National Basketball Association (Nov. 1, 2007). The union expressed some concern about the agreement subsequent to its formation. It never challenged the agreement, however. The probable reason for this lack of challenge is that the union is not unhappy with the agreement's operation.

In contrast, the National Hockey League Players Association (NHLPA) was a full participant in the construction of the player transfer agreement between the NHL and the IIHF. Jeffrey P. Gleason, *From Russia with Love: The Legal Repercussions of the Recruitment and Contracting of Foreign Players in the National Hockey League*, 56 BUFF. L. REV. 599 (2008).

bargaining process. It involved a matter that the parties were required to negotiate collectively. And it concerned only the parties to the collective-bargaining relationship.[128]

None of these characteristics defined the negotiation of the NBA–FIBA Agreement.[129] Accordingly, it is questionable that this accord between domestic and foreign entities has a sufficiently close relationship to genuine collective bargaining to justify application of the nonstatutory labor exemption.[130]

The argument for application of the exemption must rest on the notion that the union 'could have' addressed the agreement, as its terms affected conditions of employment. The rules governing movement of players from Europe to the United States have effects on the wages and working conditions of current and future[131] NBA players and may affect the job security of players as well. Moreover, we are clearly not dealing with a case in which the NBA is alleged to have conspired with its players' union to drive some competitor out of the market for professional basketball, i.e. the kind of case where antitrust scrutiny would surely not be precluded. This argument is logically coherent in light of the extensive reach of the exemption articulated in *Brown*. But is not a scenario where the union is not a party to the agreement with a third party, has not participated in

---

[128]   *Brown*, note 124 *supra*, at 250.

[129]   This statement requires one qualification. It *may* be that all or some of the terms of the agreement constituted a mandatory subject of bargaining. The question of whether the league was obliged to engage the union did not arise at the time. But see Stephen F. Ross and Robert B. Lucke, *Why Highly Paid Athletes Deserve More Antitrust Protection than Ordinary Unionized Workers*, 42 ANTITRUST BULL. 641, 675–8 (1997) (whether challenged employer agreement relates to mandatory subject of bargaining under labor law is wrong question; ultimate inquiry should be whether the trade restraint facilitates the purposes of the NLRA; significance and value of distinctions drawn in labor law between mandatory and permissive subjects of bargaining is open to question). See also Noll, note 73 *supra*, at 617 (insistence that players choose either unionization or antitrust but not both as their sole weapon to combat monopsonization of sports leagues likely to be a bad policy outcome.)

As demonstrated *infra*, these conditions also did not characterize the agreement between MLB and the NPB. See text accompanying notes 172–5 *infra*.

[130]   See *Reed* v. *Advocate Health Care*, No. 06-C3337, 2007 U.S. Dist. LEXIS 22816 (N.D. Ill. March 28, 2007) (multi-employer conduct outside context of collective bargaining scenario not entitled to exemption). Following *Brown* – a case that largely focuses on the issue of *when* the labor exemption becomes available – the question these circumstances present is whether all antitrust claims are precluded whenever a union is not decertified (or defunct, or had its recognition properly withdrawn). A positive answer to that question would mean that labor law would trump antitrust law on matters unrelated to the collective bargaining agreement in all circumstances. Faced with this result, Professor Gould responds: 'My view is that that bridge, which the Court may cross in the years to come, at present is a bridge too far.' William B. Gould IV, *Globalization in Collective Bargaining, Baseball, and Matsuzaka: Labor and Antitrust Law on the Diamond*, 28 COMP. LAB. L. & POL'Y J. 283, 300, n. 66 (2007).

In her dissenting opinion in the *Brown* case in the D.C. Circuit Court of Appeals Judge Patricia Wald argued that the rule later adopted by the Supreme Court creates incentives unhelpful to the bargaining process. One of these negative consequences is that some 'employees will be encouraged to decertify their unions rather than risk unilateral multiemployer imposition of terms at impasse.' *Brown* v. *Pro Football, Inc.*, 50 F.3d 1041, 1065 (D.C. Cir. 1995).

[131]   See *Clarett* v. *Nat'l Football League*, 369 F.3d 124 (2d Cir. 2004); *Wood* v. *Nat'l Basketball Ass'n*, 809 F.2d 954 (2d Cir. 1987) (argument that individuals who were not current members of bargaining unit cannot be regulated by collective bargaining agreement rejected; potential employees are within purview of labor exemption).

its negotiation, and has not been notified of that negotiation and been given an opportunity to participate one that is 'sufficiently distant in time and in circumstances from the collective-bargaining process ... [so that] permitting antitrust intervention – [would] not significantly interfere with that process?'[132] To apply the exemption to this situation in the name of collective bargaining strikes me as an unwarranted reach, one that is unnecessary to avoid subversion of fundamental principles of federal labor policy.[133] That conclusion is reinforced if one recognizes the likely (undiscussed) adverse effects of *Brown* on consumers.[134]

RULE OF REASON ASSESSMENT ON THE MERITS

As the Sherman Act likely reaches the agreement, the next issue is the identification of the relevant market. When sports league practices have been subjected to antitrust challenge, whether by a member of the organization, a contractual partner, or an employee, the league has typically argued – generally unsuccessfully – for an expansive definition of the relevant market. For example, the NFL has contended that the relevant product market is not that for professional football, but rather that for all football, college and pro, or for all sports, or even for all entertainment.[135] The strategic reason for this effort is apparent – the more expansive the market definition the less consequential the challenged practice. Here, though, it seems clear that the relevant market is the (worldwide) market for basketball players. The focus is not on the league product but rather on the market for raw materials – players' services.[136]

---

[132]   *Brown*, note 124 *supra*, at 250.
[133]   In a situation where the arrangement results from the unilateral action of the two associations' executive offices with no union input sought or received – and it is a situation replicated in the origins of the MLB–NPB Agreement – it is quite a stretch to view the arrangements' terms as having been constructively bargained for.
[134]   Ross and Lucke, note 129 *supra*. The authors argue that in reconciling antitrust and labor policies the court incorrectly ignored consumer interests. The *Brown* decision, they contend, will harm sports fans (consumers) in two ways, neither of which is mentioned in the court's opinion. First, the decision increases the chances that management efforts to impose unreasonable trade restraints will produce strikes and other industrial disruption. Second, the restraints imposed by management that would be subject to antitrust challenge but for *Brown* will reduce competitive balance among teams in a league, thereby decreasing the quality and entertainment value of the product. The basic flaw in the opinion, they assert, is its failure to appreciate the distinctive economics of professional sports as compared with the typical unionized industry. Because labor market restraints in the sports setting can also significantly affect product quality – through the inefficient allocation of players among teams, particularly via restrictions that harm competitive balance by making it more difficult for inferior teams to improve – the public interest in competition ought to be sacrificed only when the benefits of labor peace are likely to be achieved. Ross (2003), note 64 *supra*, at 577–8.
[135]   See, e.g., *Los Angeles Memorial Coliseum Comm'n* v. *Nat'l Football League*, 726 F.2d 1381, 1393 (9th Cir. 1984) (Raiders claim relevant market consists of NFL football in Southern California; NFL argues market is all forms of entertainment across entire country). See also *Nat'l Collegiate Athletic Association* v. *Board of Regents of the University of Oklahoma*, 468 U.S. 85, 90 (1984) (college football broadcasts constitute separate market).
[136]   Of course, restraints on pursuit of foreign players affect the quality of the product available to American basketball consumers. Since the 1992–93 season the number of foreign-born players in

The anticompetitive effect of the basketball agreement is straightforward. The parties have agreed to buy on only certain terms. More precisely, in stipulating that players under contract are not to be approached in pursuit of their present services, they have agreed not to deal with suppliers of the service for a period of time. (One result of this collective arrangement is that a buyer can be comfortable in not talking with a player because he knows that other buyers will not be talking to players.) The leagues undoubtedly would note that the terms of their agreement simply track the existing contractual obligations. But that response would likely be inadequate. Antitrust law generally does not care about inducement of breach of contract.[137] Of course, some breaches may be efficient.[138] If a breach does, in fact, take place, the law of contracts is available to respond to it. Under antitrust law justification of an arrangement that improves the leagues' status beyond that provided by contract law requires some (pro-competitive) connection to product quality.[139]

---

the NBA has increased from 21, representing 18 countries, to 83, from 36 nations and territories, in the 2009–10 season. *Season Opens with Record-tying 83 International Players*, http:// www.nba.com/2009/news/10/27/international.players/index.html (international players = 22% of NBA population). Sixty percent of the NBA's foreign players come from Europe. Moreover, one-quarter of the 24 players who participated in the 2006 All Star Game were foreign-born. Greg Boeck, *Team-first, Back-to-Basics Foreigners Changing NBA*, USA TODAY, Apr. 20, 2006, at 1A. See generally JOZSA, note 83 *supra*, at 112–19, 251–2. For a brief history of foreign players in the NBA, see Harlan Schreiber, *Hoops Analyst: A History of Foreign Players in the NBA*, at http:// www.hoopsanalyst.com/eurohistory.html.

As with MLB, the inclusion of international athletes boosted television ratings of NBA games, particularly in the foreign countries and cities where those players had previously performed. JOZSA, note 83 *supra*, at 16. In the past decade most North American sports leagues have been characterized by increased recruitment and expanded employment of foreign or non-native American athletes in the United States. See, e.g., JOZSA, note 83 *supra*, at 147, 149 (composition of NHL players).

137   See generally *PermaLife Mufflers, Inc.* v. *Int'l Parts Corp.*, 392 U.S. 134 (1968) (no doctrine of clean hands); Herbert Hovenkamp, *The Antitrust Enterprise: Principle and Execution: An Introduction*, 31 J. CORP. L. 287, 291 (2006) ('Punishing unfair behavior is not antitrust's role. Its purpose is to make markets perform more competitively …').

138   See, e.g., E. ALLAN FARNSWORTH, *ET AL.*, CONTRACTS 7–8 (6th ed. 2001) (the economics of remedies, efficient breach).

139   A recent European soccer case is instructive. In 1999 Nicolas Anelka announced that he no longer wished to honor his contract to play for Arsenal in the UK and wished to move to an Italian team, Lazio. Anelka had 4 years to run on his contract. Arsenal was not prepared to release him and Lazio was not ready to pay the sizable transfer fee that Arsenal required. The argument was made that to prevent a player from terminating his employment agreement (and paying damages), as the transfer system did, is as much an impermissible restraint on a player's freedom of movement as the situation in *Bosman*, where a player was prevented from moving to another team on the expiration of his contract. There was no authoritative assessment of this argument, as the dispute was settled. Gardiner and Welch, note 80 *supra*, at 121–2. See generally Andrew Caiger and John O'Leary, *The End of the Affair: The 'Anelka Doctrine' – The Problem of Contract Stability in English Professional Football*, in PROFESSIONAL SPORT IN THE EUROPEAN UNION: REGULATION AND RE-REGULATION 197 (Andrew Caiger and Simon Gardiner eds., 2000); Bell, note 12 *supra*; STEPHEN WEATHERILL, *Annotation [Bosman Case]*, in EUROPEAN SPORTS LAW: COLLECTED PAPERS 87, 113 (2007) (transfer system applicable to in-contract players violates Article 48 of EC Treaty). For the conclusion that such industry behavior – more particularly, the blocking of player transfers where those players have unilaterally terminated their contracts and fulfilled relevant

An instructive analogy to the claim that the agreement simply operates to prevent and remediate breaches of contract and therefore should be deemed reasonable is present in the case of *Fashion Originators Guild (FOGA)* v. *FTC*.[140] There a group of manufacturers of women's garments and textile fabrics joined together to protect their creations from copying by other manufacturers. To eliminate this form of competition by other manufacturers, the organization's members agreed to decline to sell their products to retailers who sold copied garments. This concerted refusal to deal was intended to deny the alleged design 'pirates' access to adequate retail distribution facilities and thus to narrow the outlets to which garment and textile manufacturers could sell and the sources from which retailers could buy. Most significant for our purposes was the court's response to the offered justification that the scheme was designed to protect the defendants' intellectual property rights and defend them from unauthorized copying. After noting that the question of whether copying of dress designs is tortious is a matter of state law, the court states that the designers' collective arrangement would be illegal even if the conduct were tortious under the laws of every state. In other words, elimination of design 'piracy' would not justify the boycott under scrutiny even if copying were a tort under the law of every state.[141]

Put somewhat differently, the Guild is not authorized to act as self-appointed condemnor of design 'pirates' and to determine, and enforce, a rule as to what copying is or is not permissible. It is true that FOGA involved the severe restraint of a boycott that elicited – and would likely elicit today – application of the *per se* rule while the basketball accord would be assessed under the rule of reason. But the same concerns about extra-governmental law making – here in the context of contract rather than tort law – are clearly present.[142]

The parties might counter that the collective agreement not to approach players aims to prevent the disorder of litigation, particularly in-season litigation, the potential decline in player motivation that the prospect of such approaches might induce, the administrative disruption that the curtailed behavior might produce, and the negative impact on fans'

---

obligations under national employment law – constitutes a violation of EC competition rules, see Pons, note 90 *supra*.

[140]   312 U.S. 457 (1941).

[141]   *Ibid.* at 468. HOVENKAMP, note 38 *supra*, at 272:

> [E]ven if such [intellectual property] rights existed, the defendants would not have been permitted to pursue them by means of a boycott but instead would have had to assert them in a court that could determine both the validity of the claimed rights and the factual issue of infringement.

[142]   In its opinion the court noted the Guild's complex regulatory machinery, including an elaborate system of trial and appellate tribunals that operated to determine whether a particular garment was in fact a copy of a Guild member's design. FOGA, note 140 *supra*, at 462–3. *FOGA*, in which the guild members tried to give themselves the 'intellectual property' protection that the legislative and judicial branches had denied them, is one of a number of cases in which courts have struck down industry efforts at self-regulation on the ground that the restraints imposed constituted 'private government.' 1 PHILLIP E. AREEDA AND HERBERT HOVENKAMP, ANTITRUST LAW 505 (2nd ed. 2000). See AREEDA AND KAPLOW, note 100 *supra*, at 405 (judges unquestionably hostile to private lawmaking; hostility is historical fact that also enjoys support in principle). The basketball agreement contains an arbitration provision for the resolution of disputes that might arise about the contract status of players

identification with their team.[143] These effects are surely possible and concern about them can be seen, at least in part, as tied to a desire to offer a better product. Thus, administrative confusion may affect the planning needed to produce an improved product. Moreover, the security of the relationship between team and supporter and the wider local community may be undercut.[144] At the same time, the force of this kind of argument should be discounted. Skepticism about the incidence and import of these effects is probably warranted in light of the judicial rejection of similar arguments in non-antitrust cases involving new leagues that signed players for future services[145] and in light of the existence of contractual remedies.

A stronger, and more basic, justification for the basketball accord lies in a contention about the ties between the two leagues. More particularly, it can be claimed that the smooth operation of the foreign leagues, which, for example, provide valuable player training, is important to the quality of the American league. This focus on the (present) interaction between the two leagues, and particularly on the training function provided by the European leagues, points, in turn, to a critical question about the proper conception of their market relationship, the answer to which has marked consequences for antitrust analysis. Put simply, are the European leagues competitors of the NBA or suppliers of the NBA? If the parties to the accord are competing with each other for talent, then the accord is properly viewed as a horizontal agreement that limits competition for raw materials, an agreement that traditionally and properly elicits reservations under antitrust analysis. Furthermore, justification for the agreement would have to lie in the creation of a better product for both parties. On the other hand, if the foreign league functions as a supplier of raw materials, the relationship would properly be seen as vertical and, thus, be easier to defend. For example, a rule limiting the timing of when the NBA can sign a player from a foreign league could aim to insure that the training league stays in business. And the arrangement could be seen as contributing to a better NBA product, one that permits it to better compete with other entertainment offerings.

This question of the relationship between the leagues is an empirical one, the answer to which may change over time (with corresponding legal consequences). Presently, and

---

[143]   A practice in a very different setting that is largely rooted in a desire to avoid program disruption is that of the Association of American Law Schools (AALS) that urges member schools to make an offer of an indefinite appointment as a teacher during the following academic year no later March 1. See text accompanying notes 39–40 *supra*. Similarly, faculty members are urged not to resign later than March 15 to accept a position at another law school during the next academic year. The stated objectives of the practice are to give a school sufficient time to make arrangements to find another instructor to offer the instruction given by the departing teacher, to not frustrate the reasonable expectations of students and to not otherwise disrupt the school's educational program.

[144]   See Gardiner and Welch, note 80 *supra*, at 125–6:

[I]t is undesirable to allow players to move – a l'Anelka – as and when they think fit. This is detrimental to the employer but this is not the central problem. The key specificity with respect to professional football is the relationship between club and supporter and the wider local community ... For many football supporters their sense of self-identity is fused with the identity of their club. Loyal fans of football clubs – big and small – should be allowed some sense of security through the knowledge that players under contract cannot just leave the club at the drop of a hat.

[145]   See text accompanying notes 19–20 and 78 and notes 20, 28, and 78–9 *supra*.

historically, the answer to the question of market definition, of who competes with whom, is that the foreign leagues are suppliers, rather than competitors of, the NBA in the labor market.[146] That is, the movement of high-quality basketball players goes in one direction – from Europe to the United States.[147] American players do play in Europe, but they are generally players who are not talented enough to play in the NBA[148] or NBA players who are now in the declining years of their careers.[149]

---

[146]   See, e.g., Joseph D. Robbins, *Katash: Lior Eliyahu is Perfect NBA Prospect*, JERUSALEM POST, June 20, 2006, available at http://www.jpost.com/servlet/Satellite?cid=1150355529073& pagename=JPost%2FLPArticel%2FShowFull (player prospects placed on teams in home countries to grow stronger and develop further before attempting to play in NBA); Didier Primault, *European Professional Basketball in Crisis: 1992–2002*, in HANDBOOK ON THE ECONOMICS OF SPORT 530 (Wladimir Andreff and Stefan Szymanski eds., 2007) (an appendix of the American labour market); Victor A. Matheson, *European Football (Soccer)*, in HANDBOOK OF SPORTS ECONOMICS RESEARCH 118, 123 (John Fizel ed., 2006) (NBA sole purchaser of athletic talent within its sport; pay in foreign leagues only fraction of American counterpart). See generally Michael Solove, *From Tel Aviv to the Space Needle, by Way of Slovenia*, Play, N.Y. TIMES SPORTS MAGAZINE, Nov. 2006, at 58 (players from outside the United States play a different game and bring needed elements of skill and cleverness that have all but disappeared from the American style). Cf. Chris Miller, *Comment: Hockey's Cold War – Russia's Defiance of the IIHF and the Evgeny Malkin Saga*, 17 SETON HALL J. SPORTS & ENT. L. 163, 187–8, nn. 174, 195 (2007) (questionable that NHL and Russian Super League are in direct competition since NHL is world's premier hockey league and Russian teams do not usually sign players directly away from NHL rosters). But see Kenneth L. Shropshire, *Thoughts on International Professional Sports Leagues and the Application of United States Antitrust Laws*, 67 DENV. U. L. REV. 193, 201 (1990) (overseas basketball leagues have served as negotiating alternative for NBA players; threat of playing in another country used in basketball negotiations); Heather E. Morrow, *The Wide World of Sports is Getting Wider: A Look at Drafting Foreign Players into U.S. Professional Sports*, 26 HOUSTON J. INT'L L. 649, 690 (2004) (foreign players immediately accepted as NBA-caliber athletes).
   In football, the CFL may be similarly characterized as a minor league that feeds its best players to the NFL; and legal assessment of the relationship between the two leagues should reflect this characterization. While the CFL plays on a larger field and has other rule differences that produce distinctions in strategy and the optimal combination of player skills, many CFL players, after proving their quality, move on to the NFL. Noll, note 64 *supra*, at 535. If the rules of two leagues are dramatically different, cross-league player exchanges are less attractive. *Ibid.* at 543. But see generally Michael Schwirtz, *A New Miracle on Ice: Russia is Luring Back N.H.L. Stars*, N.Y. TIMES, Feb. 29, 2008, at A1 (Russia's professional league expects to catch and surpass the NHL as the world's premier hockey league); Jeff S. Klein, *Matters of Finance and Safety Unsettled as Season Begins*, N.Y. TIMES, Oct. 2, 2009, at B9 (NHL is locked in battle with Russian Kontinental Hockey League over player signings and, ultimately, control over the lucrative European market).
[147]   See generally Neale, note 72 *supra*, at 7 n. 6 (pressure for US–Japanese baseball competition and US–Canadian football competition is low because it is not widely believed that the Japanese or Canadians might win). However, signing foreign players is one way for American sports leagues to tap into new markets across the globe and to broaden their geographical appeal, and this practice points to some overlap in player and fan base. See, e.g., JOZSA, note 83 *supra*, at 16.
[148]   See generally Primault, note 146 *supra* (European leagues are an appendix of the American labour market). But see Robert McG. Thomas, Jr., *Ferry Will Play for Rome Team Instead of Signing with Clippers*, N.Y. TIMES, Aug. 2, 1989, at A17; GREENBERG, note 22 *supra*, at 3–107–08. The movement of Brian Shaw, though not a star player, might be viewed as an exception to this proposition. See *Boston Celtics, LP v. Shaw*, 908 F.2d 1041 (1st Cir. 1990). A more notable exception to this pattern of movement was the recent move of Josh Childress, the Atlanta Hawks' top reserve last season, to the Greek club, Olympiakos. *From N.B.A. to Europe, Player Reverses a Trend*, N.Y.

MLB–NPB AGREEMENT

Much of this analysis of the NBA–FIBA Agreement has application to an assessment of the legality of the United States–Japanese Player Contract Agreement,[150] the present accord between MLB and the Japanese baseball leagues that provides for the transfer of

---

TIMES, July 24, 2008, at C16 (Childress can make more money overseas than as a restricted free agent in the NBA; strength of euro against dollar gives international clubs the resources to pursue high-level American players.) For the suggestion that such moves will be unexceptional in the future, see Posting of Sam Smith to HoopsHype NBA Blog, http://blogs.hoopshype.com/blogs/smith/ 2008/07/22/the-great-escape/ (July 22, 2008, 07:23 EST); Chris Mannix, *My Big Fat Greek Deal*, SPORTS ILLUSTRATED, Aug. 4, 2008, at 22. See also Andy Katz, *Jennings Goes Pro, Signs with Pallacanestro Virtus Roma*, ESPN.COM, July 17, 2008, http://sports.espn.go.com/ncb/news/ story?id=3491998 (high school star passes up college to play professionally in Europe); Ian Whittell, *The Lure of Europe – Fact and Fiction*, http://sports.espn.go.com/nba/news/story?page=euroam factfiction (last visited July 6, 2009) (though options of lower-level NBA players have significantly broadened, signings of Childress and Jennings do not mark end of NBA as we know it).

Were foreign leagues to become authentic comparable sources of substitute professional opportunities for basketball players, the likely result of the more competitive market for player services – as with the existence of a rival domestic league – would be an upward shift in player compensation and change in the collective bargaining relationship between the NBA and the NBPA.

[149]   Foreign leagues regulate the employment of players from abroad in other ways. One contemporary example is a parallel set of exclusionary rules, one in football and the other in basketball. The CFL has a by-law, instituted in the spring of 2007, that prohibits a team from signing a player currently under suspension in the NFL. FIBA has a similar rule that respects NBA suspensions and bans employment of suspended NBA players. (The rule that bars an NFL player serving a suspension from signing a CFL contract was a response, in part, to criticism over the 2006 signing by the Toronto Argonauts of running back Ricky Williams, who was under suspension by the NFL for drug use. Rick Matsumoto, *Vick Won't Find a Home in CFL*, TORONTO STAR, Aug. 22, 2007, at S4, available at LEXIS, News Library, TSTAR File.)

Do the CFL and FIBA exclusionary rules run afoul of United States antitrust law? The initial question is whether American law would reach this regulation that bans access to a foreign market. Here, as a matter of substantive jurisdiction and/or comity, it is doubtful that a United States court would subject the foreign leagues' practices to a rule of reason assessment.

As previously noted (see text accompanying notes 92–5 *supra*), the reach of American antitrust laws is not limited to conduct occurring within the boundaries of the United States. Anticompetitive conduct that affects United States domestic or foreign commerce may violate those laws independent of where that conduct occurs or the nationality of those involved. But that extraterritorial reach is circumscribed by statute and judicial doctrine. The Foreign Trade Antitrust Improvements Act (FTAIA), 15 U.S.C. § 6a (2000), removes foreign commercial activity from the ambit of the Sherman Act unless that activity has a direct, substantial, and reasonably foreseeable effect on exports of goods or services from the United States. Is the effect of the suspension rules 'substantial'? While the employment markets for professional football players beyond the CFL and for professional basketball players beyond the FIBA-sanctioned leagues are limited, the effect of the rule would likely be regarded as insubstantial. Though theoretically all NFL and NBA players are affected, only a very small number would move between the leagues in the absence of the rule. Whether viewed through a de minimus or proportionality lens, a small portion of the foreign market is affected.

The 'substantiality' conclusion is reinforced by considerations of comity. The alleged offenders are foreign entities whose principal places of business are located abroad. Also, there is no explicit purpose to harm American commerce. Moreover, the significance of effects on the United States is relatively small as compared with the effects in Canada and Europe; and conduct abroad, rather than conduct in the United States, is central to the violations charged. In addition, both Canada and

Japanese players to MLB.[151] The agreement governs the movement of non-free agent players between the two leagues. The cornerstone of the agreement is the posting system. Under that system American clubs are allowed to bid for a Japanese player, made available by a Japanese team, with exclusive negotiating rights going to the club that submits the highest bid.[152]

---

the European Union have active antitrust regimes (and adequate incentive to police anticompetitive conduct engaged in there). These considerations suggest that an American court should decline to exercise Sherman Act jurisdiction on comity grounds. See text accompanying notes 195–9 *infra*.

What would be the antitrust status of the foreign leagues' rules if United States law were, in fact, applicable? It seems clear that if these rules reflected not unilateral conduct but agreement between the American and foreign leagues, such an agreement would violate the Sherman Act. The American league would be looking to extend the geographical reach of its disciplinary action without a convincing justification that the player's employment abroad would damage its product and market here. See generally text accompanying notes 41–6 *supra* (MLB's ban on employment of former Mexican League players).

Though the CFL and FIBA are undoubtedly motivated, in part, by a desire to maintain a good relationship with their American counterparts – the CFL, e.g., has received financial support from the NFL – no formal agreement to honor suspensions presently exists. What justifications, beyond the maintenance of good relations, might the foreign leagues offer for their rules that bar employment? Is the rule's anticipated effect the production of a better product? Tarnishment would be a principal concern. Thus, the CFL does not want to be seen as a repository for castoffs. The underlying assumption is that employment of those under suspension, in particular drug users, would damage the marketability of the league's product. This assertion is surely plausible. In an analogous situation, arbitrators passing on the 'just cause' of discipline of baseball players for drug use have accepted the contention that such behavior may well harm the sport through its threat to athletes' playing abilities and the increased chance of a dangerous involvement with criminals who sell the drugs, an involvement that could lead to control of the player (either because of addiction or because of the risk of exposure). See, e.g., *Kuhn* v. *Major League Baseball Players Ass'n (Willie Wilson, Jerry Martin)*, Panel Dec. No. 54 (April 3, 1984) (Bloch, Arb.) (player use of drugs a matter of legitimate collective concern; perception of taint potentially damaging).

But what of an employment ban triggered by a suspension for behavior, particularly off-field behavior, that is not drug-related, e.g, for offensive speech or for engagement in dog fighting? In these situations, as well, the league can surely assert that its product will be blemished. See generally Lewis Kurlantzik, *John Rocker and Employee Discipline for Speech*, 18 LAB. LAW. 439 (2001); Marvin F. Hill, Jr. and Mark L. Kahn, *Discipline and Discharge for Off-Duty Misconduct: What Are the Arbitral Standards?*, in ARBITRATION 1986: CURRENT AND EXPANDING ROLES 121 (Walter J. Gershenfeld ed., 1986). However, reflection on the claim points to the uncomfortable fact that a tarnishment justification is difficult to contain and its vulnerability to expansiveness makes it a candidate for pretextual use. (In its difficulty of containment and potential for expansion it resembles the common assertion that athletes are 'role models.') In any case, the underlying factual assertion of market protection can be contested with proof of a lack of nexus such that the market for the league product would not be harmed by employment of a suspended player. After all, it is not patent that a player's off-field misconduct, at least all off-field misconduct, affects the league's pocketbook.

Does the CFL's reliance on the NFL's decision and its failure to conduct its own, independent inquiry affect the analysis of the antitrust legality of its behavior? Presumably, if it had to defend the reasonableness of its practice, the CFL would contend that the NFL is in a much better position to assess the player's conduct, as witnesses and other relevant evidence are more readily available to it. More generally, the presence or absence of due-process like regularities or explanations – e.g., notice and an opportunity to be heard – in a decision-making process that denies access to a prospective employee cannot determine antitrust liability. In the absence of a relevant regulatory regime, the antitrust laws do not impose a requirement of process. Compare *Silver* v. *New York Stock Exchange*,

Under the agreement's provisions, during the off-season Japanese teams can post the names of players they are willing to make available. Any interested American team can then submit a bid. The MLB Commissioner determines the highest bidder and that team has 30 days to try to sign the player. The offer represents the amount to be paid to the Japanese team if the American team does sign the player. Thus, if the American team and the player come to terms, the Japanese team is paid the bid, and the player moves to the United States. If the Japanese club finds the bid unacceptable or the American club fails to sign the player after reaching agreement with his team, the player's name is removed from

---

373 U.S. 341 (1963) with *Northwest Wholesale Stationers, Inc.* v. *Pacific Stationery & Printing Co.*, 472 U.S. 284 (1985). A claimant must introduce evidence of an antitrust violation under the rule of reason quite apart from any lack of procedural fairness in the method of his exclusion. However, the absence of process may be relevant in considering whether a proffered justification is a sham. 8 HERBERT HOVENKAMP, ANTITRUST LAW 324–32 (2nd ed. 2005). See also *Is the 'Ricky Williams Rule' About to Be Sacked?*, Posting of Marc Edelman to Sports Law Blog, http://sports-law.blogspot.com (Aug. 25, 2007, 13:23 EST) (less restrictive alternatives exist for the CFL to prevent entry of troublesome players; league can review candidacy of prospective players on case-by-case basis). (A potential problematic aspect of the exclusionary rule's operation is that while it prohibits suspended NFL players from playing in the CFL, CFL players who engage in similar conduct may not necessarily be suspended.)

Whether a FIBA ban based on a NBA suspension violates European Union competition law or related national law is an independent question. *Re Federation Internationale de Basketball*, 117 F. Supp. 2d 403 (S.D.N.Y. 2000) (German court preliminarily enjoins FIBA ban of Stanley Roberts on grounds that its drug policy was unenforceable under German law because it was not reflected in its charter; Roberts also contended that FIBA should not be permitted to rely on the NBA's determination.)

For an example of a different sort of foreign league restriction on player employment, see text accompanying note 192 *infra* (Japanese Professional Baseball League rule limiting number of foreign players per team).

150   Perusal of the FIBA–NBA Agreement leaves the reader with the distinct impression that the draftsmen of the document were very much aware of potential antitrust issues. Reading the MLB–Japanese Professional Baseball League Agreement does not produce the same reaction.

As a practical matter it is unlikely that the baseball accord will be subjected to antitrust challenge, as the logical claimant to assert the claim in the United States would be a Japanese baseball player. Thus, Daisuke Matsuzaka might have sued on the theory that the negotiated process restrained him (and others in Japan) from pursuing his vocation. Realistically, such a suit is improbable. But see generally William B. Gould IV, *Baseball and Globalization,* 8 IND. J. GLOBAL LEGAL STUD. 85, 120 (2000) (antitrust actions filed by dissatisfied Japanese, Korean, and Australian players).

151   For an account of prior Japanese–American understandings and the discord they produced, see Robert Whiting, THE MEANING OF ICHIRO (2004).

152   Two other routes to MLB for a Japanese player exist. One is to obtain an outright release; the other is to exercise his rights as an international free agent after playing nine full seasons. A key element of the agreement is that each side will respect the other's rights to players.

The route to free agency is an arduous one. Japanese players become international free agents only after they spend at least 150 days on a Division 1 roster for nine seasons. In fact, most players never become free agents and those that do take a mean 11.5 years. See Minoru Nakazato and J. Mark Ramseyer, Bonuses and Biases in Japanese Baseball 8 (Discussion Paper No. 589, Harvard John M. Olin Discussion Paper Series, June 2007); Robert Whiting, *MLB's Effect on Japan: NPB Players in Need of Strong Union like MLBPA* (pt. 4), THE JAPAN TIMES, Apr. 14, 2007, available at http://search.japantimes.co.jp/cgi-bin/sb20070414cl.html (free agency rules are model of obfuscation designed to frustrate player from choosing freely where he wants to work). See also Whiting, note 151 *supra,* at 84–5, 87–95, 142 (history of reserve clause and free agency in Japan).

the available list and is not eligible to be posted again until the following year.[153] In this situation the major league team is refunded its posting fee.[154]

The baseball accord is more restrictive in some respects than the NBA–FIBA Agreement and less restrictive in other respects. It is more restrictive in that it prohibits any communication between the potential employer and the player and in that it requires a payment to the team in order to gain access to the player. It is less restrictive in that it

---

[153]   For an assessment of the potential problems in contract enforcement posed by the posting system, see Casey Duncan, *Stealing Signs: Is Professional Baseball's United States-Japanese Player Contract Agreement Enough To Avoid Another 'Baseball War'?*, 13 MINN. J. GLOBAL TRADE 87, 109–112 (2003).

The MLB–NPB Agreement does not address the signing of either country's amateur players. The recent courting of a high-profile Japanese pitching prospect by major league teams has strained relations between baseball entities in the two countries, as Japanese officials allege that there is an established understanding that places amateurs there off limits to major league clubs. Alan Schwarz and Brad Lefton, *Japanese Are Irked by U.S. Interest in Pitcher*, N.Y. TIMES, Nov. 20, 2008, at B12. Whether or not, in fact, a gentleman's agreement that precluded offers from Major League teams before an amateur played, or even signed, with a Japanese team existed is unclear. See *ibid*. Were there such an agreement limiting recruitment of amateur players in each country by professional teams in the other, that restrictive arrangement would violate the Sherman Act.

[154]   The same rules govern the movement of players from the United States to Japan. However, the posting mechanism has never been invoked with respect to the move of an American player under contract to the Japanese leagues.

MLB, on the other hand, has been able to attract major Japanese stars such as Hideki Matsui (Yankees) and Ichiro Suzuki (Mariners). The result has been the generation of enormous Japanese media coverage of and fan interest in the American game. The financial benefits for MLB, in the form of greatly increased licensing sales and broadcast revenues, have been considerable. ANDREW ZIMBALIST, IN THE BEST INTERESTS OF BASEBALL? 191–2, 234 n. 45 (2006). See JOZSA, note 83 *supra*, at 16. In fact, more generally, the use of foreign baseball players has become a productive strategy for MLB to globally promote and expand the sport. For an historical list of posted players and the results of the process in their cases, see *Posting System*, at http://www.baseball-reference.com/bpv/index.php?title=Posting_System. The movement of Japanese players is part of a broader phenomenon whereby the proportion of MLB players who were born outside the United States has been measurably increasing. In fact, the import of foreign players, along with the league's interest in global sponsorship and licensing agreements and its opportunities to broadcast its teams' games abroad, led MLB to restructure its international business activities into one organizational unit (MLBI–Major League Baseball International) in the late 1980s. The other U.S. professional sports leagues have formed similar units within their organizations. JOZSA, note 83 *supra*, at 30, 42.

When major leaguers first began to compete in the Japanese League, they most often were at the end of their careers. In the past decade a change has occurred in the composition of the players moving from the United States to Japan, and the movement of players between the two countries has become more common and more nuanced. ALAN M. KLEIN, GROWING THE GAME: THE GLOBALIZATION OF MAJOR LEAGUE BASEBALL 166–7 (2006). Thus, players are now more often mid-career players who have been unable to secure an everyday role on a major league team. Often, these players choose to go to Japan so they will have a chance to play and contribute every day. They also realize a substantial increase in salary. However, while a player may make substantial contributions to his team, he is unlikely, as a foreigner, to ever be fully accepted. Paul Mrokzka, *Major League Baseball Players in Japan – Strangers in Paradise*, at http://ezinearticles.com/?Major-League-Baseball-Players-in-Japan–Strangers-in -Paradise&id=192531. See generally KLEIN, *supra*, at 125–68 (cultural tension producing ambivalence about American players). A unique exception to this pattern was Bob Horner, who at the age of 29 went to play in Japan while still in his prime. See Alexander Wolff, *A New Kind of Orient Express*, SPORTS ILLUSTRATED, May 18, 1987, at 28. See also ROBERT WHITING, YOU GOTTA HAVE WA 5–26 (1989).

permits the potential employer to bid for a player who is presently under contract. This posting system[155] was constructed to benefit the Japanese team owners, as it allows them to maintain the integrity of their game and to control the flow of players to the United States.[156] Is the agreement a violation of the Sherman Act?

---

[155]   For criticism of the shortcomings of the posting process and suggestion of improvements that would make the process a more efficient arrangement that correctly determines both the player's value and the value of the posting team's contract rights, see Allan T. Ingraham, *A Fair Posting Process for Japanese Professionals Entering Major League Baseball*, ENT. & SPORTS L., Winter 2007, at 1. See generally Duncan, note 153 *supra*, at 117–22 (proposed modifications); Gould, note 130 *supra*, at 293–4; Gould, note 150 *supra*, at 115 (problems with Japanese agreement). One possible direction of improvement from the players' perspective would be to permit a player to be 'redrafted' by another club should the club that originally selected him fail to sign him within a limited time. This alteration in the posting system that would allow a player to re-enter the system during the designated posting period if contract negotiations fail is analogous to the rules governing the baseball draft under which an unsigned player goes back into the 'draft pool' after 6 months. See Major League Baseball Official Rules §§ 4(h)–(j) (2005); Leonard Koppett, *Baseball's New Draft*, N.Y. TIMES, Feb. 28, 1965, § 5, at 2. For comparison of the posting system to the transfer fee system in European soccer, see DUANE W. ROCKERBIE, PECULIARITIES OF THE MAJOR LEAGUE BASE-BALL POSTING SYSTEM (2006).

[156]   The agreement prevents the loss of non-free agent players without any compensation to the teams. Moreover, the requirement of team consent to both the initial posting and to the acceptability of the bid amount provides teams with significant control over the release of their players. However, the increased popularity of the United States game in Japan has led to a diminution in the popularity of the Japanese game in recent years. ZIMBALIST, note 154 *supra*, at 191.

The Japanese Professional Baseball Players Association never ratified the posting agreement. In fact, it was never consulted about its imposition by the owners.

Interestingly, the agreement imposes no limit on the number of players who can be posted over a period of time. Compare note 84 *supra* (IIHF–NHL Agreement, annual limit on transfers). Such limits can dampen competition. Thus, a MLB team will recognize that, at some point, it does not have to worry about other teams competing for Japanese players. However, these kinds of limits might reflect a justifiable concern about possible large-scale turnover of a team's roster in a short period of time with the consequent negative effect on fan identification. In the present situation such a limit is unnecessary both because the Japanese team controls whether or not to post a player and because there are not enough high-quality Japanese players of interest to MLB to raise the concern. The agreement does provide, though, that if the team with exclusive negotiating rights is unable to come to terms with the posted player, that player cannot be posted again until the following November.

The attitude of the Japanese baseball establishment to the movement of players to and from MLB is one of marked ambivalence. On the one hand, they take pride in the display of excellence by Japanese players in the United States. On the other hand, the increasing foreign attention and the steady outflow of talent from Japan fuels a perception, and self-perception, of the NPB as a feeder organization for MLB, helpless to stop the move of the league's best players out of the country. See Robert Whiting, *MLB's Effect on Japan: Is the MLB Destroying Japan's National Pastime?* (pt. 1), JAPAN TIMES, Apr. 11, 2007, available at http://search.japantimes.co.jp/print/sb2007041cl.html. Moreover, while economic gains may accrue from the employment of foreigners, the concern persists that such employment may have a corrupting influence on cherished traditions and on team harmony. See David Goldblatt, *Off Base*, TIMES LITERARY SUPPLEMENT, June 22, 2007, at 24 ('Japan's position is ... ambiguous, as the two baseball cultures and their professional leagues compete and cooperate for labour, kudos and television audiences in a complex dance of mutual incomprehension'). See generally Whiting, note 151 *supra*, at 73 (non-economic conflict, example of difference in Japanese and United States attitudes towards contracts and human relations).

The initial question, again, is jurisdictional. With respect to import commerce – the importation of player services – the standard test is whether the conduct was meant to produce and did in fact produce some substantial effect in the United States.[157] The answer is not as incontrovertible as in the basketball context. A few Japanese baseball players have moved to the United States,[158] but the potential for more large-scale movement is apparent.[159] The quality of the best Japanese players and the draw of the competition and exposure of the American major leagues make it likely that the future will see a rise in player mobility.

With respect to personal jurisdiction, the key questions about legitimacy of service and constitutionality of asserted federal judicial authority are the same as with FIBA. Thus, does the Japanese Professional Baseball League (NPB) have the requisite contacts with the United States so that haling it into court would not be fundamentally unfair?

It is doubtful that the required contacts exist. The NPB does not maintain an office or any other permanent address in the United States. Moreover, it has no internet presence here.[160] It is true that owners of particular teams operate internationally and do business in the United States. Unlike the typical ownership arrangements of American sports franchises, which are controlled by individuals or groups of individuals, the Japanese baseball clubs are generally owned by large corporations and serve to advertise the products and services of their corporate owners.[161] For example, Lotte Group, owner of the Pacific League Chiba Lotte Marines, is a major South Korean–Japanese conglomerate

---

[157]   See text accompanying notes 92–4 *supra*. Though the agreement applies to the export of services of MLB players as well, that application, at this point in time, is only hypothetical. See note 154 *supra*.

[158]   As of 2007 31 Japanese players had made the transition to MLB. See *Japanese Players in the Majors*, http://sports.espn.go.com/mlb/asia/news/story?id=2232362 (last visited Sept. 30, 2007).

[159]   Though to date the number of Japanese players joining MLB teams has been relatively small, there are likely to be more postings in coming years:

> Japanese players are good. Bobby Valentine, who manages in Japan, said three years ago that every starting position player in Japan could make a major league team. And the pitching there is getting better and better, as was proven again this past March when Japan, led by [Daisuke] Matsuzaka, won the 2006 World Baseball Classic.

Tim Kurkjian, *Posting Process Needs To Be Altered*, ESPN THE MAGAZINE, Dec. 15, 2006, available at http://sports.espn.go.com/mlb/columns/story?columnist=kurkjian_time&id=2697354.

See also WHITING, note 151 *supra*, at 261–2 (reasons why movement of players to the United Stated certain to continue). For a brief historical account of the movement of Japanese players to the United States, see Jim Albright, *Why Haven't We Had More Japanese Players in the Majors?*, at http://baseballguru.com/jalbright/analysisjalbright15.html. The posting system indicates both that MLB has the institutional power to bring about changes in Japan and that the Japanese players are now of a sufficient caliber to attract major league interest.

[160]   The league does maintain a website, but it communicates only in Japanese. There is disagreement among Japanese team owners about the desirability of marketing their game abroad. Apparently, Pacific League owners are more open than their Central League counterparts to the idea of promotion to North America. Generally, though, NPB has been averse to dealings with North America.

[161]   See Whiting, note 151 *supra*, at 89–91 (ballclub ownership not primarily concerned with making a profit; system of corporate sponsorship v. business orientation). Thus, unlike American pro teams, Japanese professional baseball teams are usually named after their corporate owners or sponsors rather than the cities in which they play.

with major operations in the United States. Similarly, Nippon Meat Packers, Inc., owner of the Hokkaido Nippon Ham Fighters, maintains production facilities and a sales operation in the United States. However, there is no reason to attribute these non-baseball-related activities to the NPB or to disregard the ownership structure. Thus, it is unlikely that personal jurisdiction over the Japanese Baseball League can be achieved constitutionally.

While an American court likely cannot assert jurisdiction over the NPB, the MLB–NPB Agreement would still be subject to antitrust scrutiny. There remains an agreement among the 30 major league teams that they will not bid for Japanese players except pursuant to the terms of the agreement.[162] And there is no impediment to jurisdiction over MLB and its constituent franchises. However, before facing the antitrust merits a potential litigant must confront the additional obstacle posed by the unusual status of MLB under federal (and state) antitrust law. As a result of a set of three Supreme Court decisions ('the trilogy'),[163] it is commonly understood that 'the business of baseball' is exempt from antitrust scrutiny.[164] Determination of whether this 'exemption' precludes the challenge requires analysis of 1) the scope of the exemption as a matter of judicial precedent and 2) the effect of the Curt Flood Act of 1998[165] on the extent of the exemption.

The contours of the exemption are particularly imprecise as it is no longer attributable to a limited federal authority over interstate commerce; grounded in neither principle nor policy, it is simply an historical aberration. Thus, standard forms of legal reasoning that might be invoked – for example, *cessante ratione legis, cessat et ipsa lex* – are of no aid, as there is no underlying rationale to guide delineation of the exemption's limits. The result is some uncertainty as to which aspects of the sport come within the grant of immunity. Courts, however, have consistently refused to extend the reach of the exemption to baseball's dealings with outside parties, such as merchandisers,[166] concessionaires,[167] and broadcasters.[168] Though one could argue that an arrangement affecting the player labor market is integral to the sport, an agreement with a foreign league appears closer to these precedents involving dealings with outside parties than to an arrangement tied to baseball's internal league structure, such as a rule about franchise relocation.[169] Indeed, it is difficult to defend the extension into the international domain of what is an historical

---

162   MLB's (and its teams') status as a party to the agreement is important not only jurisdictionally but also remedially. See text accompanying notes 190–1 *infra*. These points would apply to the NBA–FIBA Agreement as well.

163   *Flood* v. *Kuhn*, 407 U.S. 258 (1972); *Toolson* v. *New York Yankees, Inc.*, 346 U.S. 356 (1973); *Federal Baseball Club* v. *Nat'l League*, 259 U.S. 200 (1922). See note 44 *supra*.

164   See, e.g., *Flood* v. *Kuhn*, 407 U.S. 258, 285 (1972) ('Congress had no intention of including *the business of baseball* within the scope of the federal antitrust laws' (emphasis added)).

165   15 U.S.C. § 26b (2000).

166   See *Fleer* v. *Topps Chewing Gum & Major League Baseball Players Ass'n*, 659 F.2d 139 (3rd Cir. 1981).

167   See *Twin City Sportservice Inc.* v. *Charles O. Finley & Co. (Oakland Athletics)*, 365 F. Supp. 235 (N.D. Cal. 1972), *rev'd on other grounds*, 512 F.2d 1264 (9th Cir. 1975).

168   See *Henderson Broadcasting Corp.* v. *Houston Sports Ass'n (Houston Astros)*, 541 F. Supp. 263 (S.D. Tex. 1982).

169   See Posting of Gabe Feldman to Sports Law Blog, http://sports-law.blogspot.com/2008/11/mlb-japanese-baseball-and-us-antitrust.html (Nov. 20, 2008, 12:16:00 EST) (court should reject

quirk whose oddity is no longer defended on the merits. Accordingly, it is unlikely that the baseball exemption would immunize the MLB–NPB posting agreement from antitrust scrutiny.[170]

Consideration of the applicability of the nonstatutory labor exemption to the baseball agreement would parallel the analysis of the exemption's possible application to the NBA–FIBA accord.[171] Thus, has there been such union involvement in the fashioning of the posting agreement so that antitrust scrutiny should be precluded? Preclusion is a difficult conclusion to reach.

The Major League Baseball Players Association (MLBPA) is not a party to the MLB–NPB Agreement. Moreover, the union played no significant role in the negotiation or conclusion of the pact, a pact with a foreign entity that is not a party to the collective bargaining relationship.[172] Professor Gould, in examining the nonstatutory labor exemption issue, put forth the assumption: 'the MLBPA was presumably advised, notified, and given an opportunity to participate.'[173] That assumption is in error. In fact, the union was not given an opportunity to participate,[174] and the restraint was made outside the collective bargaining process. Under these circumstances the agreement between domestic and foreign employers does not have a sufficiently close relationship to genuine collective bargaining with a union embracing the workers of the agreeing employer(s) to justify application of the immunity from antitrust prosecution for labor activities.[175]

---

application of baseball exemption in situation where MLB has entered an agreement with a non-MLB party).

[170]   This conclusion (about the treatment of an agreement with a third party) is reinforced by the court's characterization of the exemption as 'aberrant' and by the exceptional nature of any antitrust immunity. See WEISTART AND LOWELL, note 5 *supra*, at 496–500 (exemption should be confined to essential aspects of league's sports function). See also Ross (1990), note 64 *supra*, at 471–4.

[171]   Has. See al accompanying notes 117–94 supra

[172]   The Japanese players' union also had no involvement in the negotiation.

[173]   Gould, note 150 *supra*, at 117.

[174]   Telephone Interview with Donald Fehr, Executive Director, MLBPA (Aug. 22, 2007). At most there were a few communications about peripheral matters. The question of whether MLB was obliged to engage the union did not arise. See note 129 *supra*. Fehr, however, has indicated that the posting system is likely to be an issue for union attention in future years. See Liz Mullen, *Upshaw: Pension Issue Beyond Ditka's Grasp*, SPORTS BUSINESS JOURNAL, May 29–June 3, 2007, at 18.

The Nippon Professional Baseball Players Association (NPBPA), the Japanese players' union, also was not consulted when the agreement was drafted and was not a party to its ratification. As with its American counterpart, no input was sought or received from the union. Whiting, note 151 *supra*, at 147.

[175]   See note 130 *supra*. See also Jesse Crew, *In Irabu's Footsteps: Baseball's Posting System and the Non-Statutory Antitrust Exemption*, 7 VA. SPORTS & ENT. L.J. 127 (2007). For a statement and rejection of other possible supports for a conclusion that the nonstatutory labor exemption applies, see Gould, note 130 *supra*, at 299–300. As noted previously (see note 134 *supra*), the conclusion that the exemption should not apply is strengthened if one believes that *Brown* is likely to produce adverse consumer effects.

The posting system has been criticized because it limits a player's freedom of choice, prohibiting him from cutting the best deal possible for himself.[176] But this kind of liberty curtailment is not a concern of the antitrust laws, which focus instead on the impact of a practice on the operation of markets.[177] Moreover, theoretically the player was rewarded for the contingency of the auction process when he signed his contract.

The restrictive character of the arrangement is clear enough, as it constrains bidding for Japanese players[178] and is magnified by the major restraints on mobility contained in the Japanese Uniform Player Contract.[179] Under the agreement employers of athletic services agree only to pursue players pursuant to the limitations of the agreement. And the prohibition on speaking with players adds a significant constraint, as a team would wish to communicate with a player both to assess whether he would be happy moving to the United States and to determine what bid to submit.[180]

Is this agreement 'reasonable' within the meaning of the antitrust laws?[181] A conclusion of reasonableness is doubtful. Comparison of the posting system to the rookie draft and consideration of judicial treatment of challenges to the draft may be instructive. Each of the four major American sports leagues conducts an annual draft, and while there are variations across the sports, the basic structure of the draft is straightforward. Its function is to allocate new players among the existing league teams. The draft's purported purpose is to equalize playing talent among the teams within the league, and the selection process is designed to enable the least successful teams to obtain the best of the new players

---

[176]   See Elliott Z. Stein, *Coming to America: Protecting Japanese Baseball Players Who Want To Play in the Major Leagues,* 13 CARDOZO J. INT'L & COMP. L. 261, 266, 273–4, 291 (2005); Crew, note 175 *supra*, at 133–4 (player has no choice with regard to team with which he can negotiate).

[177]   See generally Gary R. Roberts, *Antitrust Issues in Professional Sports,* in 3 LAW OF PROFESSIONAL AND AMATEUR SPORTS § 21:16 (Gary A. Uberstine and Jeffrey K. Pressman eds., 2007) (judge or jury's sense about whether rule is fair to players or reasonable in some generic sense of that term irrelevant to rule of reason inquiry). But see Ingraham, note 155 *supra* (criticizing inefficiencies of present posting process).

[178]   See Gould, note 130 *supra*, at 297 (gravamen of antitrust complaint re restraint of access by Japanese players to American market).

[179]   Free agency did not reach Japan until 1993. Player agents were barred from negotiation sessions until 2001, and even when finally permitted their role was quite limited. These conditions, in part, reflected the fact that Japanese players and their union were (and are) far more submissive than their American counterparts. See, e.g., Whiting, note 151 *supra*, at 88–95 (union a cooperative wa-oriented association; appearance of free agency not a result of union action).

[180]   See KLEIN, note 154 *supra*, at 142–3 (most American teams think twice before entering posting system).

[181]   Another way of posing the question is through the language of monopolization. See 15 U.S.C. § 2 (2000). Thus, assuming that the Japanese league has monopsony power – that is, for most players no other realistic option exists – and that a single buyer may impede efficient resource allocation by setting lower prices for the purchased service and using fewer resources than it would in a competitive market with many buyers, a conclusion that this agreement is being used to sustain that power is plausible. The question then becomes whether the arrangement is commercially necessary. In the end, the required analysis is similar to that of the rule of reason under section 1 of the Sherman Act.

Casey Duncan argues forcefully that the posting system does not adequately protect the NPB's interests and may even contribute to the decline of the league. See Duncan, note 153 *supra*, at 113–15. While his points suggest that the agreement is misguided, they do not appear to bear on the antitrust analysis.

entering the league.[182] Thus, proceeding in reverse order of their finish from the prior season,[183] each team selects a player from the pool that is available that year; and the process is repeated in subsequent rounds. Since the team's right is exclusive in the particular league, the consequence of the arrangement is that there is effectively only one buyer for the player's services. A player's choice is to negotiate a contract to play with the team that selected him or not play in the league at all. When challenged, courts have found the draft, and its restriction on competition for player services, to be a violation of the Sherman Act.[184] One significant difference between the posting system and the rookie draft, though, is that although both limit the player to negotiation with only one team, in the posting process all major league teams have the opportunity to bid for the right to deal exclusively with the player.[185]

The owners, presumably, would stress the need to keep the raw material in order for the Japanese league to prosper; they fear an exodus of talent and fan attention.[186] Moreover,

---

[182] This rationale is rooted in a collective interest in the promotion of on-field sporting competition. The presence of a severe and prolonged imbalance among teams could threaten league stability by undermining a fundamental aspect of the product, uncertainty of outcome. However, there is good reason to believe that the draft is an ineffective mechanism in promoting equalization and that, in light of the fact that draft choices may be traded, its actual effect with respect to distribution of athletic talent is insignificant. See DEMMERT, note 79 *supra*, at 25–40. Whether or not one finds this rationale for the draft persuasive, this justification for the prevention of competition for new players carries no weight when assessing the acceptability of an *inter-league* agreement such as the MLB–NPB accord. That accord undercuts the fans' interest in seeing the best players.

[183] Accordingly, the team with the best record is the last to pick a rookie. The NHL and NBA conduct a lottery for drafting position among the teams that miss the playoffs, but this mechanism is still heavily weighted towards the teams with the worst records that season. The lottery system for the first round of picks was introduced by leagues to address the moral hazard problem, i.e. low-ranked teams that intentionally lose end-of-season games in order to secure the first pick.

[184] See *Smith* v. *Pro Football, Inc.*, 593 F.2d 1173 (D.C. Cir. 1978) (draft had severe anti-competitive effects and no demonstrated procompetitive virtues); *Robertson* v. *Nat'l Basketball Ass'n*, 389 F. Supp. 867, 890–95 (S.D.N.Y. 1975) (preliminary ruling – difficult to conceive of any theory pursuant to which college draft could be saved from Sherman Act condemnation). See generally *The Super Bowl and The Sherman Act*, note 44 *supra*, at 420–25.

[185] In 2006 Daisuke Matsuzaka, the premier Japanese pitcher, was posted and the Boston Red Sox acquired the right to deal with him by bidding $51.1 million dollars. The Red Sox then entered a contract with Matsuzaka for 6 years under which the team agreed to pay the player $52 million. Presumably the total of the two payments represented the value the Red Sox placed on having Matsuzaka on the team. The division of that total between player and Japanese team per se is of no concern of the antitrust laws. Rather the laws' focus is on anti-competitive allocative restrictions on the labor market, and therefore the division scheme is of interest only to the extent it is structured in a way that may have restrictive effect. For example, a scheme under which the player receives 90% of the posting bid may discourage teams from posting players and thereby letting them move. Presumably, the combined bid amount and contracted player salary will be closer to the free market wage than the player salary resulting from the rookie draft.

[186] To date no Japanese player has instituted a legal action, either in Japan or the United States, to challenge the legality of the posting system. Most of the Japanese players who have moved to the major leagues have arrived via free agency and not through the posting system. See Crew, note 175 *supra*, at 129, 134–5 (possible explanations for lack of challenge). Moreover, professional baseball in Japan has functioned largely free from the constraints of antitrust regulation. The Japanese government has never attempted to enforce the antitrust laws against the country's two professional basketball leagues. JEROLD J. DUQUETTE, REGULATING THE NATIONAL PASTIME 137–8 (1999).

as in the basketball situation, where foreign leagues function as suppliers of talent and the movement of high quality players goes in one direction,[187] it is in the interest of MLB to keep the Japanese (and Latin American) leagues operating in order to train players.

However, while less restrictive than the rookie draft, the extent of limitation exceeds what is necessary to achieve permissible objectives, and less restrictive alternatives are available. First, the accord imposes a full-fledged tampering rule, thereby reducing competition among employers in the buying of athletes' services. Teams are prohibited from speaking with players without permission from the employer. As we have seen, there is a plausible justification for a tampering rule.[188] But that rationale is grounded in a concern about conflicts of interest *within* a league. The rationale is unpersuasive in an inter-league context, such as that between MLB and NPB. Second, the restrictions go beyond what is needed to produce respect for existing player contract rights. Controversies about the contract status of a player can be handled with the kind of arbitration mechanism incorporated in the NBA–FIBA Agreement.[189]

REMEDIAL ISSUES

In antitrust actions brought against foreign defendants problems of remedy can be substantial.[190] In litigation challenging the NBA–FIBA or MLB–NPB Agreement, however, these difficulties, in particular the potential complications attendant to controlling foreign activity by the decree of an American court, would be significantly lessened. The reason for this reduction is the presence of a domestic defendant in both cases, a defendant against whom relief may be directed.[191] Moreover, an injunctive remedy against the United States defendant will effectively restrain the operation of the challenged agreement.

---

[187]   Shropshire, note 146 *supra*, at 204 ('if a court does not perceive the Japanese league as an alternative, then competition may not be viewed as being greatly affected'). See generally Neale, note 72 *supra*, at 7 n. 6 (pressure for United States–Japanese competition is low because it is not widely believed that the Japanese might win.)

[188]   See text accompanying notes 75–9 *supra*.

[189]   To the extent that the compensation to the posting team is conceived of as (re)payment for its investment – see generally Nakazato and Ramseyer, note 152 *supra*, at 9, 10, 15 (salary structure, including seeming salary shortfall, reflects recoupment of initial training costs) – there is no necessary correlation between the amount the team receives from the posting process and the amount the team invested in the player's development. See also Harrie A. A. Verbon, Migrating Football Players, Transfer Fees and Migration Controls 10 (CESifo Working Paper No. 2004, May 2007) (no guarantee that soccer transfer fees implied the optimal allocation).

[190]   See, e.g., AREEDA AND KAPLOW, note 100 *supra*, at 158–9. With respect to public antitrust enforcement, if the Department of Justice or the Federal Trade Commission believes that it may encounter difficulties in obtaining effective relief, the agency may seek to resolve its concern by working with foreign authorities who may be examining the transaction. GUIDELINES § 3.122, illustrative example D.

[191]   See generally 1 WILBUR L. FUGATE, FOREIGN COMMERCE AND THE ANTITRUST LAWS § 3.20 (5th ed. 1996) (effect of judgment on rights of parties not before the court – foreign parties to contracts adjudged illegal). This point would not apply to a challenge to the Japanese rule limiting the number of foreign players on a team. There no domestic defendant exists, and a claimant might face the unenviable situation where all actors are foreign and without sufficient persons or assets in the United States to coerce compliance.

JAPANESE LIMITS ON FOREIGN PLAYERS

The United States–Japanese Player Contract Agreement, and the posting system it establishes, is not the only restriction on the international movement of baseball players between the United States and Japan. Japanese baseball has, and has long had, a limit on the number of foreign players any one team may employ. That limit is presently four players per team.[192] Obviously, the effect of this rule is to limit employment opportunities for American and other non-Japanese players.

---

[192] The restriction permits a maximum of three position players or three pitchers. There cannot be four position players or four pitchers at one time. Three position players and one pitcher, one position player and three pitchers, or two of each are permissible.

Foreign players in Japan have been mostly, but not exclusively, Americans; thus, in the last decade Latin American players, such as Alfonso Soriano, have played in the Japanese leagues. See, e.g., Whiting, note 151 *supra*, at 141–5. In 2002 the breakdown of the country of origin of foreigners playing in Japan was: United States–38 players; Venezuela–4; Puerto Rico–3; Brazil–3; South Korea–3; Dominican Republic–2; Panama–2; Taiwan–2; China–1; Mexico–1; Canada–1; England–1. Wayne Graczyk, *62 Foreigners in Japan Pro Ball; At Least One More on the Way*, WEEKENDER ONLINE, available at http://www.weekender.co.jp/new/020405/baseball-foreign-020405.html (last accessed, October 24, 2006). For a summary account of the history of importing foreign players from the 1950s on, see Masaru Ikei, *Baseball, Besuboru, Yakyu: Comparing the American and Japanese Games*, 8 IND. J. GLOBAL LEGAL STUD. 73, 78–9 (2000).

Quota systems are not distinctive to Japanese baseball. Prior to the seminal *Bosman* case, Case C415/93, *Union Royale Belge Des Societies De Football Association (ASBL)* v. *Jean-Marc Bosman* [1996] All E.R. (E.C.) 97, [1996] 1 C.M.L.R. 645 [hereinafter *Bosman*], such systems existed in many European national soccer leagues and also in the Union of European Football Associations (UEFA) club competitions. Only a limited number of foreign players could play in a particular match. For example, in the UEFA club competitions, only three foreign players could play for a team. Rachel B. Arnedt, *European Union Law and Football Nationality Restrictions: The Economics and Politics of the Bosman Decision*, 12 EMORY INT'L L. REV. 1091, 1104 (1998). See also 2008 MLS Player Rules & Regulations § I(A)(i) (number of international players on club roster limited to eight). Similar quotas presently exist in European and associated basketball leagues. Thus, the Israeli professional basketball league recently introduced a rule, imported from the Russian league, which states that at any given time two Israeli players must be on the court for each team. Allon Sinai, *Dan Shamir Thrown into the Hapoel Jerusalem Cauldron*, JERUSALEM POST, Nov. 5, 2006, at 11. See also *What Next for Hockey?*, GRAND RAPIDS PRESS, Feb. 18, 2005, at E1 (European hockey leagues limit number of North American players they can sign). And the CFL has long employed a quota system to insure that a minimum number of roster spots go to Canadian-born players. Neil Longley, *The Professional Football Industry in Canada: Economic and Policy Issues*, in INTERNATIONAL SPORTS ECONOMICS COMPARISONS 209 (Rodney Fort and John Fizel eds., 2004). The *Bosman* decision, which fundamentally altered the governance of sport in Europe, held quota systems to be illegal. It condemned rules under which soccer clubs could field only a limited number of professional players who are nationals of other Member States as contrary to the principle of prohibition of discrimination based on nationality. (Bosman's principal argument was that the existing transfer system violated his rights of freedom of movement under Article 39 of the EC Treaty by preventing him from securing employment with teams in other Member States. His club had effectively prevented him from moving to a French team by imposing an excessive transfer fee for his services.) The ruling of the European Court of Justice produced an enormous increase in international player mobility. STEFAN KESENNE, THE ECONOMIC THEORY OF PROFESSIONAL TEAM SPORTS 94 (2007); Robin C.A. White, *Free Movement of Persons and Sport*, in THE REGULATION OF SPORT IN THE EUROPEAN UNION 33, 44–6 (Barbara Bogusz, *et al.* eds., 2007) (of 643 players registered to play in British Premier League 232 were not from the United Kingdom). Soccer clubs were then able to play as many foreigners from other European Union states as they

An obvious question, then, is whether this restriction, which goes well beyond an anti-tampering rule in its impact, violates the Sherman Act. An answer first requires examination of whether American courts have, or would exercise, jurisdiction over a challenge to this restriction that bars access to a foreign market. As previously noted, the reach of American antitrust laws is not confined to conduct that occurs within the boundaries of the United States; anticompetitive conduct that affects United States domestic or foreign commerce may violate those laws independent of where that conduct

---

wished, although limits on players from outside the European Union could still be imposed. Geoff Pearson, *Fact-Sheet One: The Bosman Case, EU Law and the Transfer System*, http://www.liv.ac.uk/footballindustry/bosman.html (last accessed Aug. 24, 2006). These quotas on non- European Union athletes have themselves been subject to recent challenge. See *Player Quotas in EU Ready To Fall?*, DEUTSCHE WELLE, Jan. 20, 2005, at http://www.dw-world.de/dw/article/0,2144,1463136,00.html (last accessed Aug. 28, 2006). Indeed, a series of cases has extended the anti-discrimination principle to nationals from countries that had entered into Association or Cooperation Agreements with the European Union. See *Malaja v. Federation Francaise de Basket-Ball*, Conseil d'Etat [CE] [highest administrative court] Dec. 30, 2002, Rec. Lebon 485 (Fr.); Case C-438/00, *Deutscher Handballbund eV v. Maros Kolpak*, 2003 E.C.R. I-04135; Case C-265/03, *Simutenkov v. Ministerio de Educacion de Cultura and Real Federacion Espanola de Futbol*, 2005 ECJ CELEX LEXIS 115 (Apr. 12, 2005) (agreements contained employment non-discrimination clauses for third-party nationals legally employed in European Union member states). See also Bernhard Schmeilzl, Lilia Malaja and Maros Kolpak, Unrestricted Professional Athletes Within Europe and Beyond? Current Developments and Future Perspectives in the Area of Freedom of Movement in Sports (Nov. 2003) (unpublished LL.M. dissertation, University of Leicester) (on file with author). *Bosman* and its underlying principle have not been uniformly applauded, and there have been ongoing organizational attempts to frustrate the central precepts set forth in the case. See David W. Penn, *From Bosman to Simutenkov: The Application of Non-Discrimination Principles to Non-EU Nationals in European Sports*, 30 SUFFOLK TRANSNAT'L L. REV. 203, 226–8 (2006); Jesse Gary, *The Demise of Sport? The Effect of Judicially Mandated Free Agency on European Football and American Baseball*, 38 CORNELL INT'L L.J. 293, 303–304 (2005); David Bond, *Scudamore Criticises Blatter's Foreign Quota Plans*, THE DAILY TELEGRAPH, Jan. 15, 2008, at 3; Kerr, note 80 *supra*, at 111–13 (interaction between market forces and national structures in collective European sports). See also Arnedt, *supra*, at 1091–2, 1110–15 (plausible arguments that nationality restrictions are pro-competitive and enhance consumer welfare). However, it appears that European soccer fans are more concerned with the quality of the team on the field than with a player's ethnic makeup. See Gary, *supra*, at 321, 324; Amikam Omer Kranz, *The Bosman Case: The Relationship Between European Union Law and the Transfer System in European Football*, 5 COLUM J. EUR. L. 431, 446–8 (1999) (lifting of restrictions has led to increased skill and performance; nationality of individual players dissociated from sporting identity of soccer clubs).

Bosman illustrates the complex intersection of the competing interests of players, domestic professional sports teams, national federations, and international sports governing bodies. The decision represents a turning point in EU policy towards sport. But the weakness in the ruling is that it stressed the incompatibility of the previous soccer transfer structure with the basic economic provisions of the EC Treaty without providing guidance on how to resolve the issues. Erika Szyszczak, *Is Sport Special?*, in THE REGULATION OF SPORT IN THE EUROPEAN UNION 3, 12 (Barbara Bogusz, *et al.* eds., 2007).

The practices challenged in *Bosman* and the league responses to the decision raise the general question of whether there is a conflict of interest between the needs of sport and the general EU treaties guaranteeing the free movement of goods and people. See, e.g., Stephen Weatherill, *On Overlapping Legal Orders: What is the 'Purely Sporting' Rule*, in THE REGULATION OF SPORT IN THE EUROPEAN UNION 48 (Barbara Bogusz, *et al.* eds., 2007). *Bosman's* long-term implications are still to be fully worked out. See generally Verbon, note 189 *supra* (in an unrestricted market free migration of soccer players will be Pareto efficient only under special circumstances).

occurs or the nationality of those involved. However, that extraterritorial reach is limited by statute and judicial doctrine. The FTAIA removes foreign commercial activity from the ambit of the Sherman Act unless that activity has a direct, substantial, and reasonably foreseeable effect on exports of goods or services from the United States.[193]

The effect of the Japanese league's restriction is direct and foreseeable, but is it substantial? In light of the number of employment markets for professional baseball players, a conclusion of substantiality appears dubious. Rather the effect appears slight.[194]

Even if the FTAIA does not bar jurisdiction – a doubtful conclusion – a court would consider whether the doctrine of (international) comity should preclude the exercise of authority. This doctrine, which might lead an American court not to apply American law even though it has the constitutional authority to do so, is rooted in respect for the significant interests of foreign sovereigns in transnational business activity and the avoidance of damage to relations between the United States and foreign governments. The parameters of comity are unclear. The best-known case to address the comity analysis presents a multifactor balancing test – a jurisdictional rule of reason – to be used in determining whether an American court should decline to exercise Sherman Act jurisdiction on comity grounds.[195] Under this approach, in assessing whether the American interests are too weak and the foreign harmony concern too strong to justify an extraterritorial assertion of jurisdiction, the elements to be weighed include:

> [T]he degree of conflict with foreign law or policy, the nationality or allegiance of the parties and the locations or principal places of business or corporations, the extent to which enforcement by either state can be expected to achieve compliance, the relative significance of effects on the United States as compared with those elsewhere, the extent to which there is explicit purpose to harm or affect American commerce, the foreseeability of such effect, and the relative importance to the violations charged of conduct within the United States as compared with conduct abroad.[196]

---

[193]   15 U.S.C. § 6a (2000).

> This Act shall not apply to conduct involving trade or commerce (other than import trade or import commerce) with foreign nations unless –
>
> (1) such conduct has a direct, substantial, and reasonably foreseeable effect –
>
> (A) on trade or commerce which is not trade or commerce with foreign nations, or on import trade or import commerce with foreign nations; or
> (B) on export trade or export commerce with foreign nations, of a person engaged in such trade or commerce in the United States ... .

[194]   See generally GUIDELINES § 3.122, illustrative example E.
[195]   *Timberlane Lumber Co.* v. *Bank of America*, 549 F.2d 597 (9th Cir. 1976).
[196]   *Ibid.* at 614. See generally RESTATEMENT (THIRD) OF THE FOREIGN RELATIONS LAW OF THE UNITED STATES § 403 (1987) (a state may not exercise substantive jurisdiction when doing so would be 'unreasonable' considering 'all relevant factors'). As critics have noted, the flexibility of *Timberlane*'s balancing approach is bought at the cost of considerable complexity. While the court noted numerous factors, it did not offer a metric for assessing the weight of each or how they should be traded off against each other. The result is a method that is cumbersome, often indeterminate, conducive to lengthy and expensive discovery and therefore burdensome to litigants and courts. AREEDA AND HOVENKAMP, note 102 *supra*, at 369, 382–6.

A central concern in comity situations, that of clash with foreign law or policy,[197] is absent from this case, as the challenge is to a baseball league regulation, not a governmental mandate. Moreover, the alleged offender is a non-citizen whose business is located abroad. In addition, the significance of effects on the United States is relatively small as compared with the effects in Japan. On the other hand, the foreseeable effect is to inhibit American export commerce, and there is little reason to think that the objective sought to be achieved by the invocation of United States law will be achieved by foreign enforcement.[198] In sum, this case appears to be one in which a court should decline to apply American antitrust law on comity grounds.[199]

Assuming *arguendo* that a player challenging the Japanese restriction on the number of permitted foreign players surmounted both the substantial effect hurdle of the FTAIA and that of comity, would he have a winning case on the merits? Does the Japanese limit violate the rule of reason? On the one hand, the rule constitutes a concerted refusal to deal; all the Japanese teams have agreed not to hire foreign players. On the other hand, the league is likely to contend that the rule's purpose is not to exert anti-competitive influence on player salaries. Rather, it is designed to define a certain kind of product for sale, that product being Japanese baseball.[200] However, rather than simply pursuit of physical homogeneity and resistance to internationalization, the rule likely represents a desire to preserve a traditional approach to the game that emphasizes certain values including team harmony (*'wa'*).[201]

---

[197]   See *Hartford Fire Insurance Co.* v. *California*, 509 U.S. 764 (1993). The opinion in *Hartford Fire* might be viewed as eliminating, or at least substantially narrowing, the inquiry into limits dictated by considerations of comity. See *ibid.* at 812 (Scalia, J., dissenting). However, federal appeals courts continued to refer to comity considerations: see, e.g., *Metro Industries, Inc.* v. *Sammi Corp.*, 82 F.3d 839, 845–47 (9th Cir. 1996), and the Guidelines formulated in 1995, 2 years after the *Hartford* decision, direct the antitrust enforcement agencies to consider international comity in determining whether to assert jurisdiction to investigate or bring an action. See GUIDELINES, § 3.2. In *F. Hoffmann-LaRoche Ltd.* v. *Empagran S.A.*, 542 U.S. 155 (2004), the court confirmed that *Hartford Fire* did not hold that the only comity limit was when foreign law compelled conduct in violation of United States antitrust law, but rather held that this was the only comity issue raised in that case. Moreover, *Empagran* also indicates a willingness to apply principles of comity not only case by case but to reach a general statutory interpretation.

[198]   There is overlap between the *Timberlane* factors – e.g., the comparison of effects in the United States and abroad – and the 'substantial' effect inquiry under the FTAIA. See *Timberlane Lumber Co.*, note 195 *supra*, at 610–13.

[199]   Of course, even if a court were prepared to exercise this prescriptive jurisdiction, a claimant in this kind of situation may face serious difficulties in establishing personal jurisdiction or in obtaining effective relief. See text accompanying notes 160–1 *supra*.

[200]   It is likely that in its origins this rule reflected an element of racial prejudice. See Whiting, note 151 *supra*, at 148–60 ('Gaijin'). See also Sinai, note 192 *supra* (Israeli basketball rule requires each team have two Israelis on court at all times).

[201]   Reaves, note 81 *supra*, at 4, 75, 86–7, 156:

> [T]he Japanese want their game to be different. They want – and work tirelessly to perpetuate – a 'Japanized' version of baseball. They want their cultural values to be mirrored in the style of play – in the sacrifice bunts in the first inning, in rigorous practice sessions and homage to managers, in tie games, and in organized cheers. They cherish those values and desperately want their Asian neighbors to admire and emulate them in every way – including the way baseball is played.

See ROBERT WHITING, THE CHRYSANTHEMUM AND THE BAT 36–67 (1977) ('Baseball samurai

This rationale of product differentiation has elicited a sympathetic response from courts in other athletic settings. Thus, the NCAA has defended its complex of 'amateurism' rules that prohibit athlete compensation and the hiring of agents as necessary to distinguish its product, college athletics, from professional sports and to offer consumers a choice between the two.[202] This product definition rationale, combined with the relatively small impact on employment opportunities, suggests that the foreign player rule would, and should, survive antitrust scrutiny.[203]

---

style'); WHITING, note 154 *supra*, at 70–73, 78–110 (practice of group harmony or *wa* most dramatically differentiates Japanese game from American; it is connecting thread running through all Japanese life and sports); WHITING, note 151 *supra*; see generally Robert K. Fitts, *The Evolution of Japanese Baseball Strategy,* 36 THE BASEBALL RESEARCH JOURNAL 61 (2008) (strategic differences in how American and Japanese professionals play game); Ikei, note 192 *supra*; Dom Amore, *East Moves West,* HARTFORD COURANT, April 1, 2007, at L11. See also WHITING (1977) *supra* ('Baseball in Japan appears to be the same as the U.S. version – but it isn't'). But see generally Gary, note 192 *supra* (soccer fans more interested in quality of team than players' ethnicity); WHITING, note 154 *supra*, at 325, 328–9 (major leagues strong because open to all ethnic groups; Japanese game stagnant because it limits outside participation). For an historical account of the status and fate of American players in Japan, see WHITING, note 151 *supra*, at 48–73. The Japanese restriction, of course, stands in sharp contrast to the operation of MLB where there are no such limits. It is possible for a major league team to field a lineup of players born outside the United States. Indeed, at the beginning of the 2004 season players born outside North America composed more than one-quarter of all big league rosters.

Presumably, the pursuit of these national values and the definition of a separate product of Japanese baseball have some connection to the distinctive character of team ownership under which teams exist as promotional tools to advertise the products and services of their corporate owners.

 [202] See, e.g., *Nat'l Collegiate Athletic Ass'n* v. *Board of Regents,* 468 U.S. 85, 101–102 (1984) (colleges can agree to set of restraints designed to differentiate 'amateur' college sports from minor-league professional sports); *Banks* v. *NCAA,* 977 F.2d 1081 (7th Cir. 1992). See also Arnedt, note 192 *supra*, at 1113, 1119–22 (nationals-only soccer is distinct brand of soccer and restrictions on player nationality are necessary for this brand to exist; sport as an expression of culture). But see Peter Kreher, *Antitrust Theory, College Sports, and Interleague Rulemaking: A New Critique of the NCAA's Amateurism Rules,* 6 VA. SPORTS & ENT. L.J. 51, 83–4 (2006) (NCAA rules anti-competitive, standardizing amateurism across all conferences limits, rather than expands, consumer choice).

 [203] However, the Japanese history of racial bias toward the outsider ('*gaijin*') and resistance to globalization point to the difficulty of assessment of whether the purpose of the rule limiting the employment of foreign players is to preserve a distinctive cultural approach to the sport or is an instance of exclusionary provincialism.

The Japanese Players Association supports the rule, arguing that without it Japanese baseball would be overrun by foreign imports, given the somewhat lower level of play in Japan. WHITING, note 151 *supra*, at 150, 271–2. Whatever the political resonance of this argument, it is not a winning justification for antitrust purposes.

It is noteworthy that in *Bosman* the argument that teams must have a number of national players to insure that the team's supporters will identify with the club was rejected. That decision, though, was based on the right to freedom of movement within the European Community rather than on European competition law. But see Opinion of Advocate General Lenz, *Bosman*, at ¶ 262 (perfectly clear that effect of transfer rules at issue in case is a restriction of competition within the meaning of Article 81(1)). See generally Pons, note 90 *supra*, at 83–5.

I am not aware of any challenge under Japanese competition law to either the player limit rule or to the MLB–NPB Agreement. As a general matter, American antitrust policy, substantively and remedially, is more aggressive than the policy of many other countries, often censuring behavior that other countries view as legal. HOVENKAMP, note 55 *supra*, at 766.

14 European regulation of media rights

Chris Watson and Christine Graham

INTRODUCTION

This chapter analyses the effect of media rights regimes and certain regulatory arrangements on the sporting world in various European jurisdictions. Although European Union (EU) law applicable to the exercise of sports-related commercial rights is in the early stage of quite rapid evolution, to date it has had a significant impact in a number of areas, including:

1. ticket sales arrangements under EU competition law;
2. restrictions on broadcasting output and broadcasting new media in relation to the English Premier League;
3. collective sales of football broadcasting rights in the Ukraine;
4. the right to short reporting[1] from the perspective of the owner of exclusive rights in Austria; and
5. ambush marketing.

A common element in each of these areas is that the convergence of various methods of content delivery has come so rapidly in recent years that the law is at least as much in arrears of events as many commercial industry participants. The areas, discussed in the following five sections, consider a chronologically wide range of commercial rights from the staging and reproduction of sporting events, to the creation of a sports league, to the sale of tickets, to the marketing of a live event and ending with a reproduction of highlights.

The first section, on the treatment of joint sales of sporting event tickets under EU competition law, tracks the development of the Commission's thinking from an initial *laissez faire* approach to a stricter and more structured analysis of the possible anti-competitive terms and effects of collective sales arrangements. The second section considers the marketing of the UK Premier League and the history of its treatment by UK regulators. It identifies the fact that regulators treat sport as a special case, the 'specificity of sport'; there is a strong public interest in general availability of particular sporting content which has led to various forms of *ex ante* regulation which are rarely seen other than in relation to sport. The third section analyses the early days of collective sales of football rights in the Ukraine; it identifies the struggle between competing commercial interests and how this plays out against a background where the national laws and

---

[1] A Short Report is defined in Recommendation No. R (91) 5 of the Committee of Ministers of the Council of Europe as 'brief sound and picture sequences about a major event such as to enable the public of the secondary broadcaster to have a sufficient overview of the essential aspects of such an event'.

competition policy are both at a formative stage. The fourth section considers a specific aspect of sports law broadcasting, the right to short reporting of key sporting events. It discusses the definition of 'short reporting' and the exercise of the right against the background of European legislation and the jurisprudence of the Austrian courts applying it. The final section considers a very current aspect of sports law, ambush marketing. This is starting to be seen as a serious threat to the value of rights granted by sporting organisations and has recently provoked a considerable amount of jurisprudence and analysis. This section reviews various different techniques of ambush marketing and how each is considered in relation to the exclusive rights granted by sporting associations around the world.

1. TICKET SALES ARRANGEMENTS UNDER EU COMPETITION LAW

Introduction

When implementing commercial ticketing arrangements, national associations and organising committees of major sports events (World Cup, Champions League, Olympic Games, etc.) are considered to be acting as 'undertakings' under European law. Thus, they must fully comply with the principles of competition law expressed in Articles 101 and 102 of the Treaty on the Functioning of the European Union (TFEU) (formerly Articles 81 and 82 of the EC Treaty – the new numbering is used below unless otherwise stated) and cannot (Article 101) conclude agreements the effect or object of which is to prevent, restrict or distort competition or (Article 102) abuse a dominant market position. As was confirmed by the European Court of Justice (ECJ) in its 2006 judgment in the *Meca-Medina* case[2] the specific requirements of Articles 101 and 102 are fully in force in the field of sport.

In applying European competition law to ticketing arrangements, the Commission's decisions to date have focused on three topics: (i) exclusive distribution agreements; (ii) territorial restrictions, and (iii) restrictions in payment methods.

Exclusive Distribution Agreements

Exclusive distribution is the most restrictive form of limited distribution, as there is only one undertaking entitled to distribute the supplier's products in the entire EU. The key concern generally identified by the Commission with regard to this kind of agreement is the foreclosure of the competing distributor. The Commission took the opportunity to apply these principles in the sector of sport in the case of the International Federation of Football Associations (FIFA) World Cup in Italy.

For the 1990 FIFA World Cup in Italy, the organisers conferred on an Italian company the global exclusive rights to combine stadium tickets with package tours. It also allowed the company to present itself as the exclusive agent of the local organising committee. The

---

² Judgment of the Court of 18 July 2006, *David Meca-Medina and Igor Majcen* v. *Commission*, C-519/04 P, ECR, 2006, Page I-06991.

consequence of these exclusive rights was that there was only one tour operator able to acquire entrance tickets from the local organising committee for the purpose of putting together and selling package tours that included such tickets. The only package tours including entrance tickets available on the market were thus those put together by the Italian undertaking. Other tour operators were only able to offer package tours that were much less attractive, as they did not include ground entrance tickets. Among them was a Belgium company that wanted to sell World Cup package tours including transport, accommodation and entrance tickets to the stadia, and which lodged a complaint before the Commission.

In its Decision of 27 October 1992,[3] the Commission determined that global exclusive rights granted by these agreements had the effect of restricting competition between tour operators in the EU within the meaning of Article 101.

Article 101 prohibits agreements and other collusive behaviour between undertakings and association of undertakings that restrict competition (by effect or by object) and affect trade between Member States. In other words, undertakings are to compete with each other, and not to cooperate to influence market conditions to the detriment of competition and, ultimately, of consumers. Pursuant to Article 101(2) any agreement or practice contrary to Article 101 is void.

Notwithstanding the nullity sanction under Article 101(2), if the four conditions provided for in Article 101(3)[4] are fulfilled, then the agreement or practice at stake will be exempt from the prohibition. The agreement:

- must contribute to improving the production or distribution of goods (of services) or to promoting technical or economic progress;
- must allow consumers a fair share of the resulting benefit;
- must not impose on the undertakings concerned restrictions which are not indispensable to the attainment of these objectives; and
- must not afford undertakings the possibility of eliminating competition in respect of a substantial part of the products in question.

The restrictions could not be justified under the exemption criteria at Article 101(3) on stadium safety grounds, given that a number of tour operators fulfilling the same criteria as the Italian company could have competed on the market without jeopardising spectator safety. The Commission considered that as the only package tours including ground entrance tickets available on the market were those put together by the Italian company, and since the other tour operators were only able to offer packages that did not include ground entrance tickets, the latter suffered considerable competitive disadvantage *vis-à-vis* the Italian undertaking. The remaining possible option for travel agencies to sell package tours that included match entrance tickets was to obtain such package tours from only one tour operator, which would have meant extra work and extra costs for them.

---

³   Commission Decision of 27 October 1992 relating to a proceeding under Article 85 (the original article number for the current Article 101) of the EEC Treaty, Cases IV/33.384 and IV/33.378 – Distribution of package tours during the 1990 World Cup, O.J. 1992 L 326/ 31.

⁴   Article 101(3) aims at ensuring that no anti competitive agreements or practices generating substantial efficiency gains are condemned.

The Commission considered the potential market condition without exclusive rights granted to the undertaking at stake. Travel agencies would in that case have been able to choose between a number of tour operators and possibly obtain more favourable terms, thus enabling them to gain a competitive edge over other travel agencies and offer a lower price to end consumers.

Consequently, the Commission ruled that the exclusive rights had the effect of restricting competition between travel agencies within the Community. The Commission did not impose fines because, among other reasons, it was the first time it had taken action on the distribution of tickets for a sporting event.

Territorial Restrictions

The Commission has taken as its guiding principle that ticketing arrangements should ensure that all consumers have reasonable access to entry tickets. The case where the Commission confirmed this position relates to the 1998 World Cup held in France.[5] Immediately after the event, the Commission initiated proceedings with regard to the ticketing arrangements implemented by the Comité français d'organisation de la Coupe du monde de football 1998 (CFO), the body responsible for the technical and logistical organisation of the World Cup. The competition concern was that in 1996 and in 1997 the purchase of individual tickets and Pass France 1998[6] was conditional on the requirement that the purchaser provided a postal address in France.

The Commission scrutinised the various means of purchasing tickets and their accessibility for the general public and examined whether this requirement was compliant with the abuse of dominance rules under Article 102. It determined that the CFO was an undertaking in a dominant position on the market for the sale of blind[7] tickets and Pass France 1998 in the period between 1996 and 1997, as the CFO was the sole outlet for such tickets at that stage. The CFO contended that the requirement to provide a postal address in France was not contrary to Article 102 because it did not affect the structure of competition in the given market, and did not imply any commercial or competitive advantage for itself. The Commission rejected this argument, considering that this provision 'can properly be applied where appropriate, to situations in which a dominant undertaking's behaviour directly prejudices the interests of consumers notwithstanding the absence of any effect on the structure of competition'. The Commission followed the position taken by the ECJ in the earlier *Continental Can* case.[8]

The Commission further stated that the evidence that a dominant undertaking has secured for itself a financial or competitive advantage as a result of its actions is not

---

[5] Commission Decision of 20 July 1999 relating to a proceeding under Article 82 of the EC Treaty and Article 54 of the EEA Agreement, Case IV/36.888 – 1998 Football World Cup, O.J. 2000 L 5/55.

[6] This package comprised five or six separate match tickets at a single stadium.

[7] The use of the term 'blind' is due to the fact that that the period 1996–97 preceded the group draw so that it was not possible to know the composition of the first phase groups and hence the identities of participating teams.

[8] See Judgment of 21 February 1973, *Continental Can*, Case C-6/72 (1973) E.C.R. 215, para. 26, where the court held that: 'The distinction between measures which concern the structure of the undertaking and practices which affect the market is not decisive, for any structural measure may influence market conditions if it increases the size and the economic power of the undertaking.'

essential to a finding of abuse and that the effect of the CFO's behaviour was 'to discriminate against residents outside France, which indirectly amounted to a discrimination against those consumers on grounds of nationality, contrary to fundamental Community principles'. The Commission insisted that the CFO bore a serious responsibility as a dominant undertaking on a defined product market not to limit ticket sales and concluded that the CFO's 'conduct cannot, in this case, be considered to fall outside the scope of Article 82 on the grounds that the CFO, as a dominant undertaking, failed to derive a commercial or other advantage from its actions'.[9]

The Commission thus concluded that the implementation of those ticketing arrangements represented an abuse of the CFO's dominant position in accordance with the specific wording of Article 102(b), in that it had limited 'production, markets or technical development to the prejudice of consumers'.

Recognising that 'ensuring effective security at football matches is essential and may, in particular circumstances, justify the implementation of special tickets sales arrangements by tournament organisers', the Commission proceeded objectively to assess the claim that a French postal address was an excessive or necessary condition for receiving tickets in order to achieve security objectives, concluding that the requirement at stake was excessive. The CFO had failed to take into account the generally peaceful nature of consumers purchasing tickets at a time when the identities of participating teams are not known, and the Commission imposed a symbolic fine of €1000.[10]

It is noteworthy that in this case Article 102 was used as a broad prohibition of conduct by a dominant firm which violated non-competition related objectives. The Commission held that discrimination on the basis of nationality by a dominant firm selling tickets did not fall outside the scope of Article 102, 'notwithstanding the absence of any effect on the structure of competition', which demonstrates that the provisions of the Treaty on competition law may be used as a tool to achieve the EU authorities' internal market policy objectives.

Restriction on Payment Methods

The Commission has also examined credit card exclusivity arrangements in two cases: the VISA exclusivity for ticket sales via the Internet for the Athens Olympic Games in 2004 and the MasterCard exclusivity for direct sales of tickets for the World Cup 2006 granted by the German Football Association (DFB). It should be noted that both cases were closed without a formal decision but after a close dialogue between the stakeholders.

In the Athens Olympic Games, tickets ordered via the Internet directly from the organising committee (ATHOC) could only be paid for with VISA cards. The Commission deemed that this exclusivity did not constitute an infringement of Articles 101 or 102 if consumers had reasonable access to tickets via alternative sales channels that did not require payment with VISA card. According to the Commission, such an alternative

---

    9 Paragraph 102.
    10 The Commission did not impose a heavy fine because the abusive ticketing arrangements as implemented by the CFO were similar to those adopted in previous World Cup finals tournaments and the CFO could not have easily relied upon previous decisions of the Commission or case law of the Court in order to ascertain their responsibilities under competition rules. The Commission also took into account the constructive attitude taken by the CFO in its dealings with the Commission.

supply channel for the general public was available, in that tickets could be bought from any National Olympic Committee in the EEA, where other payment methods were accepted. ATHOC nevertheless agreed to make changes by considerably improving the information available to consumers on all options for the purchase of tickets and by intervening with the National Olympic Committees. The steps taken by ATHOC were considered satisfactory; the Commission did not receive any complaints on this issue, and the case was subsequently closed without a decision.

The World Cup case related to the MasterCard exclusivity arrangements for tickets intended for the general public for the World Cup 2006. Direct ticket sales by DFB for the World Cup 2006 could be paid for by three means: (i) with MasterCard credit card; (ii) direct debit from a German bank account; or (iii) international (cross-border) bank transfer. For the third of these means of payment, there were allegedly significant costs for consumers, particularly in countries outside the Eurozone, such as the UK. A UK consumer organisation lodged a complaint in March 2005 against FIFA, DFB and MasterCard.

In this case, the Commission followed the same guiding principle as in the Olympic Games case, i.e. that there should be reasonable access to tickets for all consumers in the EEA. The Commission requested the implementation of a viable alternative to direct sales by DFB in order to ensure reasonable access to tickets for the World Cup 2006 for consumers who did not have access to a MasterCard payment service. This alternative could take the form of (i) other payment forms for direct sales by DFB (*i.e.* more than one credit card and/or bank transfers without prohibitive additional costs for the consumer) or (ii) other sales channels for which there was no credit card exclusivity.

Following discussions, changes were introduced in the ticket sale arrangements, whereby more payment methods were accepted as of the Second Ticket Sales Phase. Fans based in non-Eurozone countries in the European Economic Area (EEA) were able to pay for tickets by making a domestic bank transfer in their local currency. This added another payment method to the three payment methods that were already available. Consumers were informed of these modified arrangements and of the different ways of obtaining tickets on the event website. FIFA and DFB also took the initiative to make the improved payment arrangements available retroactively for tickets sold during the first ticket sales Phase, thus providing a consumer-friendly and cost-effective payment method for all ticket purchasers. In light of these changes, the complaint was withdrawn and the case was closed without a decision.

Conclusion

The Commission's early leniency when dealing with ticket sales arrangements, caused by the absence of case law on the topic, has now changed. Any undertaking wishing to organise a sporting event should strictly comply with competition law given that the Commission is expected to be stricter, as it has set precedents which enable undertakings within the sports sector to anticipate the consequences of their actions.

2. RESTRICTIONS ON BROADCASTING OUTPUT AND BROADCASTING NEW MEDIA IN RELATION TO THE ENGLAND PREMIER LEAGUE

Modern sport has become a major generator of cash flow. Whether it is £10 million for a winner-takes-all cricket match, £80 million for one player or $1 billion or more of career earnings through winnings and endorsements, money has continuously flowed towards sport in increasingly remarkable figures. Nowhere is this more striking than in relation to broadcasting rights.

Application of Competition Law to Football Media Rights

The collective sale of media rights (also commonly referred to as the collective selling of broadcast rights) is an agreement among members of a league that specifically prevents teams from competing individually to sell rights to matches. The concept of the collective sale of media rights has gained popularity in recent years in the EU jurisdictions and elsewhere. It has been widely applied in particular to the organisation of the national football leagues or championships, when the football clubs sign an agreement on the pooling up and the subsequent sale of the rights to their matches through a selected common entity, for example, a football association.

Although collective sale had been used for years in England to sell rights to a limited number of matches to the BBC or other free-to-air broadcasters, competition law concerns did not arise until the introduction of pay-TV into the UK, which brought dramatic financial benefits to the clubs and the broadcaster. In 1992 Premier League (PL) clubs agreed to sell all broadcast rights collectively and BSkyB (Sky) paid £191.5 million to secure the exclusive rights to screen 60 PL matches for five seasons (the remaining 320 games would not be televised live within the UK). In 2009, Sky paid more than £1.62 billion for 115 PL matches from 2010 to 2013 while Setanta Sports Holdings Ltd (Setanta), Sky's main competitor, paid £159 million for 23 PL matches from 2010 to 2013. The PL netted £1.78 billion in return for its broadcasting rights, which was an increase of 5% over the previous rights package and well ahead of inflation. In fact, if the original figure had only risen in line with inflation, it would stand just short of £300 million rather than rising by £1.5 billion.

While this money can benefit the sports industry, the knock-on effect is that it is becoming increasingly difficult for the competition authorities to balance the contradictory needs of the rights holder, the broadcasters and the consumer. The enormity of this task becomes apparent when you consider the ultimate aims of the rights holders and the broadcasters juxtaposed against the competition authorities' primary duty to the consumer. The rights holders want to ensure maximum profit when selling their rights while the broadcasters want exclusivity to ensure they can compel the consumer to buy their offering. It is these drivers that have resulted, amongst other things, in both rights holders and broadcasters challenging the 'free-to-air' sporting events that exist in the UK and elsewhere. In the midst of regulating these competing interests, the competition authorities must adhere to their principal duty, which is to promote the interests of consumers by, where appropriate, promoting competition. If this duty is carried out effectively and competently, the promotion of competition should deliver greater choice and greater value for money for the consumer. However, in order to achieve this, the competition authorities have to temper the aims of both the rights holders and the broadcasters.

The competition authorities' desire to balance the needs of the rights holders, broadcasters and consumers is not evident in relation to other industries. This is known as the 'specificity of sport', a phrase which refers to the differences and nuances of the sporting industry which are not seen anywhere else. The European Commission first coined the phrase in its White Paper on Sport[11] (the White Paper) in which it focused on the 'specificity of sport' stating that it could be approached through 'two prisms':

- The specificity of sporting activities and of sporting rules, such as separate competitions for men and women, limitations on the number of participants in competitions, or the need to ensure uncertainty concerning outcomes and to preserve a competitive balance between clubs taking part in the same competitions;
- The specificity of the sport structure, including notably the autonomy and diversity of sport organisations, a pyramid structure of competitions from grassroots to elite level and organised solidarity mechanisms between the different levels and operators, the organisation of sport on a national basis, and the principle of a single federation per sport.[12]

It is this specificity of sport which has lead to the EU, the European Commission and the ECJ altering their approach to sporting cases and sporting bodies when considering the application of established case law and established legislation. Furthermore, it has caused the EU to consider sport when legislating in a way in which it would not do for other industries.

As a result of the specificity of sport, a fine balancing act must be performed between regulating sporting events, facilitating free competition and protecting that the rights of consumers, sports clubs and companies, as well as broadcasting rights, especially given the surge in new media that is available.

The collapse of Setanta illustrates this point. The PL and the Scottish Premier League were not paid the instalments due under contracts for their rights. Consequently, the football clubs were not paid their share either. In addition, as Setanta's rights were bought up by Sky and ESPN, which will more than likely sell them to an existing UK pay-TV provider, there is a reduced choice for the consumer. Setanta's collapse shows graphically how these different groups are intertwined despite their differing interests.

With that in mind, although the issues discussed will affect all areas of sports broadcasting in the UK, it is easier to focus on the application of competition law to the PL due to its considerable prominence in the UK, the rest of the EU and indeed the world.

Articles 101 and 102 TFEU (formerly Articles 81 and 82 of the EC Treaty) were brought into force in the UK through the Competition Act 1998 (which came into force on 1 March 2000). The British statute likewise contains effects-based prohibitions on anti-competitive agreements and abuse of market dominance, and also created a UK Competition Commission (the Commission). The Commission, which replaced the Monopolies and Mergers Commission on 1 April 1999, was created under section 45 of the Competition Act 1998. However, it is the Enterprise Act 2002 which governs the majority of its powers. All of the Commission's inquiries are undertaken as a result of a

---

[11] The White Paper on Sport, COM(2007) 391 Final.
[12] *Ibid*, p. 13.

reference from another authority, the majority of which come from the Office of Fair Trading. The Commission has the power to conduct in-depth inquiries into mergers, markets and the regulation of the major regulated industries. (It was as a result of one of these inquiries that the predecessor to the Competition Commission prevented Sky's attempted purchase of Manchester United in 1999.)

Two Current Cases: *Murphy* and *QC Leisure*

British pubs are particularly hard hit by the current arrangement whereby PL games are collectively sold to a small number of rights holders in a manner designed to maximise the value of the rights. Because PL games are sold at a lower price in Europe, where they face more effective economic competition with other domestic football leagues, publicans are among the consumers most interested in using technology to find economic alternatives to the UK rights holders.

Two pending cases concerning broadcasting output could have a significant impact on the position of rights holders, and consequently on the issue of how much money broadcasters will have to pay to obtain those rights. Karen Murphy,[13] a publican, was prosecuted for broadcasting PL matches on a foreign decoder in her pub and QC Leisure[14] was prosecuted for supplying foreign decoders to publicans.

In both cases it was argued as a defence that the PL's exclusive contracts with broadcasters throughout Europe infringed competition law by:

- restricting the ability of a broadcaster to screen live pictures outside its own designated territory; and
- restricting the ability of consumers or companies either to view – or to purchase – decoders to view live PL matches from any source other than a national broadcaster.

The PL argued that it was permissible to put such restrictions in place in order to protect the value of its broadcasting rights; the broadcasting rights retain their value precisely because they relate to content which is both live and exclusive.

The outcome of these two current ECJ cases could have a very substantial impact on how rights holders sell their rights in the UK and throughout the rest of Europe. If the ECJ were to side with the publicans, then the value of the rights would drop, because consumers would be able to watch broadcasts from any Member State providing coverage, and this seepage between Member States would devalue the live product. It was argued by the publican that the foreign decoder was not an 'illicit' device under Council Directive 98/84/EC (the Directive) and so the domestic measure under which she was prosecuted (section 297(1) of the Copyright, Designs and Patents Act 1988) could not apply as it would infringe Article 3(2)(a) and/or (b) of the Directive.[15] The publican also contended that the export ban contained in the broadcasting licences fell within the prohibition in Article 81(1) of the EC Treaty as being an agreement which was liable to affect trade

---

13   *Murphy* v. *Media Protection Services Ltd* [2008] F.S.R. 33.
14   *Football Association Premier League Ltd* v. *QC Leisure* [2008] F.S.R. 32.
15   Article 3(2)(a) restricts the provision of protected services, or associated services, which originate in another Member State; Article 3(2)(a)(b) restricts the free movement of conditional access devices.

between Member States and which had as its object or effect the prevention, restriction or distortion of competition within the Common Market. As such, the publican submitted that the export ban was prohibited and automatically void by virtue of Article 81(2). Conversely, the PL relied upon the ECJ's seminal *Coditel* cases[16] from the early 1980s, which established, in the context of film distribution, the right of the content owners to grant absolute territorial protection to a broadcaster. The outcome of these cases will either completely change how rights holders sell their rights or serve to strengthen their position and increase the value of their rights.

The Sector Regulator: Ofcom

The Office of Communications (Ofcom) began an investigation into pay-TV in early 2007. Following consultations, Ofcom issued a report in late 2008 and drew the following conclusions:

- Pay-TV users base their choice on the content, not the platform. Ofcom noted that it was PL matches and first-run movies – both of which are not free-to-air – that were of particular importance to consumers. Sky has market power in both these areas, offering a wide range of PL matches and a wide range of 'Box Office' movies.
- Sky's market power in these areas caused two concerns for Ofcom. First, Sky is likely to limit the distribution of such content and Ofcom believes that it is already limited. Secondly, Sky may be able to set wholesale prices above their competitive level.
- Ofcom considers that markets where competition is weak do not deliver the best outcomes for consumers. A market lacking in competition is likely to result in reduced choice, reduced retail innovation, reduced platform innovation or higher prices; Ofcom used the example of video-on-demand to highlight this point. Ofcom believes that as a result of Sky's market power, the UK has a strong track record of technical innovation in areas which play to the strengths of Sky's satellite platform, but this is not the case for an innovation such as video-on-demand which does not contribute to the strengths of Sky.
- In consequence, Ofcom proposed that Sky should be required to provide wholesale designated premium channels on regulated terms. Ofcom would use its sectoral powers under sections 316–18 of the Communications Act 2003 to put in place such an obligation.

Before taking action under section 316, Ofcom is required under section 317(2) of the Communications Act 2003 to consider 'whether a more appropriate way of proceeding in relation to some or all of the matters in question would be under the Competition Act 1998'. With this in mind, Ofcom explained that the limited wholesale availability of Sky's premium content could be explained by Sky's reluctance to wholesale to retailers on other platforms at a price that would be lower than the price at which Sky would need to wholesale to itself on those platforms. If this was the reasoning behind Sky's decision not

---

[16] *Coditel SA* v. *Ciné Vog Films SA*, Case 62/79 (1980) E.C.R. 881, ECJ; *Coditel SA* v. *Ciné Vog Films SA (Coditel II)*, Case 262/81 (1982) E.C.R. 3381, (1983) F.S.R. 148, ECJ.

to supply, it might well not constitute abusive behaviour and it would not be appropriate to take action under the Competition Act 1998. Ofcom's concern as a sectoral competition authority and regulator with a forward-looking duty to actively promote competition remains though.

Ofcom also highlighted that any wholesale must-offer remedy would need to include a number of detailed conditions governing the terms and conditions of wholesale supply. The most obvious of these conditions concerning a form of *ex ante* pricing rule. Ofcom would need to set a pricing rule in a way which took account of the lack of scale of potential new entrants. This may require an approach to cost analysis and therefore a price which could not be imposed under Ofcom's Competition Act 1998 powers.

Finally, Ofcom identified a lack of incentive for Sky to supply its wholesale Core Premium channels at prices that other retailers could afford and surmised that this would lead to reduced competition between retailers and between platforms which would damage the interest of consumers. Taking this and the reasons discussed above into account, Ofcom concluded that it would not be appropriate to rely on its powers under the Competition Act 1998 as its sectoral powers would be better equipped to deal with the apprehension that competition would not develop in the manner that best served consumers.

Section 316 allows Ofcom to intervene on an *ex ante* basis to ensure fair and effective competition, where appropriate, either by inserting new conditions into Broadcasting Act 1990 licences pursuant to section 316(1), or by taking action under section 316(3) in relation to an existing licence condition. As Sky holds television licensable content service licences under the Broadcasting Act 1990 for its premium sports and movie channels, those channels are therefore deemed to be 'licensed services' for the purpose of section 316. As a result, Ofcom can take appropriate action under section 316 to ensure fair and effective competition in the provision of those channels, and any services provided for purposes connected with those channels.

There were 26 responses to the report, which came under attack most notably for its market definition. In defining the market, Ofcom focused on wholesale markets rather than the downstream markets. Sky believes that Ofcom's failure to consider the relevant downstream markets has led it, implicitly, erroneously to consider downstream issues as though the relevant market were the retail supply of pay-TV services, where the only competition faced by pay-TV retailers came from other pay-TV retailers. In reality, Sky argued, competition among existing pay-TV retailers and providers of free-to-air television services is a key factor that drives observed market outcomes.

Sky, who were predictably by the far the most critical of the report, also responded to Ofcom's finding that the industry was lacking in innovation by stating that: 'Ofcom is proposing to impose new and highly intrusive regulation into the audiovisual sector, at a time when it is more competitive than ever before, and characterised by rapid and pervasive change in both the technologies used to deliver services to consumers, and the services that are actually delivered to consumers.' It was not a difficult argument to put forward given Sky's recent progress in providing high definition (HD) TV, which is widely available on a number of different platforms, and launching a Sky TV internet service on which subscribers can watch several Sky channels including Sky Sports.

If the Ofcom proposal were to be carried through, Sky is certain to contest it and a mighty legal battle would ensue. However, if Ofcom succeeds, this would increase competition for Sky, and have an effect on the PL as it would lose control over the onward sale of rights by Sky; this would see the value of those rights reduced in the UK and in Europe as the PL could no longer guarantee exclusivity.

The 'Crown Jewels'

Rights holders have been able to profit from selling their rights to broadcasters for many years now but in the UK, as in most other EU countries, there is still a listed set of events from which they are unable to maximise their profit.

At a European level, under Article 14(1) and (2) of the Audiovisual Media Services Directive[17] (AMS) a Member State may prevent broadcasters having exclusive rights to certain listed events that are regarded by that Member State as being of major importance for its society. In order to exercise this right the Member State must draw up a list of all such events and notify the Commission. The original AMS came into force on 19 December 2007 as an amendment to the Television without Frontiers Directive (TVWF).[18] Member States were required to implement it by 19 December 2009, and on 5 May 2010 the codified version of the AMS superseded the TVWF.

In the UK, the Independent Television Commission (ITC) Code on Sports and Other Listed Events is a series of regulations that are designed to protect the availability of live coverage of the so-called Crown Jewels in sport. The origins of the code derive from the Broadcasting Act 1996, Part IV. The Broadcasting Act 1996 offers no definitive guidance as to what these events should be and although the then Home Secretary Kenneth Baker had devised a list in 1991, the Act required the ITC to create a permanent list. In 1997, an ITC advisory committee drew up an initial list of free to air events. This was then revised in 1999 resulting in two groups of events: Group A which has full live coverage events protected; and Group B which has secondary coverage (e.g. highlights) events protected. Group A includes such events as the Grand National, the Olympic Games and the FA Cup Final. Group B includes cricket test matches played in England, Six Nations Rugby tournament matches involving home nations and the Ryder Cup. The events in Group A are deemed to meet all of the necessary criteria set out by the committee and have a 'national resonance' which means they must be freely available for the public to view.

This list has come under attack from both FIFA and the Union of European Football Associations (UEFA), who have challenged the European Commission's approval of the listing of all 64 matches of the FIFA World Cup and the entire UEFA European Championships Finals tournament in the UK and in Belgium.[19] FIFA and UEFA want to overturn a decision made by the European Commission under the TVWF (now replaced by the AMS). FIFA and UEFA believe that the listing of all matches is not proportionate and that the Commission is mistaken in finding that matches not involving the national

---

[17]   Directive 2010/13/EC of the European Parliament and of the Council of 10 March 2010 amending Council Directive 89/552/EEC on the coordination of certain provisions laid down by law, regulation or administrative action in Member States concerning the pursuit of television broadcasting activities.

[18]   Council Directive 89/552/EEC on the coordination of certain provisions laid down by law, regulation or administrative action in Member States concerning the pursuit of television broadcasting activities, 3 October 1989 as amended in Directive 96/36/EC of the European Parliament and of the Council.

[19]   T-68/08.

teams of England, Scotland, Ireland or Wales should be considered events of major national importance in the UK. FIFA and UEFA have also put forward arguments that the listing prevents the granting of exclusive licences to broadcasters and is an infringement of competition law. FIFA and UEFA have been prevented from licensing new entrants who wish to use premium sports broadcasting to establish themselves in the European football broadcasting market which has in turn reduced the value of FIFA's and UEFA's rights.

If FIFA and UEFA were successful in their challenges, this could open the door for rights holders in the UK to challenge the status of other listed events. Rights holders obtain a high value for their rights because the packaged auction price is dependent on the features of territorial and broadcaster exclusivity. If a rights holder in the UK were successfully able to challenge the Crown Jewels list it would then be able to grant territorial and broadcaster exclusivity. For example, Wimbledon, the FA Cup and the Olympics could all be sold much more profitably around the world than they are now. In fact, in December 2008 the International Olympic Committee (IOC) did not award its rights to the European Broadcasting Union for the 2014 Winter and 2016 Summer Olympics as it felt it could earn more money from selling them to individual broadcasters.

In June 2009, the Department of Culture, Media and Sport (DCMS) instructed an independent panel to review the UK's Crown Jewels list. The panel was led by David Davies, a broadcaster and the former executive director of the Football Association; the panel's report was published December 2009. The panel considered that listed events should have a 'special national resonance and not simply a significance to those who ordinarily follow the sport concerned'. The report concluded that there is still a place for a free-to-air list in the UK, but that it may not be so relevant in the future of changing media. The report also recommended that there should be a single list, rather than the current Group A and Group B lists. Following the publication of the report, the DCMS issued a consultation asking for any views on the report and the free-to-air regime in the UK generally. The consultation ended in March 2010 and the DCMS sought to deliver a decision before 6 June 2010.

However, in July 2010 the Minister for Sport and the Olympics, Hugh Robertson, said that the government would wait until 2013 to review the list again. This decision was greeted with much relief, particularly from the England and Wales Cricket Board and the Lawn Tennis Association, as any moves to add sporting events such as the Ashes to the Crown Jewels list would lead to a substantial drop in income from ticket sales and, more importantly, from the sale of broadcasting rights.

At the time of writing the DCMS has noted that it did not have time to implement any legislation before the general election took place. Therefore, the future of the Crown Jewels list remains uncertain, with the Conservative party promising to reduce the list for the benefit of many sport associations such as FIFA.

Exclusivity and Collectivity

The challenges facing Ofcom and the European Commission are not necessarily new: the issues discussed above have been played out by the Commission and the PL, who have long been at loggerheads regarding the sale of PL television rights. The Commission claims preventing Sky owning all of the rights is for the benefit of the ultimate consumer, the football fan, and that, by bringing an end to Sky's monopoly, it is ensuring better access to live games. On the other hand, the PL claims that it is securing not only the best deal for its constituent members, the clubs, but it is also brokering a deal that is in the best interests of football as a whole, including the fans. The key issues are collectivity and exclusivity.

Collectivity, in this scenario, is where a group of clubs act together to form a league, play in competitions and negotiate commercial deals as one entity. The European Commission claims that by limiting the number of live games that can be televised, and thereby maximising its revenues, the PL is abusing its position as a monopoly supplier. The PL would argue that its commercial agreements need to be organised collectively in order to manage the interests of its 20 members and to help it maintain as level a playing field in respect of the distribution of the revenues received. This is particularly relevant when you consider the different approach in countries such as Spain, where all of the clubs negotiate broadcasting rights contracts individually, and in the Ukraine, where there is a combination of individually negotiated deals and collective agreements.

In the Ukraine, discussed in more detail below,[20] there is a collective broadcasting deal in place for the majority of the clubs in the Ukrainian Premier League with individual broadcasting deals for the larger clubs. Therefore, although it is possible for there to be individually negotiated deals or a combination of collective and individual deals this can have negative side effects, as illustrated by the continued dominance of successful clubs such as Barcelona, Real Madrid and Dynamo Kiev which generate record amounts of revenue compared with the less successful clubs in their respective leagues. The PL approach allows for a fair distribution of the income and, in theory at least, helps to maintain the competitiveness of the league and therefore the product which the PL is selling, itself.

Exclusivity in this context is the means by which a broadcaster can effectively guarantee large audiences for a popular product. Broadcasters can ensure that consumers can only view the event through one medium. This enables a satellite broadcaster such as Sky to generate subscriptions from consumers with the knowledge that they cannot get the programme elsewhere. This arrangement benefits the PL as it maximises its revenue potential.

Reconciling exclusivity and collectivity with promoting consumer choice and increasing competition in the broadcasting market was the difficulty facing the European Commission. The worry remains, however, that the Commission, in claiming to act in the best interests of consumers, may perhaps be chasing something which is not possible to achieve. Similarly, the PL in continuing to promote the idea of collective sale must recognise that although there is a definite advantage to a collective sale, in terms of benefiting the league (product) itself, the PL has to be careful to ensure the legality of such a sale, something which it currently achieves by selling the rights to all of the games, on behalf of all the clubs, in packages as discussed below. However, the PL may be forced to consider alternative methods for ensuring the sanctity of the competition as the continued dominance, or at the very least perceived dominance of Sky may make the current position anti-competitive, so in order to avoid falling foul of competition law clubs may have to sell their broadcasting rights individually. One way in which the PL could allow

---

[20] Section 3. Collective sales of football broadcasting rights in Ukraine, *infra*.

individual sales but ensure the sanctity of the league is to make clubs give a fixed percentage of any revenue they generate from the sale of their broadcasting rights and then distribute the collective money between the clubs, with a formula agreed so that the bottom clubs receive a bigger share than the top clubs. In effect, the amount they receive would be inversely proportional to their league position and thereby help the smaller clubs to keep pace.

Since 1992 Sky has maintained exclusive rights to the PL games for a variety of reasons. However, for the 2007–10 rights package, the European Commission was determined that Sky would not have exclusive rights and so Sky would be unable to take control of all the rights on offer,[21] something which has continued in the 2010 13 rights issue. The European Commission to a degree was able to balance exclusivity and collectivity. Despite that, Sky holds five of the six packages available (the other deal package available through ESPN) and so still holds enormous power. In addition, consumers would argue that it costs more to them now as they have to pay a separate monthly subscription to ESPN which would not have been the case if Sky had exclusive coverage.

So, while the European Commission did succeed in widening the choice to consumers and limiting the exclusivity, it may not have had the entirely positive consequences it had hoped; this is the case, particularly if you consider the failure of Setanta which, by being unable to generate enough subscription revenue, went bust, and thereby deprived the collective clubs of much needed revenue. Striking the right balance with regard to such diverse interests is something which the UK competition authorities will need to carefully consider in the future.

Future Regulatory Issues: IPTV

In the last few years there has been an upsurge in new media, which has in turn affected how the general public watch television programmes, whether it be live sporting events, first-run movies or re-runs of previously aired programmes. The influx of new media and the rollout of broadband have meant that most of the general public now has access to the live Internet streaming of television (IPTV) almost anywhere. IPTV can be viewed via, amongst others, Sky TV player, BBC iPlayer and 4OD. As well as being available online, BBC iPlayer, one of the most popular IPTV sites, can be viewed through an Xbox 360, the Nintendo Wii, the PlayStation 3, the iPhone, the iPad and iTouch and several other mobile phone devices. Sporting events, broadcast by Sky, can now be viewed live over the Xbox LIVE network, on mobile phones and even in '2nd life', a virtual world online.

Over the last few years, the availability to receive broadcasts in a variety of forms and from a variety of locations has increased dramatically. However, the wide availability of new media, coupled with the growth of new technologies, mean that it is becoming increasingly difficult for rights holders and broadcasters to retain control of their rights. For instance, the PL has long been at odds with Internet sites streaming live PL football, and has won court judgments against five websites for illegally streaming live PL footage.

The prominence of IPTV, particularly BBC iPlayer, which has over a million weekly users, has led to concerns over its regulation and its place in the market. The regulation of

---

[21]   *Distribution of Package Tours during the 1990 World Cup* IP/05/1441.

IPTV should give an indication of how new media will be regulated going forward. There are three key regulatory issues for IPTV:

- Do IPTV providers require a licence from the broadcasting regulator to provide an IPTV service?
- Are IPTV providers required to comply with the various broadcasting codes that govern the transmission of various types of content, include restrictions on advertising, access to electronic programme guides, etc?
- Should there be a standard set of regulations dealing with IPTV, and new media in general, or because of the speed by which new media and new technology is advancing, should each be dealt with on an *ad hoc* basis?

The first and second issues will be determined by whether or not IPTV is regulated as 'television licensable content' under the Communications Act 2003. The relevant provisions were clearly not drafted with IPTV in mind and, in the absence of case law, it is difficult to say whether IPTV services must be licensed. One may speculate that the closer a service looks and feels to 'normal' television, the more likely it will need a licence. The AMS goes some way to reducing the uncertainty surrounding the licensing regime for IPTV. The AMS introduced new regulations for providers of linear (broadcast) and non-linear (video-on-demand) services and extended regulation to television-like services such as IPTV and mobile television.

Although the implementation of the AMS answers at least some of the current concerns surrounding IPTV, there is still uncertainty as to how regulation will deal with the next generation of technology. IPTV has been a mainstream service now for three years, yet no significant regulation dealing with it emerged until recently; three years is a long time in terms of technological advances. Rather than expect legislation to provide direct answers for all the issues arising from new media, it might be more efficient, both in terms of speed and how effectively that example of new media is regulated, if the government were to delegate to a body such as Ofcom the power to regulate instances of new media without the need for legislation. Legislation will always be playing 'catch-up' with new media and new technology. Having an organisation that can regulate new media and new technology quickly and effectively could protect consumers, rights holders and broadcasters.

Conclusion

The UK sports broadcasting landscape may be about to change. Traditionally, rights holders have been able to charge high prices for their rights because they can provide territorial and broadcaster exclusivity. This in turn has meant that broadcasters have been able to dictate prices to consumers who often have very little option when it comes to receiving sports broadcasts. However, if the ECJ sides with the publicans and Ofcom's recommendations are put in to place, rights holders will lose some of the features that have enabled them to sell their rights for such high prices. Consequently, consumers will have more choice and lower prices as Sky will be forced to license the rights it has acquired to their competitors at wholesale prices. While there are clear benefits to consumers, the fact that less money will be going to the PL and other rights holders means less money for the clubs and for highly paid international talent with the result that fewer talented sports stars will play in the UK; it will also mean less money for grass roots sport.

Despite these potential changes, the continued growth of new media could mean that any changes made in the future could be made redundant shortly afterwards: if regulation does not keep pace with new media, then rights holders and broadcasters could find that the value of their rights and their products plummet. As discussed earlier, this has a knock-on effect within the sport and ultimately might degrade the product offered to the consumer.

Balancing the needs of rights holders, broadcasters and consumers is already extremely difficult and will become increasingly more so. Ensuring that these needs are balanced may mean that rights holders and broadcasters may have to re-evaluate how they sell their products, particularly in light of the two cases before the ECJ and Ofcom's recent recommendations. It is also imperative that any new regulations and developments keep pace with new media to ensure that rights holders and broadcasters retain control of their product and receive a fair price whilst still allowing consumers a choice of products and providers and value for money.

3.   COLLECTIVE SALES OF FOOTBALL BROADCASTING RIGHTS IN UKRAINE

General Overview

Despite its sometimes unregulated status, the issue of the collective sale of media rights in the Ukraine involves many of the legal and competition policy issues discussed above with regard to the UK and is controversial in a country of 48 million people, many of whom take a keen interest in football. The broadcasting of Ukrainian football championship matches highlights a history of changing TV broadcasters, changing broadcasting rights principles and even changing the championship structure itself.

As of 2003 the exclusive broadcast rights to the Ukrainian football championship belonged to the Inter TV channel and subsequently to the First National TV channel. These broadcasting channels have always been available free-to-air in the territory of the Ukraine. The most serious attempt to impose the collective sale of broadcasting rights in the Ukraine was in 2009 when the Ukrainian Premier League (PL) was formed. To date, the application of competition law to collective sales discussed above in the context of English football has not been applied to agreements among Ukrainian clubs.

Current Ukrainian Football Unions – a Brief Overview

On 15 April 2008, the managers of the leading Ukrainian football clubs signed a protocol to establish the Union of the Professional Football Clubs of Ukraine, the Ukrainian Premier League. On 20 June 2008, the Ukrainian Premier League became the collective member of the Ukrainian Football Federation in order to comply with the FIFA/UEFA requirements under which only one national federation can be recognised. Currently the PL is the collective member of the Ukrainian Football Federation uniting the top level of professional football clubs, representing and protecting their lawful rights and interests and acting on behalf of the clubs in their relations with the Ukrainian Football Federation. Accordingly, the 2008–09 football season championship was held under the auspices of the Premier League, and the 2009–10 football championship season is being held under an Agreement on the Organising and Carrying out of the 2009–10 matches between the clubs of the PL.

In June 2009, a lawsuit was filed with the Kyiv Administrative District Court by the Dnipro Football Club seeking the invalidation of the PL registration. The request was granted by the court, which issued an order requiring the liquidation of the registration on some very formalistic grounds – namely due to the fact that its charter did not contain the fields of activities in which it intended to engage. The court also stated that the newly established PL was established as a so-called 'union of companies' and controversially declared that the PL could not have been registered in that form without providing any grounds. However, the PL was not formally dissolved upon the above ruling; the situation was instead resolved when the PL amended its charter to comply with the demands of Dnipro Football Club, and as a result, the higher courts overturned the ruling. As of the time of writing, the conflict appears to have been settled.

Current Situation with Media Rights to the Ukrainian PL Matches

The Ukrayina TV and Radio Broadcasting Company obtained the media rights for the Football Championship for the 2009–10 and the 2010–11 seasons during the competition organised by the PL in June 2009. Under the conditions of the proposal submitted by the Ukrayina TV and Radio Broadcasting Company, 20% of the matches were to be aired by the Ukrayina pan-Ukrainian TV channel, with two additional matches from each stage of the championship to be aired by the First National pan-Ukrainian TV channel. Additionally, four matches of the championship were to be aired by the Futbol cable TV channel.

Clubs which have become members of the PL are required to agree to transfer to the PL all the broadcasting rights to matches in which they participate. However, unlike the case in England, several leading Ukrainian football clubs, including Dynamo Kyiv and Dnipro, have refused to transfer the broadcasting rights to their matches. Instead, matches involving these clubs are currently aired by the TET TV Channel.

In December 2009, the PL sold to IMG the international broadcasting rights to the matches of 11 members of the PL. The contract covered several seasons, beginning with the 2011–12 season. Again, unlike a true collective sale, the agreement does not cover rights for five Ukrainian clubs, including Dynamo Kyiv. Under the contract, worldwide broadcasting rights to matches are sold by IMG worldwide, except for Russia, where the broadcasting rights are sold directly by the PL itself.

Some of the matches of the leading Ukrainian football clubs (including the Cup matches) have been broadcast by Ukrainian radio stations, in particular by Radio Era FM, which broadcasts in all major Ukrainian cities. No significant deals have been signed for the broadcast of the Ukrainian Premier League matches on the major Ukrainian mobile phone networks. However, the Futbol TV channel has been offering some broadcasts on its website.[22] These broadcasts have been available in the Ukraine only.

---

[22]   http://footballua.tv/online.

Ongoing negotiations with regard to collective sales take place in the shadow of a Ukrainian competition law that is still in its relatively early stages of development; the currently effective primary law in this area being adopted in 2001 (the Law of Ukraine No. 2210-III 'On the Protection of Economic Competition'). Therefore, the practice of applying this law in many areas is still relatively limited.

The collective sale of media rights (when the identical conditions apply to all clubs selling the rights to their matches) could formally be considered to be falling under Article 6 part 2 of the above Law, namely 'concerted anti-competition actions'. It could qualify as setting the prices or other conditions on the acquisition or sale of goods, and preventing or removing other sellers/buyers (i.e. television companies) from the market. The above concerted anti-competition actions are prohibited by the same law (Article 6 part 4).

However, there are potentially a number of exceptions in the same law which make it possible to consider the effective contract on the collective sale of media rights concluded between the PL, the Union of Professional Football Clubs and the closed joint-stock company Teleradiokompaniya Ukrayina in 2009 for airing the Ukrainian football championships in 2009–10 and 2010–11 as being compliant with effective Ukrainian legislation. First, the concerted anti-competition actions should lead to a significant restriction of competition in the whole market or its significant part. However, under the term of the contract, six matches are to be shown on the TV, two of them free-to-air on the national TV network First National Channel and at least 20% of the matches shown on the Ukrayina TV channel are also free-to-air. (By way of contrast, the initial collective sale of English PL games to Sky were shown only via the satellite provider.) It could therefore be difficult to argue that the competition in the market is restricted. Besides, the market is not yet really dominated, as some prominent Ukrainian football clubs have decided not to participate in the collective sale of rights. They have preferred instead to conclude contracts with other channels, such as TET channel, which does not belong to the group of companies controlled by the closed joint-stock company Teleradiokompaniya Ukrayina.

A major exception for concerted anti-competition actions is the case where such actions serve the 'scientific, technical or economical development' (Article 10 Part 1 of the Law). It is established in the contract that the Futbol channel transmitting the bulk of matches would be using the modern quality TV equipment, using an increased number of TV cameras and increasing the statistics information for the TV viewers, etc. Thus it could reasonably be argued that even if there was a case of concerted anti-competition actions, it served the technological and economical development of both the Ukrainian TV broadcaster and Ukrainian football sport and was therefore exempt from the requirement to stop such actions.

Thus, the overall conclusion would be that the current state of collective sale of media rights by Ukrainian football clubs is in compliance with governing Ukrainian legislation. Additionally, under the information available, no complaint has been currently filed with the Anti-Monopoly Committee of Ukraine (the authority protecting economic competition in Ukraine) regarding the collective sale of media rights; the Anti-Monopoly Committee of Ukraine being the body capable of starting an investigation on its own initiative, as it has frequently done in the past. In addition, the exact terms of the contract concluded between the PL and Teleradiokompaniya Ukrayina are not subject to disclosure to third persons and have therefore not been made public.

4. THE RIGHT TO SHORT REPORTING FROM THE PERSPECTIVE OF THE OWNER OF EXCLUSIVE RIGHTS IN AUSTRIA

New media such as Internet, IPTV and Media on Demand services are increasingly putting pressure on old and established media such as television broadcasts. One reaction of the established industries is to offer content that is not easily made available in the media, where right holders face multiple problems such as piracy and illegal downloads. Consequently, broadcasting rights for attractive sports events have gained importance both on a national as well as an international level. If the public shows significant interest in a certain sports event (most typically important premium association football league games), the organisers may generate huge proceeds by adapting an auction process by which several television broadcasters compete. Hence the Austrian TV market, which was until recently dominated by the Austrian national broadcaster (ORF), was shaken when a company called Premiere (from now on referred to as Sky) acquired the exclusive broadcasting rights to the top two divisions of the Austrian Bundesliga, as well as further premium soccer games, for €42 million, for a period of three years.

If a broadcaster purchases TV rights allowing it to broadcast sports events on television, the nature and extent of the exclusivity of these broadcasting rights are of crucial importance. The exclusivity may be an area of conflict with other broadcasters and their interest in informing their viewers about what has happened in particular sports events.

There are two sources of law that govern the balancing of this issue. Domestically, Austria promulgated an Act on Exclusive Broadcasting Rights (FERG). Today, this law must be read together with the Community-wide AMS,[23] discussed above, which coordinates certain provisions laid down by law, regulation or administrative action in Member States concerning the provision of audiovisual media services.

Under Section 5 of the FERG, any broadcaster has the right to use the broadcasting signal of the owner of the broadcasting rights, in order to adapt it into a short report for the purpose of informing the public about certain sports events. Because rights holders perceive this significantly limits the value of the exclusive rights they purchased, this issue has been heavily contested in numerous court proceedings, with regard to how extensively the right to short reporting in Section 5 of the FERG should be interpreted. For this reason, the character and extent of exclusive broadcasting rights were disputed, since the exclusive broadcasting rights to the T-Mobile soccer league were assigned by the ORF to the German pay-tv broadcaster Sky in 2004 for the first time. This dispute is one of first impression the right of short reporting had not been previously regulated under domestic Austrian law, nor was it covered by the European TVWF[24] (the directive preceding the AMS), nor does the AMS harmonise short reporting rights.

---

23 Note 17 *supra*.
24 Note 18 *supra*.

According to Article 15 of the AMS, Member States have to take care that events of general interest which are subject to the exclusive TV licence of one TV station will receive mandatory access to the TV signal of the exclusive rights holder, thus being enabled and entitled to make short reports for the sole purpose of information, and nothing further. The access to the TV signal shall be granted in a fair, reasonable and non-discriminatory way.

This rule is very similar to Section 5 of the FERG. Whereas Section 5 of the FERG refers to general interests, the AMS refers to interest of major importance. The EU also determines that the owner of the exclusive broadcasting rights has to provide the signal and not just the right of access (as the German legislation provides). According to AMS Article 4, Member States may alternatively establish an equivalent system which achieves access on fair, reasonable and non-discriminatory basis through other means.

Highest Degree of Exclusiveness

From an international point of view, the acquisition of sports broadcasting rights is a risky investment for broadcasters, since in most Member States of the EU organisers of reputable events charge high fees for broadcasting rights, depending on the quality of the sports event. Generally, a broadcaster will not be able to acquire exclusive sports broadcasting rights from one organiser for a period longer than three years; for any longer periods, the European Commission may assume the agreement to be anti-competitive.

The greatest degree of exclusivity is granted where the broadcaster that acquires the broadcasting rights is entitled exclusively to broadcast all the live, or at least the essential, matches. Other forms of broadcasting rights, for example, those which are commonly known as 'magazine rights', are also of considerable value; they allow the holder to report on one or more games of the football league in an entertaining manner, with editorial reports as well as comments and interviews. Magazine broadcasting occurs after live broadcasts, generally with a considerable time delay.

Whereas live broadcasting and magazine rights are subject to licence agreements, short reporting rights are prescribed by Section 5 of the FERG, which is now related to Article 15 of the AMS. It serves as a basis for short reports whose emphasis lies on information and not on entertainment. Short reports are characterised by shortness, a lack of repetition and the fact that only basic game situations are being broadcasted. As a principle, short reporting rights as they are regulated by law should also be conceded by means of agreements. It is quite understandable that the owner of exclusive rights should wish to reduce reporting by a third party, since any 'extension' of short reporting rights would lead to a reduction in value of exclusive rights. Contrary to the provisions of Section 5 of the FERG, the Federal Communications Office (BKS)[25] and the Austrian Administrative Court (VwGH)[26] allow the owner of the broadcasting signal to charge for costs of production of the broadcasting signal, as well as compensation costs for the broadcasting rights of exclusive graphical material listed in short reports by broadcasters as it is in keeping with constitutional requirements. If it proves impossible to reach an agreement, the BKS is appointed to facilitate a settlement, and if this cannot be achieved,

---

25   BKS 9.9.2004, GZ 611.0003/0023-BKS/2004.
26   VwGH 20.12.2005, 2004/04/0199, ecolex 2006, 112 = MR 2006, 39.

the BKS has to decide whether short reporting rights should be allowed. Decisions of the BKS may only be appealed to either the VwGH or the Constitutional Court (VfGH), for annulment.

Duration of the Right to Short Reporting

The FERG, which follows Recommendation No. R (91) 5 of the Committee of Ministers of the Council of Europe, prescribes that the right to short reporting must not exceed 90 seconds per event. For a long time it was unclear whether the term 'event', used in relation to games of the Football League, covered the entire weekend of matches (a 'round') or whether each game should be considered an event. The BKS initially decided that the term 'event' represented the entire round of matches; accordingly one short report with a maximum length of 90 seconds had to cover all the matches of a round. Since the 'event' is taking place on two days, mostly Saturdays and Sundays, for which case the Act allows a maximum of 90 seconds to be shown per match day, only a 180-second maximum for short reports for each round of matches was allowed.

The VwGH was presented with the question whether the maximum length of 90 seconds prescribed by law for each short report applied to each match day or to each individual match. In its decision dated 20 December 2005[27] the VwGH stated that, contrary to the view of the BKS, each individual match represented an event which was subject to short reporting rights. The terms of the right of short reporting therefore had to be revised and for this reason the VwGH entirely overruled the decision of the BKS.

Following the VwGH's decision, the BKS decided that the duration of a short report must be limited to the time sufficient to communicate the essential information about a game. Consequently only the most essential scenes of a match are allowed to be shown, for a maximum of 10 seconds each, and it must be decided on a case-by-case basis whether the maximum aggregate duration for a short report (90 seconds) may actually be used in full. The BKS established a detailed catalogue of game-deciding scenes. This changed the structure of the right of short reporting, but due to that decision more extensive short reports have been made impossible.

Both the owners of the exclusive rights, Sky, and the ORF filed complaints at the VfGH contesting these decisions. The VfGH overruled the decision of the BKS, upheld both complaints and the case was referred back to the BKS. The VfGH held that a free of charge access to the TV signal infringed the constitutional rule of equality before the law and infringed the constitutional right to private property. Moreover, the VfGH decided that a broadcasting company has the right to choose which scenes are of interest to present to the public. Otherwise there would be an infringement of the freedom of expression. The maximum duration of time for a short report for an individual game cannot be exactly derived from the decision of the VfGH, but a period of 20–40 seconds per scene, but in total not exceeding 90 seconds per game seems to be appropriate (by keeping the same fee). The VfGH also upheld the complaint of the ORF, because in the court's opinion, the limitation to a certain catalogue of game scenes would strongly impact the freedom of broadcasting.

---

27   VwGH 20.12.2005, 2004/04/0199, ecolex 2006, 112 = MR 2006, 39.

In summary, it can be said that the VfGH exercised a careful weighing up of interests between the owner of exclusive rights and the interest of the broadcaster to short reporting. Broadcasters are free in their choice of game scenes, but the maximum duration of a short report about an individual football match has to be under 90 seconds, rather than between 20 and 40 seconds.

Waiting Period

The owner of the exclusive rights has a legitimate interest in preventing a broadcaster entitled to short reporting from broadcasting at the same time as the owner of exclusive rights. However, a short report serves the purpose of providing information, which means that the waiting period may not last too long. The BKS[28] decided that broadcasting the short report may not start before the game begins and may only begin at the earliest 30 minutes after the regular playing time. The AMS does not contain any terms regarding the duration of the waiting period. Therefore, the Member States are free to determine such duration.

Nature of the Right to Short Reporting

From the point of view of the owner of exclusive rights, a preferable limited interpretation of the legal licence on 'short reporting rights' will appear reasonable. On that basis there is no space for editorial presentations by the editor except for informative explanations. Game scenes have to be reduced to the level of information. Repetitions of game scenes are prohibited, as well as slow motion and other digital effects that do not serve the purpose of information but constitute entertainment. The length of short reports, however, is calculated only by the time of visual coverage using the broadcasting signal of the owner of exclusive rights. Hence introductory moderation of the short report, notifications about the Football League table and the goal-scoring list are not considered as part of the report; they are not considered to add time to the maximum duration of the short report.

Permitted Broadcasting Format for Short Reports

There is no doubt that short reports may be shown in news formats and sports news formats. However, there is argument about whether a broadcaster who is entitled to short reporting should also be entitled to broadcast a short report in a sports entertainment program whose emphasis is not only on information but also on entertainment. The VwGH decided that the broadcast of a short report in a sports entertainment programme was prohibited.

Fee

According to the BKS and VfGH the owner of the exclusive right gets the costs for the signal production but also the proportionate licence fee has to be replaced by the broadcaster who is entitled to broadcast short reports.

---

[28]   BKS 3.2.2006, GZ 611.003/0006-BKS/2006.

Delivery of Signals and Quality

The FERG (Section 5 Paragraph 2) and the AMS require the owner of exclusive rights to transfer the signal to the entitled broadcaster. There have been disputes as to how and at what level of quality the signal must be transferred to the entitled broadcaster. In both cases there are several possibilities. The signal can be transferred from a satellite to a magnetic videotape recording and/or directly transferred by carriage from the owner of the exclusive rights. Either kind of signal transfer requires cooperation from the owner of the exclusive rights and also from those parties who control admission into the stadium or place of the event. Any broadcaster who is entitled to short reporting must feature the name or emblem of the owner of the exclusive rights. This is also determined by the AMS (Article 15(3)). Alternative systems may also be established, which achieves access on a fair, reasonable and non-discriminatory basis through other means (Article 15(4) of the AMS). Austria adheres to the right to access of the signal.

What degree of public awareness is a precondition to trigger a right of access to the output of the exclusive broadcaster?

The AMS requires events of major interest to be determined by the Member State. According to Section 5 Paragraph 1 of the FERG, the right of short reporting only exists in relation to events of general public interest. This right exists if the event is likely to be of large interest to a major proportion of the public in Austria or in other Member States of the EU.

Prospect and Criticism

Both on the (Austrian) national level as well as on a community level, the right of access to information for important events is regulated sufficiently. Article 14 of the AMS states that Member States shall safeguard the national provisions for the right of the exclusive rights owner to access a broadcasting signal in cases where there is a general public interest in an event. Regrettably, the directive insists on giving access to the signal produced by the exclusive broadcaster although all broadcasters have the capacity to send the signal. They do not wish to send the signal themselves, because recording the whole game merely to transmit a few seconds of it would require a huge expense. For this reason, broadcasters wish to forward these expenses to the owner of the exclusive rights. The German legislation, which allows the entitled broadcaster to produce its own signal, would have been sufficient. It seems questionable from the prospective of national constitutional law that no appropriate licence fee may be charged for the signal or the use of the signal to produce short reports for information purposes. Only the production of the signal may be reimbursed by a minimum fee. Austrian legislation does contain the principle of fair use. The conditions of gratuitous acquirement (e.g. for teaching purposes) do not apply because the purposes of the benefits have commercial character. On the other hand, the VwGH grants compensation due to constitutional requirements. Unless broadcasters find appropriate licence agreements, the right of short reporting and news access will remain contentious matters.

5. AMBUSH MARKETING: A BRITISH PERSPECTIVE[29]

Ambush marketing can be defined as the attempt by a company to profit from the goodwill or popularity of a particular event by creating an association between the company and that event, without permission from the relevant organisation and without paying the fees required to become an official sponsor.[30] The process has been described metaphorically speaking as follows:

> Imagine you throw a party and invite heaps of brilliant, interesting people. Imagine your roommate fails to help with the planning or the cost. Imagine the night of the party, your deadbeat roomy shows up and claims co-sponsorship. Imagine watching in awe as the freeloader takes credit for your expenses and effort. Now imagine that party just cost you $20M.[31]

In the last two decades ambush marketing has become a highly controversial issue: opinions on it range from 'parasitism'[32] and 'achieving an undeserved advantage'[33] to 'smart business'.[34] Advocates of all positions argue strongly for their particular case. This section explores how the law views such activities.

Background

The Olympic Games, as well as the World and European Championships in popular sports, are very important commercial events not only from a sporting point of view but also from a marketing perspective. The organisers generate most of their returns through sponsorship fees and the sale of broadcasting rights. Additionally, many other companies recognise the economic potential of such events and aim to exploit them through their own means and strategies.

Although ambush marketing is not limited to sporting events,[35] these have been the main targets to date. The perceived attributes connected with sports competitions are, for example, 'international, competitive, dynamic, successful, fair, qualitative', so that, for instance, companies that are Olympic sponsors are described as 'leaders in their industry',

---

[29]   This topic is also discussed, with regard to other countries, and in particular with regard to a specific statute barring ambush marketing in South Africa, in Chapter 18, *Legal Aspects of International Event Sponsorships*, of the Handbook by Tone Jagodic.

[30]   Steve McKelvy and John Grady, 'Ambush Marketing: The Legal Battleground for Sport Marketers' (2004) 21 WTR Ent. & Sports Law 8, 9; Tony Meenaghan, 'Point of View: Ambush Marketing: Immoral or Imaginative Practice?' (1994) 5 Journal of Advertising Research 77, 77.

[31]   Abram Sauer, 'Ambush Marketing: Steals the Show' (2002) at http://www.brandchannel.com/features_effect.asp?pf_id=98 (accessed 25 May 2007).

[32]   Nick Bitel, 'Ambush Marketing' (1997) 5 (1) Sport and the Law Journal 12, 12; Geoffrey Brewer, 'Be Like Nike' (1993) Sales and Marketing Management, September, 67, 68.

[33]   Michael Payne, 'Ambush Marketing: The Undeserved Advantage' (1998) 15 (4) Psychology and Marketing 323, 325.

[34]   Jason K. Schmitz, 'Ambush Marketing: The Off-Field Competition at the Olympic Games' (2005) 3 Nw. J. of Tech. & Intell. Prop. 203 at http://www.law.northwestern.edu/journals/njtip/v3/n2/6/ (accessed 24 May 2007).

[35]   Ambush marketing might affect every event that provides economic potential for companies and is dependant on sponsorships. Nick Bitel, note 32 *supra*, mentions the Notting Hill Carnival as an example on p. 13.

'dedicated to excellence', 'socially responsible' and 'innovative'.[36] Moreover, the audience of sports events is enormous. Obviously, it is the goal of any marketing department to capture for a company's products the positive emotions of enthusiastic spectators world-wide. Consequently, recent years have seen huge increases in the fees paid for the rights to sponsor major events. These sums are no longer affordable for the majority of companies. Many see ambush marketing as the only alternative method to compete for the profitability arising from the event.

The Nature of Sponsorships

Successful ambush marketing campaigns, however, undermine the value of sponsorships; that value lies in exclusivity. Official sponsorship takes the form of a commercial agreement or arrangement whereby a sponsor pays a certain sum of money and/or provides certain products, services or other facilities to the sponsored party. In return the sponsor is granted certain rights of association with the sponsored party or its product which culminates in an improved perception of the brand.[37] The event's positive impact on the public is exploited by the sponsor to improve its brand image and to increase the public awareness of its corporate identity. A consequence of this is that the more companies that associate themselves with the event, the lesser is the 'share of voice'[38] of each undertaking; gaining a competitive advantage is becoming more of a challenge within a cluttered market place.

However, as no direct legal 'right of association' or 'sponsorship right' exists *per se* under which exclusivity may be granted, the organisers of events seek to protect the sponsors indirectly and provide exclusivity by creating and licensing logos, official endorsements and symbols for advertising purposes. But this assistance often turns out to be limited in its effect, since many forms of symbol are not regarded as subject to intellectual property law protection and thus are free to be used by competitors without authorisation.[39] Even if the organiser manages to secure a legal monopoly over certain marks, ambushers are imaginative enough to use other, often equally effective, means to associate themselves with the event.

If competitors are able to draw attention to their products by association as well as the official sponsor and thus even appear as one, without having paid substantial sums, most of the significant benefit of the acquired sponsorship right is lost.

---

[36]   Payne, note 33 *supra*, 326.

[37]   See Simon Gardiner and Mark James, *Sports Law* (3rd edn, Routledge Cavendish, London 2005) 507.

[38]   That is the relative portion of inventory available to a sponsoring company within a certain market.

[39]   See for the 'England rugby rose': *RFU and Nike* v. *Cotton Traders Ltd.* [2002] E.W.H.C. 467; for 'WM '94 / World Cup '94' in Germany: OLG Hamburg (1997) SpuRt. 172; for 'Fussball WM 2006' in Germany: BGH (2006) G.R.U.R. 850.

Although the IOC and BOA (British Olympic Association) have already registered 'London 2012' as a Community trade mark in every class of goods and services (Community Trade Mark Registration No. 3422921) and an application for '2012' is pending (Community Trade Mark Application No. 4482147), it will be interesting to see if these survive considering the German decisions.

Ambushing Tactics

Ambushing companies use different tactics to create an unauthorised association with the event to capitalise on its goodwill, reputation and popularity. First, there is the unauthorised use of protected names, devices or symbols, sometimes referred to as 'direct ambush marketing'. However, ambush marketers rarely make use of such campaigns since these actions usually infringe intellectual property rights and are so easily prevented. Instead, rather more subtle campaigns are pursued. These can be divided into two main categories, namely 'ambush marketing by intrusion' and 'ambush marketing by association'.

Intrusion

Intrusion campaigns aim to seize an opportunity to bring the ambushing company to the audience's mind, thereby taking advantage of the mass appeal of the event. These campaigns will usually occur in close proximity to the physical location of the event and/or major transportation routes leading into and out of that location to distribute the marketing message to the stream of visitors effectively. Strategies may include: (i) securing as much advertising space as possible around the venues and throughout the entire city, (ii) distributing products around the venue bearing the company mark, such as shirts, caps or flags, in advance of a competition or (iii) flying over the event with a helicopter bearing a banner.

However, alerted by several successful campaigns of this kind, event organisers have taken safeguarding measures in most cases. The modern practice is to keep the areas around sporting venues free for official sponsors. Prior to the 2006 World Cup in Germany, FIFA together with the National Organisation Committee and the host cities agreed upon 'controlled areas' of about one kilometre around the stadiums, including the airspace above the venues, to impede competing campaigns. These areas had to be kept free of 'non-official' advertisements, commencing two weeks before the start of the competition. All stadiums were requested to be 'clean', that is free of any advertisement, when handed over to FIFA. Likewise, the IOC imposes upon the host city of the Olympic Games the obligation to comply with its 'clean city' policy when the city enters into the 'Host City Contract'. As a result of these types of restrictions being exercised at most big sports events today, ambush marketing by intrusion will not be legally practicable as far as enclosed venues are concerned in the future.

Association

Greater difficulties can arise when fighting ambush marketing by association. These campaigns aim to enable the public to recall the event by indirect reference to it. As a result, the event is used as a means of communication to promote the ambusher's own products. An example often quoted in this context is the very successful play on words which was used by American Express in the lead-up to the Winter Olympics in 1994 in Lillehammer to compete with VISA, namely: 'If you are travelling to Norway you'll need a passport, but you don't need a Visa!' Several campaigns were launched in Germany during the 2006 FIFA World Cup. The German airline 'Lufthansa', for instance, provided many of its planes with a 'football nose' to the disadvantage of Emirates Air, the official sponsor.

Legal Protection against Ambushers

The populist argument that such campaigns should not be prohibited, as these are the sort of ideas that make people smile and contribute positively to an event, does carry a certain weight. In legal terms, when discussing legal means of restricting ambushing campaigns, one must take into account the laws on free competition and freedom of expression. These concerns explain why intellectual property law does not extend to cover every potential economic benefit that might result from an investment in innovation or creativity. The public's interest in participation and the need to offer protection of rights and investment both need to be taken into consideration and balanced. It is not appropriate therefore to prohibit every kind of association of competitors, as the target of gaining the public's attention without causing any kind of false perception is the essential function of such advertisement. Hence, the provisions of any legal or regulatory regime should leave some latitude to allow companies to refer to the event, but nevertheless deter them from going too far. As a result, the law should prohibit campaigns which are likely to cause appreciable harm to the sponsor and/or the organiser.

Legal Situation in the UK

In the UK, event organisers cannot for this purpose rely on a proprietary right in the event itself, even if that right or the event has been interfered with by a third party.[40] In the absence of any such proprietary legal 'event right' vesting in the organisers, one must rely on traditional causes of action to succeed against ambushers in the UK. In consequence, passing off is the primary remedy against ambush marketing by association.

The essence of passing-off is actual or probable deception resulting from confusion of the ultimate consumer.[41] However, evidence of confusion can rarely be provided and surveys may easily paint a false picture in cases of sponsorship. Generally, studies suggest that consumers are not concerned, and so are not materially confused, about who officially sponsors the event.[42] Additionally, one research project came to the conclusion that consumers who do not recognise the official sponsor tend to believe the event is sponsored by a renowned brand they use instead.[43] Consequently, brands with high penetration tend to be automatically linked to sponsorship. Against this background consumer confusion cannot be the only factor taken into reliance in order to achieve satisfactory legal protection against ambush marketing.

Although there has not yet been a case dealing explicitly with ambush marketing in England, cases decided in Canada and New Zealand provide useful authority since the principles relating to passing-off in these Commonwealth countries are very similar to

---

[40] See *Victoria Park Racing* v. *Taylor* (1937) 58 C.L.R. 479; upheld in *Moorgate Tobacco Co. Ltd.* v. *Philip Morris Ltd.* (1984) 156 C.L.R. 414.

[41] See *Hodgkinson & Corby Ltd.* v. *Wards Mobility Services Ltd.* (1995) F.S.R. 169; *Phones 4u Ltd. and Another* v. *Phone4u.co.uk Internet Ltd. and Others* [2005] E.W.H.C. 334.

[42] Lori Bean, 'Sports Sponsorship, Confusion and the Lanham Act' (1995) B.U.L. Rev. 1099, 1128; John Voortman, 'Trademark Licensing of Names, Insignia, Characters and Designs: The Current Status of the Boston Pro Hockey per se Infringement Rule' (1989) Marshall Law Rev. 567, 572–3; *Boston Athletic Ass'n* v. *Sullivan*, 867 F.2d 22 (1st Cir. 1989).

[43] Pascale Quester, Francis Farrelly and Rick Burton, 'Sports Sponsorship Management: A Multinational Comparative Study' (1998) 4 (2) Journal of Marketing Communications 115, 118.

those in England. In the Canadian case *National Hockey League et al. v. Pepsi-Cola Canada Ltd.*[44] (the *NHL* case), Pepsi launched a marketing campaign during the league's finals playoffs in spring 1990 and thereby ambushed the official sponsor Coca-Cola. The campaign consisted of a contest called the 'Pro Hockey Playoff Pool'. The public was invited to purchase Pepsi's products and obtain bottle cap liners or specially marked scratch-off cups that revealed, after scratching a hypothetical statement in relation to a certain playoff result of a NHL team, the possibility to win a prize if this statement turned out to be correct. Pepsi used the city name of the team, as opposed to the NHL teams' trademark names (e.g. 'New York' instead of 'New York Rangers'). The contest was advertised by means of TV advertisements and tags hung on Pepsi's bottles showing an ice hockey goalkeeper wearing a shirt bearing the Pepsi logo. The front and the back of the tags displayed a disclaimer dissociating the contest from the NHL. This disclaimer appeared on all printed promotional material and also at the bottom of the TV screen during the first seven seconds of the commercials.

The court held that there was neither trade mark infringement, unlawful interference with NHL's contractual relations nor passing-off. As regards the latter, the court found that, if there was any likelihood that the campaign would create a false impression in the public's mind that the NHL endorsed Pepsi's products, it was minimal. However, in the end the disclaimers were found to have sufficiently prevented any kind of association with the NHL. A survey produced by the NHL, showing that those interviewed had been misled, was seen as unrepresentative and therefore inadmissible. It is noteworthy that the court came to these conclusions even though the counsel for Pepsi formally conceded that the city names were intended to refer to the respective NHL teams and that the term 'Pro Hockey Playoff' was a reference to the Stanley Cup playoffs.

In *The New Zealand Olympic and Commonwealth Games Association Inc. v. Telecom New Zealand Ltd. and Another*[45] (*New Zealand Olympic Games Association* case) the defendant ambushed the official sponsor Bell South, a recent entrant into the very competitive telecommunications market in New Zealand. Telecom New Zealand therefore commenced a campaign consisting of the following newspaper advertisement:

RING   RING   RING
RING   RING
WITH TELECOM MOBILE YOU CAN TAKE YOUR OWN PHONE TO THE OLYMPICS

The words 'RING' were coloured in the same way the Olympic rings are depicted. The plaintiffs complained that the advertisement would convey an impression that there was some association or connection between Telecom and the Olympic movement or the New Zealand Olympic team. They had applied for an interim injunction, claiming passing-off and misleading practices under the Fair Trading Act 1986. Due to time constraints, reliable consumer evidence as to such an alleged confusion was not obtainable. Evidence was limited to the opinions of staff or experts. Inevitably the experts of each party came to different conclusions as to whether this advertisement conveyed an impression of some association or connection between the Olympic Movement and Telecom New Zealand.

---

[44]   (1992) 70 B.C.L.R. (2nd) 27.
[45]   (1996) F.S.R. 757.

However, the court found it unlikely that readers would assume that 'this play on the Olympic five circles' must have been authorised by the Olympic Association, or indicated sponsorship of the Olympics as 'it quite simply and patently is not the use of the five circles as such'. It disagreed with the plaintiffs' allegation that, because Telecom New Zealand sponsored events regularly, consumers were more likely to view this advertisement as a further part of that sponsorship.

It is obvious that the key problem of a passing-off claim in cases of ambush marketing continues to be how to show that there has been a misrepresentation. The judge in the *New Zealand Olympic Games Association* case stressed that the issue 'comes near the borderline' and 'it would not have taken very much in the way of changes to result in a different outcome'. Nevertheless, the reluctance to grant injunctive relief prevailed. He rather added that 'it may be this outcome that illustrates the need for additional protection by way of legislation'.

The necessity for such additional legislation has been recognised in other jurisdictions and was, for example, dealt with in detail when London applied to organise the 2012 Olympics. In accepting the 'Host City Contract', the London Organising Committee for the Olympic Games undertook to provide methods for securing the requisite protection against ambush marketing. As a result, the London Olympics Bill was published just eight days after London was chosen as host city and eventually became the London Olympic Games and Paralympic Games Act 2006. The legislation authorises the Secretary of State to issue regulations that 'shall aim to secure compliance with obligations imposed on any person by the Host City Contract'. It is said that this Act will ensure greater protection for official sponsors than has been seen at any previous Games. But at the same time it illustrates in a telling way the shortcomings of the common law in preventing ambushing campaigns.

Side Glance at Germany

It is striking that there was no demand for an *ad hoc* law on the occasion of the 2006 Football World Cup in Germany, since the German Act against Unfair Competition (UCA) already provided what was considered to be a satisfactory basis for appropriate protection. It prohibits not only misleading activities, but also other exploitative behaviour even where it is devoid of misleading effect. Both causes of action have been successfully applied by FIFA to certain ambush marketing scenarios in Germany.[46]

Conclusions

It is perhaps not surprising that the most stable legal environment support the longest-lived methods of exploitation of sporting rights. Thus the television broadcasting of live football, which has been occurring for decades, had allowed the evolution of a relatively stable regulatory environment troubled primarily by factual issues such as leverage of market power. This is applicable both to broadcast restrictions and to ticket sales arrangements.

---

[46] *FIFA* v. *Sunkid GmBH,* 3–08 O 98/05, LG Frankfurt (08.09.2005, unreported); *FIFA* v. *Kabri-Vino Italiano* 36 O 5/06 KfH, LG Stuttgart (13.01.2006, unreported); *FIFA* v. *Carlsberg Deutschland GmbH* 33 O 219/06, LG Köln (15.08.2006, unreported).

However, the arrival of new technology and human creativity in the field of marketing have brought new issues to a much older form of exploitation of sporting rights – the staging of sporting events. Less surprisingly, new technology has bought new legal challenges and it is here that the law is developing most rapidly and so less predictably.

It is also clear that the inflow of money and the degree of public interest in sporting events are not diminishing; indeed bigger investments are seen on a daily basis, and these investments will require increasing detailed and robust legal regimes for their analysis and protection. The next ten years will see a major growth and development of the law in this area.

The enactment of the London Olympic Games and Paralympic Games Act 2006 as a response to the IOC's demand to provide protection against ambush marketing can in fact be seen as a 'declaration of bankruptcy'. It is an acknowledgment that the existing rules should be abandoned and that there is a need for revision. Despite the low threshold of mere association which is likely to undermine freedom of commercial expression, it is not a satisfactory solution, however, to let *ad hoc* legislation paper over any cracks in the legal system. Ambush marketing must be regulated generally, not on a day-to-day basis. Hence, it is time to reconsider the view that passing-off is an appropriate counterpart to other European unfair competition rules. Rigid adherence to the requirement of showing consumer confusion ignores the realities of the sport business market.

CONCLUSION/AFTERWORD

It is striking to observe how many aspects of the sports industry have been at the forefront of new law, and indeed regulation, as regards the marketing and sale of rights. It is a truism that the creative and marketing sectors are so often found at the cutting edge of legal development; it is their mission to be in the forefront of commercial life, to test and transgress boundaries and to create new models. That has emphatically been the case in relation to sports rights, where the number of open, undecided issues has if anything increased rather than reduced over the period of time to which the analysis in this chapter relates.

It is also noteworthy what a broad spectrum of the activities of sports marketing and sales are affected by these legal developments; very few aspects of the law and regulation sports business remain unmodified even over a few years. It is clear that the rapid evolution of sports business models and their legal treatment are set to continue, as convergence of content and delivery mechanisms finally and undeniably arrives and content truly becomes king of communications.

15 Intellectual property rights in sports: a comparative overview of the USA, UK, and Italy

Lucio Colantuoni and Cristiano Novazio

1. INTRODUCTION

1.1. Background

Traditionally, 'intellectual property' connotes a legal system of protection of immaterial goods that have significant economic importance: it refers to the result of human creativity and imagination such as, for example, artistic and literary works, industrial inventions, and trademarks. Intellectual property rights (IPR) influence three dimensions of a community: socio-cultural, economical, and environmental. Copyright and image rights particularly affect the cultural/artistic process, to the point that they can influence the freedom of expression. Patents and trademarks become such an integrated part of the product and of the industrial/commercial processes that they regulate significant and economically relevant aspects (production, use and circulation).

Intellectual property can be divided into two categories: industrial property, which includes inventions (patents), trademarks, industrial designs, and geographic indications of source; and copyright, which includes literary and artistic works such as novels, poems and plays, films, musical works, artistic works such as drawings, paintings, photographs and sculptures, and architectural designs. The copyright may subsist in creative and artistic works (e.g. books, movies, music, paintings, photographs, and software) and give the copyright holder the exclusive right to control reproduction or adaptation of such works for a certain period of time. A patent may be granted for a new, useful, and non-obvious invention, and gives the patent holder a right to prevent others from practicing the invention without a license from the inventor for a certain period of time.

The trademark is a distinctive sign which is used to distinguish the products or services of different businesses.

In this chapter, we will analyze the specific role of IPR regulation in the sport industry, comparing the American, English, and Italian legal systems. Of course, the American legal system can be defined as the true forerunner of marketing applied to sport. In particular, the absolutely innovative legal review on the image rights of celebrities established by American law represented a significant turning point, which has significantly influenced the European experience. In addition, legal practices such as licensing and merchandising have constituted for several decades a fundamental component of sports law in the United States and, therefore, they have a high level of sophistication and complexity that are not found in other jurisdictions. The English legal system is also of great interest, in particular for its peculiar approach to the issue of image rights, which are protected through the doctrine of passing off. The analysis of the Italian system in the field is also important, because, through a careful interpretation of the labor law, it combines the personal and financial aspect of the image right.[1] In practical terms, then, for several years, the Italian clubs have been trying to develop a more targeted marketing policy, though at still low levels, especially when compared with that of other rich countries.

1.2. The Importance of IP Rights in Sports

IPR are important in business generally and in the sport business in particular. They have a value and importance on their own, and also as marketing tools. The branding of sports, sports events, sports clubs and teams, through the application and commercialization of distinctive marks and logos, is a marketing phenomenon that, in the last 20 years, has led to a new lucrative global business of sports marketing.[2]

A growing part of the economic value of sports is linked to IPR. In an increasingly globalised and dynamic sector, the effective enforcement of IPR around the world is becoming an essential part of the health of the sport economy. The use and exploitation of intellectual property (IP) in a sports business context in itself is unremarkable. IPR within sport have become an extremely important asset, as is the case for many modern commercial businesses. In the post-Second World War period, as the influence of the cinema and, later, television grew, so, slowly, did the status of the professional footballer as a sports and television personality who could sell commercial products through advertising, sponsorship, and merchandising. In fact, the commercial exploitation of the image rights of famous sports persons is a big business. Equally, licensing and merchandising rights in relation to major sports events, such as the International Federation of Football Associations (FIFA) World Cup and the Olympic Games, are 'hot properties', commanding high returns for the rights owners and concessionaires alike.[3] Likewise, sports broadcasting and new media rights are also money-spinner.

Football (I use here the term as used in most of the world, to refer to Association Football, or soccer) is arguably one of the most important sports in the world, and the marketing of football has become an increasingly important issue, as clubs and product owners need to generate more revenue from the sport. In a wider context, football marketing has also become a benchmarking standard for other sports to learn from worldwide. The greatest sports clubs have been developed and marketed as brands around the world and these brands are worth million dollars and a significant contributor to the value of a club, in terms of earnings, shareholders dividends, and capital appreciation.[4]

In a high-profile event, such as the Olympic Games, many people would be keen to capitalize on the potential that such an event has to offer. This view on profitability is shared both by the organizers as much as the business community. In relation to the commercialization of sports events, it is essential to have trademarks, copyrights, or

---

[1]   In the Italian law image right is considered a particular right. This right regards the personal aspects (such as the person's proper name), which are by nature inalienable, but the Italian law also consents the commercial exploitation of such right, under licence.

[2]   S. GARDINER, *Sports Law*, Third Edition, 2006, p. 400.

[3]   I. BLACKSHAW, *Sports licensing and merchandising – the legal and practical aspects*, in 2002, 1 International Sports Law Journal 22–5.

[4]   I. BLACKSHAW, *Protecting and exploiting sports image rights*, in 2005, 3–4 International Sports Law Journal 43.

other legal protection of event marks and logos. Otherwise, there is nothing that an event organizer can exploit for business purposes, like media or merchandising rights, which provide a lucrative source of income for sport in general and sports event in particular.

In sum, the role played by IPR in connection with the organization and promotion of sporting events and the commercial exploitation of sports persons and team is a crucial and significant one and is not be underestimated. Indeed, without exploitation of such rights, many major sports events could not be staged – as there would be nothing that could be commercialized and exploited and, therefore, no financial returns available for defraying the costs. As with the granting and commercial exploitation of all IPR, attention to detail is the key to their success; as also is a holistic approach, especially one that reflects and respects the special characteristics and dynamics of sport.

2. THE INTERNATIONAL DISCIPLINE OF THE INTELLECTUAL PROPERTY RIGHTS

The intrinsic characteristics of IPR – that they can circulate with extreme facility outside national borders – has led to a strong acceleration of previous initiatives to achieve international harmonization. This section reviews past and recent international agreements.

The Paris Convention for protection of industrial property,[5] signed in Paris on March 20, 1883, constitutes one of the first treaties on IP. Under the provisions on *national treatment*, the convention provides that, as regards the protection of industrial property, each contracting State must grant the same protection to nationals of the other contracting States as it grants to its own nationals. Nationals of non-contracting States are also entitled to national treatment under the convention if they are domiciled or have a real and effective industrial or commercial establishment in a contracting State. The Convention provides for the *right of priority*[6] in the case of patents (and utility models, where they exist), marks, and industrial designs. This right means that, on the basis of a regular first application filed in one of the contracting States, the applicant may, within a certain period of time (12 months for patents and utility models; six months for industrial designs and marks), apply for protection in any of the other contracting States. The convention also provides a few *common rules* which all the contracting States must follow. No application for the registration of a mark filed by a national of a contracting State may be refused, nor may a registration be invalidated, on the ground that filing, registration, or renewal has not been effected in the country of origin. Once the registration of a mark is obtained in a contracting State, it is independent of its possible registration in any other country, including the country of origin; consequently, the lapse or annulment of the

---

[5]   The Paris Convention was revised at Brussels in 1900, at Washington in 1911, at The Hague in 1925, at London in 1934, at Lisbon in 1958, and at Stockholm in 1967, and it was amended in 1979.

[6]   One of the great practical advantages of this provision is that, when an applicant desires protection in several countries, he is not required to present all his applications at the same time but has six or 12 months at his disposal to decide in which countries he wishes protection and to organize with due care the steps he must take to secure protection.

registration of a mark in one contracting State will not affect the validity of registration in other contracting States.

The Berne Convention for the Protection of Literary and Artistic Works,[7] signed in 1886, is the oldest international treaty in the field of copyright. The aim of the Berne Convention, as indicated in its preamble, is 'to protect, in as effective and uniform a manner as possible, the rights of authors in their literary and artistic works'. The convention established for the first time mutual recognition of the copyright between contracting States. Every literary or artistic work, whatever its form of expression (books, pamphlets, conferences, allocutions, dramatic or dramatic-musical works, choreographic or pantomimic works, musical composition with or without words, cinematographic works, design works, photographic works, applied art works, etc.), created by subjects of different nations who adhere to the convention, can be protected by the copyright. The convention recognizes the protection of the copyright in its economic and moral terms, and also defines its temporal duration which can, however, vary from country to country.

The convention rests on three basic principles. First, there is the principle of *'national treatment'*, according to which works originating in one of the member States are to be given the same protection in each of the member States as these grant to works of their own nationals. Secondly, there is *automatic protection*, according to which such national treatment is not dependent on any formality; in other words, protection is granted automatically and is not subject to the formality of registration, deposit, or the like. Thirdly, there is an autonomous protection under the convention's provisions, because the exercise of the rights granted is independent from the protection granted in the country of origin of the work. Independently of the author's economic rights, Article 6b provides for 'moral rights' – that is, the right of the author to claim authorship of his work and to object to any distortion, mutilation, or other modification of, or other derogatory action in relation to, the work which would be prejudicial to his honor or reputation. Article 7 lays down a minimum term of protection, which is the life of the author plus 50 years after his death.

These two conventions, conducted in the ambit of the World Intellectual Property Organization (WIPO),[8] only supplied a general picture, and any State can provide

---

7   The first major revision took place in Berlin in 1908, and this was followed by the revisions in Rome in 1928, in Brussels in 1948, in Stockholm in 1967, and in Paris in 1971.

8   The WIPO Convention, the constituent instrument of WIPO, was signed at Stockholm on July 14, 1967, entered into force in 1970, and was amended in 1979. WIPO is an intergovernmental organization that became in 1974 one of the specialized agencies of the United Nations. WIPO has two main objectives. The first is to promote the protection of intellectual property worldwide. The second is to ensure administrative cooperation among the IP unions established by the treaties that WIPO administers.

In order to attain these objectives, WIPO, in addition to performing the administrative tasks of the unions, undertakes a number of activities, including:

(i)   normative activities, involving the setting of norms and standards for the protection and enforcement of IPR through the conclusion of international treaties;

(ii)   program activities, involving legal technical assistance to States in the field of intellectual property;

(iii)   international classification and standardization activities, involving cooperation among industrial property offices concerning patents, trademarks, and industrial design documentation; and

protection remains within its border in honor of the principles of territoriality.[9] The international community, however, did not have a single source for IP obligations and norms until the 1994 Uruguay Round of the General Agreement on Tariffs and Trade created the World Trade Organization (WTO) and included the Agreement on Trade-Related Aspects of Intellectual Property Rights (TRIPS). The significance of the TRIPS Agreement is threefold. It is the first single, truly international agreement that:

- establishes minimum standards of protection for several forms of IP;
- mandates detailed civil, criminal, and border enforcement provisions; and
- is subject to binding, enforceable dispute settlement. TRIPS, in effect, lays the groundwork for a strong and modern IPR infrastructure for the world community.

TRIPS requires all member nations to adopt, through the promulgation of a national law, a system for the protection of IPR, defining a minimum standard in 20 years. The agreement is designed to reduce distortions and the impediments in international commerce, balancing the need to promote a sufficient and efficient protection of the IPR without becoming an obstacle to the legitimate exchanges.

The main objective of TRIPS is the protection and the respect of the IPR in a wider context of promotion of technological innovation, of transfer and spread of technology, to mutual advantage of the producers, and of the consumers of technological knowledge. It applies to all fields of IP, substantive and procedural. TRIPS also fixes precise rules for measures to be adopted at the frontier against counterfeiting and piracy. The protection of the TRIPS agreement is wider than any other previous IPR world norm. Up to today, it conforms the rules of protection of all the states members of the WTO, except the group of the 49 less advanced countries that have time – until 2016 – in order to adapt themselves.

In the international landscape there are other treaties dedicated specifically to the matter of IP, such as:

- Patent Cooperation Treaty (PCT). the treaty makes it possible to seek patent protection for an invention simultaneously in a large number of countries by filling an 'international' patent application.[10]
- Madrid Agreement Concerning the International Registration of Marks, and the Protocol Relating to the Madrid Agreement: the Madrid system for the registration

---

(iv)   registration activities, involving services related to international applications for patents for inventions and for the registration of international marks and industrial designs.

[9]   The international structure based on the two conventions left huge margins to the national legislators.

In tribute to the national treatment principle, the protection that each country assigned to its own residents had to be extended to the other member States; but the premises and the measure of the protection remained consigned, in conformity with the territoriality rule, to the determinations of each juridical system.

[10]   In matter of patents many agreements have been made throughout the years: the Convention on the Unification of Certain Points of Substantive Law on Patents for Invention, signed in Strasbourg on November 27, 1963; the Patent Cooperation Treaty, signed in Washington on June 19, 1970; the Agreement on the International Classification of Patents, signed in Strasbourg on March 24, 1971; the European Patent Convention, signed in Munich on October 5, 1973; the Treaty

of international trademarks offers the owner of the trademark the possibility to protect its brand in numerous countries (members of the Madrid Union) simply presenting the request directly in his national or regional patent office.[11]

- Geneva Copyright Treaty: the Contracting Party must ensure that enforcement procedures are available under its law so as to permit effective action against any act of infringement of rights covered by the treaty. Such action must include expeditious remedies to prevent infringement and remedies which constitute a deterrent to further infringements.[12]

3. INTELLECTUAL PROPERTY RIGHTS IN THE FIELD OF SPORT

IPR have an unchallenged value and they are very important in business generally and in sports in particular. The World Bank's Global Economic Prospects Report for 2002 confirmed the growing importance of IP for today's globalised economies, finding that 'across the range of income levels, intellectual property rights (IPR) are associated with greater trade and foreign direct investment flows, which in turn translate into faster rates of economic growth'.[13]

The phenomenon is so important that the Sports Rights Owners Coalition (SROC), which includes 37 sports institutions – from soccer's Premier League and FIFA to cycling's Tour de France to World Snooker – seeking international treaties to 'protect and promote the special nature of sport' and its IPR in a fast-changing digital world. In particular, the purpose of the SROC is to enable:

- discussion and sharing of best practice on key legal, political, and regulatory issues;
- raising awareness of new developments and innovation in sports rights; and
- sport to take joint action to protect and promote their rights.

---

on the International Recognition of the deposit of Microorganisms for the Purposes of Patent Procedure, signed in Budapest on April 28, 1977; and the Patent Law Treaty signed in Geneva on June 1, 2000.

[11]   Numerous are the agreements made to regulate the many aspects of the trademarks right: the Nice Agreement Concerning the International Classification of Goods and Services for the Purpose of the Registration of Marks, signed on June 15, 1957, reviewed in Geneva on May 13, 1977; the Vienna Agreement Establishing an International Classification of the Figurative Elements of Marks, signed on June 12, 1973; the Nairobi Treaty on the Protection of the Olympic Symbol, signed on September 26, 1981; the Trademark Law Treaty, adopted at Geneva on October 27, 1994; and the Treaty on the Law of Trademarks, signed in Singapore on March 27, 2006.

[12]   In matter of copyrights many agreements have been made: the Rome Convention for the protection of performers, producers of phonograms and broadcasting organisations, adopted on October 26, 1961; the Universal Copyright Convention, signed at Geneva on September 6, 1952, revised at Paris on July 24, 1971; the Convention for the protection of producers of phonograms against unauthorized duplication of their phonograms, signed on October 29, 1971; the Convention relating to the distribution of programme – carrying signals transmitted by satellite, adopted at Brussels on May 21, 1974; the Geneva Convention for the registration of audiovisual work, signed on April 18, 1989; the WIPO performances and phonograms treaty, adopted at Geneva on December 20, 1996.

[13]   See http://usinfo.state.gov/products/pubs/intelprp.

In fact, SROC members are looking to national governments and international treaty organizations such as the European Union, WTO and WIPO to:

● fully recognize, protect, and promote the special nature of sport and sports rights;
● provide comprehensive protection for sports rights, including their names, logos and marks, outlaw ambush marketing and ticket touting/scalping; and
● create a regime for sports betting that enables sport to protect its integrity, and establishes a fair return.

In the international sport area, the mark is undoubtedly the IPR that finds the greatest application. A great variety of entities may be used as trademarks, obtaining a different protection in connection with the national law system of reference. An important exception is surely constituted by the Olympic Movement Symbol (five interconnected rings in blue, yellow, black, green, and red) that have special trademark protection on international and national level.

In the sport application, the following entities have been object of registration as marks:

● the name – such as soccer players Michael Owen and Eric Cantona;
● the nickname – such as Paul Gascoigne 'Gazza' and David Seaman 'Safe Hands';
● the image – such as Formula 1 stars Jacques Villeneuve and Damon Hill;
● the sporting slogans and mottoes, such as Erik Cantona, the soccer player, who registered the slogan 'Ohh aah Cantona' as a trademark;
● the sport club names and logos;
● the distinctive autograph of a famous athlete;
● the name and associated logos of sport events; and
● the mascot of a sport club.[14]

The main problem with trying to use trademark law to protect against the unauthorized use of a celebrity's name or image is that that use is likely to be merely descriptive of the character of the goods to which the name is attached, rather than an indication of trade origin, and therefore not an infringement of the trademark owner's rights.[15] For example, the owner of the copyright of footage of Alan Shearer playing football could include his name in the packaging of a video of that footage, notwithstanding the fact that Shearer's name is registered as a trademark, because it would be being used merely to describe what was inside the packaging, not to indicate that Alan Shearer himself had produced or authorized the production of the video. Alan Shearer is one of those famous footballers who have been allowed to register their names as trademarks; in contrast, Mark Hughes' application to register his name was rejected on grounds of lack of distinctiveness. To circumvent such lack of distinctiveness, some players have registered nicknames.[16]

Copyright and patent law can also find application in the specific field of sports. Copyright protects:

---

[14] GARDINER, note 2 *supra*, 405.
[15] J. TAYLOR, S. BOYD, AND D. BECKER, *Image rights*, in Adam Lewis and Jonathan Taylor, Sport: law and practise, 2003.
[16] *Ibid.*

- the name of a sport event – usually it is not qualified for protection as literally works, but when it has a distinctive logo it may qualify as artistic works;
- the music of a sporting event, for example, the music that introduces the Union of European Football Associations (UEFA) Champions League transmission benefits from copyright as a musical work;
- the photographs of sportspersons and sport events can benefit from copyright protection as artistic work. Patents may be obtained in connection with building and operations of new sports installation and facilities, for example, the case of golfer Bernard Langer, who has registered the patent of the inverted putting grip, and the former basketball player Kareem Abdul Jabbar, who obtained the patent for the sky hook scoring shot.

3.1.   Image Rights in Sports

In the sport market there is another category of rights which needs to be protected and it concerns, specifically, athletes' personality rights, such as name and image rights. This kind of right, known in different jurisdiction by a variety of names, including right of publicity (United States), right of privacy (United Kingdom), and right of personality (Italy), stand in a difficult juridical qualification zone that presents certain connections with the right of IP. There are two aspects to image rights' protection. There are those who wish to control the use made of their image as a form of privacy. There are others, like sportsmen, with a high reputation, who wish to control the use made of their image as its affects their income.

In the United States the right of publicity, is defined as intellectual property and whose infringement constitutes an offence and the practice of unfair competition. Historically, the American courts refused to recognize a celebrity right to privacy. Later, the courts stated that all private individuals had a basic right to be left alone and they started to recognize a right of privacy as a way to protect private individuals against outrageous and unjustifiable infliction of mental distress by the press and advertisers. Afterwards, it became obvious that to prevent the unfair enrichment of others off a celebrity reputation, the right to privacy was extended to include the right of publicity. Therefore, the American courts legitimated a commercial view of the image rights; this evolution is reflected in the linguistic tenor of some of the numerous statutes that have given an expressed protection norm, as it is testified by the Personal Rights Protection Act of Tennessee, where 'every individual has a property right in the use of his name, photograph or likeness in any medium, in any manner' (Section 47-25-113).

In the United Kingdom it appears very difficult to protect the name and image of famous persons because there is no specific law protecting personality rights. Famous people have to rely on a rag-bag of law, such as trademarks and copyrights law and the common law doctrine of passing off. The passing off[17] doctrine is intended to protect the good commercial reputation of all those economic activities that do not possess the

---

17   The tort of passing off protects the goodwill and reputation of individuals and companies, which arises as a result of their business activities. The claimant must show that there has been misrepresentation and the public has been deceived into believing that the goods or service of the trader are those of the claimant. Damage as a result of the passing off must also be established.

necessary characteristics to obtain the full protection from IPR (such as patents, marks, and copyrights). Three elements and required to constitute a case of 'passing off', namely:

- reputation or goodwill acquired by the claimant in his goods, services, name, or mark;
- misrepresentation by the defendant leading to confusion (or deception), causing
- damage to the claimant.

In substance, for the British, the image's rights technically do not exist, but they acquire a status similar to IPR.

Italy[18] had traditionally qualified image rights only as a right of personality. Through American influence, however, it is nowadays defined as a right of double nature, personal and patrimonial. Although embracing the American thesis, the Italian system has followed a different juridical path.

In the United States the right of publicity was a judge-made common law creation that has anticipated the subsequent recognition through legislation. In the Italian system the image right constitutes a codified right (Art. 10 Civil Code (abuse of other people's image) and art. 96–97 L.D.A. (disposition on copyright)), that remained the same even after the above influence. The Italian courts, in short, have only supplied a different interpretation of a norm that has never been changed.

Particularly, the image rights of professional athletes constitute, nowadays, an essential component of sport marketing. In fact, endorsing products or lending image has become to some athletes more lucrative then their professional contract. At the root of this commercial mix is the athlete, whose value is his or her image over which, at the outset at least, the athlete has complete ownership. This is a developing area of law, which can be broadly understood by reference to what rights rest in a person (normally famous) to exploit the rights that arise from their own image or personality. It is, to some extent, founded in copyright and trademark but generally arises out of the imposition of a contractual obligation or reservation to the person involved of certain rights that stem from the use of that person's name or image. In fact, many sport organizations are adept at leveraging this asset to their own benefit by forging commercial relationships with their athlete members and, in turn, using the athlete's visibility to forge marketing relationships with sponsors and others. Clubs want to maximize their assets to please their shareholders and within these assets there are the brands and images of their players. To control these assets they need to acknowledge their existence contractually.

The case of football player David Beckam is emblematic, because his face sells products worldwide and makes significant revenue for his club. When he played in the United Kingdom he had two agreements, one for him playing football and another with regard to what parts of his image the club could use. David Beckham had enhanced his salary in his contract by effectively drawing additional income out of his contract because of the perceived enhancement to Manchester United of his association with the club's products

---

[18] For a complete examination of the image rights in the Italian legal order see L. FERRARI, in I. Blackshaw and E.C.R. Siekmann, Sports image rights in Europe, 2005, p. 187. See also D. HARRINGTON, *Image rights – overview of protection in key markets*, 2002, 9(2) Sports Law Administration & Practice 11, 12.

and services. Manchester United agreed to allow Beckham to preserve his image rights and allowed him the freedom to choose his own endorsements. In return, the club paid him (via his image company) £33 300 a week for the club to use his image on club merchandise.[19] At Real Madrid, Beckham gave up a large chunk of his image rights (and subsequent income); in his current contract with the Los Angeles Galaxy of Major League Soccer in the United States, Beckham will keep 100% of the income generated from the use of his image.[20]

Even the standard FA Premier League player contract makes precious little reference to the subject of image rights. Specific arrangements with particular players are usually dealt with by way of an addendum to the standard contract, negotiated on a case-by-case basis. Within Italian professional football, the problem of the ownership of the rights of commercial exploitation of the player's image was removed or resolved. In recent years Italian football has adopted the practice of the so-called naked contracts, imported from the world of Formula 1, under which a player that binds himself to a football club for his sports performance, allows, through compensation, the rights of commercial exploitation of his image. Thus the club becomes the sole holder of the image rights of the players.

Football clubs do not always manage to acquire player image rights because, especially for outstanding athletes, it is often more convenient to manage these rights personally (*Del Piero*) or give them to a third party (*Nesta*). In other cases, the player allows the club the right of commercial exploitation of his image only in certain areas, for example, in printed media and television, and retains for himself the rights of exploitation on other media such as the Internet (*Totti*).

One difficulty is understanding the extent to which the clubs can incorporate their players' names and images in their own commercial programs without risking a writ. Many deal with the issue under their terms and conditions of participation in an event. Wimbledon Tennis Club, for example, obtains the right from all players for the use of their name, voice, likeness, and biographical information – for the purpose of promoting the tournament – and the right to require players to participate in reasonable promotional activities for the tournament. This type of provision is reasonably standard but appears unlikely to allow the event organizer to use or authorize third parties to use players' names in connection with event-based products, such as video games, or with event sponsors' activities.

Assuming that image rights do become a species of IP, whether in law or in practice, one of the key practical questions will concern the precise circumstances in which such rights may be infringed. If a third party (a pirate merchandiser or a rival sponsor) uses any of the licensed player signs without the player's consent, whether the player or the authorized licensee can do anything about it depends on whether the courts in the jurisdiction concerned recognize any legal right in the player's image or with regard to other specific references to the player, under IP, advertising, and privacy laws. The existence of goods and services bearing the individual's name or image (and therefore the possible implied suggestion that the individual has approved or endorsed the products), without authorization, can in some cases seriously damage the value of a sporting personality's licensing

---

[19]   A. Braithwaite, *Image rights – do they exist and who should own them?*, http://www.sportandtechnology.com/features/0035.html.

[20]   See http://www.sportsbiz.wordpress.com.

rights in his image. Not only does the individual suffer the loss of royalties he might have earned but also his image may depreciate in value by the affixing of his name and image to inferior goods or materials. It may also deprive him of another lucrative endorsement contract due to loss of exclusivity.[21] Many jurisdictions now protect athletes against these harms, and the underlying trend towards a proprietary right in a personality will remain. Image rights will become a permanent part of the sports marketing spectrum, alongside TV rights, sponsorship rights, and merchandising rights.

3.2. TV Rights in Sports

Sport has overwhelming global appeal transcending national, cultural, religious, and gender boundaries, as well as socio-economic class. Of potential revenue streams in sports marketing, which include sponsorship, merchandising, endorsement of products and services, and corporate hospitality, the most important and lucrative one is the sale and exploitation of sports broadcasting rights around the world, which contributes huge sums to many sports and sports events. The best illustration of how much sports programming has increased in value over the years is the National Football League (NFL).[22] In 1962, the NFL signed its first national television contract for a total of $4.65 million a year, or $320 000 for each team. In 2010, the 32 NFL teams earned a total in excess of $20 billion in rights fees.

The United States has a much more diverse set of sports leagues available for broadcasting than any other part of the world. There are major professional sports leagues for baseball, American football, basketball, and hockey, which have been in existence for decades and which have lucrative broadcasting contracts with various commercial broadcast networks, local broadcast stations, direct broadcast satellite services, and cable networks. In addition, college basketball, college football, professional soccer, professional golf, professional tennis, and automobile racing enjoy wide broadcast exposure. The importance of media rights in the European football is exemplified by the English FA Premier League, which has sold its broadcasting rights for the 2007–10 seasons for a record sum of £1.7 billion.[23] In Italy, the profit for the 2008–10 seasons in 'Serie A' has been about €1.4 billion in total, while the forecast for the 2010–16 seasons is about €900 million per year.

The exploitation of broadcasting rights in football is so valuable and important that many leading football clubs, such as the English Club Manchester United, now operate their own television channels for the benefit of their fans and also their commercial sponsors, made possible with the advent of digital TV.

---

[21] C. STEELE, *Personality merchandising, licensing rights and the march of the turtles*, in 1997, 5(2) Sport and the Law Journal 14.

[22] NFL produces an annual series of interrelated football games involving all of its 28 member clubs, annual division championship race, a nine-game post-season playoff tournament, and ultimately a Super Bowl game and league champion. See, on this point, G.R. ROBERTS, *The single entity status of sports league under s.1 of the Sherman Act: an alternative view*, in 1986, 60 Tulane Law Review 562, 569.

[23] I. BLACKSHAW, *The importance of IP rights in sport*, in 2008, 3–4, International Sports Law Journal 146.

Among the legal issues raised in the commercialization and exploitation of sports broadcasting rights are the following:

- the ownership of sports broadcasting rights, including the position of individual sports persons, teams, clubs, venue owners;
- the different methods of protecting them, including copyright;
- the different methods of exploiting them, including collective selling and buying, as well as 'pay per view' and 'free to view' arrangements;
- the so-called new media rights, including the 'streaming' of sports broadcasts on the Internet (so-called 'webcasts') and on the so-called 'third generation' mobile phones; and[24]
- the impact of the European and National Competition Rules on the broadcasting of sports events.[25]

There is a widespread agreement that the broadcast of sports events constitutes a copyrighted work. The focal point of the discussion about the nature of sports media rights is in the determination of the moment starting from which a broadcasting of a sports event receives its copyright protection. In other words: can an event itself be protected by copyright law, or it is only its broadcast which receives its IP law protection?[26] The former would increase revenue of the holders of those rights and stimulate long-term strategic investment in the industry. On the other hand, if sports media rights are protected only as broadcasting rights, it would create incentives for the competitors of exclusive rights holders to seek the ways to exploit sports events, by creating an alternative content, which might be of interest to particular segments of audience.[27] This aspect has been the object of many debates, and the majority of the authors stated that sports media rights have to receive their copyright protection already at the stage of sports performance.[28] It must be clear that copyright as such is not an absolute right. It can be compromised, limited, or overruled by other rights and public interests, such as, for instance, the right to fair competition, the right to information, the right to access to artistic heritage, the right to coherent cultural development, the right to innovations and expansion of new forms of media products, fair use, sports parody, etc.[29] New formats for content delivery have become a very attractive way to reach viewers, and their share of the media market has increased exponentially. Digital technology diversifies consumer choice. For some groups of consumers, new media platforms can be seen as a partial

---

[24]   See W. FISHER, *Nothing but the internet*, in March, 1997, 110(5) Harvard Law Review 1.

[25]   *Ibid.*

[26]   O. ANDRIYCHUK, *The legal nature of premium sports events: IP or not IP – That is the question*, in 2008, 3–4 International Sports Law Journal 52.

[27]   *Ibid.*

[28]   See *ibid.*, 52. For the author, such an owner-friendly approach is justified by the legal argument summarized by the claim that 'each commercially attractive event of an artistic nature, regardless of predictability of its results and its aesthetic creativity, shall be granted a copyright status'. In the United States, the actual sports performance is not protected by copyright; only the video representation or the audio commentary is. However, other common law rights protect some of the clubs' interests. See, e.g., *National Basketball Ass'n* v. *Sports Team Analysis*, 105 F.3d 841 (2d Cir. 1997).

[29]   *Ibid.*

substitution of traditional ones. In this situation, technological tensions are unavoidable, in particular, if the traditional broadcaster is not interested or simply unable to provide its content via the new media. In the domain of premium sports, those tensions are even more severe, inasmuch as sports media rights constitute the major driving force for development of new media platforms. Usually, the companies which operate in this market are not able to obtain the rights to broadcast sport events, because most of these rights are distributed by event organizers on the principle of exclusivity. This model is seen as a main requirement of traditional media, which prefer obtaining all media rights to sports events, even if some of them are not exploited in their entirety.[30] This helps them to preserve *status quo* and does not allow dissemination of media rights between many potential content operators. For example, in Italy, during the 'Serie A' season 1998–99, the most important TV broadcasters (RAI, Mediaset, and Telemontecarlo) signed an agreement to share some of the TV rights concerning the football matches. The AGCOM (the Authority that guaranties the equity in the broadcasting market), with its sentences n. 6633 and 6662 on 3 December 1998, stated that the agreement was against the market rules because – *de facto* – it left out other competitors. Nowadays, with a new law in the matter of TV rights in sport (D.Lgs. 9/2008), applicable from the 2010–11 season (not only in football but also in all professional sports), TV broadcasters will be forbidden to own more than one platform right. Each broadcaster can only buy one of the rights on the market (e.g. it can buy the satellite broadcasting rights but not the digital broadcasting rights which it could eventually license to others).

Finally, EU competition rules significantly affect sports broadcasting rights, particularly the vexing legal questions of the collective selling and collective buying of those rights. The leading 2003 Decision of the Commission,[31] involving the collective selling of the broadcasting rights to the UEFA European Champions League, has been used as a 'template' in subsequent sports broadcasting cases at the national level, and also the unresolved legal questions regarding the matter of the so-called 'organisational solidarity'[32] in sport -considered to be legally and politically sensitive – are of crucial importance to. The European Commission may grant exemptions to restrictive agreements when they contribute to improving the production or distribution of goods or to promoting technical or economic progress. Following the objections expressed by the Commission, UEFA proposed a new system of collective sales that neutralized the Commission's concerns and resulted in a final decision of exemption from EU competition law. This new policy will allow UEFA to continue to sell, through a call for tenders, its rights over the Champions League, making football affordable for a greater number of broadcasters, Internet and telephony operators and allowing clubs to commercialize on an individual basis part of the above-mentioned rights, such as the right to exploit pre-recorded broadcast and to use the contents of the archives, for example, for the production of videos, thus providing and improved and diversified offer. The European Union's

---

[30]   ANDRIYCHUK, note 26 *supra*, 65.

[31]   European Commission Decision, July 23, 2003, *Uefa CL*, in GUCE L 291/25, November 8, 2003, para. 124.

[32]   In Italy, the law (D.Lgs. 9/2008) states that 10% of the TV rights revenues is devolved to the minor league and to other sports (the so-called organisational solidarity), while the remainder must be divided in the following way: 40% in equal parts among the championship competitors, 30% based on the sport club audience and 30% based on the obtained success.

approach expressed in UEFA's case was approved in cases on Bundesliga[33] and Premier League,[34] where the Commission has recognized the legality of patterns of negotiation and sale of television rights. That said, however, it is good to point out that, under Article 295 TCE (European Union Treaty), the harmonization cannot be extended to the proprietary regime relative to the existence of the law. This rule requires that the proprietary regime be left unjudged in the member States. On point, in its decision in the UEFA case, the Commission expressly stated that the determination of the titularity of those rights is exclusive responsibility of the national law.

4. LICENSING IN SPORTS

Because IP shares many of the characteristics of real and personal property, associated rights permit IP to be treated as an asset that can be bought, sold, licensed, or even given away at no cost. Licensing and merchandising are generic names given to agreements which provide for the use of the name, logo, trademarks, livery colors, and other properties of and relating to a person, club, or organization to brand or publicize goods and services that are not directly connected with the core business of that person, club, or organization. A licensing agreement is a legal contract between two parties, known as the licensor and the licensee. In a typical licensing agreement, the licensor grants the licensee the right to produce and sell goods, apply a brand name or trademark, or use patented technology owned by the licensor. In exchange, the licensee usually submits to a series of conditions regarding the use of the licensor's property and agrees to make payments known as royalties.[35]

For enterprises that own IP assets, licensing out to potential merchandisers may provide them the following benefits:

- First, licensing out IP rights (such as brands, designs, or artworks) to other companies can generate lucrative license fees and royalties. It also allows a business to enter new product categories in a relatively risk-free and cost-effective way.
- Merchandising is also an invaluable marketing tool, as it increases the merchandiser's brand exposure, enhances the brand's image, and leads it to new markets. For sport teams, for example, merchandising helps foster a sense of belonging amongst their fans, who feel proud to wear their team's merchandised goods, such as T-shirts and caps.
- Merchandising may also be an effective tool to attract sponsorship for special events, as it strengthens the association between the sponsor's brand and the event. It is common for organizers of football matches, art exhibitions, music concerts,

---

[33]   European Commission Decision, January 19, 2005, *Bundesliga*, in GUCE L 134/46, May 27, 2005, para. 4.

[34]   European Commission Decision, March 22, 2006, *FA Premier League*, in GUCE C 7/18, January 12, 2008, para. 5.

[35]   For a complete study of a licence agreement see B.B. SIEGAL, *Merchandise licence agreement: an overview of key provision*, http://www.alabar.org/sections/intellectualproperty/pdf/BruceSiegal-LicenseAgreements.pdf.

benefit dinners, etc. to authorize sponsors to manufacture and sell merchandise that bears the event's trademark or symbol.[36]

Advantages for the licensee include:

- Companies that manufacture low-priced mass goods may make their products more eye-catching, glamorous, fun, and attractive by using a well-known brand, famous character, artistic work, or other appealing element on them.
- Companies that launch a new product on the market may advertise their product by associating it with a personality or fictional character in whose reflected light it will appear more attractive.

Sport licensing is reputed to be worth more than $125 billion in global sales, with the United States, Far East and Western Europe representing 85% of the global licensing market. The success of sports licensing depends not only on negotiating the best possible commercial and financial arrangements, but also on the careful drafting the license agreements to reflect the particular circumstances and dynamics of the sporting events to which they relate.[37] Sports licensing agreements are similar to other licensing agreements, but several different considerations arise. If the logo that is being licensed relates to a particular event, there will also be a specific prohibition against using or permitting the logos from being used in any manner contrary to public morals, or which compromises or reflects unfavorably on the good name, goodwill, reputation, standing, and image of the sport body, its event, and the sport itself.[38] Likewise, the grant of rights will be made subject to the rules of the sport body concerned; for example, in the case of an Olympic merchandising program, the Olympic Charter. Even the consequences of termination or expiration of the license agreement are particularly important in the case of a license of a sport event logo. Due to the cyclical nature of sports events, for example, the FIFA World Cup takes place every four years, the circulation of out-of-date merchandise can cause confusion and thus commercial and marketing problems. It is usual, therefore, to include a provision in the license agreement requiring the licensee to clear the market of licensed products/stocks within six months of termination or expiration, after which any remaining products/stocks should be destroyed.[39] Furthermore, attention also needs to be paid to the financial and fiscal provisions of the agreement, especially, where the sports licensing program is an international one transcending several national boundaries.[40] Finally, it is advisable to include a 'dispute resolution clause' referring disputes to arbitration or mediation, as sport bodies and sports persons prefer not to 'wash their dirty sports linen in public' but to settle their disputes privately, quickly, inexpensively, and effectively.[41]

---

[36]   L. VERBAUWHEDE, Consultant SMEs Division WIPO, *Savvy marketing: merchandising of intellectual property rights,* http://www.wipo.int/sme/en/documents/merchandising.htm#P8_112.
[37]   I. BLACKSHAW, *Licence to thrill,* in 2000, 5 Sport and Character Licensing 6–8.
[38]   GARDINER, note 2 *supra,* 438.
[39]   *Ibid.*
[40]   BLACKSHAW, note 23 *supra,* 149.
[41]   *Ibid.*

Where sports personality licensing is involved, the agreements also need to contain a so-called 'morality clause' to guard against and deal with all kinds of foreseeable contingencies affecting the value of the association with the sports personality. In particular, endorsement contracts require protection if the endorser is affected by doping offenses, loss of form or performance, or scandals.

As clubs increasingly become marketing-oriented, licensing is an extremely important tool. In particular, the clubs have realized that such licensing deals would not be possible without a comprehensive IP protection regime. The top clubs operate a strict, zero-tolerance approach to IP infringement. Some clubs, like Manchester United, are severe in punishing common counterfeits, such as hats and scarves. The Trade Marks Department actively looks for counterfeits, and wherever possible raids the manufacturing source. Different enforcement procedures are in place depending on the territory, but many of the club's anti-counterfeiting procedures are consistent throughout the world. For example, all Manchester United Merchandising Limited products bear security labels. These labels prevent counterfeiting and they also assist the authorities to differentiate between a genuine and a fake article.

As for many brand owners, the Internet poses a huge problem for Manchester United, and the club's Trade Marks Department monitors it on a daily basis using word- and image-recognition software, and by conducting ad hoc searches. As a football club with many child fans, it is particularly vigilant against pornographic websites that use the club's trademarks to lure visitors. The Trade Marks Department also works closely with other football and fashion brands when it comes to policing their IPR online.[42]

5.   MERCHANDISING IN THE SPORT INDUSTRY

Merchandising is one of the most powerful contemporary forms of marketing and brand extension available to brand owners today and it is being used in ever-increasingly sophisticated ways. Industry analysts estimate the value of the global market for sales of licensed merchandise is in excess of $170 billion per year and sport accounts for about 11% of the global market.[43]

The licensing of IPR in connection with sport and sporting events is becoming an ever more popular phenomenon. Sports licensing and merchandising programs offer a wide range of possibilities including:

- sports events and team logos and emblems ('logo licensing');
- sports events and team mascots ('character licensing');
- sports stars licensing ('personality licensing'); and
- sports clothing and footwear licensing ('product licensing').

Copyright, logos, patents, and trademarks are licensed to persons or organizations who wish to exploit a name, reputation, event, or personality and thus merchandising of

---

[42]   See article in IP review online, April 2006, http://www.cpaglobal.com//ip_review.
[43]   A. KOLAH, *Maximising the value of licensing & merchandising,* 2005, http://www. sport business.com.

natural and international sports events, emblems and mascots, and personalities is now the norm for many major sporting events.

Merchandising in sports area has undergone an incredible development during the end of the 1980s and the beginning of the 1990s. In the field of merchandising, the United States pre-empted everyone with the experiment of the NFL, which in 1963 was the first sports organization that formally and officially defined a licensing program for all its affiliates. Nowadays, the sport licensing industry ranks as one of the top revenue producers in the licensing world.

Elsewhere, merchandising is growing in importance as a potential source of additional revenue for sports clubs, but remains under-utilized, especially in Europe. This is especially true in Italy, where revenues currently account for only 25% of total revenues. More specifically, according to estimates provided by the Italian Soccer League (*Lega Calcio*), revenues derived from merchandise account for only about 3% of the total revenues of Serie A teams. In England, in 1990, following the National League Baseball Association example, Arsenal was one of the first clubs to register its name, to stop traders outside the football ground selling the club logo at an undercut price. Following this, the League and all individual clubs now jealously protect 'official' club and League products from reproduction or imitation by non-club producers. All top clubs now have extensive club shops or superstores; some have a number in different locales selling exclusive, official club products.

Nowadays, television and the popularity of sport has meant clubs coming to terms with a much more complex and lucrative financial environment and many top clubs are turning to marketing and 'branding' as a means of maintaining and extending their competitiveness. A brand is a fundamental resource for clubs and brand management is a key strategy for professional sports teams. Marketing and branding are increasingly important in the sports industry. A football club has a number of likely advantages over other branded products:

- brand loyalty – fans rarely switch allegiance between clubs and their products;
- brand longevity – football appeals to all age groups and increasingly across the social classes; and
- low marketing expenditure – football has little need to spend on marketing its product because of its established position in the marketplace.[44]

Although some sports clubs are now exploring the commercial potential of a successful merchandising strategy, built around a strong brand, only a small number of clubs have the potential to become global brands, i.e. the brands which will be recognized and valued all round the world. The case of Manchester United is emblematic. Manchester United has its own brand nature and has adopted its own strategies for expansion of marketing activities. There is a lot of 'crossing over' in football merchandising due to the diversity of product areas. These include 'core' merchandising, financial services, and fast-moving consumer goods, all under different departments, leading to possible fragmentation of a 'brand' strategy. Brand management is extremely important in this case due to the

---

[44] S. HOWARD-R.SAYCE, *Branding, sponsorship and commerce in football*, http://www.le.ac.uk/ sociology/css/resources/factsheets/fs11.html.

possibility of 'brand dilution' caused by having a wide variety of such products. The Manchester United brand encompasses a range of goods that have evolved as a result of its prominence in its core activity of being a successful football club brand. There has been a Manchester United Nintendo game and also Manchester United mineral water, beer, and even tomato sauce. In the club's official shop one can purchase a United Monopoly game – and much, much more. Growth in marketing activity has coincided with the team progression on the pitch and with increased television coverage at home and overseas.

The strategy of the English club is based on the strengthening of the trading network in new and emerging markets; the attention of the management is particularly concentrated on the Far East and North America. In this regard, to increase the degree of penetration of its mark in the American market, Manchester United has signed a contract with the New York Yankees, a leading Major League Baseball club. The agreement provides for the sale of T-shirts and gadgets of Manchester United in the shops of the Yankees around the United States and vice versa. It is clear that the two sports clubs rely so much on the degree of loyalty of their fans to be able to sell the products of their partners.

In general, in order to develop the merchandising is absolutely necessary to increase the visibility of the club to conquer new fans. In this regard, clubs must move in different directions:

- participate in international competition and get victories;
- organize stages, summer schools, and tours in order to be able to entrench their brand in these markets;
- increase their visibility through the Internet;
- create sales points in their respective cities and a series of corners at major shopping centers;
- buy foreign players, which allows clubs to increase their visibility within the countries of origin of those players; and
- buy a symbol player of international fame who can gather transversal popularity.

Because of the globalization of economy, the competition on foreign markets has dramatically increased and it is essential for the clubs to expand their market through strategies whose final aim is to internationalize the mark. Being global is the major objective of sport brands in general and of professional football clubs. For this reason, Chelsea F.C. participated, with some of its most representative players, in an important Indian movie dedicated to the football club. This will serve to reach the Indian football market, not yet 'attacked' by the big European football club and the choice of the movie is motivated by the fact that India is the most important movie producer after the United States. Another important example is that of the Barcelona club that has managed to combine local and universal dimension of its brand perfectly, on the one hand through initiatives that promote the protection of human rights in the world and, on the other, by maintaining a strong connection with the local reference (Catalonia). Symbolic, in that sense, was the choice of the official sponsor, the Barcelona club was for years the only European club to refuse sponsorship for the official uniforms and in 2006 the logo that appeared for the first time on the '*blaugrana*' shirt during a Champions League match was not that of a multinational or a large private group, but that of UNICEF, with which the

Barcelona club has established a partnership that includes the use of football players as testimonials.[45]

6. JUDICIAL CASES IN THE SPORT CONTEXT

The contribution of the jurisprudence has been of fundamental importance for the application of IPR to sport. The American jurisprudential contribution is particularly influential mostly in consideration of the fact that the principles asserted in such system have influenced various European juridical cultures.

6.1. American Cases

Through the first half of the twentieth century, publicity-based lawsuits were filed based upon rights to privacy, and courts would allow non-consented use of a person's image where the person had attained fame. Typical of this was the 1941 case of *Davey O'Brien*.[46] O'Brien was a famous college football player who sued to recover for the use of his persona on a calendar that advertised Pabst beer. O'Brien claimed he would never lend his name to advertise alcohol, but the court denied relief, stating that he had lost his right to privacy by his prior achievement of fame.

In 1953, in *Haelan Laboratorie Inc* v. *Topps Chewing Gum Inc.*,[47] the jurisprudence extended the right of privacy to include a right of publicity, which was officially recognized. In this case, Haelan, a chewing gum manufacturing company, entered into various contracts with professional baseball players, who provided the company the exclusive right to use the players' photographs in connection with the sale of its chewing gum. In addition the contract also stated that the players agreed not to grant any other gum manufacturer a similar right during the terms of the contract. So, when Topps, a rival chewing gum manufacturer aware of the terms of Haelan's contract, deliberately entered into contract with various players to use their photographs in connection with sales of Topps' gum, the defense was that the contract between Haelan and the players was no more than a release by the player, which gave Haelan the right to use the photographs. In rejecting Topps' argument, the Second Circuit Court of Appeals stated that, in addition to and independent of the right of privacy, a man has the right in the publicity value of his photographs, i.e. the right to grant the exclusive privilege of publishing his picture.

With the right to prevent the unauthorized use of a persona established, the ability to manage the persona or defend against its misuse is aided by knowledge of the right's parameters. The courts and statutes seem reluctant to create a list of specifically protected rights to publicity, because a finite list of protected elements of one's identity would only invite marketers to discover new ways to appropriate.

The court in *Abdul-Jabbar* v. *General Motors* stated that, '[a] rule which says that the right of publicity can be infringed only through the use of nine different methods of

---

[45] F. BOF, F. MONTANARI, and S. BAGLIONI, *Il calcio tra contesto locale ed opportunità globali. Il caso del Barcellona FC, més que un club,* in 2007, Vol. III, Fasc. 2 Rivista di diritto ed economia dello sport 36.

[46] *O' Brien* v. *Pabst Sales Co.*, 124 F.2d 167 (5th Cir. 1941).

[47] *Haelan Laboratories, Inc.* v. *Topps Chewing Gum, Inc.*, 202 F.2d 866 (2d Cir. 1953).

appropriating identity merely challenges the clever advertising strategist to come up with the tenth'.[48] The appellate court addressed the question of whether an individual has a right to publicity in their former name. (Abdul-Jabbar was identified through his years at UCLA and in his early years in the NBA with his birth name, Lew Alcindor.) General Motors ran an advertisement during the 1993 National Collegiate Athletic Association (NCAA) men's basketball tournament, which created an association between the three consecutive years of Alcindor's being named most outstanding player in the NCAA tournament, and the same number of consecutive years (three) that the Oldsmobile 88 had been named Consumer Digest's 'Best Buy'. The commercial showed no visual image of Alcindor, the person; it only showed a graphic of the name. The district court ruled against Abdul-Jabbar, finding that he had abandoned his use of the name and therefore General Motors' use of it could not be construed as an endorsement. The appellate court reversed and remanded stating that the 'right of publicity protects celebrities from appropriations of their identity not strictly definable as "name or picture"'. The court held that 'by using Alcindor's record to make a claim for its car, GMC has arguably attempted to "appropriate the cachet of one product for another"'. This means that a person's former name can remain attached to their persona and warrant protection when the appropriator sufficiently attempts to link their product to that name.

At this point, a reflection seems appropriate: the creation of this new, subjective right has helped the chances of protection for celebrities, but it is equally true that this right has little typical content, which can imply hidden dangers in court, especially when put in conflict with other rights regulated by norms and protected.

It is well settled that use of a player's persona for news-reporting purposes is not an infringement of the right of publicity. This is obviously so, as countless images are exposed daily via various news sources. Despite this First Amendment protection, limits do exist pertaining to the use of newsworthy images of sports figures.[49] On occasion, news entities use video clips, sound bites, or photographs from their news items for use in other commercial contexts. In *Joe Montana* v. *San Jose Mercury News*,[50] the question arose as to whether a newspaper may republish its front sports page and sell it for a profit. The San Francisco 49ers had won their fourth Super Bowl. The following day, the newspaper published a 'Souvenir Section' devoted exclusively to the 49ers as a 'team of destiny', with an artist's drawing of Montana's image was on the front page. At a later date, the front page was produced in poster form and sold to the general public. Montana thereafter filed suit for common law and statutory commercial misappropriation of his name, photograph, and likeness. The issue before the court was whether there was an infringement of Montana's right of publicity or if the republication was entitled to First Amendment protection. The court looked to prior case law that stood for the proposition that, 'a person's photograph originally published in one issue of a periodical as a newsworthy subject ... may be republished subsequently in another medium as an advertisement for the periodical itself, illustrating the quality and content of the periodical, without the person's written consent'. Citing several other supporting cases, the court recognized that 'the right of publicity has not been held to outweigh the value of free expression', and

---

48   *Abdul-Jabbar* v. *General Motors*, 75 F.3d 1391 (9th Cir. 1996).
49   B. M. ROWLAND, *An athlete's right of publicity*, in 2002, 76, Florida Bar Journal, Part 10.
50   *Montana* v. *San Jose Mercury News Inc.*, 35 USP.Q. 2d 1783, 1785 (Cal. App. 1995).

'[a]dvertising to promote a news medium ... is not actionable under an appropriation of publicity theory so long as the advertising does not falsely claim that the public figure endorses that news medium'. Therefore Montana lost his claim because the poster did not constitute an endorsement of the San Jose Mercury News by him. It follows from *Montana* that the media may not take the athlete's image from its use in a newsworthy context for use in commercial materials if the image is an unauthorized endorsement. However, the media can use the formerly newsworthy image for self-promotion otherwise.

In a most recent case, *ETW Corp.* v. *Jireh Publishing*,[51] the court allowed the unauthorized use of another's trademark when the sign is used in an artistic expression. The incident involved the golfer Tiger Woods, who sued Jireh Publishing for publishing a painting, created by Rick Rush, entitled 'The Masters of Augusta' and portraying the image of the golfer, all in order to commemorate his victory in the Masters Tournament of Augusta (Georgia). Woods and his exclusive licensing agent, ETW Corporation, complained a breach of competition rules, trademark rights, and, precisely, the right of publicity. By contrast, Jireh argued that Rush's artistic work was protected by the First Amendment and that it did not violate the Lanham Act in relation to trademarks. The Ohio federal district court rejected Woods' argument that the print was 'merely sports merchandise' unworthy of the First Amendment protection. Instead, the court found that the print sought to convey a message, and that message was a unique expression of an idea, rather than the mere copying of an image. The court decided that the print was protected by the First Amendment and dismissed the case. The Sixth Circuit US Court of Appeals affirmed the decision, stating that the image of Woods was only used to describe the content of the painting, which is allowed by the Lanham Act when it is used legally and in good faith with a descriptive function. In essence, the court stated that the right of publicity had to be considered significantly limited in the social interest of the freedom of artistic expression.

6.2. UK Cases

The British situation is of particular interest because it represents one instance of a developed country resisting the inexorable creation of new and expansive IPR, at least in this one domain. The Copyright, Designs and Patents Act 1988 (CDPA 1988) defines copyright to include (s. 3) 'literary works' other than a dramatic or musical work, which is written, spoken, or sung. This obviously covers news, articles, magazines, and books. So, for example, copyright subsists in the vast amount of original written material generated about sport, including rules and regulations, match reports, newspapers, and so on. Information itself, such as football results, is not subject to copyright, but the way the information is expressed may be.

In *Football League Ltd* v. *Littlewoods Pools Ltd*,[52] the House of Lords held that copyright subsisted in the League's fixture list because it was not possible to separate the arrangement of fixture from the mere making of the chronological list of fixtures, and even if it had been possible, the preparation of the chronological list itself involved sufficient labor, skill, and expertise to justify copyright protection. As a result, pools

---

[51]   *ETW Corp.* v. *Jireh Pub. Inc.*, 332 F.3d 915 (6th Cir. 2003).
[52]   *Football League Ltd* v. *Littlewoods Pools Ltd* [1959] 1 Ch 650–1.

companies, betting offices, and the media have had to enter into royalty-based license agreements for the right to reproduce such fixture lists. Literary works can also encompass databases. The literary work comprised by a database is original if, by reason of selection or arrangement of its contents, the database constitutes the author's own intellectual creation.

The FA Premier League and Football League, which between them organize the top four divisions of professional football in England, have formed a separate company, Football DataCo Ltd, to secure, protect, and exploit the commercial value of data generated by the matches they organize. In addition the Scottish Premier League and Scottish Football League have each appointed Football DataCo Ltd to perform the same role in respect of their competitions. This involves the traditional licensing of pools companies, betting offices, and the media to reproduce the fixture lists, as well as the gathering of statistical data from a game for exploitation on a real-time basis using the Internet and mobile telephony, and also on a long-term basis in form guides for betting, interactive television, and fantasy football games. The value is created and protected by means of copyright and database law in relation to the data that is generated for exploitation by Football DataCo Ltd. It is also created and protected by requiring members of the media and public seeking access to football matches to agree, via press pass terms and conditions for the media, and ticket conditions, and ground regulations for the public, not to seek to create and/or transmit data about the match for commercial exploitation, on a 'real-time' basis or otherwise. As mentioned above, the copyright work is infringed when someone, other than the copyright owner, gives rise to one of the restricted acts in relation to the whole of the work or also only to a substantial part of it.

Whilst it is usually obvious what constitutes the whole of a work, the question of what constitutes a substantial part of a work can be problematic. The approach the court has adopted is that the question of what constitutes a 'substantial part' is a qualitative rather than a quantitative question. In *Ladbroke (Football) Ltd* v. *William Hill (Football) Ltd*,[53] Lord Pearce said that the question as to what is substantial must be decided by quality rather than quantity. Additionally, the parts of a work copied will not amount to a substantial part if the parts copied were not in themselves original.

The law in this area should also be seen in the light of the law relating to incidental inclusion of copyright works. There is another category of infringing act known as 'secondary infringement'. The category of secondary infringement generally relates to commercial use of infringing copies of a copyright work. Secondary infringers are often also prosecuted in the criminal court. In contrast to the position under CDPA 1988, ss. 16–21, secondary infringement under ss. 22–26 requires a mental element on the part of the infringer: the infringers must know or have reason to believe that they are dealing with infringing copies of a work. In 1997, in *LA Gear Inc* v. *Hi-Tee Sports plc*, it was stated that the test as to what a defendant 'has reason to believe' is an objective one. It requires a consideration of whether the reasonable man, with knowledge of the facts that the defendant had knowledge of, would have formed the belief that the item was an infringing copy. This is important for many reasons, not least because, under CDPA 1988, s. 97, if it can be shown in an action for infringement of copyright that at the time of the infringement the defendant did not know, and had no reason to believe, that copyright

---

53   *Ladbroke (Football) Ltd* v. *William Hill (Football)* [1964] 1 WLR 273.

subsisted in the work to which the action relates, the claimant is not entitled to damages. There is provision in s. 97 for the court to award damages notwithstanding the defendant's lack of knowledge if the infringement is flagrant and the defendant has benefited from the infringing activity. In such a case, the court may award 'such additional damages as the justice of the case may require'.

Dealing now with trademark, s. 1 of the Trade Marks Act 1994 (TMA 1994) defines a trademark as 'any sign capable of being represented graphically which is capable of distinguishing goods or service of one undertaking from those of other undertakings. A trademark may, in particular, consist of words (including personal names), designs, letters, numerals or the shape of goods or their packaging'. This definition is not exhaustive: a distinctive color or combination of colors or a distinctive sound or smell may constitute a trademark, so long as it is capable of being represented graphically.

There are certain grounds of absolute refusal of registration under TMA 1994. For example, a mark will not be registered if it is devoid of distinctive character. Thus, 'Aspirin' is a generic mark, insufficiently distinctive of its manufacturer to be recordable as a trademark. Nor will a mark be registered if it consists exclusively of signs or indications that serve to designate the kind, quality, quantity, intended purpose, value, geographical origin, or other characteristics of goods or services. In addition, there are certain specially protected emblems, such as royal arms and insignia, national flags and emblems, and coats of arms granted by the Crown.

Those comparatively straightforward examples have been supplemented in recent law by some considerably harder cases. A famous example arose in *Trebor Bassett* v. *FA*.[54] Trebor Bassett manufactured candy sticks into which it inserted cards bearing a photograph and description of famous footballers. This included certain member of the England football team wearing the national team strip which bore the Three Lions logo, which was a registered trademark of the Football Association. The Football Association sought to restrain this use and Trebor Bassett applied to the court on the basis that it was entitled to a declaration that such use was not 'use' in the sense of trademark use which was therefore restrained by TMA 1994. It was held that the correct answer was a commonsense one and that in the mere depiction of the England shirt in a photograph, which as a necessary consequence included a depiction within that photograph of a trademark, there was not an affixation in any real sense of a trademark to goods or their packaging as referred to in TMA 1994.

A further case of perhaps even greater importance in this context is that of *Arsenal* v. *Reed*.[55] Mr. Reed was a street trader who sold merchandise displaying Arsenal Football Club's trademarks on a stand which displayed, however, a disclaimer of any formal connection between Mr. Reed and Arsenal Football Club or any official endorsement by the club of the goods he sold. It stated that this was unofficial merchandise. This effectively denied Arsenal the opportunity to suggest that there existed any likelihood of confusion, either in the context of passing off or in the context of s. 10 of TMA 1994. However, Arsenal held registrations of its trademarks for goods of an identical nature to those sold by Mr. Reed. The first limb of trademark infringement, namely an identical mark used in connection with identical goods or services to those for which the registered

---

[54]   *Trebor Bassett* v. *FA* [1997] FSR 211.
[55]   *Arsenal Football Club Plc* v. *Matthew Reed* [2003] EWCA Civ 96.

mark holds its registration, therefore, seemed to be made out. Mr. Reed argued, however, that his use of the trademark was not use trademark sense. In other words, the trademarks when displayed upon the goods sold by him were not 'badges of origin', i.e. badges which identified the goods as being those of Arsenal Football Club, but rather 'badges of allegiance'. As a result, the finding of the court was that the use by Mr. Reed of the Arsenal trademark did not constitute trademark infringement. It is an authority that sent some shockwaves through the law generally and its direct appropriateness and relevance to sport will be immediately apparent. As a result certain questions were referred to the European Court of Justice by the trial Judge, Laddie J. First, is it a defense to an action for infringement that the use complained of does not indicate the trade origin of the goods? Secondly, if so, would the fact that the use would be perceived as a badge of support, loyalty, or affiliation to the proprietor be a sufficient connection to indicate trade origin?

The judgment of the European Court[56] is not the clearest. The court was concerned less with whether the use complained of was 'trademark use' and more with whether the use by the third party, affects or was likely to affect, the functions of the trademark. The principal function of the trademark in this context is to indicate trade origin. Where the use of the sign in question by the third party is liable to affect the guarantee of the origin of the goods, the trademark proprietor must be able to prevent this and it is immaterial whether or not the sign is perceived as a badge of support for or loyalty or affiliation to the proprietor of the mark. When the case was referred back to the High Court, Laddie J. said that the European Court in reaching its determination had trespassed into matters of fact and therefore had exceeded its jurisdiction. He upheld earlier view that then was no infringement. The matter then went to the Court of Appeal. The Court of Appeal was given the somewhat unenviable task of trying to untangle what had become, with all respect to the learned judges involved, something of an unedifying judicial spectacle. The Court of Appeal found that the European Court of Justice had not disregarded the conclusions of fact made by Laddie J. but did find that in the circumstances which had been found by Laddie J. to exist the conduct and use of the mark by Mr. Reed was liable to jeopardize the guarantee of origin.

Whilst this resolution of the case was treated in many quarters with some relief, it is likely that there may be further judicial consideration of these topics before long. At the present time, what had seemed to be a major danger to brand owners in the particular context of sport has been allayed to a greater or lesser extent. In *Eddie Irvine* v. *TalkSport Limited*,[57] the High Court undoubtedly paved the way for a more effective legal protection for sporting personalities whose names and image have been misappropriated by the advertising industry, without the necessary consent or license to do. Talk Sport had doctored a photo of Irvine in an advertising brochure; it had manipulated the photo to look as if Irvine was holding a portable radio which had the words 'Talk Radio' on it. Irvine claimed that this amounted to false endorsement of the TalkSport radio station. Irvine's claim was upheld. The judge, Laddie J., found that the law of passing off could apply to cases of false endorsement because Irvine had a significant reputation/goodwill and TalkSport's actions gave rise to a false message which would be understood by a not insignificant section of its market that its goods had been endorsed, recommended, or

---

56   Case C-206/01, *Arsenal Football Club Plc* v. *Matthew Reed* (13 June 2002), ECJ [7].
57   *Eddie Irvine* v. *Talk Sport Limited* [2002] EWHC 367 (Ch).

approved by Irvine. It was held that Irvine had a property right in his goodwill through which he could protect his image from unlicensed appropriation or endorsement of a third party's business. In this case, the court unequivocally recognized for the first time that a well-known sportsperson can prevent third parties from exploiting his name or image in circumstances where members of the public will be confused into thinking that the sportsperson concerned has endorsed or in some way authorized or licensed such use by that party, which was not, in fact, the case.[58]

6.3. Italian Cases

The application of new laws regarding trademarks in the sports context[59] have occupied Italian courts. In 1991, the Inferior Court of Turin resolved a controversy between *Juventus F.C. S.P.A. and the Juvena Produits de Beautè S.A.*,[60] a company that produces cosmetic products, aiming to establish to what degree the Juvena brand could be protected in the comparison with the Juventus mark, adopted later by the Homonym soccer club. The judge considered the brand of the claimant Juvena as weak mark and, consequently, the protection was limited: light variations and differences are sufficient to exclude the confusion between marks. It is obvious, therefore, that the Juventus mark, registered in recent times by the Homonym soccer club, used as a sign to distinguish, *inter alia*, cosmetic and perfumery's products, cannot be confused with the previously adopted Juvena brand, because this brand introduces a variation of relief regarding the first sign and, secondly, it is a complex mark, also constituted by figured elements and by denominative characters. Later, as always relating to soccer, the Court of Novara[61] considered the denomination of the headline 'Super Inter' illicit, because it may be confused with that of the official magazine of the F.C. Inter (Inter Football Club professional football team), forbidding the production and sale of gadgets with the name or the signs of the soccer team, both registered marks, without the authorization of the club.

The new law on marks, in the attempt to directly protect the evocative function of famous trademarks, has established (in art. 21), that, 'If well-known, they can be registered only by the subject having right to, or with his approval   the signs used in artistic, literary, scientific, political and sport field, the denominations or acronyms of public manifestations and those of no profit agencies and associations, and their characteristic signs'. There is a reference to this norm in a sentence of the Court of Modena, called to resolve a controversy between FIFA (International Football Federation) and ISL Football AG (a Swiss company),[62] over who was entitled to use the logo of the World Cup, held in the United States 1994. The Act introduces a new category of signs as marks that may be registered, assuring the exclusive right to the author of the notorious mark or its licensee, in exception to the principle of the freedom to register marks. According to

---

[58]   The case is analyzed by J. TAYLOR, *Commercialisation of sports proprietary rights*, in Sports Properties, King's College, London, Lecture, November 6, 2006.

[59]   For a complete examination of the Italian cases, see L. COLANTUONI, *Merchandising*, in I Contratti, 2006, nn. 8–9, p. 827 *et seq.*

[60]   Trib. Torino, 30 luglio 1991, in Giur. It., 1991, I, 844 ss.

[61]   Trib. Novara, 24 giugno 1996, in Aida Rep., 1997, voce IV 3.2.

[62]   Trib. Modena, 26 giugno 1994, in N.G.C.C., 1995, I, 99 ss.

the tribunal, there is nothing that forbids the owner of a notorious mark, that is, the subject that has taken the mark to notoriety, to consent others to register the mark in his place rather than to avail himself of the right commercially to take advantage of the license system. In such case, the subject that had the consent to register the mark detains all the rights connected with its ownership, among others the right to forbid the use to non-authorized third parties. Consequently, according to the judge, only the Swiss company would have been authorized to ask the protection offered by the new law on marks in order to react to the undue use of the logo of the manifestation.

Recently, Italian jurisprudence has faced two analogous cases that regard the protection of the mark of soccer clubs that had been excluded from the Italian championship for financial reasons. The first decision, adopted in April 4, 2006 by the Inferior Court of Naples, Intellectual Property Department, regards the case of *Salernitana Sport Spa* v. *Salernitana Calcio 1919 Spa*, both acting in soccer. The action was brought regarding the violation of a series of IPR, including the Salernitana trademark. The judge applied the distinction between strong marks and weak mark, of jurisprudential derivation. In Italian law, a strong mark means the mark constituted by a original name completely separated from the product or service that characterizes it, while weak marks are constituted by common names, that often identify or evoke the product or the service. The weak mark, having a low distinctive capacity, is protected only in the case of its integral counterfeit and therefore it is sufficient to bring a small change to exclude the forgery; the strong mark, on the other hand, having an elevated originality, has an extensive protection because infringement to trademark is recognized even in presence of relevant changes.

Following the above-mentioned rules the judge stated the weakness of Salernitana mark, because this denomination is explicitly referred to the city of Salerno, where the club owns the local soccer club. The word Salernitana indicates the citizens of Salerno, without any creative elaboration and therefore it must qualify as weak mark. In this specific case, the differential element, although minimum, of the word 'Calcio 1919' was declared sufficient to exclude trademark infringement.

The second decision,[63] adopted on April 11, 2007 by the Inferior Court of Bologna, Intellectual Property Department, resolved the controversy between Spal Spa, a successful soccer team of the past, owner of the S.P.A.L. (*Società Polisportiva Ars et Labour*) trademark and Spal 1907 Ferrara that, in application of the Italian sport law, took over the first club, ruled out for financial reasons from the Italian Championship Serie C. The court qualified the SPAL trademark as weak, because it was formed by the association of common words and therefore the small changes of 'Spal 1907 Ferrara' have excluded trademark infringement. In any event, the judge did not consider it necessary to compare the two marks, because the old Spal nowadays does not have any role in a sport context; it is not enrolled in any championship (not even amateur), with nothing to offer on the market and therefore it cannot obtain the protection of the trademark law.

Regarding athlete's images rights, the Inferior Court of Milan handled a controversy between the soccer player Sandro Mazzola and Bambole Franca Sas,[64] a company that had launched on the market dolls that reproduced the semblance of the soccer player, who

---

63   The case is analyzed by C. NOVAZIO, *Tutela del marchio e disciplina del titolo sportivo*, in 2007, 2–3 Rassegna dir. ed economia dello sport 402 ss.
64   Trib. Milano, 25 novembre 1974, in Riv. dir. sport., 1974, 237.

had been very famous in the 1970s. The manufacturer asserted that the commercialization of the dolls was justified by the notoriety of the soccer player. Rejecting the manufacturer's defense, the court stated that principle of art. 97 L.D.A. serve to protect a public interest and not to favor merely lucrative private purposes, as placing in the market dolls with the semblance of a famous sportsman.

In another case, in 1976, the Inferior Court of Modena[65] decided the controversy between Panini and two famous Italian boxers (Giuseppe Ros and Fernando Atzori), whose images had been reproduced in an album of stickers. Panini's defense was based on the facts that the two boxers were famous, that the images reproduced events that had taken place in public (boxing matches), and that the profit purpose of the publication was not enough to render the use of the pictures illicit; moreover the publication had the purpose to inform. The court has sanctioned the commercial character of the publication of the album binder and of the closed envelopes containing the stickers, the operation did not appear to be run with the only purpose of informing the collectors on the lives and deeds of the champions. To confirm this matter, two reasons were invoked: the first was the large number of stickers one had to buy to complete the collection and the second the artificiality of the system; the envelopes, in fact, were not numbered and had no indications of their content, reasons that clearly showed the preponderance of the lucrative purposes over the information purposes.

In 1978, the Court of Appeal of Bologna,[66] reversing the previous finding, found it lawful to use the image of the two boxers, recognizing that the collection of stickers had an informative and didactic-cultural scope. In fact, the court has observed that the sticker collection not only offers a way to collect and conserve the images of many athletes, but also a way to have personal information, such as age, place of birth, etc. and information about the most significant achievements of the athletes' careers.

The same problems have been addressed, in 1981, by Court of Appeal of Genoa[67] in a dispute between Flash Spa and two professional soccer players of the Fiorentina football club (Mauro Della Martira and Ennio Pellegrini), regarding the non-authorized publication and the commercialization of stickers with the images of the above-mentioned players. In this case, the court decided the notoriety of the figured players and the informative and instructive scopes of the publication, moreover coexisting with an unavoidable lucrative gain, led to considering legitimate the behavior of Edizioni Flash. These three ultimate decisions are the expression of a jurisprudential guideline that considers lawful the unauthorized publication of someone else's image, when public information prevails over the financial purposes.

Recently, the Italian jurisprudence decided on the controversy concerning the unauthorized use of the personality rights of the soccer player David Trezeguet. This decision, adopted by the Inferior Court of Turin,[68] Intellectual Property Rights Department, is strictly tied to the Italian conception of the name's right as a right of personality. The controversy originated from the initiative of the Soccer Shirt Srl that produced and put in

---

[65]   Trib. Modena, Sez. III, 17 gennaio 1976, in Riv. dir. sport., 1976, 240.
[66]   App. Bologna, 21 aprile 1978, in Foro pad., 1978, 296.
[67]   Corte d'Appello di Genova, 24 febbraio 1981, in Riv. dir. sport., 1982, 564.
[68]   Trib. Torino, sez. spec. proprietà industriale e intellettuale, 20 gennaio 2006, in Riv. dir. ind., 2006, II, 356 ss.

commerce, also through its own Internet site, a line of sportswear containing the name and the last name of the French soccer player, under contract for Juventus. The manufacturer observed that in 2005, between the stages of the litigation, there was a verbal agreement having as its object the production and commercialization of the line of sportswear in question. Receiving the appeal proposed by the soccer player, the court stated that, even if the conclusion of the verbal agreement could have been proved, the manufacturer could not continue to use the name of the athlete because, presenting the appeal, Trezeguet had, in fact, countermanded his assent. The judge affirmed that in regard to personal and unalienable rights such as the name and image, the consent of its use constitutes a unilateral agreement having as object not the right but its exercise; even if the consent can be occasionally inserted in the agreement, remains separated from it and it can be revoked.

7. CONCLUSIONS

7.1. General Remarks

Intellectual property plays a critical role in furthering economic progress and the welfare of the world's citizens. The reason is simple. Intellectual property typically is both a key input into and a byproduct of successful innovation, which is a principal factor in fostering a dynamic, growing economy. In this context, IP licensing is generally efficient because it enables firms to combine complementary factors of production, reduce transaction and production costs, and reduce free-riding by others. Intellectual property, therefore, is a highly valued asset, and it has been granted substantial legal protection by the nations of the world. It is important that those protections are preserved.

In general terms, even for effect of the above mentioned international agreements, the differences between common law and civil law in the field of IP have remarkably decreased. Unfortunately, the complexity of the issues sometimes hinders achievement of a complete international harmonization, and notwithstanding the great advances that have been made, there still remain significant areas of divergence both in substantive law and in procedure. First, the vital area of enforcement has so far remained largely outside the compass of international regulation and harmonization, and remains subject to the greatest diversity. Secondly, although IP/antitrust issues have occupied the attention of courts for some time, a number of open questions remain. Nonetheless, in the United States, certain basic principles have emerged that help to define the scope of IPR, its enforcement, and its licensing. For example, antitrust laws permit a patent owner to use litigation to enforce the statutory right to exclude others from making, using, or selling a patented invention. Similarly, the general rule is that, with limited exceptions, the owner of IP, similar to any other property, may refuse in the United States to license that property.[69] Finally, there is a common thread that runs through the above discussion of copyrights, patents, and trademarks. Promoting cultural development, fostering innovation and growth, and protecting public health and safety are all commonly held goals.

---

[69]   J.F. RILL and M.C. SCHECHTER, *International antitrust and intellectual property harmonization of the interface*, 2003, 34 Law & Pol'y Int'l Bus. 783.

The United States undoubtedly differs from other jurisdictions on the antitrust legality of various license restrictions. The different approaches have the potential of forcing industry to navigate its way through disparate, and possibly conflicting, rules on the permissibility of licensing restrictions. A rationalization and convergence of approaches is needed to remove the cloud of uncertainty that has befallen licensing restrictions, and thereby spare industry the kind of protracted litigation that accompanies uncertainty.

In the information age, with technology advancing at an accelerating rate, simply implementing the TRIPS Agreement is not enough to establish a robust IP system. Advances in information technology, biotechnology, and other fields require the updating of national and international laws that protect IP. Fortunately, WIPO has led the way in developing new international norms to meet these challenges. WIPO also has led the way in simplifying and streamlining the procedures for seeking, obtaining, and maintaining rights in multiple countries. Through its 'Global Protection Services' and its harmonization treaties, it saves creators and national IP offices a great deal of time and effort. WIPO also makes available its excellent technical assistance for establishing and improving IPR systems worldwide. Countries should look to both the WTO and WIPO when crafting their IPR systems. However, global harmonization of principles and standards affecting the IP is unlikely to be achieved in the near future. Against this backdrop, it is less than surprising that efforts to date to seek convergence have been few and the accomplishments limited. Nonetheless, useful foundations have been laid, and there is reason to believe that some progress can be made.

7.2. The Sports Industry and IP Rights

IPR in sports represent a central issue that needs continuous study, because of new applications deriving from praxis that offer many possibilities of exploitation of these rights, but, at the same time, they raise the risk of infringements. New technology is continually affecting all sports, making information and viewing available to fans through several different mediums – no longer just TV and radio. In particular, the Internet is rapidly advancing the progress of sports technology, while simultaneously sparking a number of copyright and trademarks infringement issues. In fact, the Internet is very difficult to regulate and has been generally describes as 'the new wild west' and also 'the world's photocopying machine'. As a source of information it is a particularly valuable communications and marketing tool for sport, not least sports clubs and personalities. As with all leading sports clubs, Manchester United has its own website, ManUtd.com and is reputed to receive some 8 million 'hits' a month from a worldwide fan base of some 25 million.[70] Anyway, the Internet has also developed into an important vehicle for the sale and purchase of a wide variety of goods and services – 'e-commerce' – including sporting ones.

In order for both the sports industry and the IPR owners to benefit from the remarkable potential the Internet holds, the two sides need to strike a balance – one that will require some give and take on both sides. All professional sport leagues have been notoriously stubborn when it comes to issues of IPR infringement – after all, it is how they make most of their money. But they often fail to look at the big picture; compromising on certain

---

[70] GARDINER, note 2 *supra*, 424.

issues would actually increase their revenue, if they could find a way to appease the fans and the infringers. Often, the alleged IPR violations are incredibly lucrative ideas created with the sports fan in mind. Sports leagues and franchises will need to approach these ideas with much more of an open mind in the future – and doing so will allow for a new era of sports to emerge.

As far as the current status of IPR in sports, progress is being made – very slowly. For every settlement and agreement reached between sports leagues and IPR infringers, there are ten times as many lawsuits with immovable parties on both sides. This is due in part to the fact that many of these technological advancements have not been the product of a gradual progression. Most took the sports industry by surprise, and rather than welcoming new ideas and concepts, they felt threatened and defensive. As such, they pushed hard to make sure no one else was getting a piece of their profits. What they did not realize was that doing so only opened the door for criticism, and shed a negative light on the industry.

There is another innovative subject related to IPR in the field of sports. Recently, the specialized doctrine has raised the interesting question whether the 'sports moves' (movements) that athletes adopt in some disciplines, such as rhythmic gymnastics and synchronized swimming, can enjoy protection under the IP law.

Generally speaking, as said, sport is now big business, and big business demands this protection. Entire industries exist to sell and promote goods and services at sporting events and for use by sports participants. Players in this vast market may benefit from the efficiency of fixed property rights, as the 'fuel' that drives these market transactions. A key element of that fuel is the sports moves themselves, and patents, copyrights. and trademarks may provide the best tools for securing those rights.[71] It could be argued that new 'sports moves' could be caught by the ambit of the *ratio* of patent law, as long as they involve strong efforts by the inventor and they are so innovative that by their constant us they can benefit sport. However, the satisfaction of the *ratio* test is not sufficient at all, because the all patent law imposes very strict condition to grant a patent.

In respect of the copyrights, even if theoretically a 'sport move' could be considered to be a dramatic work, 'sport moves' could not be protected by copyrights law, since the spontaneity and the uncertainty of outcome that sport moves involve are inhibitory factors for its application. This is not the case, though, for the routine-orientated sports such as rhythmic gymnastics, synchronized swimming, and ice dancing. Athletes in these sports devise complex sets of movements that are intended to be performed with a high level of accuracy during competitions.[72] Anyway, the difficult trade off between recreational and commercial component of the sport and the implications deriving from the acceptation of a similar theory do not concur to answer with absolute certainty these

---

[71]   See R.M. KUNSTADT, F. SCOTT KIEFF, and R.G. KRAMER, *Are sports moves next in IP law?*, in National Law Journal, May 20, 1996, 1. *Contra*, see, M. WALSH, *Patently ridiculous, some say; people dunk basketballs. people lift boxes. Should the Patent Office protect their 'inventions'?*, in Legal Times, August 19, 1996, S32.

[72]   A. VAGELIS, *The legal protection of sports moves in UK and US law*, 14th World IASL Congress in Sports Law: an emerging legal order, November 27–9, 2008, Athens. A similar argument regards even the tactics and the plans that sport coaches use in order to make their athletes win. In football, basketball, and other sports, these tactics are of pivotal importance for the victory and quite often some kind of novel tactics invented by a coach are adopted by other coaches throughout the world.

innovative questions, even if it seems rather excessive to expand IP to sports tactics and moves, and this for the following reasons:

- first, human movements are infinite and furthermore infringements could happen anywhere at any time,
- secondly, the infringement could hardly be controlled as well as proved; and
- finally, it is unreasonable to prevent recreational players and athletes from using a certain move, method, or strategy or to impose the rigid sanctions provided by the law on the athletes infringers.[73]

In conclusion, it is absolutely necessary to make one last observation regarding the peculiarity of the sports world in IPR issues.

Football clubs are being given the same broad powers over their IPR as any other business, which has therefore allowed the protection of almost every sport related aspect. On this point, it is important recognize the significant differences between a normal business enterprise and a sporting club. For instance, most businesses are run purely for financial gain and their existence has very little impact upon the lives of anyone who does not work for the company. Its customers have no sense of loyalty or passion towards the company and merely purchase a service or product in a standard transactional sense. However, football fans are the customers of sports clubs and a very different relationship between the customer and the company (club) exists. The IPR regime is effectively a system of 'private gain in service of the public good' which is a particularly inappropriate system in regards to sport and more specifically football. In fact, the IPR justifications are unpersuasive in the sporting sphere due to sports' different characteristics and origins, and their full enforcement serves merely an economic purpose which preys on the vulnerability of fans.[74]

The origins of sports lie rich within the public domain, therefore restricted access to the materials is in truth unjustifiable beyond a weak economical argument. Sporting material is vital for a community and its residents whilst also being vital as to help develop the sports stars of tomorrow. So, it is vital that sport is recognized as more than a business. Sports companies constitute a 'unicorn' in the enterprising landscape, that depends on the fact that, alongside the exercise of economic activity, even relevant, there are still sports clubs and that are subjects which provide a sport show, as such.

---

[73]   *Ibid.*

[74]   S. HAGAN, *Intellectual Property Rights in Sport,* http://www.kent.ac.uk/law/ip/resources/ip_dissertations/2005–06/Stefan-Hagan.doc.

16 Recent sports-related issues in US intellectual property law

Anthony J. Dreyer

Licensing and sponsorship rights unquestionably have become among the most important sources of revenue to professional and amateur sports entities, as well as to many professional athletes. Yet these revenue streams – and the intellectual property rights from which they arise – are under continuous attack from third parties who seek to appropriate for themselves the value and goodwill associated with sports entities and athletes.

In the United States, recent litigation reflects the continuing struggle over the extent to which sports leagues, teams, and athletes are able to prevent the unauthorized use of their intellectual property rights. Whether it is a sports league's right to exploit all broadcasts of its games or the colors and uniforms of its teams, or an athlete's right to prevent others from using her persona for commercial gain, intellectual property rights have been and will continue to be a heavily litigated subject for professional sports leagues, teams, and athletes, as well as third parties looking to profit from those commercial rights without a license or permission.

This chapter focuses on five principal areas of sports and intellectual property law that recently have received significant attention in the press and U.S. courts. First, a series of recent cases involving the unauthorized use of sports team colors and team uniforms are examined. Next, the chapter looks at the recent right of publicity litigation, and the growing tension between an athlete's right to control the commercial use of his or her persona and the free speech rights of those seeking to use athletes' persona for commercial endeavors that involve some speech-related aspect, including fantasy sports games and videogames.

The chapter will also examine ambush marketing – a growing trend in sports marketing in which an entity seeks to associate itself with a sports team, league, or sporting event, despite the fact that the entity has not paid a sponsorship fee for that right. In addition, this chapter examines recent efforts by sports entities to restrict media access to sporting events and the use of information obtained from those events, ostensibly so that the sports entity can itself commercially exploit that information. Finally, the chapter discusses an emerging threat to all sports leagues and teams: the unauthorized live streaming of sports broadcasts over the Internet.

I. THE PROTECTABILITY OF TEAM COLORS AND TEAM UNIFORMS

Trade dress litigation involving collegiate and professional sports is driven by the fact that many teams are identifiable not only by their team names and logos (which may be entitled to traditional trademark protection) but also by their distinctive color patterns or

designs.[1] Recent court decisions examining these issues reflect both (i) a general acceptance among U.S. courts that team color combinations – particularly those of popular
professional and collegiate teams – are powerful source identifiers; and (ii) a willingness
by these courts to protect team colors against unauthorized use.

A. General Principles

1. Trade dress protection

Trade dress is a device used 'to identify and distinguish' a person's goods and/or services
'from those manufactured or sold by others and to indicate the source.'[2] However,
whereas 'trademarks' are generally comprised of words, names, logos, or symbols,[3] trade
dress encompasses the 'total image and overall appearance of a product' or its packaging.[4] A product's trade dress may include its size, shape, color or color combinations,
texture, or graphics.[5] By way of example, a manufacturer's logo printed on a golf club may
be a trademark by identifying that manufacturer as the creator of the club, while the
colors of that club and the club's overall appearance may constitute trade dress serving
the same function.[6]

Federal trade dress protection under U.S. law is set forth in § 43(a) of the Lanham Act.[7]
To qualify for protection, trade dress must be (i) used in commerce;[8] (ii) distinctive; and
(iii) nonfunctional.[9] The 'used in commerce' test can be met by the sales of goods under
the mark and advertising under the mark.[10] Like trademarks, protectable trade dress must
'be capable of distinguishing the applicant's goods from those of others.'[11] To satisfy this
requirement, the trade dress must be either inherently distinctive or have acquired
'secondary meaning.'[12]

A trademark or trade dress is inherently distinctive when its 'intrinsic nature serves to
identify a particular source of a product.'[13] Inherently distinctive marks are creative or
imaginative and 'have minimal natural or necessary conceptual connection with the

---

[1]   See, e.g., *Major League Baseball Props., Inc.* v. *Salvino, Inc.*, 420 F. Supp. 2d 212 (S.D.N.Y.
2005), *aff'd*, 542 F.3d 290 (2d Cir. 2008); *Tex. Tech Univ.* v. *Spiegelberg*, 461 F. Supp. 2d 510 (N.D.
Tex. 2006); *Bd. of Supervisors for La. State Univ. Agric. & Mech. College* v. *Smack Apparel Co.*, 550
F.3d 465 (5th Cir. 2008) (involving team colors serving as trademarks), *cert. denied*, 129 S. Ct. 2759
(2009).

[2]   15 U.S.C. § 1127.

[3]   *Ibid.*

[4]   *Sunbeam Prods., Inc.* v. *West Bend Co.*, 123 F.3d 246, 251 (5th Cir. 1997), *overruled in part on
other grounds by TrafFix Devices, Inc.* v. *Mktg. Displays, Inc.*, 532 U.S. 23 (2001).

[5]   *John H. Harland Co.* v. *Clarke Checks, Inc.*, 711 F.2d 966, 980 (11th Cir. 1983).

[6]   See *Callaway Golf Co.* v. *Golf Clean, Inc.*, 915 F. Supp. 1206, 1215 (M.D. Fla. 1995).

[7]   15 U.S.C. § 1125(a).

[8]   For federal protection to apply under the Lanham Act, the mark must have been used in
interstate commerce. 15 U.S.C. § 1127.

[9]   See *ibid.* See, e.g., *Two Pesos, Inc.* v. *Taco Cabana, Inc.*, 505 U.S. 763 (1992).

[10]   15 U.S.C. § 1127.

[11]   *Two Pesos*, 505 U.S. at 768.

[12]   *Ibid.* at 769.

[13]   *Ibid.* at 768.

products they mark.'[14] In the context of trademarks, for example, the name 'Pepsi' is inherently distinctive because it bears no relationship to soft drinks or the act of drinking, generally; the word 'Pepsi' is wholly arbitrary. However, a name such as 'honey roasted peanuts' would obviously describe the product and thus lack inherent distinctiveness.

If the trademark or trade dress is not inherently distinctive, then it must have acquired 'secondary meaning' in order to obtain protection.[15] As the Supreme Court has explained, '[t]o establish secondary meaning, a manufacturer must show that, in the minds of the public, the primary significance of a product feature or term is to identify the source of the product rather than the product itself.'[16] For example, if a particular company produces golf balls that always come in royal blue, hexagonal packaging, over time this packaging could become strongly associated with that particular company in the mind of the public; if so, it will have 'acquir[ed] a distinctiveness' as identifying that company as its source.[17]

In determining whether particular trade dress has achieved secondary meaning, U.S. courts consider such facts as (i) the length and manner of use of the mark or trade dress, (ii) volume of sales of products bearing the trade dress, and (iii) the amount and manner of advertising.[18] Direct consumer evidence such as consumer surveys is often used in trade dress litigation to demonstrate that an appreciable portion of the relevant consumer population associates the trade dress at issue with a particular source.[19] Trade dress based on product design features (as opposed to those based on product packaging) must always obtain secondary meaning to qualify for protection.[20] Further, as discussed in greater detail below, colors require secondary meaning to be protected because they cannot be inherently distinctive.[21]

Unlike trademarks that are written words or graphic symbols, trade dress such as product design or packaging may simultaneously serve as a source identifier and provide a utilitarian function.[22] In order to prevent trade dress owners from obtaining a perpetual monopoly on a useful function, U.S. trademark laws require that product designs or packaging be 'non-functional' to be protectable as trade dress.[23] The 'traditional test' for functionality asks whether a product feature is essential to the use or purpose of the product, or whether it affects quality or cost.[24] If either of these standards is satisfied, the

---

[14]   Graeme B. Dinwoodie, *Reconceptualizing the Inherent Distinctiveness of Product Design Trade Dress*, 75 N.C. L. REV. 471, 486 (1997).

[15]   *Two Pesos*, 505 U.S. at 769.

[16]   *Inwood Labs., Inc. v. Ives Labs., Inc.*, 456 U.S. 844, 851 n.11 (1982).

[17]   *TrafFix Devices, Inc. v. Mktg. Displays, Inc.*, 532 U.S. 23, 28 (2001).

[18]   See *Pebble Beach Co. v. Tour 18 I Ltd.*, 155 F.3d 526, 541 (5th Cir. 1998), *overruled in part on other grounds by TrafFix Devices, Inc. v. Mktg. Displays*, 532 U.S. 23 (2001); *Bd. of Supervisors for La. State Univ. Agric. & Mech. College v. Smack Apparel Co.*, 550 F.3d 465, 478 (5th Cir. 2008), *cert. denied*, 129 S. Ct. 2759 (2009).

[19]   See, e.g., *Pebble Beach*, 155 F.3d at 541; *Tex. Tech Univ. v. Spiegelberg*, 461 F. Supp. 2d 510, 523 (N.D. Tex. 2006).

[20]   *Wal-Mart Stores, Inc. v. Samara Bros., Inc.*, 529 U.S. 205, 212 (2000).

[21]   See *Qualitex Co. v. Jacobson Prods. Co.*, 514 U.S. 159, 163 (1995).

[22]   *Wal-Mart*, 529 U.S. at 213. An example of functional trade dress would be the color orange for a safety vest, since the color 'functions' to make its wearer highly visible to others.

[23]   See *Qualitex*, 514 U.S. at 164.

[24]   *Inwood Labs., Inc. v. Ives Labs., Inc.*, 456 U.S. 844, 851 n. 10 (1982).

feature is likely functional and thus not entitled to trade dress protection.[25] For example, a company selling safety vests could not likely claim trade dress in the bright orange color of the vest because the product's color is essential to its purpose of making the wearer visible to others.

2. Trade dress liability

Under the Lanham Act, there are two forms of trade dress liability: infringement and dilution. A defendant infringes if its product or packaging is likely to cause confusion 'as to the affiliation, connection, or association of such person with another person, or as to the origin, sponsorship, or approval of his or her goods, services, or commercial activities by another person.'[26] The concern here is twofold: (i) the trade dress owner loses revenue because sales are diverted to the infringer, and also goodwill in the trade dress because the owner does not control the quality of the infringing good; and (ii) consumers are potentially deceived into buying goods from the third party under the mistaken belief they are purchasing a product authorized by the owner of the mark.[27]

The Lanham Act also provides for liability when a trademark is diluted.[28] Dilution law is not based on the likelihood of confusion, but rather, is designed 'to protect the quasi-property rights a holder has in maintaining the integrity and distinctiveness of his mark.'[29] Therefore, only 'famous' marks may be diluted; famous marks are those that are 'widely recognized by the general consuming public of the United States as a designation of source of the goods or services of the mark's owner.'[30] There are two different types of dilution: blurring and tarnishment.[31] Dilution by blurring occurs when third parties use a mark in a way that would lessen the strong association that consumers feel for that mark. Dilution by tarnishment occurs when a mark is used in a way that 'harms the reputation of the mark.'[32]

---

[25]   In *TrafFix Devices, Inc. v. Marketing Displays, Inc.*, 532 U.S. 23, 33–4 (2000), the Supreme Court added a second dimension to the test for functionality. The court explained that even if a product feature was not essential to the use or purpose of the product and would not affect quality or cost, the feature could still be functional if exclusive use of the feature would put competitors at a 'non-reputation-related disadvantage.' *Ibid.*

[26]   15 U.S.C. § 1125(a)(1)(A).

[27]   See, e.g., *Bd. of Supervisors for La. State Univ. Agric. & Mech. College v. Smack Apparel Co.*, 438 F. Supp. 2d 653, 657–58 (E.D. La. 2006), *aff'd*, 550 F.3d 465 (5th Cir. 2008), *cert. denied*, 129 S. Ct. 2759 (2009). Although the test for determining likelihood of confusion varies somewhat between federal circuits, all generally apply a similar multi-factor analysis, including: (i) the strength or recognition of the mark or dress allegedly infringed, (ii) the similarity between the two marks or dress, (iii) the similarity and quality of the owner and alleged infringer's products or services, (iv) the identity of the retail outlets and purchasers, (v) the identity of the advertising media used, (vi) the defendant's intent, (vii) the sophistication of the purchasers, and (viii) any evidence of actual confusion. See *ibid.* at 659–61.

[28]   15 U.S.C. § 1125(c).

[29]   *Kellogg Co. v. Toucan Golf, Inc.*, 337 F.3d 616, 628 (6th Cir. 2003).

[30]   15 U.S.C. § 1125(c)(2)(A).

[31]   15 U.S.C. § 1125(c).

[32]   15 U.S.C. § 1125(c)(2)(B), (C).

3.   Color as trade dress

In *Qualitex Co.* v. *Jacobson Products Co.*,[33] the United States Supreme Court recognized the protectability of the green-gold coloring of the plaintiff's dry cleaning pads. The court stated that, '[c]olor alone, at least sometimes, can meet the basic legal requirements for use as a trademark. It can act as a symbol that distinguishes a firm's goods and identifies their source, without serving any other significant function.'[34] However, the court held that color always requires secondary meaning to be protectable.[35]

B.   Sports Trade Dress/Uniform Cases

One of the largest sources of revenue for professional sports teams and university athletic departments is league- and team-related merchandise. Trade dress protection (and in some instances, trademark protection) allows teams to prevent third parties from diverting potential revenue streams by using the teams' distinctive colors or uniform designs.

1.   Team colors

Professional sports teams, as well as colleges and universities with major sports programs, often – through widespread press and media coverage – become synonymous with particular color schemes. With that recognition comes an increasing need to prevent goods or merchandise by third parties from appropriating those team or school colors for their own financial gain.

In *Board of Supervisors for Louisiana State University Agricultural & Mechanical College* v. *Smack Apparel Co.*,[36] four public U.S. universities[37] filed suit against a clothing producer who, without authorization from the universities, created and sold T-shirts that incorporated the schools' colors and made reference to the schools' geographic locations, specific athletic events, or historical accomplishments.[38] The court first considered the issue of protectability, recognizing that a trademark may include a combination of elements, and accepting the universities' argument that the combination of team color and other indicia could be protectable.[39] Then, after examining the schools' long, historic use of the colors in varied contexts, the court found that the color schemes had acquired secondary meaning in the minds of fans and other consumers.[40] The court also noted that the defendant acknowledged that it had intentionally 'incorporated the Universities' color schemes into its shirts to refer to the universities and call them to the mind of the

---

33   514 U.S. 159 (1995).

34   *Ibid.* at 166. Similarly, the pink color of home insulation has been found to be protectable trade dress because there are no functional reasons for other brands to color their insulation pink, and the color in that context has come to signify a specific producer by acquiring secondary meaning. See *In re Owens-Corning Fiberglass Corp.*, 774 F.2d 1116, 1122–8 (Fed. Cir. 1985).

35   See *Qualitex*, 514 U.S. at 163–4.

36   550 F.3d 465 (5th Cir. 2008), *cert. denied*, 129 S. Ct. 2759 (2009).

37   Louisiana State University, Ohio State University, the University of Southern California, and the University of Oklahoma. See *ibid.* at 471–2.

38   *Smack Apparel*, 550 F.3d at 472.

39   *Ibid.* at 476.

40   *Ibid.* at 476–7.

consumer,' demonstrating that even the defendants themselves understood that the colors had secondary meaning.[41]

Having determined protectability, the court then found in favor of the universities on the question of infringement, applying the multi-factor test for likelihood of confusion.[42] In particular, the court emphasized that the defendant's intent in using the universities' colors was to 'obtain a "free ride" by profiting from confusion among the fans of the Universities' football teams who desire to show support for and affiliation with those teams.'[43] The court disapproved of the defendant's 'inten[tion] to take advantage of the popularity of the Universities' football programs and the appearance of the school teams in the college bowl games.'[44]

The court also rejected the defendant's affirmative claim that the colors were functional (and thus not protectable) because the shirts merely 'identif[ied] the wearer as a fan and indicate[d] the team the fan is supporting.'[45] Although team uniforms function to allow players to differentiate between their own team and their opponent, the use of specific team colors on *fan merchandise* serves no such purpose.[46] On this basis, the court rejected Smack's functionality defense.[47] Similarly, in *Texas Tech University* v. *Spiegelberg*,[48] Texas Tech University successfully enforced trade dress protection for its scarlet and black color scheme against the owner of a local store named 'Red Raider Outfitters.' In so holding, the court rejected the defendant's argument that the use of colors on shirts and other apparel was functional, explaining that '[t]he fact that a knit cap is scarlet and black ... does not affect the quality of the cap or its ability to keep one's head warm.'[49]

In *Major League Baseball Properties, Inc.* v. *Salvino, Inc.*,[50] the issue of team colors as protectable trade dress was also considered. The defendant produced stuffed, plush bears, which were sold at a variety of retailers, including concession stands at Major League Baseball (MLB) stadiums.[51] The bears displayed the names and numbers of individual major league players, were produced in team colors that correlated to the specific MLB teams for which the athletes identified on the bears played, and incorporated the logos of MLB teams.[52] Some of the bears also included the home city or state of the team in block letters.[53] Although the use of the player names was licensed by the Major League Baseball Players Association, the defendant had not licensed the team uniforms from MLB, which asserted claims of trademark and trade dress infringement, including the unlicensed use of MLB team color patterns.[54]

---

[41]   *Ibid.* at 477.
[42]   *Ibid.* at 483–4.
[43]   *Ibid.*
[44]   *Ibid.* at 482.
[45]   *Ibid.* at 487.
[46]   *Ibid.* at 486.
[47]   *Ibid.* at 486–7.
[48]   461 F. Supp. 2d 510 (N.D. Tex. 2006).
[49]   *Ibid.* at 520.
[50]   420 F. Supp. 2d 212 (S.D.N.Y. 2005), *aff'd*, 542 F.3d 290 (2d. Cir. 2008).
[51]   *Ibid.* at 217.
[52]   *Ibid.*
[53]   *Ibid.*
[54]   *Ibid.* at 218.

The court declined to rule on summary judgment on whether the colors had achieved secondary meaning, finding that a genuine issue of fact remained.[55] However, the court found that the use of the specific team colors was not functional because it did not 'represent an "advance in the useful arts, the [colors] merely function ... to identify a bear with a particular [baseball player]."'[56]

2. Uniforms

In addition to colors, uniforms in and of themselves have been found protectable under U.S. law. In *Dallas Cowboys Cheerleaders, Inc.* v. *Pussycat Cinema, Ltd.*,[57] the main character of a pornographic film was a cheerleader depicted in a uniform with elements that were nearly identical to those worn by the Dallas Cowboys Cheerleaders: white boots, white shorts, blue blouse, and white star-studded vest and belt.[58] The plaintiff did not hold any registrations for the uniform, but claimed that the uniform constituted protectable trade dress because it was recognized by the public as belonging to the Dallas Cowboys Cheerleaders, and that the defendant's use of the uniform infringed on and diluted that trade dress.[59] Although the court found that each element of the uniform was functional on their own, because each was designed and fitted to allow free movement,[60] the specific combination of these elements that constituted the Dallas Cowboys Cheerleaders' uniform was arbitrary and served no purpose other than as a source identifier,[61] and constituted protectable trade dress because the combination held secondary meaning.[62]

The plaintiff also prevailed on its claims of infringement and state law dilution and infringement.[63] First, the court found dilution by tarnishment because the use of the cheerleaders' distinctive uniform in a pornographic film could damage public perception of the mark.[64] The court also concluded that a likelihood of confusion existed because even if the public did not believe that the Dallas Cowboys Cheerleaders had produced the film, consumers could be misled into believing the plaintiff had approved the use of its trademark.[65]

In contrast, *NBA Properties, Inc.* v. *Dahlonega Mint, Inc.*[66] held that unlicensed cards depicting some NBA players in full uniform, including the display of trademarked team

---

[55]   *Ibid.* at 223.
[56]   *Ibid.* at 222 (alterations in original) (quoting *Warner Bros., Inc.* v. *Gay Toys, Inc.*, 724 F.2d 327, 332 (2d Cir. 1983)). Following the court's decision, a consent judgment was entered dismissing all of Salvino's claims with leave to appeal the district court's entry of summary judgment in favor of MLB Properties on Salvino's antitrust counterclaims. See *Major League Baseball Props.* v. *Salvino, Inc.*, 542 F.3d 290, 309 (2d Cir. 2008).
[57]   604 F.2d 200 (2d Cir. 1979).
[58]   *Ibid.* at 202–203.
[59]   *Ibid.* at 202–203 and n. 3.
[60]   *Ibid.* at 203.
[61]   *Ibid.* at 203–204 and nn. 4–5.
[62]   *Ibid.* at 203–204 and n. 5.
[63]   See *ibid.* at 205.
[64]   See *ibid.* ('[I]t is hard to believe that anyone who had seen defendants' sexually depraved film could ever thereafter disassociate it from plaintiff's cheerleaders.').
[65]   See *ibid.*
[66]   41 F. Supp. 2d 1341 (N.D. Ga. 1998).

logos and designs, did infringe, while team uniforms without logos (although registered) were found *not* to be distinct marks because they had not been used in commerce by the plaintiffs.[67] Moreover, in considering whether the uniforms without logos were confusingly similar to the plaintiffs' infringed marks (the uniforms with logos), the court found consumers were not likely to be confused because the conspicuous removal of the logos would likely inform the consumer that the cards were unlicensed.[68]

C. Conclusion

The cases above demonstrate a general, if not unfettered, willingness among U.S. courts to protect against the unauthorized use of team uniforms and colors. But questions remain, such as the geographical reach of sports-related trade dress. *Texas Tech* described the university's color scheme as having secondary meaning for goods sold in the town in which the school was located, explaining, correctly, that trademark rights are territorial in nature.[69] Additionally, while *Smack Apparel* attributed secondary meaning to Louisiana State University's purple and gold color scheme without specific geographic limitation, that same color scheme may be associated with other teams in different parts of the country.[70] If two teams share a common color scheme, will that prevent either from gaining trade dress protection? May both protect the scheme when it is combined with other information related to the team, or used in a different sport and/or league?

The *Smack Apparel* court's use of the phrase 'other indicia' to define the trademark at issue may be based upon a view that (at least in some instances) colors alone without any other context may not have secondary meaning, as many teams and universities share the same colors. Although the universities provided examples of the 'indicia' that are part of their trade dress, the phrase may be viewed by some as vague.[71] In this regard, U.S. courts have ruled 'that a plaintiff seeking to protect its trade dress ... must articulate the design elements that compose the trade dress.'[72] Trade dress protection will only be granted when there is a relatively precise definition of what constitutes the trade dress.[73] The question of how precisely teams must describe what constitutes their trade dress may affect how broadly teams can protect their colors in the future.

Lastly, defendants have at times attempted to raise their First Amendment rights to free speech as a defense to trade dress claims.[74] The court in *Dallas Cowboys Cheerleaders* rejected that argument, declining to apply first amendment protection based on the film's

---

[67]   *Ibid.* at 1345, 1347 n. 5.

[68]   *Ibid.* at 1349.

[69]   *Tex. Tech Univ.* v. *Spiegelberg*, 461 F. Supp. 2d 510, 524 n. 2 (N.D. Tex. 2006).

[70]   See *Bd. of Supervisors for La. State Univ. Agric. & Mech. College* v. *Smack Apparel Co.*, 550 F.3d 465, 472, 476–7 and n. 34 (5th Cir. 2008), *cert. denied*, 129 S. Ct. 2759 (2009). For example, the Los Angeles Lakers use a purple and gold color scheme similar to LSU, but do so in professional basketball.

[71]   See *ibid.* at 473–4.

[72]   *Yurman Design, Inc.* v. *PAJ, Inc.*, 262 F.3d 101, 116 (2d Cir. 2001).

[73]   See 1 J. THOMAS MCCARTHY, MCCARTHY ON TRADEMARKS AND UNFAIR COMPETITION § 8:3 (4th ed. 2010).

[74]   See *Dallas Cowboys Cheerleaders, Inc.* v. *Pussycat Cinema, Ltd.*, 604 F.3d 200, 205–206 (2d Cir. 1979).

'adult' content and, more importantly, based on the fact that the court was protecting private rights and not censoring the content.[75]

II. RIGHT OF PUBLICITY AND SPORTS

For the individual athlete, perhaps no intellectual property is as important as his or her right of publicity: it gives an athlete the exclusive right to capitalize on the fame achieved through talent and hard work on the courts or fields. While the right of publicity is not recognized under federal law, and not uniformly recognized in each state in the United States, it has gradually achieved acceptance by many state courts and state legislatures. However, U.S. courts are now grappling with the right of publicity on numerous fronts, most notably as to the interplay between the right of publicity and the First Amendment, as well as with respect to the evolving technology means through which a person's name or likeness can be exploited.

A. General Principles

1. Overview
The right of publicity is defined as 'the inherent right of every human being to control the commercial use of his or her identity.'[76] U.S. law did not explicitly recognize a right of publicity until 1953 when a leading U.S. court recognized that, 'a man has a right in the publicity value of his photograph, i.e. the right to grant the exclusive privilege of publishing his picture, and that such a grant may be validly made "in gross."'[77] In the typical *prima facie* case for a right of publicity violation, the claimant must prove: (i) the use of his or her persona (including name, likeness, or voice), (ii) for a commercial purpose, (iii) without permission.[78]

The right of publicity is an offspring of the right of privacy and is a state right.[79] Although the two rights are often confused, the right of privacy is a personal right addressing the indignities one endures when one's privacy is invaded, while the right of publicity is more akin to a property right that addresses the damages one incurs when his or her persona is misappropriated.[80] Although right of publicity claims most typically are raised by celebrities and professional athletes, in most states the right is an inherent right of every citizen.[81]

2. State variations
To date, more than 20 states have recognized a right of publicity in their common law,[82] and several others have statutory provisions that either explicitly protect a right of

---

[75]   See *ibid.* at 206.
[76]   1 McCarthy, note 73 *supra*, § 1:3.
[77]   *Haelan Labs., Inc.* v. *Topps Chewing Gum, Inc.*, 202 F.2d 866, 868 (2d Cir. 1953).
[78]   See 1 McCarthy, note 73 *supra*, § 3:2.
[79]   See *ETW Corp.* v. *Jireh Publishing, Inc.*, 332 F.3d 915, 952–4 (6th Cir. 2003).
[80]   See 1 McCarthy, note 73 *supra*, § 1:7.
[81]   *Ibid.* § 1:3.
[82]   *Ibid.* § 6:3.

publicity or are broad enough in their language to encompass such a right.[83] Ten states have 'privacy' statutes that may be interpreted so that the right of publicity is embodied within the statute.[84] Thus, in total, at least 30 states recognize some form of the right of publicity.

However, variations from state to state create conflicts and confusion as to what, precisely, the right of publicity protects. For example, states vary with respect to descendability of one's right of publicity. Nineteen states recognize a post-mortem right of publicity either by statute or common law, meaning that one's right to publicize is descendable; however, the duration of a post-mortem right of publicity varies in length from 20 years to 100 years.[85] On the other hand, states such as New York and Wisconsin reject a common law post-mortem right of publicity.[86] Some states recognize the right only in celebrities,[87] while others recognize the right as belonging to all citizens.[88]

To avoid the patchwork nature of the right of publicity, a growing number of commentators have advocated for a uniform federal right of publicity.[89] A federal right – like that of the federal copyright and patent laws – would preempt state laws that conflict with each other and the proposed federal right, but would still be subject to First Amendment considerations.[90]

3. Right of publicity licensing and group licensing in sports

As a property right, the right of publicity is transferable, either through assignment or license.[91] Assignment is the sale of the right and the transfer of title in one's right of publicity, whereas a license grants a licensee certain rights, but title still remains with the licensor.[92] To exploit the associational fame, the sports industry developed a concept called 'group licensing' which allows both the team and athletes to promote themselves

---

[83]   *Ibid.* § 6:3 and n. 8 (listing states).

[84]   *Ibid.* § 6:3 and n. 9 (listing states).

[85]   See 2 MCCARTHY, note 73 *supra*, § 9:18.

[86]   See *Antonetty* v. *Cuomo*, 131 Misc. 2d 1041, 1046, 502 N.Y.S.2d 902, 905 906 (Sup. Ct. Bronx County), *aff'd mem.*, 125 A.D.2d 1010, 509 N.Y.S.2d 443 (1st Dep't 1986); *Hagen* v. *Dahmer*, No. 94-C-0485, 1995 WL 22644, at *4 (E.D. Wis. Oct. 13, 1995)

[87]   See, e.g., 42 PA. CONS. STAT. ANN. § 8316(a) (West 2007) (extending protection in Pennsylvania only to those whose identity 'has commercial value').

[88]   See, e.g., N.Y. CIV. RIGHTS LAW § 50 (McKinney 2009) (extending protection in New York to 'any living person').

[89]   See, e.g., Marci A. Hamilton, *et al.*, Symposium, *Rights of Publicity: An In-Depth Analysis of the New Legislative Proposals to Congress*, 16 CARDOZO ARTS & ENT. L.J. 209, 210 (1998) ('[O]ur Task Force has … initiated discussion aimed at producing its own federal right of publicity statute … The subcommittee generally believes that a uniform body of law is desirable in this area, compared to the patchwork quilt with which the people of the United States are now afflicted.') (comments of Steven M. Getzoff, then Chair of the American Bar Association's Joint Task Force on federalizing the right of publicity); Alice Haermmerli, *Whose Who? The Case for a Kantian Right of Publicity*, 49 DUKE L.J. 383, 477 (1999) (recognizing that '[t]here appears to be a general consensus that a uniform right of publicity is sorely needed,' and that '[i]t also appears that most advocates of uniformity believe that preemptive federal law, rather than a uniform code or model state statutes, would more readily achieve that goal.').

[90]   See Richard S. Robinson, *Preemption, the Right of Publicity, and a New Federal Statute*, 16 CARDOZO ARTS & ENT. L.J. 183, 204–205 (1998).

[91]   See 2 MCCARTHY, note 73 *supra*, §§ 10:10, 10:13, 10:17.

[92]   *Ibid.* § 10:17.

synergistically.[93] Group licensing agreements involve individual players assigning their group licensing rights to a licensee (typically the players' union) that thereafter has the right to license the players' names, signatures, pictures, likenesses, and other biographical information in connection with group licensing programs.[94] Athletes typically retain the right to license their name and likeness on an individual basis.

B. Right of Publicity in Sports: Early Case Law

As noted, in 1953, the Second Circuit was the first court to recognize a right of publicity.[95] In *Haelan Laboratories, Inc. v. Topps Chewing Gum, Inc.* the plaintiff (Haelan) sued the defendant (Topps), a rival gum manufacturer – for inducing a baseball player to grant Topps a license to use the player's photographs in connection with its gum sales.[96] Haelan claimed that Topps' inducement invaded Haelan's exclusively licensed right to use the baseball player's pictures for commercial use.[97] Topps argued that Haelan's licenses were releases from liability for invasion of privacy, and because the right of privacy is a personal right, they were not assignable.[98] The Second Circuit affirmatively recognized the right of publicity separate and distinct from the right of privacy.[99]

Yet, courts have not uniformly used the 'right of publicity' label after *Haelan Laboratories*. For example, Arnold Palmer and three other professional golfers sought an injunction and damages for the use of their names and likenesses on profile sheets used in a board game.[100] Defendant claimed that because 'the information contained in the profiles [was] readily obtainable public data,' they were not prohibited from reproducing it.[101] The court held that although publishing biographical data of well-known individuals is not a violation of the right of privacy, nonetheless, one does violate that individual's privacy rights by capitalizing on that information.[102]

Only three years later, yet another court recognized the right of publicity in the context of athletes. In *Uhlaender v. Henricksen*, Negamco, a game manufacturing company,

---

[93]   See Gary R. Roberts, *The Legality of the Exclusive Collective Sale of Intellectual Property Rights by Sports Leagues*, 3 VA. J. SPORTS & L. 52, 59–60 (2001).

[94]   *CBS Interactive Inc.* v. *Nat'l Football League Players Ass'n, Inc.*, 259 F.R.D. 398, 402–403 (D. Minn. 2009). '[A]ny entity that wants to use the publicity rights of more than a specified number of players (usually six or more) for any commercial purpose must [purchase that right on a collective basis from the players' union], and not by negotiating individual licenses with those players individually.' Roberts, note 93 *supra*, at 60.

[95]   See *Haelan Labs., Inc.* v. *Topps Chewing Gum, Inc.*, 202 F.2d 866, 868 (2d Cir. 1953).

[96]   *Ibid.* at 867.

[97]   *Ibid.*

[98]   *Ibid.*

[99]   *Ibid.* at 868.

[100]   See *Palmer* v. *Schonhorn Enters., Inc.*, 96 N.J. Super. 72, 74, 232 A.2d 458, 459 (Ch. Div. 1967).

[101]   *Ibid.* at 76, 232 A.2d at 460.

[102]   See *ibid.* at 79, 232 A.2d at 462. The court drew from *Gautier* v. *Pro-Football, Inc.* in reaching its conclusion: "While one who is a public figure or is presently newsworthy may be the proper subject of news or informative presentation, the privilege "does not extend to commercialization of his personality through a form of treatment distinct from the dissemination of news or information."' *Ibid.* at 78, 232 A.2d at 461 (quoting *Gautier* v. *Pro-Football, Inc.*, 304 N.Y. 354, 359, 107 N.E.2d 485, 488 (1952)).

produced and sold games that employed the names and statistics of MLB players to allow customers to manage fictional teams they assembled according to their strategic decisions.[103] When Negamco refused to enter into a licensing agreement with the Major League Baseball Players Association, the latter brought suit for unauthorized appropriation and use of proprietary information for commercial profit.[104] Negamco tried to characterize the action as an invasion of privacy involving only incidences of personal harm, rather than unauthorized appropriation, which involves pecuniary loss.[105] The court rejected this argument and, like the *Palmer* court, determined that Negamco's use of the players' statistics and biographical information was in fact an unauthorized appropriation.[106]

C. Right of Publicity in Sports: Recent Developments

Although the right of publicity has now attained wider recognition in the law, the advent of the Internet and other forms of digital media has raised new considerations in the sports context, particularly relating to fantasy sports leagues and other forms of entertainment. In addition, courts continue to grapple with the tensions between the First Amendment and the interests protected by the right of publicity.

1. The right of publicity and the First Amendment

Gridiron.com, Inc. v. *National Football League Players Ass'n, Inc.*[107] rejected a First Amendment defense to a right of publicity claim. The case involved the group license between the National Football League Players Association (NFLPA) and National Football League Players, Inc. (NFLPI), which covered 97% of the National Football League players (NFL players).[108] Gridiron.com (Gridiron) induced over 150 NFL players to grant Gridiron a license to use their images in conjunction with Gridiron's fantasy sports website, which also included news and information about the players.[109] The NFLPA and NFLPI claimed that Gridiron induced the players to breach their contract with the NFLPA.[110] They also claimed that Gridiron tortiously interfered with their group license agreement as to the rest of the players because the website contained links to nearly every player's website in the NFL.[111]

The court found that Gridiron's use of the players' images was not protected by the First Amendment.[112] The court observed that the defendant's purpose was to produce a commercial product: a website used to help sell advertisements.[113] The court found that its

---

[103]   See *Uhlaender* v. *Henricksen*, 316 F. Supp. 1277, 1278 (D. Minn. 1970).
[104]   *Ibid.* at 1278–9.
[105]   See *ibid.* at 1279–1.
[106]   See *ibid.* at 1281–3.
[107]   106 F. Supp. 2d 1309 (S.D. Fla. 2000).
[108]   *Ibid.* at 1310–11.
[109]   *Ibid.* at 1311, 1313.
[110]   *Ibid.* at 1311.
[111]   *Ibid.* at 1311, 1313.
[112]   *Ibid.* at 1315.
[113]   *Ibid.* at 1314–15.

activities interfered with the NFLPA's licensing agreement and thus infringed on its licensed right of publicity.[114]

In contrast, the Sixth Circuit reached a different conclusion in a different context in *ETW Corp.* v. *Jireh Publishing, Inc.*,[115] finding the defendant's use of Tiger Woods' likeness was protected by the First Amendment. In 1998 artist Rick Rush created a painting entitled *The Masters of Augusta*, which commemorated Woods' victory at the Masters Tournament in Augusta, Georgia.[116] The painting was later reproduced and sold by Jireh Publishing as part of a limited edition lithograph set. ETW (Mr. Woods' licensing agent) sued Jireh alleging trademark infringement, dilution, unfair competition, deceptive trade practices, and violation of Woods' right of publicity.[117]

The Sixth Circuit concluded that the First Amendment preempted any possible state law right of publicity claim. The Sixth Circuit found that Rush's work had substantial informational and creative content – 'a collage of images [depicting] a historic event in sports history and ... convey[ing] a message about the significance of Woods's achievement' at the Masters golf tournament – which outweighed any negative effect on ETW's market for licensed merchandise.[118] Accordingly, the work was entitled to full protection under the First Amendment.[119]

A similar result was reached in *C.B.C. Distribution & Marketing, Inc.* v. *Major League Baseball Advanced Media, L.P.*[120] C.B.C. brought an action against Advanced Media (and later the MLBPA as an intervenor) for a declaration that C.B.C. could use the names and information of the baseball players without license in connection with the sale of their fantasy baseball products.[121] Advanced Media counterclaimed, asserting that C.B.C.'s fantasy leagues violated the players' rights of publicity, which were exclusively licensed to Advanced Media by the players' association.[122] On appeal from a district court decision in favor of C.B.C., the Eighth Circuit held that C.B.C. *was infringing* on the players' rights of publicity.[123] It found that use of the players' names and statistical information was used as a symbol of their identity and that the use was for profit which amounted to commercial advantage.[124] However, the court concluded that the First Amendment preempted the state law right of publicity.[125] In so holding, the Eighth Circuit emphasized that C.B.C. was using information such as player statistics that was

---

[114]   See *ibid*.
[115]   332 F.3d 915 (6th Cir. 2003).
[116]   *Ibid*. at 918. In the foreground, the painting displays three views of Woods in golfing positions. The Augusta National Clubhouse is in the background, and, above the clubhouse, are likenesses of past, famous golfers (including Arnold Palmer, Sam Snead, and Ben Hogan) looking down on Woods. *Ibid*.
[117]   *Ibid*. at 918–19.
[118]   *Ibid*. at 938.
[119]   *Ibid*.
[120]   505 F.3d 818 (8th Cir. 2007).
[121]   *Ibid*. at 820.
[122]   *Ibid*.
[123]   *Ibid*. at 822–3.
[124]   *Ibid*.
[125]   *Ibid*. at 823–4.

already in the public domain, and that fantasy leagues were entertainment and thus, protected speech.[126]

CBS Interactive Inc. v. *National Football League Players Ass'n, Inc.*[127] continued the trend away from enforcing an athlete's right of publicity where First Amendment concerns are implicated. CBS Interactive (CBSI) operates a fantasy sports league under the domain name CBSSports.com. CBSI argued that it did not need a license from NFL players, relying on *C.B.C. Distribution.* The NFLPA tried to distinguish *C.B.C. Distribution* by claiming that CBSI's use of the players' information amounted to 'greater exploitation of publicity rights than the use in *C.B.C. Distribution*' because CBSI packaged information more comprehensively for commercial exploitation.[128] The court, however, rejected this distinction,[129] as well as the NFLPA's argument that CBSI's use of player information gives rise to a fact issue regarding whether consumers may mistakenly believe that the players endorse the website.[130] Finally, the court rejected NFLPA's argument that while the Eighth Circuit was influenced by the public interest in baseball as a national pastime, it was not clear that the public followed football in 'equal ... degree' and so the players' information deserves weaker First Amendment protection.[131] The court found the football/baseball contrast to be 'a distinction without a difference.'[132] Thus, *C.B.C. Distribution* controlled and entitled CBSI to judgment as a matter of law on First Amendment preemption grounds.[133] Not surprisingly, as a result of these cases, other fantasy sports league providers are seeking to avoid licenses with professional athletes or their associations.[134]

---

[126]   See *ibid.* at 823 (citing *Cardtoons, L.C.* v. *Major League Baseball Players Ass'n*, 93 F.3d 959, 969 (10th Cir. 1996)). A similar result was reached in *Gionfriddo* v. *Major League Baseball*, 94 Cal. App. 4th 400, 114 Cal. Rptr. 2d 307 (2001). There, the court found that MLB's use of player names and statistics for websites, documentaries, and programs was protected by the First Amendment. See *ibid.* at 411–14, 114 Cal. Rptr. 2d at 315–18.

[127]   259 F.R.D. 398 (D. Minn. 2009).

[128]   *Ibid.* at 418.

[129]   *Ibid.* at 417–18.

[130]   *Ibid.* at 418–19. The *E1W* court similarly rejected a false endorsement claim.

[131]   *Ibid.* at 419.

[132]   *Ibid.*

[133]   *Ibid.* On May 28, 2009, NFLPI and NFLPA filed a notice of appeal in *CBS Interactive.* See *Defendants' Notice of Appeal, CBS Interactive, Inc.* v. *Nat'l Football League Players Ass'n, Inc.*, No. 0:08-cv-05097 (D. Minn. May 28, 2009). After the filing of a joint stipulation to dismiss, the Eighth Circuit dismissed the appeal pursuant to Federal Rule of Appellate Procedure 42(b). See *CBS Interactive, Inc.*, No. 09–2438, Judgment at 1 (8th Cir. Nov. 12, 2009). More recently, the District of Minnesota held that the NFL's use of the names and likenesses of retired NFL players in NFL Films' documentaries constituted commercial speech (at least for purposes of a motion to dismiss), and thus, did not preempt the players' right of publicity claim. See *Dryer* v. *Nat'l Football League*, 689 F. Supp. 2d 1113, 1115–21 (D. Minn. 2010).

[134]   For example, Yahoo! Inc. filed a declaratory judgment action against the NFLPA and the NFLPI in the District Court of Minnesota to establish that Yahoo! Inc. is either not violating players' rights of publicity or, if it is, then the rights are preempted by the First Amendment or preempted by federal copyright law. See *Complaint, Yahoo! Inc.* v. *Nat'l Football League Players Ass'n, Inc.*, No. 0:09-CV-01272 (D. Minn. June 1, 2009). The action was later dismissed pursuant to claimant's notice of voluntary dismissal without prejudice. See *Yahoo! Inc.* v. *Nat'l Football League Players Ass'n, Inc.*, No. 0:09-CV-01272, Order of Dismissal at 1 (D. Minn. July 7, 2009).

2.   Videogames – the next digital frontier

In 2009, Sam Keller, a former college football quarterback, filed a class action complaint on behalf of similarly situated collegiate athletes against Electronic Arts (EA), the National Collegiate Athletic Association (NCAA) and the NCAA's licensing company in California (the 'Keller Complaint').[135] The Keller Complaint alleged that EA 'extensively utilizes actual player names and likenesses' with full knowledge of the NCAA's licensing company and the NCAA.[136] The Keller Complaint further alleged that EA's NCAA videogames violate the collegiate players' rights of publicity.[137] EA moved to dismiss, arguing that its use of the claimant's likeness was protected under *C.B.C. Distribution* and the First Amendment.[138] The district court denied EA's motion, holding that: (i) unlike the fantasy baseball game at issue in *C.B.C. Distribution*, the success of EA's game did not 'depend on updated reports of the real-life players' progress during the college football season'; and (ii) First Amendment protection was not available where EA merely copied the claimant's likeness verbatim without adding any transformative elements that warrant First Amendment protection.[139]

D.   Conclusion

As the cases above show, the right of publicity in sports continues to be a hotly contested and evolving area of jurisprudence. Until recently, it was generally accepted that commercial users of athletes' names and likenesses were required to pay a licensing fee. Yet, with the Internet, fantasy leagues, and perhaps even videogames, the trend appears to be towards finding against athletes or licensees due to First Amendment implications preempting and overriding those rights in the sports context. Where the First Amendment boundaries will be drawn remains to be seen.

---

[135]   See *Class Action Complaint, Keller* v. *Electronic Arts, Inc.*, No. 4:09-cv-01967-CW (N.D. Cal. May 5, 2009).

[136]   *Ibid.* at 3–4. Such conduct is in contravention of NCAA Bylaw 12.5 which specifically prohibits the commercial licensing of an NCAA athlete's identity.

[137]   See *ibid.* at 17–18.

[138]   Videogames have been accorded First Amendment protection by some U.S. Courts. See, e.g., *Interactive Digital Software Ass'n* v. *St. Louis County*, 329 F.3d 954, 957 (8th Cir. 2003); *Am. Amusement Mach. Ass'n* v. *Kendrick*, 244 F.3d 572, 574 (7th Cir. 2001). In a recent, unpublished decision, a California district court dismissed on First Amendment grounds, a false endorsement claim brought under the Lanham Act by former NFL great Jim Brown against videogame publisher Electronic Arts. See *Brown* v. *Electronic Arts, Inc.*, No. 2:09-CV-01598 (C.D. Ca. Sept. 23, 2009). The court found that EA's use of a Jim Brown lookalike player in its John Madden videogame series was protected under the First Amendment, and thus not actionable under the Lanham Act. The court declined, however, to address Brown's state law right of privacy/publicity claim. The case is now on appeal to the Ninth Circuit.

[139]   *Keller* v. *Electronic Arts, Inc.*, 2010 WL 530108, *4–*7 (N.D. Cal. Feb. 8, 2010) (appeal pending).

III. THE GROWTH IN AMBUSH MARKETING

A. What is Ambush Marketing?

In the sports context, ambush marketing broadly refers to a party's attempt to capitalize on the goodwill of a sports team, league, event, or athlete without authorization and without paying a sponsorship fee.[140] The ambushing company often will use promotional campaigns that try to create or suggest an association with the sports entity, event, or athlete.[141] Ambush marketing can also occur when a company's sponsorship of an event is limited to a defined market, but the company promotes its association with the event outside the boundaries of its defined market.[142] It will often (but not always) occur when a rival has paid significant sums to become an official sponsor or licensee.

Ambush marketing can take several forms. The most obvious cases involve clear trademark infringement or false claims of sponsorship, such as a company using a sports league's trademarks to suggest that it is affiliated with the league, when there is, in fact, no such association.[143] As discussed below, victims of these forms of ambush marketing can most easily rely on the protection of trademark and false advertising laws.[144]

More prevalent and troublesome cases of ambush marketing occur when the ambusher does not impermissibly use another's trademarks,[145] but instead simply uses creative advertising to associate itself with the event.[146] Four common ambush marketing strategies are: (i) purchasing advertising time prior to or during the event broadcast; (ii) conducting consumer sweepstakes or promotions related to the event; (iii) negotiating sponsorship arrangements with teams or athletes competing in events; and (iv) advertising near sporting venues.

---

[140] Jason K. Schmitz, *Ambush Marketing: The Off-Field Competition at the Olympic Games*, 3 Nw. J. Tech. & Intell. Prop. 203, ¶ 5 (2005). But see Mark R. Lyberger and Larry McCarthy, *An Assessment of Consumer Knowledge of, Interest in, and Perceptions of Ambush Marketing Strategies*, 10(2) Sport Marketing Q. 130, 131 (2001), stating that, '[t]he perception that marketers are trying to benefit by expending a fraction of the cost paid by official sponsors is erroneous.' At the 1996 Olympic Games, MCI, in its ambush marketing efforts, outspent official sponsor AT&T by $5 million. *Ibid.*

[141] Steve McKelvey, *NHL v. Pepsi-Cola Canada, Uh-Huh! Legal Parameters of Sports Ambush Marketing*, 10 Ent. & Sports Law 5, 5 (1992).

[142] 5 McCarthy note 73 *supra*, § 27:66.

[143] See, e.g., *Nat'l Football League* v. *Coors Brewing Co.*, No. 99–7921, 1999 WL 1254122 (2d Cir. Dec. 15, 1999) (discussed in more detail below).

[144] See Stephen Townley, D. Harrington, and N. Couchman, *The Legal and Practical Prevention of Ambush Marketing in Sports*, 15(4) Psychology & Marketing 333, 335 (1998) (noting that clear legal remedies exist for those activities traditionally considered piracies, including trademark infringement, where an ambushing party uses the registered or unregistered trademarks of a sport organization, and false claims of sponsorship, where an ambushing party falsely claims to be an official sponsor or supplier for a particular event or team).

[145] See Robert N. Davis, *Ambushing the Olympic Games*, 3 Vill. Sports & Ent. L.J. 423, 430 (1996); see also Schmitz, note 140 *supra*, ¶ 6 ('Purely defined, ambush marketing does not involve counterfeiting or the illegal use of trademarks, tradenames, or symbols.').

[146] See 1 James B. Astrachan, Donna M.D. Thomas, George Eric Rosden and Peter E. Rosden, The Law of Advertising § 10.07[3][a] (2011).

1.   Broadcast sponsorship and advertising

Ambush marketers often seek to avoid expensive official sponsorship fees by sponsoring the broadcast of the event, rather than the event itself. For example, although McDonald's was an official sponsor of the 1988 Calgary Winter Games, Wendy's sponsored ABC's broadcasts of the Olympics.[147] Similarly, when Fuji secured the official sponsorship for the 1984 Games, Kodak responded by sponsoring the ABC broadcasts.[148] Sponsorship of the network broadcast allows the ambusher to associate with the event without paying event sponsorship fees, which may be more costly than the price of broadcast airtime.

Alternatively, ambush marketers may choose to purchase advertising time for spots airing prior to the event broadcasts. At the 1992 Winter Olympic Games, American Express arguably 'ambushed' Visa, the official credit card for the Games, by purchasing advertising time near the event broadcasts, and running a series of advertisements on major networks featuring winter sports athletes.[149] The advertisements – which were conducted without use of any Olympic trademarks or symbols – told viewers that, 'to enjoy the fun and games they don't need a Visa.'[150] The International Olympic Committee (IOC) threatened to bring suit against American Express, but ultimately did not do so.[151]

Often, such cases are not litigated because (i) broadcast sponsorship and advertising are typically viewed as separate promotional advertising opportunities from the underlying event;[152] and (ii) official sponsors are often provided the first right of refusal to purchase exclusive advertising rights to the broadcast of the events.[153] If the sponsor chooses not to purchase the exclusive advertising package, one can argue that it has effectively forfeited its right to protection from this form of ambush marketing.[154]

2.   Commercial promotions

A second common ambush marketing tactic involves conducting consumer sweepstakes or promotions in connection with sporting event themes and locations, or through the use of event tickets. In *National Football League* v. *Governor of Delaware*,[155] the state of Delaware created a lottery paying winners proceeds based on the results of National Football League (NFL) games. The lottery cards referred to the following week's games, using the teams' city names, instead of the teams' trademarked names.[156] The District Court of Delaware held that the State did not misappropriate the NFL's goodwill, nor was there any trademark infringement, as the state of Delaware did not utilize the NFL's name

---

[147]   See Lori L. Bean, *Ambush Marketing: Sports Sponsorship Confusion and the Lanham Act*, 75 B.U. L. REV. 1099, 1104 (1995).

[148]   Dean Crow and Janet Hoek, *Ambush Marketing: A Critical Review and Some Practical Advice*, MARKETING BULL., 2003, art. 1, at 2, available at http://marketing-bulletin.massey.ac.nz.

[149]   See Davis, note 145 *supra*, at 425.

[150]   *Ibid.*

[151]   See Bean, note 147 *supra*, at 1104.

[152]   See Crow and Hoek, note 148 *supra*, at 3–4.

[153]   See Stephen M. McKelvey, *Atlanta '96: Olympic Countdown to Ambush Armageddon?*, 4 SETON HALL J. SPORT L. 397, 406 (1994).

[154]   *Ibid.* at 406 n. 34. In addition, sports properties are sometimes reluctant to alienate potential future sponsors.

[155]   435 F. Supp. 1372, 1375–6 (D. Del. 1977).

[156]   *Ibid.* at 1380.

or any of its service marks.[157] However, the court, finding that there was at least partial consumer confusion, did require the State of Delaware to place a disclaimer on tickets and advertising materials in an effort to negate any association of the lottery with the NFL.[158]

More recently, in *National Collegiate Athletic Ass'n* v. *Coors Brewing Co.*,[159] the NCAA brought suit against Coors, alleging that its commercial promotion – in which Coors provided NCAA Men's Basketball Final Four tickets as a prize – created an improper association between Coors and the NCAA.[160] Although the case settled, thus providing no precedent, it was one of the first litigated challenges to unauthorized ticket giveaways in the context of ambush marketing.[161]

3. Sponsorship of individual teams and athletes

The third ambush marketing technique is the use of sponsorship deals with teams or athletes to create an impression of association with the entire sporting event or league. For example, in 1988 when Kodak was an official sponsor of the Olympic Games, Fuji responded by sponsoring the U.S. Swimming team.[162] Similarly, the Dallas Cowboys sold the 'pouring rights' to its stadium to Pepsi despite the NFL's sponsorship agreement with Coca Cola.[163] Similarly, during the 1992 Barcelona Games, Adidas signed a sponsorship agreement with Australian swimmer Ian Thorpe, ambushing Nike's official sponsorship of the Australian Olympic team.[164]

4. Advertising at the venue

A fourth ambush marketing method often used is the placement of advertisements in and around the sporting venue where an event is being held, including on buses, billboards, and the like. For example, during the 1992 Barcelona Games, Nike – which was not an official Olympic sponsor – displayed large murals of U.S. basketball team players on Barcelona buildings.[165]

---

[157]   *Ibid.*

[158]   *Ibid.* at 1380–1.

[159]   No. IP 02–1325-B/S, 2002 U.S. Dist. LEXIS 21059 (S.D. Ind. Oct. 25, 2002).

[160]   Edward Vassallo, Kristin Blemaster, and Patricia Werner, *An International Look at Ambush Marketing*, 95 TRADEMARK REP. 1338, 1341 (2005). The NCAA brought claims based on breach of revocable license and unfair competition. The former claim related to language found on the back of the ticket; the latter claim alleged that Coors's promotion attempted to create public confusion as to an association and affiliation between Coors and the NCAA. *Ibid.*

[161]   *Ibid.*

[162]   Crow and Hoek, note 148 *supra*, at 2; see also Stephen McKelvey and John Grady, *An Analysis of the Ongoing Global Efforts to Combat Ambush Marketing: Will Corporate Marketers 'Take' the Gold in Greece?*, 14 J. LEGAL ASPECTS SPORT 191, 214 (2004) (describing the 1992 Barcelona Games where, while Reebok held the official Olympic sponsorship position, Nike sponsored the U.S. basketball 'Dream Team').

[163]   Paul O'Sullivan and Patrick Murphy, *Ambush Marketing: The Ethical Issues*, 15(4) PSYCHOLOGY & MARKETING 349, 352 (1998).

[164]   See Crow and Hoek, note 148 *supra*, at 5.

[165]   Davis, note 145 *supra*, at 426.

B. Legal significance

Although ambush marketing occurs frequently, there remains little direct legal precedent discussing the issue of ambush marketing. The reasons for limited precedent in this area are unclear but may include: (i) the relative recency of the phenomenon; (ii) the fact that ambush marketing campaigns are typically short in duration such that the cost incurred in pursuing litigation is disproportionate to the benefit of obtaining a legal remedy; and (iii) the availability of First Amendment and fair use defenses.[166]

1   Trademark claims

Where an ambush marketer uses another's trademark, the Lanham Act provides a cause of action for infringement for both registered and unregistered trademarks.[167] As noted above, trademark infringement action under the Lanham Act requires a showing that: (i) the claimant possesses a valid trademark and (ii) the defendant's unauthorized use of a mark is likely to cause confusion with the claimant's mark.[168]

As also noted above, a claimant may establish likelihood of confusion by demonstrating that the defendant's mark is likely to cause confusion as to the source, sponsorship, or endorsement of goods or services, or, as to the affiliation or association of the parties.[169] For example, in *National Football League* v. *Coors Brewing Co.*,[170] Coors used the phrase 'Official Beer of the NFL Players' in an advertising campaign corresponding with the beginning of the upcoming football season.[171] Coors entered into a sponsorship agreement with Players, Inc., a marketing company associated with the NFL Players Association; however, it did not obtain a trademark license from the NFL.[172] The Second Circuit affirmed the lower court's holding – in the context of a preliminary injunction application – that the NFL was likely to succeed in demonstrating that Coors infringed the NFL's trademark, since its advertising campaign resulted in widespread consumer confusion as to whether Coors was an official NFL sponsor.[173]

However, one of the difficulties in challenging ambush marketers under the Lanham Act is that, often times the ambusher does not use the claimant's trademarks.[174] In such cases, the primary potential claim is confusion as to sponsorship, endorsement, affiliation or association.[175]

---

[166]   McKelvey, note 141 *supra*, at 5.

[167]   Schmitz, note 140 *supra*, ¶ 11. If the marks at issue are famous, the conduct may also give rise to a trademark dilution claim.

[168]   See 1 ASTRACHAN, *ET AL.*, note 146 *supra*, § 10.07[3][a].

[169]   15 U.S.C. § 1125(a)(1)(a).

[170]   No. 99–7921, 1999 WL 1254122 (2d Cir. Dec. 15, 1999).

[171]   *Ibid.* at *1.

[172]   *Ibid.* Miller Brewing Company and Anheuser Busch were the authorized NFL sponsors.

[173]   *Ibid.*

[174]   Schmitz, note 140 *supra*, at ¶ 11. As noted, factors generally considered in determining whether a likelihood of confusion exists include: (i) strength of the claimant's mark; (ii) similarity of the marks; (iii) similarity of the products or services; (iv) evidence of actual confusion; (v) consumer sophistication; and (vi) the defendant's intent to confuse the consuming public, i.e. bad faith. See *Polaroid Corp.* v. *Polarad Elecs. Corp.*, 287 F.2d 492, 495 (2d. Cir 1961).

[175]   See 1 ASTRACHAN, *ET AL.*, note 146 *supra*, § 10.07[3][a]. While few cases directly address the issue of ambush marketing, several trademark infringement actions could also raise ambush

2. False advertising

A relevant case in this area, *Mastercard International Inc.* v. *Sprint Communications Co.*,[176] while not a pure ambush marketing case, suggests that ambushed corporations may resort to a claim under section 43(a) of the Lanham Act for false advertising. Different from a trademark infringement claim, a false advertising claim under section 43(a) requires: (i) that the defendant made a false or misleading description of fact or representation of fact; (ii) in interstate commerce; (iii) in connection with goods or services; (iv) in commercial advertising or promotion; (v) when the description or representation misrepresents the nature, qualities or origin of a person's goods, services or commercial activities; and (vi) that the claimant is likely to be injured by these acts.[177]

Mastercard obtained exclusive rights to the 1994 World Cup 'World Cup '94' trademarks on all card-based payment devices.[178] Sprint entered into a similar agreement to use the 'World Cup '94' trademarks in its telecommunication advertisements and promotions.[179] When Sprint used the 'World Cup '94' trademarks on calling cards, Mastercard brought suit for false advertising under section 43(a).[180] The District Court for the Southern District of New York found that Sprint's use of 'World Cup '94' marks on calling cards was likely to mislead consumers as to which entity was officially sanctioned by the World Cup to use its marks on calling cards.[181] Mastercard was granted injunctive relief, prohibiting Sprint from using the World Cup marks on its calling cards.[182] As official sponsors enter into new markets, expanding the products and services they offer, the *Mastercard* precedent may be used to prevent sponsors from exceeding the bounds of their sponsorship packages.

3. Unfair competition

An alternative avenue for relief from ambush marketing tactics is by claiming that the ambusher has improperly implied that an entity is officially associated with a sports organization or event, giving rise to an unfair competition claim through misappropriation of goodwill.[183] Such a claim requires a showing that the claimant is the owner of the right or event being ambushed, and that the false representation appropriated or damaged its goodwill.[184]

The claim is far from a 'silver bullet' however. In *National Football League* v. *Governor of Delaware*, as discussed above, the district court rejected the NFL's misappropriation of

---

marketing concerns. See, e.g., *WCVP-TV* v. *Boston Athletic Ass'n*, 926 F.2d 42, 46 (1st Cir. 1991) (holding that Channel 5's use of the trademarked words 'Boston Marathon' in connection with its broadcast of the event was not likely to cause confusion because the words were merely used to describe the event); *Boston Athletic Ass'n* v. *Sullivan*, 867 F.2d 22, 34 (1st Cir. 1989) (holding that use of the Boston Marathon logo on unlicensed T-shirts was likely to cause consumer confusion).

[176] No. 94 CIV. 1051, 1994 WL 97097, at *3 (S.D.N.Y. Mar. 23, 1994), *aff'd*, 23 F.3d 397 (2d Cir. 1994).

[177] See 5 MCCARTHY, note 73 *supra*, § 27:24.

[178] *Mastercard Int'l*, 1994 WL 97097, at *1.

[179] *Ibid.*

[180] *Ibid.* at *1, 3.

[181] *Ibid.* at *4.

[182] *Ibid.* at *5.

[183] See Townley, note 144 *supra*, at 338.

[184] See 1 ASTRACHAN, *ET AL.*, note 146 *supra*, § 10.07[3][c].

goodwill claim.[185] The court reasoned that defendant's lottery was simply profiting off the demand for collateral services of NFL games, and such activity did not constitute a misappropriation of NFL's property.[186] While courts have in the past refrained from extending unfair competition claims to ambush marketing practices, in the right circumstances an unfair competition claim may remain a viable litigation tool for sports organizations, particularly where the 'ambusher' is careful to avoid the use of trademarks.[187]

C.   Potential 'Ambush Marketing' Defenses

1.   First Amendment
A free speech defense under the First Amendment may be available to ambush marketers faced with legal action. Commercial speech, as is typically associated with ambush marketing campaigns would likely be considered, is entitled to some First Amendment protection.[188] However, such protection does not extend to protect false or misleading commercial speech that misleads as to the source or the content of the work.[189] Ambush marketing often straddles the line between legitimate First Amendment protected expression and misrepresentation as to sponsorship or affiliation. For example, in connection with the 2002 Winter Games, a religious organization distributed pamphlets displaying five colored fish in the form of the Olympic rings, and used the words 'Sowing the Seed in Salt Lake City – the New Testament Souvenir – Winter Games Salt Lake City, Utah.'[190] The United States Olympic Committee (USOC) appears not to have challenged the conduct, presumably because of a potentially viable First Amendment defense and because of the unlikelihood that consumers would believe that the USOC was sponsoring a religious group.[191] However, those ambush marketing campaigns which more explicitly misrepresent the origin or sponsorship of goods or services will likely be unable to successfully invoke a First Amendment defense.[192]

2.   Fair use
The fair use defense allows a defendant to use a protected mark if used 'otherwise than as a mark … fairly and in good faith only to describe the goods or services.'[193] The fair use defense would not likely apply to cases where there is clear evidence that the defendant

---

185   453 F. Supp. at 1378; see also *National Hockey League* v. *Pepsi-Cola Canada*, 70 B.C.L.R.2d 27 (Can. 1992) (rejecting plaintiff's claim of unfair competition, referred to under Canadian law as the tort of passing off), *aff'd*, 2 B.C.L.R.3d 3 (Can. 1995).
186   *NFL* v. *Governor of Delaware*, 435 F. Supp. 1372, 1378 (D. Del. 1977).
187   Anita M. Moorman and T. Christopher Greenwell, *Consumer Attitudes of Deception and the Legality of Ambush Marketing Practices*, 15 J. LEGAL ASPECTS SPORT 183, 186 (2005).
188   See 5 MCCARTHY, note 73 *supra* 4, § 27:68.
189   *Ibid.*; see also *Rogers* v. *Grimaldi*, 875 F.2d 994, 999 (2d Cir. 1989).
190   McKelvey and Grady, note 162 *supra*, at 208.
191   *Ibid.*
192   See Bean, note 147 *supra*, at 1121.
193   15 U.S.C. § 1115(b)(4). See also *New Kids on the Block* v. *News Am. Publ'g, Inc.*, 971 F.2d 302 (9th Cir. 1992) (involving newspapers which used New Kids on the Block trademarks in connection with a call-in survey about New Kids band members; the court held that the fair use defense applied).

intended to create an association with the rights holder, which is unlikely to be considered as a good faith undertaking. For example, in *National Football League* v. *Coors Brewing Co.*,[194] Coors contended that its use of the phrase 'Official Beer of the NFL Players' in an advertising campaign constituted fair use. The Second Circuit rejected Coors' fair use defense, stating that, '[t]he record [was] transparent that Coors [which had signed a sponsorship agreement with the NFL Players Association] wanted to capitalize on the goodwill inherent in the NFL trademark and focused on the endorsement and marketing power of the mark, not its descriptive sense.'[195]

3. Disclaimers

National Football League v. *Governor of Delaware*[196] establishes that in at least some forms of ambush marketing, a disclaimer may be used to avoid liability. When Delaware instituted a state lottery using city names, rather than NFL trademarks, the court noted that no statement suggested that the NFL authorized the lottery.[197] However, given that the public believed that the NFL sponsored or authorized the lottery, the court mandated the use of a disclaimer on all lottery tickets and advertising.[198] While courts often declare inconspicuous disclaimers ineffective,[199] a more conspicuous use of a disclaimer may, in some cases, serve as a potential defense to claims against ambush marketers.[200] However, not all courts recognize the ability of disclaimers to dispel consumer confusion.[201]

D. Impact of the Ted Stevens Olympic and Amateur Sports Act of 1998

The Olympic Games, perhaps more than any other sporting event, is targeted by ambush marketers.[202] Because the USOC historically has not received government support for its Olympic program, sponsorship revenue is of primary importance.[203] In 1978, Congress enacted the Amateur Sports Act, later amended as the Ted Stevens Olympic and Amateur Sports Act of 1998 (OASA).[204] The OASA grants the USOC exclusive control over the

---

[194] No. 99-7921, 1999 WL 1254122, at *1 (2d Cir. Dec. 15, 1999)
[195] *Ibid.*
[196] 435 F. Supp. 1372 (D. Del. 1977).
[197] *Ibid.* at 1380.
[198] *Ibid.* at 1380-1.
[199] See, e.g., *Univ. Ga. Athletic Ass'n* v. *Laite,* 756 F.2d 1535, 1547 (11th Cir. 1985) (holding that when a trademark has been exactly replicated, use of an inconspicuous disclaimer does not remedy the likelihood of consumer confusion).
[200] In one of the few cases specifically addressing ambush marketing, *National Hockey League* v. *Pepsi-Cola Canada,* the Supreme Court of British Columbia held that Pepsi had used sufficient disclaimers in the promotion and advertisement of its 'Pro Hockey Playoff Pool' to prevent consumer confusion as to NHL sponsorship or association. 70 B.C.L.R.2d 27 (Can. 1992). Although decided under Canadian law, the Supreme Court of British Columbia relied heavily on U.S. case law with respect to the use of disclaimers in ambush marketing campaigns. See McKelvey, note 153 *supra,* at 427-8.
[201] Steve McKelvey and John Grady, *Ambush Marketing: The Legal Battleground for Sport Marketers,* 21 ENT. & SPORTS L. 8, 11-13 (2004) (suggesting that an increasing number of courts disfavor disclaimers to remedy consumer confusion).
[202] Schmitz, note 140 *supra,* ¶¶ 5-6.
[203] McKelvey and Grady, note 162 *supra,* at 200-201.
[204] 36 U.S.C. § 220506.

Olympic marks in the United States.[205] Protection given to the Olympic marks differs from normal trademark protection in two significant respects. First, the USOC is not required to show that a contested use is likely to cause consumer confusion in order to obtain relief.[206] Second, an unauthorized user of the Olympic marks, under the OASA, does not have the statutory defenses available in a Lanham Act case.[207] Given the broad protection granted to the USOC, the USOC has aggressively pursued infringers and ambush marketers.[208]

Statutory and judicially created exceptions exist to the OASA's broad grant of control to the USOC. First, under the grandfather clause, persons using the Olympic marks prior to September 21, 1950 may continue to do so without violating the Act.[209] Second, courts have carved out an exception from the USOC's exclusive rights for non-commercial speech. For example, in *United States Olympic Committee* v. *American Media, Inc.*,[210] the United States District Court for the District of Colorado held that claims brought under the provision 'for the purposes of trade and to induce the sale of goods' pertained only to commercial uses.[211] The court found that defendant's use of the Olympic marks in connection with the *Olympics USA* magazine constituted non-commercial speech, and thus did not violate the Act.[212] Despite these two exceptions, the USOC's control over the Olympic marks is, and will likely remain, fairly broad.

E.   Proactive Measures to Prevent Ambush Marketing

Many solutions exist to prevent (or at least limit the impact of) ambush marketing. Cease and desist letters should be sent promptly once an organizer or sponsor learns of potential ambush tactics.[213] Second, event organizers can purchase all billboard advertising space around a venue and lease the billboards only to official sponsors.[214] Third, official sponsors can purchase the advertising time before and during the event broadcast to

---

205   *Ibid.*
206   *San Francisco Arts & Athletics, Inc.* v. *U.S. Olympic Comm.*, 483 U.S. 522, 531 (1987).
207   *Ibid.*
208   See Moorman and Greenwell, note 182 *supra*, at 190, providing an example in which the Salt Lake City Organizing Committee required a corn farmer who had created crop circles in the shape of the Olympic rings to remove the symbol or pay the required licensing fee.
209   36 U.S.C. § 220506(d)(2) ('A person who actually used ... ['Olympic,' 'Olympiad,' 'Citius Altius Fortius,' or any combination thereof] for any lawful purpose before September 21, 1950, is not prohibited by this section from continuing the lawful use for the same purpose and for the same goods or services.').
210   156 F. Supp. 2d 1200 (D. Colo. 2001).
211   *Ibid.* at 1203, 1205.
212   *Ibid.* at 1203, 1209; see also *Stop the Olympic Prison* v. *U.S. Olympic Comm.*, 489 F. Supp. 1112, 1114, 1121 (S.D.N.Y. 1980) (holding that use of the term Olympic, and the symbols of the rings and torch, did not violate the Act because the poster was not used 'for the purpose of trade,' or 'to induce the sale of any goods or services, or to promote any theatrical exhibition, athletic performance, or competition').
213   See 1 ASTRACHAN, *ET AL.*, note 146 *supra*, § 10.07[5].
214   Vassallo, *et al.*, note 160 *supra*, at 1353. In 1997, bidding nations for the 2004 Olympics were informed that bids would be rejected unless the organizers promised to buy all billboard space within city limits for the month during which the Olympics was held. Athens' winning bid included such a provision, despite the anticipated $10 million cost. *Ibid.*

prevent competitors from using such broadcast time to falsely associate with the event.[215] Fourth, educational campaigns can be used to inform the public that event or team marks cannot be used without a license.[216] The goal is for the public to 'recognize ambush marketing when it occurs, to see it as damaging and thus to react negatively to it.'[217] Finally, event organizers can take steps to prevent ambush marketer's merchandise from being displayed in or near the venue.[218] The listed proactive measures can help blunt the effect of a wide range of ambush activities, from a competitor giving away sample products near the venue to sophisticated television campaigns.

IV. THE CONTINUING FIGHT OVER MEDIA ACCESS

As the ability to generate income through websites and other digital media grows, both sports event organizers and the media are staking claims to this lucrative industry. Local and national media, as well as sports leagues and individual teams, now each have their own websites, which compete to provide Internet users with real-time information about the status of sporting events. However, given the inherent time-sensitivity of this information in the Internet age, the ability of an event organizer to monetize such information often rests on the ability to maintain control long enough to take advantage of its value. As a result, this data, which could include facts about pitch counts, number of downs, aces, and faults, etc., is of tremendous value, but often only to those who make use of it first.

In an effort to protect the legal right to control this time-sensitive information, event organizers are increasingly restricting who has access to this information and what can be done with it, ultimately limiting the avenues through which content is available to the public. In recent years, event organizers have gone so far as to entirely bar news journalists of freestanding websites,[219] eject bloggers,[220] and to reshape the language used in press credentials.

---

[215]   *Ibid.* at 1354. However, ambushers will still have the opportunity to buy advertising time on the national network's local affiliates. *Ibid.*

[216]   See, e.g., Scott A. Bearby, *Marketing, Protection and Enforcement of NCAA Marks*, 12 MARQ. SPORTS L.J. 543, 546 (2002) (describing the NCAA's annual educational campaigns to inform the public why use of NCAA marks such as 'Final Four' requires the NCAA to take action).

[217]   Vassallo, *et al.*, note 160 *supra*, at 1354.

[218]   See Schmitz, *supra* note 141, ¶¶ 13–14 (describing Athens strict regulation whereby spectators were prevented from carrying food and drink from competitors into the venue, and were required to wear clothing inside out or be denied admission if the spectators appeared to be wearing the merchandise of an official sponsor's competitor for the purpose of attracting attention).

[219]   See George D. Gabel, Jr. and Craig D. Feiser, *Sports Credentialing and the Battle over Competitive Coverage*, 19 COMM. LAW 21, 21 (2001). In 1998 the IOC refused to accredit online journalists for the Nagano Olympics, and in 2000 the NCAA denied credentials to online reporters wishing to cover the March Madness Tournament. *Ibid.*

[220]   Rick Bozich, THE COURIER-JOURNAL Reporter Ejected From U of L Game (June 11, 2007), available at http://www.courier-journal.com/apps/pbcs.dll/article?AID=2007706110450.

A.   Copyright Law and Media Access

Through copyright law, Congress has accorded protection to the telecasting of live games,[221] but it has become fundamentally clear since *NBA* v. *Motorola* (discussed below) that the facts relating to underlying games themselves do not warrant the same protection.[222] Thus, because the underlying facts in a copyrighted work are not considered copyrightable, a third party wishing to use those facts need not obtain a license.[223] Therefore, scores and statistics broadcast during the course of a sporting event do not themselves come under the umbrella of copyright protection, unlike the broadcast itself.

B.   *NBA* v. *Motorola*

NBA v. *Motorola* is in many ways the watershed ruling which defines where a sports leagues' ability to control third parties' use of game-related information ends and the public domain begins.[224] The original conflict between the NBA and Motorola came about through technological progress, in much the same manner as the advancement of the Internet and live blogs gave rise to the 'Louisville Blogger' incident discussed below.

In 1995, the NBA filed suit against Motorola to enjoin Motorola's use of a pager system, called SportsTrax, to display up-to-the-minute information about the progress of NBA games.[225] SportsTrax used reporters to follow NBA games on live television or radio and provide information via personal computer to relay the information being received to the SportsTrax pagers.[226] The NBA was also working on its own pager system at the time, called Gamestats, which broadcast the same type of data. Thus, the NBA claimed that SportsTrax's use of the same information constituted unfair competition through commercial misappropriation.

Ultimately, the U.S. Court of Appeals for the Second Circuit found that the unauthorized use of game statistics gathered via public sources such as television or radio did not

---

[221]   See, e.g., H.R. Rep. No. 94–1476, at 52 (1976), reprinted in 1976 U.S.C.C.A.N. 5659, 5665 (noting that the work of a camera man and director of the broadcast of a sporting event constitutes the creation of a copyrightable work of authorship, but implying through omission that the game itself being televised does not).

[222]   *National Basketball Ass'n* v. *Motorola, Inc.*, 105 F.3d 841, 846 (2d Cir. 1997) (stating that 'the underlying basketball games do not fall within the subject matter of federal copyright protection because they do not constitute "original works of authorship" under 17 U.S.C. ¶¶ 102(a)' (citation omitted)).

[223]   This premise, known as the fact/expression dichotomy, was articulated by the U.S. Supreme Court, and rigorously restricts the protection given to underlying facts within a copyrighted work by discerning between copyrightable material and non-copyrightable material, in that 'no author may copyright facts or ideas; rather the copyright is limited to those aspects of the work, termed 'expression,' that 'display the stamp of the author's originality.' *Feist Publ'ns, Inc.* v. *Rural Tel. Serv. Co.*, 499 U.S. 340, 350 (1991) (citation omitted).

[224]   See 105 F.3d at 849–50.

[225]   *Ibid.* at 843.

[226]   *Ibid.* at 844.

amount to misappropriation or violate the NBA's broadcast rights. The court painstakingly scrutinized the claim through a copyright preemption analysis, as well as a 'hot-news' misappropriation claim.[227] The court pointed out that the fact gatherers were not within the stadium, and that in recording these statistics from information in the public domain they had not misappropriated anything that was the subject of copyright. The court also ruled that the facts underlying sports games cannot themselves be copyrighted. Thus, once the broadcast is in the public domain, news sources may expend their own resources to collect and transmit purely factual information about the game by watching the broadcasts themselves, and not infringe any copyright held by a sports event organizer.[228] However, the *Motorola* court left this precise issue open to future litigation, noting: 'if the NBA were in the future to market a rival pager with a direct datafeed from the arenas – perhaps with quicker updates than SportsTrax and official statistics – then Motorola's statements regarding source might well be materially misleading.'[229]

C. Contract Law and Media Access

In the wake of *Motorola*, sporting event organizers have employed, with greater frequency, contractual restrictions on the ability of event attendees to disseminate information about the event. These contractual restrictions come in various forms, including press passes, licensing contracts, and the terms and conditions on the back of admission tickets.

When sporting events occur on private property to which the general public does not have unfettered access, the law permits organizers to place non-discriminatory restrictions upon those who enter.[230] Restrictions are generally implemented by issuing tickets for general admission, which include express terms and conditions that limit conduct, access, and/or the use of certain information obtained at the event (including facts, digital information, or photographs). The ticket itself, if not a contract, is at least evidence of one.[231] Dating far as back as 1886, courts have recognized that '[a] theatre ticket is simply a license to the party presenting the same to witness a performance to be given at a certain time, and being a license personal in its character, can be revoked.'[232] Courts have since affirmed this notion, as well as recognized that the ticketback contracts printed on them are freely and fully enforceable.[233]

---

[227]   *Ibid.* at 852 (concluding that 'only a narrow 'hot-news' misappropriation claim survives preemption for actions concerning material within the realm of copyright').

[228]   *Ibid.* at 853–4.

[229]   *Ibid.* at 855.

[230]   See, e.g., *Morris Commc'ns Corp.* v. *PGA Tour, Inc.*, 235 F. Supp. 2d 1269, 1274–5 (M.D. Fla. 2002), *aff'd*, 364 F.3d 1288 (11th Cir. 2004).

[231]   See *Jacksonville Bulls Football, Ltd.* v. *Blatt*, 535 So. 2d 626, 629 (Fla. Dist. Ct. App. 1988) (stating 'it is considered evidence of the contract between the proprietor and the ticketholder, entitling the holder to attend a specified performance at a specified date and time').

[232]   *Purcell* v. *Davis*, 19 Abb. N. Cas. 301, 304 (Sup. Ct. N.Y County 1886); see also *Aaron* v. *Ward*, 203 N.Y. 351, 354, 96 N.E. 736, 737 (1910) (holding that a theater ticket was a revocable license, and that one who gained admission by possession of a ticket was subject to expulsion if the proprietor revoked the license).

[233]   *Soderholm* v. *Chicago Nat'l League Ball Club, Inc.*, 255 Ill. App. 3d 119, 124–5, 587 N.E.2d 517, 522 (1992) (stating '[e]ach individual ticket permits the holder to enter the ball park on the date

As the highest New York state court recognized over a century ago, '[t]he law does not prevent the proprietor of a theatre from making reasonable regulations for the conduct of his business and imposing such reasonable conditions upon the purchasers of tickets as in his judgment will best serve the interests of that business.'[234] The court also propounded a set of factors in deciding whether a ticketback clause was valid.[235] Indeed, ticketbacks are rarely voided, and are typically done so only for unconscionability, or other common law contract defenses such as vagueness.[236]

Exclusive credentials and licenses are granted for different platforms to disseminate the facts of the game.[237] These media credentials often are granted only after a formal application process. Recently, sports event organizers such as the NCAA have included a variety of media platforms (such as TV, Radio, Internet, Videoboard, and Internet Live Statistics) as within the scope of their ticketback language.[238] Event organizers in this capacity do have some right in determining who may distribute or publish news generated within their private arena, as discussed in detail below.

D.   *Morris* v. *PGA Tour*: Media Restrictions are Put to the Test

Morris Communications Corp. v. *PGA Tour, Inc.*,[239] addressed the enforceability of media restrictions regarding information gathered by the event organizer and provided to the media at the event.[240] The PGA Tour developed a real-time scoring system (RTSS) that recorded scores from each hole, gathered from volunteers around the golf course using hand-held devices that relayed this information to PGA Tour computer technicians who then posted the scores on the 'pgatour.com' website and also transmitted the scores to an on-site media center. This allowed the PGA Tour, as well as the media in the on-site media center, to monitor the play and scores around the entire golf course. One reason for the success of the RTSS system was that the PGA Tour did not allow event attendees to use

---

and at the time stated on the ticket for the specific purpose of attending the identified game and sitting in the specified seat, subject to all terms, conditions and policies established by the Chicago Cubs').

[234]   *Collister* v. *Hayman*, 183 N.Y. 250, 254, 76 N.E. 20, 21 (1905).

[235]   See *ibid.* at 255–6, 76 N.E. at 21–2 (listing factors in determining whether a ticketback clause, which denied access based on the breach of a ticketback assignability clause, would be held valid: (i) whether the condition violated a statute or was against public policy; (ii) whether the regulation reasonably served the interests of the business; (iii) whether the business operated under a franchise from the state, and therefore had an obligation to accept customers; (iv) the reasonableness of the restraint upon assignability of the property; and (v) whether a certain class of persons was excluded).

[236]   See HOWARD J. ALPERIN AND ROLAND F. CHASE, 364 MASSACHUSETTS PRACTICE SERIES TM CONSUMER LAW § 30:33 (2d ed. 2009).

[237]   See *Shubert* v. *Nixon Amusement Co.*, 83 N.J.L. 101, 102, 83 A. 369, 369 (N.J. 1912) (holding that a theater ticket creates only a revocable personal license, so that for the ejection of the purchaser without unnecessary force no action in tort will lie, but only an action in contract for the price of the ticket and incidental damages).

[238]   See, e.g., 1 National Collegiate Athletic Association Quick Reference Guide to Broadcast Rights, available at portal.ncaahome?WCM_GLOBAL_CONTEXT=/broadcast/media/broad casting/broadcasting+manual/quickref.

[239]   *Morris Commc'ns Corp.* v. *PGA Tour, Inc.*, 364 F.3d 1288 (11th Cir. 2004).

[240]   *Ibid.* at 1291–2.

hand-held devices or cell phones, which could replicate the PGA's RTSS system; as a result, compiling the same information without RTSS would be nearly impossible.[241]

Access to the media center at PGA tournaments was also contractually restricted to only those members of the media who had obtained press credentials from the PGA Tour. Those credentials included the PGA Tour's On-Line Service Regulations (OLSR), which contained the following restrictions: (i) media organizations must delay publication of scores on their website until (a) 30 minutes after the actual shot occurred, or (b) the information has become part of the public domain by being posted on pgatour.com; and (ii) credentialed media organizations are prohibited from selling or syndicating to third parties the scoring information they receive in the media center, unless they obtain permission to do so from the PGA Tour.[242] The credentials also made clear that noncompliance could result in the offending party having its media credentials revoked.[243]

After Morris was denied the ability to syndicate the information provided by the RTSS and disregard the OLSR, it filed suit. The district court found (and the Eleventh Circuit affirmed), that the PGA Tour did not violate section 2 of the Sherman Act by controlling the use of real-time golf scores through credentialing.[244] The PGA Tour court analogized the PGA Tour's property right to the property rights in the 'ticker cases' of the 1900s which held:

[P]laintiff's collection of [stock] quotations is entitled to the protection of the law. It stands like a trade secret. The plaintiff has the right to keep the work which it has done, or paid for doing, to itself ... The plaintiff does not lose its rights by communicating the result to persons, even if many, in confidential relations to itself, under a contract not to make it public.[245]

The Eleventh Circuit affirmed this ruling,[246] relying upon the more recent decision in *ProCD, Inc.* v. *Zeidenberg*[247] for the proposition that courts recognize the ability of compilers of information to limit the use and dissemination of that information through contract.[248] After finding that the PGA Tour did have a property right in the scores, the court held that 'the PGA Tour controls the right of access to that information and can place restrictions on those attending the private event, giving the PGA Tour a property right that the Court will protect.'[249]

---

241 *Ibid.*
242 *Ibid.* at 1291 n. 3.
243 *Morris Commc'ns Corp.* v. *PGA Tour, Inc.*, 117 F. Supp. 2d 1322, 1325 (M.D. Fla. 2000).
244 364 F.3d at 1295.
245 *Morris Commc'ns Corp.* v. *PGA Tour, Inc.*, 235 F. Supp. 2d 1269, 1281 (M.D. Fla. 2002) (quoting *Bd. of Trade of the City of Chicago* v. *Christie Grain & Stock Co.*, 198 U.S. 236, 250–1 (1905)), *aff'd*, 364 F.3d 1288 (11th Cir. 2004). In the early 1900s the Supreme Court dealt with similar issues allowing the trading board to contractually restrict the release of continuous quotations of futures prices unless express permission of the trading board was granted.
246 *Ibid.* at 1279 nn. 19 and 20.
247 86 F.3d 1447, 1451 (7th Cir. 1996).
248 235 F. Supp. 2d at 1298.
249 *Ibid.* at 1281.

E. *NBA* v. *NY Times*

In another important, although less widely publicized case involving sports event organizers' ability to use credentials to restrict media action, the NBA challenged a violation by the New York Times (NY Times) of the terms of the NBA's media credentials. The case involved NY Times photographers sent to cover NBA games through the use of media credentials. These credentials, which explicitly limited the use of the photographs for 'news coverage of the game' only, read as follows:

> The use of any photograph, film, tape or drawing of the game, player interviews or other arena activities taken or made by the accredited organization or the individual for whom this credential has been issued shall be limited to news coverage of the game by the organization to which this credential is issued, unless expressly authorized in writing by the NBA.[250]

When the NY Times sold these photographs to the public at a profit the NBA brought suit claiming that the NY Times sale was a violation of the terms of the press credentials.

Unlike *Motorola*, which involved information in the public domain, *NBA* v. *NY Times* dealt with restrictions on what the media could do *outside* the arena with information gathered *inside* the arena. The NBA argued that in obtaining credentials, members of the press are consenting to a contract with the NBA for a limited license that conditions access to the arena on the media organization's agreement to restrict its use of any film or photographs of the game to 'news coverage.'[251] The NY Times moved to dismiss on copyright preemptive grounds, arguing that it held the copyright to its photographers' photos, and that the NBA could not restrict those rights. The court, in denying the NY Times' motion to dismiss, concluded that the issue was one of contract and not copyright, and that the NBA has demonstrated *prima facia* evidence of a binding contract.[252]

F. Blogging and Access

Recently, the ability of sports event organizers to restrict the flow of information from a sporting event via copyright was put at issue when a reporter was ejected for posting live game updates onto his blog. In 2007, Brian Bennett, a Louisville Courier-Journal sports reporter who had been keeping a real-time blog of the University of Louisville baseball team's playoff games on the Courier-Journal's website, was thrown out of the NCAA tournament.[253] According to a memo circulated one hour before the game, the NCAA considered Bennett's blogging to be a 'live representation' of the game and a violation of his NCAA media credentials.[254]

Following the incident, the NCAA managing director of public and media relations stated that the information released to the media after the eviction of Bennett that indicated an absolute ban on blogging was incorrect. However, the NCAA reiterated that

---

[250]   *Complaint, NBA* v. *N.Y. Times Co.*, No. 602858–2000, at 15 (Sup. Ct. N.Y. County July 7, 2000).

[251]   *Ibid.* at 2.

[252]   *Transcript of Record, NBA* v. *N.Y. Times Co.*, No. 602858–2000, at 5 (Sup. Ct. N.Y. County Feb. 21, 2001) (unpublished transcript of record).

[253]   See NCAA says live updates via blog limited to score, time remaining only, June 21, 2007, available at http://sports.espn.go.com/ncaa/news/story?id=2912100.

[254]   Bozich, note 220 *supra*.

blogging was still in violation of the NCAA policy because it contained play-by-play details.[255] The NCAA has, so far, avoided litigation on this issue, and it has since stated that 'in-game updates to include score and time remaining in competition are permissible by any media entity whether credentialed or not.'[256] It has also changed its policy on blogging, by revising its press policy to include a separate section within its Media Credentials policy that deals solely with blogging.[257]

This new NCAA policy on blogging states that a 'blog may not produce in any form a "real-time" description of the event.'[258] Real-time is defined by the NCAA as 'a continuous play-by-play account or live, extended live/real-time statistics, or detailed description of an event.'[259]

Although no legal claim resulted, the issue of whether a live blog constitutes a 'live representation' may well be the subject of litigation in the near future. Moreover, with technology presenting new ways of depicting the display of live sports events, it is quite possible that as a digitally imaged representation of a real time game, or frequent photo or video blogging, could in fact be deemed a live representation and infringe broadcast rights.

G. Conclusion

Decisions such as *PGA Tour* and *NBA v. NY Times* suggest that through the use of contractually based credentials, sports event organizers can control the distribution of factual information gathered within a private arena, including facts distributed via blogs. Absent such contractual restrictions however, *Motorola* teaches that control over the dissemination of real time information is likely limited at best once the information has entered the public domain. The inherent limitation of credentialing, however, is that only those who have accepted the contract restrictions – such as event attendees and members of the press – are bound by them.

V. DIGITAL COPYRIGHT ISSUES RELATING TO THE UNAUTHORIZED BROADCAST OF SPORTING EVENTS

Advances in technology often present intellectual property owners with new ways to monetize their rights, but also create new threats to those rights. Sports intellectual property owners are no different. Recent technological advances have enabled live sporting events to be streamed over the Internet and the mobile web. Although live streaming presents a potential revenue source for U.S. sports leagues, it also presents a host of new challenges: many of the technological advances that make live streaming possible also enable third parties to engage in the unauthorized streaming of sporting events often for free. Compounding the problem for U.S. sports leagues and broadcasters

---

[255] Andrew Wolfson, *NCAA Clarifies Live Blogging Policy*, THE COURIER-JOURNAL, June 21, 2007, at 1C.
[256] See Bozich, note 220 *supra*.
[257] NCAA Blogging Policy, available at http://www.ncaa.org/wps/ncaa?ContentID=638.
[258] *Ibid.*
[259] *Ibid.*

is the fact that many of the websites offering 'pirated' sporting events operate offshore, ostensibly beyond the reach of U.S. courts.

A. Overview: the Protections Accorded under U.S. Copyright Law

The exclusive broadcast rights of sporting event organizers and broadcasters that are most frequently implicated by broadcast piracy are those of public display and public performance under the U.S. Copyright Act.[260] The Act explicitly includes broadcast transmissions within the ambit of its definition of public performance / display, stating that:

> to perform or display a work 'publicly' means
>
> …
>
> (2) to transmit or otherwise communicate a performance or display of the work … to the public, by means of any device or process, whether the members of the public capable of receiving the performance or display receive it in the same place or in separate places and at the same time or at different times.[261]

Thus, at least one U.S. court has concluded that the unauthorized retransmission of a sports broadcast into another country is subject to a claim under U.S. law where at least some part of the conduct occurs in the United States.[262] In *PrimeTime 24*, a satellite broadcaster (PrimeTime) made unauthorized retransmissions of NFL games to Canadian – but not American – subscribers. Although such conduct did not violate Canadian law, the court accepted the NFL's argument that its public performance/display rights were violated when PrimeTime captured or 'uplinked' the NFL broadcast from a U.S. source and sent it to the PrimeTime satellite.[263] The court first examined relevant legislative history and Congress's statement that each and every method by which images or sound comprising a performance or display are picked up and conveyed is a "transmission," and if the transmission reaches the public in any form, the case comes within the scope of U.S. copyright laws.[264] The court thus concluded that 'a public performance or display includes "each step in the process by which a protected work wends its way to its audience."'[265] Consequently, the Second Circuit held that uplinking to a satellite was as much of a public performance or display as downlinking to a viewer, and that PrimeTime was liable for infringing the NFL's copyrighted football broadcasts.[266]

An example of a downlinking challenge, disposed of mere months before *PrimeTime 24*, was *NFL* v. *TVRadioNow Corp.*[267] Shortly thereafter, a Canadian website (iCraveTV)

---

[260] See 17 U.S.C. § 106(4) and (5).

[261] 17 U.S.C. § 101.

[262] See *Nat'l Football League* v. *PrimeTime 24 Joint Venture*, 211 F.3d 10 (2d Cir. 2000).

[263] *Ibid.* at 11–12.

[264] *Ibid.* at 12 (quoting H.R. Rep. No. 94–1476, at 64 (1976), *reprinted* in 1976 U.S.C.C.A.N. 5659, 5678).

[265] *Ibid.* at 13 (citation omitted).

[266] *Ibid.*

[267] 53 U.S.P.Q.2d 1831 (W.D. Pa. 2000).

captured television broadcasts from U.S. sources and engaged in their illicit retransmission, streaming them over the Internet.[268] These unauthorized broadcasts included both prerecorded television programs as well as live sporting events, causing both traditional studios and sports leagues (e.g., the NFL) to file a lawsuit alleging copyright infringement of their exclusive rights of public performance and display.[269] Because there was extensive evidence that the retransmissions made on iCraveTV's website could be and were viewed within the United States, the court found that the defendant was engaged in copyright infringement within U.S. borders.[270]

B. Live Nation Motor Sports: Mere Linking Means Liability

As *PrimeTime 24* and *iCraveTV* demonstrate, an expansive interpretation of public performance and display, encompassing every stage of the transmission process in '*all conceivable forms and combinations* of wired or wireless communications media,'[271] portends potential liability for unauthorized retransmitters operating in digital as well as more traditional formats – provided that at least some aspect of the conduct occurred in the United States. A more recent case, *Live Nation Motor Sports, Inc.* v. *Davis,*[272] demonstrates that merely directing Internet users to an infringing website or video clip also gives rise to liability under U.S. copyright law.

SFX Motor Sports, Inc. (SFX), the promoter and producer of motorcycle racing events (Supercross), also produced live television, radio, and free audio Internet (webcast) broadcasts of its races. In *Live Nation Motor Sports*, SFX claimed that Davis infringed upon its public display and performance rights in the webcasts merely by providing links to those webcasts on his website.[273] In considering this matter of apparent first impression, the court found that Davis's provision of an unauthorized hyperlink to SFX's webcasts was indistinguishable from PrimeTime 24's unauthorized satellite uplinking of NFL television broadcasts.[274] Accordingly, summary judgment was granted to the claimant on the issue of infringement of its 17 U.S.C. § 106(4) and (5) public performance and public display rights.[275]

Live Nation Motor Sports suggests that – absent a strong fair use argument[276] – unauthorized linking to freely accessible web broadcasts of sporting events can result in infringement liability. Hyperlinking may prove to be the least of broadcast copyright

---

[268] See *ibid.* at 1834.

[269] See *ibid.*

[270] See *ibid.* at 1834–5.

[271] *Nat'l Football League* v. *PrimeTime 24*, 211 F.3d 10, 12 (2d Cir. 2000) (emphasis in original) (quoting H.R. Rep. No. 94–1476, at 64).

[272] 81 U.S.P.Q.2d 1826 (N.D. Tex. 2007).

[273] See *ibid.* at 1828–30 ('Davis admits to providing an audio webcast "link" to the racing events on his website ... [T]he court determines that the unauthorized "link" to the live webcasts that Davis provides on his website qualifies as a copied display or performance of SFX's copyrightable material.').

[274] See *ibid.* at 1830.

[275] See *ibid.* at 1830–1.

[276] The defendant in *Live Nation Motor Sports* made such an argument, but the court rejected the defense, finding no evidence that defendant's use of the webcast was for criticism, news reporting, teaching, or any other recognized purpose. *Ibid.*

holders' worries, however, as an explosion of new Internet-based hardware and software technology has made it easier than ever before to transmit and receive unauthorized broadcasts.

C. Emerging Technology and its Effect on Copyright Holders' Control over Broadcasts

1. New devices – the Slingbox

The Slingbox is a brick-sized device that connects both to a purchaser's home Internet network modem or router and to the origin of his or her television signal.[277] The device then compresses the television signal and makes it available over the Internet via the purchaser's home network. As a result, when the purchaser downloads the required Slingplayer software onto an Internet-connected computer or mobile PDA device (e.g., an iPhone or Blackberry) he or she can use the device to watch television anywhere in the world as if at home.[278]

The Slingbox, and similar computer card technology, raises red flags for sports leagues that reap financial benefits from the licensing of their broadcasts. Consider the situation of a hypothetical MLB fan on a vacation or business trip abroad. If he or she can open up his laptop, access the Internet, and watch MLB games just as easily as if in front of a television at home, why would they pay for league-sponsored online game broadcasts?[279] Furthermore, were Slingbox use to become widespread even only domestically within the United States, the valuations behind regional licensing agreements, as well as the incentives behind broadcast blackouts,[280] would be vitiated. The effect is a double-whammy that could potentially significantly lower the value of sports leagues' exclusive broadcasting rights.

In terms of potential copyright infringement liability, it remains somewhat unsettled as to whether the user is even making unauthorized copies of the protected sports broadcasts, and thus violating the exclusive right of reproduction. On the one hand, the broadcasts are not being stored on the hard drive of the viewer's computer and therefore are arguably not 'fixed' under the definition of the statute. However, courts have held that copies made in a computer's RAM – such as those temporary files that a viewer's computer would make of the broadcasts – are indeed fixed and thus infringing if

---

[277]   See Sling Media, *How Does the Slingbox Work?*, http://support.slingmedia.com/get/HLP-005430.html (last visited June 23, 2010).

[278]   See *ibid.*

[279]   See MLB.com, *Subscriptions*, http://mlb.mlb.com/mlb/subscriptions/index.jsp (last visited June 23, 2010) (offering TV quality out-of-market live baseball game broadcasts for an annual fee).

[280]   The term 'blackout' refers to a certain sporting event being broadcast in some areas but not in others. See, e.g., ESPN.com, *ESPN FAQ-why is a game that I see listed as being televised on an ESPN Network not available in my area?*, http://sports.espn.go.com/espn/news/story?page=help/espn-faq#blackout (last visited June 23, 2010). ('In most cases, ESPN is contractually obligated to protect the interest of a local television outlet that has rights to the game. For Major League Baseball, this will be the case throughout the season for select games on Mondays and Wednesdays. Our Sunday Night Baseball games are exclusive and seen nationwide on ESPN. When a blackout is in place, alternate programming is provided to the areas affected. Please Note: for satellite subscribers, the alternate and/or regionalized programming is available to viewers on an alternate ESPN channel. Please check with your provider for channel number.').

unauthorized.[281] Furthermore, the exclusive right of public performance could also be implicated by the retransmission of the broadcast over the Internet.[282]

Even if a Slingbox user's activity was found to infringe the owner of a sports broadcast's copyright, however, there is still a consideration as to whether or not such activity would fall under the rubric of fair use.[283] One commentator posits that the defense is probably unavailable, applying fair use analysis to the hypothetical of her mother using a Slingbox to view Pittsburgh Panthers basketball broadcasts:

> Mom's purpose is consumptive rather than transformative. The material she's copying and transmitting ... is a televised sporting event ... [and therefore] among the most valuable broadcasts that copyright protects. She's copying and transmitting entire programs, and her doing so undercuts the market for online and mobile phone products that copyright owners target to viewers like her.[284]

Some argue, however, that SlingMedia would not be liable for infringement under the inducement standard because it has taken affirmative steps – such as forbidding public performances in its end-user license agreement, making efforts to prevent users from recording broadcasts onto their hard drives, and only allowing one computer or mobile device to view transmissions from a given Slingbox at a time – in order to protect the interests of copyright holders.[285]

---

[281]   See, e.g., *MAI Sys. Corp.* v. *Peak Computer, Inc.*, 991 F.2d 511, 518 (9th Cir. 1993) ('Peak's loading of copyrighted software into RAM creates a "copy" of that software in violation of the Copyright Act.'); Jessica Litman, *Lawful Personal Use*, 85 TEX. L. REV. 1871, 1901 and n. 174 (2007) (applying *MAI* to the Slingbox context and concluding that if a court followed *MAI* it would probably find that Slingbox created unauthorized reproductions of copyrighted material). But see *Cartoon Network LP* v. *CSC Holdings, Inc.*, 536 F.3d 121, 139 (2d Cir. 2008) (holding that playback transmissions of DVR copy of television programs were not 'public performances' under the U.S. Copyright Act), *cert. denied*, 129 S. Ct. 2890 (2009).

[282]   See Litman, note 281 *supra*, at 1901.

[283]   The fair use defense, which allows an individual to make unauthorized use of copyrighted expression under certain circumstances, is codified at 17 U.S.C. § 107, reproduced here:

> Notwithstanding the provisions of sections 106 and 106A, the fair use of a copyrighted work, including such use by reproduction in copies or phonorecords or by any other means specified by that section, for purposes such as criticism, comment, news reporting, teaching (including multiple copies for classroom use), scholarship, or research, is not an infringement of copyright. In determining whether the use made of a work in any particular case is a fair use the factors to be considered shall include – (1) the purpose and character of the use, including whether such use is of a commercial nature or is for nonprofit educational purposes; (2) the nature of the copyrighted work; (3) the amount and substantiality of the portion used in relation to the copyrighted work as a whole; and (4) the effect of the use upon the potential market for or value of the copyrighted work. The fact that a work is unpublished shall not itself bar a finding of fair use if such finding is made upon consideration of all the above factors.

[284]   Litman, note 281 *supra*, at 1901.

[285]   See Michael Bartley, *Slinging Television: A New Battleground for Technology and Content Holders?*, 48 IDEA 535, 553 (2008).

2. P2P, guerrilla websites, and the difficulty of enforcement

Another area of concern for sports broadcast copyright holders involves the proliferation of peer-to-peer (P2P) file-sharing and live video-streaming networks.[286] P2P networks are characterized by their decentralized nature, with users' computers communicating directly with one another rather than through centralized servers.[287] These networks are extremely efficient because they do not require the acquisition of expensive storage space for servers, file requests and retrievals travel directly from user to user without being routed through a centralized location, consumption of bandwidth is borne more evenly by all members rather than solely by a server proprietor, and a malfunction on one computer does not disable the entire operation as a server glitch would in a more traditional network.[288]

Unfortunately for copyright owners, however, P2P networks can be (and are) easily employed by those seeking to duplicate and disseminate unauthorized copies of music, movies, books, or any other type of media that can be digitized, including live sports broadcasts.[289] Most troublesome is the fact that the features that make P2P networks so efficient and decentralized are also the features that make them nearly impossible to regulate, as content flows briskly from user to user with no central mediator to filter out the protected material from the unprotected.[290]

The emerging predominant force in the illicit P2P sharing of sports broadcasts – and of all other pirated television broadcasts, for that matter – is known as SOP (Streaming Over P2P).[291] These networks work as follows:

> The primary source of programming is from individuals who route signals from their home cable or satellite accounts onto SOP networks. To do this, one only needs to have a personal computer equipped with a PC-TV tuner, ... broadband internet access, and an SOP service's 'broadcast software' downloadable [for free] from a service's website.[292]

The ease with which broadcast piracy can be accomplished, coming at little to no extra cost beyond a computer and Internet access, has led to a veritable 'open door' through which any type of programming can be distributed by anyone, regardless of copyright protection.[293] On the receiving end of these SOP broadcasters are the end user/consumers of SOP broadcasts, who need only download free SOP software in order to access a plethora of unauthorized content.[294] P2P allows unauthorized re-broadcasters and end users to share the burden of bandwidth, creating a seamless network through which data – up to and including live broadcasts – may flow with only negligible delay.

Moreover, the diffuse nature of SOP networks, combined with the general variance of copyright protection worldwide, creates an intractable problem from the perspective of

---

[286]   See generally, Michael J. Mellis, *Internet Piracy of Live Sports Telecasts*, 18 MARQ. SPORTS L. REV. 259 (2008).

[287]   See *MGM Studios, Inc.* v. *Grokster, Ltd.*, 545 U.S. 913, 918–20 (2005).

[288]   *Ibid.*

[289]   *Ibid.*

[290]   *Ibid.*

[291]   See Mellis, note 286 *supra*, at 260.

[292]   *Ibid.* at 262.

[293]   *Ibid.*

[294]   *Ibid.* at 263.

U.S.-based broadcast content owners such as sports leagues. First, as many SOP services lack sufficient nexus to the United States, U.S. copyright holders are essentially left with no U.S. litigation-based remedy.[295] Second, as many countries do not grant the same copyright protection to live broadcasts as the United States does, enforcement authorities in those countries have no motivation or grounds upon which to stop SOP services and broadcasters within their borders.[296] Finally, the proliferation of so-called 'guerrilla websites,' which aggregate links to SOP services and broadcasts, allows completely unsophisticated users to find and access SOP transmissions with the simplicity of a Google search.[297] While recent development in U.S. law such as the *Live Nation* case have recognized that unauthorized linking – even to authorized broadcasts – could be direct copyright infringement, that is of little help if the 'linker' cannot be subject to personal jurisdiction in the United States.[298] Similarly, lawsuits against such sites for secondary liability based upon *Grokster*-type inducement theories may likely fail for lack of U.S. connections.[299]

Criminal penalties for copyright infringement, while less frequently employed, have recently gained traction in the struggle between P2P users and copyright owners.[300] The most notable occurrence of this involves the guerrilla website ThePirateBay.org, which facilitated both illicit and legal file-sharing by aggregating and organizing links to locations where shared works can be found and downloaded with P2P software.[301] The site had approximately 20 million users worldwide.[302] In early 2009 the website's proprietors, all Swedish residents, were prosecuted by Swedish authorities under a statute that penalizes anyone who takes actions which involve the infringement of copyright.[303] The four principals of ThePirateBay were subsequently convicted and, in a result hailed by industry groups, each sentenced to one year in prison. They were also ordered to pay approximately $3.6 million dollars in damages and fines.[304] High-profile, international criminal trials such as the *Pirate Bay* case offer some hope for U.S. broadcast copyright owners seeking to shut down international piracy networks such as SOP. Nonetheless, the

---

[295]   See *ibid.* at 265–6 (describing a SOP network in which the SOP service operator is located in China, the location of an individual 'broadcaster' is in Canada, the victim of sports piracy is in the United States, distribution of the signal is worldwide, and a 'guerrilla website' pointing Internet users to broadcast streams is located in the Netherlands). But see *NFL* v. *TVRadioNow Corp.*, 53 U.S.P.Q.2d 1831, 1834–5 (W.D. Pa. 2000) (court found sufficient nexus between Canadian Internet service engaging in the unauthorized streaming of sports broadcasts into the United States for jurisdiction in part because two advertisers on the site had U.S. addresses).

[296]   See Mellis, note 286 *supra*, at 266.

[297]   See *ibid.* at 263.

[298]   See *Live Nation Motor Sports, Inc.* v. *Davis*, 81 U.S.P.Q.2d 1826, 1830 (N.D. Tex. 2007) (determining that defendant's unauthorized linking to claimant's webcasts constituted 'a copied display or performance of ... copyrightable material').

[299]   See *MGM Studios, Inc.* v. *Grokster, Ltd.*, 545 U.S. 913, 936–7 (2005) (describing the inducement rule).

[300]   For the U.S. provisions related to criminal infringement, see 17 U.S.C. § 506.

[301]   See Eric Pfanner, *Four Convicted in Sweden in Internet Piracy Case*, N.Y. TIMES, Apr. 18, 2009, at B2, available at http://www.nytimes.com/2009/04/18/business/global/18pirate.html (last visited June 23, 2010).

[302]   See *ibid.*

[303]   See *ibid.*

[304]   See *ibid.*

scarcity of such trials, and the uncertainty as to whether they would occur in other countries such as China, leave doubt as to whether these types of proceedings will ultimately solve the file-sharing problem.

Even in countries with well-developed bodies of copyright law, there can still be unpredictability when it comes to enforcement of the copyright in broadcast.[305] A 2008 decision by an Israeli district court, interpreting that country's newly implemented copyright statute, reversed long-standing Israeli precedent related to its old copyright statute by refusing to find copyright in live soccer broadcasts.[306] In *Football Ass'n Premier League Ltd.* v. *Anonymous*, the Tel Aviv district court denied a Premier League request seeking the identity of the operators of a website that captured English Premier League broadcasts and illicitly rebroadcast them.[307] The judge reasoned that the requisite originality standard of the Israeli copyright statute was not satisfied by a work comprised of a filmed sporting event.[308] Should this interpretation of the originality standard be upheld in subsequent Israeli (or other international) decisions, it would mark a break with the current international trend toward greater copyright protection for sports broadcasts.

D. Conclusion

The developments described in the foregoing sections paint a potentially troublesome picture for the owners of sports broadcast copyrights. On the one hand, U.S. law protecting their copyright interests in broadcasts is quite strong. On the other hand, however, technological innovation and the exploitation of weak copyright protection in certain jurisdictions outside the United States make it harder than ever to stem the growing tide of broadcast infringement. Any solution to these issues likely will require coordination amongst content owners, cooperation on the international level through diplomatic efforts that incorporate stronger copyright protection, and a concentration of resources toward the development and deployment of counter-infringement technology.

---

[305]   See International Intellectual Property Alliance (IIPA), *Israel 2009 Special 301 Report on Copyright Protection and Enforcement*, http://www.iipa.com/rbc/2009/2009SPEC301ISRAEL.pdf (last visited June 23, 2010).

[306]   See *ibid.* at 205. The website is still operating, pending appeal.

[307]   See *ibid.*

[308]   See *ibid.*

17 Image rights

Steve Cornelius

1. INTRODUCTION

The second half of the twentieth century was marked by an unprecedented growth in the entertainment industry – not only as far as theatre, film, music and fashion were concerned, but also sport. It was especially during the 1950s and 1960s that the world was first confronted with the concept of the superstar. Film stars such as James Dean and Marilyn Monroe, models such as Twiggy, musicians such as Elvis Presley and the Beatles and sport stars such as Pele and Muhammad Ali set new standards of fame and virtually overnight changed our society, our values and the way in which we viewed ourselves and others.

One of the consequences which stems from these developments is that the outward image and physical attributes of the individual have suddenly become commodities. The advertising world takes notice of the popularity enjoyed by the stars and realises the value of associating merchandise or trade marks with superstars. On the one hand, this leads to a whole new source of income for the superstars themselves and hopefully increased profits for the enterprises that associate their services or products with the stars. But, on the other hand, it leads to difficulties when the attributes of a person are apparently used without consent. And it is precisely this unauthorised usage which poses new questions to the law. Should the law protect the individual against unlawful use of his or her image? If so, to what extent should such protection be granted?

At first glance the answers to these questions seem rather simple. But closer analysis reveals a controversy which makes the whole matter quite complex. First, we have to determine to what extent the individual should be protected against the unlawful use of his or her image. Exactly which attributes of the individual should enjoy protection? Is it only the hereditary traits, such as physical features and voice? Or should other acquired attributes, such as handwriting, autograph, skills, qualifications, experiences or even habits and customs, opinions and points of view also be protected?[1] And what about apparent attributes, such as when a fictitious *persona* is created? To what extent should they be protected?[2]

Secondly, if protection should indeed be granted, what is the legal nature of such protection? Does the individual have any subjective right which is worthy of protection? If so, what is the nature and extent of such right?

And against whom do these rights apply? After all, it is well known that different people may have the same name or that people may naturally by coincidence or artificially by

---

[1] McGee, Gale and Scanlan 'Character merchandising: aspects of legal protection' 2001 *Legal Studies* 226 at p. 230.

[2] *Ibid.* p. 231.

design look or sound alike. Does protection of a particular person's right to identity mean that the rights of all other persons with similar attributes will be affected thereby? And how long should this protection last? As long as the individual is alive? But stars such as Elvis Presley, Marilyn Monroe and James Dean still earn millions of dollars even decades after their apparent demise. Should the rights then devolve on the estate of the individual? And if it can devolve, can it also be traded during the lifetime of the individual?

Thirdly, protection of the individual's right to identity must be weighed against the fundamental right to freedom of expression. Can an artist be sued merely because a subject in a portrait purposefully or coincidentally looks like a particular individual? Can a newspaper or magazine be sued because a photo of an individual appears next to a news report which involves that individual? And where does that leave the cartoonist who pokes fun at famous people?

These questions require a fundamental analysis of the principles involved, first, to determine whether there is indeed a right to identity and, secondly, to define the nature and extent of such a right.

2. HISTORICAL DEVELOPMENT

Ancient legal systems already recognised certain personality rights but were generally only concerned with protection of individuals against physical assaults. As such, the Twelve Tables of early Roman law provided for a variety of physical impairments for which predetermined compensation could be claimed in delict or tort.[3] These principles would eventually form the basis on which the *actio iniuriarum* would develop during the Roman Republic.[4] During this period, the focus in the Roman law of personality rights shifted from physical assault to *contumelia* or insult as the basis for unlawfulness.[5] Eventually Roman law reached the stage where any insult through word, act or conduct could be actionable. This ranged from physical assault to cases of insult where no physical attack took place.[6] Eventually, it was decreed that:

> [t]he Praetor outlaws that which could lead to insult for another. So whatever one does or says to embarrass someone else that gives rise to the *actio iuniuriarum*.[7]

Roman law consequently reached the stage where a variety of personality rights were recognised and any infringement of a person's body, honour or dignity could in principle found a claim with the *actio iniuriarum*.[8] And more significant from a modern perspective

---

[3]   *Leges Duodecim Tabularum* VIII.1–4. See also Zimmermann, *The law of obligations: Roman foundations of the civilian tradition* (1990) p. 1050 *et seq.*

[4]   Zimmermann, note 3 *supra*, p. 1050.

[5]   Borkowski *Roman law* (2003) p. 348; Van Zyl *History and principles of Roman private law* (1983) p. 343; and Neethling *Persoonlikheidsreg* (1998) p. 51.

[6]   *Digest of Justinian* 47.10.1.1 *et seq.*

[7]   *Digest of Justinian* 47.10.15.27 (current author's translation). The original text reads: 'Generaliter vetuit Praetor quid ad infamiam alicuius fieri. Proinde quodcumque quis fecerit vel dixerit, ut alium infamet, erit actio iniuriarum.'

[8]   *Digest of Justinian* 47.10.1.2.

is that the scope of the *actio iniuriarum* could be extended on the strength of the general *boni mores* (or legal convictions of the community) test to cover situations not previously envisaged under that remedy.[9] However, it seems that unauthorised use of another person's name or image was only actionable if such use would also amount to an insult, as when someone wrote, published or performed a poem or song that ridiculed someone else.[10]

The *actio iniuriarum* was also received into medieval European legal systems.[11] Voet[12] explains that *iniuria* consisted of any infringement of a person's good name or reputation. It could be committed through acts, words, writings or collusion with another. But it seems that insult was still a requirement if someone wished to succeed with a claim for the unauthorised use of his image.[13] The focus was solely on privacy and dignity, rather than a concern with unfair appropriation of economic value derived from the image of another. From these concepts the modern concepts of privacy and dignity developed in the private or civil law of many modern legal systems.[14] From there only a small adjustment in focus was required to deal with commercial exploitation of an individual's image.

While Roman law influenced English law, there was no reception of Roman law into English law as occurred in other medieval European systems.[15] The civil-law countries were influenced much more extensively by Roman law than England and the influence of Roman law became in England secret, and, as it were, illicit.[16] This was the result of resistance to the reception of Roman law in England, which started in 1234 AD when Henry III prohibited the teaching of Roman law in the law schools of London.[17] While the nations of Western Europe adopted Roman law as their own, the English lawyers chose to reinvent or reproduce Roman law.[18]

In early English law, royal justice was a favour which had to be specifically granted by the king. A party who wished to originate a suit in the king's courts consequently first had to obtain a royal writ from the king's Chancery to authorise commencement with the action.[19] As a result, early English law followed a procedural approach, as opposed to a principles-based approach followed in other European systems.

Where one person suffered a wrong at the hands of another, this was in certain cases seen as a disturbance of the King's peace and the wronged party could obtain the writ of trespass. Initially, three kinds of trespass were recognised: battery or assault, taking goods

---

[9]   Neethling, note 5 *supra*, p. 55.
[10] *Digest of Justinian* 47.10.15.27.
[11] Voet *Commentarius ad Pandectas* 47.10.7; Pothier *Traité des Obligations* 116, 118; Lessius *De Iustitia et Iure, Ceterisque Virtutibus Cardinalis Libri Quatuor* 2.7.5.19; Durandus *Speculum Iuris* 4.4.2.15; Ubaldi *Commentaria Corpus Iuris Civilis* 9.2.41.
[12] Note 11 *supra*, 47.10.7.
[13] *Ibid.* 47.10.7.
[14] Zimmermann, note 3 *supra*, p. 1050 *et seq.*
[15] Baker *An introduction to English legal history* 2nd ed. (1979) p. 33 *et seq.*
[16] Jenks *Short history of English law* 3rd ed. (1924) p. 5.
[17] *Ibid.* p. 20.
[18] Baker, note 15 *supra*, p. 27.
[19] Baker, note 15 *supra*, p. 49; Jenks, note 16 *supra*, p. 47.

and entering land or a house.[20] Trespass was soon modified to extend its scope to various other wrongs.[21] As a result, different writs or actions were developed for different wrongs.[22]

In particular, the trespass of battery or assault was developed to include malicious prosecution which related to any abuse of judicial processes.[23] Abuse of process was seen as a deceit and this eventually gave rise to the writ of deceit.[24] This in turn provided the basis on which modern torts such as passing off could be developed in English law. [25] The English law of torts in the modern sense only developed in the nineteenth century. [26]

Towards the end of the eighteenth century in the United States, the Fourth Amendment, which dealt with unreasonable searches and seizures, introduced the concept of personal sovereignty.[27] This in turn gave rise to the systematic protection of domestic privacy in various state courts and the imposition of penalties for criminal trespass, which in turn gave rise to civil remedies against intrusions by strangers.[28] In 1880, this process gained substantial momentum with the publication of an article in which Samuel Warren and Louis Brandeis[29] sought to extract a right of privacy from the protection afforded by common law copyright, on the grounds that the protection afforded to the expression of thoughts merely amounted to enforcement of the more general right of each individual to be left alone.[30] The right to privacy at common law was first recognised by the Supreme Court of Georgia in *Pavesich* v. *New England Life Insurance Co.*[31] and this provided the impetus for courts in other states to follow suit.[32] Significantly, many of the early cases on the right to privacy dealt with the unauthorised taking or publication of photographs depicting the aggrieved parties. This provided the logical basis, then, for the eventual protection of image rights in various US states.

3.   COMPARATIVE ANALYSIS

From an analysis of various legal systems, it is apparent that there are mainly two approaches to protection of the individual against unauthorised use of his or her image. This distinction also generally coincides with the distinction between continental systems

---

[20]   Reeves *History of the English law from the Saxons to the end of the reign of Philip and Mary* 3rd ed. (1814) p. 84 *et seq.*

[21]   *Ibid.* p. 88 *et seq.*

[22]   Lunny and Oliphant *Tort law* (2010) p. 2.

[23]   Burdick *The law of torts: a concise treatise on the civil liability at common law* (1905) p. 2.

[24]   Reeves, note 20 *supra*, p. 90.

[25]   Carty *An analysis of the economic torts* (2001) p. 131 *et seq.*

[26]   Burdick, note 23 *supra*, p. 1.

[27]   Originally the Fourth Amendment only restricted the power of the Federal Government until the US Supreme ruled in *Mapp* v. *Ohio* 367 US 643) that it was also applicable to state governments.

[28]   Glenn *The right to privacy: rights and liberties under the law* (2003) p. 47 *et seq.*

[29]   'The right to privacy' 1890 *Harvard L.R.* p. 193.

[30]   Beverley-Smith *The commercial appropriation of personality* (2002) p. 146 *et seq.*

[31]   50 S.E. 68.

[32]   See, e.g., *Smith* v. *Suratt* W.L. 1024 (Alaska); *Mabry* v. *Kettering* 117 S.W. 746 (Arkansas); *Thayer* v. *Worcester Post Co.* 187 N.E. 292 (Massachusetts); *Vassar College* v. *Loose-Wiles Biscuit Co.* 197 F. 982 (Missouri); *Flake* v. *Greensboro News Co.* 195 S.E. 55 (North Carolina); *Harlow* v. *Buno Co.* 36 Pa. D. & C. 101 (Pennsylvania).

where the law is largely codified and systems that are generally based on common law. In some systems, the matter is regulated by statute, while there are attempts in other systems to afford protection within the confines of existing common law measures of mainly the law of tort or delict. There is, however, also a third category of systems where both statutory and common law measures are applied to protect the individual against unauthorised use of his or her image.

3.1 Common Law Protection

English law is one of the systems where the common law approach is followed to protect the individual against unauthorised use of his or her public image. The approach which the English courts have followed thus far is to apply existing principles of *tort* and determine to what extent the individual should be afforded protection, if at all.

In particular the *tort of passing off* is relevant in this regard. There are two requirements that must be satisfied before a party can succeed with a claim based on the tort of passing off. First, at the time when the conduct complained of took place, the claimant should already have acquired some measure of fame and, secondly, the conduct complained of must be of such a nature that it would create an impression with a significant portion of the proposed market that the claimant endorses, recommends or approves the product of the defendant. It is particularly this second requirement which is problematic in the majority of cases.

Consequently, the court ruled in *Elvisly Yours* v. *Elvis Presley Enterprises*[33] that the unauthorised use of Elvis Presley's name and image is not unlawful since it would not create confusion amongst the public. Consumers purchase the curios simply because they contain the image of Elvis Presley and not because they come from a particular source or because the people are led to believe that Elvis, wherever he may be, endorses the particular products. The second requirement is therefore not satisfied.

On the other hand, the claimant succeeded in *Irvine* v. *Talksport Ltd.*[34] Without consent from the claimant, the defendant altered a photograph of the claimant so that it seemed as if he held a radio to his ear. The caption next to it read 'Eddy Irvine listens to Talksport'. The court ruled that the advertisement clearly created the impression that the claimant endorsed or approved the defendant's radio broadcasts and could therefore confuse the public. The claimant was world famous as a racing driver and the other requirement to succeed with a claim based on *passing off* was therefore also satisfied.

English law affords the individual only limited protection where the attributes of that person are used without permission in a way which cannot be reconciled with the true image of that person. There is as yet no protection against commercial appropriation of an individual's image. The implication of the English precedents is that a party may freely use the image of a famous person without permission to promote its goods or services, just as long as it is done in a way which does not create the impression that the famous person endorses, recommends or approves the product of the defendant.

By contrast, the approach to the protection of the individual against unauthorised use of his or her image in French law is more susceptible to change and development. In spite

---

[33] (1997) R.P.C. 543.

[34] [2003] 2 All E.R. 881 (CA).

of the fact that French law is mainly codified, the French approach to the commercial exploitation of the individual's image is closer to a common law approach than a statutory approach. A person's right to decide over the commercial exploitation of his or her image is not mentioned at all in any of the French codifications, but is rather based on precedents which derive the protectable interest from other legal grounds, such as the right to privacy,[35] as well as the honour and reputation of the individual.[36] According to the French approach, the public image of a famous person embodies a personality interest, although it also encompasses a proprietary interest. Any unauthorised use of a famous person's image for commercial gain therefore amounts to an infringement of that person's personality as well as proprietary rights.

Even before the proliferation of the mass media, before the general use of photography and in the absence of any clear right to identity in the French law at the time, the foundation for the protection of the individual against unauthorised use of his or her image was laid in French law. The *Tribunal Civil de la Seine* had already decided in 1858[37] that no one could create and publish a lifelike portrait of a famous actress on her death bed, without the consent of her family. The next logical step was to extend the same protection also to the living.

In time, French law would reach the position where the image of any famous person could not be used for commercial gain without that person's consent.[38] This development culminated in 1993 in a case before the *Tribunal Civil* where the famous football player Eric Cantona instituted a claim against the publishers of the magazine *But*.[39] A special edition of *But*, exclusively dedicated to Cantona, was published. The court ruled that, due to their fame, people living in the public eye give tacit consent that they may be photographed in public and that the subsequent photos may be published within reasonable bounds. Although the photos of Cantona printed in the special edition of *But* were all taken in public places, the purpose of the special edition was not to inform the public, but rather to exploit the image of an undoubtedly famous person for commercial gain and consequently obtain profits for the publishers. Such commercial exploitation exceeds the bounds of reasonable use and may only take place with the prior consent of the person who is portrayed.

It is not only the image of a famous person which is protected in French law. In 2000 the *Tribunal Civil* in Nanterre ruled that the unauthorised use of tennis star Amelie Mauresmo's name as an Internet domain name amounted to unlawful appropriation of her personality rights and was therefore unlawful.[40]

Various jurisdictions in the United States also follow a common law approach to protection against the unauthorised use of an individual's public image.[41] In New York, the matter first received attention when the Court of Appeals held in *Mackenzie* v. *Soden*

---

[35]   a. 9 Code Civil.

[36]   a. 12 Code Civil.

[37]   *Affaire Rachel* 1858 D.P. III 62.

[38]   *Sarl Pleins Feux Editions c/Fignon – Cour de Cassation*, 3 April 1987.

[39]   Verheyden 'France' in Blackshaw and Siekmann *Sports image rights in Europe* (2005).

[40]   T.G.I. Nanterre D. 2000 somm. 275.

[41]   Unlike most countries, even federal ones, the US Supreme Court's jurisdiction is limited to federal constitutional and statutory law and common law claims are determined in the final instance by the supreme courts of each of the 50 states.

Mineral Springs Co.[42] that the unauthorised use of an opinion and autograph attributed to a well-known physician amounted to infringement of the appellant's privacy which justified injunctive relief against the respondent. At first glance this seems to be a typical case of passing off, as it would be in English law, but the court placed less emphasis on the potential to mislead and more on the right of the appellant to protect his status and reputation as physician.

In a subsequent case, *Robertson* v. *Rochester Folding Box Company*,[43] the majority of the court, however, ruled that the right to freedom of expression in the First Amendment was of greater importance than any rights which the individual may have had to prevent unauthorised use of his or her image in an advertisement. This case caused a public uproar which in turn led to amendment of the New York Civil Rights Law to regulate the right to identity and the protection thereof.

Against this background the *locus classicus* relating to the right to use a person's attributes in the United States, *Haelan Laboratories Inc* v. *Topps Chewing Gum*[44] came before the Second Circuit Court of Appeals. The appellant contracted with various baseball players for the exclusive right to use their images in the marketing of the appellant's chewing gum. In spite of this, the respondent did the same in the marketing of its chewing gum. The court held that, apart from the statutory right to privacy in the New York Civil Rights Law, a right to publicity could also be derived from the common law of New York. The court explained that where the image of a famous person was used without consent in advertisements or for commercial purposes, it was not usually the honour or dignity of the person which was affected, but the patrimonial state in that the individual was not compensated for such use or because the individual's ability to exploit his or her own image elsewhere was diluted. The fee which a person can command for the use of his or her image depends to a substantial extent on exclusivity and any conduct which compromises such exclusivity detracts from the individual's ability to exploit his or her image.

The Second Circuit Court of Appeals eventually held in *Pirone* v. *MacMillan*[45] that the court had erred in *Haelan Laboratories*[46] since the right to identity was only recognised by statute in New York and there was no distinguishable common law right to identity in New York.[47] By this time, however, *Haelan Laboratories*[48] had already served internationally as authority and led to the recognition of a common law right to publicity in more than thirty of the US states, mainly as the tort of violation of the right to publicity.[49]

---

[42]   18 N.Y.S. 240.

[43]   171 N.Y.S. 538.

[44]   202 F. 2d 866.

[45]   894 F. 2d 579.

[46]   Note 44 *supra*.

[47]   See also *Chimarev* v. *TD Waterhouse Investor Services Inc* 280 F. Supp. 2d 208; *Myskina* v. *Conde Nast Publications Inc* 386 F. Supp. 2d 409; *Messenger ex rel Messenger* v. *Gruner Jahr Printing and Publishing* 94 N.Y. 2d 436; *Freihofer* v. *Hearst Corporation* 65 N.Y. 2d 135; *Novel* v. *Beacon Operating Corporation* 446 N.Y.S. 2d 118; *In re Dora P* 418 N.Y.S. 2d 597 and *Kiss* v. *County of Putnam* 398 N.Y.S. 2d 729.

[48]   Note 44 *supra*.

[49]   See, e.g., *Allison* v. *Vintage Sports Plaques* 136 F. 3d 1443 in Alabama (framing and resale of collectors' cards depicting sports stars are unlawful); *Olan Mills Inc.* v. *Dodd* 353 S.W. 2d 22 in Arkansas (use of person's image on advertising brochure without consent is unlawful); *Venturi* v.

In *Allison* v. *Vintage Sports Plaques,*[50] Judge Kravitch of the federal appeals court for the Eleventh Circuit summarised the common law position succinctly.[51] She explained that in Alabama, as in various other jurisdictions in the United States, the right to the use of a person's image is protected under the tort of invasion of privacy. This tort can be committed in any one of four ways. First, privacy is violated through access to the plaintiff's physical and intimate secludedness, secondly, through publication in conflict with generally accepted norms of decency, thirdly, through publication which places the plaintiff in a false light and fourthly through unauthorised use of the plaintiff's image for commercial gain. The third category is also known as the 'tort of false light publicity', while the fourth category is also known as the 'tort of commercial appropriation'.

The basis for the protection of the right to identity in terms of these measures is the financial interest of the individual and not merely human dignity as one would expect with invasion of privacy. To succeed with a claim under commercial appropriation, the plaintiff must prove that the respondent used the plaintiff's identity, that the use of the plaintiff's identity holds commercial or other gain for the respondent, that the plaintiff's

---

Savitt Inc. 468 A. 2d 933 in Connecticut (claim by golf player for unauthorised use of photograph in advertisement fails because plaintiff could not prove intent to cause harm); *Vassiliades* v. *Garfinckel's Brooks Bros.* 492 A. 2d 580 in the District of Columbia (plastic surgeon and publisher who published 'before' and 'after' pictures of patients violated privacy of patients, whether they are famous or not); *Martin Luther King Jr. Center for Social Change Inc.* v. *American Heritage Products Inc.* 296 S.E. 2d 697 in Georgia (court prohibits unauthorised sale of statuettes made to the image of King); *Fergerstrom* v. *Hawaiian Ocean View Estates Inc.* 441 P. 2d 808 in Hawaii (property developer may not use pictures of purchaser and construction of house in advertising brochure without consent); *Johnson* v. *Boeing Airplane Co.* 262 P. 2d 808 in Kansas (employee who tacitly agreed to have photograph taken next to aircraft and for such photograph to be used in advertising brochure forfeits claim against employer); *Prudhomme* v. *Proctor and Gamble Co.* 800 F. Supp. 390 in Louisiana (advertising showing impersonator of famous chef violates privacy of chef); *Lawrence* v. *A.S. Abell Co.* 475 A. 2d 448 in Maryland (use of newspaper clippings with picture of babies in advertising for newspaper does not violate privacy of mothers or babies); *Carson* v. *Here's Johnny Portable Toilets Inc.* 698 F. 2d 831 in Michigan (unauthorised use of famous person's name is unlawful if that person can be identified); *Candebat* v. *Flanagan* 487 S. 2d 207 in Mississippi (reference to particular person's motor vehicle collision without consent in advertising is unlawful); *Haith* v. *Model Cities Health Corp.* 704 S.W. 2d 684 in Missouri (employer may not use the names of medical practitioners which it employs in advertising without their consent); *Gilham* v. *Burlington Northern Inc.* 514 F. 2d 660 in New Jersey (where a company owns the copyright in a picture of an individual the company may consent to the use of that picture on the cover of a magazine); *Benally* v. *Hundred Arrows Press Inc.* 614 F. Supp. 969 in New Mexico (publication of photograph showing Navajo natives in a book on the life and work of a photographer is not unlawful); *Reeves* v. *United Artists Corp.* 765 F. 2d 79 in Ohio (right to publicity is not heritable and lapsed on the death of a famous boxer); *Martinez* v. *Democrat-Herald Publishing Co.* 669 P. 2d 818 in Oregon (picture of student with history of drug abuse in article on drug use on campus does not violate rights of student); *Gee* v. *C.B.S. Inc.* 612 F. 2d 572 in Pennsylvania (where record company owns copyright in music it may use the name and image of the singer on the record cover); *Staruski* v. *Continental Telephone Co.* 581 A. 2d 266 in Vermont (employer may not use picture of employee in advertising without consent); and *Crump* v. *Beckley Newspapers Inc.* 320 S.E. 2d 70 in West Virginia (picture of female coal miner in article on women in the coal mines is not unlawful).

50   136 F. 3d 1443.

51   Under US law, when a federal court is deciding a common law issue, it is bound to follow the specific decisions of the state supreme court for the state whose common law applies. Thus, the federal court in *Allison* was predicting how the Alabama Supreme Court would define the scope of the tort of invasion of privacy.

image was used without consent and that the plaintiff will suffer loss or prejudice as a result. In this regard, a court would look at the commercial damage to the business value of the human identity or the extent to which the plaintiff is deprived if he or she does not receive money for authorising the use of his or her image.

The court also compared the tort of commercial appropriation with the tort of violation of the right to publicity which applies in other states that follow a common law approach and concluded that the difference was merely semantic. The extent of the right to publicity was eventually determined and expanded in various judgments across the United States so that the right applies irrespective of whether the person concerned is famous or not and even public and political figures may be protected against commercial exploitation of their images.

In Georgia the court held in *Martin Luther King Jr Center for Social Change Inc* v. *American Heritage Products Inc.*[52] that the unauthorised production and sale of statuettes of the late civil rights activist, was unlawful. The court held that the right to publicity was heritable, that the right applied irrespective of the fame of the individual concerned[53] and that even public and political figures were protected against commercial exploitation of their image.

In *Carson* v. *Here's Johnny Portable Toilets Inc.*[54] the *Sixth Circuit* in Michigan held that a famous person's right to publicity could be violated if his or her identity was consciously used without consent for commercial gain. The court further held that the identity of a person was used where the person could be identified even if only a part of the person's name was used. This case is significant since it was not so much the name or image of Johnny Carson that was exploited, but rather the distinctive 'Here's Johnny' introduction that could be heard at the beginning of each episode of the *Johnny Carson Show*. Likewise, according to *Prudhomme* v. *Proctor and Gamble Co.*,[55] the right to publicity of a person is also infringed upon where an impersonator or double of that person appears in an advertisement, as long as it is clear that the person can be identified as the one which the impersonator or double tries to emulate.

In *Vassiliades* v. *Garfinckel's Brooks Bros*[56] the court in the District of Columbia warned, however, that the right to publicity was not absolute. There are in fact certain grounds of justification which a party may raise to show that the unauthorised use of an individual's image is actually lawful. The first justification which is relevant here is consent, whether it is given expressly or tacitly.[57] This justification for the use of an individual's image is self-explanatory as the controversy surrounding the commercial exploitation of the individual's image centres mainly around the unauthorised is of the individual's attributes. In addition, in any claim based on the use of a person's attributes, there are always a variety of interests that have to be weighed against each other. On the one hand, the individual has a right to privacy, an interest in being left in peace and not be exposed to inappropriate publication, as well as an interest in being protected against

---

[52] 296 S.E. 2d 697.

[53] These principles have been confirmed in other cases. See, e.g., *Fergerstrom* v. *Hawaiian Ocean View Estates Inc.* 441 P. 2d 808.

[54] 698 F. 2d 831.

[55] 800 F. Supp. 390.

[56] 492 A. 2d 580.

[57] *Johnson* v. *Boeing Airplane Co.* 262 P. 2d 808.

commercial exploitation. On the other hand, there is the right to freedom of expression as provided for in the First Amendment and the public interest in the free flow of information, not only in respect of dissemination of news, but also with regard to everyday human activities.[58]

One result of this is that the courts recognise incidental use as justification. In *Lawrence* v. *AS Abell Co.*[59] the court of appeal in Maryland held that the use of newspaper clippings with photographs of babies in advertisements for the newspaper did not infringe on the privacy of the babies or their mothers. The court in New Mexico held in *Benally* v. *Hundred Arrows Press Inc.*[60] that publication of a book on the life and work of a photographer did not violate the rights of a group of Navajo whose photos appeared in the book. Similarly, publishing a photo of a student with a history of drug abuse next to a report on drug use on local university campuses was, according to the Oregon court in *Martinez* v. *Democrat-Herald Publishing Co.*,[61] not unlawful.[62]

The First Amendment also provides the basis for a further justification which is known as parody. Although an image rights dispute is between private parties, the state action necessary for First Amendment protection exists where a state law right-of-publicity claim exists only insofar as the courts enforce state-created obligations that were never explicitly assumed by one of the parties.[63] The Supreme Court in the United States places a high premium on freedom of expression and in *Hustler Magazine* v. *Fallwel*[64] the bounds of parody and decency were tested to the extreme. The court ruled that the publication of a composite picture in which a famous evangelist and *Hustler* opponent apparently has sexual intercourse with his own mother was protected under the First Amendment and that the evangelist was a public figure who could be exposed to criticism and comment to an even greater extent.[65] In spite of the apparent free reigns which the Supreme Court gave in the *Hustler* case to poke fun at famous people, parody as justification is not unlimited. In *White* v. *Samsung Electronics America Inc.*[66] the majority of the court held that advertising is not protected under the First Amendment and the individual's interests weigh more when his or her image is used without consent to promote or market the defendant's products.[67] The mere fact that a party aims to make a profit is, however, not sufficient to deny protection under the First Amendment. The test

---

[58]   *Vassiliades* v. *Garfinckel's Brooks Bros.* 492 A. 2d 580.
[59]   475 A. 2d 448.
[60]   614 F. Supp. 969.
[61]   669 P. 2d 818.
[62]   See also *Gee* v. *CBS Inc.* 612 F. 2d 572 in Pennsylvania where the court held that a record company which owned the copyright in music could use the name and image of the artists on the record cover and *Crump* v. *Beckley Newspapers Inc.* 320 S.E. 2d 70 in West Virginia where the court held that a picture of a female coal miner in an article on women in the coal mines is not unlawful.
[63]   *C.B.C. Distribution and Marketing, Inc.* v *Major League Baseball Advanced Media, L.P.*, 505 F. 3d 818 (8th Cir. 2007).
[64]   485 U.S. 46.
[65]   See also *Hoffman* v. *Capital Cities/A.B.C.* 255 F. 3d 1180 that deals with a composite picture of the actor Dustin Hoffman in a scene from the film *Tootsie*. The body of Hoffman, which was clothed in a seductive red evening gown in the original footage, was replaced with the hairy muscular body of a man in a silk dress. The court held that the publication was justified as parody.
[66]   971 F. 2d 1395 (television advertisement imitated popular television game show).
[67]   *Fergerstrom* v. *Hawaiian Ocean View Estates Inc.* 441 P. 2d 808.

to determine whether the use of an individual's image can be justified as parody and whether it amounts to commercial exploitation revolves around the question whether the person's image is used for any purpose other than to secure commercial gain from the popularity or reputation of the person concerned.[68]

Similarly, in *C.B.C. Distribution and Marketing, Inc.* v. *Major League Baseball Advanced Media, L.P.*[69] the Court of Appeals for the Eighth Circuit held that the fantasy leagues, in which the plaintiff used the names of athletes from various professional leagues without their permission, were protected under the First Amendment even though the plaintiff did so for commercial gain. The court held that First Amendment protection prevailed over any right to publicity protection which Missouri law could provide to the defendants.

A different common law approach is followed where the attributes of a person is used without consent for commercial purposes in South Africa. In *Van Zyl* v. *African Theatres Ltd*[70] the defendant wrongly advertised in a local newspaper that the plaintiff, a famous singer, would appear at the defendant's theatre. While the claim failed because the plaintiff did not succeed in proving *animus iniuriandi* or actual damage, it is significant that neither the court nor counsel for the defendant questioned the basis for the claim, namely the unauthorised publication of the plaintiff's name. Judge Watermeyer[71] expressly stated that the plaintiff would probably have succeeded had he, from a factual point of view, followed a different approach and satisfied the burden of proof.[72]

In *O'Keeffe* v. *Argus Printing and Publishing Co. Ltd*[73] the matter was again put under the microscope. In this case the plaintiff succeeded with a claim where the respondent used a photo of the plaintiff aiming a pistol in an advertisement for an arms dealer without her consent. Judge Watermeyer, with whom Judge President De Villiers concurred, held that publication of a person's photo and name for the purposes of advertising constitutes a violation of that person's identity and consequently the person's *dignitas* so that it can found an action with the *actio iniuriarum*. Of particular interest in this case is that the respondent, inter alia, opposed the claim on the basis that in the case of infringement of the *dignitas* a party can only succeed with a claim if there was also an insult. Judge Watermeyer considered this argument and concluded that insult or derision was not a requirement to found liability for injury to dignity with the *actio iniuriarum*.

In *Grütter* v. *Lombard*[74] the Supreme Court of Appeal got the opportunity to investigate further the rights of the individual with regard to the commercial exploitation of his or her image. The appellant and respondents practised as attorneys on common premises under the name 'Grütter and Lombard'. In 2005 the appellant terminated his ties with the respondents and went into partnership with another attorney under the name 'Grütter

---

[68]   *Zacchini* v. *Scripps-Howard Broadcasting Co.* 351 N.E. 2d 454.
[69]   505 F.3d 818.
[70]   1931 C.P.D. 61.
[71]   As he then was.
[72]   He states at p. 69: 'The reason why he thought the plaintiff was to blame was because a false explanation of his failure to appear was given by the defendants, and if damages had been claimed for the publication of that explanation, then plaintiff might have succeeded, but that is not the form of action which has been chosen.'
[73]   1954 3 S.A. 244 (C).
[74]   2007 4 S.A. 89 (SCA).

and Grobbelaar'. The respondents nevertheless continued to practise under the name 'Grütter and Lombard'. The appellant demanded that the respondents cease the use of the name 'Grütter' in the description of their practice, but they refused. The trial court dismissed the application and that gave the Supreme Court of Appeal the opportunity to consider the matter.

It is significant that the appellant did not claim any exclusive right to use the name 'Grütter', nor did he allege that the respondents made themselves guilty of passing off. The appellant merely made the case that it was well known that he was one of the persons to whom the name 'Grütter and Lombard' referred and that he no longer wished to be associated with the firm now that his relationship with it had ceased. In a unanimous judgment Judge Nugent referred with apparent approval to the judgment in *O'Keeffe*[75] and concluded that *O'Keeffe*[76] rested in violation of the right to privacy. This is, however, a loose interpretation of the judgment in *O'Keeffe*[77] and Judge Watermeyer only once mentioned the right to privacy in relation to the unauthorised use of a person's image and only when he discussed the position in the United States. In *Grütter*[78] Judge Nugent nonetheless held that privacy is merely one of a variety of interests that enjoy recognition in the concept of personality rights in the context of the *actio iniuriarum*. The interest which a person has to protect his or her identity against exploitation cannot be distinguished therefrom and is similarly encompassed by that variety of personality rights which is worthy of protection.

The right to identity can in this context be violated in one of two ways. First, a person's right to identity is violated if the attributes of that person is used without permission in a way which cannot be reconciled with the true image of that person, similar to the false light publicity tort in US law. Apart from the unauthorised use of a person's image, this kind of infringement also entails some kind of misrepresentation concerning the individual, such as that the individual approves or endorses a particular product or service or that an attorney is a partner in a firm, while this is not the case. The unlawfulness in this kind of case is found in the misrepresentation concerning the individual and, consequently in violation of the right to human dignity.

Secondly, the right to identity is violated if the attributes of a person is used without authorisation by another person for commercial gain, similar to the commercial appropriation tort in US law. Apart from the unauthorised use of the individual's image, such use also primarily entails a commercial motive which is exclusively aimed at promoting a service or product or to solicit clients or customers. The mere fact that the user may benefit or profit from any product or service in respect of which the individual's attributes have incidentally been used, is not in itself sufficient.[79] This violation of the right to identity therefore also entails unauthorised use of the individual's attributes with a commercial

---

[75]   Note 73 *supra*.
[76]   *Ibid.*
[77]   *Ibid.*
[78]   Note 74 *supra*.
[79]   In *Wells* v. *Atoll Media (Pty) Ltd and another* (11961/2006) [2009] ZAWCHC 173 para. 49 Judge Davis explained that: 'the appropriation of a person's image or likeness for the commercial benefit or advantage of another may well call for legal intervention in order to protect the individual concerned. That may not apply to the kinds of photographs or television images of crowd scenes which contain images of individuals therein. However, when the photograph is employed, as in this

purpose, whether it is done by means of advertisement or the manufacture and distribution of merchandise covered with the attributes of the individual. The unlawfulness in this case is mainly found in infringement of the right to freedom of association and commercial exploitation of the individual.

There is, however, one important question relating to the right to identity which is not considered in the *Grütter* case,[80] and that relates to the question whether the individual, apart from the personality right, also has a proprietary interest in his or her identity which is worthy of protection. This apparent *lacuna* in the *Grütter* case[81] should not pose any difficulty at all. Even in common law[82] it was already accepted that violation of personality rights can also lead to economic loss and there is sufficient authority which indicates that damages can be awarded in such circumstances to an individual whose personality rights have been violated.[83]

This holds important consequences with regard to the right to identity. As personality right, the right to identity attaches to the individual and cannot devolve or be traded. As proprietary right, the right to identity is distinct from the individual and forms an immaterial asset in the estate of the individual. It can be inherited and the individual can trade the right.

There is a further problem which is only touched upon as an aside in the *Grütter* case.[84] Judge Nugent makes it clear that the right to identity is not absolute, but does not discuss this aspect of the right to identity any further. However, it goes without saying that the use of a person's attributes must be unlawful before a claimant will succeed with any delictual (tort) claim. In other cases, where satisfaction or damages were claimed due to infringement on the *dignitas*, the courts have already recognised certain grounds of justification which would mean that the apparent violation of personality rights would indeed be lawful.

With any action due to infringement of a subjective right, a variety of conflicting interests must be weighed against each other. With the use of a person's image, the rights to identity, human dignity and freedom of association of the individual must often be weighed against the user's right to freedom of expression. Although Neethling[85] also correctly states that public policy can justify an apparent violation of the right to identity, it would in my opinion also make sense to consider the other grounds on which infringement on the *dignitas* can be justified. These grounds include consent,[86] truth and public interest,[87] fair comment[88] and jest.[89]

---

case, for the benefit of a magazine sold to make profit, it constitutes an unjustifiable invasion of the personal rights of the individual, including the person's dignity and privacy.'

[80] Note 74 *supra*.
[81] *Ibid.*
[82] *Digest of Justinian* 9.2.5.1 and Voet, note 11 *supra*, 47.10.18.
[83] *Fichard Ltd* v. *The Friend Newspapers Ltd* 1916 A.D. 1; *Bredell* v. *Pienaar* 1924 C.P.D. 203; and *Caxton Ltd* v. *Reeva Forman (Pty) Ltd* 1990 3 S.A. 547 (A).
[84] Note 74 *supra*.
[85] Note 5 *supra*, p. 315.
[86] Neethling, Potgieter and Visser, *Deliktereg* (2006) p. 89.
[87] *Ibid.* p. 313.
[88] *Ibid.* p. 315.
[89] *Ibid.* p. 317.

Consent as justification for the use of a person's image is self-explanatory, not only because of the rule *volenti non fit iniuria,* but also because the controversy surrounding the use of a person's image mainly centres on the unlawful use of the individual's attributes. The other grounds of justification, namely truth and public interest, fair comment and jest, remind one of the grounds of justification such as *incidental use* or *public interest news reporting* and *parody* that are recognised elsewhere in the world in respect of apparent infringement on the right to identity. In addition Neethling also indicates correctly that the public interest in art can in appropriate cases justify the use of a person's image.

Although the precedents in South Africa relating to the right to identity do not distinguish between the famous and the not-so-famous, a person's fame or lack of fame will in all likelihood probably play a part in calculating the amount of satisfaction or damages that will be awarded to an injured party.

3.2   Statutory Protection

As far as statutory protection against the unauthorised use of the individual's public image is concerned, the Germans are the leaders who already paved the way more than a century ago. The history of German measures to protect the individual against unauthorised use of his or her image is remarkably similar to French law in this regard. The German reaction, however, was, in typical German style, more formalistic.

Upon the demise of Otto von Bismarck, photographers entered the death chamber and took photos of the deceased Iron Chancellor. To prevent publication of the photos, legal action was taken against the photographers concerned. The *Reichgericht* found that the photographers made themselves guilty of criminal trespass to obtain the photos and that it would be contrary to public interest to allow publication of the photos in those circumstances. Consequently, dissemination of the photos was prohibited.[90]

An important consequence of this case was the promulgation of the *Kunsturheberge-setz*[91] in 1907, which provides in article 22 that images may only be disseminated or displayed with the consent of the person depicted. The individual's right to his or her image can devolve and can, for a period of no more than 10 years after the death of a person, be enforced by his or her spouse, life partner, children or parents.[92] In 1965 the *Urheberrechtsgesetz* was promulgated. It repealed the *Kunsturhebergesetz*, with the exception of the part on the protection of a person's image, which still applies with minor amendments.

For the purposes of article 22, an image can consist of any recognisable depiction of a person's external appearance, irrespective of the medium on or in which it takes place.

---

[90]   *Amtliche Sammlung des Reichsgericht in Zivilsachen* 45 170.

[91]   Or, to be more precise, the *Gesetz betreffend das Urheberrecht an Werken der bildenden Künste und der Photographie.*

[92]   Article 22 provides: 'Bildnisse dürfen nur mit Einwilligung des Abgebildeten verbreitet oder öffentlich zur Schau gestellt werden. Die Einwilligung gilt im Zweifel als erteilt, wenn der Abgebildete dafür, daß er sich abbilden ließ, eine Entlohnung erhielt. Nach dem Tode des Abgebildeten bedarf es bis zum Ablaufe von 10 Jahren der Einwilligung der Angehörigen des Abgebildeten. Angehörige im Sinne dieses Gesetzes sind der überlebende Ehegatte oder Lebenspartner und die Kinder des Abgebildeten und, wenn weder ein Ehegatte oder Lebenspartner noch Kinder vorhanden sind, die Eltern des Abgebildeten.'

However, it is important that the person depicted must show that there are reasonable grounds on which it can be assumed that he or she will be recognised from the image.[93] The *Bundesgerichthof* held that performance on the sports field will as a matter of fact lead to identification of the person depicted, even where a football goalkeeper was only photographed from behind in the goalposts.[94] The *Landgericht* in München even held that a dummy of Boris Becker which appeared in an advertisement amounted to unlawful exploitation of the tennis star's popularity.[95]

The *Bürgerliches Gesetzbuch* further protects every person's right to his or her name. Article 12 provides that a person whose name is used without permission by another person may demand that such usage should cease and can for this purpose apply for an interdict.

The right to protect his or her image against unauthorised use, is, in terms of German law, a personality right which vests in each individual's right to self-determination over his or her person and body and therefore vests in the individual. This right survives the individual and can devolve so that his or her relatives can protect the individual concerned against unauthorised use of his or her image and/or to profit from such use.

German law also recognizes a number of grounds to justify the use of a person's image. Consent is important here since article 22 of the *Kunsturhebergesetz* and article 12 of the *Bürgerliches Gesetzbuch* expressly refer to absence of consent as requirement for liability. In this regard, article 22 of the *Kunsturhebergesetz* provides that where someone was compensated for the use of his or her image, it is presumed that person concerned has consented to the use of his or her image.

In addition article 23 of the *Kunsturhebergesetz* provides that it is justified in certain cases to use the image of another person. These exceptions mainly deal with the public interest in the free flow of information and relate to use of someone's image in respect of current history, depictions where the person is shown only as part of the scenery or locality and images of meetings, riots and similar events in which the person depicted took part.[96]

Dutch law similarly provides protection against unauthorised use of an individual's image. The *Auteurswet* protects the individual against unauthorised publication of his or her portrait. The explanatory memorandum to the *Auteurswet* explains that the concept 'portrait' can be defined as any depiction of a person's face with or without any other

---

[93] *Pariser Liebestropfen* 1971 *N.J.W.* 698 B.G.II. Urt. v. 26.1.1971–V.I.Z.R. 95/70 (München).

[94] *Fußballtor* 1979 *N.J.W.* 2205 B.G.H. Urt. v. 26.6.1979–V.I.Z.R. 108/78 (Frankfurt).

[95] L.G. Urt. v. 27.3.2003 Z.U.M. 416/2003 (München) and O.L.G. Urt. v. 05.02.2003 Az. 16812/2002 (München). See also Gelinger 'Germany' in Blackshaw and Siekmann, note 39 *supra*, p. 110.

[96] Article 23 provides:

Ohne die nach § 22 erforderliche Einwilligung dürfen verbreitet und zur Schau gestellt werden:

1. Bildnisse aus dem Bereiche der Zeitgeschichte;
2. Bilder, auf denen die Personen nur als Beiwerk neben einer Landschaft oder sonstigen Örtlichkeit erscheinen;
3. Bilder von Versammlungen, Aufzügen und ähnlichen Vorgängen, an denen die dargestellten Personen teilgenommen haben;
4. Bildnisse, die nicht auf Bestellung angefertigt sind, sofern die Verbreitung oder Schaustellung einem höheren Interesse der Kunst dient.

parts of the body, irrespective how the depiction was made. In the *Ja Zuster/Nee Zuster* case[97] the *Hooge Raad* held that a clear similarity between the image and the appearance of the subject must exist before there can be talk of a portrait. The absence of such a similarity is conclusive and the fact that the public may or may not relate the image to the subject makes no difference. It is also not required that the subject must be known to or be identified by any person who may encounter the portrait.[98] A clear rendition of the face is also not a requirement.[99] In this way the *Kantongerecht* Harderwijk held in the *Kramer/ Burnham* case that depiction of a certain ice skater's distinctive posture is sufficient to classify that depiction as a portrait.[100]

An important question was posed to the *Rechtbank* Amsterdam in the *Millecam/Escom* case.[101] Millecam, a television star in the Netherlands, instituted a claim against Escom based on an advertisement pamphlet with a photo of a model who is a Millecam impersonator. Millecam argued that publication of the photo infringed on her portrait rights. However, the court ruled that, in spite of the fact that the public would in all likelihood associate Millecam with the advertisement, the image still portrayed a particular model and could therefore only be a portrait of the particular model and no one else. As a result, Millecam did not succeed with her claim against Escom. This is clearly distinguishable from the position accepted in the United States.[102]

When a portrait is commissioned by the subject, copyright in the portrait vests in the subject and the portrait may as a matter of course not be published without the consent of the subject.[103] Most instances where the image of a person is used without consent, however, entail cases where the depiction is not commissioned by the subject. In such cases, section 21 of the *Auteurswet* provides that publication of the portrait is not authorised insofar as the subject, or after demise of the subject, one of his or her surviving dependants, has a reasonable interest in opposing publication.

The requisite interest can take one of two forms. First, there is the interest in privacy. A subject can oppose publication of a portrait if the subject can show that such publication will infringe on his or her right to privacy. By the nature of things, famous people, such as politicians and film and sport stars, must endure invasion of privacy to a greater extent. But there are limits and when they are exceeded it can form the basis for a claim. Therefore, when a magazine stated on its cover that a football player had a homosexual relationship with a singer, but the article in the magazine declared the opposite, it was held that there was a breach of the football player's privacy.[104]

---

97   1970 *N.J.* 220.
98   *Naturistengids* 1988 *N.J.* 277.
99   *Ibid.*
100   Kollen *Bundel Sport en Recht: Wetgeving, Regelgeving en Jurisprudentie* (2004) p. 680.
101   1995/7 *Informatierecht* 137.
102   *Onassis* v. *Christian Dior – New York Inc.* 472 N.Y.S. 2d 254.
103   Articles 19 and 20 *Auteurswet*.
104   *Vondelpark* 1988 *N.J.* 1000.

Secondly, there is a commercial interest. Dutch law recognises the fact that the image of a famous person has become a commodity.[105] In the *t Schaep met de Vijf Pooten* case,[106] the *Hooge Raad* lay down two requirements before an individual could claim a commercial interest.

First, the individual concerned must already have obtained some fame from practising his or her profession. The concept 'profession' is not interpreted narrowly, so that even amateur sports people, who do not strictly speaking practise sport as their profession, are included here if they have gained some fame from participation in their sports.[107]

Secondly, there must be a commercial exploitation of such fame. This aspect was clearly explained in the *De slag om het voetbalgoud* case.[108] A book, entitled *De slag om het voetbalgoud*, filled with photos of the players in the Dutch football team that played in final of the 1974 World Cup tournament, was published. This in itself did not violate any of the players' rights as it merely amounted to a factual report on a contemporary matter of public interest. However, the publishers sold the entire print run of the book to a company which used the book as part of its marketing campaign. The *Rechtbank* Haarlem held that this latter aspect amounted to commercial exploitation with the result that it infringed on the players' portrait rights.

In the United States, some jurisdictions also rejected a common law approach in favour of codification to protect the right to identity.[109] Paragraph 63.60.010 of the Washington Code provides that each individual or personality holds a proprietary right in his or her name, voice, signature, photograph or likeness. Such proprietary right survives the individual or personality and can be transferred *inter vivos* by contract or *ex lege* or post mortem by will or intestate succession. The right exists irrespective of whether it was commercially exploited during the lifetime of the individual or personality.[110]

The right to identity is stated in more negative terms in the vast majority of other jurisdictions, in other words the various codes prohibit the unauthorised use of a person's image. Article 5, paragraph 50 of the New York Civil Rights Law provides that it is unlawful to use the name, portrait, picture or voice of any living person for advertising or

---

[105]   *Teddy Scholten* 1961 *N.J.* 160.

[106]   1979 *N.J.* 383.

[107]   *Arnold Vanderlijde* 1994 *N.J.* 658.

[108]   1974 *N.J.* 415.

[109]   Some states only recognise statutory protection against unauthorised use of a person's image. These include Indiana (art. 32-13-1-1 *et seq* of the Indiana Statutes); Massachusetts (ch. 4, para. 3A of the Massachusetts General Laws); New York (art. 5, para. 50 of the New York Civil Rights Law); Virginia (arts 8.01–40 and 18.2–216.1 of the Code of Virginia) and Washington (para. 63.60.010 *et seq* of the Revised Code of Washington).

[110]   Paragraph 63.60.010 provides: 'Every individual or personality, as the case may be, has a property right in the use of his or her name, voice, signature, photograph, or likeness, and such right shall be freely transferable, assignable, and licensable, in whole or in part, by any otherwise permissible form of *inter vivos* or testamentary transfer, including without limitation a will, trust, contract, community property agreement, or cotenancy with survivorship provisions or payable-on-death provisions, or, if none is applicable, under the laws of intestate succession applicable to interests in intangible personal property. The property right does not expire upon the death of the individual or personality, as the case may be. The right exists whether or not it was commercially exploited by the individual or the personality during the individual's or the personality's lifetime.'

commercial purposes without the prior written consent of that person.[111] The provision is transgressed if there is conduct which, first, speaks of an intention to benefit from the name or identity of a person or, secondly, if it could have the effect that a party will benefit from using the name or identity of another person.[112] In *Onassis* v. *Christian Dior – New York Inc*[113] the court held that even the use of an impersonator can infringe on the rights of the individual if it is clear that the person can be identified as the individual who the impersonator is imitating.

The protection in terms of this provision is based on the right to privacy and as such it apparently creates a personality right[114] which can apply during the lifetime of the individual but cannot protect the image of any deceased person.[115] Consequently, such right also cannot be traded during the lifetime of the individual.[116] In *Lombardo* v. *Doyle Dane & Bernbach Inc.*[117] the court distinguished between the personality right which is expressly protected in paragraph 50 and a proprietary right in a person's image which can be derived from that provision.[118] While the latter can indeed not devolve or be traded, the position in respect of the former is the opposite. New York may not offer common law protection against the unauthorised use of an individual's image,[119] but it does recognise the common law grounds of justification of consent,[120] incidental use[121] and parody.[122]

---

[111]   Paragraph 50 provides: 'A person, firm or corporation that uses for advertising purposes, or for the purposes of trade, the name, portrait or picture of any living person without having first obtained the written consent of such person, or if a minor of his or her parent or guardian, is guilty of a misdemeanour.'

[112]   *Nebb* v. *Bell Syndicate* 41 F. Supp. 929. See also *People on Complaint of Maggio* v. *Charles Scribner's Sons* 130 N.Y.S. 2d 514.

[113]   472 N.Y.S. 2d 254.

[114]   *Alexandre* v. *Westchester Newspapers* 9 N.Y.S. 2d 744; *Chaplin* v. *National Broadcasting Co.* 15 F.R.D. 134; *Rosemont Enterprises Inc* v. *Random House Inc.* 294 N.Y.S. 2d 122; and *Schumann* v. *Loew's Inc.* 135 N.Y.S. 2d 361.

[115]   *Shaw Family Archives Ltd.* v. *C.M.G. Worldwide Inc.* 434 F. Supp. 2d 203.

[116]   *Ibid.*

[117]   396 N.Y.S. 2d 661.

[118]   See also *Rosemont Enterprises Inc.* v. *Urban Systems Inc.* 340 N.Y.S. 2d 144.

[119]   *Chimare*v. v. *T.D. Waterhouse Investor Services Inc.* 280 F. Supp. 2d 208; *Myskina* v. *Conde Nast Publications Inc* 386 F. Supp. 2d 409; *Messenger ex rel Messenger* v. *Gruner Jahr Printing and Publishing* 94 N.Y. 2d 436; *Freihofer* v. *Hearst Corporation* 65 N.Y. 2d 135; *Novel* v. *Beacon Operating Corporation* 446 N.Y.S. 2d 118; *In re Dora P* 418 N.Y.S. 2d 597; and *Kiss* v. *County of Putnam* 398 N.Y.S. 2d 729.

[120]   *Myskina* v. *Conde Nast Publications Inc* 386 F. Supp. 2d 409; *Ruffino* v. *Neiman* 794 N.Y.S. 2d 228; and *Noble* v. *Town Sports International Inc* 707 N.Y.S. 2d 89.

[121]   See *Namath* v. *Sports Illustrated* 39 N.Y. 2d 897 (magazine clippings with pictures of football star Joe Namath in advertisement for *Sports Illustrated* does not infringe on the player's privacy); *Rand* v. *Hearst Corp* 298 N.Y. 2d 405 (it not unlawful to quote verbatim a book review by Ayn Rand on the back cover of the book concerned); and *Delan by Delan* v. *CBS Inc* 458 N.Y.S. 2d 608 (where psychiatric patient was briefly shown in an hour-long program on alternative treatments for people with mental disorders, the rights of the patient concerned were not violated).

[122]   *Walter* v. *NBC Television Network Inc* 811 N.Y.S. 2d 521 (airing a photograph of someone during a comedy time-slot is not unlawful); and *New York Magazine Division of Primedia Magazines Inc* v. *Metropolitan Transit Authority* 987 F. Supp. 254 (advertisement for a magazine which states that the magazine is the only good thing in town for which the mayor has not yet claimed credit, is lawful).

By contrast Chapter 214, paragraph 3A of the Massachusetts General Laws and paragraph 9-1-28 of the General Laws of Rhode Island, which are formulated in the same terms, are more elaborate.[123] They provide, first, that any person whose name, portrait or picture is used without written consent for the purposes of advertising or trade may institute an action in the high court to prohibit such use. Furthermore, the injured party may claim damages up to three times the value of the actual damages suffered.[124] This aspect aims to protect the individual so that the commercial value of his or her name, portrait or image cannot be exploited to the advantage of someone else.[125]

The two provisions also expressly indicate that consent is a justification for the use of a person's image. In addition, the two provisions create two other interesting exceptions. Where a professional photographer exhibits photos in the course of his or her profession, the photographer does not contravene the provisions. It is also permissible to display or publish the name and portrait of an author, composer or artist in relation to his or her work. And although it is not expressly mentioned, the courts in Massachusetts[126] and Rhode Island[127] also recognise incidental use and parody as grounds of justification.

3.3 Common Law and Statutory Protection

Some jurisdictions in the United States of America follow a twofold approach where both statutory and common law measures are applied to provide protection against the

---

[123]   Both para. 3A and para. 9-1-28 provide: 'Any person whose name, portrait or picture is used within the commonwealth for advertising purposes or for the purposes of trade without his written consent may bring a civil action in the superior court against the person so using his name, portrait or picture, to prevent and restrain the use thereof; and may recover damages for any injuries sustained by reason of such use. If the defendant shall have knowingly used such person's name, portrait or picture in such manner as is prohibited or unlawful, the court, in its discretion, may award the plaintiff treble the amount of the damages sustained by him. Nothing in this section shall be so construed as to prevent any person practicing the profession of photography from exhibiting in or about his or its establishment specimens of the work of such person or establishment, unless the exhibiting of any such specimen is continued after written notice objecting thereto has been given by the person portrayed; and nothing in this section shall be so construed as to prevent any person from using the name, portrait or picture of any manufacturer or dealer in connection with the goods, wares and merchandise manufactured, produced or dealt in by such manufacturer or dealer which such person has sold or disposed of with such name, portrait or picture used in connection therewith; or from using the name, portrait or picture of any author, composer or artist in connection with any literary, musical or artistic production of such author, composer or artist which such person has sold or disposed of with such name, portrait or picture used in connection therewith.'

[124]   This first aspect of the provision is also essentially the same as para. 8.01–40 of the Code of Virginia. Paragraph 18.2–216.1 of the Code of Virginia also makes it an offence to use the name, portrait or picture of another person without permission for advertising or trade.

[125]   *Tropeano* v. *Atlantic Monthly Co.* 400 N.E. 2d 847.

[126]   *Morrell* v. *Forbes Inc.* 603 F. Supp. 1305 (picture of fishermen in news report on organised crime in the fishing industry is not unlawful); and *Tropeano* v. *Atlantic Monthly Co.* 400 N.E. 2d 847 (the mere fact that a publisher earns a profit from distribution of a magazine does not in itself make publication of photographs unlawful).

[127]   *Leddy* v. *Narragansett Television L.P.* 843 A. 2d 481 (displaying picture of fire chief in advertisement for program on fire fighters is not unlawful, even if it forms part of a clip which is aired repeatedly to advertise the program concerned).

unauthorised use of an individual's image.[128] For example, in California article 3344 of the Civil Code provides that it is unlawful for one person to use the name, voice, autograph, photo or likeness of someone else for purposes of advertising, trade or solicitation of customers or clients, without consent. An injured party may, in terms of this provision, cumulatively claim damages, the profit which the wrongdoer gained from the use of the person's image, as well as punitive damages.[129] The protection is not limited to famous people, but is at the disposal of anyone whose image is used without consent.[130] Article 1449 of the Oklahoma Statutes contains essentially the same provision.

Apart from the extensive statutory provisions to protect the individual against unauthorised use of his or her image, common law protection is also recognised in California[131] and Oklahoma.[132] In *Porten* v. *University of San Francisco*[133] the court explained that the right to identity can also be protected by means of the tort of invasion of privacy. This tort can be committed in one of four ways. First, privacy is breached through violation of the claimant's physical and intimate seclusion, secondly, through publication contrary to generally accepted norms of decency, thirdly, through publication which places the

---

[128]   The mixed approach is followed in California (compare art. 3344 of the Civil Code and *Michaels* v. *Internet Entertainment Group Inc.* 5 F. Supp. 2d 823); Florida (compare art. 540.08 of the Florida Statutes and *Zim* v. *Western Publishing Co.* 573 F. 2d 1318); Illinois (compare the Illinois Right of Publicity Act and *Douglas* v. *Hustler Magazine Inc.* 769 F. 2d 1128); Kentucky (compare art. 391.170 of the Kentucky Statutes and *Foster-Milburn Co.* v. *Chinn* 120 S.W. 364); Nebraska (compare art. 20–202 of the Nebraska Revised Statutes and *Carson* v. *National Bank of Commerce* 501 F. 2d 1082); Nevada (compare art. 597–770 *et seq.* of the Nevada Revised Statutes and *People for the Ethical Treatment of Animals* v. *Berosini Ltd* 895 P. 2d 1269); Oklahoma (compare art. 1449 of the Oklahoma Statutes and *McCormack* v. *Oklahoma Publishing Co.* 613 P. 2d 98); Tennessee (compare art. 47-25-1101 *et seq.* of the Tennessee Code and *Elvis Presley International Memorial Fund* v. *Crowell* 733 S.W. 2d 89); Texas (compare art. 26.001 *et seq.* of the Texas Property Code and *National Bank of Commerce* v. *Shaklee Corp.* 503 F. Supp. 533); Utah (compare art. 76-9-407 of the Utah Code and *Cox* v. *Hatch* 761 P. 2d 556) and Wisconsin (compare art. 895.50 of the Wisconsin Statutes and *Hirsch* v. *S. C. Johnson and Sons Inc.* 280 N.W. 2d 129). Although the exact formulation of the various provisions differs from one state to the next, the underlying principles are essentially the same. As a result, I only refer to a few examples.

[129]   Subdivision (a) provides: '(a) Any person who knowingly uses another's name, voice, signature, photograph, or likeness, in any manner, on or in products, merchandise, or goods, or for purposes of advertising or selling, or soliciting purchases of, products, merchandise, goods or services, without such person's prior consent, or, in the case of a minor, the prior consent of his parent or legal guardian, shall be liable for any damages sustained by the person or persons injured as a result thereof. In addition, in any action brought under this section, the person who violated the section shall be liable to the injured party or parties in an amount equal to the greater of seven hundred fifty dollars ($750) or the actual damages suffered by him or her as a result of the unauthorized use, and any profits from the unauthorized use that are attributable to the use and are not taken into account in computing the actual damages. In establishing such profits, the injured party or parties are required to present proof only of the gross revenue attributable to such use, and the person who violated this section is required to prove his or her deductible expenses. Punitive damages may also be awarded to the injured party or parties. The prevailing party in any action under this section shall also be entitled to attorney's fees and costs.'

[130]   *K.N.B. Enterprises* v. *Matthews* 78 Cal. App. 4th 362.

[131]   *Michaels* v. *Internet Entertainment Group Inc.* 5 F. Supp. 2d 823; *Abdul-Jabbar* v. *General Motors Corp.* 75 F. 3d 1391.

[132]   *McCormack* v. *Oklahoma Publishing Co.* 613 P. 2d 98.

[133]   64 Cal. App. 3d 825.

claimant in a false light and, fourthly, by using the image of the claimant for commercial gain without consent.

The justification of incidental use[134] and public interest news reporting[135] are recognised by statute and common law, while the courts also recognise parody as justification.[136] An important policy consideration was mentioned in this regard in *Winter* v. *DC Comics*.[137] The purpose of protecting the image of the individual, whether by statute or common law is not censorship, but to prevent others from usurping the commercial value of a person's image through commercialisation of such person's name, voice, signature, photo or picture.[138]

The mere fact that a person's name, voice, signature, photo or picture is used in a commercial medium sponsored or financed with advertising is therefore not conclusive. The test is indeed whether there is a direct relationship between the advertising and the use of the person's attributes.[139]

4. CONCLUSION

It is clear that all modern legal systems recognise the concept of image rights in one form or another, whether in the context of privacy, personality, patrimony, veracity or a combination of these factors. However, it is significant that the extent of protection differs drastically from one jurisdiction to the next.

When the attributes of a person is used without consent for commercial gain, the level of protection ranges from the bare minimum of English law, to elaborate protection and punitive measures applicable in California, with most jurisdictions falling somewhere in between.

---

[134] Compare art. 3344 (c) and *Johnson* v. *Harcourt Brace Jovanovich Inc.* 43 Cal. App. 3d 880.

[135] Compare art. 3344 (d) and *Daly* v. *Viacom Inc.* 238 F. Supp. 2d 1118. See also *Montana* v. *San Jose Mercury News Inc.* 34 Cal. App. 4th 790.

[136] *Comedy III Productions Inc.* v. *Gary Saderup Inc.* 21 P. 3d 797; *Cardtoons L.C.* v. *Major League Baseball Players Association* 95 F. 3d 959.

[137] 69 P. 3d 473.

[138] Note 136 *supra*.

[139] Subdivision (e) provides: '(e) The use of a name, voice, signature, photograph, or likeness in a commercial medium shall not constitute a use for which consent is required under subdivision (a) solely because the material containing such use is commercially sponsored or contains paid advertising. Rather it shall be a question of fact whether or not the use of the person's name, voice, signature, photograph, or likeness was so directly connected with the commercial sponsorship or with the paid advertising as to constitute a use for which consent is required under subdivision (a).'

18 Legal aspects of international event sponsorship
Tone Jagodic

INTRODUCTION

The business of sports is one of the fastest growing industries in many countries. All over the world, many people participate as players and spectators in a variety of sporting activities, creating opportunities for the marketing of a company's goods and services. An important part of the business of sports is sports marketing, which revolves around the understanding of a consumer's behavior and the motivating of target markets to purchase goods and services.

Sports marketing is simply any sales or publicity-related activity associated with an organized sporting event (or events), its personalities or the celebrity lifestyle of its participants. There are two components of sports marketing: the marketing *of* sport and marketing *through* sports. This includes, but is not limited to, endorsements, print media, broadcast media, billboards and news media. Sports marketing is needed because it helps sport organizations to obtain financial resources necessary for survival and to provide economic incentives to feature the best possible sporting competition. Nearly every professional team or athlete participates in some kind of marketing or promotion. The modern sports marketer is charged with one simple responsibility: to increase the sources of revenue.

The history of sport marketing is interesting and rich in many fields. It reflects the stage of the development of sport, economy, political situation, media, globalization trends, commercialization and other areas. Successful marketing activities reflect the status of different sports on both a global and a national scene. Some international federations have been very successful in finding a good relationship with the media which has made some sports or sport events even more popular. If we know that sponsoring is, along with the revenues from broadcasting rights, the most important marketing tool for sport organizations, then it is logical that specialization of sponsorship has already made steps forward. On the other hand, sponsorship has become a subject of scientific examination in different areas.

In this chapter we deal with the questions of the comparison between sponsorship and advertising activities in sport, advantages of sponsorship, basic characteristics and legal categorization of a sponsorship contract and ambush marketing. Apart from theory, we mention some examples from the practice of different national Olympic committees' (NOCs') programs within the Olympic marketing. As sponsorship is very wide and complex, it was necessary to make a selection of themes which might be interesting especially for those who work practically with sponsorship on a daily basis.

BACKGROUND OF SPONSORSHIP AND SOME INTERESTING LEGAL QUESTIONS

The economic impact of sponsorship is growing steadily. In the last 10 years, the International Olympic Committee (IOC) revenues from marketing have nearly doubled. In the quadrennial 1993–96 it generated US$2.6 billion and in the period 2001–04 it generated US$4.2 billion. From the standpoint of developed international sports organizations, sponsorship has become the second most successful marketing tool, with selling of the TV rights in first place. In the last quadrennial, the IOC has generated US$2.2 billion from selling the TV rights, which represents more than half (53%), apart from the revenues from sponsoring (The Olympic Programme (TOP) and domestic sponsorship together US$1.4 billion) which creates 34% of the marketing cake.[1] Bearing in mind that many sport organizations, especially on the national level, are unable to sell TV rights, sponsorship represents the most important marketing tool for sport organizations.

Sponsorship also represents a warranty for the independence and sovereignty of sport organizations. As sponsorship is the most important financial source for the majority of sport organizations, it is obvious that legal protection of sponsorship is vital. There are different existing legal instruments available and a successful anti-ambush marketing strategy has developed in recent years. Sponsorship combines principles of universality and adaptability. From the sponsor's geographical aspect there are different levels – from worldwide, to regional, national and local level sponsorship.

Many legal and practical questions are open. An interesting question could be raised if we try to determine a sponsorship relationship. For continental lawyers, an initial question concerns whether the relationship is governed by commercial or civil codes. In any event, an important question is to identify those legal instruments that are available in case of breach of the contract.

We can find more questions regarding the:

- legal nature of sponsorship;
- definition of sponsorship agreement and the question of codification of sponsorship agreement;
- sponsorship in comparison with advertisements and other commercial or economic activities;
- exclusivity on the side of sponsor;
- position of sponsored subjects in the contract with more subjects;
- possible conflict of interests in contract between the athlete, national federation and NOC;
- most dangerous violations of sponsorship contracts; and many others ...

The majority of sport organizations seek to establish sponsorship relations with a sponsor. In many cases some fundamental elements are not clear as to the subject of the contract. It is therefore necessary to make distinction between advertising and sponsorship, endorsement and individual athlete sponsorship, licensing in relation to sponsorship

---

[1] Statistics from the Olympic marketing fact file, http://www.olympic.org.

contract and some others. I would like to tackle some of these dilemmas in this chapter. Before examining open questions a brief look at the history of sport sponsorship might be useful.

A BRIEF HISTORY OF SPONSORSHIP

Sport and sponsorship have a strong relationship dating from ancient times. The athletes who competed at the Ancient Olympic Games were awarded with large prizes and preparations for the Games were paid by others. The first advertisement for a sports competition was published in 1631 by a French newspaper and in 1852 the New England Railroad Company helped to prepare the rowing competition between the teams of Harvard and Yale Universities. The first sponsored sports radio program, *The Everyday Hour*, was aired in 1924 and one of the oldest sponsored sport competitions was the Indianapolis road race in 1911.

A very big step forward in modern sports sponsorship was represented by the creation of the IOC marketing program, called The Olympic Programme (TOP). Created in 1985, TOP is the only sponsorship with the exclusive worldwide marketing rights to both Winter and Summer Olympic Games. Sponsor support is crucial for the staging of the Games and the operations of every organization within the Olympic Movement. Partner support is not only relevant during the Games period; it provides vital technical services and product support to the IOC, organizing committees of the Olympic Games (OCOGs) and NOCs, benefiting athletes, coaches and spectators.

TOP introduced exclusivity as a strong tool for both parties that puts sponsorship on a higher level and brings into sport much more money than before. Many international sports organizations followed the principle of exclusivity and developed it in their own way. On the other hand, exclusivity provoked specific activities of unauthorized parties to enter the relationship with sport subjects, known as ambush marketing.

CATEGORIES OF SPONSORSHIP

There are many approaches to dividing sponsorship into different categories. Some claim that sponsorship depends on the type of sponsors, the characteristic type of the service provided for sponsors, the category of sport activity (sport for all, competition sport and elite, top sport sponsorships), the aim and the direction of sponsorship and many others. Usually, sponsorship is divided into three categories:

- legal entities (corporate sponsorship);
- events; and
- individual athletes.

The most common sponsored party is a legal entity created by private law, such as a sport club, an association, a federation, an NOC, a national sports confederation, a foundation, a pool, an agency or some other private legal entity.

ENDORSEMENT

Endorsement is the promotion of a company's product by means of personal recommendation of an individual who is sufficiently well known and respected that he or she can influence the purchasing pattern of sections of the consumer public. In a sense, a personality sponsors the company's product, and is paid for doing so. It is a much simpler commercial agreement than sponsorship, and is a means whereby that personality can extend his or her own program of self-promotion to increase his or her earning capacity and to maintain a profile in the public eye. Endorsement is a form of specialized advertising by the manufacturer of the endorsed product.[2] This form of sponsorship[3] has been introduced and developed in the USA, but is quickly getting its space in Europe.

Studies have shown that consumers are more likely to purchase products endorsed by athletes than products not so endorsed. Athletes are the role models and consumers tend to believe athletes, especially those with a positive public image. It is estimated that companies in the USA spend close to US$1 billion on athlete endorsements each year, and for a good reason.

Consumers choose to purchase products that are known, guaranteed and convenient. Companies believe that consumers are more likely to purchase a certain product if an athlete says it is appropriate or beneficial. A product or a brand may be weak, but an athlete's reputation gives it credibility. Numerous athletes have become 'celebrities' due to the increase in endorsements and the companies that have sponsored them. The business of sports endorsements has come a long way since the 1970s. The growing market of endorsements is larger now because of the vast changes in technology. Television allows athletes to be seen, the radio allows athletes to be heard and the Internet allows information on athletes to be downloaded. Therefore, endorsement companies have benefited a great deal due to the large growth of technology.

This high input from technology is tremendously beneficial to companies because an athlete will always be seen, and if an athlete is seen then so will be the product. Society has become so influenced by the figures that are put in front of it that people may forget the main attractive traits of sports figures: they are skilled and talented individuals. This allows a certain product to be seen regularly and allows the viewer to get to know the athlete and the companies that are endorsing them.

Product retention will be high because of the association of the product with the celebrity. The company objectives will be reached because the company will grow as a result of the increase in the popularity of the product. The idea that the consumer thinks, 'if he or she likes that product, then I should like that product too' is what makes endorsement such a highly effective marketing-communication instrument. Because celebrities possess high public profiles and significant influence on their audience and fans from the wide reach of advertising, these two marketing-communication tools will create a strong marketing-communication strategy. The job of a campaign is to transform the need of the target groups into the needing of the product. A celebrity will give a company

---

[2]   See also H. Stallard, M. Abel, G. Nuttal, Bagehot on Sponsorship, Endorsement and Merchandising, 2nd rev'd edn. London, Sweet & Maxwell, 1998, Ch. 7, Endorsement.

[3]   In theory it is not clear whether endorsement is only one type of sponsorship of an individual athlete or if it is a special legal relationship of an athlete with a commercial partner.

a competitive edge. An endorsement of a product by a celebrity is very influential on the public's opinion of the product.

The relationship between sponsorship of an individual athlete and endorsement is open to discussion. Even if we do not go deeply into endorsement we can find out some differences and specialities of both arrangements. The most important characteristic of endorsement is the promotion of a product, a service, a name or some other element of a company (sponsor). On the other hand, sponsorship is more 'sporty' oriented as a sponsor tries to identify its image with successful sporting results of its sponsored subject. If an athlete gets a royalty for his or her commercial efforts for the benefit of his or her client, a sponsor often gives prizes to its sponsored athlete for outstanding sports achievements. There are also more differences between both types of relationship of an athlete with a commercial partner but, on the other hand, the basic positions of both arrangements are similar. It is therefore justified to claim that endorsement is only a very specific type of an individual sponsorship contract.

THE IMPORTANCE OF THE MEDIA IN SPONSORSHIP

The impact of commercialization of sport is setting the pace of modern sponsorship. The development of media (especially electronic) introduced new and revolutionary methods that put sports subjects in a totally new and challenging position, where they are forced to follow new directions and guidelines of capital that has entered sport in recent years. Top athletes need sponsors; both athlete and sponsor are dependent on the TV media, which enables them the proper communication on global level. Nowadays, the selling of TV rights represents the most important marketing tool for international sport organizations ahead of the transfer of rights of intellectual or industrial property as a basis of sponsorship. The differentiation of selling of TV rights, on the one hand, and sponsorship, on the other, represents a big opportunity for sport subjects to exploit their products commercially in both ways. The selling of TV rights is a special right of sport subjects which enables them to collect huge amount of money from broadcasting organizations. On the other hand, TV coverage of sport competition brings the same sport event into a much higher level and offers the organizer the possibility of further commercial exploitation of its product. The fact that that their logos, emblems and other signs are visible to the TV audience is a great attraction for sponsors, which brings sponsorship into a completely new position.

How they are represented on TV is therefore very important for sponsors. Visual presence of different sponsor signage is a vital element of the contract of selling TV rights and the sponsorship contract of a sports organizer. There are some threats to the power of the TV for sponsorship. It is always more reassuring to buy conventional advertising time on a TV network than to commit a portion of a budget to sponsorship. New worldwide TV networks might thus represent a threat to international sponsorship.[4] It is therefore very important to establish the differences between TV advertisements during a sport event covered by the TV, on the one hand, and the effects of visible signs of sponsors of the same event, on the other.

---

4   Global Television Report, IOC, 2001.

Sponsorship and TV Advertisements

One of the major problems that the marketing world faces is how to market a new product to the consumer successfully. There are numerous different tools or instruments that a marketer has to choose from, ranging from direct marketing to sponsorship. The term that is used for the solution of this problem is marketing-communication. Marketing-communication is defined as a mass communication from a company to its customers, in order to inform the customers about brands, products and services, and to give them a favorable impression about these products and services. To accomplish the goal of marketing-communication, a marketing-communication instrument or discipline needs to be designed. This instrument is defined as a specific form of marketing-communication with its own media, expertise and organization. The instrument can combine many different media in attempt to reach the consumer. Two very popular and highly successful marketing-communication instruments are sponsorship and advertising. These two tools can be combined to create a marketing-communication campaign that appeals to consumers and that inspires consumers to purchase the product or products in the campaign. Advertising during sport events covered by the TV represents an interesting issue in several senses.

What makes the differences between advertisements broadcast during time breaks of a sport competition and the effects of visual presence of sponsor's signs, which are visible during the entire sport competition? The basic difference is that visual signs of sponsors do not represent an advertisement activity, and from here on we can distinguish legal differences of both activities. For example, a logo of a sponsor visible on a shirt of an athlete does not represent classic advertisement activity, and is therefore not limited by many legal rules governing advertising.

The advertising sector is substantially regulated in Europe by both community-wide legislation as well as national legislation of the EU member states. The sport sector is regulated by the Television without Frontiers Broadcasting Directive (89/552/EEC, amended by Directive 97/36/EC) with detailed time and other limitations for different situations. It means that an advertiser has to obey the rules governing 'television advertising.' On the other hand, the position of a visually presented logo of a sponsor on a sport of an athlete during sport competition is completely different.

Legal rules of advertising do not regulate the signs of sponsorship visible during sport competition, which was has also been clearly underlined by the European Court of Justice. In the case *Bacardi France SAS, formerly Bacardi-Martini SAS* v. *Television francaise 1 SA (TF1), Groupe Jean-Claude Darmont SA and Girosport SARL*,[5] the court interpreted Council Directive 89/552/EEC to exclude advertising resulting from billboards visible on screen during the retransmission of sporting events. As it explained:

> ... by the definition given in Article 1(b) of Directive 89/552, 'television advertising' comprises 'any form of announcement broadcast in return for payment or for similar consideration by a public or private undertaking in connection with trade, business, craft or profession, in order to promote the supply of goods or services, including immovable property, or rights and obligations, in return for payment.'

---

[5]   Case C-429/02 (ECJ).

Under Article 10(1), 'television advertising shall be readily recognisable as such and kept quite separate from other parts of the programme service by optical and/or acoustic means.' The first sentence of Article 11(1) provides that 'advertisements shall be inserted between programmes' and Article 11(2) states that 'in programmes consisting of autonomous parts, or in sports programmes and similarly structured events and performances comprising intervals, advertisements shall only be inserted between the parts or in the intervals.' In this case, the indirect television advertising for alcoholic beverages resulting from hoardings visible on screen during the retransmission of sporting events does not constitute a separate announcement broadcast in order to promote goods or services. For obvious reasons, it is impossible to show such advertising only during the intervals between the different parts of the television broadcast concerned. The images on the advertising billboards that appear in the background of the pictures broadcast, in a random and unpredictable fashion according to the requirements of the retransmission, do not have any distinct character in that context. Such indirect television advertising cannot, therefore, be regarded as 'television advertising' within the meaning of Directive 89/552/EEC, and accordingly the directive is not applicable to it.

On the other hand, signs of a sponsor visible during a sport competition broadcast on TV could be limited by other factors. Usually, there are limitations for a sponsor laid down by the rules of a sport organization responsible for the event. In some sport events, however, sport organizations do not allow any kind of advertising, as in the case of the IOC with the Olympic Games. According to Rule 53 of the Olympic Charter: 'no form of advertising or other publicity shall be allowed in and above the stadium, venues and other competition areas which are considered as part of the Olympic sites. Commercial installations and advertising signs shall not be allowed in the stadium, venues or other sports grounds.' The only 'exemption' is the sign of the equipment or the producer of sport clothes which are allowed to certain limitations. In addition, Olympic Charter Rule 41 restricts advertising giving the IOC exclusive image rights: 'Except as permitted by the IOC Executive Board no competitor, coach, trainer or official who participates in the Olympic Games may allow his person, name, and picture or sports performance to be used for advertising purposes during the Olympic Games.' The Olympic Games are the only big international sport competition with absolute restriction of advertising. All other international sport competitions allow certain types of advertisement within sport venues.

ADVANTAGES OF SPONSORSHIP

There are many specialities of visual presentation of sponsorship that, compared with 'classical' advertising, pose major challenges for sports. The most important is the attraction of sporting events primarily characterized by their commercial potential due to public attention. Marketing analyses prove that public attention during the TV advertising breaks is far from the standard of the prime time of sport events; many viewers even change the TV channel during the commercial breaks. Sponsorship basically seeks to focus on the corporation and is less product-oriented. Comparison of the cost of regular TV advertising with the sponsoring cost, which generates the less concentrated but equally effective TV exposure, shows that constant sponsorship reference gets the message home effectively and economically.[6]

Together with the development of TV, sponsorship developed in new ways. Visual coverage of sponsor logos and other insignia through the TV is an excellent opportunity for sponsorship that is considered not to constitute advertising under strict regulations adopted by the EU directive and in the national legislation of EU member states. As the effect of a sponsor's logo is much more effective than advertising itself, sponsors are interested in concentrating on prime time sport event sponsoring. Other advantages are that the sponsor does not need to pay the broadcasting company in addition to the sponsored subject, and that this kind of promotion has no time limits, unlike advertising. On the other hand, such promotion cannot be described as a proportional marketing tool of advertising as it represents only one segment of the regular method of advertising.

DIFFERENT POSSIBILITIES FOR A SPONSOR

It is logical that the differences between sponsorship and advertising are of crucial importance for a sponsor that has to decide how to invest its money optimally. Even when a business decides to use sponsorship, it has to choose whether to sponsor:

- an athlete;
- a team;
- a club;
- a sport federation;
- an organizer; or
- a specific media that covers a competition.

A sponsor can choose how to use an athlete's image. It can decide to create an advertisement with an athlete (endorsement) during the TV break of a sport competition without sponsoring a sport event, or to use the athlete's image in other kinds of promotion that are different from regular advertising. The most important factor for a sponsor is the evaluation of the effects of particular activities, as it should bear in mind the commercial objectives it is trying to achieve.

A sponsorship contract with the elements of TV coverage should be properly structured. It typically is a bilateral agreement between the sponsor and the organizer, specifying the television exposure of visual signs promoting the sponsor. The broadcaster is typically not a party to the agreement. From the standpoint of an athlete, his or her sponsor is primarily not in a relationship with the organizer or a broadcasting company, so the obligation of the sponsor is only towards the athlete. A sponsor and an athlete have to define all the necessary elements of the visibility of the sponsor's signs on the TV. Although sponsors must pay broadcasters for TV advertisements transmitted within the time limits for advertisements during TV breaks only.

---

[6]   Stallard, Abel, Nuttal, note 2 *supra*, p. 7

The above-mentioned possibilities can be presented diagrammatically as shown in Figure 18.1.[7]

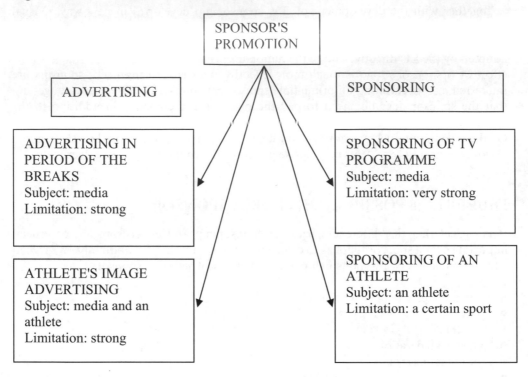

Figure 18.1

The described options show four different possibilities for a sponsor. The decision of a sponsor depends on its specific aim. It is clear that sport subjects will prefer the last two options, which include them as subjects of the relationship. The best way to achieve their involvement is to show the sponsors all the benefits of sponsorship in comparison with 'classical' advertising.

DEFINITION OF A SPONSORSHIP CONTRACT

There are many different legal definitions of a sponsorship agreement. The Code of Sponsorship of the International Chamber of Commerce (ICC) provides a real foundation that can be useful for different sport organizations. Following the ICC International Code on Sponsorship, the definition of sponsorship agreement is:

---

[7]   For clarity: an athlete in the scheme represents also other sports subjects (sport organizations such as clubs, federations, etc.); a limitation means a legal framework consisting of the EU law and the national law which sets a different kind of limitation.

… any commercial agreement by which a sponsor, for the mutual benefit of the sponsor and a sponsored party, contractually provides financing or other support in order to establish an association between the sponsor's image, brands or products and a sponsorship property in return for the rights to promote this association and/or for the granting of certain agreed direct or indirect benefits.[8]

After analyzing different parts of the above definition, we can put the most important elements into the scheme shown in Figure 18.2.[9]

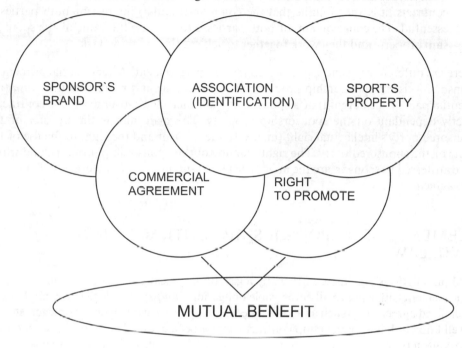

Figure 18.2

Analyzing these elements it can be seen that three elements are specific for sponsorship and differ from the elements of other known legal contracts.

1.   The basic connection represents the association between a sports property and a sponsor brand as a tool to transfer the image of a sport subject to a sponsor. It is, of course, necessary to establish a commercial agreement with the possibility to promote that connection (the identification between the value of a sports subject and a sponsor's entity) in the awareness of the public.

---

8   Code of Sport Sponsorship, http://www.iccwbo.org.
9   Note that using the Olympic rings does not mean any kind of misuse of the protected intellectual IOC right or even any kind of ambush activity. It is only a simple attempt to put the elements into a scheme which represents logical connections among different parameters of sponsorship and can be easily remembered.

2.   The right to promote the identification between a sponsored party and a sponsor is tightly linked to media exposure, as it provides public identification of the sponsorship subjects' relationship. The promotion of sponsorship in media by a sponsor can increase the value of the sponsorship property and that is also the main aim and interest of both parties. Both parties try to achieve the public awareness of a close connection between them.

3.   Both parties look forward for common, mutual benefit. Compared with some other contracts, it is very unique that the common (mutual) interest of both parties is essential. The common aim of both parties is to increase the value of the sponsorship property and they work together to achieve this common task.

There are different characteristics of a sponsorship agreement. A very special element of sponsorship is the sponsorship property, which is unique and represents the *causa* (the essential part of the bargain) of a sponsorship contract. The substance of the contract is strictly dependant on the sponsorship property. The main aim is the transfer of the sponsored party's intellectual right (image) to the sponsor and the right to the use of the name of the sponsored party. The rights coming out of sponsorship property, and which are transferred to sponsor, are the most typical and significant characteristics of sponsorship agreement.

ELEMENTS OF A SPONSORSHIP CONTRACT UNDER CIVIL LAW

Civil jurisdictions regulate contracts by legislation, typically a civil code containing the basic elements applying to all enforceable obligations, and specific legislation applying to specialized agreements (such as a sales agreement, labor bargain, agency contract, etc.). It is well known that a sponsorship contract has not been codified yet (and hence sponsorship contracts are known as 'inominative contracts' in civil jurisdictions). It seems that the nature of the relationship is still 'moving forward' and it would not be appropriate to stop the development of this modern contract with formal codification. Apart from that it is also obvious that sponsorship contracts are very common in practice and it is therefore recommended that the basic legal principles which are suitable for the interpretation of the relationship are established. Being a modern contract of autonomous commercial law, it should be noted that all basic principles of commercial civil law should apply to it – the principles of autonomy, equal rights of parties, conscientiousness and honesty, prohibition of misuse of the rights, prohibition of making harm, commitment to fulfill obligations, solidarity in collaboration, peaceful resolving of disputes and some others. A sponsorship contract is a contract between two or more parties, an obligatory, consensual, non-formal, sinalagmatic and commutative civil law contract. Among the common characteristics of the contracts of autonomous law, it is functional and heterogeneous with practical economical meaning, at some lower levels standardized and has a normative nature.

Apart from those principles, some other specific legal elements should be considered when examining a sponsorship contract. The parties' relationship often cannot be subsumed into one of the established, known and already codified types of contracts.

Many sponsorship relationships are very complex, and besides essential structural elements also contain many additional and subsidiary elements, all with the aim to optimize the effects of the main component of the contract. After analyzing some NOC sponsorship contracts, it could be concluded that the main object of the sponsorship is the transfer of the sponsorship property of the sponsored subject into the sphere of the sponsor, which is usually combined with the right to use the name of the sponsored party. Most of the contracts include an exclusivity clause, the obligation of the sponsored party for legal protection, the common interest of both parties with the aim of enlarging the value of the object of the contract, a clause of confidence, the wish to achieve a long-term relationship, the common care of successful public communication and the wish to renew the expiring contract.

Typically, sponsors seek to achieve their goals through a tight connection with public appearances of both parties, all with the particular aim of identifying and recognizing the sponsorship relationship. One of the most specific and typical elements of sponsorship is the active role and position of the sponsor with its task to take advantage of the sponsorship property, using the rights acquired from the sponsored party. It seems that the most specific and typical element of sponsorship is the manner of the identification between the entity of a sponsor and the value of a sponsored subject (sponsorship property).

Most of the contracts are connected with some obligations of other relationships, especially of a sponsored party. In the world of commercial top sport, sponsors will normally have different relationships with the athlete and his or her club, federation and NOC, all with their own sponsors, and therefore it is of the utmost importance to balance these different interests.

Substantive Legal Elements

If we accept that the recognition of a special and specific sponsorship value of the sponsored subject by the sponsor is the preliminary condition of the sponsorship contract, we have to take into account that this specific value has emerged out of sport. This specific value of a sport subject is hard to find elsewhere, which is why it is so attractive for a commercial subject. The commercialization of sport has introduced certain new values from the world of sport and launched them to the public by modern ways of communication.

The foundations of sponsorship in legal sense are:

- personality rights of the athletes;
- intellectual rights of sport organizations; and
- special *sui generis* rights of the organizer of a sport competition.

A sponsor's goal in using a sponsored subject with specific attributes is to achieve certain positive effects. The main object of the sponsorship is the sponsorship property, which gives the sponsor a specific, original and individual approach to the commercial market and to target particular costumers, which is quite different from other conventional means of advertisement or propaganda. Sponsors invest huge amounts of money into sponsorship as they believe that they will be making a good investment that will bring them certain commercial effects.

Sponsorship property is materialized in different shapes and forms. Its speciality is a specific distinction which gives it another character, much different from other similar values. This particularity involves a touch of a class, extraordinariness, attraction, extreme popularity and fame and reputation, maybe even a kind of a genius. It is the perception of this value system by the public and the environment in which we live that is the final target of the sponsors. The exceptional value of sponsorship which makes a sponsor ready to make a contract is made by the public. Celebrities are famous for a certain reason and that is why they are attractive for sponsors. The same applies to famous sports teams, clubs, organizations and sport competitions that constitute a certain valuable brand which will be sought by sponsors. The meaning of the brand of the Olympic Games is much more than just a picture of five rings, because people recognize this mark as a symbol of an exceptional international sport competition, with the best athletes, sport heroes, Olympic legends and tradition, the Olympic ideal and philosophy, what makes it so popular all around the world.

THE IMPORTANCE OF THE PUBLIC AND THE ROLE OF THE MEDIA

Sponsorship property is essentially dependent upon the public perception; its value is determined by the way the public recognizes it. Sponsorship property is original and attractive to the public and the costumers, which is why it is so important for sponsors. The interaction with the public and the identification of a sponsor with a sponsored subject in the view of the public is the most important aim of a sponsor. It is obvious that a sponsor definitely needs the media to achieve its intention. Competitive sport can only survive and develop with adequate media coverage, providing the necessary input to a major sport event and bringing it to the forefront of current news. Sporting competitions could be attractive for media as such, but that is only the first element. A sponsor will want the public to associate it with a famous athlete or club, otherwise its investment is not economically justified. The role of the media is crucial and sponsorship is especially in this element different from other similar commercial contracts. Media is a part of a sport event, not just an instrument of advertising as it is the case in regular advertising contracts.

SPECIFIC MODUS OF EXERCISING RIGHTS OF A SPONSORSHIP CONTRACT

One of the differences from other contracts is the way the sponsored subject is connected with a sponsor in the public eye. In contrast to a licensing agreement, which enables the use of a licensed subject without any necessary connection between the parties, the essential element of sponsorship is the emphasis of the relationship between the parties of the contract. The aim of a sponsor is to build a publicly recognizable relationship between a sponsor and a sponsored subject. The task of the sponsor is the promotion of the relationship that represents the focus of the contract itself. A connection is built in a special way by the sponsors, who use protected rights of intellectual property of a sport organization or the personal rights of an athlete with the intention to make the public aware of their close relationship. The theory is accomplished in several examples in praxis. For example, sponsorship contracts of the NOCs of Great Britain, Germany, Austria, and Slovenia all give a sponsor its right to acquire an association with the Olympic team of the respective NOC.

LEGAL CHARACTERISTICS OF A SPONSORSHIP CONTRACT

Most sponsorship agreements are long term, strictly confidential and strive for a successful public relationship. Sponsorship contracts are complex as they consist of many different activities which are supposed to assist the principal core of the contract with the aim to optimally emphasize the commercial benefits of the agreement. Practical economics and functional heterogeneity are the vital elements as we can see in some other modern inominative contracts.

A distinction must be drawn between sponsors and suppliers. Many sponsorship contracts have more than two parties. A lot of contracts with two parties are connected with other contracts and consist of some obligations of the subjects who are not contractual parties (athletes have to fulfill some obligations on behalf of a sport organization). A sponsor is entitled to certain rights of a sponsored party, but it is up to its determination and decision to activate those rights in a way that it would bring the expected benefits to it. The evaluation of the contract is vital; inactive role of sponsor exploitation of its rights should not be relevant for the value of the contract. The execution of sponsor's rights is important and depends on the sponsor's ability to exploit its position. The obligations of a sponsored party can be split in three directions:

- cession of its rights to a sponsor;
- fulfillment of different services; and
- efforts to transfer its image to a sponsor.

Exclusivity is becoming a very important element of a sponsorship relationship. In these cases, the sponsor's right of exclusivity represents the most important element from the sponsor's point of view. The exclusivity of a sponsor represents an essential element of the contract; the sponsor's priority is to try to create a distinction from its business competitors. There is a clear distinction between the exclusivity of a sponsor in a sponsorship agreement and a contract of selling of the TV rights. Both rights represent two different groups of rights coming from different rights of sponsored subjects. Practical reasons demand an balance between the interest of sponsors of a sport event and the sponsors of the TV. Both parties should respect different limitations regarding the substance of the contract; a sponsor must particularly take care of legal restrictions, imposed by law. A clear distinction should be made between the organizer of a sport event and an athlete or team competing at that event, as they will both have their own sponsors with different interests.

It is questionable whether endorsement is a type of sponsorship contract of an individual athlete or it represents its own type of contract. There are many differences between both types of the contracts of an individual personality, especially in the USA, and that is why most of the American literature deals with the two separately. In Europe the distinction is not as clear as endorsement has not developed as much as it has in the USA.

LEGAL NATURE OF A SPONSORSHIP CONTRACT

The relations of sponsorship are hard to subsume within one of the known types of contract, so every contract must be carefully analyzed. They consist of different rights and obligations which are typical for some other contracts. It is an inominative contract and it is not legally codified. As a special contract, a non-typical (non-formulaic) model of contract, each contract is a specific and individual one. Only some sponsorship agreements can be subordinated or compared with other nominative contracts.

A licensing agreement is required for some sponsorship contracts that are based on intellectual property. Sponsorship is a new legal instrument which consists of more integrated and connected relations; it is not a 'compound' contract. In some cases, it can be regarded as a 'mixed' contract if the provisions match with the regulations of some known nominative contract. In its essence it is a *sui generis* contract with typical characteristics and structure so that it is possible to make a distinction between other contracts.

Apart from sponsorship of sports organizations, sponsorship of individual athletes has another specific nature as they are mostly not based on intellectual industrial rights but rely more on personal property rights.

Analyzing the elements of some of the NOC sponsorship contracts[10] reveals that some sponsorship contracts have similarities with licensing as the main object of the contract is an intellectual right. TOP and the NOC contracts are based on the value of the Olympic rings. The image of the Olympic rings as a world-famous trade mark makes the essence of the contract in a way which looks as it would be a licensing agreement. A closer look into the structure of TOP contract proves the thesis of making a distinction between this sponsorship agreement and an ordinary licensing contract.

The basic difference lies in the way the object of the contract is used. As a licensee is trying to use the trade mark itself, the sponsor is trying to connect the trade mark with its own name, brand or product. It is very common that sponsors use the Olympic rings together with their own brand names and logos (a composite logo), trying to raise the image and value of their own brand. Beside the elements which are very close to the elements of a licensing agreement, TOP agreement gives a sponsor many other rights which are not common for an ordinary licensing agreement. Some of the elements (ticketing, hospitality and merchandising) are also structural parts of a sponsorship agreement. Some elements of other contracts can be found in certain sponsorship agreements, such as a sales agreement, a lease, a labor contract, the selling of the TV rights, joint venture and some others. The most important fact is that the sole right to use the brand name is only one part of the essence of the contract; far more important is how successfully a sponsor uses this intellectual property. One of the most specific and relevant elements is the exclusivity of sponsors. A sponsorship contract has developed exclusivity as a special element of distinction between sponsors which is recognized by the public as a close link between the sponsored subject and the sponsor, and not with other brand competitors. Ambush marketing (whereby the sponsor's competitors *are* linked to the sponsored subject) is a very specific attempt to diminish the value of sponsorship and NOCs have been developing special ways and legal means to protect and defend sponsorship property from it.

---

10 NOCs of Austria, Germany, Great Britain and Slovenia.

SOME CASES OF SPONSORSHIP IN PRACTICE

The Olympic Programme (TOP)

The marketing program of the IOC was created after the Olympics in Los Angeles in 1984 and became one of the key factors of the great value and importance of the IOC today. The legal nature of TOP contract is unique. Basically, it is a sponsorship agreement with all the structural elements of any sponsorship. The strength of TOP sponsorship program is evident in the fact that the program enjoys one of the highest sponsorship renewal rates of any sports property. TOP companies receive exclusive marketing rights and opportunities within their designated product category. They may exercise these rights on a worldwide basis, and they may develop marketing programs with various members of the Olympic Movement – the IOC, the NOCs and the OCOGs.

In addition to the exclusive worldwide marketing opportunities, partners receive:

- use of all Olympic imagery, as well as appropriate Olympic designations on products;
- hospitality opportunities at the Olympic Games;
- direct advertising and promotional opportunities, including preferential access to Olympic broadcast advertising;
- on-site concessions and franchises and product sale and showcase opportunities;
- ambush marketing protection; and
- acknowledgement of their support through a broad Olympic sponsorship recognition program.[11]

What Makes TOP Contract so Special?

First of all, it is the nature of the contract and the subjects it involves. TOP contract is one of those contracts known in international law as contracts with a special character. It is multinational and requires a very clear definition of the legal system which is used for different partners from different countries. TOP consists of many single contracts, like a puzzle, and involves a lot of subjects of very different legal status. That is very characteristic of TOP and it makes the whole system very interesting in the legal sense. TOP consists of many documents that must be examined in order to understand the relationship correctly. Undoubtedly, TOP represents a complex system of connected contracts, which must be adjusted. The signing of the contract requires well-developed formal procedures and a sophisticated and logistically well-organized procedure. The timing of the signings of different partners might be of the extreme importance for the whole system itself. A special allocation of the money that comes out of the contract is not typical for an ordinary contract. In this sense, the IOC has developed a very sophisticated system, the 'Olympic Solidarity', which includes some hundreds of beneficiaries. Through that, the Olympic Solidarity is also a part of TOP system. On the part of the sponsors, the exclusivity of sponsors has been developed in a very sophisticated way where also many

---

[11]   www.olympic.org.

elements from the economy were used. Certainly, there are also other elements to be examined in this contract from a legal aspect.

TOP consists of many contracts. Primarily, the IOC and TOP sponsors sign tripartite contracts with the NOCs. Apart from that, each NOC signs contracts with its own national sponsors, but these contracts have to observe the rights and obligations of the initial TOP contracts. They are secondary contracts but it is essential to find out that the system can only work if all the contracts are 'compatible'.

Questions Related to a Sponsor of an Individual Athlete Regarding other Obligations of the Athlete

As an athlete is preparing for a big international competition, he or she is engaged in legal relations with different partners. He or she is connected with a sports club, a national and international federation, an NOC and the IOC, and the sponsors of all of them. As Fasel[12] stresses, a professional athlete has loyalties to his or her sport, club, national team, fans, agent, sponsors and players' union. That can create problems if the relations are not very clear and precisely formulated. If the athlete wishes to take part in international sports competitions, he or she becomes a part of different sport systems and has to follow particular obligations. There are some open legal questions such as:

- Who is the owner of commercial rights of international sports competitions?
- What kind of obligation does an athlete have to obey when preparing for the Olympics?
- How is it possible to solve the possible conflict of interests of different sponsors of sports subjects?

An Example of an 'Olympic Games Contract' of an NOC

Commercialization of sport has merged sport and business. Nearly all important sport subjects have their own sponsors with different interests. Sport subjects are involved in different relationships. An athlete could be a member of his or her club, a national federation and an NOC of his or her country. As all of them have their own sponsors it is necessary to establish how the rights of all these sport subjects are preserved, as they are all important for 'sports reproduction'.

There are different models and methods of tackling the problem of the conflict of commercial interests of different subjects in the period of the preparation for the Olympic Games. Many NOCs seek to establish proper relations with a federation and an athlete, signing an agreement during the preparation for the Games.[13] There are two general ways. In some cases, an NOC signs a separate contract with the federation (the NOC of Norway) and an athlete (the NOCs of Great Britain, Norway, The Netherlands, Belgium) or includes all parties in the same contract (the NOC of Latvia, the NOC of Slovenia). It

---

12   Presentation of Rene Fasel, 'Who owns the ice hockey players', EOC Technical seminar, Ljubljana, October 2005.

13   During the EOC technical seminar in October 2005 in Ljubljana, 'Who owns the athlete', the NOCs of Great Britain, The Netherlands, Belgium, Latvia, Norway and Slovenia presented their models of contracts with the national federations and athletes.

this case, it is tripartite agreement with the rights and obligations of an NOC, the national federation and an athlete. In the case of the Belgian NOC, the federation gets a copy of signed agreement between an NOC and an athlete.

It is interesting to examine the reasons why the NOC of Latvia does not sign a separate agreement with the national federation or an athlete but makes instead a tripartite contract. In the case of making a contract with the federations, they are solving their financial problems on an athlete's account (the federations getting the money for funding athletes from the NOC directly), financially and morally manipulating 'disobedient' athletes, the financial flow is not coordinated and the NOC's control over sports work, attraction of sponsor funding and advertising, disappear. In case of a contract between an NOC and an athlete only (when the national federation is not party to the contract), some negative impacts are recognized, such as uncoordinated financial flow, the weak position of coaches, unclear obligations and responsibilities of national federations, not sufficiently regulated advertising activities, use of purchased sports equipment and some others. Tripartite agreements between the NOC, national federation and athlete can solve these problems, as the interests of all subjects are considered and fixed in the same document.

The basic criteria to select an athlete to be included in the contract are set by the NOC and are based on certain achieved sport results. After the signing of a contract an athlete is given the status of an Olympic candidate or a member of an Olympic team, which brings him or her certain rights and obligations. The NOC of Slovenia signs a three-part contract in which, in the preparation period, an athlete is entitled to get special rights such as logistical support, financial support via national federation, pocket money (scholarship, funding), health care and special health insurance, training at the National Institute for Sport and consultations in legal and marketing matters. In the competition period, an athlete is entitled to clothing and equipment, transportation, accommodation and accreditation, medical and physical therapeutic care, lawyers' costs in possible legal procedures, pocket money and prize money if he or she wins a medal.

On the other side, an athlete is obliged to respect the IOC and NOC rules, sign the Olympic declaration which includes the IOC eligibility code, make every effort to achieve the best possible result, follow the instructions of a team leader, respect fair and decent behavior towards the Olympic team, the NOC and sponsors and obey anti-doping rules and ignore attempts at doping. Similar obligations and rights of an athlete are stipulated also in other contracts of the NOC.

Commercial Obligations of an Athlete

The NOC usually signs a contract with the athletes preparing for the Olympic Games with regard to the athletes' commercial obligations. Regarding the athletes' relation with their sponsors, they are obliged to respect the IOC rules regarding advertisements. They must inform the NOC about their personal sponsors, wear the official Olympic clothes, allow the NOC to use their image for the promotion of the NOC sponsors, follow the instructions of medal ceremonies protocol and fulfill some other common obligations. If an athlete does not respect those rules it is the NOC which is under pressure from its sponsors and has to react properly so as not to harm its own position.

It is obvious that the Olympic Charter Rule 41 is very strict. Except as permitted by the IOC Executive Board, no competitor, coach, trainer or official who participates in the Olympic Games may allow his or her person, name, picture or sports performance to be used for advertising purposes during the Games.[14] The commercial use of athlete's images during the Games may only be made in a congratulatory or generic manner. Such communications may not refer directly to the use of any product or service that enhances performance in practicing or competing in sport and may not refer to the competitor's performance at the Games, except in the case of congratulatory communications. At no time can the use of an athlete's name, image or likeness be used to make reference to the official product of the athlete. Reference to the athlete's biography may be used in a factual manner. The athletes must appear dressed in either their national team uniform, past Games national Olympic team uniforms or in generic, unbranded clothing. Athletes may wear a uniform that is branded with the sponsor's trademarks or any other commercial mark other than the approved manufacturer trademark.[15]

This means that different rights might be in conflict. An image right of an athlete represents his or her own personal right, on the one hand, while, on the other, the rights of sporting organizations are based on intellectual property rights. The IOC original right of the use of the Olympic image has its background in the Nairobi Treaty on the protection of the Olympic symbol.[16] (It is interesting that the Nairobi Treaty only covers the use of the Olympic rings (Olympic symbol), and not the word and other expressions of the word Olympic.) An NOC's right to send an athlete to the Olympic Games emanates from the IOC Olympic Charter, on the one hand, and, on the other, an NOC has the right over its own Olympic symbols as an intellectual property right, which is transferable to its sponsors.

The IOC grants the use of the word Olympic to an NOC in the contract which is integrated in TOP. The Olympic emblem shall mean a design, as approved by the IOC, integrating the Olympic symbol with another distinctive element. Olympic designations shall mean any or all of the designations which indicate a sponsor relationship with a member of the Olympic Movement or an Olympic Team, such as 'Official Partner', 'Sponsor', 'Supplier', 'Licensee', 'Product', 'Service of' and so on.[17]

In praxis, some NOCs (Great Britain, The Netherlands and Belgium) implicitly regulate the transfer of image (portrait) right for the use of an NOC during the Games. Without an athlete's permission it would not be possible to exploit his or her image right commercially, and an NOC would not be able to use athlete's images for the commercial purposes of its sponsors.

Position of an Athlete and the IOC Eligibility Code

A typical case of limitations caused by the rules of governing sport organizations which reflects interests of individual athlete and its sponsor is the IOC 'eligibility rule'. This

---

14   Olympic Charter, Rule 41, Bye-law para. 3.
15   Presentation of the IOC Managing Director Timo Lumme, 'Changes and Challenges within the Olympic Market', EOC technical seminar, Ljubljana, October 2005.
16   Nairobi Treaty on the protection of the Olympic symbol, issued on 26 September1981 in Nairobi.
17   Definition from the contract between the IOC and an NOC.

governs the participation of athletes in the Olympic Games and comprises the basic information about the Olympic Rules and Regulations including the World Anti-Doping Agency (WADA) Anti-Doping Code and refers to the Court of Arbitration for Sport. The Eligibility Code is the basic element not only for the participation of athletes in the Olympic Games but also for the cooperation between athletes, their NOCs and their stakeholders.

The Eligibility rule (Rule 41 of the Olympic Charter) sets criteria for obtaining an Olympic accreditation. To be eligible for participation in the Olympic Games, a competitor, coach, trainer or other team official must comply with the Olympic Charter as well as with the rules of the international federation (IF) concerned, as approved by the IOC, and the competitor, coach, trainer or other team official must be entered by his or her NOC. These individuals must notably:

- respect the spirit of fair play and non-violence, and behave accordingly; and
- respect and comply in all aspects of the World Anti-Doping Code.

As it is stated in the By-law to Rule 41, each IF establishes its sport's own eligibility criteria in accordance with the Olympic Charter. Such criteria must be submitted to the IOC Executive Board for approval. The application of the eligibility criteria lies with the IFs, their affiliated national federations and the NOCs in the fields of their respective responsibilities.

The Eligibility Code might be problematic from the standpoint of the right of an athlete. If he or she does not agree with the code he is not permitted to take part in the Olympic Games. After the *Meca-Medina & Majcen*[18] case it is questionable what would be the position of the European Court of Justice if it examined the Code. The importance of the *Meca-Medina & Majcen* case is reflected in its citation in the European Commission White Paper on Sport.[19] In Chapter 4.1. it is stated that specifics of sport have to be taken into consideration in the sense that restrictive effects on a competition that are inherent in the organization and proper conduct of competitive sport are not in breach of the EU competition rules, provided that these effects are proportionate to a legitimate genuine sporting interest pursued. The necessity of a proportionality test implies the need to take into account the individual features of each case. It does not allow for the formulation of general guidelines on the application of competition law to the sport sector.

It is obvious that the Code creates the fundamental criteria for athletes to be able to compete at the Olympic Games. The participation of an individual athlete at the Olympic Games is purely of a sporting nature but could also be regarded as an activity with economic consequences. If anti-doping rules could be the subject of the Community law as regarded in the *Meca-Medina & Majcen* case, it would mean that other purely sporting rules such as the IOC Eligibility Code per se also could not be excluded from common rules. In other words, restrictions involved in the Eligibility Code should be inherent and proportionate with regard to the sporting objectives pursued.

---

[18] Cases T-313/02 and C-519/04 *Meca-Medina and Majcen* v. *Commission*.
[19] EU Commission, White Paper on Sport, 11 July 2007 COM(2007) 391 final, http://www.europa.eu/sport.

The best way to resolve a possible conflict of interests of different sponsors of sports subjects is an agreement, which must be reached in due time. The preparation period for the Olympic Games is an ideal opportunity for the stakeholders of such a mission to resolve the possible problems on time. The praxis of different NOCs preparing contracts with the NFs and athletes proves that very effectively. An athlete is regarded as a contractual party with his or her rights and can resolve the relations with his or her business-related partners in good time.

The holder of the right which is linked to a sport competition is the most important. As a clear example of autonomous sports law it is obvious that the governing body of a particular sport is entitled to settle the rules that all the involved subjects have to obey. After the *Meca-Medina & Majcen* case it is, of course, important to follow the European Court of Justice principle that all sport rules are subject to Community law. In view of the restrictions they cause, the rules set by sporting organizations are inherent and proportionate with regard to the sporting objectives pursued. There might also be restrictions if those rules were in conflict with the basic principles of human or some other common rights. Provided those basic principles are not violated, the autonomy of sport is secured.

AMBUSH MARKETING

Definition

The development of top sport with all the consequences of commercialization brings new dimensions regarding the legal protection of the different parties involved. Sponsorship, as an important and, for many countries, main tool for new sources of money for sport, sets some standards which should be strictly protected. One of the main characteristics of sponsorship is exclusivity, which makes sponsorship for sponsors so attractive. The abuse of sponsorship rights, especially exclusivity, could dangerously harm the relationship between the sponsor and sponsored party.

When the value of the exclusive rights for which the sponsor has bargained is seriously eroded by marketing by a rival, this is often referred to as 'ambush marketing'. Ambush marketing tends to contrast with the general run of commercial conflicts in sport, in that it consists of an unauthorized association by businesses using one or more elements of their business (usually their name, a trade mark or a particular product or service which they supply) with an event, team or individual. Ambush marketing operates by claiming or inferring a false relationship between the ambush marketer and the rights owner, without that rights owner permission.[20]

Ambush marketing occurs whenever an advertiser uses an event to its advantage without paying 'admission' – the sponsorship fee. Most of the time, ambush marketing is legal, profitable and very effective. Ambush marketing reduces the impact of official sponsors. Consumers, who are primarily concerned with receiving the benefits of both officially licensed marketing and ambush marketing, are often confused as to the identity of an event's official sponsors. Consumers are able to identify the sponsor's line of

---

[20]   R. Verow, C. Lawrence, P. McCormick, Sport Business and the Law. Bristol, Jordans, 1999, p. 278.

business, say a credit card company, but they will not be able to say exactly which the sponsor of the event is.[21]

The International Chamber of Commerce (ICC) International Code on Sponsorship follows the well-established ICC policy of promoting high standards of ethics in marketing via self-regulatory codes intended to complement the existing framework of national and international law. The ICC International Code on Sponsorship was first issued in 1992, as an expression of the business community's recognition of its social responsibilities in respect of marketing activities and communications. Under article 4 of the code, no party should seek to give the impression that it is a sponsor of any event or of media coverage of an event, whether sponsored or not, if it is not in fact an official sponsor of the property or of the media coverage.

Sponsors and sponsored parties, as well as other parties involved in a given sponsorship, should avoid imitation of the representation of other sponsorships where such imitation might mislead or generate confusion, even if applied to non-competitive products, companies or events (article 3).[22]

There are different classifications of examples of ambush marketing. Most of the ambush activities could be selected in one of the following categories:[23]

- unauthorized use of intellectual property rights;
- advertising;
- broadcast sponsorship;
- joint promotions;
- competitions and promotions;
- pourage agreements; or
- corporate hospitality and ticketing.

Legal Protection of Ambush Marketing

As ambush marketing represents a dangerous attack on sport sponsorship, some governments have decided to pass special legislation. Following pressure from the organizers of the Cricket World Cup, the South African government has introduced legislation banning ambush marketing both before and during the tournament. The Merchandise Marks Amendment Act 2002 is drafted in very broad terms to cover what the South Africa calls both 'ambush by way of intrusion' and 'ambush by way of association'.[24]

Under the new law, officially passed on 17 January 2003, the relevant government minister is empowered to designate an event as protected. Any unauthorized person who then uses their brand in relation to the event in a way which seeks to derive 'special promotional benefit from the event' will be guilty of a criminal offence. Specifically, the Act states:

[21]   V. Fisher, International Sponsorship. Montreal, Symbiose Publishing, 1995, str. 45.
[22]   ICC International Code on Sponsorship, http://www.iccwbo.org.
[23]   Classification followed by Verow, Lawrence, McCormick, note 20 *supra*, p. 280.
[24]   New South African, 'Ambush Marketing' laws bite, http://www.marketinglaw.co.uk.

(2) For the period during which an event is protected, no person may use a trade mark in relation to such event in a manner which is calculated to achieve publicity for that trade mark and thereby to derive special promotional benefit from the event, without the prior authority of the organizer of such event.

(3) For the purposes of subsection (2), the use of a trade mark includes:

(a) any visual representation of the trade mark upon or in relation to the goods or in relation to the rendering of services;
(b) any audible reproduction of the trade mark in relation to the goods or the rendering of services;
(c) the use of the trade mark in promotional activities, which in any way, directly or indirectly, is intended to be brought into association with or to allude to an event ...

(4) Any person who contravenes subsection (2) shall be guilty of an offence.

The South African law represents strong legal support for sponsorship. It is common that the organizers of the most important global sport competitions try to get similar legal protection from their governments. The organizing committees of the Olympic Games in Sydney in 2000 and Beijing in 2008 and the European football championship in Portugal in 2004 were able to convince their governments to pass special laws regarding protection against ambush marketing during competitions.

Another effective way to protect sport organizations is reflected in the Nairobi Convention on the protection of the Olympic symbols which gives the legal protection of the Olympic rings globally. Similar protection of the Olympic symbols can be found in many countries where the NOCs have initiated protection of their symbols in their territories. These laws represent a fundamental legal grounding for the protection of marketing activities which use the Olympic symbols as their most important marketing tools.

Apart from special laws regarding protection against ambush marketing there are also some other legal possibilities for combating ambush marketing. The most effective are the legal means coming out of rules which govern intellectual property rights. At its most blatant, ambush marketing (also known as parasitic marketing) takes the form of actionable legal wrong such as trademark infringement or passing off. There may also be trade descriptions offences which can be dealt with by trading standards offices and the rights owners acting in unison.[25]

Exclusivity in Sponsorship Agreements

Exclusivity is common in endorsements and corporate sponsorship contracts. Ambush marketing may take any number of forms but essentially it is an attack on the exclusivity which most commercial partners of a sport seek and will, to a limited extent, obtain. Legal protection against ambush marketing is vitally important for the majority of modern sponsorships and endorsements.

The success of a sponsorship depends largely on the exclusivity granted and whether the venues in question are 'clean' venues. It is possible to grant sponsorship rights to a number of parties but they are usually limited to one per product/service category. The sponsor has to ensure that there are no existing agreements that conflict with its sponsorship.

---

25   Verow, Lawrence, McCormick, note 20 *supra*, p. 278.

The most common target of ambush marketing is the exclusivity of the sponsor. It is important to note that buying a sponsorship does not (and cannot) buy you the exclusive right to the association with the event, but merely a right to the official sponsor status plus a package of sponsorship rights.[26]

Some Examples of Ambush Marketing

As the variety of different ambush activities increases, parasitic advertisers try to find new and original ways how to obtain the advantages of the status of sponsors without paying a sponsorship fee. There is a long and distinguished history of brands that run campaigns around sporting and other events without being official sponsors. Whether or not these activities should be seen as legitimate depends to a great extent on the nature of the activity and your own point of view.[27]

Certain types of 'ambush by association' are clearly hard to defend. For instance, if your marketing materials suggest wrongly that you have official sponsor status, then you can expect trouble (see the successful 2002 case in Argentina against Pepsi for running ads featuring the words 'Tokyo 2002' and various images and text which were said to suggest a 'presumed sponsorship relationship'). And if you use registered trade marks without permission (e.g. FIFA WORLD CUP) then again you can expect some grief, regardless of any arguments as to whether this is the 'use in a trade mark sense'. Likewise, any kind of 'intrusion' ambushing which involves trespass on property or breach of ticket terms and conditions will tend to be problematic.

The rights holder needs to control, supervise and check a large area in order to ensure no unwelcome brands are promoted in, at or around the venue (e.g. the successful ambush marketing campaign by Nike at Euro 2000 where Adidas was the official sponsor. Nike put a huge picture of Edgar Davids on the side of a building next to a venue and, as a result, viewers thought Nike was an official sponsor). There are numerous ambush attempts trying to attack parties that have concluded official sponsorship agreements.[28]

Position of the Athletes

There are some questions regarding the role of the athletes in ambush activities. In principle, athletes can be (mis)used as a tool of ambush advertisers to achieve some goals connected with the attack on exclusivity of the official sponsors. Is the athlete in such a case a victim of an ambush company? Is he or she responsible along with the company? What degree of knowledge about ambush marketing should be expected from an individual athlete?

---

[26] New South African, note 24 *supra*.

[27] *Ibid.*

[28] Cases from the website http://www.marketinglaw.co.uk:
   1. Linford Christie wearing the Puma logo on his contact lenses at the 1996 Olympics, where Reebok was an official sponsor.
   2. American Express's ad campaign in the VISA-sponsored 1994 Lillehammer Winter Olympics, featuring the slogan 'If you are traveling to Lillehammer, you will need a passport, but you don't need a Visa!'.
   3. More recently, Heineken giving away branded foam megaphones and hats outside venues at Euro 2004.

In the commercial world of sport, the athletes are supposed to follow the main principles of sponsorship. Participation in advertising campaigns with the aim to harm official sponsors is not the behavior expected from professional athletes. Therefore I see no reason why an athlete would not be responsible for wrongdoing together with the 'ambush company', if all the elements of ambush marketing are proved. Many professional athletes have their own legal advisers who should be able to distinguish prohibited campaigns from common advertising.

The image of the athletes could also be the harmed by ambush marketing, either alone or together with their sports organizations. Unauthorized use of intellectual property rights regarding the image of a famous athlete is the classic case of such an abuse. One of the most important factors is to determine the relationship between the sponsors of an athlete and the sponsors of the athlete's (national) team. The athletes are involved in many different sports competitions with different rules regarding the rights of individual commercial promotion. It is vital to know who owns the rights of each competition and which rules should be followed. It is well known that the Olympic Charter proposes limited possibilities for commercial promotion. All the athletes who wish to get the accreditation for the Olympics have to sign a special Olympic declaration in which they agree to respect the rules of the Olympic Charter. Beside that the NOCs are also responsible for the behavior of their athletes and could be sanctioned for the infringements of their athletes. There have been some cases where sponsors of individual athletes made ambush marketing towards the sponsors of a national (Olympic) team.[29] Where rights and priorities are less clear, it is vital that both event organizers and athletes seek legal advice as to their rights and obligations.

There are some common legal ways to combat with ambush marketing. Prevention is crucial. It is very important that all rights holders have an active policy of the registration and protection of all intellectual property rights associated with a sport event.

Ambush Marketing and Licensing

Licensing is one of the most important sources of revenue for sports. The IOC supports different licensing programs regarding the Olympic Movement, which could be good examples in answer to the question. Licensing programs produce officially licensed products from the OCOGs, the NOCs and the IOC. These products carry the emblems and mascots of the Olympic Games or Olympic teams and are designed to commemorate the Olympic Games and the Olympic teams.

---

[29]   PepsiCo had endorsement contracts with a number of top football players participating in the Japan/Korea FIFA World Cup 2002, including David Beckham, Juan Sebastian Veron, Emmanuel Petit, Rivaldo and Rui Costa. However, unlike Coca-Cola, which has been an official sponsor of the FIFA World Cup for 24 years, PepsiCo was not an official sponsor of the tournament. During the tournament, PepsiCo ran a number of advertisements in various countries featuring the footballers on its endorsement roster in conjunction with the phrase 'Tokyo 2002' and the Pepsi logo. FIFA was able to obtain a court injunction in Argentina restraining PepsiCo from using one such advertisement, on the basis that it suggested a 'presumed sponsorship relationship' and could therefore cause confusion among consumers. FIFA is apparently taking proceedings in Ecuador in relation to similar commercials and has also locked horns with PepsiCo in Mexico: 'Fourth referee for FIFA "ambush marketing" claims against Pepsi?', http://www.marketinglaw.co.uk.

The question arises if the breach of a licensing system could also be regarded as ambush marketing. Could the production of a licensed product without the permission of a rights holder mean ambush?

Examining the licensing relationship, it is not necessary that any abuse of licensing could also mean ambush marketing. Only if the activity also has all the others signs of ambush marketing can such an activity be regarded as ambush. The production of articles without permission can be regarded as a breach of licensing agreement; the intent of the producer is not to damage the exclusivity of the license owner, but to sell products.

Dangers of Ambush Marketing

It is without any doubt that some facts regarding ambush marketing and the involvement of athletes are obvious, such as:

- ambush marketing represents one of the most serious threats to sports sponsoring;
- not all ambush marketing activities violate applicable law;
- the media (especially TV) play a decisive role of public opinion regarding the connection of a sponsor and a sponsored subject;
- exclusivity is the element of sponsorship which is most commonly attacked by parasitic companies;
- true ambush marketing is carried out intentionally, not by negligence;
- passing of special laws against ambush marketing represents very useful legal support for organizers of sports competitions;
- an athlete should be aware of his or her responsibilities;
- a precise examination of obligations in different sponsorship agreements with the sponsors of athletes and their teams should be made to avoid 'internal' ambush;
- prevention and immediate response to attempts of ambush marketing is crucial; and
- sponsors are extremely sensible and closely watch athletes' behavior in case of ambush marketing.

It could be concluded that both parties of sponsorship contracts are exposed to the danger of ambush marketing effects. New and innovative ways of ambush marketing put a pressure especially on sport subjects as to how legally to defend the values that are incorporated in the sponsorship contract. Special legislation is the best way of legal prevention and of great significance as it protects the position of both parties. On the other hand, quick and effective reaction in a case of ambush marketing can also diminish the devastating effects of parasite companies. The majority of the NOCs engage lawyers to protect their rights not only during the period of the Olympic Games but also in 'non-Olympic' periods.

CONCLUSION

The importance of a sponsorship contract is growing steadily. Its development has not yet reached the point at which legal codification would be justified. The European legal system especially tries to find the best possible options to put sponsorship contract into a certain classic legal framework. It is therefore logical that the continental theory is occupied with the imperative how to find a proper definition of different situations coming out of sponsorship.

Legal analysis of a sponsorship contract is crucial to establish suitable legal rules for a correct interpretation. As it represents a modern contract of an autonomous commercial type, it is logical to try to use the methods and principles of the common civil law. These legal instruments could be used if we cannot find a suitable rule of already known examples of the legislation regulating contracts. It is therefore very convenient, especially for European lawyers, to subsume a particular part of sponsorship under a special rule of the existing nominative contract. Apart from the legislative rules, the principles of autonomous law are also acceptable and useful.

The use of the principles of the ICC International Code on Sponsorship is justified, as they represent special rules in the field of sponsorship. These rules are abstract enough to allow broad and beneficial use in many cases. It is of special significance that the ICC code strives for the protection of public interests and the enforcement of good practice. Correct interpretation of the code cannot put a party to the sponsorship contract in a harmful position. The parties to the contract can exclude the use of code provisions, but it is not likely that they will do so. With the shortage of applicable legal rules for interpretation of a sponsorship contract, the use of those provisions is highly recommendable.

A sponsorship contract is conceived as a law by its parties as it defines those elements which seem to the parties to be the most important. The parties use the formal legal system to accomplish the economic substance that they would like to achieve. The specific structure of sport is very complex and must be linked to the different expectations of a sponsor. Mutual understanding of the positions, interests and aspirations of both parties is a crucial factor for the real and right substantial interpretation of their relationship. Heterogeneity of sponsorship contract implies an precise individual approach to interpret each contract on a case-by-case basis. As it can be regarded as a *sui generis* contract, special attention is required for the for proper interpretation of this prospective and promising contract of modern sport.

19 Players' agents

Roberto Branco Martins and Richard Parrish

INTRODUCTION

This chapter focuses on the regulation of players' agents in professional football given that the sector has the highest incidence of agent activity and that developments in football drives change in other sports. It begins with a brief overview of why agents play such a prominent role in world football. It then discusses the role of the International Federation of Football Associations (FIFA) in regulating agent activity and explains why agent regulation may be necessary despite criticisms of the regulatory model employed by FIFA. The chapter then considers the role the European Football Agents Association can play in shaping the regulatory environment. Three recent developments are then explored: FIFA's re-evaluation of its 2008 regulations, the conclusions of the 2009 European Commission Agent Study and developments in the European professional football social dialogue committee. Finally, the chapter reviews alternative models for regulating agents.

THE RISE OF AGENTS

In the English case of *Walker* v. *Crystal Palace Football Club* [1910], Farewell J. applied a new 'control test' as a common law means of distinguishing an employee subject to the control of the employer from a self-employed contractor who is not.[1] Whilst this control was principally exercised by subjugating the football player to the training regime of the club, in a wider context a maximum wage and transfer system was devised which formed part of a wider control mechanism of management over players.[2] Originating in 1891, the so-called retain and transfer system sanctioned a restrictive practice through which a club retained a player's registration even though contractual relations between the club and player had ended. The objectives of the system were to introduce contractual stability to the profession and limit the concentration of talent within a few clubs, thus promoting competitive balance within the league. The practical effect provided the club with a 'virtual monopoly over the player's services ... effectively tying him to his club until, and if, the club gave the player permission to move elsewhere'.[3]

In England, the earnings potential and labour mobility of players were enhanced following the abolition of the maximum wage in 1961 and the judgment of the High

---

[1]   *Walker* v. *Crystal Palace Football Club* [1910] 1 KB 87.

[2]   Caiger, A. and O'Leary, J. (2000), The end of the affair: the Anelka doctrine – the problem of contract stability in English professional football, in: Caiger, A. and Gardiner, S. (eds), Professional Sport in the EU, Regulation and Re-regulation, The Hague: TMC Asser Press, p. 198.

[3]   Thomas, D. (2006), The Retain and Transfer System, in: Andreff, W. and Szymanski, S. (eds), Handbook on the Economics of Sport, Cheltenham, UK and Northampton, MA, USA: Edward Elgar Publishing, p. 630.

Court in *Eastham* in 1963.[4] The retain and transfer system was eventually phased out and replaced with a system of 'freedom of contract' for players reaching the end of their contract, although a transfer fee could still be commanded for a player who declined renewal terms. Pure free agency was only introduced in England, and throughout Europe, following the 1995 decision of the Court of Justice of the European Union (CJEU) in *Bosman*.[5] The impact of the *Bosman* judgment was profound, with players benefitting from enhanced international employment prospects and remuneration packages. The CJEU further internationalised the professional player market by handing down its judgment in *Kolpak*.[6] Here, it extended some of the *Bosman* principles to non-EU workers protected by association agreements by finding a number of these agreements prevent professional sportsmen and women of a state covered by the agreement, who are lawfully employed by a club established in an European Union (EU) Member State, from being treated differently from member state nationals in terms of their working conditions, remuneration and dismissal.

Facilitating this migration of football labour are agents. An agent is a person authorised to act for another when dealing with third parties. For a fee, commonly known as a commission, an agent introduces players to clubs, either by way of a transfer or a contract renegotiation, and they introduce clubs to one another with a view to concluding a transfer. In this sense, a players' agent is merely an intermediary ensuring that the supply and demand for labour within football is met. Yet this apparently simple definition masks the complexity of the debate surrounding the merits and methods of agent regulation.

FIFA PLAYERS' AGENTS REGULATIONS

Until the 2001 revision of the FIFA player agent regulations, agents were entitled to operate as licensed FIFA agents after undergoing an oral examination conducted by employees of the national governing bodies. The agent was then required to deposit a CHF 200 000[7] bank guarantee and sign a code of conduct. The system was revised due to the growing number of agents and as a consequence of developments in international football, which saw increasing numbers of players move across frontiers. The 2001 regulations introduced a written examination and devolved the issuance of licensing to the national member associations. Since 2001 an agent is no longer technically a 'FIFA licensed agent' but an 'Agent licensed by (the national) Football Association (FA)'. The 2001 regulations were amended in 2008.

The 2008 Players' Agent Regulations stipulate that clubs and players can only call upon the services of agents who are licensed by national associations although this prohibition

---

[4]   *Eastham* v. *Newcastle United Football Club Ltd* [1963] 3 All ER 139, deciding that the retain and transfer system as operated in English football at the time was in restraint of trade.

[5]   Case C-415/93 *Union Royale Belge Sociétés de Football Association and others* v. *Bosman and others* [1995] ECR I-4921, hereafter referred to as *Bosman*, deciding that the international football transfer system and the use of nationality restrictions in European club football were incompatible with EU free movement laws.

[6]   Case 438/00 *Deutscher Handballbund e.v.* v. *Maros Kolpak*, deciding that non-discrimination rights can extend to non-EU nationals.

[7]   Swiss Francs.

docs not apply if the agent acting on behalf of a player is a parent, a sibling or the spouse of the player in question or if the agent acting on behalf of the player or club is legally authorised to practise as a lawyer in compliance with the rules in force in his country of domicile. The procedure for being granted a licence involves a formal application to the national association and a requirement to take a competence examination covering relevant national laws and the rules of football. Examinations take place once or twice a year on a date set by FIFA. If a candidate passes the examination, the applicant is required either to conclude professional liability insurance with an insurance company in their country or to deposit a bank guarantee to the amount of CHF 100 000. Every agent who passes the examination is required to sign a code of professional conduct. If the above requirements are met, the competent national association issues a licence and a register of licensed agents is created. As the license expires after 5 years, agents wishing to continue to offer their services are subject to re-examination. If the re-examination is unsuccessful, the licence is suspended until such a time as the examination is passed.

The FIFA regulations establish not only the conditions of access to the profession but also the standards of conduct expected of those subject to them. The agent is obliged to enter into written contractual relations of no more than 2 years with the player he represents. The agent is allowed to represent clubs and players although the agent must avoid any potential conflicts of interest. In addition, the agent is *a priori* presumed to be guilty of inducing a player to breach his contract with a club if the contract is breached prior to its ending and without just cause. In order to avoid sanction, the burden lies with the agent to establish his innocence in this regard. Sanctions that may be imposed on agents for violating the regulations are a reprimand or a warning, a fine of at least CHF 5000, a suspension of the licence for up to 12 months, a withdrawal of the licence or a ban on taking part in any football-related activity.

The regulations also include rights and obligations of clubs and players. Clubs are entitled to engage the services of only licensed agents and are required to specify the name of the agent in the written contract. Clubs must ensure that they pay the agents, within the scope of a players' transfer, only by means of a lump sum that has been agreed upon in advance. If clubs violate these regulations, sanctions can be imposed including a warning, fines, points deductions, transfer bans and a demotion to a lower division. Players engaging the services of agents may choose to pay the agent by means of a lump sum or a fee on a yearly basis. The fee is based on a percentage of the annual income of the player. If no agreement is reached concerning the fee, the agent is entitled to receive 3% of the annual income of the player, including any signing-on fee. If the player is responsible for a violation of the regulations, he can be warned or punished with a fine of at least CHF 5000, a match suspension or a ban on taking part in any football-related activity.

THE *PIAU* CHALLENGE TO THE FIFA REGULATIONS

The introduction of the 2001 FIFA Regulations was the product of a complaint initially lodged before the European Commission in 1996 by Multiplayers International Denmark concerning the compatibility of the regulations with EU competition law. In 1998 French agent Laurent Piau also lodged a complaint, adding that the regulations were also contrary to EU provisions on the freedom to provide services. Following the Commission's issuance of a statement of objections concerning various aspects of the regulations, FIFA introduced the 2001 version. Piau objected to the examination requirement and the requirement to take out professional liability insurance. He added that the new regulations introduced new restrictions by way of the rules on professional conduct, the use of a standard contract and the rules on the determination of remuneration. These, he argued, were in breach of EU competition law although Piau appeared to have ceased his complaint relating to the freedom to provide services.

Following the Commission's rejection of Piau's complaint in April 2002, the agent lodged an appeal before the Court of First Instance (CFI), since renamed the General Court. The CFI found that the licence system did not result in competition being eliminated, as the system resulted in a qualitative selection process, rather than a quantitative restriction on access to that occupation. This was necessary in order to raise professional standards for the occupation of a players' agent, particularly as players' careers were short and they needed protection. According to the court, the rule-making authority of FIFA was justified as there was a near total absence of national rules regulating agents and there was no collective organisation for players' agents which could be consulted.[8] Although the CFI disagreed with the Commission's assessment that FIFA did not hold a dominant position in the market of services of players' agents, the court went on to find no abuse of market dominance. On appeal, the CJEU rejected Piau's request that the Commission decision and the decision of the CFI be annulled. The CJEU did not explore the substance of Piau's claim relating to freedom to provide services, but dismissed this as a new argument which it could not address insofar as the Commission acted on the basis of Regulation 17/62/EEC and was therefore only obliged to consider competition law.

IN DEFENCE OF AGENT REGULATION

FIFA and the EU courts are not alone in identifying the need for an effective regime regulating the activities of players' agents. The 2006 Independent European Sport Review, otherwise referred to as the Arnaut Report, concluded that 'that rules concerning players' agents are inherent to the proper regulation of football and therefore compatible with Community law'.[9] Nevertheless, the Arnaut Report was unequivocal in its support for the adoption of a more rigorous regulatory regime, possibly by adopting a specific EU directive on sports agents. Such an intervention would have the benefit of addressing the concern expressed by the CFI in *Piau* that the legitimacy of a private body such as FIFA to regulate a profession such as agents is 'open to question' given that FIFA has not received a mandate from a public authority.[10] The CFI held that:

---

8   Case T-193/02 *Laurent Piau* v. *Commission of the European Communities* [2005] ECR II-209. Hereafter referred to as *Piau*, CFI.

9   Arnaut, J.L. (2006), Independent European Sport Review, available at: http://www.independentfootballreview.com/doc/Full_Report_EN.pdf.

10   *Piau*, CFI, paragraph 76.

[t]he very principle of regulation of an economic activity concerning neither the specific nature of sport nor the freedom of internal organisation of sports associations by a private-law body, like FIFA, which has not been delegated any such power by a public authority, cannot from the outset be regarded as compatible with Community law, in particular with regard to respect for civil and economic liberties.[11]

As is explained above, the Court went on to find that the rule-making power exercised by FIFA was legitimate insofar as there was an almost complete absence of national rules on player agent regulation and as players' agents were not organised collectively and consequently did not constitute a profession with its own internal organisation.

Further support for an EU directive on agent regulation came by way of the 2007 European Parliament report on the future of professional football in Europe, otherwise known as the Belet Report.[12] The report argued that a directive could include strict standards and examination criteria before anyone could operate as a football players' agent; provide transparency in agents' transactions; establish minimum harmonised standards for agents' contracts; establish an efficient monitoring and disciplinary system by the European governing bodies; introduce an agents' licensing system and agents' register; and ensure that the practice of dual representation and payment of agents by a player is brought to an end.

The Commission formally responded to these and other initiatives by publishing the 2007 White Paper on Sport.[13] The White Paper was designed to give strategic orientation on the role of sport in Europe, to encourage debate on specific problems, to enhance the visibility of sport in EU policy-making and to raise public awareness of the needs and specificities of the sector. On the question of agent regulation, the White Paper commented that:

[t]here are reports of bad practices in the activities of some agents which have resulted in instances of corruption, money laundering and exploitation of underage players. These practices are damaging for sport in general and raise serious governance questions. The health and security of players, particularly minors, has to be protected and criminal activities fought against.[14]

Consequently the Commission committed itself to 'carry out an impact assessment to provide a clear overview of the activities of players' agents in the EU and an evaluation of whether action at EU level is necessary, which will also analyse the different possible options'.[15]

The Commission's resulting agent study listed a number of ethical issues associated with the work of agents including: dual agency or conflict-of-interest situations in which the same agent acts as an intermediary in the deal between two clubs and, subsequently, in the deal between the player and their new club; problems relating to financial criminality, particularly in connection with player transfers; problems relating to human trafficking;

---

[11]   *Piau*, CFI, paragraph 77.

[12]   European Parliament (2007), Resolution of the European Parliament on the Future of Professional Football in Europe, A6–0036/2007, 29 March. (The Belet Report).

[13]   European Commission (2007), White Paper on Sport, COM(2007), 391 final. Hereafter referred to as White Paper (2007).

[14]   White Paper (2007), s. 4.4.

[15]   White Paper (2007), action point 41.

problems relating to the inadequate protection of minors; and problems relating the inadequate protection of sportspersons in general, particularly in relation to the lack of transparency within the profession.[16]

EUROPEAN FOOTBALL AGENTS ASSOCIATION

In *Piau* the Court found that FIFA's ability to regulate players' agents was partly justified insofar as no collective organisation for players' agents existed. This organisational question was resolved in 2007 with the formation of the European Football Agents Association (EFAA), a not-for-profit association established according to Dutch law.[17] EFAA is an umbrella organisation bringing together ten national agent associations including those of the 'big five' league countries. In countries where no agent association exists, EFAA assists in establishing one. Recently EFAA has accepted associated members in response to approaches from Brazil, Japan, United Arab Emirates and Indonesia. EFAA's mission is to maintain and, where necessary, introduce a high standard of professionalism, clarity and regulatory control in the profession of players' agents within the football family.[18] Specifically, the goals of EFAA are laid down in Article 2 of the organisation's statutes and focus on creating common ground amongst agents in Europe and supporting the creation of national agent associations.

At the end of 2008 EFAA drafted a list of ten urgent issues and malpractices requiring attention in European football, three of which receive attention below. First, EFAA argues that there is a need for the creation of a solid legal framework for the regulation of the activities of agents, clubs and players concerning all issues relating to transfers and representation. EFAA does not agree with the CJEU's assertion in *Piau* that there is an almost complete absence of national rules on players' agent regulation. Many states of the EU regulate the activity of sport agents through general statutory interventions or common laws such as contract law and agency work laws. Others have established a sport-specific statutory basis for agent regulation. Currently 93% of EU-based agents are regulated by a source of law or collection of rules that prevail over the FIFA Player Agent Regulations.[19] The complexity of this legal environment is aggravated by the rule-making activities of international sports federations whose rules are applicable to agents through the system of licensing. The mandatory transposition of international sports regulations by national associations has increased legal inconsistencies and has led to conflicts in the European sports sector. For example, whilst the FIFA regulations permit a player to pay for the services of an agent, Dutch law prohibits this. In Belgium, in order to practise, an agent must have a licence for the specific regions of Walloon, Flanders and Brussels,

---

[16]   KEA European Affairs (KEA), Centre de Droit et d'Economie du Sport (CDES), European Observatory of Sport and Employment (EOSE) (2009), Study on Sports Agents in the European Union, a study commissioned by the European Commission (Directorate-General for Education and Culture), Part 4. Summary and Recommendations, pp. 3–4.

[17]   More information is available at: http://www.eufootballagents.com.

[18]   *Ibid.*

[19]   Branco Martins, R. (2009), The Laurent Piau case of the ECJ on the status of players' agents, in: Gardiner, S., Parrish, R. and Siekmann, R. (eds), EU Sport Law and Policy. Regulation, Re-regulation and Representation, The Hague: TMC Asser Press.

alongside the Football Association licence. In France, foreign agents need to be registered and have a French licence in order to work in France, whereas in many other countries these limitations do not exist. According to EFAA, in order to avoid such conflicts and legal inconsistencies, effective agent regulation must pay due respect to the established hierarchy of laws based on the primacy of EU law over national law and the primacy of national law over the rules of the sports associations.

Second, EFAA argues that there should be more stringent control on the activities of unlicensed 'agents' and the activities of unlicensed exempt individuals. Furthermore, there should be better control of licensed agents working as façades for unlicensed agents. Without such control there is a diminution of the value attached to the FIFA licence issued by the national associations. This is because the activities of unlicensed agents take place beyond the control of the governing bodies, as they do not fall under any form of regulatory control. These agents are therefore able to be involved in malpractices without being sanctioned. The current regulatory framework leads to the injustice of licensed and professionally organised agents experiencing stringent restrictions on their freedom to provide services whilst unlicensed agents and exempt individuals can act with apparent impunity. The problems with the exempt individuals is a particular concern for EFAA although it notes that a number of countries have introduced bans on the activities of lawyers who, in many cases, 'sell' their signature to unlicensed agents. For example, France has introduced one such ban, and the Dutch bar association has announced that lawyers are prohibited from acting as a layman for non-licensed agents. The Portuguese bar association has warned its members to refrain from working as agents. EFAA takes the view that the governing bodies should have the authority to investigate how a players' agent uses his licence. If, having analysed the pattern of transfers negotiated by the agent, it appears that the agent uses his licence mainly to act as a façade for unlicensed agents, the proposal is that they should be sanctioned.

EFAA's third issue concerns the better protection of youth players and minors and the extent to which agents should exercise a professional influence on football players below the age of 16. EFAA considers immigration control for minors entering the territory of the EU to be a matter for further debate, and it wants to prevent parties involved in the international movement of minors from being able to 'forum shop' in order to bring minors into the EU. In addition, EFAA favours an analysis of the current system of training compensation and transfer sums which results in players becoming valuable financial commodities to clubs at a very young age, and of the question of alternative means for achieving the objectives pursued by such a system. Finally, EFAA seeks an analysis of the effects of the home-grown player rule which has been introduced by the Union of European Football Associations (UEFA) and which requires clubs to reserve a number of squad places for players trained by the club's own football academy and players trained by other clubs from the same association. A club-trained player is defined as a player who has been registered for a minimum of three seasons with the club between the age of 15 and 21, whereas an association-trained player is a player who has been registered for at least three seasons by the club or by other clubs affiliated to the same association between the age of 15 and 21. Concern has been expressed that this system may lead to an increased demand for young players as clubs seek to attract the best young talent from other countries in order qualify them as 'home-grown'.

Other issues confronting EFAA include a transparent sanctioning system for agents, players and clubs for malpractices related to transfers; a ban on the tolerance of the ownership of 'athlete's registration rights' or 'federative rights'; harmonisation and simplification in the method of the invoicing of agents' fees; uniformity in tax legislation; harmonisation of the method of payment of agents, enabling agents to be paid directly by players as well as by clubs on behalf of players; compulsory permanent education for players' agents including a yearly seminar composed, educated and controlled by the FAs and football stakeholders including EFAA; and guidelines on the 'legal and allowed' services rendered by agents to clubs.

AGENT REGULATION: RECENT DEVELOPMENTS

The future of agent regulation is likely to be influenced by three recent developments in European football, the 59th Annual FIFA Congress, the European Commission Agent Study and social dialogue in European professional football.

The 59th Annual FIFA Congress

FIFA has acknowledged that only 25–30% of football transfers are carried out by licensed agents.[20] At the FIFA Congress in 2009, the member associations of FIFA therefore voted for 'an in-depth reform of the players' agents system'.[21] This admission that the current form of regulatory control is not working has led FIFA to consider adopting a more pragmatic attitude towards the regulation of agents. A working group of the FIFA committee for club football has been established to report on the new regime. The working group is composed of representatives from the world players union FIFPro, club representatives and the FIFA legal department. Once adopted the new regulations will supersede those of 2008. Initial reports indicate that the new approach is expected to focus less on regulating agents' access to the profession, most of whom clearly fall outside the reach of FIFA's regulatory authority, and instead focus on the conduct of clubs and players, both of whom fall more directly under FIFA's control.[22] This means that anyone will be able to act as an agent but players and clubs, as the main actors, need to exercise due diligence and transparency in negotiating and concluding contracts. If they do not, they are the parties to be sanctioned. This implies that the system of licensing will be abolished with agents handing back their licences to the national associations and having any bank guarantees returned.

Given reports of numerous examples of agent abuse, the proposed deregulation of the agent profession has been criticised by those fearful of a new unregulated 'free-for-all'.[23] At the Globe Soccer conference in Dubai in January 2010, Omar Ongaro, the Head of Players' Status at FIFA, explained that members of the working group, especially club

---

[20]   FIFA Media Release (2009), FIFA Acts to Protect Core Values, 15 July 2009.

[21]   FIFA Media Release (2009), Protect the Game, Protect the Players, Strengthen Glob Football Governance, 03 June 2009.

[22]   http://www.Reuters.com, FIFA Tries to Squeeze out Unlicensed Agents, 14 July 2009.

[23]   http://www.guardian.co.uk, 'FIFA to Give up Regulating Player Agents', 12 November 2009.

representatives, asked for the opinions of other stakeholders such as the European Professional Football Leagues (EPFL) and EFAA. Having consulted these organisations, FIFA received feedback indicating that deregulation was regarded as potentially counter-productive with concern being expressed about liberalising who can practise as an agent, the lack of regulation concerning conflicts of interest and the demise of the register of agents. In response, FIFA is continuing with stakeholder consultations with a view to issuing new regulations in due course.[24]

European Commission Agent Study

In the White Paper on Sport, the Commission committed itself to 'carry out an impact assessment to provide a clear overview of the activities of players' agents in the EU and an evaluation of whether action at EU level is necessary, which will also analyse the different possible options'.[25] The study was carried out by a consortium of European research institutes and was published in late 2009.[26]

The study identified 32 sports disciplines in which up to 6140 sports agents are active. All 27 Member States of the EU had football agents operating within their territory and the commissions earned by the agents were estimated at €200 million per annum. The study identified few legal texts designed specifically to regulate the activities of sports agents, with only Bulgaria, France, Greece, Hungary and Portugal having adopted specific national laws. Among private undertakings, only the international governing bodies for basketball (FIBA), football (FIFA), athletics (IAAF) and rugby (IRB) had adopted regulations. Nevertheless, the activities of agents are also regulated through general national agency that generally provide for registration, licensing or authorisation procedures in order for agents to provide private placement services. In addition, the study identified a number of laws found in the European Treaty to be applicable to the activities of agents, including primary laws on the freedom to provide services, the freedom of establishment and competition laws and secondary legislation covering services and the recognition of professional qualifications.

The study favours a form of self-regulation for agents. It argues that the rules adopted by sports federations will best reflect the specificities of each sport within their own respective jurisdictions. In this connection the study favours the use of an examination-based licensing system for each sport. However, the study argues that in framing and implementing these regulations, the sports federations must be supported by public authorities, particularly the EU. The study indicates that the EU's support should be supporting and co-ordinating in nature, for example, taking the form of facilitating dialogue at European level. Consequently, the study does not favour the enactment of specific laws at the EU level. It argues that as only five Member States have enacted specific laws regulating the activities of agents and as these laws do not give rise to obvious restrictions in terms of service provision and establishment, a case for the harmonisation of national laws cannot be made. The study does, however, acknowledge that the lack of

---

[24] Omar Ongaro (2010), New Concept to Regulate the Activity of Intermediaries, presentation at Globe Soccer Conference, Dubai, 04 January 2010.

[25] White Paper (2007), action point 41.

[26] KEA, CDES and EOSE (2009), Study on Sports Agents in the European Union, a study commissioned by the European Commission (Directorate-General for Education and Culture).

evidence of problems with the current pattern of agent regulation may simply reflect the ease by which agents can circumvent regulation.

Social Dialogue in European Professional Football

One means of giving effect to the call contained within the Commission's agent study for the EU to play a facilitating role in agent regulation is for the issue to be discussed within the context of a social dialogue committee. Social dialogue allows for the two sides of industry representing employers and workers to discuss labour relations in a formal setting and if necessary to conclude binding agreements within the framework of Articles 153–155 TFEU (formerly Articles 137–139 EC).

A social dialogue committee for European professional football was established in July 2008 after almost eight years of preparatory work and the publication of a number of reports endorsing its establishment.[27] Before the committee could be established, the Commission was required to confirm the representativeness of the employer and employee organisations. The two representative employer social partners are the European Club Association (ECA) and the European Professional Football Leagues (EPFL). The representative employee social partner is the international football players union, FIFPro. The work programme that was agreed upon at the launch event included the development of minimum conditions in players' contracts throughout the EU and the possible conclusion of a collective agreement on these requirements. The question of agent regulation does not currently fit into this work programme. Indeed, as the social partners may only reach agreements that are able to be transposed into national guidelines or regulations if the topic is directly related to the issues mentioned in Articles 153–155 TFEU, it remains a moot point whether a social dialogue committee is an appropriate venue through which agent regulation can be discussed.

Agent regulation could form part of discussions within an 'informal' social dialogue, but this could not lead to binding agreements and would, arguably, fail to satisfy the desire for a mechanism which secures greater legal certainty within the sector than currently exists. Therefore, it seems that for agent regulation formally to form part of social dialogue discussions a deviation from the norms of social dialogue is required. Such a deviation is already evident in the operation of the football social dialogue committee insofar as the ECA has been conferred social partner status even though it does not appear to conform to the social dialogue representation criteria. These criteria state that in order to be eligible for consultation, an organisation must be cross-industry, or relate to specific sectors or categories and be organised at the European level; consist of organisations which are themselves an integral and recognised part of Member States' social partner structures and with the capacity to negotiate agreements, and be representative of all Member States, as far as possible; and have adequate structures to ensure the effective participation in the consultation process.[28] The ECA does not satisfy all of these characteristics.

---

[27]   These are listed in Commission Staff Working Document, The EU and Sport: Background and Context, Accompanying Document to the White Paper on Sport, COM(2007) 391 final, footnote 149.

[28]   Article 1 of Commission Decision 98/500/EC, Commission Decision of 20 May 1998 on the establishment of Sectoral Dialogue Committees promoting the Dialogue between the social partners at European level.

Further evidence of the somewhat unorthodox approach to social dialogue in European football is supplied by the construction of the committee. The social partners within the committee agreed to establish UEFA as an associate member and the chair of the committee and agreed to establish a rule of procedure under which items are first submitted to UEFA's Professional Football Strategy Council before being discussed in the formal social dialogue committee.[29] This somewhat unusual structure affords UEFA influence over social dialogue discussions and enables it to defend the specificities of sport during the discussions between the representatives of clubs and players. It also illustrates that the peculiarities of the football sector may require a more pragmatic application of social dialogue principles. In this connection, the Mavrommatis Report of the European Parliament stated that, '[the committee] considers that players' agents should have a role within a strengthened social dialogue in sports, which, in combination with better regulation and a European licensing system for agents, would also prevent cases of improper action by agents'.[30] This is consistent with the practice in a number of member states where private employment agencies form part of the self-regulation of their profession and participate in collective agreements with employers and employees.[31]

CONCLUSIONS

At the time of writing, the future of agent regulation remains uncertain. FIFA is currently reassessing its agent regulations and the European Commission is studying the conclusions of the agent study. Therefore a number of regulatory models may emerge in the future.

No regulation. One argument in support of freeing agency work from private regulation provided by sport governing bodies is that since agency work is a profession, agents should be allowed to provide a service subject only to regulation provided by public authorities. The counter-argument is that governing bodies possess an obvious interest in the integrity of their respective sports and provide a pattern of comprehensive qualification-based regulation which mitigates against the uncertainties of relying on measures found in national laws. Furthermore, governing bodies possess considerable knowledge and experience of their respective sport, and their role in regulating the activities of agents is important as it safeguards the specificities of sport.

EU directive on agents. Perhaps the highest level of legal certainty could be achieved by the adoption of uniform rules enshrined in an EU directive on agents. However, the case for such a directive is not yet sufficiently strong. In particular, as only five EU Member States have adopted specific player agent laws, the case for the harmonisation of existing standards may be considered premature. Furthermore, questions exist as to whether a

---

[29] 'Rules of procedure for the European sectoral social dialogue committee in the professional football sector', available at: http://circa.europa.eu/Public/irc/empl/sectoral_social_dialogue/library?l=/professional_football/2008/20080701_plenartagung/football_080702_1/_EN_1.0_&a =d.

[30] European Parliament Resolution of May 8 2008 on the White Paper on Sport (2007/2261(INI)), (The Mavrommatis Report), para. 107.

[31] Arrowsmith, J. (2009), Temporary Agency Work and Collective Bargaining in the EU, Eurofound Report, available at: http://www.eurofound.europa.eu/eiro/studies/tn0807019s/index.htm.

directive would be able to capture the diverse activity and regulatory models adopted by governing bodies in a range of sports. Finally, the EU may decide that alternative regulatory models, such as self-regulation, should be explored before it acts in this field.

Regulation by governing bodies. Regulation undertaken by governing bodies benefits from their knowledge of their respective sports and it ensures that specificity of sport arguments, such as the need to protect the integrity of the sport or the need to protect minors, is sufficiently articulated in the relevant regulations. Private regulation may, however, conflict with the superior laws of Member States and the EU, and so legal certainty cannot be guaranteed. Unilateral private regulation also does not necessarily tap into the knowledge and expertise of all stakeholders thereby potentially causing tension if good governance principles such as democracy and transparency in decision-making are not observed. In addition, the use of a licensing system for agents has proved problematic, particularly where this allows certain exempt individuals to bypass the licensing regime.

Social dialogue. The existence of a social dialogue committee for professional football offers a platform through which questions of agent regulation can be discussed by the key stakeholders. Potentially social dialogue can lead to binding agreements which can be implemented into national laws therefore creating a more uniform and specific regulatory regime. Nevertheless, agent regulation is not a 'pure' social dialogue topic because only employment related matters can lead to agreements. Furthermore, as FIFPro is a social partner and involved in the representation of players, issues of conflicts of interest may arise.

Self-regulation. This model refers to a private regulatory regime in which the governing bodies openly negotiate with relevant stakeholders, such as players, clubs and representative agent bodies, in order to draft, implement and enforce agent regulations. As such, self-regulation has the potential to benefit from expertise, legitimacy and compliance. Of course, self-regulation may not satisfy the desire of the public and public authorities to see stringent regulation imposed on a sector perceived to be corrupt. In addition, for self-regulation to work effectively, robust structures need to be in place and representative stakeholder bodies must possess the capacity and will to collaborate with one another. In this connection, bodies such as the EU could assist in encouraging dialogue within the sector. Clearly, any restrictions on free movement or competition that flow from self-regulation may be subject to legal challenge although regulation that is agreed upon openly and transparently should minimise conflict.

REFERENCES

Arnaut, J.L. (2006), Independent European Sport Review, available at: www.independent footballreview.com/doc/Full_Report_EN.pdf.
Arrowsmith, J. (2009), Temporary Agency Work and Collective Bargaining in the EU, Eurofound Report, available at: www.eurofound.europa.eu/eiro/studies/tn0807019s/index.htm.
Branco Martins, R. (2009), The Laurent Piau case of the ECJ on the status of players' agents, in: Gardiner, S., Parrish, R. and Siekmann, R. (eds), EU Sport Law and Policy. Regulation, Re-regulation and Representation, The Hague: TMC Asser Press.
Caiger, A. and O'Leary, J. (2000), The end of the affair: the Anelka doctrine – the problem of contract stability in English professional football, in: Caiger, A. and Gardiner, S. (eds), Professional Sport in the EU, Regulation and Re-regulation, The Hague: TMC Asser Press.
European Commission (2007), White Paper on Sport, COM(2007) 391 final.

European Parliament (2007), Resolution of the European Parliament on the Future of Professional Football in Europe, A6–0036/2007, 29 March (The Belet Report).

European Parliament (2008), Resolution of May 8 2008 on the White Paper on Sport (2007/2261(INI)) (The Mavrommatis Report).

KEA, CDES & EOSE (2009), Study on Sports Agents in the European Union, a study commissioned by the European Commission (Directorate-General for Education and Culture).

Siekmann, R., Parrish, R., Branco Martins, R. *et al.* (2007), Players' Agents Worldwide: Legal Aspects, The Hague: TMC Asser Press.

Thomas, D. (2006), The Retain and Transfer System, in: Andreff, W. and Szymanski, S. (eds), Handbook on the Economics of Sport, Cheltenham, UK and Northampton, MA, USA: Edward Elgar Publishing.

Index